SECOND EDITION

TURNER PUBLISHING COMPANY

TURNER PUBLISHING COMPANY
Publishers of Military History

Gamewardens History Book Committee:
John C. Williams, Senior Chief Yeoman, USN (Ret.)
 Vice President East Coast
James D. Davy, Vice President West Coast
Ron Laratta, National Treasurer

Copyright © 2000 Turner Publishing Company.
All rights reserved. Additional copies
may be purchased directly from
Turner Publishing Company.

Library of Congress Control No. 00-102778
ISBN: **978-1-68162-162-3**
Limited Edition.

Photo courtesy of James D. Davy

TABLE OF CONTENTS

Warren K. (Tom) Thomson 4

Foreword 5

Dedication 6

Tribute to Adm. Elmo Russell Zumwalt,
    Jr., (Ret.) 8

Tribute to BM1 James Elliott Williams,
    USN (Ret.) 10

Publisher's Message 11

Gamewardens History 12

Medal of Honor Citations 64

Navy Cross Citations 64

Special Stories 71

Gamewardens Veterans' Biographies
    First Edition 96

    Second Edition 132

Roster 151

Index 158

Warren K. (Tom) Thomson

Warren K. (Tom) Thomson, OSCS RET.
American River Division 573
September 1969 — November 1972

Upon arriving in country, I was assigned to River Division 573 out of Tuei Non patrolling the Vam Co Tay River (Giant Sling Shot) and the "Grand" Canal (Barrier Reef East). I was assigned as a boat captain in "Hotel" patrol. My Patrol Officer was EMC Jimmy Walker, a large "BEAR" of a man who had a heart and sense of humor even larger. We worked Tuei Non for about four months and then moved to the YRBM-16 at Tan Chau on the Mekong. From the YRBM-16 we were running north on the Mekong through the "French" Canal to the Bassac, then north to Chao Duc and then west on the Vihn Te Canal which was the Cambodia border. We patrolled for six days at a time and on the seventh we would return to the YRBM-16 (about 40 klicks) for one night in a bed and three hot meals. We worked the border for another eleven months and then moved to Rach Soi in the top of the U Minh forest. I worked Rach Soi for eighteen months and my river division turned over with River Division 515 to form Vietnamese RPD-58 in October 1970. We moved from Rach Soi to Sadec and then My Tho. I ran out of My Tho until they took all the advisors off the river. I had been in country for three years and three months. I received the Silver Star, three Bronze Stars with Combat V's, three Navy Commendations with Combat V's, the Navy Achievement award with Combat V, and the Combat Action Ribbon. I retired from the Navy July 31, 1981 and currently live in Georgetown, Texas, with my wife Nona. Since naval retirement I have worked for defense contractors and presently work at Lockheed Martin, Austin Division, on the US Navy's Tomahawk Cruise Missile System.

I am currently serving as National President of Gamewardens of Vietnam Association, my term is 1995 through 1996.

FOREWORD

My association with operation Gamewarden started on 18 December 1965 when I got orders to report for PBR training at the Naval Amphibious Base Coronado. I believe that we were the first PBR class ever. My first river section was RS 511 (First in the Delta) at Can Tho, where I was the after gunner/engineman on PBR 40 (the slowest PBR ever). My boat captain was BM1 Anderson, he taught me lot about life and I will never forget him. Our patrol officer, Lt. Norm Howell, was one of the most unforgettable leaders I have ever worked for in my entire navy career. In October of '66, I was transferred to RS 533 and was assigned as Boat Captain of PBR 149 in the RSSZ, operating out of Nha Be. In May of '67, I went back to the Delta in RS 512, which was located on USS *Jennings County* (LST 846) on the Lower Bassac. In March of '68, I was transferred to USS *Austin* (LPD 4) and ended my Vietnam service with the PBR force. While attached to TF116, I formed many lasting and great friendships that have helped and guided me through my 28+ years of Naval service. In February of 1989 I retired as a Master Chief Engineman and currently work as a Navy contractor onboard CV's and CVN's.

I would like to take this opportunity to state that my stay with the PBR forces was the greatest time in my life. Looking back, I fully realize that it was a very turbulent time in our country's history and I am very proud of each and every day and night that I was there and each and every one of my fellow members of TF116!

I urge each and every reader of this book to look beyond the political side of the Vietnam War and see the human side of it.

I am currently serving as the National President of Gamewardens of Vietnam Assoc. Inc. and still happily married to Patricia. We have two fantastic daughters and lots of grand kids.

Stephen Watson

DEDICATION

Seawolf Navy Huey of MK II PBR's RIV DIV 594, Vam Co Tay River about March 1969, on operation Giant Slingshot.

From Captain Burt Witham, USN (Ret) and Plank Owner to all U.S. Navy Personnel who served on the rivers and in support of inshore Naval Operations, especially the families of those who gave their lives, I wish you the best for you gave your best in defense of our Nation.

I salute the U.S. Navy Gamewardens of Vietnam Association for your dedicated service and honoring the memory of thse who have passed before. I am proud of the fact that you are the oldest Vietnam Veteran organization of its kind in America. I wish you contiued success and a bright future.

DEDICATION

From MasterChief Jim Davy, USN (Ret)

BMC James Elliott Williams

Adm. Elmo Russell Zumwalt, Jr., (Ret.)

It has been more than thirty years since most of us left Vietnam, yet in the minds of many it seems like yesterday. Never has a greater group of men been brought together and served in one command as those that served with Commander Naval Forces Vietnam. We were close then, and we have remained close over the years.

So, it is very hard on all of us when we lose a friend (brother), and we have lost many over the years. This past year was especially hard for Vietnam veterans and none will be missed more than James Elliott Williams and Elmo Russell Zumwalt, Jr.

For those of us who served in Vietnam and with Gamewardens...they both touched our lives in many ways; Admiral Zumwalt, as the leader we all respected and followed, and Elliott Williams as the hero we all would have followed anywhere when the going got tough. Both were heroes, both were friends and both will be dearly missed.

The Gamewardens of Vietnam dedicate this book to James Elliott Williams and Elmo Russell Zumwalt, Jr., our brothers both now serving on the staff of the Supreme Commander.

Tribute to Adm. Elmo Russell Zumwalt, Jr., (Ret.)

(Both photos courtesy of James D. Davy)

ELMO RUSSELL ZUMWALT JR., born in San Francisco, CA Nov. 29, 1920, son of Dr. E.H. Zumwalt and Dr. Frances Zumwalt. He attended Tulare (California) Union High School, where he was an Eagle Scout and Class Valedictorian; and the Rutherford Preparatory School, at Long Beach, CA before his appointment to the US Naval Academy, Annapolis, MD from his native state in 1939.

As a midshipman he was president of the Trident Society, vice president of the Quarterback Society, twice winner of the June Week Public Speaking contest (1940 and 1941), company commander in 1941, regimental three striper in 1942 and participated in intercollegiate debating. Graduated with distinction and commissioned ensign June 19, 1942 with the Class of 1943, he subsequently progressed to the rank of admiral to date from July 1, 1970.

Following graduation from Naval Academy in June 1942, he joined the destroyer USS *Phelps* and in August 1943 was detached for instruction in the Operational Training Command, Pacific at San Francisco, CA. In January 1944 he reported on board the USS *Robinson* and for "heroic service as evaluator in the Combat Information Center...(of that destroyer), in action against enemy Japanese battleships during the Battle for Leyte Gulf, Oct. 25, 1944..." he was awarded the Bronze Star with Combat "V." The citation further states: "During a torpedo attack on enemy battleships, Lt. Zumwalt furnished information indispensable to the success of the attack..."

After the cessation of hostilities in August 1945 until December 8 of that year, he commanded (as prize crew officer) HIMJS *Ataka*, a 1200-ton Japanese river gunboat with 200 officers and men. In that capacity he took the first ship since the outbreak of WWII, flying the US flag, up the Whangpoo River to Shanghai. There they helped to restore order and assisted in disarming the Japanese.

He next served as executive officer of the destroyer USS *Saufley* and in March 1946 was transferred to the destroyer USS *Zellars* as executive officer and navigator. In January 1948 he was assigned to the Naval Reserve Officers Training Corps Unit of the University of North Carolina at Chapel Hill where he remained until June 1950. That month he assumed command of the USS *Tills*, in commission in reserve status. That destroyer escort was placed in full active commission at Charleston Naval Shipyard on Nov. 21, 1950 and he continued to command her until March 1951 when he joined the battleship USS *Wisconsin* as navigator.

"For meritorious service as navigator of USS *Wisconsin* during combat operations against enemy North Korean and Chinese Communist forces in the Korean Theater from Nov. 23, 1951 to March 30, 1952..." he received a Letter of Commendation with Ribbon and Combat "V" from Commander Seventh Fleet. The letter continues: "As navigator his competence and untiring diligence in assuring safe navigation of the ship enabled the commanding officer to devote the greater part of his attention to planning and gunfire operations. His performance of duty was consistently superior in bringing the ship through dangerously mined and restricted waters, frequently under adverse conditions and poor visibility. He assisted in the planning of the combat operations...(and) piloted *Wisconsin* into the closest possible inshore positions in which maximum effect could be obtained by gunfire..."

Detached from USS *Wisconsin* in June 1952, he attended the Naval War College, Newport, RI and in June 1953 reported as head of the Shore and Overseas Bases Section, Bureau of Naval Personnel, Navy Department, Washington, DC. He also served as officer and enlisted requirements officer and as action officer of Medicare Legislation. Completing that tour of duty in July 1955, he assumed command of the destroyer USS *Arnold J. Isbell*, participating in two deployments to the Seventh Fleet. In

this assignment he was commended by the commander, Cruiser-Destroyer Forces, US Pacific Fleet for winning the Battle Efficiency Competition for his ship and for winning Excellence Awards in engineering, gunnery antisubmarine warfare and operations. In July 1957 he returned to the Bureau of Naval Personnel for further duty. In December 1957 he was transferred to the Office of the Assistant Secretary of the Navy (Personnel and Reserve Forces) and served as special assistant for Naval Personnel until November 1958, then as special assistant and naval aide until August 1959.

Ordered to the first ship built from the keel up as a guided missile ship, USS *Dewey* (DLG-14), building at the Bath (Maine) Iron Works, he assumed command of that guided missile frigate at her commissioning in December 1959 and commanded her until June 1961. During this period of his command, *Dewey* earned the Excellence Award in engineering, supply, weapons and was runner-up in the Battle Efficiency Competition. He was a student at the National War College, Washington, DC during the 1961-62 class year. In June he was assigned to the Office of the Assistant Secretary of Defense (International Security Affairs), Washington, DC where he served first as desk officer for France, Spain and Portugal, then as director of Arms Control and Contingency Planning for Cuba. From December 1963 until June 21, 1965 he served as executive assistant and senior aide to the Honorable Paul H. Nitze, Secretary of the Navy. For duty in his tour in the offices of the Secretary of Defense and the Secretary of the Navy, he was awarded the Legion of Merit.

After his selection to the rank of rear admiral, he assumed command in July 1965 of Cruiser-Destroyer Flotilla Seven. "For exceptionally meritorious service..." in that capacity, he was awarded a Gold Star in lieu of a second Legion of Merit. In August 1966 he became director of the Chief of Naval Operations Systems Analysis Group, Washington, DC and for "exceptionally meritorious service...as director, Systems Analysis Division, Office of the Chief of Naval Operations, Deputy Scientific Officer to the Center for Naval Analyses, during the period from August 1966 to August 1968..." he was awarded the Distinguished Service Medal, The citation further states in part:

"RAdm. Zumwalt, by direction of the Chief of Naval Operations, established the Systems Analysis Division and rapidly developed it into a highly effective, responsive organization. Under his leadership, the division has assisted in generating within the Navy a better understanding of requirements, problems and a more effective presentation of those requirements in major program areas which will strongly influence the combat capabilities of US Naval Forces through the next generation. (He) has displayed exceptional acumen, integrity, tact and diplomacy as personal representative of the Chief of Naval Operations, not only in dealings within the Department of Defense, but also in testifying before Congressional Committees. Among the major analyses completed under his direct supervision were the major Fleet Escort, Antisubmarine Warfare Force Level, Tactical Air, Surface-to Surface Missile and War-at Sea Studies. Additionally, under RAdm. Zumwalt's guidance, the Center for Naval Analyses has been restructured and its methodologies clearly defined with such precision as to ensure that completed studies will reflect thoroughness, comprehensiveness and accuracy when subjected to closest scrutiny..."

In September 1968 he became Commander, US Naval Forces, Vietnam and Chief of the Naval Advisory Group, US Military Assistance Command, Vietnam. President Richard M. Nixon nominated him as Chief of Naval Operations April 14, 1970. Upon being relieved as Commander Naval Forces, Vietnam on May 15, 1970, he was awarded a Gold Star in lieu of a second Distinguished Service Medal for exceptionally meritorious service. He assumed command as Chief of Naval Operations on July 1, 1970 and retired from that position July 1, 1974. In 1976 he unsuccessfully ran as a Democratic candidate for the Senate from Virginia. Later he held the presidency of the American Medical Building Corp. in Milwaukee, WI.

Adm. Zumwalt died Jan. 2, 2000 at the Duke University Medical Center in Durham, NC. His home was in Arlington, VA. He was married to the former Mouza Coutelais-du-Roche of Harbin, Manchuria and they had two sons, Elmo R. Zumwalt III, who died of cancer in 1988 and James Gregory Zumwalt; two daughters, Ann F. Zumwalt Coppola and Mouza C. Zumwalt-Weathers. He was also survived by six grandchildren.

TRIBUTE TO BM1 JAMES ELLIOTT WILLIAMS, USN (RET.)

EULOGY
BY RADM MORTON E. TOOLE, USN (RET)
16 OCTOBER 1999, DARLINGTON, SOUTH CAROLINA

Elaine, children and grandchildren of James Elliott Williams, relatives of James Elliott Williams, friends of James, friends of Elliott, fellow shipmates of "Willie".

Those of us who served for one year up the Mekong River with Boatswain's Mate First Class James Elliott Williams always called him, "Willie"…Navy people do that…they'll latch onto your name and decide, affectionately, to change it. We who served alongside him always called him Willie, even though he told us after he retired that he was *now* Elliott. We all ignored that.

Today, you and I, the crew of PBR–105, the United States Navy, and our nation have all lost a great friend, an outstanding naval leader, a genuine American hero. But he has come home to you of Darlington and Florence, South Carolina who knew him the longest…Home is the sailor; Home from the sea.

I met Willie in 1966 when he was a very long way from home during the last year of his service; a time during which most Naval careerist seek a job near their future retirement home…it is called the "twilight tour". Willie saw that his country was at war, whatever people wanted to call it. He had been in one of those "non–war" wars before, and I am reminded of that because I see his old ship's–named hat in the casket with him. In 1952, he was assigned to USS *Douglas Fox* (DD–779) during gunfire support and shore bombardment of South and North Korea. He volunteered when his ship was asked for a Boat Coxswain to shuttle U.S. and South Korean Raiders against North Korea from an island–base off Hungnam, each night for six months.

In 1966, he could see that his country's new effort, small boats, could use his experience. So, he came to the River Patrol Force. He lead young Americans who were not draftees, who were not draft–dodgers…who were volunteers one and all. He and they went to Vietnam to help the South Vietnamese people…to help keep their rivers free for them to move safely on those rivers and bring their products of fish, coconuts, rice, and bananas to market. And not to be intercepted by the Viet Cong, the Vietnamese Communists who would rob them and "tax them" and murder them in the name of something they did not believe…communism.

So, Willie came to help by serving on a 31 foot fiberglass boat: a boat specifically designed not to stop bullets, but let bullets pass through the boat. Armor would have slowed the fast boats down and would have caused shrapnel wounds. The boats were painted in camouflage to blend in with the lush jungle and coconut trees that lined the sometimes very narrow river. But, the enemy snipers could peer out and easily see the bright red, white and blue flag of the United States of America.

It had not been since the Civil War that Americans had fought a river war. Willie and the PBR–men like him in 1966 became the pioneers of 20th Century small–boat river–fighting. Some of them are here today: Willie's forward gunner Rubin Binder, who had to physically push around the unpowered twin .50 caliber guns; Willie's immediate boss, retired Commander Fred McDavitt; one of Willie's river shipmates, retired Captain and Navy Cross winner, Chester Smith.

Under Willie, PBR–105 quickly was molded into a Team, not just physically, but mentally ready to do the job. By training his crew on those twin aspects of readiness and ensuring everyone could readily and quickly do all job on board their PBR–105, Willie did more than lead…he inspired them as a team.

The Navy thought it would have Officers and Chief Petty Officers act as the Patrol Officer for two–boat Patrol. The reality of river warfare found that it was the natural leaders who became the guiding lights. It was the natural, real leadership showed by Willie that made it clear that he be given the additional responsibility as a Patrol Officer: over and above all others.

The first real combat action resulted in Willie's first Bronze Star: a Viet Cong tax collector who was nothing more than a highwayman on the river, robbing the poor people of their money to finance the VC campaign of terror and murder. He was expected to try to cross the river. Lt. McDavitt and Willie set a trap. I shall never forget Lt. McDavitt saying over the radio, "Go get him, Willie!" That action returned thousands of dollars back to the South Vietnamese people.

"Go get him." Now, that was very dangerous. Because after certain hours, no one was supposed to be on the river. But Willie still had to maneuver his boat up alongside, with the distinct possibility of a grenade being thrown into the boat, and ask the enemy for his ID card. Our boats had to take the first round.

However, Willie's first success set the tone for the entire River Patrol Force. It was professional. It was effective. It was supportive of the people. It demonstrated an ability to plan, prepare and respond in combat, if combat occurred.

And combat occurred often with Willie. The night he earned the Navy Cross, an important enemy commander sought to sneak across the river in a high–powered boat. Willie and his team spotted him. Heavy enemy fire from both sides of the river sought to protect the enemy boat. Willie could have stood–off to safety and called in support. But he knew it would be too late; the enemy would escape. He knew that to have that much enemy fire support, the enemy had to have someone big. With his support boat suppressing one river bank and his boat suppressing the other, he guided his boat alongside the enemy sampan. In a hailstorm of enemy bullets from which he was wounded in the hand and eye, he retrieved a treasure of invaluable documents from the bodies of the enemy.

On October 31, 1966 a regimental–size enemy troop movement was going on along the river; many troops in two staging areas were already in their boats and moving when Willie surprised them and waded right into them, destroying or capturing over sixty five sampans and junks, causing scores of casualties, and earning the Medal of Honor.

The History of the Navy in Vietnam has yet to be written. But no historian will every be able to talk about the war without devoting many paragraphs to Boatswains Mate James Elliott Williams and his incredible twilight tour, because no man in any war, on land, sea or air ever earned the top seven awards for combat: Medal of Honor, Navy Cross, Silver Star Medal, Legion of Merit with Combat V, Bronze Star (two) with Combat V, Navy Commendation Medal with Combat V, and Purple Heart (two).

Throughout history, there have been many famous sayings by many famous names: "I have not yet begun to fight," "We have met the enemy, and they are ours," Henry the Fifth that on every Saint Crispin's Day those who fought the French could say that they were at Agincourt.

Vietnam has never engendered such a ringing phrase. In a war and at time when the know–it–all elements of our society were saying there were no heroes, they did not know the hero we knew, who daily was doing his job up a dirty, muddy river. And what a job he did! For those who served aboard the River Patrol Boats on the Mekong River, it says it all to simply say, "I served on the river with Willie."

God be with you, Willie, on this, your last patrol.

A cast of worthy Navy men include: Adm. Chon, VN Navy; RAdm. Matthews, USN, Vice Task Force Commander; and Lt. Dick Hick, USN, River Div. 514. (Courtesy of J. Warnock)

PRELUDE

The long history of the United States Navy, 200 years-plus, is the story mainly of ships and the men who have sailed them in battle against the enemy, either the force of another power or maybe the sea itself.

The legendary John Paul Jones and his *Bon Homme Richard,* the *Monitor's* slugfest with the *Merrimac,* the disaster at Pearl Harbor, the heroic surface action at Leyte Gulf and the terror from the skies off Okinawa - all have their place in the great Navy tradition of triumph and tragedy.

The litany of action at sea could fill volumes and in fact does. The Murmansk run, Savo Island, Wonsan Harbor, it's hard to know where to stop. The great events associated with those faraway places had one feature in common. The battles were fought on blue, deep water often out of sight of land and almost certainly out of sight of the human enemy. Mention naval action and images of huge gun blasts, torpedoes hissing through the water and jets roaring from carrier decks most often come to mind.

The Vietnam War introduced something entirely different, a Navy role unique in scope, if not in kind, in the American military experience and one not likely to occur in quite the same way again. The sailors who were part of this distinct phase of their branch's combat service were warriors of the brown-water Navy, a term that enjoys instant and admiring recognition by anyone familiar with the long Southeast Asia conflict.

To the traditions of the sea service before 1966, the men who wore the black berets, led by junior officers and non-coms, added a proud chapter of their own. That is what this book is about - the sailors who fought their part of the Vietnam War on the muddy surface of rivers and canals, more specifically one group of men who took the code name of their task force's operations as their own. They were called the Gamewardens. The survivors still are.

Before that unit became a reality in the early part of the Americans' direct combat involvement in Vietnam, Navy advisers to the Vietnamese were in the small boats in the Mekong Delta. Earlier, the French carried out riverine warfare in their futile effort to defeat Ho Chi Minh's forces. Otherwise, the antecedents to American Navy in-country operations, which at their peak involved 38,000 men, are skimpy to non-existent, at least on anything approaching the scale experienced in Southeast Asia in the mid-1960s.

The Civil War had its river component, particularly on the Mississippi as both sides sougt to control the great river. Union gunboats passing beneath Confederate shoreline cannon might have represented a faint glimmer of what was to come a century later.

Earlier wars from the Revolution on included some river and lake operations.

The United States Navy had more recent river experience in China before World War II, the sinking of the gunboat Panay on the Yangtse in 1937 being the most noteworthy incident.

But the spiritual ancestors, supposedly, of combat boats that plied Vietnam's inland waterways were the PT boats. The comparison is natural in terms of size, speed, crew and perhaps firepower. However, the similarities are quickly exhausted upon closer examination. The PTs of World War II were flashy, made good movie material and might have captured the public imagination with their dash, but other than taking General MacArthur off Corregidor and being associated with the young officer John Kennedy, the contribution of the little boats in that big-ocean, big-ship war was marginal at best.

Not so the small boats of Vietnam's rivers and canals, an environment made for their kind of warfare. The work of Gamewarden, essentially a patrol and interdiction operation; Market Time, a coastal task force aimed at halting infiltration from the north by sea; and the Mobile Riverine Force, an Army-Navy joint search-and-destroy unit that in some ways resembled the large-scale amphibious operations of World War II scaled down, were integral parts of the total allied war effort in Vietnam. There was nothing peripheral about brown-water duty.

The side-by-side combat of American Army and Navy personnel on the scale seen in Vietnam was probably unprecedented in the nation's military history. Bluejackets, for what surely was the first time, routinely fought like infantrymen, firing small arms and seeing the enemy up close. Most of that action was from the decks of their boats, but not always. It was not unheard of for sailors to plunge into the jungles with rifles and medical kits to lend assistance to beleaguered infantrymen.

The United States Navy's river warriors

PBR in a high speed run on the My Tho River, to overtake a Sampan it has spotted crossing the river. All civilian craft must be checked. Official U.S. Navy photograph taken by J.C. Deckert, PHC, USN on September 18, 1966. (Courtesy of Richard E. Abbbott)

(Courtesy of Ms. Dale Drako)

were a special breed who carried out a dangerous mission and on the whole were successful in the process. The Gamewardens and the mobile river attack force essentially won the Mekong Delta region from the Viet Cong, which in 1965-66 could claim almost uncontested control of that fertile and heavily populated plain. The cost in blood and lives was high. In the chapters that follow, the story of the Navy's Gamewardens will be told in detail. It is an account the American public needs to know and the Gamewardens themselves deserve to have told.

THEATER

The Mekong River rises in Tibet, high in the snows of the eastern Himalayas, to begin its eastward journey of 2,400 miles toward the South China Sea. Its water touches or passes through Burma, China, Thailand, Laos, and Cambodia before entering Vietnam.

Just after the great river flows past Phnom Penh, the capital of Cambodia, it divides into two major streams, one retaining its name of Mekong before veining once again into three major fingers. Those three together with the single stream form the delta.

At that point, the Mekong loses its name as a river, but not its identity. Even where the Mekong as such ceased to be, the region is still known as the Mekong Delta. By the 1960s, it would be a geographical entity recognized throughout the world, nearly as famous as the Nile or Amazon, but for the unfortunate reason of long and bloody conflict.

The four delta components, from north to south, are the My Tho, the Ham Luong, the Co Chien, all from the Mekong branch, and the Hou Giang, or Bassac River, which was the second main branch created by the major split in Cambodia.

Branching off from all of these are smaller tributaries, and connecting them are canals, thus creating in the region a maze-like but extensive network of waterways. Swamps and marshes help complete a huge section of real estate that is far more wet than dry, a fact that influences the way life is carried out by the population and the way the war had to be fought there. Boats were the principal mode of travel by the Vietnamese, the rivers and canals in effect becoming the roads. Villages developed accordingly at the water's edges, stilted construction protecting against high-tide or rainy season flooding. Conventional roadways were few in the Delta, and that too had a bearing on wartime operations. In fact the only hard-surfaced road through the area was Route 4, which connected Saigon and the Ca Mau peninsula, a thumb-shaped protrusion at the extreme south end of the country bordering both the Gulf of Thailand and the South China Sea.

The Delta is an alluvial plain, one of the most fertile regions in the world and no more than 10 feet above sea level in places. Centuries of silt and mud deposits near the end of the meandering downward flow to the sea built to a depth of 200 feet in places.

The region clearly is the rice bowl of the country and is also the most populous. Its 13 provinces accounted for 80 percent of the national harvest of the grain and at the end of the 1960s, nine million people lived in the Delta,

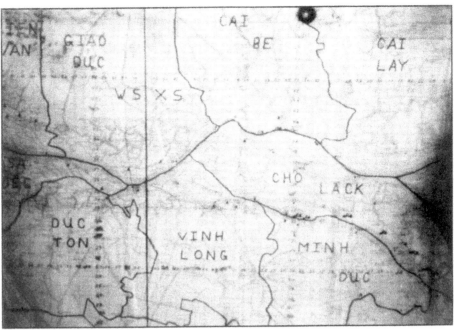

Coxswain Flat Map by GMG-3 Bill Curtis. PBR 55 River Section 523/River Division 572. (Courtesy of Bill Curtis)

more than half the population of South Vietnam. Many were crowded into the major provincial capitals, among them Vinh Long, My Tho and Can Tho.

The big rivers and their tributaries amount to about 1,700 linear miles. When another 750 miles of canals are added, the total, if stretched out into one stream, would reach from the United States East Coast to the Rocky Mountains. That gives some idea of the task facing a relatively small force of brown-water sailors and their small boats. They had to know the vast and complicated watery network sufficiently well to maintain a measure of control over it.

The canal system, as well as an extensive drainage project, was the work of the French during the colonial period. It is what makes the Mekong Delta the populous and food-producing area that it became.

The Ca Mau Peninsula is different, or at least that was so during the war. As an alluvian plain, it is newer and less well developed, good mainly for growing mangrove and nipa palm. It is tied to the northern Delta region by water, lateral canals running between the Bassac River and the Gulf of Thailand.

The Ca Mau was generally a less hospitable environment to allied forces. It was hard to get to and even harder to get into, in the words of Admiral Elmo Zumwalt, top sailor in Vietnam after late 1968. He would try to do something about that, as will be seen.

A second major locale where Gamewarden was concerned was the Rung Sat Special Zone, another Delta, smaller than the Mekong but of the utmost strategic importance. That waterway system comprised the shipping lanes to Saigon.

The Rung Sat was known as the "Forest of Assassins" owing to its notorious past as a haven for pirates and robbers. The tangle of mangrove trees and swamps within the lacework of rivers lent itself to that purpose.

The principal rivers in the Rung Sat were the Long Tau and the Soi Rap by which ocean-going vessels could navigate their way from the South China Sea to the waterfront of the South Vietnamese capital.

Due west of Saigon toward the Cambodian border was another forbidding piece of real estate known as the "Plain of Reeds." This was a marshland, dimensions 30 miles by 70 miles, most of it under from two to six feet of water depending on the season. The villages were dry only about half the time. Water vegetation, including reeds 10-feet-tall and intermingled with brambles, grew in abundance. Along the deeper channels were stands of trees.

To the north, the brown-water Navy also operated in rivers that flowed into the South China Sea. This action occurred in the I Corps Tactical Zone. Rivers of tactical importance to allied ground units were the the Perfume, Cua Viet and Cua Dai, which were vital supply links to such cities as Quang Tri, Cam Lo and Hue.

The rivers and canals of South Vietnam, especially in the Mekong and Rung Sat, were lined with thick jungle growth. As the distance increased from the sea, the waterways narrowed and vegetation became more dense. Some of the canals were too narrow and shallow to allow easy maneuvering. Among the wildlife inhabiting the river country were a variety of poisonous snakes. A sailor describing one patrol during which contact with the Viet Cong was expected made matter-of-fact mention of seeing only an occasional snake slide into the water from the banks. There were times when the men of the river fleets would have to share the water with the snakes, or at least face that potential prospect.

And always, there was the dripping, oppressive heat in the tropical land of monsoons whose northernmost point is 17 degrees north. The printed page is inadequate to convey what the men at war there felt with respect to the climate. Accounts tell of the relief, however, that was derived just from breeze that resulted from the movement of the boats.

The foregoing is a brief description of the

Mark II PBR River Division 594 in Rung Sat Zone - 1969. (Courtesy of Bill Curtis)

environment in which sailors of the United States Navy's brown-water fleet, men who for the most part had lived all their lives in the temperate zones of the United States, had to live and fight.

PRECEDENCE

Riverine warfare in some form or another dates approximately to the origin of warfare itself, for the obvious reason that internal waterways, be they rivers, canals, lakes or swamps, historically have been so crucial to the life of any society.

Thus in war, they become strategic prizes to control or obstacles to combat objectives. That was true in ancient wars of the Persians and Macedonians. It was true in the punic wars between Rome and Carthage. The Vikings were water-borne warriors.

On our own continent, water battles in the interior were prominent in the French and Indian War, the Revolution, notably the Hudson River and Lake Champlain campaigns, and the War of 1812.

The Seminole wars in Florida in the 1830s and the 1840s were the first engaged in by American forces that approximated the environment and conditions that the United States Navy would find in Southeast Asia 130 years later.

Finally, in the Civil War, riverine operations would be employed by Union forces on such a scale that the rudiments of a doctrine would emerge. If United States forces early in its Vietnam experience were to find a brown-water antecedent under the American banner, they would have to look backward one century to the war between the Blue and Gray.

A fair assertion would be that the western campaigns of that conflict would not have been won by the North, or at least in the time consumed, had it not been for the Navy's role on the rivers. The reason is easy to see. The great Mississippi River cut the continent down the middle, so control of the waterway was critical. Major tributaries, primarily the Tennessee, Cumberland and Ohio rivers also were important.

Early in 1862, a Union naval officer converted three steamers into unarmored gunboats near Cairo, IL, at the confluence of the Mississippi and Ohio. To those were added seven armored boats carrying 13 guns each and the river fleet, under Flag Officer Foote, began patrolling, raiding, transporting troops and delivering supplies. Their goal was to keep the Confederates from using the rivers for their own purposes. Gamewarden veterans will recognize the duties and objectives as being similar to their own.

The gunboats joined combat in direct support of U.S. Grant's troops in the taking first of Fort Henry on the Tennessee River and then Fort Donelson on the Cumberland, both of major strategic importance. Later, farther up the Tennessee at Pittsburg Landing, Foote's boats were credited with helping Grant salvage the bloody victory over the Southerners at Shiloh.

At about the same time, boats were engaged in a sharp engagement at Island No. 10 in the Mississippi at a horseshoe bend near the town of New Madrid, thus reducing a Confederate stronghold.

In the meantime, Admiral Farragut was pushing up from the other end of the big river, anchoring at New Orleans. Later, the two forces would meet at Vicksburg.

Twentieth Century river campaigning by American forces was done first by the United States Marines in Nicaragua in the 1920s during one of the so-called "banana wars." Later, as mentioned in the initial chapter, Navy gunboats patrolled China's Yangtse River during the 1930s.

By the time the United States Navy engaged the enemy in a full combat role on the waterways of South Vietnam, the French had carried out riverine operations in their war against the Viet Minh and then the South Vietnamese, first alone and later with the aid of American advisers, took on the role.

The conflict between the French and the communist forces under Ho Chi Minh began almost immediately upon the conclusion of World War II in the Pacific, as the Europeans attempted to re-establish their colonial control over Indochina.

The French quickly saw the need for riverine operations and by use of a makeshift fleet of junks, barges and other assorted craft carrying naval infantry into the Mekong Delta, wrested control of three provincial capitals, My Tho, Vinh Long, and Can Tho, from the guerrillas.

So impressed was French army leadership that it pressed for the formation of a more formally organized brown-water force. What emerged was the dinassauts, literally in the French an abbreviation for naval assault divisions.

These units were made up mainly of converted American and British landing craft of various sizes, the LCM, the LCI, the LCT, and the LCVP. Years later, the United States would follow something of the same pattern, though with more refinement.

To do the job on the rivers, the craft needed bolstering in both armament and armor. Most of the action by the dinassauts took place not in the Mekong but in the Red River Delta of what was North Vietnam during the later war.

Work of these convoys and columns was closely tied to infancy operations in battalion strength and involved pitched battles with Viet Minh ambushers. The boats of dinassauts engaged in difficult supply missions to infantry units over periods lasting as long as two months. The Viet Minh presented no waterborne opposition to the French riverine forces, but were formidable enemies from the riverbanks. A peculiarity of the Ho Chi Minh military was its lack of knowledge, interest or acumen during that period of naval operations in any venue. That was uncharacteristic of Asians, particularly those from a country where land transportation was so difficult and waterways so plentiful.

Several bitter Red River campaigns were fought in the early 1950s, and while the French ultimately lost, it can be said that the dinassauts undoubtedly delayed the day of reckoning and proved their value in the kind of war being waged. In fact, it might be added that French river forces may have been the single most successful aspect of the French misadventure in Inchochina during those eight years, 1946-1954.

Even before the climactic Dien Bien Phu debacle, the French began turning dinassauts over to the Vietnamese navy in the Mekong Delta.

Eventually, these came to be known as river assault groups, abbreviated RAG, naturally. They consisted initially of the converted landing craft operated by the French as patrol boats. Later an improved version of the patrol boat was brought on line to replace the aging French craft, but with a 14-knot top speed; it was a far cry from the speedy American PBRs that would come later.

Under Vietnamese control in the ensuing years, riverine operations would languish, primarily because in that country's military establishment, the Army was clearly dominant. Mainly, RAGs were reduced to performing supply missions, though not without hazards from enemy fire.

It was not until the Vietnamese navy begin to come under the influence of American naval advisers in the early to mid-1960s that a resumption of the prominence the French gave river warfare would be seen.

The Europeans in a losing cause had made a significant contribution to military doctorine as it applied to inland waterways. Now it would fall to the Americans to build on those concepts, improve and refine them with better equipment and more advanced tactics.

The first military advisors arrived in Indochina in 1950, but it was not until after the French left that the American presence and influence gradually increased. The Navy was barely represented in the early years, with just two naval officers among the 155 members of the American mission in 1955. Even 10 years later, Captain Bill Hardcastle, head of the Naval Advisory Command in the country, felt conspicuously underranked at a meeting of United States military advisory leadership. Seated with Army and Air Force officers at a high-level conference with Defense Secretary Robert McNamara, he realized he was the only officer there below flag rank, a situation described by Lieutenant Commander Thomas J. Cutler in his book, *Brown Water, Black Berets.*

Early American naval advisors were not encouraged by what they were seeing. The Vietnamese navy's strength in the Sea Force, the Junk Force and the RAG was about 6,000, many of them unfit by reason of age, health or circumstance, meaning some became involved to escape from poverty. That was particularly true of the Junk Force.

In general, the undermanned and underqualified Vietnamese navy had notable lack of success in its primary mission, which was to halt the infiltration into the South by sea and internal waterways.

The fleet of 50 patrol craft and minesweepers plus 200 riverine and amphibious types made little meaningful contribution to the effort against the communist insurgency, and even the claimed record might well have been padded for bureaucratic or political reasons.

The United States advisors recognized the problem with little difficulty, but were hard-pressed to effect change without a more active American role in the war.

Differences in culture and experience contributed to some difficulties. For instance, the Vietnamese, essentially an agrarian people, did not grasp the mechanical concepts that would be so necessary in the operation and maintenance of boats and weaponry. The Vietnamese at times took a more relaxed attitude toward the whole business than did their eager American counterparts. Rotation of United States personnel did not help matters. The Vietnamese, who had seen conflict in their homeland for many years and thought in terms of the long haul, might have had trouble understanding the commitment of someone who was there a year only to be replaced by someone new.

Nevertheless, the talent and dedication of many of the early advisors were sufficient to develop rapport and enhance the combat competence of the native countrymen.

Naval advisors in the country numbered 53 in 1961. Four years later, that contingent had grown to 235, enough to allow some officers to move down to the unit level and join the Vietnamese Navy in actual operations.

Some were assigned to Sea Force ships, some to junks and some to the River Assault Group.

As a generalization, these were exceptionally able, courageous and motivated naval officers who believed in what they were doing and went well beyond any ordinary course of duty not only to carry out combat operations against an enemy but to win over by special acts of consideration and accommodation the population they were helping to defend.

Epitomizing this group of advisors was Lieutenant Harold Dale Meyerkord, an officer whose feats elevated him to near-legendary status. In 1964 he was working with a RAG in the Mekong Delta.

His story was told in Lieutenant Commander Cutler's book, which is the source for most of what follows regarding Meyerkord. The officer, just 5-feet-nine, 150 pounds, had been the soul of aggressiveness since the days he played high school football in St. Louis and attempted the same at the University of Missouri. An Officer Candidate School product, he entered the Navy in 1960, serving first on a cruiser and then a destroyer.

Meyerkord volunteered for Vietnam in 1963 when it became apparent to him that major events of a world-shaping nature would be taking place there. The special training took six months, including Vietnamese language school, and then he was off to Southeast Asia. Captain Hardcastle assigned him as senior advisor to River Assault Group 23 based near Vinh Long 65 miles south of Saigon in the Delta.

Advisors theoretically were not combatants but the casualty figures said otherwise. During 1964, 18 of the 44 Americans assigned to Vinh Long would be killed or wounded.

Meyerkord, whose radio call sign was "Hornblower," after the fictional British naval hero, quickly built the reputation for coolness in a firefight and a willingness to press his luck in taking risks. The chief petty officers working under him expressed great admiration for the officer, albeit in somewhat worried tones because of his affinity for taking chances in which they would have to share.

Meyerkord drove himself to excel in every way. He was a near fanatic where reconnaissance was concerned, spending many hours in Army helicopters with map in hand learning the countryside and the vast network of waterways. In due time, he came to know the territory like a native.

Whatever complaints American military personnel may have had about their Vietnamese counterparts, Meyerkord added none. The rapport he shared with his opposite number, a VNN lieutenant named Hoa, was remarkable, a situation that no doubt contributed mightily to the fighting efficiency of the unit and the esprit de corps that existed among the men.

It was Meyerkord who pushed the United States Army and by extension the South Vietnamese army into greater cooperation in the field in the form of joint missions. Between the two Vietnamese services were political turf rivalries that did not aid the war effort. Meyerkord and Army Major Oscar Padgett Jr., the senior advisor to infantry regiments operating in the Delta, broke down that obstacle to the point that Army-Navy sweeps were being carried out in early 1965. These presaged the later work of the American Mobile Riverine Force, an outfit the RAG most resembled. In fact, neither the French nor the Vietnamese, in plying the rivers and canals, came particularly close to presenting a forerunner to Gamewardens in terms of tactics, mission or equipment. That would be something new and distinctly American.

A typical RAG flotilla consisted of a monitor, a command boat, LCMs, LCVPs, and the old French patrol boats, called STCAN/FOMs. The boats would disembark troops and then move to a blocking position as the ground units, plus others dropped in by helicopter, would push the Viet Cong toward the boats and their formidable array of machine guns and hand-held weapons.

During one particularly fierce firefight, Meyerkord's style, the elan that served so well in battle, was demonstrated. The old patrol boat was taking a fearful raking of automatic weapons fire, wooden splinters flying everywhere. As Meyerkord and Chief Radioman Eugene Barney hugged the deck, the officer turned to the chief and with a grin remarked, "What do you think, Chief? Is this worth sixty-five dollars?"

It took a few moments for the question to register with Barney, but when it did he laughed out loud, even in the midst of combat that could have ended his life in an instant. Meyerkord was referring to the $65 per month extra the men received as hostile fire pay.

Who would think to say such a thing in the middle of a battle? Barney wondered that too, but at the same time he thought to himself how glad he was to be serving under that kind of officer in those hard circumstances.

Meyerkord and Hoa both wore Australian bush hats in combat situations, a habit that worried and dismayed Padgett. He reminded the Navy men that an enemy would especially target anyone wearing that head gear, but of course there was no deterring them.

Meyerkord engaged in 30 firefights during his months in the brown waters, often turning defeat into victory by his initiative and boldness. On one occasion, he jumped from his boat into another to administer medical aid to two seriously wounded Vietnamese sailors and then back to his own to resume exchanging fire with the enemy. On another, he met two civilian barges on a canal and learned they had been ambushed by Viet Cong ashore. He hid his smaller boats between the barges and had them reverse course, certain the Viet Cong would attack them again. This time, the firepower of the Meyerkord force routed the communists. He once took command of a flotilla after its ranking officer had been wounded and ran the battle himself for an hour, though wounded also.

In March 1965 the RAG flotilla was having a fairly routine day on the Co Chien River and by noon was preparing to return to Vinh Long. Meyerkord had just returned from three days in

Hong Kong where he was met by his wife over from the states, and was overdue in Saigon where Captain Hardcastle was to present him with the Air Medal and the Purple Heart. Before the day was over, he would earn another.

Radio transmission from the Army told of contact with a sizable Viet Cong force. Would the boat column set up a block? The ever-eager Meyerkord got to it.

The infantry pushed Charlie toward the canal, and after a brief firefight involving the patrol boats, the engagement appeared to be over. But as the vessels moved up the waterway to find a place wide enough to turn around, they passed into the sights of the main Viet Cong force, which had set up machine guns on either side to cover withdrawal. With sudden force, automatic weapons fire tore into the boats, including the command on which Meyerkord, Barney and an Army officer named Snooks were riding.

Meyerkord was quickly hit, but continued to fire. As Barney sought to pull his officer to a position of better cover, rounds tore into both.

At the dock at Vinh Long, two Vietnamese sailors carried a litter. At the feet of the prone figure was an Australian bush hat. Major Padgett, watching the scene, then knew.

Back at Saigon, Captain Hardcastle read once again one paragraph from the March 1965 report of Military Assistance Command Vietnam:

"During an amphibious assault and destroy operation on 16 March, Lieutenant H.D. Meyerkord was killed by small arms fire. This was a great loss to the United States advisory effort. Lieutenant Meyerkord was an outstanding and extremely aggressive advisor whose acts of bravery earned the respect of all who knew him."

Meyerkord thus became the first American naval officer killed in action in Vietnam. He was awarded the Navy Cross posthumously, not for any one action but for his consistently courageous performance throughout his period of duty. Despite his excellent record, he probably was more typical than exceptional among his naval advisor peers in the field during that period of the American experience. And to a large degree, the motivation, aggressiveness and courage he brought to his job was emulated by the American riverine forces that would follow as part of the full-scale combat operations.

But before Gamewardens and other United States combatant units took over in the waterways of the Delta and the Rung Sat in 1966, another forerunner was on the scene to account for the American naval presence. The little unit was called "McLeod's Navy" and while it predated Gamewarden by a few months, its mission was much the same. It could be stated that the outfit filled the gap between the Navy's advisory role, as epitomized by Meyerkord and others, and the organized large-unit combat operation that would come with Gamewarden and the Mobile Riverine Force.

When the Navy decided in late summer 1965 that the rivers would require major league attention, as will be described in greater detail in a subsequent chapter, the idea initially was to expand the coastal patrol upstream from the South China Sea. Rear Admiral Norvell G. Ward

tapped Lieutenant Kenneth L. McLeod III for the first, largely experimental phase of river warfare.

His equipment left much to be desired. Included were four rundown old relics, LCPLs (Landing Craft, Personnel Large), two of which were in such bad shape they had to be sent to Subic Bay in the Philippines for overhaul. McLeod and his men went to work on the other two and in the best tradition of military "dog-robbers" scrounged enough material one way or another to put the old craft into shape. The crews scraped layers of paint, reinforced rusted areas, reconditioned the diesel engines, devised a way to muffle their noise and added a bristling array of armament, including .50-caliber machine guns fore and aft and .30 calibers amidships. Searchlights, some of them automobile headlights and others from tanks, were mounted. Radar was added, and to provide just the right touch of fierce aggressiveness, shark's teeth and eyes were painted on the bows. The LCPLs were ready for their mission.

Admiral Ward described that job simply: Patrol the rivers south of Saigon, where the Viet Cong were thought to be especially strong, and develop tactics for future operations. Starting in September 1965, the same month the Navy ordered 120 new river patrol boats for the operations that would follow, McLeod and his small band of cigar-chomping, ready-for-anything sailors set out in their 36-foot converted landing craft, a boat relatively slow for the task at hand. They may have been the first United States Navy vessels to fly the American Flag in combat on South Vietnam's rivers.

Other figures in this tiny fleet included the second-in-command, Lieutenant (jg) Hal Graber, a reserve officer who had quit medical school in order to join the Navy, and Boatswain's Mate Third Class Rick Chapman, lead boat coxswain who previously has served as an advisor in the Junk Force and found subsequent stateside duty so boring that he volunteered to return to Vietnam. Those two men, one of whom could have been studying to be a doctor and the other enjoying the safety and comfort of some billet in the United States, exemplified the motivation of the sailors who served in the brown-water fleet.

The unit was based at the riverfront of Saigon, from where it embarked on its night patrols into the Rung Sat, the Viet Cong infested tangle of swamps, streams and islands through which passed the main shipping channel to the capital. The South Vietnamese army would not venture into that rat's nest and the country's navy was not equipped to do so. It was left to the United States Navy to do the job.

A particular night patrol by the two LCPLs under McLeod's command in October 1965 was described by Lieutenant Commander Thomas J. Cutler in his book, Brown Water, Black Berets.

The boats, each with nine-man mixed Vietnamese-American crews, left dockside in Saigon just before dusk and headed into the Rung Sat. Their objective was to seek and check out curfew violators and deal with any other manner of trouble that might come up. Based on history of the past few weeks, that would not be unlikely. As McLeod noted as he pointed to black crosses on a map, there already had been several encounters in the Rung Sat. Going along on this

patrol was a Phoenix newspaperman, Paul Dean, to whom McLeod offered the opinion that just the presence of two small boats in the Rung Sat had unsettled the Viet Cong. The craft couldn't be everywhere, of course, but Charlie's problem was he never knew when or where the river patrol would pop up next. This was precisely the kind of thing Ward wanted to know when he ordered the patrols, and McLeod was convinced his work was proving the value of large-scale Navy river operations. He was right, of course.

As he told Paul Dean as the boats headed into the Rung Sat that October evening, "Our stated mission is basically experimental, to see if we can disrupt some of Charlie's movements in the area. If we're successful on a small scale, then the Navy will come in here and in the Mekong Delta in a big way and clean out this infestation." (From Brown Water, Black Berets - Cutler).

As the two boats passed Nha Be, the last friendly location, the glow of Saigon could still be seen off the port quarter. From this point on, the territory would be increasingly hostile and dangerous. Crewmen donned helmets and flak jackets, uncovered the guns and turned out the running lights. McLeod switched the radar on.

It did not take long to make the first contact. The metallic click of weapons being readied on the suddenly tense vessels could be heard as the crew became aware of activity ahead in the darkness. It could be harmless Vietnamese violating the night curfew, or it could be Viet Cong ready to open fire.

This time it turned out to be the former. At McLeod's order, searchlights had speared the darkness to expose a small sampan and a dinghy and when the shouted order by one of the Vietnamese aboard the lead LCPL failed to produce the desired result, a .45 caliber shot into the air did. Inspection revealed only fishing gear, so the Vietnamese were let off with a lecture about curfews and confiscation of their identification papers for further checking. While all of this was going on, the second boat had remained astern in the darkness, unable to be seen by the people in the sampan. McLeod was developing tactics as the admiral had instructed.

The scene was repeated several times as the night wore on, a routine that took its toll on the crew members, who alternately would gear themselves up for the danger of a possible firefight, only to find that prospect gone. It was an ebb and flow of adrenaline that worked to exhaust the crew physically and otherwise.

But this night would not pass with nothing more eventful than inspections of fishermen out on the river past curfew.

After the boats reached the mouth of the Soi Rap River as it empties into the South China Sea, they turned back upstream into the Dong Tranh River, which eventually merges with the Long Tau as the main channel to Saigon.

It was after 5:00 a.m., roughly 12 hours into the patrol and the two boats had penetrated upriver past the point where the banks had been defoliated. McLeod and his men expected trouble and once again made themselves ready for it.

Three contacts were detected on the lead boat's radar ahead in the still-dark river. The boats throttled up to close the distance quickly, their engines giving off a pugnacious roar. Again, it was time to "hit the lights" and now the beam revealed three motorized sampans. The light startled the men aboard, but not for long. One of them without hesitation grabbed a rifle and fired it at the lights. The American-Vietnamese force did not hesitate either. Machine gun fire spewed from LCPL-1, McLeod's boat. The Viet Cong responded with gunfire that peppered the decks of the converted landing craft.

McLeod calmly loaded a 40-millimeter grenade into a launcher and fired at the lead sampan. The direct hit eliminated the target in a shower of splinters and the other two enemy boats ran for cover in the swamps. The fight was not over, however. Hostile fire now was coming from the mangroves on the bank. Both LCPLs directed a torrent of fire onto the shore until the enemy guns were silenced, though not before LCPL-1 nearly hit the second boat commanded by Graber with friendly fire. Such is one of the hazards during the melee of close combat in the dark.

It was a victory. One enemy sampan had been destroyed with loss of all hands, Viet Cong ashore likely suffered casualties and the friendly force was all but unscathed. Only the correspondent Dean could be counted as a casualty and that a burn on his elbow from a tracer passing closely by.

It took another seven hours for the return trip to Saigon and even then, cleaning of weapons and checking of engines preceded the much-needed sleep. The crew had survived another night in the Rung Sat.

Lieutenant Ken McLeod's Bronze Star listed September 1 through November 4 as the period in which he carried out his missions in the Rung Sat. His citation said his units came under enemy fire more than 20 times over the two-month course, which ended, incidentally, the month before the Navy officially organized Task Force 116, the Gamewardens, to carry out the fight on a large scale as McLeod had envisioned.

San Diego newspapers only reported McLeod's decoration, which attracted attention of another kind. Again, we rely on Lieutenant Commander Cutler's *"Brown water, Black Berets,"* for this special insight into some of the homefront attitudes these brave men had to endure.

This is the letter McLeod received: "Congratulations on your decoration for cowardly heroism in Viet Nam. The United States Christian Crusaders are doing a wonderful job massacring the people and devastating their people with no bombers to bomb back and no warships to fight the mightiest navy in the world.

"Killing unarmed people in unarmed fishing junks should be worth the Congressional Medal. Fighting a country that cannot fight back - must be fun."

McLeod's reaction is unrecorded, but he would be less than human if he didn't wish for a least a moment that the author of that masterpiece could have spent one frightful night with him on a LCPL in the Rung Sat, though he certainly wouldn't have wanted to depend on that ilk in a fight.

Riverine warfare had come a long way since the time of the ancients, the American Revolution and this country's Civil War. The French added their refinements, as did the Ameri-

can advisors with the Vietnamese. Now "McLeod's Navy" contributed a final refinement before full-scale Navy operations would begin.

EQUIPMENT

The fleet of small craft that carried out the war in the rivers and canals of South Vietnam, augmented by some ocean-going vessels, eventually came to be about as varied as that of the traditional deep-water Navy. To a degree, the brown-water component of the branch had its counterparts in the large-ship fleet.

A major example was the PBR (Patrol Boat, River), the vessel of most prominent use in Operation Gamewarden and truly the workhorse of brown-water operations. The same label has often been attached to the destroyer, and in their own contexts, the two vessels are similar. Both are small compared with their fleet fellows, and rely on speed, maneuverability and muscular armament. The versatility of the PBR, like the destroyer, enabled it to do many jobs. And it carried a punch disproportionate to its size.

The next step up was the Swift boat, (Patrol Craft, Fast), which was more than 50 percent longer than the PBR - a "cruiser" perhaps.

To push the analogy between brown - and blue-water fleets a bit further, river operations employed converted LCMs, a landing craft, as ATCs (Armored Troop Carriers) to ferry infantry to points of debarkation and retrieve the troops when the operation was over. In a large-scale amphibious invasion, the rough equivalent would have been the APA, a large attack transport. Finally, the joint Army-Navy operations in the Mekong Delta took along their own "battleships," Monitors on which was mounted a 105-millimeter howitzer for heavy artillery support of action on the ground.

The river and inshore fleet included an array of fighting and auxiliary craft, many of them landing types developed for World War II

and adapted, often with major modifications, for riverine warfare.

Other craft were conceived and built specifically for the purposes of the Vietnam operation, a significant challenge to the Navy that at the outset found itself confronting a combat mission without the kind of vessels needed to carry it out or for that matter a corporate doctrine for doing so.

For the best example of this, we return to the PBR. Initial Gamewarden activity was carried out on old LCPLs (Landing Craft, Personnel Large), 36-foot vessels reconditioned for the rigors of a new war and modified by mounting .50 and .30 caliber machine guns and installing a radome mast. Special French mufflers were used to help quiet the diesel engines. However, it was soon seen that the LCPLs were not the boats to carry out the Gamewarden mission, so Navy planners lent themselves to the task of getting a replacement type to the war zone.

The Navy wanted a shallow draft, quiet-running boat about 30 feet in length and capable of 30 knots, one weighing about 10,000 pounds and able to operate at a range of about 150 miles.

Among the pleasure boat manufacturers listening to a briefing on specifications in Washington was the owner of Hatteras Yacht Company of High Point, North Carolina, Willis Slane.

As Lieutenant Commander Thomas Cutler described the scene in his book, *"Brown Water, Black Berets,"* Slane interjected that one of his hulls matched the Navy's requirements closely and that he could build a prototype in about a week for the Navy's inspection.

By putting his plant into a full-court press in procurement and production, by working himself and his employees to the edge of endurance, Slane was able to accomplish exactly what he said he would do. The 28-foot boat, capable of 30.5 knots and with a range of 165 miles, was ready. At top speed, it would draw only nine inches of water.

(Courtesy of John K. Ferguson)

19

The demonstration went well enough to prompt the Navy to buy the prototype for further testing. For Hatteras, however, the story had an unfortunate end. Slane died of a heart attack that night and another firm later won the contract to build the boat. The Navy was obliged to open up the bidding and the contract was won by United Boatbuilders of Bellingham, Washington. The boatyard would deliver 120 boats costing about $75,000 each by April 1966, five months hence.

The PBR would be 31 feet long, the size of an existing Bellingham hull. Material was lightweight fiberglass, which had the further virtue of being resistant to the teredo worm. Displacement was 14,600 pounds, somewhat heavier than the Navy originally envisioned. The power source was two 220-horsepower General Motors engines. Bellingham matched Hatteras in the shallow-draft department, nine inches.

Maneuverability was exceptional. The boat was equipped with two Jacuzzi water jets to provide thrust and steering through nozzles located on the stern just below the water line. The PBR was able to reverse course within its own length at full throttle by a 180-degree rotation of the nozzles. At top speed, about 28 knots, the boat could halt dead in the water in three lengths. It was a remarkable successful design that required only a short gestation period, from conception to delivery, reflective of the urgency of war. The late Willis Slane, though he didn't live to see it, deserves a fair share of credit for that success.

Armament on the new PBR consisted of twin .50-caliber machine guns in an open mount forward, a single .50 mounted on the fantail, and mounts on either side amidships for either an M-60 machine gun (7.62 millimeter) or an MK-18 grenade launcher. Initially, the fantail gun was a single .30 caliber, but ammunition problems forced the change to the .50-caliber. Ceramic armor protected the coxswain's and weapon's station.

Radar was a Raytheon 1900N model, and communication was provided by two AN/VRC-46 FM radios.

All in all, it was a compact, serviceable little boat that over the course of several years in South Vietnam, mostly in the Mekong system, would carry thousands of bluejackets and junior officers into action that varied from long tedious patrols to fierce bursts of combat. At $9,000,000 the total cost of the initial procurement of 120 boats, the PBRs represented a lot of military hardware for the money, as wartime price tags go. As with most of the floating equipment that would fight in the foliage-lined waterways of Vietnam, the traditional Navy gray was put aside. The PBRs sported a dark green paint job.

The original order of 120 would turn out to fall far short of the needs of the protracted war. For one thing, additional craft were needed for training crews in California. By 1968 250 PBRs were on station in Vietnam.

An improved Mark II model costing $90,000 each was introduced that same year, a little faster and bigger and with a slightly lower profile. The new model was 11 inches wider and a foot longer. Small refinements were in evidence throughout the vessel, including better communications arrangements, electrically fired machine guns, better muffling of engine noises, and

Forward .50s on a Mark I PBR - River Section 523 on Cho Chin River - September, 1968. Photo by GMG-3 Bill Curtis. (Courtesy of Bill Curtis)

better protection for gunners. Another new feature was the addition of aluminum gunwales to lessen the damage the earlier model had experienced from bumping against sampans.

Fouling of the engine from the organically rich waters of the Delta was one major reason for the updated version of the PBR. Accumulations of plant life and micro-organisms on the fiberglass hull also cut down on speed and efficiency of the boats, and there was insufficient time for maintenance to combat that problem.

Most of the improvements were a direct result of suggestions by veterans who had been fighting from the decks of the PBRs. The Mark II was not the product of mere theoretical thinking. One river sailor, Engineman Third Class Robert B. Summerhill, liked what he saw when the Mark II appeared, as he remarked: "It looked like we were going a lot faster than we really were. The hull was flatter to give us a shallower draft than the other boats and it threw out more spray."

The PACV (patrol air cushion vehicle), a hovercraft, was employed for a time in Gamewarden in an area west of Saigon called the Plain of Reeds, a marshland covered with water from which grew aquatic grass and reeds. PAVCs were 39 feet long, 34 feet wide and could skim over the surface at the blinding speed of 70 knots. Their gas turbine engine, which drove the lift fan and propeller, was so noisy that the vessel seldom was able to achieve surprise. Its speed, however, compensated for the disadvantage in most encounters. Machine guns and grenade launchers provided the armament.

Three PAVCs were assigned to Gamewarden for operations in the Plain of Reeds. By comparison to the economy model PBRs, the million-dollar hovercraft fell far short of justifying its cost.

Minesweeping was a major function of Gamewarden, mostly in the Rung Sat Special Zone, the web of rivers that comprised the main shipping channel from the South China Sea to Saigon.

Two types of vessel did that tough, vital job and ensured that enemy mining would not block the water lifeline to the South Vietnam capital. The larger was the Minesweeping Boat (MSB), a 57-foot wooden hull craft. The diesel engines could drive the boat through the water at 14 knots. Skippered by a chief or first-class petty officer, the MSB carried a crew of seven. Firepower was provided by a single .50 caliber machine gun mounted in an elevated tub aft, and single .30 caliber machine guns on either side of the forecastle.

The smaller vessel, designated MSM (minesweepers, medium) was a converted LCM-6. Sweeping mines was just one of several tasks to which the landing craft was adapted in riverine operations. Developed originally to put troops and equipment ashore during amphibious landings during World War II, the venerable M boat, as they once were called, performed a variety of utility chores in the fleet Navy, ranging from delivering supplies in port to ferrying liberty parties. Now the Navy was finding other uses for the craft, usually after modification, in Vietnam's rivers, canals and harbors. In fact, when all the river craft and their variety of uses in the waterways of Vietnam are taken into account, it was the LCM in its different models that was the most adaptable, and that was true even before the American Navy was on the scene. The French and Vietnamese navies were employing converted M or Mike boats in abundance also. World War II and Korean War sailors, if they had looked in, would have been surprised at the way the landing craft were being used and may have barely recognized them. Gamewarden was not all surface units. The Navy knew that air cover would be needed for the PBRs and minesweepers, and helicopters were the obvious answer. However, the sea service's stock, mostly anti-submarine craft, consisted of equipment that was too big, heavy and expensive to perform the needed tasks over the inland waterways.

The Army had the right helicopter for air cover in the UH 1B Iroquois, informally known as the Huey. These open-door choppers were mainstays in the Army as gunships and would be the same for the Navy in Gamewarden.

The Army lent the Navy 22 Hueys, which the Navy renamed Seawolves, the label by which the squadron also would be known.

Initially, the Army manned and maintained the Seawolf helicopters until naval personnel could be trained. In a phased changeover, the Navy assumed the gunship operation.

The outfit, Helicopter Attack (Light) Squadron Three (HAL-3), comprised three detachments, which served as mobile bases for Gamewarden.

The Iroquois, made by Bell Helicopter Co., was 53-feet long, was powered by a single engine and could carry up to 4,000 pounds at maximum speed of 90 knots. The crew consisted of pilot, co-pilot, crew chief gunner and door gunner. Its firepower was potent. Ordnance included four M-60 machine guns fired by the co-pilot in the direction the craft was heading, 14 2.75-inch rockets controlled by the pilot and two hand-held M-60s fired by the two gunners, who also each had an M-79 grenade launcher.

The Seawolves also performed aerial reconnaissance and medical evacuation.

Augmenting the helicopters in supporting Gamewarden operations from the air was a squadron of fixed wing planes, 14 OV-10A Broncos, dubbed "Black Ponies." These were twin-engine, propeller-driven aircraft that could remain in the air two to three hours at 180 to 200 knots. They were designed to take off and land within a short distance.

Their mission was close support, for which the Black Ponies were impressively endowed with up to 2,400 pounds of ordnance. Armament included M-60 machine guns, 20-millimeter cannons, SUU-11 Gatling-type miniguns, and 2.75 and 5-inch rockets, the latter packing a knockout punch with 48-pound warheads in three configurations, depending on whether the job was removing foilage and structures, going after dug-in targets or scattering shrapnel above the ground to cut down personnel in the open. The rocket was accurate enough to be used within 100 yards of friendly troops if they were sufficiently dug in. The light machine guns, including the Gatlings, could spit out a prodigious volume of fire within 50 yards of friendly units. The six-barrel Gatling, for instance, was able to shower a position with 6,000 7.62 millimeter rounds per minute. For heavier machine gun fire, the 20 millimeters could put out 400 rounds per minute.

The Black Ponies, which arrived in Vietnam in April 1969, operated in two detachments, one from a Vietnamese air base to cover the Mekong, the other from an Army airbase to cover the Rung Sat. Together they comprised the Light Attack Squadron Four (VAL-4).

The Navy found the LSTs to be an especially useful piece of floating equipment in the Vietnam river war. These dowdy, flat-bottomed, slow-moving members of the sea-going fleet had been around since World War II, mostly as part of amphibious warfare. They took part in offshore operations during the Korean War and now were involved in Vietnam.

For Gamewarden, they served as bases for PBR units and Seawolf helicopters, one ship per task group on a three of four rotating basis. This meant PBR crewmen berthed aboard the larger ship when not on patrol. LST crewmen provided boat maintenance and general support. And when the occasion demanded it, the LSTs 40 millimeter cannon fired on enemy targets on the banks, often in direct assistance of allied combat operation. Initially, the LSTs were positioned near the mouths of the major Delta rivers, but it was quickly found that the water there was too rough for the little PBRs, so the ships were moved upstream into the interior.

Another large ship of traditional amphibious origins played a somewhat similar role in Gamewarden base support. That was the LSD, landing ship, dock, or floating drydock, as they were sometimes called.

The Swift boat, officially Patrol Craft, Fast, was developed out of the Navy's need for an appropriate vessel to augment United States Coast Guard WPBs in the Market Time Operation, the close-in coastal interdiction designed to halt seaborne infiltration from North Vietnam into the south.

As with the PBR, once again it was the commercial boat industry that provided the answer. The Navy found that Stewart Seacraft of Burwick, Louisiana, had built a 50-foot aluminum alloy boat that was being used principally to carry oil-rig crews out to off-shore installations.

The company was enlisted to build a combat version, the first four of which Stewart delivered in 40 days despite more than 50 modifications required by the Navy. The Swift's two diesel engines could push the boat through the water at 28 knots. Displacing 19 tons, the vessel drew just three and one half feet.

The armament consisted of a twin .50 caliber machine gun in a tub atop the pilothouse. On the fantail was an 81-millimeter mortar mounted piggyback-fashion over a .50 caliber machine gun.

Eighty-four Swifts had been sent to Vietnam by November 1966. Initially, they were allocated to Market Time, which was essentially a salt-water operation. But the versatile Swifts, big enough for coastal waters and adaptable to inland waterways, also found themselves in the narrower confines of the rivers.

The crew consisted of a junior officer and five enlisted men.

As indicated, Market Time was a Navy and Coast Guard operation, the latter service's two

Capt. R. Beckwith showing R. Adm. Daniel Gallery a minigun mounted on a Seawolf gunship - 1969. (Courtesy of Reynolds Beckwith)

classes of cutters making their presence felt along the coasts in preventing as much contraband as possible from finding its way to the Viet Cong in the south.

The larger of the Coast Guard vessels were the WHEC, about the size of a Navy destroyer escort radar (DER), which also participated in Market Time. The smaller cutter was 82-foot WPB.

The third of the three major riverine task forces was the Mobile Riverine Force, which required possibly the most varied small-craft fleet.

The converted LCMs as troop carriers, ATCs, was mentioned earlier. The boats could transport platoon-sized units from base camp to the landing point. Once having accomplished that, the ATCs, armed with 20 millimeter cannon, .50-caliber machine guns and two grenade launchers were capable of giving fire support to troops after putting them ashore. The ATCs, showing an admirable versatility, also were used as medical aid stations, the smallest hospital ships in the world, some said, and were equipped with bladders for refueling other vessels, thus becoming the river equivalent of the fleet oiler.

The monitors and other boats in the river fleet were equipped with a defensive grated shield that caused incoming rocket fire to explode before doing structural damage.

A Mobile Riverine Force column typically would include monitors and command communication boats, CCBs. LSTs were used for fire support also. Floating barracks ships, some self-propelled, some not, provided living quarters when Army troops and Navy boat personnel were at the base. Flagships of this force were the USS *Benewah* and USS *Colleton*, both APBs.

The monitors and CCBs, as other craft of the line as it were, deserve a closer look. Both also were converted LCM-6s, but they did not retain the front ramp. Instead, their bows were tapered to cut through the water better.

The monitors were heavily armed, carrying the same machine guns and grenade launchers as the ATCs and in addition a 40-millimeter cannon, and an 81-millimeter mortar. They also were equipped in some instances with flamethrowers, as were some ATCs, which led naturally to the coinage of their nickname: zippo.

The CCBs differed from the monitors mainly in the replacement of the mortar with a command console where radio communications could be maintained. The CCBs served as the flagships of any operation, a floating command post for the Army battalion commanders as well as the naval office in charge.

Unlike most of the Mobile Riverine Force's fleet, which consisted of old craft converted, modified and adapted for the immediate use, the assault support patrol boat (ASPB) was especially designed and built for the job it did.

The Alpha boat was a short name for the 50-foot craft, which boasted a strengthened hull that would be more resistant to underwater explosions. The alpha was capable of 16 knots, and because the exhaust was expelled into the water and not the air, the boat was exceptionally quiet, an advantage offset in part by maintenance difficulties.

The Alpha was equipped to be tough in a fight. It came with an 81-millimeter mortar and 20-millimeter cannon in addition to the usual package of grenade launchers and machine guns. The boat had multiple uses, from patrol, to reconnaissance, to escort to counter-ambush. The ASPB carried a crew of seven.

The Navy SEALS (Sea Air Land), in actuality commandoes, operated at times from vessels peculiar to their mission. Light Seal Support Craft (LSSC) and Seal Team Assault Boat (STAB) were prominent in that category. The latter was a high-speed patrol craft armed with light machine guns and a 40 millimeter grenade launcher. Similar to the STAB was the Boston whaler as part of the SEALs' fleet.

The LSSC turned out to be the best SEAL craft, with its low profile, Jacuzzi-powered water jet pump and 30-knot speed.

The foregoing is not a complete roster of the equipment that made up the river and close-in coastal fleet during the Vietnam War, but it is representative and includes the major fighting craft. In addition to those vessels mentioned were still other landing-type craft, support vessels and yard auxiliaries.

It is worthy of note that to carry out river warfare required a prodigious number of boats and ships of varied kinds. The adaptability of the Navy was impressive, inasmuch as so many old craft were used in wholly different ways than their original designers might have had in mind. Innovation also must rate high. Finally, the speed with which floating stock needs were identified, procurement was arranged, production was achieved and the material means of war sent to the combat zone should not go unnoticed.

TRAINING

Navy boot camp was never like this. That might have been the uppermost thought in the minds of sailors during much of their training for service on Vietnam's rivers, canals and outer shores. As much as conditioning and drills can ever prepare military personnel for the real thing,

(Courtesy of Kenneth A. Delfino)

UH-1C Huey of HAL-3 Seawolf at Ben Lul S.U. Note P.A.C.U. in background - 1970. Photo by Dan Fuller.

the Navy's regimen was designed to do the job and to a large extent accomplished its objective. Surviving the physical and psychological rigors was a stern challenge in itself.

The experience of one young sailor, Dave Roever, as described in his book, *Welcome Home, Davey,* may typify the training program experienced by many of the men.

Roever, who served about six months on a river patrol boat in 1969 until he was grievously burned by an exploding white phosphorous grenade, provides in his book not only a graphically detailed description of river combat, but of the events that preceded it.

What follows in this chapter, as it pertains to his training and initial exposure to Vietnam, is drawn from Roever's book. His combat experience will be treated later.

Dave Roever was not your stereotypical macho guy spoiling for military action. As a youth, by his own admission, he would rather run than fight. And when the draft board beckoned, his enlistment decision was not one designed to put him into the jungles of Vietnam, or so he thought. On the other hand, being a devoutly religious person and an aspiring clergyman, he could have had a ministerial exemption for the asking. He did not choose that route either.

This look at Dave Roever at the time of his transition from civilian to military status to trained fighting man early in 1968 is informational to typify the river training experience. But it also is directed to another important point, that the men who ultimately performed so capably and courageously in close combat with the enemy were not at the outset thought to be extraordinary, and certainly did not think of themselves as such.

Many were drawn from the ranks of enlisted men on the basis of need. Roever for one did not volunteer for in-country Vietnam duty, or for any Vietnam assignment for that matter, except the lesser of the two hazards before him as he prepared to ship out to the war zone. It didn't matter anyway. He got the other one. Other than that, the only act of volunteerism he performed was raising his right hand at swearing in. The Navy took it from there. It is true that many of the sailors who manned the small boats in Vietnam were volunteers for that hazardous work, and it was not uncommon for crewmen to extend their tours beyond the normal year. Many also were senior petty officers who had served in the deep-water fleet. But there were many Dave Roevers as well, men who simply had joined the Navy, and found themselves, in their first real duty after training, caught up in more than they had ever bargained for.

After boot camp in San Diego, Roever was schooled as a missile technician, not exactly apt preparation for what he would be doing. Upon graduation from the latter, he and most of his class learned they would be going to Vietnam to fill the ranks of a river patrol division that had suffered 90 percent casualties.

Training for that duty lasted 12 weeks, starting at the Navy Inshore Operations facility in Coronado, California. Even before that regiment began the trainees' self-esteem had grown. They knew they had been selected as part of an elite force, fighting men getting ready for a dangerous mission.

The first phase was strictly physical. Six days a week, a Marine major led the sailors on an eight-mile run. He would sprint the last half mile and challenge his charges to keep up. Some did. When a man went down, no one could finish the course until he got up and continued. The intention was to build a sense of peer responsibility and interdependence.

Classroom material included films of river patrol action, uncomfortably graphic for some trainees' taste. The men were taught to use weapons and radios, and most important, how to operate the boats. All crewmen would have to know every job - the gunner's, the engineman's and the coxwain's. With crews of four or five and the prospect of casualties ever-present, a high degree of cross-training was a must.

The future brown-water sailors had special introduction in techniques of inspection of Vietnamese boats they would encounter and the interrogation of nationals. They learned enough of the language to get them by and how to respect the customs of the land. For instance, they were to use two hands in passing an item to a Vietnamese and were told never to point at the soles of anyone's feet or to throw food to the children.

Training shifted to Mare Island, California, in the San Francisco Bay area, long the site of a major Navy shipyard. There hands-on boat training would take place in the swampy Delta terrain similar to that of Vietnam. The sailors learned to maneuver the craft in all of the kinds of situations they eventually would confront in southeast Asia. They were drilled in docking, making high speed turns, dealing with narrow channels so as to avoid being trapped, and an especially tricky maneuver, backing down at a speed that would not cause the craft to sink.

Combat was closely simulated at Mare Island. Maneuvers would cover three or four nights without sleep, during which boats would be loaded, unloaded, supplied, and resupplied repeatedly. Flares would light up the night and blanks would be fired from the riverbanks. The purpose was to acquaint, and then thoroughly saturate, the men with the sound of gunfire. With Dave Roever, at least, the training method worked. He noted in his book that by the time he got to Vietnam, the sound and flashes associated with the enemy fire were so familiar that he was beyond the impulse to duck and run when the real thing occurred. "My only thought was that I had two seconds. If I didn't return fire in two seconds, they would be on target and I was dead. But the instant I started returning fire, they had the same problem I did," Roever wrote.

A final and most difficult week of training, conducted on Whidbey Island in Washington State, taught survival in case of capture. It was realistic in the extreme.

The program was called SERE (survival, evasion, resistance, escape). The men were taken to the wilds, separated, and left with nothing more than a compass, topographical map and a parachute, which they used to keep warm and as a tent. They had no food or other supplies. The objective was to find their way back to a certain spot within three days while eluding men posing as the Viet Cong. Roever ate raw crab and a slug on one occasion, but mostly subsisted on the green stuff beneath tree bark that was chewable. Enough rain fell to provide water from the hollows of rocks or trees.

Another Gamewarden veteran, recalling the week of survival training that was devoid of food except any that could be found off the land, related a story that became part of the folklore of the Whidbey Island camp.

Jim Guthrie, of Bowling Green, Kentucky, who after training served as a PBR crewman with River Division 533 in 1969, recalled that one trainee on the brink of starvation concluded that a nearby resident's black cat was about the most edible morsel to be found, and acted accordingly. The hide of the cat was nailed to the wall of one of the camp's buildings, possibly as a symbol of the training program and perhaps as a reminder of the lengths man will go to in order to survive. Guthrie, along with others no doubt, wonder if the lady who owned the cat ever learned the truth about its fate.

The sailors learned, among other things, that hunger breeds ingenuity. Guthrie and his companions used their parachute risers to make nets for catching fish, and the parachute itself to make a smokehouse for the fish or game they had caught, rabbit, for instance. Other survival-week fare included crabs, shark, roots and - raw rabbit eyeball, a source of needed salt.

The game was rigged so that no trainee would make it all the way out of the woods in which he had been placed, to resume Roever's account. The idea was to see that everyone was captured. The men posing as Viet Cong were Orientals, some of whom had been prisoners of war themselves. Their expertise, as well as their appearance, North Vietnamese uniforms and accent, lent special authenticity to the experience. The enemy would employ terror propaganda on the sailors. The rules were scrupulous in that the facades were seldom dropped, and then only to let a trainee know he had gone too far in his resistance and had been killed. What a difference between this war and previous ones, notably Korea. The country was shocked in 1953 to learn that many American POWs had been totally unprepared for the enemy's psychological tactics. A new word entered the national vocabulary: brainwashing. It wouldn't happen this time, if the military establishment could help it. Every cruelty, subtle or otherwise, that the Vietnamese communists might inflict on American prisoners, was anticipated.

What the resistance sailors were taught consisted of refusal to answer questions, refusal to obey orders and standing straight, shoulders back, jaw thrust, eyes front and impassive. Sometimes the group would shuffle and kick dust in a show of defiance.

The prisoners were held in a compound enclosed by a high chain-link fence rimmed with razor wire. For most of the first night, the men stood. There was no food and their issue of clothes were tattered and buttonless. The guards harassed the prisoners nearly constantly, slapping them around at will. It got worse. One method designed to break the prisoners was to soak a black canvas bag, put it over the men's head and tie it around their necks. They naturally thought they were going to suffocate. Panic would set in to the point of loss of bladder control.

The trainees found themselves crammed into small pine coffin-like boxes, just big enough for them if they were bent into the position of a contortionist. Sometimes two men were forced into a vertical box where they had to stand nose-to-nose for hours. It was no place for the claustrophobic.

Not everyone could endure. One enlisted man cracked from the stay in the coffin. An Army lieutenant colonel, after a week of starvation, found hunger more than he could bear and tried to climb the fence after an orange the guards had thrown there. On the brink of completing the program, he was dropped.

Even one of the guards lost control in an incident involving Roever. The sailor had endured several episodes of the wet-bag-over-the-head ploy without breaking. Each time the bag was removed, the Viet Cong impersonator would ask Roever his mother's name, whereupon he would simply grin. Finally, the guard, apparently in frustration, put the bag on Roever's head one more time and then punched him in the face with all his strength. The blow brought blood. The guard, apparently pulled from the program, wasn't seen around the camp after that.

The psychological tricks used against the prisoners were designed to destroy their faith in their country, their families, their religion. The guards would go into detail about the sexual escapades of American presidents, the idea being to diminish the will of the servicemen to fight for that brand of leadership.

One of the worst ordeals for the prisoners was the way the enemy would try to drive a wedge between them. It was one thing to endure on your own behalf, but when resistance caused pain for a buddy, that was different.

Roever experienced exactly that. Each time he refused to tell the guard his mother's name, his partner, who was standing with his head against the wall, would be forced to step farther away. Finally, he was standing at a 45-degree angle, his body quaking in spasms. Roever never gave in and his fellow prisoner finally fell to the floor. The sailor had won the battle of wills, but at a cost to him, in terms of guilt, and to his friend, in physical discomfort. All Roever could do was whisper his apology.

The final indignity involved food. The famished trainees watched guards prepare a kettle of stew, which of course smelled delicious. When it was finished, the guards asked the men if they were ready to capitulate on some point. When they refused, the guards urinated in the stew and then overturned it onto the ground. Ironically, the Army officer who lost control over the orange had passed the milestone with the stew.

At last, soldiers in American uniforms with American weapons burst into the compound. "Liberation" day had arrived. The flag was raised and the bugler played *Battle Hymn of the Republic*. The week had been so realistic, the simulated guards so good at their jobs that the men actually felt they were prisoners of war now being freed.

The survival training ostensibly was never put to use by most of the men, perhaps by none of them, but that is not exactly true.

The value of the program went far beyond the practical lessons of resistance and endurance learned by the Vietnam-bound sailors. A bond had been fashioned among the men, one that can be forged only through shared experience of danger or ordeal. The fact that in the war zone, these sailors would not be serving together but with others, strangers yet, made no difference, because all of them knew that all of the rest had undergone and survived the same training. That was the bond that helped hold the fighting units together. Roever, referring to his compatriots in training, wrote, "We would have died for each other." Now he was ready for Vietnam and combat, where he like others would be willing to die for his buddies.

For most men making the trans-Pacific journey to Vietnam and war, the mode of travel was similar - usually a chartered commercial jet airliner. For instance, Roever made the flight on a Pan Am Boeing 707 under contract to the military. Navy Lieutenant Jim Morgan, also bound for PBR duty, reached Vietnam a couple of months earlier by a Braniff 707.

Before Vietnam, men did not go to war in such fashion, on an airliner complete with pretty stewardesses in attractive apparel whose job it was to help make war-bound men enjoy their last few hours of peace.

In times past, soldiers and sailors left civilization behind at the dock in some stateside port and sailed across one ocean or another in a cramped troop ship or a warship ready for business. For the fighting men in Vietnam, the trappings of normal life stayed with them nearly to the point of landing, which may have made the change for them all the more rude and abrupt.

For all the similarities of one man's arrival to another, the initial impressions and thoughts were highly personal.

Like Roever and Guthrie, Morgan remembered the cheerful stewardesses trying to make the trip as upbeat as possible. For the officer, on his way to river patrol boat duty in the area around Saigon, it didn't take. The realization hit him during the last two hours of the flight that he had but a short time before his life would be on the line. An All-American hot dog snack was offered. Morgan wasn't hungry. He would pass.

At Tan Son Nhut airport, Morgan was not prepared for the fact that the moment he stepped off the plane, he was junior to everyone already on the ground in terms of time served there and time left to go. It was not a circumstance he was allowed to overlook.

His case of nerves was not helped when he ran into some men he had trained with for PBRs in the States - they had arrived a couple of days earlier - and the talk turned to casualties already suffered.

But it got better. At the Bachelor Officers' Quarters that evening, Morgan was relaxing when the Armed Forces Vietnam news came on featuring a good-looking blonde weather girl. The news crew did ridiculous things like throw water on her if she predicted rain, and finally, Morgan wrote in *The Vietnam Experience, A War Remembered*, the absurdity of such antics in a war zone struck him. His sense of humor took over and his nerves settled down.

For Guthrie, who had been kissed for good luck by a stewardess on the stop at Guam where the females got off, his first breath of Vietnam air was a staggering experience. "We thought we would pass out. The heat, the humidity, and the stench of decay was so overwhelming it made us weak-kneed and lightheaded," was his recollection.

As he stepped off the planes in new fatigues and full of youthful energy, Guthrie could not help but notice a line of "haggard old men in faded fatigues" waiting to board for the return trip to "the world," as the servicemen in-country called home.

"The old men at the airport, as it turned out, were the way I looked when my time came to leave Vietnam. I had become one of those old warriors," Guthrie recalls. He was 22 years old at the time of his departure. In a sense, the day he arrived in Vietnam, he looked at his own reflection, one year later.

Roever described his arrival at Saigon. When the plane's doors opened that January day in 1969, the heat and odor hit him, like it did Guthrie, square in the face, and for him too, the starkest sensation was reserved for the eyes. At the airport waiting to be loaded on an eastbound plane, were the stacks of bullet-shaped, aluminum coffins. They held the bodies of men who, like Roever and the other passengers, had likely arrived a few weeks, a few months or maybe a year earlier and smelled the same odors and saw the same sights and wondered what their own return trip would be like.

A blue school bus carried the arrivees to customs and then to downtown Saigon where they would stay in a rundown old French hotel, the Annapolis, for the three days of orientation. More so than in most wars, servicemen in Vietnam had to learn how to survive the non-combat phase of their tour. Some things never change, however. The new arrivals were given the benefit of VD films in all their lurid and frightening detail.

With an issue of jungle uniform and other gear, Roever, like so many before and after him, was ready to join the war. The preliminaries were over.

GAME ONE

Astute observers of the nature of the intensifying war in South Vietnam in the early 1960s had no illusions about the seriousness of the infiltration problem; nor had they many doubts about what it would take to counteract it.

As early as June 1961, the bare beginnings of serious United States advisory involvement, Chief of Naval Operations Arleigh Burke expounded on need for the United States Navy to take responsibility for policing and patrolling the rivers and canals in the country.

But the author of the definitive work on the subject, which would be cited repeatedly over the subsequent years, was Navy Captain Phil Bucklew.

By default Bucklew led an eight-man fact-finding mission on infiltration in January 1964. He originally was to have been the number two man in a nine-member party, but the admiral in charge fell ill and it was left to Bucklew, temporarily detached from a base in California, to carry on. What he would discover and report formed the basis for the Market Time Operation offshore and anticipated Gamewarden as well. It took some time, but most of the recommendations in the Bucklew report eventually were followed.

The Bucklew team was nothing if not thorough. Its members visited villages, rode rivers and canals, peered across the national boarder into Cambodia, talked with the people. They roamed the countryside and learned much. They saw Viet Cong flags, for instance, planted virtually side-by-side-with those of the South Vietnamese. They saw evidence of the enemy's presence and influence in the Cambodian sanctuary.

But mainly what the party learned was that South Vietnam was something of a sieve where the smuggling of equipment, supplies and personnel were concerned. It could come by sea, overland through Laos and Cambodia or by way of the elaborate network of waterways that were part of the Mekong River system. Some of the transactions were effected first down to the coast to the river mouths and then upstream into the interior of the Delta.

Bucklew was at pains to remind the readers of his report the makeup of the Oriental mind. Where Westerners are impatient and efficient, not so the Asiatics. He pointed out that the Vietnamese found it no great imposition to dismantle a weapon and bury the components in different places against the day it would be needed, or that taking ammunition apart and hiding the pieces among fish being shipped was an acceptable inconvenience.

Furthermore, the Viet Cong blended quite easily with the population. A Viet Cong might work in the fields by day and spend the night moving to his destination. Dealing with a people who would insinuate themselves and their equipment this way was no small task.

The need for stepped-up infiltration from Ho Chi Minh's standpoint came when the Communists decided to more nearly standardize their small-arms weaponry in the South. Up to this point, the Viet Cong were fighting with a variety of weapons, French, Chinese, American, etc., all of different caliber, which made ammunition a problem.

The decision for uniformity, so that most ammunition could be used in most rifles, put obvious pressure on the smuggling operation.

At this stage of the war, it would be fair to say that the Viet Cong, if they didn't own the Mekong Delta, at least were able to exercise significant control in that most crucial of sections, the populous and fertile rice bowl of the country.

As one indication of their deleterious effect on the countryside, in 1964 South Vietnam was a major exporter of rice, 80 percent of which grew in the Delta. By 1967, the country was a huge importer of the grain that grew in such abundance and the Viet Cong were getting most of it.

It is worth knowing that for the most part, the Viet Cong were not what Americans often were led to believe during the war and for that matter still assume to be true, if they think about it at all.

To understand this, events immediately after the Indochina War must be recalled. After the French lost in 1954, one of the terms of the subsequent agreement was the partition of Vietnam, supposedly temporarily, at the 17th parallel. A 300-day regroupment period was allowed during which time Vietnamese were allowed to cross the border, north or south, free from interference and settle on the other side.

Figures vary, but by one conservative count, 800,000 Vietnamese voted with their feet to leave Ho Chi Minh's paradise and live in the South. No more than 100,000 migrated the other way and many of them were Viet Minh who were south of the line when the war ended.

What is more important is the fact that among those 800,000, or maybe a million, north-to-south trekkers were Ho loyalists who formed the nucleous or the actual body of the major Viet Cong cadres in South Vietnam. The great majority of the people who moved south did so for legitimate reasons, and it can't be denied that some of the Viet Cong were indeed indigenous to the area.

But the significance of the free infiltration of Communists during the regroupment period as a deliberate tactic by Ho Chi Minh to undermine the government of the South cannot be overlooked. Without them there is serious question whether the genuine rebels could have mounted a threat to the Saigon administration.

So the idea of the Viet Cong representing a popular citizens' uprising against an oppressive government is far from accurate. The Viet Cong fought like guerrillas and so they were guerillas, but in politics and to a great extent in their place of origin they might as well have been wearing the uniform the North Vietnamese regulars.

The Bucklew report then was something of a genesis. It recognized the strength of the Viet Cong and their ability to be continually resupplied, and it had some recommendations, among them a tight sea blockade employing United States Navy units as well as South Vietnamese, which came to pass as Task Force 115, codename Market Time.

The Bucklew report also recommended riverine operations, including the ultra-bold measure of trying to halt infiltration from Cambodia at the border. Patrols by regular United States Navy units didn't happen right away, and serious efforts near Cambodia not for nearly five years.

Bucklew was cited and recalled in the institution of Gamewarden about two years later. A few more things had to happen first, however, notably the Gulf of Tonkin incident, and the congressional action by that name that came to be the legal authorization for full-scale combat operations by United States regular forces independent, if necessary, of the Vietnamese military.

Large-scale entry by the United States into river warfare presented a three-fold problem: lack of patrol craft, lack of crews trained in the kind of work that would be required and absence of any established doctrine on the subject.

Reasons for that were understandable. Very little of the United States Navy's experience in this century pertained to rivers. The nature of the modern wars this country had fought before Vietnam did not lend themselves to or require river operations by the Navy. World War I and Korea, both essentially static conflicts across fixed lines, had no place for a river Navy. Rivers in those wars were for crossing and the infantry did that. Even the more fluid Pacific jungle warfare of World War II presented no comparison to the problems faced by the allies in Vietnam.

Thus, in terms of training, tactics, strategy, equipment, personnel and structure, the Navy would have to start at the first square. If history was to provide any help at all, it would have to come from the Civil War, and indeed it did. The

Navy dug one century into the musty past and boned up on how the Union had used gunboats and river tactics on the Mississippi and elsewhere to its advantage.

Otherwise, it was a matter of starting anew and employing trial and error. As one observer noted, there were obvious disadvantages in having to initiate a combat operation in such circumstances, but it was a blessing of sorts as well. The Navy, unencumbered by any river tradition, or "it's always been done this way" syndrome, was free to innovate, to use and refine what would work and discard what would not.

The speed with which the service moved from conception to reality, and the ultimate effectiveness of the operation, is a tribute to the Navy's adaptability to a novel situation and its ability to get things done.

The urgency was the product of the situation. The Viet Cong had put their own priorities on the rich and populous Delta and on the strategically situated Rung Sat. In 1965, they were moving in and through these regions with virtual impunity in battalion-sized units. They levied taxes on the population and menaced the South Vietnamese army. Resupply was no problem. The Rung Sat was a major Viet Cong training and staging area.

The South Vietnamese navy, even with the help of American advisors, did not have the muscle or the leadership necessary to counter the Viet Cong in the waterways of Mekong or the Rung Sat.

The harsh truth, one that had now become clear to the Americans, was that the war could not be won if the Viet Cong were allowed to exercise unchallenged control of the rivers.

Pursuant to Bucklew, Operation Market Time, the coastal patrol and surveillance effort against seaborne infiltration, had begun, first by ships and planes of the Seventh Fleet and, as of August 1, 1965, under the command of Rear Admiral N.G. Ward, Chief, Naval Advisory Group, Saigon.

It was Ward who contemplated expanding Market Time into the Delta and the Rung Sat and with that in mind initiated the studies that confirmed the Viet Cong's stranglehold on those two areas.

When Secretary of Defense Robert McNamara authorized the procurement of craft and other necessities to undertake riverine warfare, events were on the move.

The month after Ward took over Market Time, a brass-plated conference was convened in Saigon to draft the river plans. Sitting in were the Chief of Naval Operations, the Commander-in-Chief, Pacific; the Commander-in-Chief, Pacific Fleet; Commander, United States Military Assistance Command, Vietnam; and the Chief, Naval Advisory Group.

Among the decisions made, one was very concrete and direct: the early acquisition of 120 patrol boats, anticipating operations the following year, which was carried through as envisioned. There followed the episode with Willis Slane, of High Point, North Carolina, and the ultimate contract to a Washington state boatyard to build the PBRs, as described in an earlier chapter.

It did not take long after the September conference for the naval leadership to realize that keeping the river patrol operation under Market Time would not work. The job was far too big and far too different from coastal patrols for that. A separate task force would have to be formed.

Thus it was that Task Force 116 came into being on December 18, 1965. Officially called River Patrol Force, its code name was Operation Gamewarden, and the nickname "Gamewardens," stuck.

The unit might have had another monicker if some of the rather morbid early speculation had turned out to be true. In the winter of 1966, even before the task force had become a reality, Assistant Chief of Naval Operations Leroy V. Swanson, speaking at a luncheon, had this to say: "Some observers have ventured the opinion that this force should be labeled the 'Divine Wind Squadron.' However, we don't feel it will be all that bad." The reference, of course, was to the kamikazes, the Japanese word for "divine wind." River patrol was not a suicide mission, but as the casualty lists would show, the hazards of the operation were considerable.

The original command structure had Gamewarden, like Task Force 115, Market Time, under Admiral Ward as an integral part of the Naval Advisory Group. Later, after the admiral also was named Commander Naval Forces Vietnam, Gamewarden was shifted from the advisory to the operational side.

While boats were being built in Washington and the first crews were undergoing training in California, activity in Vietnam that winter was devoted to preparation for their arrival.

First came the search and procurement of land for seven shore bases and establishment of the logistical and operational apparatus for the unit.

Naval Support Activity Saigon was formed to provide supply, personnel and maintenance support for Gamewarden, which freed the task force commander of everything but operational responsibilities.

Task Force 116 was divided into two task groups, 116.1 assigned to the Delta and 116.2 to the Rung Sat. Each was headed by an officer of commander rank who doubled as the senior naval advisor for his respective zone.

River Squadron 5 also came into being to coincide with Task Force 116. Naval organization typically follows two distinct but parallel lines. Administrative units are squadrons, divisions and sections (later flotillas, squadrons and divisions). The task forces, task groups, task units and task elements are operational in nature, concerned with the mission at hand. Dual command situations often occur. For instance, at one point, the same officer commanded Task Group 116.1, the operational river unit in the Mekong, as well as River Division 51, an administrative unit.

Generally, the numerical designation of units follows in logical progression. Squadron 5 was composed of divisions 51, 52, etc., and divisions were made up of sections with a third digit added. For instance, sections in Division 52 would be designated as 521, 522, and so forth.

The operational chain of command for Gamewarden under the commander of naval forces in Vietnam, Admiral Ward at the outset, were the Task Force 116 commander, and then the task group commanders. Initially, as mentioned, there were two task groups but eventually this number grew to five mainly to reflect the size of the Delta operation. In January 1968, the organization was changed to the following: Task Group 116.1 on the Bassac River, Task Group 116.2 on the Co Chien and Task Group 116.3 on the My Tho. The Rung Sat task group then was designated as 116.4. By mid-year, the fifth task group, 116.5 was added for the upper Delta region.

Under each lower Delta group were PBR and helicopter units, a SEAL detachment and its supporting unit and an LST unit.

The upper Delta group had only PBR and helicopter elements and the Rung Sat group featured a mine countermeasure unit instead of the LST.

Administratively, the chain of command started with the Amphibious Force, Pacific, through River Squadron 5 and then the divisions and sections as described above. At the division level, operational and administrative authority merged. A separate administrative branch covered the LST force under the Landing Ship Flotilla whose commander reported directly to Commander, Amphibious Force, Pacific.

In 1969, the administrative organization for Gamewarden was ratcheted upward one notch. Thus River Squadron 5 became Patrol Flotilla 5, what had been divisions became squadrons, and what had been sections became divisions. Again, this was a reflection of the expanding importance of the river operation, which called for officers of higher rank to take command at different levels of the structure.

An organizational change of significance occurred in May 1966, when Gamewarden, while still in its infancy, got its own commander for the first time. He was Captain B.B. Witham Jr. whose appointment relieved Admiral Ward of direct responsibility for the task force. The first commander of River Squadron 5 was Commander Kenneth Rucker. When the squadron later was upgraded to flotilla, the task force commander doubled as flotilla commander as well.

From the start, the plan was to provide floating bases centered on refitted old LSTs. In fact, that eventuality had been foreseen as early as 1962. But in late 1965, those LSTs were not ready, so as a consequence the first mobile river patrol bases were a fleet LST, the *Floyd County* (762) and three fleet LSDs (Landing Ship Dock), the *Belle Grove* (2), the *Comstock* (19) and the *Tortuga* (26). Each was equipped with a temporary helicopter deck so that the early PBR crews would have some air gunship support. The first of the vessels to be ready was the *Tortuga*, which was deployed in May 1966 with PBRs to the mouths of the Bassac and Co Chien rivers. In keeping with the cautious practice at the time, which would change radically as the war progressed, the sea-going LSD did not enter the rivers proper.

BASES

The Navy envisioned a combination of land and floating bases for its PBR patrols. The latter would be of two kinds, those built around sea-going ships and others that were called non-self-propelled bases. Either way, they were movable.

The fixed bases were thought to be better equipped for the array of support services that would be needed, but the mobile bases were considered more secure from enemy attack. In either case, security was a major consideration and the Gamewardens essentially were required to take care of that matter themselves, though the bases ashore were integrated with local security forces.

The land bases were moved from time to time to reflect the changing situations and the needs of the moment, as were the mobile bases, not just for security, but as part of the learning process in this new style of warfare.

In the early winter of 1966, when Gamewarden was nothing more than an organizational reality, and even that in embryonic form, one of the main matters for attention was the basing. Initially, the aim was to establish bases that would be within about 50 miles of the PBRs' patrol areas, an attainable goal with the combination of shore and floating bases. Planners had to deal with the complication of boats arriving in the theater before the bases were ready for them.

Search and procurement of real estate for seven land bases were undertaken during the winter. These were the selected sites: Cat Lo and Nha Be in the Rung Sat; My Tho on the river

PCFs at N.S.D. Qui Nhon - 1969. (Courtesy of Richard Sidote)

of the same name; Vinh Long on the Co Chien; Long Xuyen and Can Tho on the Bassac, and Sa Dec in the upper Mekong.

Three criteria were applied. A main consideration was readiness and availability for use. All were sites of either Vietnamese or military installations and only Sa Dec was not the location for a Vietnamese River Assault Group base. That site, however, was a Vietnamese army divisional headquarters and in the Sa Dec Canal within the compound was a boat base. A railroad large enough to haul a PBR also would be put to good use.

Second, a good reason existed to have Gamewarden units operate out of Vietnamese navy bases, because at that time, the task force was under the Naval Advisory Group and the two task group commanders doubled as senior advisors for their areas. Having the units of both countries based at the same place greatly facilitated the advisory function.

Third, the locations were selected for strategic reasons. The Navy planners took into account that the three LSTs eventually would be on station, one each supposedly at the mouth of the Bassac, Co Chien and Ham Luong rivers. The objective was to base the PBRs where they could provide the broadest patrol coverage and be in the best position to interdict Viet Cong activities. From a logistical standpoint, all could be reached by air or water.

Choosing the bases was the first step. Preparing them was the second and that is where the Navy's Seabees went to work. They, together with civilian construction crews, began dredging out channels and converting the encampments into semi-permanent facilities. Metal Butler Buildings and "hootches" rose rapidly. The latter were barracks of screen and louvered walls, appropriate for the tropics.

For perimeter security, observation towers and concertina wire appeared. Sandbagged bunkers were built as protection against incoming fire, sometimes referred to by the men as "mail call."

My Tho did not have room for a new base, so Ammi barges, floating pontoons, were towed in as mooring facilities and nearby hotels were leased for berthing, mess and headquarters spaces.

Those seven bases were the initial arrangement. It did not stay that way. For instance, the Cat Lo base in the Rung Sat was closed as soon as Nha Be was ready in June 1966. The latter, centrally located in the Saigon and Rung Sat areas, became the largest PBR base in Vietnam as home to all 40 boats originally assigned to the Rung Sat. Cat Lo, however, continued to serve as a Market Time base.

The Bassac River base of Can Tho was another that Gamewarden left fairly soon. The move mainly was precipitated by the Vietnamese who wanted to shift their RAG operation upstream to Binh Thuy to improve security. The United States unit actually beat its ally to the new location even before the facility was ready and functioned for a while in Spartan accommodations. It was a combination shore and floating arrangement across the road from the Binh Thuy airfield, which was the target of frequent attacks. The Gamewarden base there was completed in June 1967 and it became the second largest PBR base in the country, serving 30 boats.

The other original Bassac River base, at Long Xuyen, also was abandoned in 1967 and the units there redeployed to Tan Chau just below the Cambodian border. The base there was a floating facility, YRBM 16. This style of barge, (Repair, Berthing, Messing), was one of the non-self-propelled water-borne bases referred to earlier.

The reason for the move was the lack of activity at Long Xuyen, contrary to expectations at the onset. The area turned out to be one of the most pacified in the entire Mekong Delta and in fact was the only provincial capital not attacked during the Tet Offensive.

However, the new location was not much more productive of contact than Long Xuyen, so three months later, in July 1967, the YRBM and its PBRs were moved down-river to Binh Thuy and then in September to Ben Tre on the Ham Luong River.

Still another shift occurred in mid-1968 when the fixed land base at Vinh Long was replaced by one afloat, an activated APL, another variety of non-self-propelled facility. The APL, however, remained in the Vinh Long area. The change was occasioned by an experience during Tet when the Viet Cong overran Vinh Long. The PBR crews were berthed two kilometers from the piers and most of them were cut off from the boats by the enemy attack.

Eventually, the Gamewardens would have five floating non-self-propelled bases. Mobile bases were the preferred arrangement because they could be moved frequently, and were, if only a short distance. One of the Viet Cong's tactics was to place mortar-aiming stakes to help correct fire. The short, frequent moves were designed to thwart the enemy's effectiveness in that regard.

Gamewarden also moved its headquarters several times during the course of the operation, starting first in Saigon and shifting then in order to Nha Be in the Rung Sat, Tra Noc near Can Tho and finally to Binh Thuy on the Bassac.

If land basing remained in somewhat a state of flux in the first couple of years of the Gamewarden operation, the same was no less true of the water bases able to move on their own power.

In the early going, the LSDs and the fleet LST would have to do until the four old but specially outfitted LSTs arrived, and that was nearly a year away.

The first inclination of the Navy was to place the sea-going ships off the mouths of the major rivers, but well out into the South China Sea. Behind that decision was both an assumption and a fear, the assumption that the big, clumsy vessels would be unable to maneuver in the confined internal waterways, and the fear that if they tried, they would also be excessively vulnerable to hostile fire from the close range afforded by river banks, mines and sabotage.

However, the Navy found it had little choice. The high seas, especially during monsoon, made it virtually impossible for the little PBRs to operate off-shore. One was lost in the effort. So the LSTs were moved up into more sheltered waters. It turned out that the Navy's misgivings were overdrawn and the ships were able to function quite well.

"Ski." Mark II PBR in Rung Sat Zone - River Division 594. (Courtesy of Bill Curtis)

(Courtesy of Kenneth Delfino)

As a matter of fact, as the war progressed, the LSTs edged ever farther upstream and eventually plied all four of the major rivers with ease and even sailed into the narrow secondary waterways. These seagoing vessels found themselves 100 miles from any ocean, penetrating the country as deeply as the Bassac-Mekong crossover near the Cambodian frontier.

The ever-changing nature of the rivers, with shifting shoals, were, to be sure, navigational hazards and LSTs were known to run aground. But the difficulties were taken into account and the Navy took an uncommonly tolerant view of those missteps.

The Navy's river pilots had gotten good at their jobs. For example, one took an LST safely up the treacherous Ham Luong River at night, a feat worthy of special mention by knowledgeable officers.

The four recommissioned LSTs that would join Gamewarden were the *Garrett County* (786), the *Harnett County* (821) the *Hunterdon County* (838) and the *Jennings County* (846). The first to arrive was the *Jennings County* in November 1966; the others followed shortly thereafter in 1967.

The LSTs had been equipped with a helicopter landing pad with lights for use day or night. A machine shop had been installed in the tank well, and the latest in electronic and communication equipment had been added. Booms were capable of lifting the PBRs. The LSTs served as berthing and messing quarters for the PBRs. They were in all respects a full-service floating base, within the limitations of their spaces, of course. Because of the modification and the many uses to which the ships were being put, the hulls were crammed with little room to spare.

At the start, the LSTs were the best PBR bases in Vietnam. The fixed bases ashore were still in the process of development, but eventually their advantages began to show through. The space restrictions on the LSTs could never be changed, but as the land bases expanded, they afforded more stowage, repair and living spaces than the LSTs could and became the better sites. In recognition of that, PBR units were rotated between LSTs and the fixed bases ashore, whether land or non-self-propelled floating, so that they would more or less share equally the maintenance advantages the LSTs could not provide.

The contribution of the old landing ships and their crews must not be underestimated, however.

The four LSTs rotated in such a way that one always would be off-station for maintenance requirements of its own, usually in Japan or the Philippines. The other three would be stationed in the rivers, one each in the Co Chien, the Bassac and the Ham Luong.

The constant moving to obtain more advantageous positioning or as a security measure did not make life easier for the LST sailor. Every time the river was transited, the crew was called to general quarters, which meant donning helmets and flak jackets and maintaining an alert for any hostile activity.

The PBRs, for which the crews were responsible, came and went at all hours of the night. It was a 24-hour operation. Likewise "flight quarters" exacted a continual demand on the crew. Either for routine patrols or emergency scrambles, alerts might be sounded six to 10 times a day.

Maintenance of the PBRs was a demanding responsibility. The little boats had a hard life. Their engines and weaponry were sorely taxed by the nature of the combat operations and of course they were hit by enemy fire a lot. Sometimes engines or electronic equipment had to be

overhauled and sections of the fiberglass hulls rebuilt. Keeping the PBRs in fighting shape was the task of the base maintenance crews. That often would entail lifting the seven-and-one half ton boats by boom and lowering them down through the tank deck hatch, which seemed barely large enough. It was a task that required much skill.

The helicopter units took care of their own maintenance, but the LST sailors were responsible for keeping the choppers fueled and armed and performed direction during landing operations.

Life on a Gamewarden LST was not all auxiliary-type work as might be typical of "rear areas" in a war zone. As the men who fought that war know, there were no rear areas.

The LSTs were called upon to provide fire support for various operations. Her armament of 40-millimeter cannon, essentially an anti-aircraft weapon in the blue-water Navy, was heavy ordnance on the rivers and the Viet Cong more than once felt their sting.

Two incidents make the point that the LSTs were combatant as well as support ships. The *Jennings County* in May 1968 was credited with killing 17 enemy and destroying many Viet Cong structures during a gunfire mission.

But it worked the other way too. In September of the same year, the *Hunterdon County* came under intense rocket and recoilless rifle fire in a mid-Delta ambush. Two crewmen were killed and 25 were wounded. Damage was extensive to the superstructure, the PBR crane and one PBR. So the Navy's worries about the LSTs' vulnerability were not entirely without foundation, but on balance, the big vessels served their purpose far better by being upstream in the rivers.

The LSTs also did their part in the more pacific aspect of the Vietnam mission. Their personnel participated in the Medical Civil Action Program by going into the villages and tending to various medical needs. They also performed such services as fixing broken rice mills and repairing clothing, often sent by the sailor's families to the people of South Vietnam.

None of the Gamewarden bases, regardless of type, were self-sufficient indefinitely. They were supported and supplied from their parent

command in Saigon. Routine resupply of bulk items was accomplished by way of LSTs, AKLs, a small cargo ship, or various yard or landing craft such as YFs, YFRs, YFUs, and LCUs.

Higher-priority items got to their destination by air, either helicopters or fixed wing craft flying out of Saigon. Commander S.A. Swartztrauber wrote a chapter, *River Patrol Relearned,* for Frank Uhlig Jr.'s *Vietnam: The Naval Story,* In which he described the course a typical urgently needed PBR part might take to get to an LST on the Bassac River. The part would be taken from the Naval Support Activity warehouse in Saigon and flown by NSA helicopter or C-117 from Tan Son Nhut to the Vietnamese air base at Binh Thuy. PBRs at that base then would carry the part south as part of their regular patrol to the northern boundary of the lower Bassac patrol area, where a PBR from the LST needing the part would rendezvous and make the pickup, but also as part of regular patrol operation.

The PBRs were loaded on victory ships in Puget Sound, Washington, and off-loaded at one of three Vietnamese ports at Saigon or the Rung Sat area. They were outfitted at the Cat Lo and Nha Be bases in the Rung Sat and underwent shakedowns there. In April, the first PBR combat patrols were undertaken by Gamewardens in the Rung Sat.

The PBR, as it would turn out, was a marvelously adaptable craft to the purposes set out for it, but in the beginning the Navy was not so sure, and in fact experienced considerable grief.

As reported in an earlier chapter, the hull had been designed by a Bellingham, Washington, boatyard for a pleasure craft, one to be used in clean and peaceful waters, presumably by gentle handlers who were not inclined to be reckless with a considerable personal investment.

Now the PBR had gone to war, to patrol muddy, silty, vegetation-choked rivers, canals, ditches, and creeks. The boats would be roughly driven at high speeds in tropical temperatures and above all, would be shot at. More than that, maintenance and repair would have to take place under wartime conditions.

Shortly after the first PBRs arrived, a board convened by the Navy command in Vietnam concluded that the boats had a life expectancy of six months in the combat zone due to corrosion, hard use and hull deterioration. The recommendation was for complete re-engineering.

Nevertheless, despite the pessimistic outlook, the same boats that were delivered in March 1966 were still operating four years later, and some looked and ran better than they did when they were new.

The reason is a tribute to the Navy's ability to learn maintenance and improve its techniques. That was particularly true with regard to fiberglass repair. Logistical performance improved also so that replacement parts for pumps and engines were expedited through the supply system.

Before that stage was reached, however, the original PBR fleet developed problems that gave cause for grave doubts of the boats' suitability for the job given them. It had to do with speed. While the Jacuzzi jets were designed to propel

Ha Tien - 1969-70 Advisory Team 55, PBR 532. (Courtesy of Robert Rubio)

the boats at about 28 knots, within a couple of years average PBR speed was down to about 13 knots, and some were as slow as 11.5. knots. That would not do, of course, because speed was the PBR's most effective defensive weapon.

Causes of the trouble were multiple. Erosion of the impellor blades had caused the Jacuzzi pumps to deteriorate. Moreover, stryrofoam that had been stuffed into the bow had become waterlogged to the point that the boats were displacing an excessive amount of water. The purpose of the styrofoam was to ensure that the craft would float even if flooded. Finally, poor fiberglass repair had fouled the hull plane, which cost the boat speed.

While the Navy was struggling with this problem, the second generation of PBRs, the Mark II, began arriving, and in them was found part of the solution. The new model had more advanced and more powerful water-jet pumps, and when it was discovered that they could be adapted for Mark I model, the propulsion problem essentially was resolved. The saturated styrofoam was removed from the boats, dried out and reinstalled into newly sealed hulls that would be less susceptible to the same kind of problem. Finally, the boat crews and maintenance personnel had mastered the art of repairing fiberglass, so that the difficulties more or less were smoothed out all at the same time. In fact, the reconditioned Mark I models, which not long before had represented a speed liability, now were capable of 30 knots, faster than original, and commanders had to be admonished to throttle back to 27 knots until structural adjustments could be made, lest damage occur.

Commander S.A. Swartztrauber, in *River Patrol Re-learned*, summed up the skills borne of necessity this way: "There is very little the enemy can do to a PBR that cannot be fixed by local maintenance crews."

One hundred and twenty boats were in the first allocation, 80 destined for the Mekong Delta and 40 to the Rung Sat, based on the best estimates of need at the time.

Both the number of boats devoted to the task and the distribution between the two main locales would change drastically as time passed. It did not take long for the Navy to determine that 80 boats were woefully inadequate to cover the vast Delta, and by the following year the number had risen to 155 and in 1968 to 250. The original ratio of 2-to-1 Delta-to-Rung Sat in due time was changed to 6-to-1, again based on need. Of the total PBR inventory in South Vietnam, 20 were assigned to Combat Tactical Zone I near the North Vietnamese border and another 10 were held for the overhaul and battle damage pool. Though by 1970, maintenance techniques had advanced to the point that boats were not likely to wear out, more than a dozen had been stricken from the register as unsalvageable or damaged beyond repair.

From the beginning of Gamewarden operations, the PBR units were set up in 10-boat sections, stationed at either a floating or fixed base. First four and then five divisions were formed under River Squadron 5, which comprised the entire Gamewarden PBR force, and the sections, usually four or five, fell under the divisions.

The mission of Gamewarden could be simply stated: interdict Viet Cong's resupply efforts, logistical movements and recruitment of soldiers. Further, the goal was to disrupt tax collections, more accurately extortion, exacted from the population by the Viet Cong and deny them, to the extent possible, the virtually free use and sanctuary of the Mekong Delta and Rung Sat the communists had been accustomed to. Toward the end, the PBR force would enforce the nighttime curfew and monitor the heavy daytime traffic.

Combat of a fierce and sudden nature would naturally arise from those activities, but Gamewarden was not a search-and-destroy outfit.

The task set out for Gamewarden was daunting indeed. As mentioned in previous chapters, the Viet Cong enjoyed nearly uncontested primacy in the Delta when the Gamewarden units arrived. The best estimate was that 75 percent of the population of the Delta was controlled or at least intimidated by the Viet Cong. The latter factor is important to consider. The Delta was inhabited by peasants, fishermen, and merchants, mostly, simple people whose main goal was to live in peace and extract a living from the rice paddies, streams and the commerce they supported. Perhaps they were ambivalent or indifferent to the government in Saigon. It would be surprising if most were not. So it should have been natural to expect these Vietnamese unless they were unusually political and loyal to the South Vietnamese government, to at least make a show of sympathy for the strongest presence in their region - and in 1965 that was the Viet Cong. That didn't make the population communist, just fearful and practical. In *The History of the Vietnam War* by Charles T. Kamps, Jr., an unattributed quotation was descriptive of the Delta and the ambivalence that marked its villages: "This the most densely populated area of all Vietnam. You can't walk five steps down here without stumbling on a gaggle of ducks, some kids and an old lady selling soda pop. One old man near Dong Tam doesn't know where his village stands. The kids are helping Americans fill sandbags, the young men are off with the Viet Cong guerrillas and the women are doing the laundry for the soldiers."

The number of Viet Cong and their sympathizers in the Delta was estimated by one source at 80,000 in 1965. Of those, 30,000 were thought to be regular troops and the rest part-time guerrillas capable of operating in units as large as battalion size.

The intricacy of the Viet Cong military organization belied the image of a ragtag band of adventurous revolutionaries loosely bound together. Colonel Victor Croizat, United States Marine Corps, in his book, *The Brown Water Navy*, put the number of Viet Cong troops in the Mekong at 70,000, organized along the following lines: one guerilla squad per hamlet, one guerrilla platoon per village, a separate company per district and one battalion per province, with corresponding reserves at the regional level.

This force made war against both the government of Saigon and the South Vietnamese military by various direct and insidious means. The strategy was to take control of the central Delta in order to isolate the capital and then fan out from there to the peripheral provinces.

The well-trained, well-led army considered itself secure in several strongholds, including the Rung Sat, the Coconut Grove in Go Cong Province, the Cam Son Secret Zone west of My Tho, the U Minh Forest on the western coast, and the Seven Mountains region near the Cambodian border. These areas had the effect of being safe islands from which the Viet Cong could stage and launch attacks, and move troops in, out and through without interference.

Thus the Task Force 116 sailors would be fighting an enemy on the latter's home turf, where he had had a long head start in entrenchment. The Viet Cong, even if they were not indigenous to the Delta, as indicated in a previous chapter, were for the most part veterans of the long war with the French and then the South Vietnamese, a period ranging over 20 years. They knew guerilla warfare, they knew the territory, they were cunning and they were patient.

Furthermore, the Viet Cong, in the Delta and everywhere, were an enemy who in every respect looked exactly like the friends of the allied cause, a situation the Viet Cong of course exploited at every turn, by dressing and acting like farmers and simple folk going about their business.

That included the main mode of transporta-

Loaded Sampan on Cho Chin River - 1968. River Section 523. (Courtesy of Bill Curtis)

(Courtesy of Charles E. Baxter)

Forward EOC at Tinh Binh. The kids made it worthwhile. "Kids are kids." (Courtesy of Jeffrey J. Warnock)

tion, sampan or junk, the two most common native boats found on the many rivers, canals, creeks and other waterways of the Delta.

The Vietnamese had rather precise working definitions of the two kinds of boats. A junk was so designated if it was wide enough for a water buffalo to ride at right angles to the bow and stern, in other words standing athwartship. If the boat was so narrow the animal had to stand the long way, that was a sampan.

To appreciate the task facing the Gamewarden sailors, the nature of the waterways in Delta life had to be understood. In every respect they were the highways of the region. That's how people traveled, moved merchandise and in general conducted their ordinary affairs.

During the day, the rivers would be choked with boat traffic and to the unpracticed eye, at least, there was little to distinguish a harmless Vietnamese family in daily pursuit of commerce from Viet Cong attempting to move weapons or food to comrades in arms.

That briefly was the situation into which the fledgling Gamewardens operation was injected in the early months of 1966. The inaugural Delta PBR patrol was on May 8 of that year when boats of Section 511, moved out from Can Tho on the Bassac River.

One of the first operational decisions, to which the Navy generally would adhere throughout, was to patrol in pairs. The standard rotation of the five teams in a 10-boat section was for one to work during the day, three at night and one to remain at the base.

Each section was responsible for about 30 linear miles of waterway and zones were established so as not quite to overlap, though they came close enough that at times patrols from different divisions would see each other.

The two boats would operate in line from 400 to 600 yards apart. This distance was devised as providing the best balance for mutual fire support and maximum radar coverage during night patrols. The boats also were far enough apart to deprive Charlie of the chance for getting two boats with one barrage in an ambush.

Since much of what the PBR patrols did was to intercept and inspect boats, the doctrine became quite precise. The PBR conducting the search would always approach at an angle that allowed the most guns to be brought to bear on

the possible target. Commanders usually tried to carry out this activity as close to midstream as possible to increase the range from either bank. The PBR would not tie up to the sampan or junk, so that freedom of motion was always maintained.

The second PBR would cover the near shore in particular, but would position itself so that it could fire on both if necessary. The boat conducting the search always had one of its .50 calibers trained on the bank opposite the activity.

If the contact was at night, meaning the chance of hostility was greater, the PBR would approach at high speed without lights and then suddenly illuminate the suspect craft. If the Vietnamese aboard showed no sign of belligerence, everyone would be ordered to show himself before the PBR came alongside.

Gamewarden personnel had not read any of this in a manual. They had learned by doing and in effect were writing the manual as they went along.

Searching sampans was probably the most tedious and at times unpleasant work the Gamewarden sailors had to do. What made it less rewarding still was the fact that in most cases, contraband was not found. In those instances, providing their identification papers were in order, the Vietnamese would be allowed to go on their way. That does not mean this phase of the operation was fruitless, however, because the mere knowledge by the Viet Cong of the new American naval presence in the Delta and the inspections being conducted forced the enemy to alter his behavior.

Crawling into the lower spaces of a sampan, not knowing what to expect, was surely no easy matter for the PBR crewmen. Different situations might cause different reactions. One sailor, knowing the cargo space would be alive with cockroaches, could barely bring himself to enter. It could get worse than that. One of the Viet Cong's favorite tricks was to tack the tail of one of Vietnam's many poisonous snakes to the bottom of hold, knowing that some unwitting American sailor would come up and the reptile would be in an ugly mood.

Besides the sweltering heat, uncomfortable conditions and onerous physical labor associated with searching boats, the Americans, with their well-developed sense of personal privacy

and property, knew they in effect were invading the homes of people in their own land, people who presumably had committed no offense. But it was war and it was necessary if the population was not to be victimized in an even worse manner. In some ways, the operation was counterproductive to the non-combat objective of the United States forces, which was pacification of the region by winning over the population.

Some of the Gamewarden sailors saw the situation in more positive terms than that, however. The statement of a young lieutenant, as quoted without attribution in *Brown Water, Black Berets,* from an article in *True* magazine in February 1968, is worth repeating here: "I'm still new here and maybe I'll change my mind. But the way I see it, this Vietnamese family is off in a sampan to catch a few fish, and here comes this rugged green boat shooting a shot across the bow. It's carrying a lot of tall, round-eyed white men wearing thick armored vests with all sorts of weapons, who board their boat - which is their home - and search through everything."

"Then just when they are most terrified, these huge Americans give the kid a bar of candy and the father a pack of cigarettes, and smile and wave them on. The next time we pass that sampan on the river, the family waves back. I swear to God that means something to me. You can talk all you want about your firefights, but I think this other kind of thing might add up to more in the end."

The American tradition of the kind Yank was long and well-earned, and the Navy officer's comments proved it was not dead in Vietnam. Tough fighting men did not necessarily lose their ideals.

While endless inspections and searches were the normal daytime routine for the PBR crews, at night there were far less traffic to deal with, but it was more likely to be hostile. In fact, if the nighttime curfew imposed on the civilian population had been strictly obeyed, any movement on the river at night could be presumed to be unfriendly and the Gamewardens could have saved themselves the anxiety and danger of letting the Viet Cong first reveal themselves.

Unfortunately, the curfew was not always kept and the Americans knew that. Again, it might have been hard for the Vietnamese to be told that they couldn't enter their own rivers, maybe to fish, in their own boats. For whatever reasons, curfew violations were not that uncommon, and sometimes that could have the tragic consequences of unoffending Vietnamese coming under friendly fire because of the difficulty in establishing their identity and intentions. It was the nature of war, and particularly this war.

The different objectives of the Viet Cong and the Gamewardens task force helped shape the conflict. The Viet Cong mainly wanted to retain the freedom of movement and operation it had previously enjoyed. The Americans were trying to interfere as much as possible. Consequently, the United States Navy was more eager to fight than was Charlie, and to the extent that the Viet Cong initiated combat, it demonstrated the effectiveness of Gamewardens interdiction effort.

The Viet Cong was nothing if not a clever and cunning enemy. As the PBR crews developed tactics and methodology, the guerillas were learning also.

For instance, they studied the Navy's patterns on the river, and would wait hidden on the heavily foliated shore for a patrol to pass and then cross.

During the day, the Viet Cong were even more subtle. By mingling with the heavy sampan traffic that was normal, the communists might avoid detection by the sheer odds against being one of the boats selected for inspection.

The Viet Cong hid contraband beneath the cargo a boat might normally be carrying. As the step-up in United States activity increased, the Viet Cong was obliged to employ such devices as hiding material beneath the boat or in false bottoms.

The enemy would set up one boat with proper identification and no contraband as a decoy. While the PBRs were detaining that boat, another, one moving supplies or personnel, could escape from the area. The sailors could divide their attention only so many ways.

A seemingly empty boat, the Viet Cong learned, was often considered less suspicious by the Americans, and might be allowed to pass. One guerilla told of carrying only explosives, and that hidden in the overhead of his boat.

The Viet Cong learned American tendencies and exploited them. They knew, for instance, that the sailors would respond to medical emergencies, so they would plant an injured Vietnamese in a boat as a distraction while the sampan carrying the contraband slipped through undetected. As a matter of fact, the Gamewarden PBRs served as water ambulance more or less regularly as the occasion demanded, not just for wounded comrades, but for Vietnamese nationals as well. All PBR crewmen were trained in first-aid, which was fortunate because among other medical requirements placed on them, they helped deliver at least eight Vietnamese babies aboard PBRs that were not able to get pregnant women to hamlet hospitals quite fast enough. Dave Roever, a Gamewarden sailor in 1969, described in his book, *Welcome Home, Davey*, how on more than one occasion he performed the humanitarian service of relieving and treating painful injuries to Vietnamese through such knowledge as he had.

The South Vietnamese government's attempt to control the enemy's use of the waterways included requiring cargo manifests and the identification papers, which would be checked against a black list when a Vietnamese boat was stopped.

Here again, however, the Viet Cong proved too wickedly adept in the art of forgery and other circumvention. They would use people with legitimate papers to move their material of war, and sometimes would steal the documentation from innocent civilians, either to use themselves or create confusion among the allies who were ever trying to sort out friend from enemy.

If the natural difficulties posed by an entrenched and crafty enemy in his home territory were not enough, other impediments, some of them artificial or politically inspired, added to problems faced by Gamewardens.

For example, early in the operation, the rules of engagement prohibited the PBRs from firing at a target unless fired upon. The implications of that order are plain to see. A suspicious boat could ignore a Navy order to halt for

Bringing school supplies to a local school in Chau Doc - 1969. Ens. Warnock and Lt. Dick Hicks. (Courtesy of Jeffrey J. Warncock)

inspection with virtual impunity, so long as it could outrun or outmaneuver the PBR. And some of the Viet Cong's motorized sampans were capable of 30 knots, which was at least as fast as the PBRs. The Navy was permitted to fire warning shots when a Vietnamese boat failed to obey an order, but if the Viet Cong in such a situation maintained sufficient discipline to avoid firing its weapon, there is little the Gamewarden crew could do to stop the enemy boat. That order, thankfully, was changed in October 1966.

Another problem had to do with merchant shipping through the navigable rivers of the Mekong system that led into Cambodia, upon which the capital, Phnom Penh, depended. A treaty between Cambodia and South Vietnam ensured free passage. As a consequence, PBRs were not permitted to stop any steel-hulled merchant ship flying a foreign flag, a restriction many exploited by off-loading cargo in midstream onto a small boat or by dropping it overboard for later recovery.

The only countermeasure available to the Gamewardens force to that tactic was to try to apprehend any craft that had taken cargo from the big ship in mid-river, but the PBRs had to wait until the small boat was no longer alongside. The rules did not make life or the accomplishments of the assigned mission any easier for the PBR sailors.

In a typical morning, when sampan and junk traffic was heavy, a PBR team might stop up to 300 boats. In an average month, the number for the entire Gamewarden task force was about 200,000 boats detected, about half that number boarded for at least cursory inspection and about half of those, roughly 50,000, for a thorough inspection.

Selections were made on the basis of experience, the presence of any suspicious tell-tale signs, or perhaps intuition.

Beside sampans and junks, some of them quite large, traffic on the rivers included water taxis, up to 60 feet in length and loaded with

passengers, any one of whom might be an armed Viet Cong ready to use his weapon on the American sailors who had boarded.

Dave Roever described the job of boat search, which he said could take all day on a large junk: "There were a million places on those vessels to hide stuff. We had to look behind everything, never knowing when we would reach into something and have our heads blown off. It was scary, especially when we were poking around down in some dark, cramped hole."

Roever recalled that the sailors looked for hidden passages and doors that wouldn't open. Weapons or other contraband could easily be hidden in the holds beneath tons of rice. The Gamewardens used long poles to poke down through the grain to determine whether anything solid could be felt. Even clothing of the occupants was checked. It could be booby-trapped.

A favorite hiding place of the Viet Cong for grenades and small-caliber ammunition, Roever learned, was in pottery canisters that were used to carry a rancid sauce made from decomposing fish. The Viet Cong relied on the typical American aversion to anything that smelled so foul, believing they would not stick their hands down into that mess. Roever wrote that he would. In fact, it was his insight that sense of smell was a Viet Cong advantage, the result of the cultural acceptance of body odor. Americans, of course, bathed regularly when they could and used deodorants and lotions, by which, Roever believed, the Viet Cong could detect their enemies when near.

In addition to the usual four-man PBR crews, civilian Vietnamese policemen often were assigned to ride the boats to serve as interpreters and to otherwise establish a Vietnamese national presence in the American operations. Because they wore a white hat, a white shirt and blue pants, they were called "white mice" by the sailors.

The policemen accompanied the patrols in which interrogation was expected. Mostly the questions were fairly simple, according to Roever,

Crew of PBR 6670 from Go Dau Ha. Picture taken at Ben Keo, near Tay Ninh - July, 1969. GMG-3 Lopresti (Steve) of Tularr, Calif., RD-1 Slimmer (Norm) of Millville, N.J., (Saufatuck, Mich.), MM-2 Bartholomew (Jeff) of Albany, N.Y. and GMG-3 Sheridan (T. J.) of San Antonio, Tex. Monkey "Charlie" Go Dau Ha RVN. (Courtesy of Norman H. Slimmer, Jr.)

such as, "Have you seen the Viet Cong?" or "What makes you think they are here?"

The "white mice" were not always loyal or trustworthy. Roever said some turned out to be Viet Cong, helping the sailors with inspections by day and shooting at them by night, as he put it. On one occasion, one of the policemen stole every weapon that wasn't bolted down from the boat.

CREWMAN

Boats, ships, weapons, hardware of all kinds, bases, supplies and organization all are vital to any war effort, obviously, but nothing gets done without the men who put themselves on the line day in and day out. Any combat commander at any level would quickly confirm that reality.

It has been the proud history of the United States military that through many wars, countless units have distinguished themselves by their achievements, courage and esprit de corps. There is reason to believe the United States Navy Gamewarden of the Vietnam War stood out in that respect, exemplifying the American fighting man.

Commander (later Rear Admiral), S.A. Swarztrauber, who himself served in a combat role on South Vietnam's rivers, wrote of PBR sailors: "Their morale is the highest of any this writer has ever seen in the service." In his article, *River Patrol Re-learned*, Swarztrauber pointed out that "in spite of poor, uncomfortable living and working conditions, rigorously long hours and constant danger, one out of every five PBR crewmen requests a six-month extension of his tour in Vietnam."

Many sailors volunteered for river duty, often out of the blue-water fleet and even straight out of training. In fact when Gamewardens was being organized, two succeeding gunnery classes at Great Lakes Naval Training Center to a man requested assignment to the outfit.

They did not do so in expectation of soft or safe duty. A PBR crewman had a one in three chance of landing on a casualty list, and many of them were wounded more than once. One commander was dismayed to observe a six percent per month casualty rate, which over a year's time would come to 72 percent, ordinarily an unacceptable loss for any military unit.

Throughout the Vietnam War, 2,663 Navy men were killed in action. Many were pilots, many were hospital corpsmen serving with the Marine Corps, a smaller number were in the deep-water fleet offshore, but a significant number were the river fighters, not a large contingent as military units go.

Detailed figures are available for 1967. That year, Gamewardens lost 39 dead and nine missing and 366 wounded. The following year, the task force collected more than 500 Purple Hearts.

In 1969, the Gamewardens task force counted 80 dead, 47 of them PBR crewmen lost in direct contact with the enemy. During that year, one of the worst in terms of casualties suffered by the unit, the SEALs lost seven men and the two air contingents, helicopter and fixed wing, 12.

The list of Gamewardens killed in Vietnam is indicative of the diversity of the force. No fewer than 26 enlisted ratings were represented among those who lost their lives. Leading that list were 38 enginemen followed closely by 36 gunner's mates, and then 22 boatswain's mates. Those figures are not surprising since piloting the boat, operating and maintaining its power

plant and manning the weapons were the three main functions aboard a PBR. But fire controlmen, radarmen, radioman, electronics technicians, machinist's mates, quartermasters, signalmen, commissarymen, yeoman, torpedomen, damage controlmen, storekeepers and others all were represented on the casualty list.

Two monuments, one in Norfolk, Virginia, and one in San Diego, California, are inscribed with the names of 251 men of Task Force 116, the Gamewardens, who lost their lives in Vietnam. That is a substantial number for a force that at any given time accounted for only about one half of one percent of the military personnel in the theater. It is a ratio, in fact, that is comparable to that of all forces over the duration of the war, which of course included front-line ground units.

The enemy paid a dear price for the casualties inflicted, however. The Gamewardens kill ratio was 40 to 1, one of the highest of any combat unit in the theater. In an average week, Gamewardens accounted for 75 enemy dead, and in 1967 alone, the Viet Cong suffered about 1,400 personnel casualties at the hands of Gamewarden surface and air units.

The PBR force also was the most highly decorated naval command of the war. Again, in 1968 alone, the Gamewardens earned one Medal of Honor, the unit's second, six Navy Crosses, 24 Silver Stars, 290 Bronze Stars, 363 Navy Commendation Medals and scores of other decorations. A Gamewarden sailor coming home was likely to be wearing an impressive array of "fruit salad" on his left chest.

Haste should be made to point out that Gamewardens was not just PBR and their crews. While Swarztrauber's remarks were specifically about the men of the patrol boats, they could apply as well to the other elements of Task Force 116, which included SEALs, helicopter and Black Pony crews, the sailors who manned the minesweepers in the Rung Sat as well as the LST and LSD crewmen and the base support personnel, whose skill and tireless efforts helped make the whole operation work. They could never rest in the security of being in the "rear," which in Vietnam hardly existed.

But to return to the PBR divisions, there were solid reasons for their extraordinary high morale and splendid motivation. The smallness of the unit and the intensity of the shared danger contributed to the special closeness a PBR crew would feel. There was also a special bond to their craft. It is axiomatic that a ship or boat is an extension of the men who serve on her, and the smaller the vessel, the truer that is. Submariners know the feeling, and so do destroyermen in the blue-water Navy. But four or five men riding a 31-foot boat into danger repeatedly over a period of months lends a whole new meaning to the relationship of men to vessel and to each other.

A remarkable aspect of that fact had to do with drug use, or rather the lack of it. Dave Roever in his book pointed out that in his experience as a PBR crewman, about six months, he was not aware of heroin, marijuana or hashish usage among his fellow sailors, though it is no secret that in the Vietnam theater as a whole, drug consumption could be a problem.

Jim Guthrie makes the same point. "Because we were team players, we didn't use drugs or smoke marijuana. But the movies depict all Vietnam veterans as dope addicts."

The reason the PBR men were an exception is not hard to understand. Units so small, whose members are so interdependent for their very lives, cannot tolerate the impairment that would naturally occur if any one of them were high on narcotics. It was a matter of self-policing by men who for reasons of self-preservation declared, perhaps tacitly, that using dope was unacceptable. Infantrymen, as an example, fought in similarly desperate situations and depended upon each other as well, but their basic units were larger. That made a difference.

Another morale factor was the huge amount of responsibility placed on PBR crewmen out of all proportion to their rank. Enlisted men were called upon to make decisions and exercise leadership in ways that would be unheard of in more traditional Navy settings. Boat captains, usually first class petty officers, were authorized to take action and demonstrate initiative that would be reserved for commissioned officers of middle ranks aboard a destroyer, for instance. The phenomenon is an interesting commentary on the character of the young American, at least this group. They craved the chance to take the lead, to make a direct and up-close contribution to their country's mission, even at great hazard to themselves. Rather than shirking responsibility, and the potential difficulties that can come with it, they coveted the opportunity. At ages 19 to 24, as many of the Gamewarden sailors were, men are not inclined to sentimentality, so at the time some of them might have rejected the loftier descriptions of their motivations. But the facts speak for themselves. And some men were unabashed about their feelings. Signalman Third Class Jere Beery, about whom much more will be learned later in the book, described his outlook in Lieutenant Commander Cutler's *Brown Water, Black Berets*: "You've got to look at the positive end of things because to think of the negative end of things is a waste of time. That's not valuable or useful information. We were volunteers. Patriots. We were gung-ho as hell. We'd look for trouble."

The black berets, incidentally, were adopted by the river sailors as their peculiar emblem, which of course made its own contribution to the sense of unit and pride. The Gamewardens did not indulge in initiation rites except one that was quite specific, and no doubt was a special moment for each sailor when his time came. A Gamewarden man was entitled to notch the back strap of his beret after he had experienced his first enemy fire. Such was the nature of river warfare that beret straps did not remain unnotched for long for most new arrivals.

The PBR crew of four, whose captain usually had been selected and specially trained in the United States, consisted also of an engineman, a gunner's mate and a seaman. All except the coxwain, or pilot at the time, were gunners during firefights.

Cross-training to a high degree was essential. Every man aboard had to be adept at handling all the weapons, working with the engines, operating the electronic gear - radar and radios - and piloting the boat.

The Navy tried to find its boat captains from the so-called deck ratings, meaning boatswain's mates, quartermasters, gunner's mates and radarmen, but the needs often were such that cooks, clerks and engineering ratings also served. The PBRs essentially adopted the submarine one-rate philosophy to the extent that what a given sailor was doing at a given time did not necessarily have a lot to do with the kind of "crow" he wore on his left sleeve.

A two-boat patrol would usually have five men aboard each vessel. In addition to the regular crew, the lead boat would carry the patrol commander, most often a chief petty officer, a warrant officer or a junior officer, up through the rank of lieutenant. The second boat would carry the English-speaking Vietnamese policeman that often was assigned to patrols, particularly when interpretation or interrogation was anticipated. Six of national policemen were assigned to each section.

Because of battle casualties and other personnel circumstances, a certain amount of "fleeting up" was necessary, meaning men assumed responsibility beyond their rank. Some highly qualified second-class petty officers became boat captains, and some first-class petty officers took command of patrols. One of the latter, in fact, distinguished himself in a singular way, becoming one of the most highly decorated Americans of the entire Vietnam war. Descriptions of his exploits will come later.

PBR duty sometimes was tedious and boring, sometimes it was violent and terrifying, but always, it was exhausting.

The average PBR sailor could count on 80 to 90 hours of patrol duty per week, about half of it at night. The PBR was underway about 40 percent of the time, and when her crews were not on the river, they spent many hours in cleaning, repairing and refueling the boat or doing maintenance on engines, electronics, weapons, and personal gear. Sleep had the last priority.

The PBR man's living accommodations varied with the kind of base his unit was billeted to, whether it was an LST, a non-self-propelled floating base, or a fixed land site. On an LST, berthing and messing was much like any shipboard existence, highly crowded. The other bases were more like barracks. Some base locations, at least, afforded the men off-base diversions.

Guthrie described life at a base camp named Tuey Nhon on a small canal. The men were issued a half cup of potable water for brushing of teeth and shaving, and showers of rationed water of ambient temperature were available. Living quarters were tents with plywood floors. Toilet facilities were a small wooden box covered with a tarpaulin and cantilevered over the river.

The diet could be monotonous when C-rations for some reason couldn't get upriver. On one occasion the river sailors had beans and peanut butter three times a day for six weeks. The mess hall was also a wooden box, bigger than the head, covered with a tarp. Metal trays were dipped in common garbage pails of water after the meals, not the most sanitary arrangement.

Ens. Warnock at Vinh Te Canal - 1969.

River Division 514 change of command (Old CO - LCDR Mulford, New CO - LCDR Roper). Shown left to right - Lt. Paul Roberts, Lt. Dick Hicks, LCDR Mike Mulford, LCDR Jim Roper and Ens. Jeff Warnock. (Courtesy of Jeffrey J. Warnock)

"That is one of the reasons we had a lot of dysentery." Guthrie says.

When the weather was dry at Tuey Nhon, a powdery dust covered everything. When it rained, the dust turned to a gummy mud as much as calf-deep.

Dave Roever's book provides a look at two types of bases. His first assignment was to Sa Dec in the upper Mekong, a compound established ashore. Living quarters were one half mile from the boats, which were tied up alongside the supply and ammunition barges. The compound was built with security in mind. Sandbagged bunkers and guard stations were strategically located. Berthing was in a wood and canvas structure designed for tropical existence. The walls came only to about eye level, leaving a space beneath the roof for air to circulate. That building, which housed the 150 men who made up the boat and support personnel, was the only one not air-conditioned in the compound, but most of the men had electric fans, which made the spaces livable at least. The head (showers and toilet facilities) was in a separate building. The compound included a library and a bar for off-duty diversions.

The second base was at Tan An, located west of Saigon on the Vam Co Tay River, a tributary of a river formed from an upstream split from the Mekong proper. A mobile barracks called an MB2 provided the berthing space. It was like a ship on the inside, with hatches and the like, but it was spacious, clean and comfortable. Here, however, with the living arrangements on the river itself, security became more of a concern, and constant vigilance against mines and other hazards was required.

Swarztrauber offered an impressive statistical perspective on the Gamewarden task force's workload in an average month. PBRs put in 65,000 to 70,000 patrol hours. Seawolf helicopters flew about 1,500 hours and SEALs launched about 60 missions. Minesweepers engaged in 75 antimine patrols, and LSTs engaged in 20 fire-support missions. The PBR and Seawolf contingents participated in about 80 firefights each. The cost to the enemy, besides the aforementioned 75 confirmed kills, included destruction of 80 watercraft and 125 structures. The proverbial difference between night and day applied literally to the PBRs. The daytime routine, described in some detail previously, was mostly inspecting river craft in search of contraband, draft-dodgers, forgers, or any other Viet Cong activity. Actual combat was far more likely after dark. But it could work the other way too, with interdiction operations at night and firefights during the day.

As with boat inspections, combat tactics had to be developed and refined as the unit matured and learned by trial and error.

At the outset, PBR tactics were less aggressive than they later would become. For instance, initially when fired upon, the boat would return fire and call for help, leaving the area until help arrived. Later it was learned that the firepower of the PBRs and the fighting skill of their crews would allow them to stand and exchange fire with the enemy, usually with success. The Gamewardens, in fact, did not lose many firefights.

Also, 'the early patrols were instructed to stay on the wide main rivers where distance to the bank afforded some security. After the PBRs began to prove their effectiveness, commanders were given discretion to venture up the narrower, and far more dangerous, secondary streams and canals.

One Gamewarden officer who had little patience with orders dictating caution was Lieutenant Commander Donald Sheppard, who arrived in 1967 to command two PBR sections, 20 boats and 130 men, on the Bassac River. It was still early in the task force's experience and the tactics that later would become more commonplace as the unit pushed up into the narrow canals, Sheppard put into place early. His approach was described in the review of his book, *Riverine*. The reviewer was John F. Wukovits, whose work appeared in August 1993 issue of *Vietnam* magazine. Sheppard, placing the most liberal interpretation possible on instructions to stay in the middle of the wide rivers, organized aggressive missions in conjunction with SEALs, Air Force, Army and Vietnamese units, with impressive results.

He emphasized the importance, however, of the more pacific work done by the Gamewarden sailors among the Vietnamese civilians, which he felt was not sufficiently appreciated or understood except, as he said, possibly by the Vietnamese themselves.

The most common form of PBR combat throughout the war was the ambush, and it worked both ways. The Viet Cong employed the tactic largely to further its main goal, and that was logistical movement, resupply, reinforcements and the conduct of its nefarious affairs among the Delta and Rung Sat populations. Of course, the guerillas considered inflicting casualties and damage on the Americans worthwhile, but if they could have gone about their business while avoiding contact with the United States Navy, they would have done so. Every Viet Cong ambush, in effect, was a message that Gamewarden was doing an effective job of forcing the enemy into changing his habits and inhibiting his movements.

The PBR force also initiated some of the fights as consistent with the objective of neutralizing the Viet Cong in the wetlands region. One way to do that was to destroy as much of the VC's war-making potential as possible.

Tactics on both sides could be intricate. The Viet Cong, fighting on home turf of long familiarity, were not to be underestimated for their cunning. They often chose times of low tide for ambush so the PBRs would have trouble maneuvering in the shallower water. The enemy, by studying the American movements, would know when a patrol was nearing its end. By attacking then, the Viet Cong surmised the sailors were most fatigued and less alert, and therefore vulnerable. The enemy was capable of digging himself into well-fortified bunkers, from which he could launch an attack and still be somewhat invulnerable to return fire, even when air support was called in. One of the favorite Viet Cong tricks, which once again relied on the fundamental decency of the Americans, was to set up fish traps. The PBR sailors, to avoid disturbing gear they assumed had been placed by Vietnamese civilians, would maneuver around it and into a place anticipated by the Viet Cong for an ambush. Or, if Charlie had massed firepower on one side of a stream, he would fire a couple of shots from the other side in hope of driving the PBRs closer to the more dangerous shore. The Viet Cong placed command-detonated mines in the water, waiting for the Americans to pass. Aiming stakes were an effective tactic. These would be driven so that they barely showed and the Viet Cong would use them to sight their weapons in advance, virtually ensuring themselves of at least initial accuracy when the PBRs would pass over a certain point. A particularly devious trick in a narrow waterway was to fell a tree across the stream in the path of the PBR and then trap the boat by cutting another tree behind it.

The PBRs were not lambs among the lions by any means. Gamewarden boats would set up ambushes of their own in areas where intelligence information or the boat commanders' judgement told them to expect enemy activity. The boats frequently would hide themselves along banks until the Viet Cong made a move, or perhaps drift quietly with the current, using a starlight scope to try to detect enemy movements.

Guthrie told of one favorite tactic when the PBR patrol wanted to set an ambush. Both boats would run at full speed to make as much noise as possible before the cover boat shut down. The lead boat then went another 100 yards and shut its engines also. "This was to make the Viet Cong lose track of one or both boats. Both boats would drift down the river until they came in contact with the river bank," Guthrie related.

A variation of this was called "engine reversing." Two PBRs would run toward each other from opposite directions. At the point of nearly passing each other, one would cut its engines as the other throttled up one engine and throttled back the other. This had the effect of creating an illusion of two boats passing, which led the Viet Cong to believe it was safe for them to cross. The boats in the meantime would have drifted to a place of advantage.

The *Illustrated History of Riverine Force* by John Forbes and Robert Williams carries some unattributed insights into ambush strategy. One PBR veteran observed that if intelligence data was sufficient, the process of selecting an ambush site was easy. It would be anywhere athwart the Viet Cong route of travel that would provide adequate concealment and field of fire. Lacking that information, however, as was more likely, the contest more nearly resembled a chess match, inasmuch as both sides knew the river and where the best crossings were. It was a matter of one trying to outguess or outmaneuver the other.

Another river fighter noted that one favorable aspect of operations on the waterways was that the sailors generally could anticipate where action would occur. Running the big rivers tended to be uneventful, but when the boats turned into one of the canals, they could expect trouble because ambush almost always occurred. But if that prospect was a near certainty, the identity of the enemy was not.

"It's hard to tell most of the time who your enemy is, because a man can be standing out in a field waving to you one day, and then you'll draw sniper fire from the same place that night," the sailor commented.

If the Viet Cong had some advantages in

stealth and familiarity with the territory, that was offset in large measure by the technological support provided the Americans and the sailor's own natural acumen and ingenuity with things mechanical.

PBR men on the line relied on their intelligence and the experience gained in the field to adapt, adjust and solve problems. They had to make exceptionally practical decisions that could make all the difference between success and failure of a mission, or even survival itself. For instance, commanders had to decide between the advantage of extra ammunition and the loss of speed the weight would cause, between the protection flak jackets provided and the effects of the heat from wearing them, between the problem of engine noise and the value of power.

The scientific community at home was a major help on the highly technical matters, developing such devices as underwater detection gear, infrared and ultraviolet spotlights and fluorescent chemical boat-marking systems. The Navy itself was giving official recognition to the new demands of river warfare. A master's thesis at the Naval Postgraduate School in Monterey, California, was entitled, *A Mathematical Analysis of Tactics in a Riverine Ambush.* Another was, *A Probability Model and Patrol Planning Device for Counter-Insurgency Operations on the Mekong River.* There is an almost unreal incongruity between such scholarly titles as those and the bare-knuckle slugfests out on a remote Southeast Asian river between machine guns, grenade launchers, rockets and recoilless rifles to which the studies would apply, but those works nevertheless probably contained solid material that, in addition to the experience in the field, contributed to the development of riverine warfare doctrine that was noticeably missing when the war began.

The sailors on the firing line were innovative also, adding their own improvements to the ways of doing things. They used small outboard engines that allowed their boats to move more quietly through the water when avoiding detection was the goal. At least one crew mounted a light machine gun on top of the boat's canopy to provide additional elevation that allowed firing over raised canal banks when the tide was low. Jury-rigged acoustical devices were put together by use of soda cans filled with pebbles and attached to trip wires strung across the stream. The Gamewardens even took a page from the American Indians' book by using bows to fire flaming arrows at combustible structures on shore. Some river boats employed real flame-throwers, but the PBR men had to improvise a lighter duty version. A photograph in *Riverine Force* by John Forbes and Robert Williams shows the unorthodox Lieutenant Commander Sheppard using a longbow to ignite a bamboo hut concealing a fortified Viet Cong bunker on a bank of the Bassac River in November 1967.

Roever described a more sophisticated tactic his team employed in an area called the Devil's Hole, an island criss-crossed by canals in the Sa Dec area that was thought to be a major Viet Cong stronghold. If the patrol made itself seen at the village at night, there would be no activity. The curfew was in effect and the Viet Cong knew better than to show themselves. So the boats cruised past the village during an after-

noon and casually dumped garbage overboard. In the refuse was a sensitive hydrophone, which sank to the bottom of the 10-foot canal. The device was attached to a thin, strong wire, about two miles worth, spooled aft on one of the PBRs. The boats moved down the canal playing out the wire until the right place was found to drop anchor and await developments. At nightfall, the amplifier aboard the boat was turned on and now the PBR men could hear what the hydrophone heard. Furthermore, they knew the precise range, because the length of wire used was measured accurately.

Sure enough, about 11:00 p.m., the sailors heard the click-click of a boat moving down the canal at the point of the listening device, which was at the intersection of two important canals. That was their signal to fire a mortar round (some river boats had mortars mounted piggy-back over the machine guns). The unsuspecting people on the boats surely were puzzled at the fact that the Americans knew where they were. One round apparently scored a direct hit, because the next day splinters from a sampan were found on the surface at that point. The crews did not worry that their targets might have been innocent villagers, inasmuch as the curfew was in place and no movement had been discovered when the boats operated in the open.

Even in cases where the Navy would seek to provoke hostile contact, the initiative usually fell to the Viet Cong for the main reason that it was easier for people traveling light to hide along the bank, where vegetation was usually heavy, than it was for the Gamewardens to hide their boats out on a river or canal.

In the Forbes-Williams book, a PBR crewman described how the Viet Cong usually got the first shot but after the first moments, all the advantage swung to the Yanks: "They've got to initiate the firefight because we couldn't see them. But it only took a matter of two second to start firing your weapon and usually when the Viet Cong hit us, maybe their first two or three rockets would be on target and the rest would go wide, or high or low - for the simple reason that as soon as they exposed themselves they were in trouble."

"They couldn't afford to stand up because when a column of boats opens up, in theory, there's about five guns working on each boat. If I jumped up and saw just one boat with two .50s and two .20s looking at me, I don't think I'd jump up too often. Out of all the firefights I've been in, I've only seen the Viet Cong once. He was behind a bunker and he decided to get up and run, which was not a very good idea because he didn't get more than two feet."

The Gamewardens could count on outgunning the Viet Cong because they knew what to expect from the enemy weaponry. The Viet Cong most often used AK-47 automatic rifles, 57-millimeter recoilless rifles and two models of rocket-propelled grenade launchers, the B-40 and the B-41. The latter was considered the more dangerous by the PBR sailors. The weapons usually were fired at exceptionally close range, though the B-40 was effective at 120 meters and the recoilless rifle at about 1,000 meters.

The Viet Cong learned to fear the grenade launcher in the boat's arsenal. A competent gun-

ner could send all 36 grenades on the way before the first one fell. A barrage of that magnitude, grenades falling in rapid succession on an enemy position, was usually sufficient to silence the opposition.

The .50 calibers were potent weapons as well, capable of spitting 500 rounds per minute from each barrel in a pattern that crossed about 500 yards out. Every fifth round was a tracer so that a gunner at night could see the path of his firing. The barrels would glow red with heat and in fact would overheat unless the gunner used the short-burst technique. The .50s were not easy to control and their range was long enough that the crewmen had to take care against hitting friendly targets ashore. Roever told how practice taught him how to adjust his firing for the pitch his PBR might experience, especially when caught in another boat's bow wave.

CLEARWATER

The PBR Navy was essentially a Mekong Delta and Rung Sat fleet, but not altogether. The little men-of-war also saw action on the rivers in the northern regions of South Vietnam, in CTZ I, or "Eye Corps," starting in 1967.

The initial operation there was by a Gamewarden task unit, but later a new task force, named only Clearwater with no numerical designation, was formed to carry out patrol efforts on the Cua Viet and Perfume Rivers. The Clearwater PBRs were part of River Division 55 and River Section 521, both administrative branches of River Squadron 5, the PBR component for Gamewarden.

Operation Clearwater, while not operationally part of Gamewarden, was formed from Task Force 116 assets and adopted the Delta operations as its prototype.

The first patrol-boat venture into the northern zone was dubbed Operation Green Wave as part of Gamewarden, albeit far afield from the principal locale of that force. Officially it was Task Unit 116.1.3.

In September 1967, the Gamewarden LST *Hunterdon County* with a 10-boat PBR section aboard arrived off Cau Hai Bay 17 miles northwest of Da Nang, ready to begin fulfilling the new Navy mission of instituting I Corps river patrol.

Green Wave did not enjoy an auspicious start. The LST could not safely enter the bay. Thus PBRs had to be unloaded in the open seas and be recovered likewise, dangerous maneuvers. The trips by the little boats to their patrol areas and back to the base ship were through high swells and heavy surf, which resulted in frequent groundings. It was the early experience of Gamewarden in the south all over again, when LSTs and LSDs tried to serve as PBR bases from off the river mouths instead of upstream in sheltered water.

Patrol in this vicinity was relatively uneventful, but after about 10 days, the Hunterdon County moved her PBRs south to the Cua Dai River about 18 miles southeast of Da Nang, and from that point, the river war became hotter for the Green Wave boats, as became apparent almost immediately. The first day, four PBRs left Coastal Group 14 headquarters after a briefing and had not moved more than 1,000 yards from the base when they came under intense automatic weapons fire. The boats withdrew at high speed, but in the process PBR 118 was hit five times and lost all the oil to its engines, damaging them so severely the craft was put out of commission. The only personnel casualty was a Vietnamese sailor who suffered a gunshot wound in the groin.

The next day, September 29, was much worse. A total of 15 separate incidents were recorded on a day described by the task unit commander as a "running gun battle." The first firefight of the day occurred just before noon when PBRs 54 and 79 were patrolling about five miles upstream near Hoi An. The boats took about 20 rounds of rifle grenade and about 200 rounds of small-arms fire, killing one crewman and wounding another.

Two other PBRs, 53 and 84, came under fire later in the day in the same area and called in Army helicopters for support. Friendly fire destroyed 15 enemy huts and bunkers. The same surface-air team encountered Viet Cong sampans, sank three of them and killed at least seven Viet Cong.

By the end of the day, Navy commanders on the scene concluded that was enough. Patrols were suspended. The main reason was that the engagements to that point had involved relatively light enemy armament and still the PBRs had their hands full. The commanders feared the

consequences if the Viet Cong decided to bring up the heavy stuff.

In terminating Green Wave a little more than a week later, a report from naval headquarters in Saigon took note of the 50-percent damage rate among the 10-boat division, from groundings or battle. Navigational hazards diminished two of the PBRs' most important natural assets, speed and maneuverability. The small boats, the report continued, were not designed to stand against the weaponry the enemy was able to bring to bear in that particular environment.

The recommendation was that PBR development in I Corps end, and as a result, the Hunterdon County loaded up her PBRs and headed back to the familiar environment of the Mekong.

The termination of Green Wave, however, did not end small-boat warfare in the northern combat zone. The PBRs, some of the same ones actually, would be back before their crews could have expected.

Early the same year, Marine Lieutenant General Lewis Walt had been asking for Navy patrol craft to protect supply movements on the Perfume and Cua Viet rivers in I Corps. The Perfume River, so called because of the fragrance of the floral abundance that grew along its banks, flowed down from Hue, the old capital of the two Vietnams. The Cua Viet farther north

connected the South China Sea with Dona Ha, from which the key base of Khe Sanh at the DMZ was supplied.

The Navy was reluctant to part with boats that already were inadequate in number to do the job required of them in the Mekong Delta and Rung Sat, but the urgency of the needs to the north was recognized and accommodated. A mobile base constructed of pontoons would be established on each of the two rivers, the first on the Perfume, and a division of PBRs, some of the same boats that had gone south after Green Wave in October, returned before the end of 1967 to join the new base, MB1, which was set up at Tan My.

The PBRs began security and population control patrols on the Perfume on January 9, 1968, much as they would be doing in the Mekong system.

The problem remained with the Cua Viet, however, where enemy pressure was growing and the supply situation to the besieged Marine outpost at Khe Sanh was precarious. Supplies were airlifted the last 20 miles to that base from Dong Ha, but the first leg was by sea from Da Nang and the dangerous second one was the 10 miles up the Cua Viet.

Conditions argued against sending more PBRs, however. The second mobile base had not been established for their berthing and mainte-

nance, and they were not considered sufficiently armored or armed for the heavy action that might come from the banks.

Consequently, Task Force 117, the mobile riverine force from the Delta, transferred a division of brawnier monitors, armored troop carriers and communications command boats to the Cua Viet to provide convoy security for the vital logistical shipments up the river.

Task Force Clearwater was formed on February 24, 1968, under the command of Captain G.W. Smith, who set up headquarters aboard MB1 at Tan My, but five days later transferred north to Cua Viet at the mouth of the river of that name.

One peculiarity of the task force and its command structure was the inter-service mix. Smith reported to an Army general and had a Marine searchlight unit in his outfit. His force also was supported by Army helicopter and signal units.

Smith broke the task force into two groups, one each for the Perfume and Cua Viet.

Before those organizational developments, however, the Tet Offensive already had changed the nature of the mission, at least for the time.

Before that coordinated country-wide attack was launched by the enemy on January 31, PBRs patrolling the Perfume and lagoons of the region had encountered only light Viet Cong activity. On that first day, personnel at the supply-loading ramp at Hue radioed that the attack was on. Eight PBRs sped upriver and when they arrived, they ran into rocket, mortar and small-arms fire from enemy troops on the north bank opposite the ramp. The PBRs succeeded in holding off the enemy until Marines moved in that evening to secure the area.

After Tet had spent itself, the American force on the Perfume River kept matters generally under control, though occasional attacks still occurred on the boats and the ramp at Hue. By

June, the area was considered pacified to the extent that the PBRs received permission to resume Gamewarden-like patrol and security operations.

Psychological tactics played a part. An officer remembered the Vietnamese in the Hue area honored the dragon as a powerful and honorable figure; therefore the PBRs began flying dragon-head flags and passing out materials with the symbol of the dragon. Predictably, the people began referring to the PBRs as "dragon boats." As in the Delta, the PBRs conducted humanitarian missions, making medical and dental aid visits to the villages. The work paid off. When the population contrasted the help the Americans provided to the massacre carried out by the communists while they were in control during Tet, the sentiment swung sharply toward the allied side. That translated into tangible cooperation, on the Perfume and the Cua Viet as well.

Through the winter and early spring, attacks continued on the Cua Viet against the river columns, a situation that prompted another change in procedure.

Ranking officers concluded the speedy PBRs were better suited after all to respond to the attacks than the more heavily armed, but slower, craft from the river assault unit. So the monitors and other elements of River Assault Division 12 were returned to the Delta - though the ATCs stayed for mine countermeasures - and a section of PBRs was deployed from the Rung Sat. Five boats arrived in May and five the following month. Other equipment changes occurred when the ATCs were relieved by LCM-6s converted for minesweeping, eight specially outfitted LCPLs (the 13-knot river patrol boats that preceded the PBRs) were sent to the Cua Viet and the three PAVCs that last had seen action in the Plain of Reeds were deployed with the Hue group. That vehicle was thought to be ideal for the marshes, paddies and lagoons, which turned

out to be the case. The vehicle proved effective in working with infantry in pursuit of enemy ground troops who could not evade the fast craft by any means. The hovercraft also were useful for medical evacuation and for extracting friendly troops in an emergency. The Navy PAVCs were sent back to the United States in mid-1969, but the Army was so impressed with their performance that service replaced them with Pack Vees of their own.

There was no PBR base at Cua Viet for the incoming boats because that location was within artillery range of the DMZ, the Navy thought better of following its original plan and establishing MB2 at Cua Viet. That facility was sent to the Delta instead.

The Cua Viet PBR division would have to undergo repair and upkeep 40 miles south at MB1, Tan My, which was reinforced with more support personnel for that purpose.

True to the United States military tradition of improvisation in the face of tough tasks, NSA at Da Nang developed an ingenious way to transport PBRs to the maintenance base. Personnel there rigged an LCM-8 in such a way that it could serve as a small floating dry dock. That was done by equipping the craft with PBR skids in the well deck and installing special plumbing to ballast and deballast the tanks.

A change in command of Task Force Clearwater brought Commander Sayre Schwarztrauber to the post in the fall of 1968 after he had spent six months as commander of River Squadron 5 in Gamewarden.

A few months into his Clearwater command, the ambush threat along the Cua Viet had all but disappeared, but mines were still a problem, as were artillery barrages against the base itself at the river's mouth.

The place was described in Cutler's book, *Brown Water, Black Berets.* It was an austere place of sandbags and half-buried quonsets where men kept their flak jackets, helmets and personal weapons close at hand.

The shelling from the DMZ was frequent, but since Cua Viet was at the far end of the artillery range, it was notoriously inaccurate. Still, the amount of ammunition being expended argued for an occasional fluke, as had happened a few months before when a direct hit was scored on the mess hall, killing the cook. Swarztrauber regretted the casualty, of course, and was also disturbed that Hanoi Hannah, the North Vietnamese version of Tokyo Rose, knew about the mess hall hit, indicating the enemy had inside contacts.

Clearwater, like its counterparts to the south, did its job according to the measurement that counted: Enemy forces were neutralized and the supply shipping got through.

A tribute was paid to the men of Clearwater by Commander R.L. Schreadley in a 1971 article, quoted in part in Cutler's book. This paragraph was devoted to the men stationed at Cua Viet: "The men at Cua Viet lived little better than moles in heavily bunkered huts burrowed down among the sand dunes. When the rain stopped falling, the sand, fine and gritty, began to blow, accumulating in drifts before the huts, sifting through the screens and under doors, finding its way into lockers and between sheets and even into the food the men ate."

Some of the young guys of YFNB-21 — YRBM-16 at Chau Doc, Vietnam. (Courtesy of Julius Hornyak)

M-60 on engine covers on Co Chin River - November, 1968. River Section 523/River Division 572. Photo by GMG-3 Bill Curtis. (Courtesy of Bill Curtis)

The routine was so difficult at that advance base that the Navy instituted a rotation system to Da Nang or Tan My so that no sailor would have to spend more than six months at Cua Viet. Schreadley took note of the high level of morale among the men that led many to volunteer to complete their tour of duty in the northern location.

The Clearwater mission was turned over to the Vietnamese navy in June 1970 and the task force as such was dissolved.

MINES

Mines were a major threat to allied shipping in Vietnam and the job of combatting it on the inland waterways fell largely to the Gamewarden task force and its small fleet of minesweepers, the 57-foot MSBs and the converted LCM-6s, redesignated MSMs.

The most critical area was the Rung Sat, because through the Viet Cong infested tangle of rivers, swamps, canals, mangroves and nipa wound the shipping channel to Saigon. The popu-lation of the 400-square-mile area was about 16,000, about 10 percent of which was considered hard-core Viet Cong, plus an unknown number of sympathizers. Most residents were peasants interested in extracting a living as rice-farmers, fishermen or wood-cutters in the tidal swamps and densely vegetated area that also teemed with alligators and snakes as well as huge shrimp. It was inhospitable territory for the out-sider, which made it a perfect Viet Cong liar. The principal rivers were the Long Tau, the major deep-water channel from the South China Sea to Saigon and the wider but shallower Soi Rap. At the confluence of those two streams was Nha Be, the principal United States Navy and Vietnam-ese base.

The Viet Cong's use of mines was both sophisticated and primitive. The enemy employed a wide variety of devices and tactics and usually could be credited with ingenuity.

However, the Viet Cong never succeeded in its major specific goal, to sink a large enough vessel to block the channel, or in its overall objective of choking off vital wartime shipping to the capital. The potential was always there, and had it succeeded, clearing the waterway would have taken days or weeks and broken a supply link central to the war effort.

As an example of the kind of damage the enemy was capable of, sappers set a mine against the hull of an American escort carrier and sank her at the dock at Saigon early in the war.

Later, mines sank two large freighters in the Long Tau, but the primary Viet Cong objective was not met. In May 1965, one cargo ship hit a mine near Nha Be, but the pilot managed to beach her before she could sink in the channel. Likewise in August 1966, the 10,000-ton freighter SS *Baton Rouge Victory* was mined 20 miles out of Saigon with the loss of seven crewmen, but that vessel was able to move out of the channel before she went down. So mine warfare in Viet-nam was serious business, especially near Saigon.

The first United States Navy river mine-sweepers, four MSBs, arrived on the Long Tau in the Rung Sat on March 10, 1966, from Da Nang to form the nucleus of a new unit, Mine Squadron 11, also designated Detachment Alpha. Gamewarden, or Task Force 116, was being formed at about the same time with a Rung Sat task group, and the mine squadron operationally was placed under that command.

The need for mine-clearing expanded con-tinually. Within the first year, eight more MSBs were shipped from the United States together with two officers and 106 enlisted men to pro-vide the manpower. In 1968, the detachment became Mine Division 112 with six MSBs and five MSMs, and a second division of the same strength, 113, was formed.

Before the growth and reorganization of the force, Detachment Alpha already had distin-guished itself on the rivers and was awarded the Presidential Unit Citation.

Some minesweeping assets were diverted to the north, away from the Combat Tactical Zones III and IV where Gamewarden had and would do the great bulk of its fighting.

Sweepers were assigned in three-boat units each to Cam Ranh Bay, Da Nang, Qui Nhon, and Nha Trang to sweep harbors, and to the Perfume and Cua Viet rivers in CTZ I near the North Vietnamese border.

On the Long Tau, the South Vietnamese navy was responsible for sweeping the channel from Nhe Be, site of the United States base, north to Saigon, a distance of nine miles. The Ameri-can minesweepers took it from Nhe Be to the South China Sea.

The level of Viet Cong resistance to the sweeping operations was indicative of the im-portance the guerrillas attached to disrupting shipping and the threat they perceived the Navy units to be to their plans.

Until early 1966, the Viet Cong had virtu-ally free rein in the Rung Sat, but at about the time the Gamewardens made their first appear-ance there, a joint United States Marine-United States Navy-Vietnamese marine amphibious expedition had the effect of at least trimming back Viet Cong dominance of the area.

The operation dubbed "Jackstay," was launched about two weeks after the arrival of the first Gamewarden minesweepers to the Rung Sat, but before the first PBRs or their crews had landed.

The Gamewarden participation in Jackstay was at most marginal, though the four MSBs were working the rivers before and during the operation and thus made a contribution. Also, the LCPL river patrols, the immediate forerunners of the Gamewarden PBRs, took part by engaging Viet Cong on the banks. The first shipment of PBRs and their still-novice crews were aboard the LSD *Belle Grove* off Vung Tau, and while the PBRs engaged in training runs, they did not participate directly in Jackstay.

Jackstay, though limited in size of the force and time committed to it, was considered a major success in challenging the Viet Cong in their most secure sanctuary. United States Marines found and destroyed large amounts of weapons and the equipment for making them, as well as tunnels and other hiding places for the Viet Cong. Enemy casualties were unknown, but they certainly were much higher than the allied losses of five men. The main value of Jackstay was in the demonstration that where the Vietnamese Army had previously been reluctant to fight, the Americans could and would, and do so effectively. It is doubtful that the Viet Cong ever felt quite so secure in the Rung Sat after that.

However, Charlie still had plenty of bite, still wanted to do as much mischief as he could with mines and was ready to engage the mine force directly when it suited his purpose. The enemy would coordinate his mine attacks with gunfire assaults from the river banks.

The favorite mine of the Viet Cong, in the Long Tau at least, was command-detonated. The explosive device itself was most often locally made from metal drums or fish buoys, to which were attached wires that ran along the bottom of the river to a concealed control point on shore, from where a Viet Cong could activate the mine at the optimum time, that is when the target allied vessel was at its closest, possibly directly over the mine. Defoliation of the banks eventually cramped the Viet Cong's style in this regard by driving the guerrillas so far off the river that they lost their vantage point.

While the mines described above required little sophistication, some more advanced Soviet-made mines also were discovered in the Long Tau River during the war.

Sweeping tactics on that waterway consisted mainly of cutting the bottom-running wires. The MSBs and MSMs both accomplished this effectively by trailing cutters on chain drags. The boats also were capable of sweeping for influence and moored mines as well.

Another effective mine countermeasure was use of grenades. Sailors learned that anything floating in the water might be a mine, whether it looked like one or not, so a grenade tossed nearby could be counted on to explode the weapon and might cause sympathetic blasts that would take out others also.

That somewhat unorthodox approach to anti-mine warfare was found to be the best tactic against a mine used with some success by the Viet Cong in the Cua Viet River to the north. The mine, which could be assembled on the river bank, would float just beneath the surface of the muddy water and thus be hard for sailors to see. The mine was nothing more than a straw basket slung from an inner tube. The resourceful enemy could fashion mines out of clothespins and toy balloons as well. These were crude devices, but they could be deadly. River sailors on the Cua Viet fired many a small-arms round at floating hibiscus plants because they resembled the Viet Cong mines.

The Viet Cong carried out an aggressive mine campaign on the Cua Viet, which was a major supply line to I Corps ground units, and to the lesser extent on the Perfume River, 40 miles to the south. The Cua Viet was close enough to the DMZ to make it a short run for the North Vietnamese to deliver the mines. The river, shallow and narrow, was susceptible to mining, and the communist tried to take full advantage of it. They managed to sink so large a vessel as an LST, and on another occasion, a large mine exploded under an ATC (converted LCM used as an armored troop carrier) and capsized it with a loss of six crewmen.

Originally, the mine-sweeping assets on the Cua Viet consisted of LCM-6s that had been locally converted for the purpose, but in 1968 as the threat became more serious, MSMs, previously converted LCM-6s as well as MSBs were moved from the Rung Sat where they had been part of Mine Division 113. The MSMs were outfitted with a device called Shadowgraph, a kind of sonar capable of detecting mines in the river. The mine threat on the Cua Viet was much greater for ships moving upriver, because the current would carry the free-floating mines toward the vessels. The downstream trip allowed the boats to drift at about the speed as the mines.

The rivers of the Mekong Delta were vulnerable to mining also, but the Viet Cong did not engage in that type of warfare there as they did in the Rung Sat and on the Cua Viet. The reason is not hard to understand. The Delta streams were less vital for allied supply, and since the Viet Cong themselves needed to use those waterways, floating or moored mines that recognized no flags would not do.

The favorite mine tactic in the Delta was use of the limpet carried by swimmers and placed against hulls. This was a threat Gamewarden and riverine forces were constantly aware of and on guard against, and with good reason. For instance, in November 1967, YRBM 16, a floating PBR base, was heavily damaged by an explo-

sion, presumably from a limpet mine, near Ben Tre on the Ham Luong River.

Some of the hottest mine-boat action took place in the Rung Sat, and it began in earnest the first year the minesweepers were on station. From the beginning of the sweep runs, sniper fire from shore was not unusual. In September 1966, Charlie threw a heavier punch at MSB 15, connecting with a 57-millimeter recoilless rifle round. The next month, the detachment lost its first boat, MSB 54, which hit a mine and sank with a loss of two dead and four wounded of the crew of seven.

Fog presented its own hazard. During the early hours of January 14, 1967, MSB 14, was sweeping in the Long Tau about 30 miles south of Saigon. Visibility was virtually nil in the thick soup, from which a Norwegian motor ship suddenly emerged. The larger vessel hit the minesweeper amidships, cutting her in two with a loss of three American sailors.

Undoubtedly the toughest day of the war for the Gamewarden's minesweeping detachment

EN-2 Jim Davy, boat captain PBR 756, River Division 593. Taken on the upper Saigon River during Operation Ready Deck - September, 1969. (Courtesy of James D. Davy)

(Courtesy of Kenneth A. Delfino)

(Courtesy of Kenneth A. Delfino)

was February 15, 1967. Tet is a term that forever is engrained in the American mind as the time of the North Vietnamese-Viet Cong offensive starting in January 1968. However, the Vietnamese celebrated their Lunar New Year annually, and evidently the communists found it a propitious time for stepped up military action.

The mid-February day in 1967 was the end of Tet in that Year of the Goat. The account that follows is based on one by Commander Cutler in *Brown Water, Black Berets.* He described the Detachment Alpha sailors rolling out of their netted bunks in the Nha Be base hootches at 5:00 a.m., trudging the raised wooden walkways in the barbed-wire encircled compound to the head and later pulling on the "uniform of the day," which might range from dungarees to fatigues or include only a t-shirt below the flak jackets.

They were ready for the day's work. It would be a hard one. A few minutes past six, MSB 49 and MSB 51 backed away from their moorings and headed down the Long Tau to begin the morning's sweep. The crews were veterans. They had conducted many sweeps and had been under fire, most recently two weeks before when an automatic weapons fusillade from the bank had coincided with the detonation astern of a mine that one of the boat's sweep gear had bagged.

The 49-boat was slightly off the bow of its companion as the two craft headed into the first big bend. Ambush awaited. From both banks recoilless rifle and machine-gun fire poured into 49. From the port side, three recoilless rifle rounds hit the boat, one of them setting the fuel tanks afire. The boat headed toward the shore so as to beach before sinking.

The 51 boat meanwhile was firing at enemy positions in support, and under the command of Boatswain's Mate First Class Hood it came in close behind its crippled mate despite withering fire in its own direction. Several PBRs were on the scene by that time, and they managed to keep the Viet Cong pinned down sufficiently that men from the 51 were able to evacuate the 49 boat's

crew, some of whom were wounded, and strip the armament form the disabled minesweeper.

Navy helicopter gunships arrived to lend fire support and they too were targets of heavy ground fire. As the choppers swept the enemy positions for about one half mile on either side, they were hit five times, but stayed in the air.

A fixed-wing air strike was called in to precede a four-company regional ground force team's sweep of the area. The troops found 10 75-millimeter recoilless rifle casings, a Claymore mine and two dead enemy soldiers.

MSB 49 was towed back to Nhe Be by LCMs and the 51 boat, now in company of MSB 32, resumed sweep operations.

At mid-morning, another two-boat team, MSBs 45 and 22, was sweeping about 15 miles southeast of their base when the 45 was struck by a command-detonated mine and sank almost immediately. Four of the five survivors pulled from the debris-covered water by the 22 boat were wounded. The search failed to locate Third Class Damage Controlman Gary Paddock, whose body was found three days later.

The day's fighting was not over for MSB 51, which had engaged in the morning's first action with the 49 boat. At 1428, the craft took two direct hits, one in the stack and one on the sweep winch, and in company with the 32 boat and two PBRs reversed course and headed north. Two miles upstream, the column ran into another ambush that led to a fierce firefight involving four more PBRs, helicopters and fixed-wing aircraft.

The casualty toll for the day was two American sailors killed and 16 wounded. The next day, action continued when MSBs 16 and 52 were attacked three and one-half miles from Nha Be.

The two days of combat persuaded the Navy to beef up the firepower of the MSBs with the installation of M-18 grenade launchers.

Additionally, another section of PBRs was added to operate from the LST *Jennings County* at the mouth of the Long Tau, and B-52 strikes

were called in to hit strategic points in the Rung Sat.

On February 16, the Commander of Naval Forces in Vietnam sent this message in recognition of the minesweeper action:

"The courageous action, bulldog tenacity, and personal heroism that the men of Detachment Alpha have demonstrated under fire is in keeping with the highest traditions of the Navy. It is singularly significant that in spite of yesterday's efforts by the Viet Cong, the river remains open and unblocked. Your resolution in continuing maximum coverage of the Long Tau with available resources is highly gratifying."

The statement was made relatively early in the mine unit's deployment in the Rung Sat, yet the observation that the crucial shipping lane remained open could have been made at any subsequent time.

The mine force would take some losses, but the ultimate test of its performance was found in the failure of the Viet Cong to accomplish the only goal that really mattered in that regard, blocking the flow of supplies up the Long Tau or Soi Rap.

By any measure, the mine divisions succeeded in their mission.

AIRWING

Not long after the inception of river patrol activity by the United States Navy in South Vietnam, commanders knew an air arm would be essential to the operation. The little PBRs, as quick and tough in the clinches as they would prove to be, were known to be entirely too vulnerable in certain situations without fire support.

Captain Burt Witham, Jr. (ret.), the first commander of Task Force 116, recalled that the initial belief was that the South Vietnamese army's artillery in the river-and-canal country would fulfill that function, but events proved otherwise.

One of the main problems, according to Witham, was the bureaucratic delays required. Channels had to be observed before a fire mission could be called, and the proper Vietnamese authorities were not always available. When hostile fire is being taken, there is not time for politics or logistical games.

So the alternative, and a better one, was attachment of air units, both helicopters and fixed-wing craft, to the task force.

By time Operation Gamewarden was conceived late in 1965 and put on line early the next year, the United States Army already had experience in helicopter combat in close support of activity on the ground. The Navy had none, meaning no personnel with the specific training required and no equipment of the type the job needed.

That would be rectified in fairly short order with the help of the Army.

The Army's gunship helicopter flown in support of infantry was the Bell UH-1B Iroquois, better known as a Huey. An inter-service agreement was reached whereby the Army was to lend the Navy 22 of those craft for use in Gamewarden, replace any that were lost, and train the Navy crews in gunship tactics. It was believed, correctly as it turned out, that what Army helos could do for troops on the ground was adaptable for the Navy in assistance to river patrol craft. In the meantime, such early helo support as the PBRs would need, Army crews would provide.

The PBRs did not arrive in Vietnam until March 1966. By then, two Army Hueys and personnel had been assigned to Task Force 116. They came from the 197th Aviation Company, which furnished the craft, crews and maintenance for Gamewarden's helicopter operations until the Navy was ready to take over, which would be in the fall of 1966.

The first operation by the Army choppers, called a Light Helo Fire Team, in support of PBRs was from the USS *Belle Grove,* LSD 2, a temporary base for the river craft and helicopters until Gamewarden LSTs became available.

Training of the first Navy crews began in June 1966 by the Army's 120th Aviation Company at Saigon when the first detachment led by Lieutenant Commander William Rockwell arrived in Vietnam. Pilots selected for this role were the Helicopter Combat Support Squadron One in Imperial Beach, California, which was formed into four detachments. Eight officers and eight enlisted men were assigned to each detachment, which reflected air crew breakdown, commissioned pilots and co-pilots and enlisted crew chiefs and door gunners. Each of the two helos in each detachment thus would have two full crews to accommodate schedules of 24 hours on and 24 hours off they eventually would follow in combat.

The gunship personnel were not unschooled in aviation, of course, but like the PBR sailors, they were soon to be entering a different environment than they might have imagined. The pilots were trained in ASW (antisubmarine warfare) patrols that employed a much heavier helicopter than the Huey and in non-combat search-and-rescue operations off aircraft carriers. The Navy determined that retraining pilots already proficient in helicopters was more efficient than waiting for fresh graduates from flight school. The enlisted men were "airdales," that is their ratings were in aviation specialties.

The Army also took on the initial burden of depot maintenance and supply of spare parts and ammunition. They Army's contribution to the Navy river mission was invaluable and not without its cost. An Army pilot was killed in September 1966 while flying a mission on behalf of Gamewarden.

The original crews were the only ones trained entirely in-country for gunship duty. Subsequently, pilots, crew chiefs and gunners underwent training at the stateside Army posts, Fort Benning, Georgia, and Fort Rucker, Alabama. The flight drills included entering narrow hollows in a dense forest that left barely enough room for the craft's blades and flying for two miles through woods similar to that to be found in the Mekong Delta.

The enlisted personnel were given brief maintenance training at Fort Eustis, Virginia. When they arrived in Vietnam, experienced Navy hands were ready to complete their familiarization. Maintenance crews also underwent stateside training at Army bases, ordnancemen, for instance, at the Aberdeen Proving Ground in Maryland, and electronics technicians at Fort Gordon, Georgia.

By the end of 1966, Gamewarden had eight Hueys arranged in two-craft fire teams, or detachments. They were deployed so that their scant number could provide maximum coverage. Detachments were assigned to Vung Tau on the coast, Nha Be in the Rung Sat, Vinh Long in the Delta and aboard the USS *Comstock* (LSD-19) cruising offshore. Vung Tau was also headquarters for HC-1, as the new outfit was designated, and those two helos were held for the maintenance pool there.

The Navy's helicopter unit reached its organizational maturity in April 1967 with the formation of Helicopter Attack (Light) Squadron 3, which absorbed all the detachments of HC-1. In September, the full complement of 22 helos initially pledged was reached. Seven two-ship fire teams were deployed to the three Gamewarden LSTs and four fixed bases by detachment number as follows: (1) LST *Jennings County*; (2) Nha Be; (3) Vinh Long; (4) LST *Garrett County;* (5) LST *Harnett County*; (6) Dong Tam; and (7) Binh Thuy. The other eight choppers were assigned to the maintenance pool at Vung Tau, the initial squadron headquarters.

The Navy's maintenance performance in the Seawolf Squadron was remarkable. When the Hueys were turned over to the Navy the craft already had had considerable flying time, and since spare parts tended to be in short supply, the Army maintenance crews had been obliged to improvise with unofficial field modifications. Thus the Navy had on its hands well-worn craft that were no longer standard in many ways. Yet the maintenance specialists succeeded in keeping the helos in the air to the maximum degree.

HAL - 3's commanding officer was a captain who reported administratively to Commander, Fleet Air, Western Pacific, and operationally to the Task Force 116 commander, in line with the Navy's system of parallel com-

(Courtesy of Kenneth A. Delfino)

(Courtesy of Kenneth A. Delfino)

mand tracks. The maintenance facility and squadron headquarters were moved to Binh Thuy in 1969.

With the commissioning of HAL-3 came a new name for both the aircraft and the men who flew and maintained them. They were called the Seawolves, and they, like the PBR men fighting below them on the waterways, adopted the black beret as their emblem.

The shared head-gear symbolized the relationship between surface and air. An untold number of PBR sailors owe their lives to the Seawolves who often would arrive in time to turn a firefight in favor of the small boats, or would evacuate a wounded man to a place of medical aid. Indicative of the respect the PBR men had for their comrades in the air was the remark by one decorated river sailor about the Seawolves: "They had only one fault - there was never enough of them."

Like the Hueys and infantrymen of the Army, the Seawolves and the PBRs developed an effective joint combat doctrine that served Gamewarden's objectives well and doubtless kept United States casualties down.

Seawolf missions fell usually into one of four categories: a scramble to respond to a river patrol under fire, medical evacuation, reconnaissance flight, or escort duty for PBR teams entering especially dangerous territory. About 80 percent of the missions were emergency scrambles.

When they were in the air, of course, the Seawolves potentially were available for any duty that might arise, including supporting riverine assault operations, assisting downed Army helicopters, and engaging in psychological projects.

The routine of the helicopters had to be carefully devised, because their flying time was limited to about 90 minutes and the average PBR patrol was 12 hours. Obviously, the helos could not provide constant air cover for the surface craft. They could be on the scene of trouble quickly, however. Generally, a patrol would be no more than 15 minutes' flight time from helicopter help, and often less than that.

The two-helo fire team was analogous to the two-boat patrol team even to the command structure. One of the choppers was designated as the lead, the other as the cover, and the pilot of the former was considered the team commander on a given mission.

Standard procedure called for the lead helicopter to fly about 100 feet above the second craft during patrols or en route to a mission location so that each would have a clear field of fire forward the moment enemy contact was made. During actual combat, the helicopters would circle over the target with each ship alternately firing or providing cover.

The great advantage helicopters had over the PBRs below was in their crews' ability to see into and on both sides of the tree lines, which frequently held Viet Cong positions and were the most common targets of the Seawolves. They were effective against sampans, junks, bunkers and fleeing troops also. Unless a close look was imperative, Seawolf pilots generally avoided tree-top flying, which put their craft in excessive danger from ground fire.

During combat, all four men aboard were actively engaged in firing. The pilot usually fired the 2.75-inch rockets, two pods of seven each, and the co-pilot handled the externally mounted M-60 machine guns. Both of those weapons could be fired only in the direction of the helicopter's heading. Thus the most effective weapons were those fired from the side doors, because they could swing in a semi-sphere. The crew chief and door gunner sprayed their targets either with M-60s or the heavier .50 calibers or launched grenades from the M-79 weapons. At first, it was feared the Iroquois frame was not substantial enough to withstand the stress from a .50 caliber machine gun, but once this was found not to be true, gradual replacement of M-60s on one side of the Seawolves was undertaken.

The HAL-3 craft worked night and day, and scrambles often interrupted the 24-hour "off" period. Night combat operations were simpler in at least one way because the source of enemy fire could be determined more easily.

One clever night tactic employed by the two-helo fire teams was to draw enemy fire by sending one craft in low over suspected Viet Cong positions with its running lights on, while the second chopper hovered darkened above. If the enemy revealed himself, he would have the considerable firepower of two helicopters to contend with. The ploy was virtually identical to one used by the PBRs on the surface.

The availability of aircraft was a continuing problem. The Army seldom had them to spare, though in April 1969, the Navy's quota was raised from 22 to 33 because of the arrival of a more advanced Army gunship helo, the 200-knot Hueycobra (AH-1G). The Navy itself received a newer model Huey, the C-type, as part of the expansion of its stock. Additionally, another detachment known as Sealords (not to be confused with a major naval operation of the same name) was formed with the UH-11 Huey, an unarmed craft called a slick.

Their main function was SEAL insertions and various utility duties such as mail runs, supply missions and personnel transfers.

Even with the added helicopters, the desired number of fire teams, about 15, was not achieved. That would have provided one team for each PBR base. Even better would have been one fire team for each PBR section. One factor that kept the Seawolves spread thinly was the expansion of their responsibilities. Early in 1971, Detachment 4 widened its scope to include an area north of Saigon, and Detachment 6 began operating in support of the 1st and 25th division's riverine forces.

The Seawolves emerged from their tours with Gamewarden as veteran combat aviators, many of whom earned as many as 25 Air Medals. Indicative of the fighting record of HAL-3 was the impressive array of decorations its men were awarded. Seawolves received five Navy Crosses, 31 Silver Stars, 219 Distinguished Flying Crosses, 15,964 Air Medals and 156 Purple Hearts.

Gunships engaged in countless fights on the way to that record. Seawolves participated roundly in the epic battle of Oct. 31, 1966, on a canal off the My Tho River, which is described in detail elsewhere in the book. The next day, overconfident Viet Cong, not yet accustomed to encountering the United States Navy from the air in this manner, were surprised at the ferocity of an attack by three helicopters the enemy thought had passed. In the end, 23 Viet Cong sampans and 25 camouflaged supply buildings had been destroyed.

In December of the same year, Seawolf gunships responding to a surface firefight involving PBRs on the My Tho, made firing runs that touched off a huge explosion. The score for the day was 15 guerrillas killed and 28 sampans destroyed.

The last day of combat for one of the original 32 Seawolf pilots was described in a chapter on the outfit by Dick Rose in The United States Navy in Vietnam, compiled by the editors of Sea Classics magazine.

Lieutenant (jg) Mike Peters, of South Bend, Indiana, was flying the cover helo for a team lead by Lieutenant Commander Sam Aydelotte, out of Vinh Long in the Mekong Delta about 55 miles southwest of Saigon.

On that morning, the two-chopper team embarked on what was to have been only an hour-and-a-half (the maximum flying time) reconnaissance mission over Viet Cong territory on the bank of the Co Chien River about two miles from the base.

The press was given a first-hand look at a day in the life of the Seawolves. In the lead helo rode a Navy correspondent and in Peters' craft was a photographer. The crews were rounded out as follows: In the lead helo were Lieutenant Commander Eugene Rosenthal, co-pilot; Jack Williamson, crew chief; and Jerry Lassiter, door gunner. Both the enlisted men were third class petty officers. Flying with Peters were Lieutenant (jg) Bill Mackie, co-pilot; and Wendell Maxwell and Robert Nunes, both of airman rank.

Thirty minutes into the flight, the team received a report that a Vietnamese army unit was under fire by a Viet Cong platoon in the Ben Tra Sector. At first, the ships found no activity below, but just after they decided to leave the area, Peters' helo began receiving sniper fire from a tree line. A smoke marker dropped by Maxwell from Peters' craft preceded rocket and machine gun attacks along the tree line by both ships.

The scrap lasted about 15 minutes, but had to be broken off so the choppers could refuel and rearm, which they did aboard the LST Hunterdon County, home base for another Seawolf detachment on the Ham Luong River.

Before the Aydelotte and Peters helicopters could return to their patrol area over the Co Chien, they were scrambled to another Ham Luong location across from the town of Ben Tre where a PBR had been hit with recoilless rifle fire, causing several casualties. Medical evacuation would be needed for one seriously wounded sailor.

Joined by two craft from the Hunterdon County detachment, the pair reached the location of the firefight. Aydelotte's helo, using a purple grenade marker, made a careful firing run against a tree line, keeping it tight because of the proximity of friendly personnel.

A Detachment 4 helicopter went in to recover the wounded man, while the remaining three continued to make rocket and machine-gun attacks in support of the stricken PBR and two others that had arrived to help. Fire-suppression efforts by the Seawolves, while helpful, were not enough, and Air Force fighter assistance was called in. The Viet Cong attack ended abruptly in the orange inferno of Napalm.

The three helicopters needed fueling and rearming once more and landed at Ben Tre Air Base for that purpose. However, Peters discovered two bullet holes in the main rotor of his craft and returned to Vinh Long for repairs. By that time, Lieutenant Bill Barnes, whose chopper had completed the medical evacuation, returned. There the airmen experienced some excitement on the ground. When a Vietnamese soldier noticed a wire running through the grass, Barnes cut it and traced it to a command-detonated satchel explosive charge hidden near some fuel drums and not far from parked helicopters. Thus major damage was averted. Ten minutes later, the air field came under a mortar barrage, but the helicopters managed to get aloft without being hit and then delivered successful rocket attacks on the source of the mortar fire.

Since their refueling and rearming had been interrupted at Ben Tre, the Seawolves had to land at Dong Tam air base to complete the job before returning to base at Vinh Long. The supposedly routine mission had taken just over four hours, and while the day cannot be called typical of the Seawolf experience, it was indicative of the kinds of situations the helicopter crews could encounter and how quickly they had to adjust and respond to rapidly changing circumstances.

For Lieutenant Peters, his last mission was a memorable one. His Seawolf boss, Aydelotte, paid him this tribute: "He'd been written up for more awards than any other man in the detachment. He'd amassed over 600 hours in the Hueys, earned the Distinguished Flying Cross and Purple Heart while serving with the Army and additional Distinguished Flying Crosses with the Navy."

Aydelotte, incidentally, was credited with developing many of the tactics employed by the Seawolves in their peculiar mission of working in close support of and coordination with the little patrol boats on the water below.

In 1967, alone, Seawolf helicopters flew 7,000 missions and were credited with 10,000 hours in the air.

The Seawolves later engaged in other major operations, including the 1968 Tet Offensive, in which they were credited with keeping some villages and hamlets out of enemy hands. Gamewarden in general and the helicopter squadron in particular had a major part of the Sealords operation and the Giant Slingshot campaigns later in the war.

HAL-3 detachments moved closer to the Cambodian border in early 1970 to help cut down infiltration, but their numbers were never sufficient for complete effectiveness. Several Seawolf units participated in the United States incursion into Cambodia in May 1970. Detachment 8, based on the LST Hunterdon County, provided the main support for naval forces. As the operation progressed, four other detachments, 3, 4, 5 and 9 were called in as were some of the "slick" Sealords, but the next month American forces were withdrawn from Cambodia and the Seawolves resumed their regular routine.

That same year, Vietnamization was in

Capt. R. Beckwith preparing to present medals to members of a HAL-3 detachment on a YRBM - 1969. (Courtesy of R. Beckwith)

progress and Vietnamese observers began flying with the Seawolves. As more Vietnamese Army and Navy units took over more of the duties on the surface, Seawolves continued to support them from the air. Finally, the order came for HAL-3 to stand down, and at Binh Thuy on January 26, 1972, the Seawolves came to an official end.

Three years earlier, when the war raged full bore, the Navy found a partial answer to the chronic shortage of air cover for brown-water operations. The Army was not parting with any of its new Hueycobras, so the Navy turned to fixed-wing help.

The craft chosen was the Rockwell OV-10 Bronco, a propeller-driven twin-engine plane designed for counterinsurgency. The Bronco had been used by the Marines and Air Force in Vietnam since the previous year for air-spotting and other functions. Incorporation of what was regarded as a lightly armed craft into the work of Gamewarden would entail heavier direct combat.

The Bronco had the qualities the Navy was looking for, heavy ordnance capacity, speed, sturdiness, short field requirements and range.

Starting with 18 planes borrowed from the Marines, some of which were used for training, the Navy set out to form an air-support squadron in the shortest time possible. The unit VAL-4 (Light Attack Squadron Four) was commissioned in January 1969 at North Island, California. The training course ran an intense 15 weeks, emphasizing gunnery, ordnance delivery, reconnaissance, coordination with river craft and jungle survival.

VAL-4 was deployed to Vietnam in March 1969 in two eight-ship sections, one at an Army base at Vung Tau to cover the Rung Sat and the other at a Vietnamese air base at Binh Thuy in the Delta. Combat operations began immediately.

Tactics closely mirrored those of the PBRs on the water and Seawolves in the air. Broncos, dubbed "Black Ponies" as an adaptation of their model name, usually flew in pairs for same reasons as the boats and the helos - mutual

support and cover - though some patrols over the Run Sat were performed singly. The variety of missions also approximated those of Seawolves. Black Ponies either conducted reconnaissance patrols seeking targets of opportunity, provided escort cover for PBRs when the boats were entering especially dangerous waterways or acted the role of fireman, responding to trouble on an emergency basis.

Combat tactics were developed as the operation progressed. The craft relied on various roll maneuvers during their firing runs to enhance their weapons' effectiveness and reduce their own vulnerability to enemy fire. One of these was called octa-flugeron. And like the PBRs and Seawolves, one of the Black Ponies' favorite tricks was approaching a Viet Cong position at night with one plane's lights out. That tactic, called "chumming," was dangerous for the lure, the low-flying Bronco with its lights on, but if it drew fire, the enemy usually paid a high price.

The Black Ponies had the rapid scramble down to a fine point, as described by pilot Kit Lavell in Al Santoli's *Everything We Had*. From the time the horn sounded, the Broncos would be airborne in six minutes. That was accomplished because the crews slept in their flight gear and the planes were ready, even to the point of having all switches on. Broncos could reach the outer perimeter of their coverage area in 20 minutes, meaning that no stricken PBR, or other besieged target, had more than 26 minutes to wait before help from the air arrived. Usually it would be much less time than that.

Compared to Seawolves, the Black Ponies had advantages and disadvantages. Their speed let them arrive over a target sooner and when they got there, they could stay longer and deliver a much more potent punch. The Zuni 5-inch rocket, called "the big stick," was especially devastating with its 48-pound warhead. The 20-millimeter cannon also gave the Black Ponies a hard kick. The Broncos also were less vulnerable to ground fire than the Hueys had become as the result of heightened Viet Cong aggressiveness and accuracy.

On the down side for the fixed-wing craft, their speed, a plus in getting to the scene, became a detriment over the target. The slower helicopters could maneuver more deftly in close fire support. The Broncos' weapons were not trainable, meaning they could be fired only in the direction of the plane's heading. The Broncos also could not operate from the shipboard bases. Their runway demands were not great, however. Designed for STOL (short takeoff and landing), the OV-10 required only 1,130 feet to get off the ground fully loaded.

The Viet Cong were not hesitant in firing on the Black Ponies. Kit Lavell estimated that 80 percent of the missions he flew resulted in hostile fire, usually from AK-47 rifles but also from .50 caliber machine guns, which could do major harm to the airplane.

Again, in the Santoli book, Lavell describes life as a Black Pony pilot. Sixty percent of his combat missions were at night and usually in bad weather. The monsoon season was bad, but the dry period when farmers burned off their land could be worse. Navigation was not easy. The Broncos were not equipped with sophisticated gear and Vietnam was devoid of navigational aids. It was seat-of-the-pants flying and the ceiling seldom got too low. If cloud cover was 100 feet, Lavell's Black Pony flew lower.

Shortly after the squadron's arrival in 1969, it took its first casualty. Lieutenant Peter Russell, a veteran combat flyer who had downed a MIG-17 in an A-1 Skyraider in November 1966, was killed when the Bronco he was piloting was hit by ground fire. The plane's back-seater was able to bring it home.

Russell's death so soon into VAL-4's mission had the effect of instilling a grim determination in the unit.

During the first year of operation, the Black Ponies flew 7,500 sorties. Because of their fire-power, range and staying power, they were effective against a variety of surface targets, including sampans, supply dumps, troop concentrations and fortified positions.

Like the Seawolves, the Broncos played a major role in the 1970 Cambodian operation, delivering critical support against heavy ground opposition that was hindering the advance.

After that operation, the Navy began to down-scale in Vietnam and the role of the Black Ponies changed. The squadron became mainly an airborne quick reaction force, flying support increasingly for Vietnamese river units in dusk-to-dawn patrols over assigned areas.

After most Navy surface personnel had left the theater, the Black Ponies took on other duties, including flying random patrols to provide assistance to any allied unit needing help on a moment's notice, flying cover missions for Vietnamese army supply convoys, carrying out surveillance reconnaissance, and doing spotter detail for naval gunfire.

The cover missions were mostly for Vietnamese river craft in the Delta, and they succeeded in virtually eliminating the attacks on the convoys from small guerilla bands.

The airborne surveillance was done mostly along the coasts to check for infiltration. On those missions, the VAL-4 backseater was replaced by an observer from Task Force 115 (Market Time), the coastal interdiction outfit. Likewise, a Marine officer usually occupied the rear seat during naval gunfire spotting missions.

Even until the end, the Black Ponies performed valuable service. Throughout 1971, while operating as a quick reaction force, the planes on many occasions assisted a beleaguered outpost and trapped friendly infantry, and broke up enemy attacks. By the end of the year, 7,000 sorties had been flown against communist positions. The Black Ponies were credited with kills of more than 2,400 North Vietnamese or Viet Cong troops at a loss of just one plane.

Squadron personnel began to rotate back to the United States early in 1972, but operations continued. In the first quarter of the year, 2,000 sorties were flown. On March 31, the lst Black Pony combat mission was a strike against Viet Cong positions. The next day, the squadron officially stood down at Binh Thuy, the last Navy squadron in-country to do so. The crews flew their Broncos to the Philippines where on April 10, VAL-4 was officially deactivated.

MONSTER

Million-dollar vehicles of strange appearance, frightening bearing, unusual capabilities and some fundamental disadvantages were transported by LSD across the Pacific Ocean in May 1966 for deployment in Vietnam.

They were the Patrol Air Cushion Vehicle, "Pack Vee" in military vernacular, generally described as a hovercraft not unlike in its maneuvers the air boats of the Everglades.

The craft was both boat and helicopter in some of its aspects, but not wholly either. It was capable of operating on land, through marshes and across water with equal ease and at astounding speeds of 60 to 70 knots.

After arrival in the war zone, the three English-made vehicles worked as part of Gamewarden out of the Rung Sat base at Cat Lo in river patrol at the wide mouths, and out of the well-deck of the LSD Tortuga in Operation Market Time, the coastal patrol and surveillance task force (115).

In neither operation did the PAVC engage in significant combat so its effectiveness as a war vessel was yet to be tested.

The opportunity came in November 1966 in Operation Quai Vat in an area called the Plain of Reeds. The mission's name was the Vietnamese word for "monster," which was the name given to PAVCs, and with good reason.

A Pack Vee zooming past at full tilt was a sight to inspire awe, or fear. The craft was large in all three dimensions, 39 feet long, 24 feet wide and 16 feet high, sent up an ominous cloud of spray and mist and emitted a frightening roar. Their crews added to the vehicle's menacing appearance by giving it a visage to match. They painted slanted cat's eyes and a shark's mouth with bared teeth across the front skirts of the vessels.

For Operation Monster, as it came to be called, the PAVCs became part of Task Unit 116.9.1, an element of Gamewarden, based at Moc Hoa, a Vietnamese army air boat base. Personnel consisted of four officers and 15 enlisted men.

The mission, as was so many undertaken in the III and IV Combat Tactical Zones in those early months of the active United States involvement, was to challenge Viet Cong hegemony in a area where the enemy believed he was essentially untouchable.

The Plains of Reeds, as described in a previous chapter, was 2,100 square miles of pure wetness north of the Mekong complex and west of Saigon. Like the Rung Sat and the Delta, it was a Viet Cong stronghold.

Depending on the season, the Plain of Reeds

(Courtesy of Joseph Dizona)

was under two to six feet of water, forcing the inhabitants to build up their villages and their roads. During times of lowest water levels, boats traveled by canals, which could be discerned by the coloration of the water. During high water, it didn't matter.

The Pack Vees were considered the ideal craft for the Plain of Reeds because they were capable of clearing most obstacles, such as dikes, walls, ditches and vegetation, including elephant grass that grew 15 feet high.

The hovercraft carried a crew of four, an officer and three enlisted men. For Operation Monster, they would take in a force of United States Army Green Berets, eight to 10 on each vessel. The soldiers rode the catwalks that ran down either side of the craft, an arrangement that had its discomforts from high winds and possible hazards, but one Green Beret was quoted as saying it was preferable to the stifling confines of Armored Personnel Carriers.

Other assets besides Pack Vees were part of Operation Monster. They included sampans, Vietnamese air boats, helicopters and fixed wing aircraft and were used in conjunction with the PAVCs. The combination of Pack Vees and helicopters seemed to work best. The helos from their vantage points could vector the high-speed PACVs with their firepower and troops into enemy areas with some effectiveness and could scout breaks in tree lines and other obstacles for the surface craft's passage.

There were limitations, however. The noise made by the hovercraft eliminated any element of surprise that might have been of value, but the speed was an offsetting factor. At 60 knots, the PACV could be on a Viet Cong position so rapidly it might not matter much if surprise had been achieved.

Operation Quai Vat lasted 16 days and had to be considered a success in its general objectives and for the PAVCs. The vehicles were credited with destroying 70 enemy structures, about the same number of sampans, capturing 11 Viet Cong and killing at least 23 of the enemy. The only serious problem they encountered was in getting bogged down one time in a stand of saplings, but the craft managed to free itself without much trouble.

In an environment like the Plain of Reeds, the PAVC clearly was an adaptable asset, perhaps the best available. Nevertheless, the PAVC's war career was short-lived. After some deployment to the north as part of Operation Clearwater, the vehicles were sent home.

SEALS

The Army has its Green Berets, the Marines have their reconnaissance units and the Navy has its SEALS. As a "commando" outfit, the SEALs need not take second to any, as the contingent that fought in Vietnam proved. No lesser observer on such matters than a member of the Australian Special Air Service, itself an elite fighting unit, commented on the SEALs: "They are the best, bar none."

SEALs - their name is an acronym for sea, air and land, the locales they are trained for - came into being in January 1962 when Teams One and Two were commissioned by President John F. Kennedy, a former naval officer himself.

Early in his administration, Kennedy recognized the need for a specially trained unit to counteract communism's "wars of liberation" in general and to fight the enemy's political-military efforts in Vietnam in particular.

The idea of a counterinsurgency unit was reinforced as a result of Maxwell Taylor's mission to South Vietnam in 1961.

Accordingly, the Navy established the two 60-man-SEAL teams, one each for the Atlantic and the Pacific fleets. They were trained to be particularly at home operating in rivers, canals, harbors, and adjacent areas.

Men joining this tough outfit were trained in hand-to-hand combat, SCUBA diving, parachuting, underwater demolition, weaponry, survival, escape and languages. Most in fact became multi-lingual. Forerunners of the SEALs were the Navy frogmen, the Underwater Demolition Team (UDT), whose main forte, as the name implies, was diving, swimming and other watery clandestine adventures. The SEALs, on the other hand, could do it all. They could operate in all venues and in Vietnam they would have to prove it.

Even before the United States military combat commitment to Vietnam, the SEALs were there. SEAL Team One's deployment began the year they were organized, first in training Vietnamese marines and American advisers and later in covert operations near the border with North Vietnam.

Though later in the war, the SEALs would operate from a special little fleet designed for its kind of river operation, as described in a previous chapter, different vessels were used early. The Navy in 1962 reactivated two Korean-era motor torpedo boats (PT) and armed them with 40 millimeter and 20 millimeter guns. Also, two modern, Norwegian-built PT-boats were bought and refitted with American equipment. These fiberglass-hulled, 80-foot-long craft were capable of 41 knots.

The PT fleet eventually reached eight and was used, among other things, to support raids ashore by the SEALs. Submarines also came into play. The Navy recommissioned two transport subs, the *Perch* and the *Sealion* to supply SEALs, collect intelligence and do rescue missions.

The growing involvement by the Navy in various counterinsurgency warfare efforts required central planning. Thus was formed in October 1963 the Naval Operations Support Group commands for Atlantic and Pacific fleets.

A SEAL platoon was 14 men, divided into squads. A typical operation was taken on in squad strength, a team of seven or sometimes six.

Generally speaking, the SEALs' missions were to penetrate in areas and perform tasks that they were beyond the reach or ability of conventional units. Often these were intelligence objectives. Counterinsurgency, seeking out and destroying enemy weapons and food supplies, and ambushes were part of the SEALs' job description.

SEALs were first attached to the Gamewardens in February 1966, when two platoons were assigned to the Rung Sat Special Zone mainly to disrupt enemy sappers trying to mine shipping in that critical water route to Saigon, and to carry out hit-an-run raids.

By mid-1968, SEAL Team One had 211 men making up 12 platoons, of which four of five typically were assigned to Vietnam - one or two at Da Nang and three in the Rung Sat with Gamewarden.

Owing to the success of the force in the Rung Sat, four more platoons, supplied by the Atlantic SEAL Team Two, were sent to Vietnam. Units were billeted with the Gamewardens at Can Tho, Nha Be, My Tho and Binh Thuy, thus putting SEALs into the central Mekong Delta for the first time.

Among their missions were reconnaissance for river-land operations and setting up listening posts deep in Viet Cong territory.

The SEALs sometimes operated jointly with their Army counterparts, the Green Berets, with whom a natural, though good-natured rivalry existed.

Work of the SEALs and Gamewardens was mutually complementary. The Gamewardens often transported the SEALs to their debarkation points and then stood by to provide fire support if needed, while the SEALs often gained information that would be helpful to the Gamewardens in their patrol and interdiction work.

SEALs also were taken into their operation areas by helicopter and picked up the same way. And too, the unit had its own fleet of craft, as described earlier. These included the STAB (Seal Team Assault Boat), Boston Whalers and the LCCS (Light Seal Support Craft). Sometimes SEALs traveled in native sampans, if their mission dictated that they try to blend in with the population.

Some of their more successful enterprises were in listening-post surveillance, during which SEALs would lie hidden on riverbanks and canals in places where the Viet Cong thought they could move without interference. By this tactic, the SEALs were able to discover enemy supply routes and lines of movement, which made subsequent ambush and interdiction operations more effective. As the SEALs developed their tactics and techniques, they were able to remain in place for up to seven days without resupply. That continuity also was valuable in observation of Viet Cong patterns.

So effective were the SEALs found to be that other commanders began requesting their services.

As a consequence, their work took SEALs into other areas of Vietnam, including even Haiphong Harbor itself. Other operations in which SEALs participated include assistance of Gamewarden in the successful defense of the city of Chau Doc in the Delta during the Tet Offensive, intelligence forays and covert missions during the joint Army-Navy Giant Slingshot Operation in 1969, and the aggressive work pushed by Admiral Elmo Zumwalt in the lower Ca Mau Peninsula, also in 1969.

More SEAL platoons and responsibilities were added even after other military units began scaling back as part of the Vietnamization process. In 1968, SEALs began training both American and Vietnamese personnel in counterguerrilla warfare and the next year, SEAL Team Two was given two more platoons.

Late in 1970, the SEALs participated in a raid on a Viet Cong prison camp with South

(Courtesy of Bill Curtis)

ARVN insertion. *(Courtesy of R.A. McMurry)*

Vietnamese militiamen. They rescued 19 South Vietnamese prisoners and captured two VC as well as documents and weapons.

That year, the SEALs began turning over duties to the Vietnamese and by 1972, the last year of active American participation in the war, the only SEALs in the country were a few advisors. Before that, however, the SEALs undertook clandestine missions into Cambodia to inspect enemy buildup along the border.

Because of the sensitive nature of much of what the SEALs did in Vietnam, a large part of the record remains classified and therefore cannot be disclosed. That necessarily limits the volume of the unit's history for public consumption.

One controversial operation that is generally known went by the code name "Phoenix." The job of the SEALs, in conjunction with the Provincial Reconnaissance Units, was to kill or capture Viet Cong leaders and political officers. The American news media and anti-war movement vehemently criticized the program as amounting to nothing more than "murder for hire."

However, Phoenix was successful in eliminating many Viet Cong commanders and thereby thwarted many attacks that would have cost American and South Vietnamese lives.

Safe in the United States, it might have been easy for protesters to believe war could be fought by the Marquis of Queensbury rules, but the perspective in the swamps and jungles was a bit different.

The Viet Cong, no matter what their garb or insignia, were soldiers in a war and the allies, including the SEALs, treated them as such.

An elite unit such as the SEALs assigned to perform feats of derring-do inevitably will produce conspicuous heroes.

One of these Senior Chief Petty Officer Robert T. Gallagher, whose exploits were described by John Forbes and Robert Williams in their book, *The Illustrated History of Riverine Force.* On March 13, 1968, Gallagher was serving with SEAL Team Detachment Alpha. The night mission on that date took his patrol, of which he was assistant leader, deep into a Viet Cong base camp. The contingent had penetrated 5,000 yards into the camp area without detection when it came upon a barracks with about 30 armed Viet Cong. A firefight ensued in which Gallagher killed five of the enemy but suffered wounds in both legs.

Because the patrol leader was even more seriously wounded, Gallagher had to take command and extricate his greatly outnumbered team from the enemy camp. He managed to lead the team 1,000 yards through the darkness before calling for evacuation helicopters. When they arrived, enemy opposition was still fierce, so Gallagher continued to expose himself to fire while directing fire from gunships and the extraction of choppers to their landing. In the process, he was wounded a second time, but nevertheless oversaw the successful evacuation of his men.

For his action that night, Gallagher was awarded the Navy Cross.

The SEALs were a small force. At no time during the Vietnam war did their number in the theater exceed 200; yet two SEALs won the nation's highest decoration, the Medal of Honor, an amazing percentage.

Lieutenant Thomas R. Norris, a SEAL advisor with the United States Military Assistance Command, performed remarkable feats of courage over a four-day period, April 10-13, 1972, in rescuing two downed pilots deep in enemy-controlled territory in Quang Tri Province. It took two trips and some subterfuge, but Norris pulled off the rescue.

According to the citation, Norris set out on the night of April 10 with a five-man patrol and after passing through 2,000 meters of hostile territory, located one of the pilots at daybreak. The party returned to a forward operating base, which that day came under heavy mortar and rocket attack. Norris then led a three-man team on two unsuccessful efforts to locate the second pilot, but on the afternoon of April 12, a forward air controller located the flier and radioed Norris. Disguised as fishermen and using a sampan, Norris and a Vietnamese traveled all night and found the injured pilot at dawn. They covered the pilot with bamboo and other vegetation for the return trip, successfully evading a North Vietnamese patrol. As they neared the forward base, the party came under heavy machine gun fire, whereupon Norris called in an air strike.

Norris' citation refers to his "outstanding display of decisive leadership, undaunted courage and selfless dedication in the face of extreme danger." Norris' action came later in the Vietnam war, after most of the active SEAL units had left the country. He was one of those remaining as an advisor; yet when the occasion demanded it, his training and dedication kicked in. He was still a SEAL.

Surely the most famous SEAL, past or present, is Joseph R. Kerrey, known politically as Bob Kerrey, former governor of Nebraska, former presidential candidate and now United States Senator.

In 1969, he was a SEAL lieutenant (jg) and what he did was described by one SEAL as "real Guns of Navarone stuff." The exploit won for Kerrey the Medal of Honor, but it cost him a leg.

On March 14 of that year, Kerrey and a five-man SEAL team were landed on an island in Nha Trang bay known to be a Viet Cong sanctuary and home to several high-ranking members of the VC's political structure.

The team's mission was to capture the officials alive and bring them out. The intelligence lode represented by these political leaders was thought to be rich.

However, the Viet Cong camp was heavily defended and worse than that, was situated on a large ledge halfway up, or down, a sheer 350-foot cliff. Kerrey, believing any direct approach from below would be virtually suicidal, decided to scale the cliff first and then descend from the top onto the nest of Viet Cong.

Kerrey divided his team into two three-man sections. They made the climb all right and then, whispering instructions to each other by radio, started back down. The operation almost went according to plan, but when the two groups were within a few feet of their objective, Kerrey's division came under heavy fire. A grenade landed at his feet, seriously wounding him, and throwing him back against some jagged rocks. Bleeding heavily and in great pain, Kerrey immediately directed his own element's fire and ordered the second group to open fire as well, catching the enemy gunners in a surprising crossfire and silencing them. This enabled the SEALs to complete the mission of capturing a bevy of important Viet Cong.

To quote from Kerrey's citation: "After successfully suppressing the enemy's fire, and although immobilized by his multiple wounds, he continued to maintain calm, superlative control as he ordered his team to secure and defend an extraction site." Kerrey, nearly unconscious, was evacuated by helicopter.

Again from the citation: "The havoc brought to the enemy by this very successful mission cannot be overestimated. The enemy who were captured provided critical intelligence to the allied effort."

One more SEAL of note should be mentioned. His name was Prince, a German Shepherd that, among other skills, had been trained to parachute.

Prince was especially useful during interrogation of Viet Cong prisoners, whose clothes he would tear off. The terrified captives were usually glad to share information after that. Prince was wounded during an operation in the Delta one night, but he recovered. And of course he was awarded the Purple Heart.

The score sheet for the SEALs during their six years of Vietnam deployment as combat soldiers is impressive. Recalling that their numbers never exceeded 200, their confirmed enemy kill was three times that, plus 300 others almost certainly killed. Besides those, the SEALs accounted for more than 1,000 captured guerrillas or detained suspects.

Those numbers must be taken as minimal in any calculation of the SEALs' impact on the war, much of which either was intangible or unknowable.

One last statistic that is truly remarkable was the SEAL casualty rate, fewer than a dozen in the entire war. That low number can't be attributed to lack of exposure to dangerous situations, so the explanation must be the SEALs' own skill and training.

Vietnam was this country's first war in which naval commandoes, excluding frog men, were used. The unit continues to function and if it has not already, it will achieve a recognition similar to that of the Army's Green Berets. The SEALs proved themselves in Vietnam.

MARKET TIME

Suspicions American and Vietnamese military leaders harbored about North Vietnamese seaborne infiltration were borne out on March 3, 1965, by what came to be known as the Vung Ro incident. The coastline of South Vietnam, from the 17th parallel to the Cambodian border on the Gulf of Thailand, is long, irregular and dotted with countless small islands a short distance offshore. In the battle between smugglers and the patrols that were mounted to counter them, the latter did not necessarily have the advantage.

An Army helicopter pilot, Lieutenant James S. Bowers, was flying a routine patrol from the central coastal base at Qui Nhon when over a small bay named Vung Ro he observed what looked like a small island, except for one thing. It appeared to be moving. Closer examination told Bowers the "island" was actually a camouflaged ship, obviously up to no good.

Air strikes and beach assaults over the next few days effectively destroyed the target, which ended up beached on its side. The 130-foot steel trawler was a floating arsenal of ammunition and weapons, plus medical supplies. Sources of the material were several Communist bloc countries, and evidence was abundant that the vessel's last voyage had originated in North Vietnam.

The proof, if any was needed, was irrefutable that the North Vietnamese were supplying guerrillas in the south from the sea.

The incident did nothing to inspire American confidence in their South Vietnamese counterparts. Though the trawler had been disabled early in the series of air strikes, it was five days before the ship and surrounding area were under friendly control, owing mainly to a seeming reluctance by the Vietnamese to move in if any risk was involved.

It was clear that a major coastal surveillance and interdiction effort would be needed and the Americans would have to take a dominant role. General William Westmoreland on the day after the Vung Ro incident asked Navy brass in the Pacific to join him in planning for counterinfiltration measures.

The Navy had the wherewithal to begin the work in the open seas well off the coast, but at the moment had no shallow-draft vessels available for patrols close to shore to augment the South Vietnamese Navy's junk force.

For the deep-water phase, the Navy put radar destroyer escorts (DERs) and full-size destroyers (DDs) on the outer barrier, and then looked to the Coast Guard for help closer to shore. The 82-foot cutter, the WPB, was considered right for the job and 26 of the ships were committed to Vietnam. The Navy's contribution to the close-in patrol would be the 50-foot PCF, the Swift boat, which arrived somewhat later than the Coast Guard vessels.

Code name for the new operation was Market Time, so-called because the principal task was sorting out contraband carriers from the legitimate marketing traffic.

At first, the patrol and surveillance operation came under Task Force 71, an element of the Seventh Fleet. However, in May 1965 the decision was made to create a new task force, 115, as of the end of July and place it under the naval advisory command in Vietnam.

Before the Coast Guard WPBs were deployed to Vietnam, their ordnance needed to be

Front of safe conduct pass.

Back of safe conduct pass.

beefed up. Twenty-millimeter cannon were replaced with .50 calibers riding piggyback on 81-millimeter mortars. Other .50s were added also.

Ordinarily, the commanding officer would be a chief petty officer, but two commissioned officers were added to the enlisted crew of nine. A further modification had to do with color. After a cutter, the *Point Orient*, was taken under fire on a moonlit night during her first patrol, it was determined the Coast Guard white wouldn't do. The craft were painted the traditional Navy gray.

By mid-summer 1965, the first 17 Coast Guard WPBs arrived in the war zone and were deployed at the extreme ends of the South Vietnamese coast. Nine were assigned to the Gulf of Thailand as Coast Guard Division 11 and eight to the waters near the 17th parallel as Division 12. Early in 1966, nine more of the 82-footers arrived as Division 13 to operate out of Cat Lo at the mouth of the system of rivers flowing down from Saigon.

The stateside crews were maintained for the new Southeast Asian duty. After special training appropriate to the mission, the Coast Guardsmen rejoined their ships.

Eighty-four Swift boats were allocated for Vietnam. The first arrived in October 1965, and the full complement was reached in November 1966. They were assigned in five division, three of them coinciding with WPB units, plus one each at Cam Ranh Bay and Qui Nhon. All were organized under Boat Squadron 1 under the command of Commander Arthur Ismay, whose first self-imposed assignment after getting the job was to return to the United States and set up a training program for the Swift boats at Coronado, California.

The Coast Guard also was given a role out on the deep-water barrier where DERs patrolled when the larger vessel, the WHEC, was assigned to the theater in early 1967.

Thus the two sea services became partners in Market Time, though under the Navy's command, with one type ship from each patrolling well offshore, and one smaller boat from each operating close in. Other Market Time vessels, both Navy, included minesweepers (MSO) and patrol gunboats (PGs).

Smuggling essentially took two forms. In one, the North Vietnamese would send trawlers southward well off the coast until an opportunity was seen to turn abruptly and make a perpendicular run to the beach. The second was represented by junks that would mingle with the normal boat traffic close to shore, which typically was heavy. The Market Time sailors had the same problem their Gamewarden compatriots faced on the rivers and canals, that is determining which boats among many to stop, which to inspect perfunctorily and which to search thoroughly.

Things were never simple. For instance, Market Time sailors had to be careful not to establish a pattern for their stops and searches, because the enemy was alert to take advantage. If a boat made it a habit to search the nearest junk at hand, the one with the contraband would hang back.

The potential hostility sailors would encounter even from innocent civilians induced the tactic of offering a reward, maybe candy or cigarettes, but that too led to unexpected results.

A Navy ship on one occasion summoned two boats for inspection and five responded.

The boat crews had to walk that fine line between vigilance and overreaction. A sudden move by a Vietnamese could be harmless, or it could be a Viet Cong going for a weapon. The sailor was under constant pressure to make the right decision, because the wrong one could mean death for himself or a friendly civilian.

Petty Officer Third Class Richard O'Mara, a Swift boat veteran of 1968-69, developed a personal skill at avoiding danger while carrying out inspections. If he saw a suspicious item, he would ask whose it was and watch the Vietnamese's eyes for a reaction, which he felt he could read. If his suspicions continued, he would instruct one of the boat's occupants to open it. Obviously, if nothing was amiss, the civilian would have no hesitancy in doing so.

Cargo was not always easy to determine as being contraband or not. A large quantity of small-arms ammunition could be assumed to be bound for the Viet Cong, but many items, food and other supplies, were not that obvious. It took experience and judgement to deal with the ambiguities.

For the small-boat patrol sailors, the so-called off-duty time could be among the most dangerous, as bases ashore were always vulnerable to enemy mortar or rocket attack. Also, the accommodations at first were primitive. The schedule was difficult, but commanders tried to arrange a modicum of relief for the men. It would average about five days off per three months.

A special problem for the WPBs and the Swifts in the Gulf of Thailand on the west coast of the Ca Mau Peninsula was the distance from any shore base, so a system was devised whereby the DERs and WHECs patrolling in the deep water offshore in effect became parent ships for the small boys for refueling, resupply and crew relief.

It was the nature of Task Force 115's work that sailors would endure tedium and boredom, long hours of patrol without incident, wearying and tense boardings and searches most often without bearing the fruit of contraband, but underlying the seemingly endless, mundane activity was a potential danger that could explode suddenly. The first year of Market Time saw some successful intervention by destroyers and destroyer escorts against infiltrators, and some firefight action by a few Swift boats. But those were the exceptions rather than the rule.

On Valentine's Day, 1966, the Navy lost its first PCF and with the boat, four of its crew.

PCF 4 was on patrol in the Gulf of Thailand late in the afternoon, another routine day of sightings, boardings, and inspections nearly finished.

As Lieutenant Commander Thomas Cutler wrote it in *Brown Water, Black Berets*, PCF 4 fell victim to two subtle hazards of war, boredom and complacency. The following account is drawn from his book.

A crewman aboard spotted an object in the water that upon closer examination was revealed to be a bamboo raft in which was fixed a Viet Cong flag.

The object had souvenir potential, always

a temptation for men at war, but these sailors, well-schooled by training and experience, were well aware of the dangers inherent in the situation. The Viet Cong were wise to American servicemen's tendencies and were clever at booby-trapping.

Nevertheless, boat commander, Lieutenant (jg) Charlie Bacon, ordered the coxswain to edge close to the raft. He took the appropriate precaution of having a few grenades tossed close to his objective. Had the raft been rigged with explosives, the grenades would reveal it, but nothing happened.

The coxswain was ordered to bring the Swift directly alongside the bobbing raft so a crewman could cut the flag loose. As a sailor, the flag pole in one hand and a knife in the other, was cutting the lashings, a tremendous explosion directly beneath the keel wracked the 50-foot craft, which bucked once and then settled quickly to the ocean floor.

The mine attack had been planned well and executed flawlessly by the Viet Cong, one of whom, watching the scene from his hiding place among the mangroves, touched the live wires together at just the right moment.

The drama was far from over. Navy Lieutenant Gil Dunn, an advisor and close friend of Bacon, was at Rach Gia close by when the Mayday call came from the Vietnamese Navy junk then on the scene. Plenty of help would soon be on the way, but the medical evacuation in the increasingly high seas proved dangerous and difficult. Two Army planes went along to search for the wreckage, an Army medical helicopter was enroute, as was Private First Class Dunn, a gunner's mate and an Army medic set out up the coast in a 15-foot runabout, a trip that would be an adventure in the heavy swells.

When Dunn's party arrived, three figures lay on the junk's deck. Two, Bacon and the radiomen, were alive. The officer had suffered a badly fractured leg, which the Vietnamese sailors had splint with an M-14 rifle.

The seas were worsening, but the Army chopper managed to get the wounded radioman aboard before the dangerously pitching and falling junk forced a wave-off.

Several further attempts failed, and finally, Bacon and the dead seaman had to be loaded onto PCF 3 for the trip back to Rach Gia and medical treatment. On the trip, Dunn noticed that his friend's other leg was swollen, and it was found to have been severely injured as well.

Bacon was devastated of course by the loss of his boat and four men, but the circumstances made it all the more painful. On the operating table, he told Dunn: "I don't hurt in my legs, Gil. I hurt right here," pointing to his heart.

The PCF-4 was raised, though at times under shore fire, and the hulk taken to Subic Bay where examinations of the damage helped toward design improvements that would make the Swift boats less vulnerable to mines.

The Coast Guard found itself in action also. Early in Market Time, September 1965, the WPBs *Point Glover* and *Point Marone* operating in the Gulf of Thailand near the Cambodian border exchanged fire with two junks in separate actions, to the communists' serious detriment. The enemy boat involved in the action was disabled in one case, captured in the other. More than a dozen Viet Cong were killed in the two encounters, but more important, large caches of arms and ammunition were recovered.

Coast Guard Division 13 operating out of Cat Lo at the mouth of the Rung Sat river system accounted for 27 Viet Cong dead, seven captured and much materiel seized during March 1966.

In one incident, the WPB *Point White* withdrew from its patrol at the mouth of the Soi Rap River in hopes of luring the enemy into the open. It worked. A 25-foot motorized sampan tried to cross, but the *Point White*, closing fast, took the enemy under fire. A spirited exchange ensued, and when the enemy did not succumb to the pounding it was taking, the cutter's skipper, Lieutenant Eugene Hickey, ordered his ship to ram the junk. Just four Viet Cong survived for capture, but one of them was a leader of the Viet Cong in the Rung Sat.

The enemy did not pose the only dangers for the men and the boats of Market Time.

One confirmed and one suspected incident of friendly fire occurred with deadly results in the area of the DMZ in August 1966. The WPB *Point Welcome* was subjected to repeated attacks by Air Force combat aircraft in the early morning darkness, leaving two Coast Guardsmen dead and wounded. The crewmen, after deciding their only salvation was to abandon ship and start swimming for shore, found themselves under mortar and automatic weapons fire while they were in the water. That attack probably came from the real enemy. Among the wounded was a journalist, Tim Page, who had decided to join the patrol on the cutter mainly to relax.

Two Swifts, PCFs 19 and 12, the WPB *Point Dueme*, and heavier warships all were attacked the same month just north of the DMZ, probably by friendly aircraft responding to reports that the North Vietnamese were operating helicopters in the area.

The PCF 19 was the first attacked, by rocket fire, and after the first round missed, at least three found their mark and sent the boat to the bottom. Four American Navy men and one Vietnamese were killed.

Swift boats operating at the mouth of the Hue River in October and November 1966 encountered another ancient enemy of the sailing man - the violence of the sea. It was the monsoon season and the 50-foot boats at times were overmatched.

The PCF 56 lost a man overboard in heavy seas late in October and search efforts failed. Two weeks later conditions worsened. A crewman of the PCF 22 also was swept over the side. PCF 77 joined the search, but the man was rescued by his own boat. For the 77, however, disaster lurked. A monstrous 30-foot wave overwhelmed the little boat, causing it to flip end-over-end. As the boat filled rapidly with water, the skipper Lieutenant (jg) David Wilbourne, stayed behind to rescue a crewmen who was having trouble getting free. Others previously had escaped the doomed boat, but Petty Officer B.A. Timmons was trapped in the after compartment. Chief Machinery Repairman W.S. Baker heroically tried to save Timmons, but before he could do so, the boat sank keel up. Those two men plus Petty Officer Harry Brock were lost.

Market Time combat sometimes involved

GMG-3 W.D. Marquis, gunner, PBR 152. (Courtesy of Kenneth A. Delfino)

the big steel-hulled trawlers that tried to carry major supply loads to the guerrillas in the south. One such occasion was in July 1967 when the trawler 459 maneuvered off Cape Batangan waiting for the chance to dash to the beach with its 90 tons of weapons, ammunition and other strategic materials, enough to supply a regiment for several months.

The Americans knew the trawler was there. They waited for the right moment to make their move, which came when the old ship closed to within five miles of the coast. Four United States vessels of different types moved in to surround the enemy. They were the DER *Wilhoite*, the WPB *Point Orient*, the PCF 79 and the gunboat *Gallup*. A tape-recorded message told the trawler of her plight and urged surrender. Flares illuminated her decks, but the ship defiantly continued toward her destination, the mouth of the Sa Ky River.

The American ships fired over the Trawler's bow from each side and when that warning was ignored, the vessels took the enemy under fire in earnest with mortars, .50 calibers and 3-inchers. A white phosphorous round from the Swift boat into the pilot house was the telling blow. The quarry ran aground at the mouth of the river, but the fight wasn't over. The crew of the trawler took advantage of a reloading lull to man its own guns, which included a 12.7 millimeter and a 57 millimeter recoilless rifle.

The exchange lasted several minutes, but with the help of helicopter gunships, the ships soon reduced the enemy to an inferno, which burned during the night. Despite the blaze, boarding parties discovered tons of ammunition intact.

Market Time continued to perform the assigned tasks, some routine, some frantic, most potentially dangerous and all important.

There is no question that the efforts at sea and close at shore seriously reduced the flow of material from north to south, depriving the guerrillas of the material they needed.

A definitive appraisal of a military operation of this sort is not easily done. For instance, after August 1969, 20 trawlers were known to have tried to penetrate the allied sea defenses,

and 19 of them failed. The record's success is tempered by what is not known, that is the possibility that some enemy ships about which the Navy or Coast Guard was never aware eluded the surveillance.

In November 1968, Market Time units detected 32,000 sampans and junks, inspected 14,000 of them and boarded 10,000 others, which are impressive figures. Since it took 200 boatloads to sustain the Viet Cong for a day, enough contraband would have gotten through only if three out of four boats Market Time did not inspect were carrying supplies for the enemy, a highly unlikely possibility. So it seems fairly certain that the coastal surveillance succeeded in choking off Viet Cong supplies to one degree or another.

Top military command gave Task Force 115 good marks. The Department of the Army concluded that Market Time forced the enemy to change its resupply tactics. Before 1966, 75 percent of the infiltration came by sea, a study estimated. By the end of that year, that had dropped to 10 percent.

General William Westmoreland's headquarters concurred in the general conclusion, and so did Admiral Elmo Zumwalt, who took over as the Navy's top commander in the theater in September 1968. "By the time I arrived on the scene, the interdiction mission had pretty much been accomplished as far as the coast was concerned."

Zumwalt's arrival was significant for Market Time, especially the Swift boat fleet, in an important way, which will be described in a later chapter.

TET

The Vietnamese celebrate their lunar new year annually, but so far as Americans are concerned, only one year counts: 1968. Mention Tet and several thoughts leap to mind, among them the countrywide pitched battle between the allied forces of the United States and South Vietnam, and the communist armies of the Viet Cong and North Vietnam.

The perception of the Tet Offensive, as it

Kenneth A. Delfino, Boat Captain, PBR-151, 1968. (Courtesy of Kenneth A. Delfino)

EN3 R.D. Dyson, engineer, PBR 151. (Courtesy of Kenneth A. Delfino)

has come to be known, has changed in the past quarter century. At the time, it was viewed as a stunning American military defeat by reason of the ferocity of the coordinated attacks, the initial setbacks, the images of the embassy in Saigon being assaulted and most of all, heavy American losses.

In actual fact, as any knowledgeable person now knows and the United States military in Vietnam was fully aware of at the time, the Tet Offensive was an unmitigated military disaster for the other side, one that seriously damaged its war-making ability, depleted its resources and resulted in grievous personnel casualties.

The only victory the Viet Cong and North Vietnamese won in Tet was the propaganda battle, but thanks to the political situation in the United States driven by public opinion that was swayed by news coverage of the war, it was enough.

A PBR sailor, Dave Roever, recalled watching a documentary on the BBC about the Vietnam War and quoted a North Vietnamese general as follows: "We lost the war in 1968 to the Americans. The Tet Offensive crushed us. But when we saw the antiwar demonstrations in America and the American youth in rebellion, we took new heart and began to fight again. The whole war turned in our favor."

The Mekong Delta was a major point of emphasis for the communist forces in launching Tet because, as noted in previous chapters, it was where the people lived and the food was grown. Further, the Delta continued to be regarded as a Viet Cong stronghold that could be exploited and consolidated in the offensive, or so the enemy planned.

That meant the Tet action would not bypass the United States and Vietnamese military units operating in the Delta, specifically the Gamewardens and the Army-Navy Mobile Riverine Force.

Commander S.A. Schwarztrauber, (new preferred spelling of name; previously Swarztrauber) a Gamewarden and Operation Clearwater officer, concludes that the Viet Cong committed a major blunder in their approach to Tet by first concentrating on the civilian population to the initial exclusion of the United States military. It was the enemy's mistaken belief that their aggressive campaign would cause the people to rally to their side in anticipation, perhaps, that the communist side was about to prevail. The

tactic did not succeed, which the Viet Cong seemingly should have known.

The reason, Schwarztrauber continued in his, *River Patrol Relearned*, was rooted in the Vietnamese belief about Tet. To them, what happened in their personal lives during the lunar period would set the tone for the remainder of the year. Consequently, they endeavored to make the days of Tet happy, cheerful and pleasant. It was supposed to be a time of celebration and a wartime offensive did not fit that pattern. The civilians were shocked and repelled by the brutality and did not react the way the Viet Cong thought they would. In the process, the guerrillas lost a certain initiative militarily at a time the American river forces would have been exceedingly vulnerable. That lapse allowed the Americans to collect themselves and go into action on the balls of their feet rather than back on their heels, figuratively speaking.

Tet, of course, was a general surprise across the country because, it being a national holiday period, a truce was supposed to be in effect.

But a least one American naval officer in Task Force 116 sensed an eery portent two days before the offensive began. There wasn't anything supernatural about Lieutenant Dick Godbehere's uneasiness. It was just an experienced hand's antenna at work.

Godbehere was a PBR patrol officer in River Section 511 on the Bassac River on January 29, 1968. That day, his boats engaged in a psychological mission, which meant a reduced speed patrol downstream toward Can Tho, a major Delta city, while a tape-recorded message was directed toward the banks and the people who lived there. It was a boring enterprise by nature and based on the pre-patrol briefing, it was expected to be uneventful. Can Tho was considered a relatively friendly region, and a few weeks before, a United States Army general concluded that the Viet Cong were suffering poor morale and that the South Vietnamese had gained supremacy over the enemy.

The patrol, a 56-mile round trip down-river and back, was as quiet as expected, more so, actually, but it was strange also.

What Godbehere and his men noticed was that everything ashore seemed normal - animals in the field, tools leaning against buildings, rice baskets swaying in the breeze, fish nets lying about - with one exception. There was no people to be seen.

For the entire patrol both ways, past hamlet after hamlet, the sailors did not see or hear another human being.

The atmosphere made Godbehere nervous and wary. "I don't like the looks of this, Boats," he said to his boat captain in an account in *Brown Water, Black Berets,* by Lieutenant Commander Thomas Cutler. "I know, sir, too quiet," was the response.

The situation, Godbehere knew, was ripe for an ambush, so much so that he ordered battle gear to be worn. The officer believed the Viet Cong were out there, unseen but there.

The boat captain suggested that the situation might have something to do with the lunar new year then impending, which made some sense. But if the civilians had gone to the temple or somewhere to worship they wouldn't have left their livestock unattended and their implements lying about. "Boats" was right about the holiday, though probably not in the way he thought. The Viet Cong were nearby, all right, but didn't attack and the people apparently were in hiding for reasons that could not have been discerned by the Americans at the time.

The patrol was completed without incident, but Godbehere dropped off to sleep still puzzling over the events of the day. Two days later, the first day of Tet, he would get his answer.

The Viet Cong indeed had been nearby as Godbehere's boats passed. They had moved into the hamlets around Can Tho four days before the holiday in preparation for the offensive and had resisted any temptation to reveal themselves by firing on the Godbehere patrol prematurely.

The offensive in the Mekong Delta was directed at 13 of the 16 provincial capitals, including Can Tho. Tet battles raged for 77 days in the country and by April 9 most of the pre-Tet conditions had been restored.

Aggressive and spirited performance by Gamewarden units and the Mobile Riverine Force at the outset of Tet prevented many towns from falling into Viet Cong hands and led to the recapture of others within a few days.

Throughout the region, the small force of boats and helicopters fought against long odds in lending their firepower to friendly units fighting desperate defensive battles.

When the attack was launched, Gamewarden units followed standard emergency procedures and all boats not already on patrol got under way.

When the fighting erupted, some PBRs with accompanying SEAL units by chance were already near the city of Chau Doc for an interdiction operation called Bold Dragon I that sought to prevent men and supplies from crossing the border from Cambodia. The boat crews, SEALs and Seawolves were credited by their fierce defense with saving that city from two Viet Cong battalions that had been led to believe they could enter to the welcome of waving flags. It was an astounding reversal for the Viet Cong against an American naval force that was grossly outnumbered.

The scene and results were similar at Ben Tre where PBRs and Navy helicopter gunships held off the Viet Cong for 36 hours, which gave friendly ground troops enough time to drive the enemy out of the city.

The Viet Cong temporarily overran Vinh Long, but PBRs were able to inflict heavy casualties on the enemy and with the LST *Garrett County* they succeeded in evacuating surviving American, Korean and Vietnamese personnel. The Mobile Riverine Base of Task Force 117 and the 9th Infantry Division contingent was anchored near Vinh Long when the initial Tet attacks were put in motion. A company of 9th Division troops joined South Vietnamese soldiers, Vietnamese river units and the Gamewarden PBRs in defending the airfield west of the city against about 1,200 Viet Cong troops.

And so it went over the Delta. PBR units were able to make a swift and effective response to the developing situation. The fighting by Task Force 116 units was intense and constant for two days, but the sailors helped blunt the worst of the Viet Cong assault until reinforcements turned the tide.

At the same time, the Army-Navy MRF of heavily armed river craft augmented by artillery was equally up to the demands of responding rapidly to the changing situation.

Early on February 1 River Assault Division 91 and barges carrying 105 millimeter howitzers moved along the Rach Ruong tributary to an area where the Viet Cong had ambushed riverine forces in December. When the enemy opened fire this time, the Americans were ready with heavy ordnance, including the anti-personnel "beehive" ammunition for the artillery pieces. A 30-minute pitched battle at close range ensued, leaving many enemy dead. The only American loss was a Navy man, the commander of a monitor, who was killed.

The next scene of riverine force action was at My Tho where the ground force landed and the boats provided fire support and blocking action at the waterfront. For 21 hours the battle raged as the Viet Cong were slowly pushed back. At the end, the tally was 115 Viet Cong killed against three American dead and 67 wounded.

The next day, the force operated in the Cai Lay area, forcing the enemy to withdraw, and on February 4, MRF returned to beleaguered Vinh Long where two to three Viet Cong battalions were reported to be operating. Reinforcing ARVN units in the area, the MRF drove the Viet Cong out of the city. Finally after eight days of continuous combat, the exhausted men of the MRF, Army and Navy, returned to their base.

The Tet offensive in the Mekong had been effectively blunted with enemy losses at the hand of the river forces put at 544, but that may understate the facts drastically. Don Oberdorfer in his book, *Tet*, wrote: "A total of 5,200 Viet Cong are reported to have been killed in the Mekong Delta and 560 captured. Whatever the accuracy of this estimate, it is clear that large numbers of the most dedicated and most experienced guerrillas and local force troops met their death in the unfamiliar cities."

The Gamewarden task force's casualties in the Tet fighting were eight dead and 134 wounded. Many PBRs and helicopters were damaged, some severely.

In some ways, the offensive marked a turning point for both river task forces. The PBRs after that time became even more aggressive, though as will be seen in later chapters, many of those crews displayed heroic stand-and-fight qualities during 1966-67 when the accepted doctrine for the unit was more passive.

For the MRF, which was awarded the Presidential Unit Citation for its work during Tet, the offensive represented a new phase in its operational life as well.

As a general observation, military leaders were agreed that to the two task forces, neither of them large in hardware or numbers of men, went the credit for saving the strategic Mekong Delta from Viet Cong subjugation in Tet.

The enormity of the enemy's military defeat was lost on neither side, but unfortunately, the American public did not realize it and the United States government, facing increasing domestic opposition in the face of American casualties, had no stomach for pressing the advantage so dearly earned by the men in uniform.

Tet will go down as one of a history's classic example of military victory being turned into a political defeat, but none of that detracts from the bravery and effectiveness of the men who fought the battle.

HEROES

The story of war, any war, is best told in the countless individual experiences of the men who did fighting - combat up close and personal.

Any such segment dealing with the brownwater Navy of the Vietnam War of necessity must start with James Elliott Williams, now 63 years old, chief boatswain's mate, retired, Conway, South Carolina.

His exploits in the Mekong Delta reach nearly legendary proportions, his decorations, which included the Medal of Honor, are possibly unrivaled in that war and most others.

In the autumn of 1966, the Gamewarden task force was less than a year old, still feeling its way in its primary task of interdicting Viet Cong troop movements, resupply, logistical maneuvers, recruitment, tax collections and other nefarious guerrilla activities.

Williams, then a boatswain's mate first class, was patrol commander of a two-boat PBR team in River Section 531 operating on the My Tho River. That responsibility usually went to a junior officer, lieutenant or less, or a chief petty

officer. That a white hat would be in charge of the patrol so early in the war was indicative of his superb qualifications. Later on, as casualties mounted, that became less unusual.

A seemingly routine event, a humanitarian interlude of the sort that PBR sailors often engaged in, turned out to have great significance for Williams' and his men and for the Navy effort in the Delta. His boat came upon and aged Vietnamese man in company of a woman who had serious sores on her legs. A crewman on the PBR, Rubin Binder, undertook to treat her, a process that took place over a period of time so that the crew and the Vietnamese pair became well acquainted, and trust developed. In due time, Williams recalled, the old man began to talk, to tell what he knew. Information was gleaned little by little but eventually the Vietnamese was able to provide some useful intelligence, which led ultimately to the recovery of, among other things, valuable Viet Cong map overlays. It was a case of a gesture of kindness, not a combat endeavor at all, paying off in a military sense.

The information developed during that incident foreshadowed to a degree what would happen on October 31, 1966. It was one of the most extraordinary incidents of the war, one in which American forces that seemingly were hopelessly outnumbered managed to thoroughly rout an enemy by dint of audacity, courage and intelligence.

That afternoon, the nine American sailors riding PBRs 105 and 99 on patrol on the My Tho River had no reason to believe the rest of the day would not be routine until their patrol suddenly came upon two sampans loaded with regular soldiers of the North Vietnamese army. Gamewarden units were no strangers to hostile action, but invariably it would be at the hands of guerrillas, the Viet Cong, operating from ambush in relatively small numbers and usually not seen. The evidence of their presence was mainly muzzle flashes and incoming ordnance. Allied ground troops sometimes encountered North Vietnamese regulars in the highlands farther north, but finding them in the Delta was highly unusual.

Williams as patrol commander was aboard the 105, which had a crew of four sailors beside him. Four men manned the second boat. The two PBRs were running at top speed at the time, the American Flags starched in the wind. For most boats, that would be 28 to 30 knots, but Williams, by removing much of the armor from around the engines of his craft, had shed weight in exchange for speed and ammo capacity. His boats were capable of racing through the water at about 35 knots.

One of his crewmen had no trouble making the identification when the PBRs had closed enough for the enemy's uniforms to be seen. In a mix of surprise, possibly alarm, the gunner declared the two sampans to be carrying regulars.

The fight was joined almost immediately. As the sampans split, one heading for the north bank and the other for the south, soldiers aboard opened fire on the approaching Navy boats. Forward machine guns on both PBRs answered in an instant. The craft pursued the southbound sampan, slowing to stabilize the firing, and within a few moments eliminated the target. The 105 boat, Williams at the throttle, came about in a skidding turn to try to catch the second enemy boat, but it reached the north shore and disappeared down an inlet too narrow for the PBRs to follow.

It was a brief, satisfactory firefight, half satisfactory anyway, and a less aggressive warrior might have been willing to call it good enough and resume the patrol.

Not Williams. For one thing, he knew the intricate stitchwork of rivers, canals, creeks and drainage ditches that was the Mekong Delta, maybe about as well as some of his enemy, and probably better than the troops from the north. Williams had been in the Delta since the previous April and was a quick study in the local geography.

As reported in Lieutenant Commander Thomas Cutler's book, *Brown Water, Black Berets*, which treats the battle in detail, Williams radioed PBR 99, "Stay with me. I know where he has to come out. We'll get 'im."

Once again, it was full throttle. The boats dashed along the riverbank for a short distance before turning into a canal and resuming flank speed.

Williams undoubtedly had been right about the sampan's destination, but as the PBRs came around a bend in the canal, they were confronted not with a single boatload of enemy soldiers, but 40 to 50 of them. They were troops of the 261st and 262nd NVA regiments. It was their misfortune that two among their fleet had made accidental contact with this small segment of the American brown-water navy.

Exactly how many soldiers were on hand is not certain, but the sampans were so loaded down with men that only a couple of inches of freeboard remained on the craft. One estimate was 15 to 20 troops on each boat, which meant the nine men on the two PBRs were facing 600 to 1,000 well-armed regular enemy infantrymen plus troops on the shore.

Both sides, as Cutler wrote it, might have been equally startled, but as on the river a short time before, the exchange of gunfire erupted almost immediately. Binder, gunner on the forward .50 caliber mount of the 105, may have been the first to pull the trigger. The NVA soldiers stood up in their boats to fire back with rifles.

For Williams, it was decision time and he had a split second to make it. Since there were no alternative lateral routes, it was either try to reverse course in the limited space available in order to escape the situation, or barrel ahead. Williams chose the latter. At this point, the PBR was less than 35 feet from the nearest sampan; the others were scattered out for perhaps 200 yards. Williams recalled what went through his mind: "Could I go right? Could I go left? No, I couldn't do either." The narrow canal, which ranged in width from 38 feet to only 14 feet, allowed no room to turn around and if Williams had tried, he would have been inviting disaster. "They would have blown us out of the water," Williams said.

In this case, the best defense turned out to be a good offense. As the two PBRs plunged at full power into the midst of the enemy sampan fleet, pandemonium broke out. Williams swerved his boat slightly left and then right to give his after gunner's grenade launcher a better angle.

The banks on both sides of the narrow canal erupted in rifle, automatic weapons and mortar fire, but the PBRs' speed caused them to miss the mark. Within seconds, the American boats reached the first of the sampans and ran right through and over them, swamping others in their wakes. This was possible because the PBRs at full speed rode exceptionally high, drawing only inches of water. Thus they were able to ride right over the heavily loaded sampans that already were almost down to their gunwales. The PBR Jacuzzi pumps left a tremendous plume of water behind them, as high as seven feet in the air. So the enemy boats that were not overrun were capsized by the turbulence.

It was a madhouse scene of overturned sampans, soldiers thrashing about in the water and weapons on either side of the bank missing the streaking American boats and hitting each other instead. "They killed a lot more of each other than we killed," Williams recalled in a recent interview. He related as one example a 57-millimeter recoilless rifle round hitting the starboard bow of his boat, going completely through and exploding on the opposite bank among enemy troops.

Of course while all of this was going on, the PBR gunners were furiously delivering their own considerable ordnance. Chattering .50 calibers and M-60s spewed thousands of rounds into the enemy targets, littering the boats' decks with brass cartridges, while grenades in rapid order arched toward the shores.

Miraculously, the two PBRs emerged on the far side of the sampan fleet unscathed except for numerous superficial gunfire punctures. The engines and all electronic equipment were still operating and there were no casualties.

The boats cleared the immediate area and the sailors began to relax a little while rearming. Williams, knowing prime targets remained behind his boats, possibly including junks loaded with ammunition and supplies, called for strikes by Seawolf helicopter gunships from a base at Long Binh. Throttled down, the boats proceeded up the narrowing canal while Williams looked for a place to turn around. As they cruised around a bend, they met a second and larger NVA contingent in sampans and junks. This group of North Vietnamese soldiers was just as surprised as the first, and Williams, who this time might have had the option of waiting for the helicopters, once again did not hesitate. Engines roared at full power and the two PBRs started running the gauntlet as before. Gunfire exploded on all sides, from the banks and from the boats, and the whole improbable scene was repeated. The fiberglass PBRs were hit repeatedly but never disabled and once again, the little men of war survived.

By this time, the Seawolves had arrived and despite the death and destruction left behind by the PBRs, the aircraft had plenty of live targets to shoot at both in the water and on the banks.

The radio exchange, as reported by Cutler, went like this: "I want y'all to go in there and hold a field day on them guys," Williams told the Seawolf commander, "Wilco," came the reply. "What are your intentions?"

"Well, I damn sure ain't goin' to stay here. I'm going back through." the boatswain's mate answered. Actually, the only way out was back by the same route the PBRs had traveled up the canal, and since Williams was not one to stand and watch a fight, he rejoined it.

The helicopters were having the "field day" requested by Williams, pouring rockets and machine gun fire into the jungle and canal in one swooping run after another. Williams had been right about the junks. Four of them disintegrated in tremendous secondary explosions that propelled debris 1,000 feet into the air.

The PBRs were in the middle of a melee not only of enemy but friendly fire, which was hitting close aboard. He said he and Commander Howard, commander of the Seawolves in the attack, shared a running joke after the battle about the number of helicopter rockets that landed no more than three or four feet from his bow. Not only that, but while everything else was going on, Williams called in 105mm Army artillery fire from a nearby battery and provided spotting information.

The battle was still raging as darkness fell, and Williams, despite the obvious hazard, had his boats turn the searchlights on. His Medal of Honor citation described the situation this way: "Now virtually dark, and although Petty Officer Williams was aware that his boats would become even better targets, he ordered the patrol boats' searchlights turned on to better illuminate the area and moved the patrol perilously close to shore to press the attack. Despite a waning supply of ammunition, the patrol successfully engaged the enemy ashore and completed the rout of the enemy force."

During the battle, an Army helicopter carrying a general showed up over the area, apparently to see if what he had been hearing over a radio was really true. When he saw the enemy bodies and the demolished and burning boats, he knew. "Well, I'll be damned. Seeing is believing," he said. After the helicopter circled over the area, the general radioed to Williams' boat: "Get that man in a flak jacket." It is not clear who among Williams' men was not properly attired, but in any case the boatswain's mate, who had survived the gauntlet against the longest of odds, was in no mood for that kind of order, even from an officer of flag rank. Williams grabbed the radio handset and replied: "Get your damned copter and your __ out of here. We're takin' care of this." The account of that exchange was taken from Cutler's *Brown Water, Black Berets*. The general didn't answer, possibly because it was obvious that what the sailor had said was true. He, his men and the Navy gunships were indeed taking care of matters.

The final tally showed staggering losses for the North Vietnamese: Sixty-five vessels destroyed, more than 1,000 men killed, and many more taken prisoner by the PBRs.

Against that toll, the two PBRs, though holed many times, were still operational, and most astonishing, their crews had suffered only two casualties, neither serious. Williams discovered a small piece of shrapnel in his side, and Binder took a bullet in his wrist, but it passed through without touching a bone. For Williams, it was the second of three wounds he would suffer during his Vietnam tour.

Binder also won the Navy Commendation Medal for his action and two other men in the patrol were awarded Bronze Stars.

The question, of course, is what such a large unit of North Vietnamese regulars was doing that deep in South Vietnam at that stage of the war. Williams surmises that the communists were planning a large-scale operation of the general magnitude that did not actually materialize until Tet, more than a year later. Whatever Regiments 261 and 262 had in mind, they were in no condition to carry out their mission after PBRs 105 and 99 were through with them.

Williams, who completed slightly more than a year in Vietnam in April 1967, was presented the Medal of Honor by President Lyndon Johnson on May 15, 1968. The final sentence of the citation was as follows: "His extraordinary heroism and exemplary fighting spirit in the face of grave risks inspired the efforts of his men to defeat a larger enemy force, and are in keeping with the finest traditions of the United States Naval Service."

Besides the Medal of Honor and the three Purple Hearts, Williams' decorations included the Navy Cross, two Silver Stars, the Navy and Marine Corps Medal, three Bronze Stars, the Navy Commendation Medal, and the Vietnamese Cross of Gallantry with Palm and Gold Star.

There may have been more highly decorated heroes of the Vietnam War than James Elliott Williams, but there surely could not have been many. It should be little or no exaggeration to call that sailor the Vietnam War's equivalent of Sergeant York and Audie Murphy.

Four months after that Halloween night action, another Gamewarden sailor earned the Medal of Honor for the unimaginably sacrificial act of covering a live grenade with his body. It was awarded posthumously to Seaman David G. Ouellet on January 30, 1968.

Ouellet served in River Division 53, the same one as Williams. His citation is the best available account of his action, so it will be related here in full:

"For conspicuous gallantry and intrepidity at the risk of his life above and beyond the call of duty while serving with River Section 532 against the enemy in the Republic of Vietnam.

"As the forward machine gunner on River Patrol Boat 124, which was on patrol on the Mekong River during the early evening hours of March 6, 1967, Seaman Ouellet observed suspicious activity near the river bank, alerted his boat captain and recommended movement of the boat to the area to investigate.

"While the PBR was making a high-speed run along the river bank Seaman Ouellet spotted an incoming enemy grenade falling toward the boat. He immediately left the protected position of his gun mount and ran aft for the full length of the speeding boat, shouting to his fellow crew members to take cover. Observing the boat captain standing unprotected on the boat, Seaman Ouellet bounded onto the engine compartment cover, and pushed the boat captain down to safety. In the split second that followed the grenade's landing, and in the face of certain death, Seaman Ouellet fearlessly placed himself between the deadly missile and his shipmates, courageously absorbing most of the blast fragments with his own body in order to protect his shipmates from injury and death. His extraordinary heroism and his selfless and courageous actions on behalf of his comrades at the expense of his own life were in the finest traditions of the United States Naval Service."

Ouellet wasn't killed instantly. He was evacuated by helicopter to Saigon where he died on the operating table. A Navy frigate later was named in his honor. At least three other Navy men aboard PBR 124 who survived that action undoubtedly honored Ouellet's memory as well from that day forward.

The same could be said of the men who owe their lives to Gunner's Mate Second Class Patrick Ford, who during a period after the Tet Offensive of early 1968 was a crewman aboard PBR 750 on the My Tho River. Enemy activity had picked up after Tet as Viet Cong forces tried to recoup their losses.

During a routine patrol, PBR 750 chased a sampan up a canal off the My Tho and as it returned to the main stream, the patrol boat came under intense rocket and automatic weapons fire. Two rockets hit the boat, setting it afire and causing a loss of control. As the craft headed for the beach, four more rockets found their mark. Ford, seriously wounded, nevertheless kept up steady fire from his gun mount until flames drove him from it. Then with his own clothes afire, he pushed other wounded crewmen over the side where they could be picked up.

The second PBR provided covering fire and reinforcements - more PBRs, Seawolf helicopters and ARVN troops - arrived to silence the enemy and allow the search for missing sailors. Two bodies were recovered, but Ford's was not. Nightfall halted the search.

A Viet Cong patrol found Ford's body washed up on the bank and staked it out in plain view in the hope of enticing more PBRs into an ambush. Before that could happen, a Popular Force chief dispatched his troops to the area, routed the guerrillas and recovered the Navy man's body.

For his bravery, Gunner's Mate Ford was awarded the Navy Cross posthumously and a frigate was later named for him.

BEERY

Another story of the horror of combat and the fighting spirit of patrol-boat sailors revolved around Lieutenant Dick Godbehere, who was mentioned earlier in the chapter on the Tet Offensive, and members of his crew, notably Third Class Signalman Jere Beery.

Godbehere was a mustang officer up from the ranks. By early 1968, he already was a veteran river fighter of more than 60 engagements with the enemy. He had been wounded the previous November, shrapnel in the jaw. He and his men on one occasion had to swim for their lives under intense small-arms fire after their PBR had been sunk in action.

The men liked serving with Godbehere. He was regarded as cool in a firefight and he once had been one of them. That always helped. And then there was his name. It was pronounced like it was spelled, and for men in combat who were an instant away from eternity, there was something comforting about "God Be Here."

His river section was 511 on the Bassac River out of Binh Thuy. On an evening in March 1968, the two-boat patrol headed downstream toward the city of Can Tho.

For Beery, it was too dark for him to see his new tailor-made camouflage uniform very well, but he looked anyway. He was proud of the outfit and his boatmates knew it. So they ribbed him about his being invisible, about his looking like a tree, and so forth.

The fighting garb of PBR men was somewhat eccentric at times. Many wore camouflaged uniforms, usually tiger strips, Marine-type fatigues, or traditional Navy dungarees. One sailor told of participating in many a firefight with only skivvies and a flak jacket on. Sometimes men wore only a bathing suit in deference to the extreme heat.

For this trip, a reporter was aboard. He would get a better story than he might have wanted, just as two newsmen had on a previous patrol with the Godbehere boat. On that occasion, as related by Lieutenant Commander Thomas Cutler in *Brown Water, Black Berets,* one reporter rested his camera on the canopy in an exposed position, ignoring the order by the boat captain to get a flak jacket on as the boat entered dangerous waters. Almost immediately, the boat was peppered by automatic-weapons fire, which caused the reporter to hit the deck at the boat captain's feet. The enemy fire had not helped the sailor's mood, so he kicked the civilian and told him to get up and get his pictures. "We ain't coming through here for you again." The only photographs obtained were a few stills by the second reporter. The boat, incidentally, ended up with 136 bullet holes in the hull.

The patrol, in total darkness, now had passed Can Tho and the upriver end of Cu Lao Mae Island. The account of the battle that would ensue is taken from Cutler's book.

A flash of light, then another told the practiced eye that B-40 rockets were being fired their way by the Viet Cong, though both were well off the mark.

The boats did not return fire immediately for two reasons. One was the possibility of friendly units in the area, the other to keep from exposing their position in the darkness prematurely. Godbehere by radio confirmed that no friendlies were about, so he ordered a firing run against the source of the rockets.

Beery on the after .50 caliber sent about 100 rounds into the enemy position and then leaned over to open another ammunition canister. At that time, two fireballs from B-40 rockets emerged from the trees and headed toward the PBR. Beery saw them coming, but thought they would miss. One didn't. It hit the gunwale on the starboard quarter. A few minutes later, a second rocket exploded against the grenade locker on the starboard side.

Godbehere saw the flash and felt the heat of the first detonation, and also felt shrapnel ripping into his legs. He was hurled to the deck, but despite his severe leg wounds, he was able to regain his feet and begin to evaluate the situation aboard his stricken boat. A gunner named Sherman had shrapnel wounds in his arm and foot, but he too was able to continue to function.

Godbehere noticed that Beery was still standing at his gun but not firing, which told the officer that something was wrong. He sent Sherman to find out and the gunner returned with this understatement: "Beery's hurt bad, Mr. Godbehere."

Painfully, Godbehere made his way aft to check on his crewman. "Where're you hit?"

"In the gut," Beery gasped. The shrapnel had disemboweled the young sailor. The intestines of the still-standing man trailed down to a pile on the deck. It was a hideous wound and a horrible sight for Godbehere and Sherman, but they maintained their coolness. The pair eased Beery down to the deck, and Godbehere carefully and gently placed the entrails back into the wounded man's abdomen. He then covered the gaping wound with a large battle dressing. In the meantime, Sherman cut away the shrapnel-shredded trouser legs of Beery's new camis, which he had been so proud of only hours before. His right leg and hip were badly chewed by metal fragments, and a large piece of shrapnel that had entered Beery's stomach was protruding from the back.

Godbehere tried to reassure Beery but he barely believed it himself. Of the sailor's most grievous wound, the officer was frank: "You're going to be all right. Your intestines just fell out. They can put 'em back for you. They do it all the time. You'll be okay."

Beery, who earlier had made a whispered request that Godbehere tell his parents what happened, now just shook his head, which produced an emotional reaction from the lieutenant. He shouted to his rear gunner that he was going to make it.

Even before starting to tend to his wounded crewman, Godbehere had ordered both boats in the patrol to withdraw from the fire zone. The second boat also had been hit many times in the engagement and both were too heavily damaged to continue the fight.

Godbehere headed them toward the village of Tra On on the east bank of the Bassac opposite the island from where the enemy had opened fire. Army advisors were stationed there and it was the best and closest place he could think of for medical evacuation. A call went out to an Air Force medical evacuation helicopter.

As the boats headed toward the village, Godbehere, his own leg wounds severe, knelt beside Beery offering encouragement and comfort to the horribly wounded man.

As Army advisors loaded him onto the stretcher at Tra On, Beery amazingly offered a thin smile and a little joke. Holding up a piece of what was left of his new camouflage shirt, he said, "I don't know how those guys managed to hit me. I thought I looked like a tree."

Both Beery and Godbehere were evacuated, never to fight in Vietnam again. Against all odds and appearances, Beery recovered from his wounds, a fact that Cutler attributes in part to the inner strength and spirit that caused him to make a light remark at a time when, for all he knew, he was at the point of death. Beery went on to become a movie stunt man and also has been doing a screen play of his experiences. He believes that was one of the purposes for which he

was spared through the help of a man named Godbehere.

As a postscript, Beery, Godbehere and others on the boat crew had not seen one another for 23 years until they met at the Gamewarden reunion in Norfolk in 1991. Beery, in keeping with his already well-established sense of humor, had the fare ready on the plates of his former comrades-in-arms - C Rations.

Another PBR sailor who survived terrible wounds to return to active and useful life was Dave Roever, about whom much has been included in this book earlier, notably his training experience.

Roever, a devout Christian before and during his time in the Navy, has become prominent in evangelistic circles, and during his ordeal in the brown waters of Vietnam, his never-wavering faith also was evident.

The summary that follows is taken wholly from Roever's book about his Vietnam experiences, *Welcome Home, Davey.*

In late July 1969, Roever had been in Vietnam for about six months, first serving aboard PBRs out of Sa Dec and then from Tan An on the Vam Co Tay River west of Saigon. The latter duty, he recalled, made Sa Dec seem like R&R.

Late in the afternoon of July 25, the PBRs moved out to an S-curve on the river where a canal intersected what was thought to be a crossing point for the Viet Cong.

The river was narrow at that point and an ambush should not have been surprising. It started with a B-40 rocket whizzing just over Roever's head. The Viet Cong obviously had been aiming at him, the forward gunner wielding the most firepower with his twin .50s, but unaccountably missed. B-40s actually are anti-tank weapons, containing a second charge after the initial penetration. They were less effective against the fiberglass PBRs because they often would go straight through and out before exploding. The hull material lacked the resistance necessary for detonation. Thirteen rockets were fired at Roever's boat and seven at the second vessel. As odd as it sounds, the sailor explained, the crews instinctively learned to count incoming rounds even in the midst of combat as a way of judging the size of the unit they were fighting.

In the ensuing firefight, Roever suffered a minor but painful shrapnel wound to the eye, and a helicopter lifted him out for medical attention at a nearby Army aid station not far from the PBR base. The idea was that Roever, after his treatment, would make his way back to the base to meet his boat and resume his duty.

But when he arrived, he was met by an astonished Lieutenant Rambo, his commanding officer, who wanted to know what the sailor was doing there. Roever, assuming Rambo did not know about the firefight and his wound, began to explain, but that was not the point of the officer's question. Rambo had heard about the action and Roever's medical evaluation of his radio, but strangely, his understanding of the wound was completely wrong. "I specifically heard that the side of your face was blown off, the trunk of your body had third-degree burns, and that your hands suffered blast damage. I heard that over the radio."

Roever and Rambo undoubtedly passed that misinformation off as a military communication

snafu, and let it go at that. Twenty-four hours later, they both might have wondered about the meaning of Rambo's words.

The PBRs returned from their engagement, but early the next morning they were to try to find the same location, look for Viet Cong bodies and neutralize any force that might remain.

About 4:00 a.m, they headed out, but finding the right place was not easy. The river banks looked pretty much alike in many localities. Nevertheless, with Roever at the helm, the boat captain thought he had found it, and ordered the boat beached nose in. A bunker could be seen 20 or 30 feet back in the brush, which the sailors assumed had been the source of the rockets the day before.

There was no way of knowing whether the enemy was still around, or if they weren't, whether the area had been booby-trapped, so caution was in order. Roever slipped from the chief's cabin to his regular station on the forward .50s and trained his guns in the direction of the bunker.

Grenades were called for, but Roever thought they were too close for the fragmentation variety, so he chose white phosphorous grenades, which would not shower the area with shrapnel, but would burn away foliage or any wires hooked up to booby traps.

When WP grenades detonate, they spread the chemical, which splashes like water. It burns extremely hot, searing everything it touches, and because oxygen is a byproduct of burning phosphorous, it feeds on itself. Water won't put out the fire. In fact, a white phosphorous grenade thrown into the water will continue to boil and bubble, giving off a glow.

Roever hurled one grenade toward the bunker, but decided it was not doing the job totally, so he picked up another. In his right hand, about six inches from his face, the grenade exploded, for no explicable reason.

What followed was an account of horror, struggle, pain and survival.

Roever heard the explosion, which deafened him, and felt the heat, but no terrible pain then, or for some time to come. What he saw in those first moments was worse than what he felt. His description:

"I looked down and saw half my face on the deck in front of me. Out of my right eye I saw flame and then nothing more; it went blind. Out of my left eye, I watched as the skin from my face shriveled on the deck like newspaper set aflame. I saw the ashes of my face blow around in a circle, and then float off into the air."

Roever's impulse was to get out of the gun tub, which he accomplished by pulling himself up by the guns themselves. They were so hot they cooked the palms of his hands, but at the time, that didn't hurt either.

Roever tumbled into the river, which at the moment seemed to be the best place to be, but as mentioned, water doesn't quench white phosphorous, so the sailor continued to burn. He first sank to the bottom and under the boat, which seemed to crush his body down into the mud, but the vessel lifted and Roever emerged on the other side. His left fist in the air, Roever's shouted words were "God, I still believe in You." It was an affirmation of faith even in the direst of circumstances.

A new man on the boat - he had been in

Vietnam only a few days - went into the river to try to help. He swam up close to the stricken sailor, who was still glowing and bubbling. Roever recalls: "I remember the bizarre look on his face. It was as though he had suddenly discovered that war really is hell; he had been dropped into an inferno, and his horrified expression seemed to say, "This is going to happen to us all."

Roever swam for shore, the newcomer following him, but not getting too close lest he himself ignite.

Roever pulled himself onto the bank and sometime later, the boat captain joined him. He also was burned.

The white phosphorous burned a hole in the trachea and Roever began breathing through his chest. The right side of his face was nearly gone, exposing his teeth and jawbone. From the waist up, he had about 40 percent third-degree burns. The injuries closely matched those described by Rambo - the day before.

When the evacuation helicopter arrived, a medic thought Roever was dead and handled him accordingly. When he called out "medic," mainly to let everyone know he was alive, the man almost fainted.

Incredibly, Roever was still burning. He set the stretcher on fire, and later at the Third Field Hospital, a MASH unit, he flared again every time more phosphorous was exposed to oxygen. Twelve days later, in Texas, smoldering phosphorous was still present.

In the meantime, Roever's survival was not altogether certain. He heard a doctor at the MASH declare he was not going to make it.

He was moved to Saigon for a one-night stopover before being shipped to Japan where sophisticated burn treatment could begin. At Tan Son Nhut Airport, hooked to an IV, Roever waited in a long line of stretchers to be stacked in the hospital transportation plane. They were all leaving Vietnam, not like they imagined or hoped, but leaving alive nevertheless. Somewhere nearby, perhaps, were more silver-colored coffins, awaiting shipment home of the kind Roever had seen six months before when he arrived.

That had been in January 1969, and the PBR war had already penetrated deep into the upper Delta near Cambodia. An episode of desperate action, outstanding heroism and supreme sacrifice is described by Cutler in *Brown Water, Black Berets*.

The date was January 20, inauguration day in the United States for a new president, Richard Nixon, an event that would have a profound effect on the war then raging in Southeast Asia. But Vietnamization was not yet started, and the men manning four PBRs and a heavily armed riverine "Tango" boat, which was a converted landing craft more formally called a monitor, were still prosecuting the war in American fashion.

On this night, boats of the column led by the Tango were chugging 50 to 75 yards apart on the Kinh Dong Tien Canal off the Mekong River near the Cambodian border, ready to interdict, interfere with or fight any enemy they encountered.

The previous night, a Viet Cong ambush in the same area had resulted in the loss of a boat and wounds to several sailors.

The canal ran parallel to the Cambodian border, so the best bet was that any enemy movement would be across the waterway and not along it.

PBR 8137 was commanded and piloted by Yeoman First Class G.H. Childress. The yeoman rating is clerical by nature and traditional Navy hands of previous wars might find it unusual to see clerks commanding small boats in direct small-arms combat with the enemy. The brown-water Navy was good at demolishing old stereotypes.

Also aboard Childress' boat was the commander of the two-PBR section, which included the one just ahead, Chief Quartermaster William J. Thompson.

The canal was narrow, the night was black, the enemy was probably nearby and nerves aboard the boats were taut. But Childress had volunteered his boat for this patrol on grounds that someone had to do it and besides, it was better than stationary assignments waiting for the chance to ambush the Viet Cong.

This time, the Viet Cong would be the ambushers and from the starboard bank the attack came with a ferocity of light and sound. Rockets hurtled out of the darkness. Automatic weapons fire tore into the little boats.

The five vessels replied in kind while Thompson called for Seawolf helicopter support.

An enemy rocket hit the 8137 in the starboard engine area; a second detonated against the coxswain's station armor plating. The first probably was enough to inflict a mortal wound on the vessel, the second sealed its fate.

Both Childress and Thompson were knocked unconscious by the second rocket, and when the boat captain revived, the boat was on fire and sinking fast. Yet the crew continued to fight back as though oblivious to their situation.

Childress tried to throttle up to clear the area, but the motors' pumps would not respond.

One of the Viet Cong's little tricks was to feed rice straw into the water upstream from where they believed PBRs were approaching. The straw, they knew, would float downstream and if enough got into the PBR's jet intakes, it would foul them. The tactic had worked in this case, so Childress used what little momentum his boat still had to nose her into the bank where the five men left the boat. They climbed up the muddy bank and took refuge in a drainage ditch that had been exposed by the low tide to await developments or plan the next move.

The other four boats having cleared the area, the firing subsided, but the enemy was between the five sailors and any surface help, not a reassuring situation.

The resumption of the firefight indicated that the boats had reversed course and were coming back through. One of them was PBR 770, commanded by Chief Boatswain's Mate Quincy Truett whose figure could be seen in the light of flares on the bow firing his M-16 rifle at nearly point-blank range at the Viet Cong machine gunners raking his boat. He motioned for the men in the ditch to get aboard.

Childress did not believe it possible for the 770 to survive the gauntlet, but on it came to attempt the rescue. On the first pass, one sailor managed to climb on before withering fire forced the boat to retire.

Again and again, the 770 returned, Truett still on the bow returning fire without yielding to the rounds hitting all around him, and helping men aboard. Finally, only Childress was left. As Truett continued to fire, the yeoman slipped and slid but clambered up the muddy bank of the ditch enough so he could grab the bow. Truett grabbed his shirt and pulled him the rest of the way.

At that point, his grip relaxed. Truett lay dead on the deck, an AK-47 wound in his throat.

Truett had volunteered for a second tour in

Members of River Division 533 meeting again after 22 years - from 1969 to 1991. Back row, left to right: Chuck Hodkins, William G. Mathis, Jim Guthrie, Jr. and James F. Woodward, Jr. Front row, left to right: Joe Gorshe, John Cozad and Del Goff. U.S. Navy Vietnam Veterans and proud Americans. (Courtesy of James Guthrie)

Vietnam, because that was where the war was. For career military men, professional warriors in service of their country, that is not such a strange thing to do. But it was courageous nevertheless.

The battle on the Kinh Dong Tien Canal was not quite over. Thompson picked up Truett's M-16 to resume the fire on the enemy positions and he too soon fell mortally wounded. He died the next day. One of the Seawolf helicopters that responded to Thompson's call was shot down. For PBR 8137, the war was not over. Salvage crews retrieved the boat and she was repaired for further duty.

For his heroism, Quincy Truett, chief boatswain's mate, was awarded the Navy Cross, and Chief Quartermaster William Thompson the Silver Star, both posthumously. Childress and his crew were awarded the Navy Commendation Medals for their roles in the battle.

On February 3, 1973, Geri Truett, widow of the fallen sailor, christened a destroyer escort named for her husband.

GUTHRIE

Jim Guthrie, who as a gunner's mate third class in 1969 served aboard PBRs in the lower Mekong Delta out of My Tho and later in the upper Delta in the Parrot's Beak area, counts among his combat experiences the terrible pain the death of a comrade can cause in such a small unit.

A boat's crew was four - five if the patrol commander was aboard - so if one man was killed and a couple wounded, the casualty rate could be called extreme.

Guthrie was not in-country long before he learned close-up what a deadly place he had come to. For orientation, the rookie Gamewarden sailor was taken for a short ride on PBR 21. Not long after that, the same boat took direct hits from B-40 rockets in the Cho Gao canal with loss of lives. There could be no illusions about this war or his place in it.

Guthrie was assigned to River Division 533, PBR 147 where he was the M-60 machine gunner.

Like every PBR man, Guthrie experienced the tedium, heat and tension of seemingly endless searches of sampans by day, the dark terror of night patrols where lack of vision combined with likelihood of enemy contact, and the explosive violence of the firefight, typically a close-range frenzied donnybrook of automatic weapons that paid off on the sheer volume of metal that could be delivered against the other side.

That is why Guthrie remarked that his only real moments of panic on those occasions came when he had to reload, knowing that for that brief interlude his boat was one crucial gun shy of full strength. When the firing had stopped and the boat moved to a safer area, the men would light their cigarettes with slightly trembling hands as the adrenalin level ebbed for the moment.

The Viet Cong were not the only hazards, physical or psychological. Vietnam was alive with snakes, a fact that stateside trainers had made the sailors aware of. They were told Vietnam had 100 species of serpent, 99 of which were venomous. One was called the five-step snake, meaning that anyone bitten would take

five steps before keeling over dead. During survival training, one of Guthrie's buddies, Dwayne Brooks, figured if he was bitten, he would just stand still and thus avoid the five-step hazard. Typical GI humor. Without it, few could have kept their sanity.

One of the night maneuvers on the Delta rivers and canals called for the PBR to drift quietly to the bank where crewman would reach for vegetation to tie off on. It was one of Guthrie's fears he would grab a snake instead, a real possibility. "A bamboo viper fell on the bow one night and I ever so quietly, but quickly, scooted my boot across the deck to kick it over the side. I said "bamboo viper" because I feared them the most. In my mind it had to be a bamboo viper."

The other fauna of Vietnam was about as forbidding. Guthrie described the huge mosquitoes that made raids even in the daytime, and of stories he had heard of nine-foot catfish, freshwater sharks, and bats with seven-foot wing spans.

Guthrie went on 138 combat PBR patrols during his tour in Vietnam and engaged in seven firefights in a six-month period, including one in which his boat came under ambush six times within 30 minutes.

Sometimes the situation encountered would be beyond the ordinary. The PBR, responding to reports of Viet Cong up a long, narrow canal, found none when they arrived, but did spot a 500-pound unexploded bomb. The crew called in a strike by a Black Pony aircraft to detonate it. The plane missed, so the pilot asked the sailors to mark the bomb, which they did with a white handkerchief. The aircraft's ordnance missed again, but the fireworks from the air apparently had the beneficial effect of keeping the Viet Cong at bay in a place where the PBRs would have been highly vulnerable to an ambush. Incidentally, the demolition work on the bomb had to be done from the ground.

Still another hazard of combat river duty was navigational. Guthrie suffered a serious and ultimately debilitating injury when his PBR ran aground one night at top speed.

The two-boat patrol had been scrambled in response to a call from a village that it was under attack by the Viet Cong. As the boats neared the village, they came to an abrupt stop, throwing everyone to the deck. Both boats were stranded on a sandbar within sight of the Viet Cong. Guthrie, suffered a fractured left heel, never walked without a limp after that night.

In the meantime, the boats were exceptionally vulnerable. All night the sailors watched the Viet Cong through their starlight scopes and the enemy watched them. When tidal water refloated the boats the next day, they returned to base. Later, captured Viet Cong related that they hadn't attacked because they thought the Americans had run aground deliberately in order to trick them. The United States Navy's evident reputation for craftiness served them well that night.

The Parrot's Beak section of South Vietnam is bounded by two rivers, the Vam Co Tay and the Vam Co Dong. Together they formed a natural barrier around the Cambodian bulge into Vietnam due west of and not far from Saigon. It was to this area that River Division

533 shifted from My Tho early in 1969. Guthrie recalls it was not hospitable territory. "The Viet Cong were as thick as palm trees growing along the river banks. We knew that because the friendly "Viet Cong fisherman-farmers' were flying the red and blue flag with the large yellow star in the center instead of the standard South Vietnamese . . . flag . . . "

As a show of strength, the Navy ran patrols of 10 PBRs rather than the standard two, but the Viet Cong responded later by aggressive ambushes against the two-boat mission. That was the occasion for the six attacks in a half-hour against Guthrie's patrol. Another attack on a Division 533 patrol led to heroic action by one of the crew, Michael Gates, who continued to fire despite being critically wounded. Gates, credited with helping save the lives of the other crew members, was awarded the Navy Cross.

Every man who goes to war probably takes away one searing memory, one particular experience, that above all others stays with him forever like some psychological brand. For Jim Guthrie, that would be the day John D. Muir, one of his closest buddies, was killed.

On August 1, 1969, PBR 147 and its covering boat were on patrol on the Vam Co Dong River when Guthrie and Muir were put ashore to investigate something unusual Guthrie had spotted. It was a camouflaged sampan, which the two sailors destroyed. They had just reboarded when the patrol officer, Torpedoman First Class W.G. Mathis, sensing trouble, instructed the pair to assume their gun positions, Guthrie the M-60 amidships and Muir the .50 caliber on the bow. At that moment, Muir yelled "Grenade!" it was his last word. The alerted Guthrie saw that the grenade had hit some clothing hanging on the coxwain's flat and fallen to the deck two feet below where he was standing. Guthrie, in jumping to the grenade, injured his hand, but managed to hurl the explosive over the side before it detonated.

In the instant Muir sounded the grenade warning, he was passing in front of Mathis on his way to his gun position. Automatic weapons fire from the bank killed him instantly and passed through, critically wounding Mathis. The patrol commander held onto Muir to keep him from falling into the water, which cost Mathis another wound.

Guthrie in the meantime got to his gun and began returning fire and shouted for the Vietnamese trainee to do the same on the aft .50 caliber. That gun had remained silent for the critical moments of initial frenetic activity aboard the PBR.

For a time, only Guthrie's M-60 was answering the Viet Cong fire, but the cover boat commanded by Engineman Second Class Joe Gorshe quickly jumped into the fray and enabled the 147, in Guthrie's opinion, to survive the ambush.

Boat commander Engineman Second Class Chuck Hodkins backed the PBR away from the bank and turned control over to Guthrie while he gave aid to Mathis and Muir. Hodkins, exposing himself to the enemy fire that remained heavy, went to the bow for a shotgun and an M-16 rifle to be used as makeshift splints for Mathis' leg. He received a scalp wound in the melee.

Guthrie radioed for a medevac helicopter, but conditions made that process more difficult than it ordinarily would have been. Guthrie couldn't read the map to give a precise location because of blood stains on it, and Hodkins couldn't be heard from the bow because of the engine noise. Finally, Guthrie radioed Gorshe on the cover boat to give the helicopter the position.

The boat headed upriver to the Vietnamese outpost where it was to meet the helicopter. Guthrie and Hodkins helped carry their boatmates and friends, the seriously wounded Mathis and the lifeless John Muir to the helicopter.

Later, after returning to the base camp, the two remaining crew members still able to function picked up the division commanders and returned to the ambush site, where evidence was discovered showing that the PBRs had stumbled onto a major enemy crossing point.

A combat death in such a close-knit and small unit as the PBR Navy was, in Guthrie's words, devastating, but the war robbed them even of the normal grieving process.

"We didn't have the luxury of grief, because that would cause us to be inefficient. We couldn't grieve our losses in Vietnam, so we held it in all these years. I have had thoughts of the ambush every night, while trying to go to sleep, for years," Guthrie has written in recent times.

There is a postscript to the story of John D. Muir, who, incidentally, was the direct descendant of the eminent naturalist and explorer John Muir, a leading advocate of the national park system early in this century. Some would call him "Father of the National Parks."

When Guthrie returned home in 1970, he went to Florida to pay his respects to Muir's family, "which by the way was one of the hardest things I ever had to do in my life."

Twenty-two years later, in 1992, Guthrie had occasion to be in Florida again, and naturally wanted to visit his friend's grave. But to his dismay, he found no mausoleum bearing John D. Muir's name and was further astonished to learn that the cemetery had put the body in a holding area for non-payment of funeral expenses.

Guthrie was determined to get to the bottom of that, of course, and he learned that the expenses indeed had been paid by Muir's parents, but someone had absconded with the money.

Guthrie enlisted the aid of Admiral Elmo Zumwalt, Jr., now retired, and Rear Admiral S.F. Gallo, then Deputy Chief of Naval Personnel, to ensure that John D. Muir, a man who had died valiantly in the service of his country, a hero who had won the Silver Star, was provided a resting place befitting him.

The officers gave it their prompt attention, and on July 20, 1993, a memorial ceremony was held for Muir.

"I shed tears at (the service), which was a much needed release of emotions I needed to experience. I felt as though weight had been lifted off my shoulders. I finally had a peaceful feeling about the loss of my friend, John David Muir," Guthrie has written.

If the full expression of sorrow came late

for Guthrie, so did recognition of his combat service. On August 1, 1992, exactly 23 years after that awful day in the Parrot's Beak, Guthrie was presented the Navy Achievement Medal, with Combat Distinguishing Device, for "sustained superior performance and bravery under fire . . ." The delay was the result of records being lost when River Division 533 was turned over to the Vietnamese in October 1969. The lapse of time did not take the luster from the decoration. "It is still a chest-pounding honor to receive recognition for your achievements . . . while in the service to the country you love," was the way Guthrie put it.

Lieutenant Jim Morgan, whose arrival in Vietnam in 1968 was chronicled in an earlier chapter, was assigned to a PBR division in the Rung Sat where the main job, in conjunction with minesweepers, was keeping the shipping channel to Saigon open.

The Viet Cong, he understood, operated a rocketeer school in the area and for graduation the trainee was to take a shot at the bridge of a cargo ship. But that would bring a call for an attack on the source by a pair of PBRs, which, as Morgan described it, meant six barrels of .50 caliber machine gun fire plus 72 grenades all were concentrated at one point. The Viet Cong were overmatched in those situations.

Morgan recalls his first firefight vividly. Early in his tour as a patrol commander, he took his two boats into a small canal outside the area normally patrolled by the PBRs, hoping to catch the Viet Cong in a crossing.

First an illumination round exploded over the boats, and then a round landed in the water between the two boats. The PBRs cranked up to head out when automatic weapons fire erupted from the port bank and another high explosives round hit ahead of the boat.

The boats returned fire, and Morgan recalls the clear impression the after gunner made squeezing off rounds in the short bursts like it was taught at school.

It turned out that the boats were exchanging fire with a friendly force, a battalion of Thai troops also waiting for the chance to ambush the Viet Cong. The Thais lost one man, but it was a case of failure of the ground units to clear the operation with United States headquarters, Morgan wrote. His account is carried in the book, *The Vietnam Experience: A War Remembered,* from which this narrative pertaining to Morgan is derived.

Morgan late in January 1969 suffered leg wounds in the Vam Co Dong River area, the Parrot's Beak section west of Saigon where the division had been moved. The night patrol had just started - it was not yet dark - when the PBR was hit simultaneously by two rockets, one in each bow. One went straight through and exploded in the river, and one hit an aluminum fuse panel, which shattered and filled Morgan's legs with shards of metal. As the officer recalled it, he heard the boom, saw the smoke filling the cockpit and felt the pressure in his legs. The first shots of the ambush had found their mark. The forward gunner was lucky to have escaped unscathed, inasmuch as the rockets passed close by on either side of him.

Morgan's pants legs had about 100 holes in them, but the wounds were not serious because

the light aluminum fragments had not dug deeply.

The Vam Co Dong River region presented more dangers to the PBR crews than had the Rung Sat. Less than two weeks before Morgan was hit, his unit lost the man who had been closest to the officer, a boat engineer who already had won the Purple Heart and Silver Star.

The streams were narrower and the foliage thicker in the upper reaches of Vietnam's river system, which added to the hazards and the stress level.

Morgan's account deals in detail with what he observed of that aspect. For instance, he wrote of a first-class petty officer who after enduring a year of patrols started going to sickbay for tranquilizer shots. In action, he was fine, but afterwards, he needed help.

A more extreme case involved a boat captain, a man with an excellent record who already had won the Silver Star. Yet during a night ambush, he came undone, calling on the radio every few second with a new message of fear and alarm. Back at the LST base, he started firing his .45 at passing sampans. The man had to be sent home early.

A lieutenant (jg) assigned to Morgan's unit didn't make it through the first day. "When I picked him up in Saigon, he said he just couldn't face going on patrol." Morgan wrote. So the officer was reassigned to a staff job.

Those incidents make the point that going out on small boats onto narrow, well-covered banks made for ambush was no easy matter, and the remarkable thing was how many were willing to do it day after day. Morgan's outfit had to take only five men off the river because they couldn't patrol any longer, even though some, maybe many, were tempted to seek relief.

Morgan told of visiting a young sailor whose boat had been hit and he had been singed from the fire. The officer surmised that the man wanted to ask for relief and then thought better of it. In any case, he continued to patrol and perform well for his remaining six months' of duty.

Morgan's own stress level rose shortly after he was wounded, when he had to pass the place of ambush for the first time.

Leaving Vietnam after a year of combat was the occasion for relief but not celebration on the part of Morgan and the others on the plane. There was a sense of unfinished business.

SEALORDS

Vice Admiral Elmo R. Zumwalt Jr. came to Vietnam in September 1968 as the naval commander in the theater and with him he brought an entirely new approach to river warfare in the Mekong Delta and adjacent areas.

Innovative, unorthodox and bold, Zumwalt had the attitude of a winner. He was a popular figure among the sailors, often mingling with the ranks without the imperius air associated with high command - a large entourage, for instance - and often injected himself into dangerous situations.

Strategically, his major contribution to the Vietnam War was a series of operations under a general campaign called Sea Lords, which stood for Southeast Asia Lake, Ocean, River, Delta

Strategy, a rather tortured acronym contrived to produce the easy-to-remember nautical label.

Sea Lords represented the incorporation of elements of all three river and coastal task forces: Market Time (115), the interdiction unit that operated offshore and in the major river estuaries, Gamewarden (116), the river patrol force, and the River Assault Force (117), which together with a brigade of the 9th Infantry Division formed the Mobile Riverine Force.

Sea Lords consisted of two phases. The first called for a barrier to be established parallel to and near the Cambodian border in the upper Delta and tying off near Saigon. A series of operations were carried out by river and combat elements, including Gamewarden PBRs, Swift boats and craft of the MRF under such code names as Search Turn, Foul Deck, Barrier Reef, and the largest, bloodiest and most significant, Giant Slingshot.

The idea was to form an actual fixed line to present a physical obstacle to enemy forces seeking to enter Vietnam from Cambodia. Vietnam was almost wholly a war without front lines, a point often noted. Fighting typically swirled in jungles, marshes and highlands, often triggered by ambushes after which troops of one or both sides would fade away. Frontal combat was the exception. Some likened the Vietnam land war to combat on the open seas, where the objective is to destroy the enemy rather than to take and hold territory. It's hard to control a big area of ocean, and it was just as hard to make geography secure in Vietnam against a force that employed guerrilla tactics and either was or looked like indigenous people. So Zumwalt's idea of a barrier, which eventually stretched from the Gulf of Thailand through the Delta to Saigon, was something new for Vietnam.

The second phase called for allied forces to push into localities previously considered Viet Cong strongholds, notably the U Minh Forest and the Nam Can areas on the Ca Mau Peninsula at the south end of the country.

Behind Zumwalt's approach was the realization that border crossings from Cambodia continued to provide the enemy with greater resupply and reinforcement opportunities than the allies could accept. Market Time has succeeded in reducing seaborne infiltration significantly and Gamewarden's interdiction work had been effective where it was carried out on the principal rivers and immediate tributaries, but the Cambodian border remained far from closed. Secondary streams, canals and the Plain of Reeds during high water were some of the routes of entry.

In one respect, the Zumwalt plan was a belated recognition of the validity of the Bucklew report four years before. Navy Chaplain Philip Bucklew, as described in an earlier chapter, led a contingent that studied the infiltration problem early in the war. Conclusions reached in 1964 led to the Market Time and Gamewarden, but Bucklew's observation that Cambodia represented a major entry point was not fully heeded until Sea Lords.

Other considerations for Zumwalt was his concern that the Navy's role in the war was inadequate, which in turn contributed to flagging morale in the service. The situation to a

degree was the natural result of the in-country force's successes. Enemy contact diminished as the Viet Cong pulled back. They lessened their own activity or became less eager to engage the American forces. Sea Lords would change at least one thing. Enemy contact no longer would be light.

Organizationally, Sea Lords was designated Task Force 194 initially under the charge of Captain Robert Saltzre, then commander of Task Force 117. Zumwalt dubbed Saltzer the First Sea Lord, the same title given to Great Britain's top naval minister. The new unit came into being on November 5, 1968.

The overall thrust of Sea Lords was to move the small boat forces deeper into the country. The Navy PCFs and the Coast Guard WPBs assumed a role on the inland waterway, wherever their crafts could float, and the Gamewarden PBRs penetrated farther upstream into the narrower canals and river tributaries. For that force, it was the final evolution from the original concept of staying in the middle of wide rivers and avoiding firefights. Now it was plying the dangerous, narrow waters and aggressively seeking out the enemy.

Even before Zumwalt took over, Task Force 115 under Captain Roy Hoffman had been deploying his Swift boats inland with some success. On one such mission, the PCFs went seven miles up the Ong Doc River in the Ca Mau Peninsula and then down a connecting canal to attack a Viet Cong stronghold. More than 100 structures and many sampans were destroyed.

About two weeks after Zumwalt took over naval forces in Vietnam, a young lieutenant set the tone for river warfare over the next year and a half and gave the admiral a chance to show his leadership mettle as well.

While naval leadership believed the best results in setting up an infiltration barrier would be achieved as close to the Cambodian border as possible, political considerations dictated otherwise. The fear of an incursion, real or alleged, into that country prompted establishment of the first line 35 to 40 miles away from the frontier between the two nations.

That meant the Rach Giang Thanh River, a small stream running very close along the Cambodian line, was off-limits to American Naval forces.

Lieutenant (jg) Michael Bernique, a PCF commander, was resting his men at the mouth of the river on the Gulf of Thailand on October 14 when he learned that a Viet Cong tax collecting station was operating upstream some distance.

Bernique, liberally interpreting his orders to permit personal initiative, decided that the circumstances justified action. He took his boat up the river, and sure enough, the Viet Cong were at work in the relaxed attitude that comes from believing the adversary will be nowhere about. The Viet Cong might have been as well aware of the American's political timidity as anyone.

The VC's complacency cost them. Too surprised by the sight of an American boat to open fire immediately, the Viet Cong were scattered in disarray when the Swift boat's guns went into action. The fleeing Viet Cong left behind three of their own dead plus a large supply of weapons, ammunition, supplies and

documents, which the Navy men liberated. The Viet Cong regrouped to challenge the Swift at a cost of two more dead guerrillas. The boat withdrew with the captured booty, and no friendly casualties.

When the Navy brass learned of the Bernique raid, they summoned him to Saigon, presumably to determine whether he should face a court-martial for disobeying orders to stay off the Rach Giang Thanh River.

As part of the process, Bernique had to appear before Zumwalt and members of his staff. At one point during the interrogation, Bernique proved himself just as unabashed in the presence of his superiors as he had been in combat. When told by an officer that Cambodia's Prince Sihanouk had accused him of firing into Cambodia and killing civilians, Bernique's reply was bold and risky under the circumstances, "Well you can tell Sihanouk that he's a lying son-of-a-bitch."

The junior officer, of course, had no way of knowing at the time what the three-star admiral seated opposite would think of that remark, but he soon found out. In a real-life scene like those written into the scripts of countless bad war movies, Bernique emerged from the room a hero instead of a candidate to stand court-martial. Zumwalt, declaring that Bernique was the kind of boat commander "we need more of," awarded the lieutenant a Silver Star on the spot.

The incident had more significance than a dramatic sub-plot of the war. Bernique's success in that raid resulted in a shift in strategy that placed the barrier up tight against the Cambodian border where the naval leadership thought it belonged from the start.

A second raid up the Rach Giang River - then dubbed "Bernique's Creek" - was launched, this time with three PCFs covered by two Seawolf helicopters. Fittingly, Bernique's Swift was the lead boat.

The mission, which carried all the way through to the west bank of the Bassac River, one of the two main streams in the Mekong system as it enters Vietnam, was uneventful after the force routed the first two Viet Cong tax collection stations.

That raid established the basis for Foul Deck, a continuing barrier operation for which a major degree of success in slowing infiltration can be assigned.

Giant Slingshot was launched on December 5, 1968, one month after the Sea Lords task force was established. The name derived from the two branches of the Vam Co River, which flows into the Soi Rap River in the Rung Sat south of Saigon. The Vam Co tributaries are the Vam Co Tay (west) and the Vam Co Dong (east). Together with the main stem, the river system resembles a slingshot. The two legs correspond to the boundaries of the Cambodian protrusion called the Parrot's Beak, which was a critical place to block communist infiltration because of its proximity to Saigon. The rivers were strategic because they fit so tightly around the Parrot's Beak, thus making them a natural barrier if forces were sufficiently deployed.

Placed in charge of Giant Slingshot was Captain Arthur Price, then commander of Task Force 116 (Gamewarden). His new unit was designated Task Group 194.9, based at Tan An, near the confluence of the two river branches. The location also was headquarters of the Third Brigade of the Ninth Infantry Division.

Price set up six base camps along the two rivers, inasmuch as PBRs and other boats would have to travel as far as 50 miles upstream from the main base.

These were designated advanced tactical support bases (ATSB) and were established at the following locations: Tra Cu, Hiep Hoa, Go Dua Ha and Ben Keo on the Vam Co Dong, and Tuyen Nhon and Moc Hoa on the Vam Co Tay. Pontoons laden with tents and other supplies were hauled upstream in the various sites.

The bases, so deep in the country, were subject to attack, but the defensive perimeter was well-fortified with stand-off fences to detonate incoming rounds, Claymore mines and trip flares. If a firefight ensued, land-based firepower and guns from the moored boats were capable of giving at least as much as they took.

An LST, the *Harnett County,* sailed upstream to Ben Luc to provide base support. The big ship was thought to be highly vulnerable in the narrow river so Zumwalt ordered all foliage chopped down within a 2,000-yard radius.

The admiral's concern was not unfounded. While anchored at Ben Luc late one night, the *Harnett County* was hit by a 107-millimeter rocket fired from the bank of the Vam Co Dong River. The projectile penetrated the outer skin and exploded in the wardroom. Shrapnel wounded three sailors and caused extensive damage, mainly from flooding caused by ruptured pipes.

Giant Slingshot as it developed became a multi-service operation. Army personnel from the 1st Air Cavalry and the 25th Infantry Division took part, as did Air Force Broncos.

Price moved five PBR sections, 50 boats in all, up into the Vam Co branches, to be combined with other assets, including Vietnamese navy river assault divisions.

Combat in the new operation got off to a hot start. One the second day of Giant Slingshot, an Army helicopter received ground fire and called for an investigation by PBRs, which also were taken under fire. The next day, patrol boats engaged in two firefights. On Dec. 14, an enemy attack on a PBR patrol resulted in six wounded and one dead, the first Navy loss in Giant Slingshot.

One of the worst stretches of water was on the Vam Co Dong between TraCu and Go Dau Ha, called "Bloody Alley," where some of the fiercest fighting occurred and the Navy suffered some of its heaviest losses. The intensity of combat and the frequency of enemy contact during Giant Slingshot, and indeed in all the barrier operations, was indicative of the density of American river forces in the area. Gamewarden PBRs had been operating in the upper Delta before but they were spread so thinly the Viet Cong could avoid contact and usually did. With the new operation and the beefed-up force, that was no longer possible.

Through the 515 days of Giant Slingshot, the river craft engaged in more than 1,000 firefights. Casualties were 38 sailors killed and 518 wounded. The total number of wounds suffered in fact exceeded the number of men involved.

The Army and Navy, like the joint unit of the Mobile Riverine Force, fought as a team in the Parrot's Beak region, though the operations took different forms than MRF's at times.

For one thing, the troop units were usually smaller, often platoon-sized rather than multi-company. The nature of the ground action was typically ambushes rather than sweep and quick extractions by the PBRs were often the rule.

A series of inter-service missions produced limited results, but one named Double Shift had strategic significance as well as tactical.

In July 1969, intelligence had it that the Viet Cong were preparing to mount a major assault aimed at the capture of Tay Ninh, Vietnam's third largest city. If they were successful, the plan reportedly was to declare a Provisional Revolutionary Government with Tay Ninh as the capital and hope for recognition from other countries. Such a military and propaganda coup would have been a major blow to the Saigon government, of course, and could have turned the entire fortunes of the war at that point.

In response, the Navy reinforced two ASTBs with 30 PBRs each, triple the normal complement, and brought into two river assault divisions, one of them a Vietnamese outfit.

Soldiers of the 25th Division were the ground unit. Double Shift lasted for 15 days. Ambushes and patrols by both Army and Navy forces over the period led to frequent fire exchanges, which by that time had become so commonplace that the military found it useful to develop and entirely new acronymic vocabulary to describe their variations. Thus for Double Shift, enemy initiated firefights (ENIFF) totalled 17; friendly initiated firefights (FRIFF), 70; and contact initiated by either side in which fire was not returned (ENENG and FRENG), 49.

The final boxscore was impressive for the allies. Thirty-four Viet Cong were confirmed killed and 90 structures or craft were destroyed against just 11 friendly wounded and eight boats damaged.

More important than those figures, however, was the fact that the Viet Cong designs on Tay Ninh were completely thwarted. The victory thus was unqualified.

In all the brown-water Navy's combat in Vietnam, Giant Slingshot probably was the occasion for more sailors assuming brief roles as ground fighters than during any other operation.

A major example of this occurred on Aug. 6, 1969, on the Vam Co Dong two miles south of Hip Hoa. After an Army observation plane spotted a column of Viet Cong soldiers walking along a canal, Seawolf helicopters and a PBR patrol from Division 552 were sent to the scene. The helicopters engaged in some brief firefights and then left. In the meantime, artillery strikes were called in and other PBRs arrived, one of them carrying an Army reconnaissance team.

The soldiers were put ashore and they stealthily disappeared into the heavy growth in search of the guerrilla troops.

The Army men soon made contact, but the enemy force was larger than they had believed. The PBRs provided covering fire on their flanks, but clearly, the recon team was in serious trouble.

It was at that point that a number of PBR

sailors on their initiative grabbed M-16 rifles, medical kits and grenade launchers and plunged into the jungle. When they reached the beleaguered troops, some of the sailors gave attention to the wounded while others, fighting like infantrymen, poured fire into the enemy positions. This was not specifically what Navy men had trained for and they were out of their normal element, but they acquitted themselves admirably in side-by-side combat with soldiers.

The force succeeded in evacuating from the jungle firefight with Army losses of two dead and four wounded, but the toll would have been much worse had it not been for the intervention of the PBR crewmen.

PBR action, while often fierce and resulting in American casualties, at times could be downright one-sided in the right way. A major example of this occurred on the upper Saigon River where two PBRs of River Division 593 waited quietly along the bank in a heavy downpour just as darkness settled over the country. The action was described in Lieutenant Commander Thomas Cutler's *Brown Water, Black Berets.*

The forward gunner of the lead boat peering through the rain and darkness was startled to see a North Vietnamese soldier not 30 yards away. It was an entire column of enemy, in fact several columns, and they, covering their faces against the deluge, did not see the boats.

The patrol commander without hesitation ordered engines of both boats started simultaneously, and the PBRs backed from the bank, their guns firing as they moved.

The surprised North Vietnamese returned fire from both banks, which sent the PBRs to the middle of the stream to obtain such protection as there was to be found.

The boats roaring through the water and firing rapidly called for help. It arrived in the form of Seawolf helicopters, Black Ponies, Army artillery and more PBRs. The battle continued for two hours. In the end, 49 enemy bodies were found. There were no friendly casualties.

Similar results were described by Engineman First Class John Babcock in an article by John Wukovitz that appeared in the April 1991 issue of *Vietnam* magazine.

Babcock, a PBR commander who experienced 172 ambush missions in his year on the Vam Co Tay River, estimated about one in five resulted in action.

On the night in question, another PBR patrol about 1,000 yards fired on and scattered a Viet Cong force, and according to procedure, withdrew because its position had been revealed.

The Babcock patrol, about which the Viet Cong were not aware, stayed put in expectation that the enemy would reappear. It did. The Viet Cong marched unsuspectingly into the boats' line of fire. About 50 were killed.

Admiral Zumwalt was determined to do something about the uncontested Viet Cong country of the Ca Mau Peninsula and the area on the Gulf of Thailand near the Cambodian border.

His first idea was reestablishment of an Army base on the peninsula, but that was roundly rejected by the service as too risky, so he proposed a floating river base. The overall American commander in the theater, Lieutenant General Creighton Abrams, overruled his IV Corps commander and gave the okay. The base and the operations that would emanate from it were called Sea Float.

Zumwalt chose as a site for the floating base the town of Nam Can City on the Cua Lon River. The location had both psychological and tactical value. Since the Tet Offensive the Viet Cong had been in control and most of the previous residents had fled. The admiral's idea was to demonstrate to the Viet Cong and to the civilians that the guerrillas did not own the city or the area.

In addition, the base was accessible by water from either the South China Sea or the Gulf of Thailand, and it secured a waterway shortcut for friendly traffic between the two salt-water bodies.

In July 1969, the components of the base were loaded onto three LSDs at Saigon and transported to the mouth of the Bo De River on the peninsula from where tugs hauled them upstream to their final destination.

The base consisted of nine ammi pontoons, in effect a giant raft about the size of a football field on which were built the various living and operational facilities that would be needed for the force of about 150 men. Helicopter landing pads were included, as were berths for the various floating stock, which included PCFs, PBRs, an LST, an LSM and a gunboat for defensive purposes. Other ordnance included 81-millimeter mortars. The eight-knot current was its own defense against swimmers.

Operations took a number of forms: ambushes and emergency responses on the combat side, and broadcasts and local assistance on the pacification side.

The tactics soon began to produce results. South Vietnamese flags began to appear and villages started to thrive once again. And that old reliable indicator of success - Viet Cong response - showed itself. The enemy employed ambushes and mining and its own brand of psychological warfare in trying to persuade the allies to withdraw.

There were substantial losses in the process, notably at the hands of North Vietnamese regulars who were considered tougher fighters than the hit-and-run Viet Cong.

One of the Swift boat commanders out of Sea Float was Lieutenant (jg) Elmo Zumwalt III, son of the in-country naval commander. Late in his tour, he returned for a second stint in the Ca Mau Peninsula. Zumwalt already had seen long and arduous action, having survived more firefights than he cared to count.

His return to Sea Float was by helicopter, and as he described it in the joint autobiography of him and Admiral Zumwalt, *My Father, My Son*, he was offered a grisly reminder that river combat was still deadly. On the deck was the body of a chief boatswain's mate who had been killed in a vicious firefight. Men on small-boat patrol were still dying.

Zumwalt in his book told of a two-boat patrol up the Dam Doi River where North Vietnamese had been particularly aggressive. The boats spotted a group of them around a campfire, and risking the possibility of a trap, they made all-out firing runs in both directions, routing the group without taking any visible return fire. The enemy was less pugnacious in the area after that.

On Zumwalt's last patrol in the Ha Tien area his Swift, PCF 35, was targeted by a mine attack that almost proved devastating. His cover boat first was slightly damaged by a wire-triggered claymore mine, and Zumwalt spotted a sampan moving out from an inlet. The officer ordered a full-speed run toward the boat, but soon two tremendous explosions buffeted the PCF and engulfed it in a huge geyser of water.

The boat did not capsize, however, and when no ambush followed, the action was over. Damage to the Swift was substantial, but before Zumwalt ordered the craft back to base, his crew followed a wire to shore where two stakes were found that served as sights for the command-detonated mines. Admiral Zumwalt suspected that the Viet Cong had set a trap specifically for the young officer, knowing who he was. Regardless, tactics such as those were indicative of the cleverness of the enemy in their ability to use crude sighting devices and lures such as the sampan.

Lieutenant Zumwalt had survived his last patrol, but the tragic story of his subsequent illness and death is nationally known. When he flew by helicopter back to Sea Float for his second duty there, he noticed how the area around the floating base had been defoliated. That made the base less vulnerable to enemy attack, for which he and all other personnel no doubt were grateful at the time.

Zumwalt wrote in his book that he experienced a skin rash there, which he then attributed to the sunshine but later learned was characteristic of exposure to Agent Orange. He also ate fruit that might have been sprayed with the chemical and bathed in the river into which the defoliant was washed.

Lieutenant Zumwalt was not the only Vietnam veteran presumed to have been stricken by Agent Orange-related illness, but the terrible irony in his case was that his own father, in the sincere belief he was saving allied lives, as he was of course, had ordered the defoliation.

The Navy's active presence in the U Minh Forest, a notorious Viet Cong stronghold, began in September 1969. That area was north of the Ca Mau Peninsula along the Gulf of Thailand coast and was bordered by the Ong Doc River.

River patrols in that region had as one objective the resettlement of the area by the civilian population.

Forces for the operation, called Breezy Cove, were a PBR division, 572, three ATCs, ASPB, monitors, the LST *Garrett County* anchored offshore, and a SEAL detachment. One of the monitors was armed with a 105mm howitzer.

Because the enemy troops frequently crossed the Ong Doc River on their way to the peninsula, contact with the United States forces was frequent, and costly to the communist forces. For the early months, the average enemy troops killed in encounters with the river Navy was bout 40, but in February 1970, the total jumped to 230 because the enemy was moving much larger units through the area.

The Sea Lords campaign was a time of innovation for the American forces. Trial was given to a squeeze-bore machine gun in which .50 caliber ammunition was squeezed through a .30 caliber barrel, giving the gun greater coverage but less range, an important consideration when firing near friendly villages.

Devices were developed to detect metal contraband and double bottoms in boats, but perhaps most remarkable was something called, colorfully enough, the "Douche Boat." That was an ATC equipped with two high pressure pumps that fed water cannons capable of disintegrating a concrete bunker.

PBRs on one occasion found it necessary to be refueled from an Army truck on a bridge above the waterway. The Army and Navy also teamed to cut days off the transit time of PBRs from one part of the theater to another. Heavy-duty Army helicopters airlifted PBRs from the Vam Co Dong River to the upper Saigon River in a matter of three hours. The roundabout trip by water would have taken four days. The tactic paid off in a major surprise for the Viet Cong, who had not been accustomed to seeing PBRs. One of the actions described above, where PBRs, Seawolves and Army artillery chopped up a enemy column, was on the upper Saigon River.

Sea Lords gave the erstwhile coastal fire of Swift boats and WPBs a taste of brown-water duty. This was called the Market Time Raider Campaign, after the name of the task force, and it succeeded in disrupting Viet Cong activity to an impressive degree.

The boldness of the Task Force 115 skipper, Captain Roy Hoffman, brought a reproof from Admiral Zumwalt, who learned the officer had been riding the lead boat in many of the raids.

The admiral ordered him to stop that risky behavior, whereupon Hoffman replied he couldn't send men into danger he himself was avoiding. He kept doing it.

Zumwalt, of course, had little grounds for discipline if example meant anything.

During Giant Slingshot, Zumwalt routinely studied combat reports and made it a point to visit areas where the action had just been hottest. He would talk to the men and award decorations on the spot.

Zumwalt on one occasion rode boats with each of two officers, one on the Vam Co Dong and one on the Vam Co Tay. A few hours after his visit, both officers were killed in ambushes.

Three Navy men who lost their lives near the Parrot's Beak were honored by the christening of destroyers bearing their names. They were Lieutenant Commander A.J. Elliot and Lieutenant Commander C.J. Peterson, the two officers with whom Zumwalt had been shortly before their deaths, and Chief Boatswain's Mate Quincy Truett, whose exploits were described in an earlier chapter.

The two year Sea Lords campaign, like others carried out by the Navy in the rivers and canals of Vietnam, was successful in meeting its military objectives.

Zumwalt's next command was as Chief of Naval Operations.

WAR DEAD

The following is a partial list of the men of Task Force 116, the Gamewardens, who lost their lives in Vietnam during that conflict:

J.L. Abrams, LT
W.L. Atkins, BM1
D.M. Agazzi, FTG3
J.A. Albrecht, MM1
R.G. Alcock, EN2
F.E. Anderson, QMC
R.W. Andrews, GMG2
F.G. Antone, SN
F.J. Apolinar, EN3
R.J. Arnold, AT1
C.M. Ashton, AE1
C.A. Baker, BM3
E.J. Baker, EN3
A.W. Barden, LT
J.B. Barton, LCDR
W.K. Batchelder, BM1
H.E. Belcher, GMG1
J.A. Belford, SN
J. Berkebile, LT
H.E. Birky, FN
R.L. Blais, EN3
H. Blandino, ETR2
F.W. Bomar, ENC
D.E. Boston, DC3
L.L. Bowles, AC1
T.L. Braden, SN
J.C. Brewton, LT (jg)
C.E. Brooks, RD1
H.E. Brown Jr., GMGSN
E.J. Brown Jr., ENFN
R.L. Brown, AMH3
Thomas L. Brown, GMG3
R.H. Burgess, SF1
J.R. Burke, ENS
R.H. Buzzell, LT (jg)
J.R. Cain, QM1

N. Cancilla, GMG3
F.H. Canur, EM2
M.P. Carr, BM3
Carriveau, GMG2
G.L. Carter, ADJAN
T.E. Carter, QM1
W.A. Cary, FN
D.C. Case, SN
H.C. Castle, LT (jg)
R.L. Castleberry, ETR2
R.L. Center, GMGSN
R.D. Childers, AOAN
D.R. Claiborne, GMG3
J. Clerkin, SM1
Gary Clark
M.J. Clifford, SN
M.E. Cline, GMG3
B.L. Coker, GMG3
R.M. Collins, LT
L.A. Cone, AMS3
W. Cosson, RD1
E.K. Cota, EN2
L.L. Cover, LCDR
H.E. Cowen, AMS1
G.R. Crabtree, GMG3
T.J. Craghead, GMG3
C.R. Crone, EN3
R.A. Crose, GMG3
O.P. Damrow, GMG3
O.A. Day, BMC
E.A. Dees Jr., GMG3
S.C. Delph, BM1
W.R. Dennis, FTGSA,
W.E. Dennis, LT
D.E. Devine, SFP2
P.J. Donavan, LT (jg)
R.L. Dock, GMG3
G.W. Doty, ENFN
H.J. Douglas, EN3
O.E. Durham, YN1
R.G Easton, GMG2
F.L. Edwards Jr., BM1
D.E. Egbert, SN

NTC, San Diego Monument. (Courtesy of William H. Curtis)

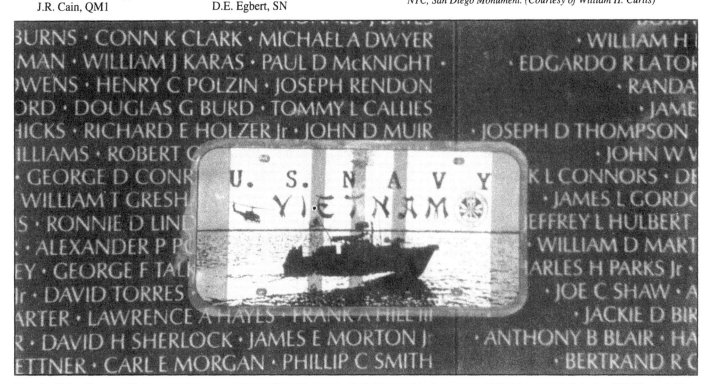

Photo by: Eldon Murray - U.S. Army, 1st Calvary - at "The Wall" in Washington, D.C. License plate designed by: GMG-3 James B. Guthrie, Jr. - U.S. "Brown" Water Navy, River Division 533 - placed under the name of GMG-3 John D. Muir who was killed in action on August 1, 1969.

T.C. Eldridge, EN2
A.J. Elliot, LCDR
F.M. Ellis, GMGSN
T.H. Emory, SM1
N.C. Estes Jr., FN
L.B. Evans, GMG3
F.L. Edwards, BM1
D.F. Fee, ADJ2
W.N. Flowers, EN2
W.V. Flynn, ENFN
Ford, BM2
P.O. Ford, GMG2
J.A. Fortino, EN3
W.D. Frahm, AMS1
E.F. Fraley, ADR2
T.J. Freund, RM1
H.L. Funk, SM3
N.G. Gage, RMC
T.E. Gilliam, LT (jg)
G.L. Giovannelli, SN
M.M. Godines, RM1
C.H. Goldbin, ADJ2
J.D. Gollahan, LT (jg)
G.J. Graham, SN
J.E. Green, LT
R.L. Green, SM1
D. Guest, AO1
D. Guest, BMC
J.A. Hangan, SA
W.C. Hagerich, RM1
C.W. Haines, RD3
D.C. Hall, GMG3
J.F. Hart, LT (jg)
D.F. Hartzell Jr., GMG3

R.A. Heintz, EN3
David P. Hoffman, EN2
L.D. Holloway, GMG2
H.B. Holmes, ENS
P.A. Holtz, SN
L.E. Hoopaugh, EN2
B.W. Hooper, LT
E.F. Houck, ETN2
J.R. Hunt, QMC
F. Jacaruso, GMGSN
D.M. Jackson, ABH1
J.D. Jamison, ABH1
J.D. Johns, FN
A.D. Johnson, SN
R.D. Johnson, LCDR
S.A. Johnson, ATN3
J.C. Jones, EN3
L.E. Jones, EN3
M.M. Jones Jr., SN
D.G. Kearney, LT (jg)
R.B. Keith, SN
H.I. Klien, LT (jg)
C. Kollmeyer, LT
R.E. Koshmaul, EN3
D.L. Kurz, EN3
R.E. Kushmaul, ENFN
R.R. Lake, GMG3
T.F. Leazer, ENFN
S.D. Ledford, EN3
D.J. Lehman, III, EN2
J.C. Lewis, BM1
L.J. Luckett, SN
J.E. Luntsford, MMC
B.W. Machen, RD2

L.A. Mahner, HM1
H.J. Maner, SM1
D.M. Mann, LT (jg)
Aubrey G. Martin, LT
H.A. Mattingly Jr., GMG2
C.A. McCaffety Jr., SM1
E.C. McGuinn, GMG3
S.W. McKinley, SN
H.M. Meute, ADJ3
J.M. Meute, GMG3
L.W. Meyer, MM2
L.J. Moe, TM1
J.S. Milamo, GMG3
R.D. Moore, SN
T.M. Moore, SA
D.E. Morgan, EN2
C.R. Moultine, GMG3
J.M. Mulcahy, LT
G. Mulrooney, BMC
R.C. Munsey, BM2
J.D. Muir, GMG3
J.T. Musetti, EN2
R.K. Neal, RM3
D.R. Nelson, ENFN
G.B. Nickerson, LT (jg)
J.A. Niemi, EN3
K.E. Norris, LT (jg)
M. C. O'Dell, GMG2
A.O. Ortiz, LT (jg)
E.L. Ott, III, ADJ1
D G. Ouellet, SN
R.E. Pace, QM2
G.C. Paddock, DC3
G.M. Page, AN

W. Paulson, CS1
E.W. Pawlowski, LT (jg)
D.G. Peddicord, EN1
W.A. Pederson, LT (jg)
C.J. Peterson, LCDR
J.R. Poe, LCDR
W.V. Potter, BM1
W.G. Pope, BM1
A.O. Prendergast, BM1
G.F. Proffer, BM1
M.C. Quinn, SN
R. Ramos, ABH2
J. Ramos, ADJ3
K.D. Rankin, EN3
J. Ratliff, AEC
R.J. Reardon, LT (jg)
A.W. Rice, GMG3
R.H. Rickli, SN
C.T. Risher, III, AMH2
E.E. Ritch, ENC
J.L. Ritter, EN3
D.R. Robertson, GMG3
R.D. Robertson, AMH3
R.D. Robinson, AMH3
J.H. Romanski, ENS
R.W. Rossignol, EM3
J.F. Rost, LT (jg)
G.H. Rush, ADJ2
P.F. Russell, LT
J.A. Sandberg, LT
J.K. Sander, ETN3
R. Saporito, EN3
M.E. Schafernocker, AO3
L.C. Schlote, BM1
J.L. Seery, LT (jg)
R.D. Sikkink, LT (jg)
D.H. Sillett, SK3
T.C. Simison, EN2
G.W. Simmers, ENC
J.L. Simon, BM1
P.T. Smith, LT
T. Smith, QMC
T.S. Stafford, SN
J.L. J. Stone, BM1
A.H. Suhr, LT (jg)
J.F. Thames, LT
W.J. Thompson, QMC
E.S. Tinnin, WO1
E.W. Tozer, ENC
F. Traini, LT
Q.H. Truett, BMC
D.L. Tucker, RD2
E.L. Tuller, GMGSN
K.E. Van Hoy, ATN1
P.L. Underwood, EN3
J.A. Wall, AO3
Wampler, BM1
G.R. Weaver Jr., EN3
D.D. Webb, EN3
M.A. Wentz, GMG2
J.B. Westervelt, ENFN
D.E. Westover, SN
A.G. Williams, GMG1
D.A. Wilson, SM1
W.R. Winters, ATR2
C.D. Witt, LT
D.M. Wobbe, AMS3
R.E. Worth, ADJ2
F.E. Wright, GMG2
G.R. Ycoco, SN

Norfolk Reunion. (Courtesy of Michael H. Bailey)

EPILOGUE

The history of Task Force 116 in particular, and the brown-water Navy of Vietnam in general, from 1966 through 1970, might be summarized thusly: The combat record, the wins and losses in direct confrontation with the enemy, would have done credit to any American military fighting unit in any war.

Whatever definition one might choose, the result was the same. The casualty ration of 30-40 to 1, and sometimes even higher, was remarkable in itself. Achievement of civilian pacification, a consideration not of concern to most previous United States military expeditions, was impressive in most cases. Where waterways and the land areas dominated by them were contested, the clear decision usually went to the Americans and not the Viet Cong or North Vietnamese. That was true in the Mekong Delta, the Rung Sat, the Parrot's Beak, the Plain of Reeds, the Ca Mau and the U Minh Forest. Granted, the American Navy took some losses, but on a head-to-head tactical basis, the enemy did not win many fights.

If the military outcome had been the deciding factor, we would be talking about the Vietnam victory today the same way we refer to the Persian Gulf war.

But of course, that was not the case. Political limitations, the propaganda victory of the communists after Tet and other such circumstances have been described in previous chapters.

Captain Burt Witham, the first commander of the Gamewarden task force, related a revealing incident from early in his command.

He recalled a State Department official accosted him with this criticism: "What are you trying to do, wreck the economy?" Witham learned the bureaucrat's complaint was that Gamewarden was succeeding in shutting down the previously thriving black market in the country.

When the Navy officer asked what was wrong with that, the State Department man retorted that the black market was the only way the population could obtain anything. The fact that the Viet Cong were the principal beneficiaries of the underground economy, as Witham was quick to point out, did not faze the man from Foggy Bottom.

How many American military commanders of any previous wars had to be saddled with that kind of interference? It was not just a political complication in this case, but one that was counterproductive to the mission at hand.

The phase-in of American military and naval participation in the Vietnam conflict began to be reverted in late 1969 as Richard Nixon's plan of Vietnamization took hold. Where Americans started as advisors to Vietnamese units and ultimately operated their own commands more or less autonomously, the native forces began to be drawn in until once again the Americans were advisors.

Task Force 194, Sea Lords, was deactivated in June 1970, but the individual operations still in progress - Sea Float/Solid Anchor, Breezy Cove, Search Turn, Barrier Reef and Blue Shark - continued under Task Force 116. Other elements of Sea Lords were turned over to the Vietnamese Navy.

Solid Anchor alone was under United States command by year's end, and on April 1, 1971, that too was handed over to the Vietnamese. It was the end of the United States Navy's involvement in-country, and thus the end of Operation Gamewarden, Task Force 116.

As further point, to reinforce the one at the outset, it should be noted that this was four years before May 1975, when the last American helicopter lifted off the embassy roof in Saigon. That is the image of war's end that most people in this country have, and it spells defeat. When the Vietnam War is routinely described as the one we lost, the 1975 fall of Saigon generally is what is meant.

But the American Navy left the country in 1971 and all combat forces were out by January 1973.

The United States Navy, and the brown-water Navy in particular, lost nothing except too many good men, and in the case of the survivors, too much of themselves.

Courtesy of Kenneth A. Delfino

MEDAL OF HONOR CITATIONS

DAVID G. OUELLET, Seaman, USN, citation for conspicuous gallantry and intrepidity at the risk of his life above and beyond the call of duty while serving with River Section 532, in combat against the enemy in the Republic of Vietnam. As the forward machine gunner on River Patrol Boat (PBR) 124, which was on patrol on the Mekong River during the early evening hours of March 6, 1967, Seaman Ouellet observed suspicious activity near the river bank, alerted his Boat Captain and recommended movement of the boat to the area to investigate. While the PBR was making a high-speed run along the river bank, Seaman Ouellet spotted an incoming enemy grenade falling toward the boat. He immediately left the protected position of his gun mount and ran aft for the full length of the speeding boat, shouting to his fellow crew members to take cover. Observing the Boat Captain standing unprotected on the boat, Seaman Ouellet bounded onto the engine compartment cover and pushed the Boat Captain down to safety. In the split second that followed the grenade's landing and in the face of certain death, Seaman Ouellet fearlessly placed himself between the deadly missile and his shipmates, courageously absorbing most of the blast fragments with his own body in order to protect his shipmates from injury and death. His extraordinary heroism and his selfless and courageous actions on behalf of his comrades at the expense of his own life were in the finest tradition of the United States Naval Service.

JAMES E. WILLIAMS, Boatswain's Mate First Class, USN, citation for conspicuous gallantry and intrepidity at the risk of his life above and beyond the call of duty as a member of River Section 531 during combat operations on the Mekong River in the Republic of Vietnam. On Oct. 31, 1966 Petty Officer Williams was serving as Boat Captain and Patrol Officer aboard River Patrol Boat (PBR) 105 accompanied by another patrol boat when the patrol was suddenly taken under fire by two enemy sampans. Petty Officer Williams immediately ordered the fire returned, killing the crew of one enemy boat and causing the other sampan to take refuge in a nearby river inlet. Pursuing the fleeing sampan, the US patrol encountered a heavy volume of small arms fire from enemy forces, at close range, occupying well-concealed positions along the river bank. Maneuvering through this fire, the patrol confronted a numerically superior enemy force aboard two enemy junks and eight sampans augmented by heavy automatic weapons fire from ashore. In the savage battle that ensued, Petty Officer Williams, with utter disregard for his own safety, exposed himself to the withering hail of enemy fire to direct counterfire and inspire the actions of his patrol. Recognizing the overwhelming strength of the enemy force, Petty Officer Williams deployed his patrol to await the arrival of armed helicopters. In the course of this movement he discovered an even larger concentration of enemy boats. Not waiting for the arrival of the armed helicopters, he displayed great initiative and boldly led the patrol through the intense enemy fire and damaged or destroyed fifty enemy sampans and seven junks. This phase of the action completed and with the arrival of the armed helicopters, Petty Officer Williams directed the attack on the remaining enemy force. Although Petty Officer Williams was aware that his boats would become even better targets, he ordered the patrol boats' search lights turned on to better illuminate the area and moved the patrol perilously close to shore to press the attack. Despite a waning supply of ammunition the patrol successfully engaged the enemy ashore and completed the rout of the enemy force. Under the leadership of Petty Officer Williams, who demonstrated unusual professional skill and indomitable courage throughout the three-hour battle, the patrol accounted for the destruction or loss of sixty-five enemy boats and inflicted numerous casualties on the enemy personnel. His extraordinary heroism and exemplary fighting spirit in the face of grave risks inspired the efforts of his men to defeat a larger enemy force and are in keeping with the finest traditions of the United States Naval Service.

NAVY CROSS CITATIONS

GEORGE AJDUKOVICH, Chief Boatswain's Mate, USN, citation for extraordinary heroism on Oct. 7, 1969 while serving as patrol officer of two river patrol boats in a night waterborne guardpost on the Muo Hai Canal, Republic of Vietnam. When an enemy grenade was thrown from the bank of the canal and landed on the craft in which Chief Petty Officer Ajdukovich was embarked, he immediately seized the grenade and clasped it to his body in an attempt to protect the lives of his fellow crewmen. Seconds later, when the deadly missile failed to explode, he hurled it into the canal where it detonated underwater almost instantly. With his two patrol boats now under a heavy concentration of automatic-weapons fire from four enemy positions on the river bank, Chief Petty Officer Ajdukovich requested air support and immediately directed a devastating barrage of suppressive fire while leading his units clear of the kill zone. Unable to make any further firing runs on the entrenched enemy force when one of the patrol boats became disabled Chief Petty Officer Ajdukovich's patrol illuminated and mortared the hostile area until air cover arrived on the scene and then continued illumination of the target area to help maximize the effects of the air strike. By his valiant fighting spirit, inspiring leadership and selfless devotion to duty, Chief Petty Officer Ajdukovich was greatly instrumental in leading his patrol to safety without sustaining a single personnel casualty. His heroic initiative was in keeping with the highest traditions of the United States Naval Service.

TIMOTHY D. ALSPAUGH, Seaman, USN, citation for extraordinary heroism during operations against an armed enemy in the Republic of Vietnam on Sept. 25, 1969. Seaman Alspaugh was the after fifty-caliber machine gunner aboard River Patrol Boat 677, which had inserted in a night waterborne guard post on the north bank of the Cai Lon River in support of interdiction operations in Kien Giang Province. His boat was acting as cover boat and had taken a position about fifty yards astern of the patrol's lead boat, with its starboard side to a heavy growth of nipa palm along the river bank. Shortly past midnight, after several hours of waiting quietly in the darkness to detect enemy movement on the water, Seaman Alspaugh observed what he believed to be a sampan on the river upstream from his boat. Alerting his Boat Captain and bringing his machine gun to bear over the port quarter, he was concentrating on the barely, visible craft when he was struck on his left side by an object which he instinctively recognized as a grenade thrown from the underbrush. He immediately shouted a warning to his fellow crewmembers, at the same time bending down to search for the grenade, which had come to rest on the pump covers on the far side of his gun mount. Despite the extreme darkness and the imminent danger of an explosion, Seaman Alspaugh succeeded in locating the grenade and quickly threw it back into the small clearing from which it had been thrown. Even before the grenade exploded near the enemy's position, he was firing his fifty-caliber machine gun into the brush, continuing until the boats were clear of the area. Because of Seaman Alspaugh's quick reaction and disregard for his own personal safety, the patrol escaped without casualty. His extraordinary courage and selfless devotion to duty reflected great credit upon himself and were in keeping with the finest traditions of the United States Naval Service.

HAROLD L. BAKER, Radioman Second Class, USN, citation for extraordinary heroism in action on the night of Dec. 20, 1970 while serving as the rear security for a five-man SEAL patrol on an interdiction mission deep within enemy territory in the Republic of Vietnam. Immediately after inserting ashore, the patrol came under withering enemy fire from automatic weapons, grenades and rockets, mortally wounding the patrol leader and the weapons man and critically wounding the patrol's radioman and Vietnamese guide. Although he was not wounded, Petty Officer Baker found himself in the river waters struggling to keep his head above the surface. Through sheer determination, he pulled himself and the body of a fallen comrade onto the bank and then returned a heavy volume of automatic weapons fire toward the enemy in an effort to stave off an assault on the squad's position. Subsequently, Petty Officer Baker administered lifesaving first aid to the two wounded members of the patrol and directed the recovery of the bodies of the patrol leader and the automatic weapons man. By his great personal valor and fighting spirit in the face of heavy, enemy fire, he upheld the highest traditions of the United States Naval Service.

ROBERT E. BARATKO, Lieutenant (jg), USNR, citation for extraordinary heroism on Sept. 15, 1970 while serving as the aircraft commander of an attack helicopter, attached to Helicopter Attack (Light) Squadron Three, during operations against enemy forces in the Republic of Vietnam. Lieutenant (jg) Baratko participated in a mission to provide cover for a medical evacuation helicopter which had previously attempted to evacuate several seriously wounded in the face of intense enemy fire. As his plane and three others entered the evacuation area, the surrounding treelines erupted with intense fire which downed two aircraft and seriously damaged a third. Lieutenant (jg) Baratko's aircraft sustained several critical hits, including one through the fuel tank. With the only flyable attack helicopter on the scene, he provided gun-ship coverage while the medical evacuation helicopter eventually succeeded in rescuing the downed crews. As he was flying this coverage, Lieutenant (jg) Baratko's plane was again subjected to heavy fire and sustained several more hits. After the medical evacuation helicopter departed the area, Lieutenant (jg) Baratko flew to a nearby landing strip with his fuel supply practically exhausted. By his perseverance and great personal valor in the face of almost overwhelming odds, he was directly instrumental in saving the lives of several of his shipmates. His selfless and determined efforts were in keeping with the highest traditions of the United States Naval Service.

BARRY W. ENOCH, Chief Gunner's Mate, USN, citation for extraordinary heroism on April 9, 1970 in connection with operations against enemy forces in the Republic of Vietnam. While serving with a detachment of SEAL Team ONE, Chief Petty Officer Enoch was the senior advisor and radioman/grenadier to a combined United States Vietnamese SEAL combat patrol against the Viet Cong infrastructure leaders in Long Phu District, Ba Xuyen Province. After insertion and patrolling to the target area, Chief Petty Officer Enoch observed six armed Viet Cong attempting to evade. Rushing forward and exposing himself to hostile fire, he succeeded in accounting for three enemy casualties. The SEALs then came under intense B-40 rocket and automatic weapon fire. Realizing that his small force was surrounded, Chief Petty Officer Enoch deployed his men in a defensive perimeter and although under intense fire, continually shifted position to more effectively employ his weapon, relocate his men and survey the enemy's locations and tactics. Although his radio was damaged by enemy fire, Chief Petty Officer Enoch directed fixed-wing and helicopter air strikes on the enemy's positions, some strikes as close as twenty meters to his position. With his men running low on ammunition and still encircled, Chief Petty Officer Enoch directed air strikes on the shortest route between his position and the river and then led the patrol through the enemy encirclement before the latter could close the gap caused by the air strikes. By his heroic and decisive efforts in the face of almost overwhelming odds, Chief Petty Officer Enoch was directly responsible for the safe extraction of the patrol members and upheld the highest traditions of the United States Naval Service.

PATRICK O. FORD, Gunners Mate Second Class, USN, citation for extraordinary heroism on June 21, 1968 while serving with friendly forces engaged in armed conflict against the communist insurgent (Viet Cong) forces in the Republic of Vietnam. Petty Officer Ford was serving as after machine gunner on a River Patrol Boat (PBR) which was ambushed during a combat patrol by a Viet Cong force using rockets and heavy machine guns. The enemy rocket fire disabled his craft and started a fire on board, causing the PBR to go out of control and head for the shore line directly in front of enemy firing positions. Although seriously wounded, Petty Officer Ford returned a continuous volume of fire into the Viet Cong positions. Realizing that his boat was out of control and in the face of point-blank hostile fire, he assisted three of his more seriously wounded shipmates from the PBR into the water. Only after insuring that all the surviving crew members had left the boat did Petty Officer Ford give any thought to his own safety. He was the last man to leave the boat. As a result of his heroic actions and fearless devotion to duty, Petty Officer Ford saved the lives of two of his shipmates, gallantly sacrificing his own in doing so. His extraordinary heroism under fire was in keeping with the highest traditions of the United States Naval Service.

TERRENCE J. FREUND, Radioman Second Class, USN, citation for extraordinary heroism in action on October 26, 1966 while serving with the United States River Patrol Force, near An Lac Thon Village, Republic of Vietnam. As forward machine gunner on board River Patrol Boat Forty during a combat patrol on the Bassac River, Petty Officer Freund was instrumental in preventing an enemy battalion from crossing the river and assisted in the dispersal of that force. By determined and accurate gunfire, he repeatedly suppressed enemy fire from the river banks during the hotly-contested action. When an attempt to capture an enemy craft resulted in the recovery party being forced into the river by hostile fire, Petty Officer Freund's covering fire was instrumental in their rescue. Although mortally wounded, he continued to fire into enemy positions so that his craft and other friendly forces could be extricated from their perilous positions close to the enemy. By his heroic conduct, he enabled his unit to retire from the action without further loss of life or damage. Petty Officer Freund's performance distinguished him among his gallant comrades, contributed to a victory over the enemy and was in keeping with the highest traditions of the United States Naval Service.

GARY G. GALLAGHER, Yeoman Third Class, USN, citation for extraordinary heroism on October 10 and 11, 1968 while serving with friendly foreign forces engaged in armed conflict in the Mekong Delta region of the Republic of Vietnam. Distinguishing himself by his exemplary leadership and selfless courage, Petty Officer Gallagher, serving in the capacity of reconnaissance Unit Adviser, led his unit in a capture mission deep into an enemy-controlled area. As the operation progressed and the unit began picking up prisoners the unit split and advanced on both sides of a small canal in an effort to capture "additional members of the Viet Cong infrastructure. At this time, an earlier-acquired captive made a warning sound to his comrades in the vicinity. Immediately, heavy fire from a numerically-superior enemy force was encountered by the separated half of Petty Officer Gallagher's patrol unit. In order to prevent his prisoners from escaping, he forced them to lead the way while crossing the canal to assist his stricken troops. Rallying his reconnaissance unit, Petty Officer Gallagher boldly exposed himself to the hostile fire while directing return fire on the enemy. His driving determination to succeed in his mission served to inspire his men and resulted in the temporary neutralization of the enemy attack. Petty Officer Gallagher then led a hasty, yet professionally executed, withdrawal - with his entire unit and all prisoners-of-war intact. Before concluding the extraction phase, he administered lifesaving first aid to a seriously wounded companion and carried the man over eight kilometers to safety. Petty Officer Gallagher's heroic response while leading this Vietnamese force, his demonstrated initiative and valor and his selfless dedication under concentrated enemy fire were in keeping with the highest traditions of the United States Naval Service.

ROBERT T. GALLAGHER, Senior Chief Interior Communications Electrician, USN, citation for extraordinary heroism on March 13, 1968 while serving with SEAL Team Detachment ALFA engaged in armed conflict against the communist insurgent forces (Viet Cong) in the Republic of Vietnam. Senior Chief Petty Officer Gallagher served as assistant patrol leader for a SEAL night combat operation deep in an enemy battalion base area. His patrol penetrated 5,000 yards into the Viet Cong base camp, locating a large barracks area occupied by approximately 30 well-armed insurgents. Senior Petty Officer Gallagher led three men into the barracks. When discovered by a Viet Cong sentry, the patrol came under heavy enemy fire. Although wounded in both legs, Senior Chief Petty Officer Gallagher accounted for five enemy Viet Cong killed. Discovering that his patrol leader was seriously wounded Senior Chief Petty Officer Gallagher took command and led his patrol 1,000 yards through heavily occupied enemy territory to an open area where he radioed for helicopter support. He continually exposed himself to heavy enemy automatic-weapons fire to direct friendly, helicopter gunships and extraction ships. While assisting his patrol to the evacuation point, Senior Chief Petty Officer Gallagher was again wounded, but, despite his multiple wounds, succeeded in leading his men to a safe extraction. By his courage, professional skill and devotion to duty, he was directly responsible for the safe withdrawal of his patrol and for killing a large number of the enemy in their own base area. His heroic achievements were in keeping with the highest traditions of the United States Naval Service.

MICHAEL L. GATES, Engineman Third Class, USN, citation for extraordinary heroism on July 10, 1969 while serving with friendly foreign forces engaged in armed conflict against the North Vietnamese and Viet Cong communist aggressor forces in the Republic of Vietnam. As Boat Engineer of a River Patrol Boat, Petty Officer Gates served with River Division 533 which was patrolling the upper reaches of the Vam Co Dong River in a special holding operation to protect Tay Ninh City from expected heavy enemy attack. While settling into waterborne guard-post positions, the units came under heavy automatic-weapons fire. During the first volley, Petty Officer Gates fell to the deck with a serious bullet wound which temporarily paralyzed the lower half of his body. When the units cleared the ambush only to come under a second enemy attack. Petty Officer Gates, despite his severe wound, grabbed a grenade launcher and from his prone position on the deck of the boat, returned the enemy's fire until the boats again cleared the ambush. After he was transported to the flight deck of a troop carrier to await medical evacuation by helicopter, the enemy once more ambushed the boats. Lying on his back completely exposed to enemy fire, Petty Officer Gates manned an M-16 rifle which he had requested and proceeded to assist his shipmates in suppressing the enemy fire. His great personal valor, dauntless initiative and inspiring devotion to duty in the face of grave personal danger were in keeping with the highest traditions of the United States Naval Service.

GREGORY O. HAMPTON, Seaman, USN, citation for extraordinary heroism on Aug. 20, 1969 while serving with friendly foreign forces engaged in armed conflict against enemy aggressor forces in the Republic of Vietnam. As an M-60 machine-gun operator, Seaman Hampton took part in a two-boat night patrol on the Vam Co Dong River. When sounds of approaching personnel on the beach were detected, his unit held its fire, due to lack of visibility, until a better target could be obtained. Suddenly, a hand grenade was tossed aboard his patrol boat and landed in the darkness. Quick to act, Seaman Hampton called to all personnel to take cover, dived across the wet slippery deck, succeeded in locating the lethal weapon and hurled it over the side of the patrol boat. As the grenade hit the water, it exploded and showered the craft with water and shrapnel. Seaman Hampton then manned the M-60 machine gun and began to deliver suppressive fire on the suspected enemy position until his boat could clear the kill zone. His craft received one rocket round close aboard as it cleared the zone. Discovering that no damage had been inflicted, the patrol boat returned to make a second firing run on the enemy position. By his daring initiative, unfaltering courage and heroic spirit of self-sacrifice in the face of almost certain death, Seaman Hampton was directly instrumental in saving many lives, along with his patrol boat. His unswerving devotion to duty was in keeping with the highest traditions of the United States Naval Service.

WILLIAM E. HAYENGA JR., Fireman, USNR, citation for extraordinary heroism on Feb. 4, 1968 while engaged in armed conflict in the Republic of Vietnam. During Operation BOLD DRAGON I, Fireman Hayenga, as engineman on board River Patrol Boat (PBR) 731, partici-

pated in a four-PBR combat patrol on the Rach Hong Nhu River to assist a Vietnamese unit pinned down by a Viet Cong company. When PBR 728 was hit by three rockets and forced to beach in the middle of the ambush site, PBR 731, having also taken a direct rocket hit, returned to the stricken boat to attempt rescue of its crew. One crew member was rescued shortly after beaching. Realizing the gravity of the situation, Fireman Hayenga volunteered to search for the four missing crew members. Unarmed, he jumped ashore and made his way upstream toward the partially-sunken boat in search of his comrades. Finding no one on board the boat, he continued his search among the numerous thatched hutches along the river bank and succeeded in locating two of the crewmen hidden in a drainage ditch. Both men were in a state of shock and one had sustained a serious leg wound. Assisting the wounded man and urging the other onward, Fireman Hayenga started to lead them back to PBR 731. Enemy fire was so effective at one point that the men were forced to crawl approximately thirty yards across an open space. On the other side of the clearing, Fireman Hayenga found a third crew member who was disoriented and in a state of shock. Upon reaching the embankment leading down to PBR 731, he sent the two ambulatory sailors to the boat and once they were aboard, assisted the wounded man down the embankment and onto the boat. The Boat Commander of PBR 728 made his way to the rescue PBR approximately two minutes later, thus completing the rescue operation. Fireman Hayenga's heroic actions in the face of intense enemy fire were directly responsible for saving the lives of three of his comrades and were in keeping with the highest traditions of the United States Naval Service.

DONALD C. KINNARD, Chief Hospital Corpsman, USN, citation for extraordinary heroism while engaged in armed conflict against enemy forces in the Republic of Vietnam on Jan. 20-21, 1970. During this period, Chief Petty Officer Kinnard was serving with Underwater Demolition Team Twelve, Detachment Golf and operating with the Second Battalion, Fifth Mobile Forces Command during a sweep and clear mission in the Ca Mau peninsula. On one occasion, Chief Petty Officer Kinnard was singled out as a target by an enemy force while he was attempting to beach a damaged sampan from which three of the enemy had leaped into the water and escaped. His courageous action resulted in the capture of the sampan and enemy weapons. On another occasion, when his unit was subjected to intense enemy rocket, machine-gun and automatic-weapons fire, Chief Petty Officer Kinnard was wounded in the arms and legs by shrapnel from an enemy hand grenade. He immediately hurled several hand grenades across a canal into enemy positions. During the ensuing battle, he was suddenly attacked by one of the enemy who had crept up behind him. After several minutes of a fierce hand-to-hand struggle, Chief Petty Officer Kinnard succeeded in overcoming his attacker who was later identified as a North Vietnamese Army Lieutenant. By his personal courage and inspiring devotion to duty, Chief Petty Officer Kinnard contributed materially to the success of a vital mission and upheld the highest traditions of the United States Naval Service.

DAVID R. LARSEN, Gunner's Mate Third Class, USN, citation for extraordinary heroism on Aug. 2, 1969 while serving with friendly foreign forces engaged in armed conflict against North Vietnamese and Viet Cong communist aggressor forces in the Republic of Vietnam. Petty Officer Larsen was serving as a gunner's mate aboard River Patrol Boat (PBR) 775 which was part of a two-boat night waterborne guard post stationed on the upper Saigon River. Operating in conjunction with the patrol six-man ambush team which was providing bank security for the guard post, engaged four enemy soldiers who were part of an estimated 35 to 50-man force that returned the contact with accurate rocket fire, killing or critically wounding all but one member of the six-man ambush team. One man from the team managed to call for the PBR crewmen's help. Armed with a machine gun and several ammunition belts. Petty Officer Larsen hastened to the assistance of the ambush team. As he led his small force ashore, he saw three enemy soldiers about to overrun the friendly position. He immediately, rushed down toward them, firing his machine gun and single-handedly turned back the enemy assault killing at least one of the enemy. Petty Officer Larsen then maintained a one-man perimeter defensive position and although under continuous enemy fire. succeeded in discouraging further enemy attacks until additional help arrived. Later, armed with three different weapons, Petty

Officer Larsen was the first man to take his post on the perimeter established to provide security for the medical evacuation helicopter. By his extremely, courageous one-man assault in the face of direct enemy fire, Petty Officer Larsen was responsible for saving the lives of three fellow servicemen and for protecting his shipmates as they administered aid to the wounded. His valiant and inspiring efforts reflect the highest credit upon himself and the United States Naval Service.

CECIL H. MARTIN, Mineman First Class, USN, citation for extraordinary heroism on the night of Nov. 21, 1968 while serving with River Division 531 during riverine unit operations against enemy aggressor forces in the Mekong Delta region of the Republic of Vietnam. As Senior Boat Captain of a two-boat patrol Petty Officer Martin was transiting from Rach Soi to Rach Gia, in conjunction with a concentrated patrol program adopted for the SEA LORDS interdiction campaign in the lower Delta, when his patrol came under heavy enemy attack on all sides. During the initial hail of fire, his cover boat received two direct rocket hits, wounding all personnel aboard and causing the craft to veer out of control and run aground directly in front of enemy firing positions. Petty Officer Martin ordered his coxswain to reverse course and reenter the ambush area to rescue the cover boat's crew members. As his unit approached the stricken craft Petty Officer Martin directed effective counterfire and placing his boat between the beleaguered craft and the blazing enemy batteries, took command of the precarious rescue effort. While affording exemplary leadership and inspiration to the members of his surprised and battered patrol element, he directed the major fire suppression efforts of his gunners, personally manning and firing a machine gun at crucial intervals. Additionally, Petty Officer Martin rendered first aid to casualties, extinguished a fire in the beached craft, advised his commanding officer in the Naval Operations Center of the seriousness of the situation and coordinated the transfer of wounded personnel to his unit. Through his courageous and determined fighting spirit, he succeeded in safely extracting his men undoubtedly saving numerous lives. His great personal valor in the face of heavy and sustained enemy fire was in keeping with the highest traditions of the United States Naval Service.

ROBERT O. PORTER, Chief Gunner's Mate, USN, citation for extraordinary heroism on June 10, 1970 while serving with River Division 513 as patrol officer of a two-boat patrol on the Giang Thanh River in the Republic of Vietnam. Having established a night waterborne guard post in support of interdiction operations, Chief Petty Officer Porter, after several hours of waiting, detected activity in the underbrush near his boat. Quickly alerting his crew to the imminent danger, he was concentrating on a muffled sound in the bushes when a hand grenade landed on the boat and the bank of the river erupted in fire directed at his craft. Chief Petty Officer Porter instantly yelled "grenade" and then dashed through the intense enemy fire, picked up the grenade and hurled it back onto the beach. In a matter of seconds the grenade exploded, showering the boat with a deadly hail of shrapnel and wounding him in the face. Ignoring his wounds, Chief Petty Officer Porter directed accurate suppressive fire against the enemy positions until they were silenced. In risking his own life to protect the lives of his shipmates, he displayed the highest order of valor, dedication and selflessness, thereby upholding the finest traditions of the United States Naval Service.

CHESTER B. SMITH, Signalman First Class, USN, citation for extraordinary heroism in action against communist insurgent forces in the Republic of Vietnam, while serving with River Patrol Section 531 on Dec. 11, 1966. As Patrol Officer on a PBR combat patrol on the Mekong River. Petty Officer Smith pursued a sampan, with three Viet Cong aboard, into a narrow canal where the sampans occupants, aided by eight other Viet Cong along the canal banks, opened fire on the patrol boat. Petty Officer Smith promptly directed his crew in returning suppressive fire which accounted for eight Viet Cong killed. Bringing in his cover boat from the main river, Petty Officer Smith reentered the canal where he came upon a company-size Viet Cong force preparing to board forty sampans. The enemy opened fire on the patrol boats, but were completely repulsed and demoralized by Petty Officer Smith's sudden attack, causing them to retreat in confusion. At least two of the enemy were confirmed as killed. While still returning the heavy fire the Viet Cong were directing at him, Petty Officer Smith systematically destroyed

their water transport and equipment. After extracting his patrol to rearm, he reentered the canal for a third time and personally directed his machine gunners in silencing six enemy weapons positions. Petty Officer Smith then vectored a US Navy helicopter in a rocket run on a cleverly camouflaged bunker. A large secondary explosion resulted completely destroying an enemy ammunition cache. When the overall four-hour engagement had ended, Petty Officer Smith's PBR's had accounted for fifteen enemy confirmed killed, twenty-eight enemy sampans sunk, twelve damaged, three captured and an enemy ammunition cache destroyed. His daringly aggressive actions, outstanding initiative, extraordinary courage and gallant leadership were in keeping with the highest traditions of the United States Naval Service.

NORMAN B. STAYTON, Aviation Structural Mechanic Third Class, USN, citation for extraordinary heroism on March 26, 1971 while serving as second gunner in the lead aircraft of a light fire team from Helicopter Attack (Light) Squadron THREE, flying convoy escort along the Can Gao Canal, Kien Giang Province, Republic of Vietnam. Petty Officer (then Airman) Stayton was participating with his fire team in providing overhead cover for a boat convoy when one of the boats carrying 9,000 gallons of explosive jet fuel struck a mine, detonating the fuel. Two enemy rockets then struck the boat, following which burning fuel spewed across the water. When he observed a wounded man struggling to shore to escape the flames and the hail of enemy bullets hitting the water, Petty Officer Stayton alerted his pilot, took the initiative and dived from the hovering helicopter into the burning canal to carry a life preserver to the survivor. Although immediately wounded in the leg, Petty Officer Stayton nonetheless succeeded in reaching the victim, who had sustained serious burns and was in a state of shock and shielded him with his own body while attempting to tow him to the recovery site. Thwarted in five attempts to reach the hovering helicopter rotor downwash, Petty Officer Stayton, although close to complete exhaustion, managed to wave his arms and get the attention of a river assault craft which proceeded to rescue both men. By his valiant and persevering efforts in the face of intense enemy fire and almost insurmountable circumstances, Petty Officer Stayton was directly instrumental in the rescue of a seriously wounded fellow serviceman. His heroic actions were in keeping with the highest traditions of the United States Naval Service.

GUY E. STONE, Chief Shipfitter, USN, citation for extraordinary heroism on Jan. 27, 1970 during operations against the enemy in the Republic of Vietnam. Engaged in clearing a graveyard of booby traps for a detachment of Underwater Demolition Team TWELVE during a bunker-destruction sweep near the Vinh Dien River, Chief Petty Officer Stone suddenly discovered eight of the enemy hidden in the grass. The hostile troops opened fire with weapons and began hurling hand grenades. Yelling a warning to the other members of his team, Chief Petty Officer Stone, without a weapon at that moment, took cover behind a mound and proceeded to direct the fire of his companions. Subsequently, in the face of the hostile fire, he raced to within fifteen feet of the enemy and hurled three grenades into their midst. Observing two of the enemy soldiers retreating, he exposed himself to the hostile fire to borrow a weapon from a team member and shoot the fleeing soldiers, accounting for a total of six enemy dead and two captured. Chief Petty Officer Stone's instinctive reactions saved two United States and two Vietnamese Naval personnel in his team from certain death. His exceptionally courageous and heroic actions and selfless efforts on behalf of his team members were in keeping with the highest traditions of the United States Naval Service.

ROBERT J. THOMAS, Radarman Second Class, USN, citation for extraordinary heroism on March 23, 1969 while serving with SEAL Team Detachment ALFA, Seventh Platoon, during combat operations against communist aggressor forces in the Republic of Vietnam. Embarked in a Seawolf helicopter on a visual reconnaissance and strike mission on Da Dung Mountain near the Cambodian border when the aircraft was struck by enemy ground fire and crashed in an exposed rice paddy, Petty Officer Thomas was thrown from the wreckage, sustaining multiple injuries. Fighting off the stunning effects of shock, he immediately moved to the aid of the helicopter crewmen who were still in the burning aircraft. Despite the intense flames and the heavy gunfire from both the mountain and a nearby tree line, Petty Officer Thomas managed to remove one of the crewmen to safety and with the aid of another man who had been dropped onto the site by an accompanying helicopter, succeeded in freeing the trapped pilot from the flaming cockpit. Petty Officer Thomas then made a gallant attempt to rescue the two remaining men trapped beneath the twisted metal, discontinuing his efforts only when driven back by the exploding bullets and rockets of the burning helicopter. After moving the two previously rescued men to a greater distance from the crash site, Petty Officer Thomas realized that Viet Cong troops were steadily advancing on his position. He selflessly threw himself upon the body of one of the wounded men and began returning the enemy fire. His deadly accuracy accounted for a least one enemy dead and held the aggressors at bay until an Army rescue helicopter landed. By his valiant efforts and selfless devotion to duty while under hostile fire, Petty Officer Thomas upheld the highest traditions of the United States Naval Service.

QUINCY H. TRUETT, Chief Boatswain's Mate, USN, citation for extraordinary heroism on the night of Jan. 20, 1969 while serving with River Division 551, engaged in armed conflict against North Vietnamese and Viet Cong communist aggressor forces on the Kinh Dong Tien Canal in the Republic of Vietnam. As Patrol Officer of two River Patrol Boats (PBR's) in company with an Armored Troop Carrier (ATC) and two other PBR's Chief Petty Officer Truett was aboard the fourth boat in the column when the entire unit came under intense enemy fire. PBR 8137, the boat ahead of Chief Petty Officer Trued, was taken under extremely heavy fire and began to burn forcing the five occupants aboard into the water. Observing the men struggling to reach the safety of a ditch, Chief Petty Officer Truett ordered his PBR into the area of the burning craft to recover the men in the water. Without regard for his own personal safety, he deliberately exposed himself to the blistering enemy fire, positioning himself on the bow of his boat to provide covering fire and to assist the men from the water. Because of several bright fires from grass huts burning along the canal bank Chief Petty Officer Truett was completely visible to the enemy during the entire rescue. Mortally wounded after he had helped rescue the last man from the water, Chief Petty Officer Truett, by his outstanding valor, concern for his shipmates' safety and inspiring devotion to duty, contributed directly to the safe recovery of the crew of PBR 8137. His selfless efforts were in keeping with the highest traditions of the United States Naval Service.

JAMES R. WALKER, Lieutenant, USN, citation for extraordinary heroism on Sept. 14, 1968 while serving with Helicopter Attack (Light) Squadron THREE, Detachment THREE, during operations against enemy aggressor forces in the Republic of Vietnam as the Fire Team Leader of a Light Helicopter Fire Team which was called in to support United State's naval forces that were under heavy attack on the Mekong River, Lieutenant Walker, upon arrival at the scene of the enemy ambush, immediately commenced his attacks against the entrenched hostile emplacements on both sides of the river. After diverting the intense enemy fire from the badly-damaged ships to himself and his fire team, he continued to press his attacks and was able to suppress much of the Viet Cong fire. With his ammunition expended, Lieutenant Walker was preparing to leave the scene of action to rearm when he was informed of the need of an immediate medical evacuation of a critically-wounded crewman aboard a severely-damaged fighter. Realizing that no medical-evacuation aircraft could approach the crippled ship due to the heavy fire, Lieutenant Walker courageously volunteered to attempt the evacuation, in the face of the withering hail of bullets and with full knowledge that the ship had no landing capabilities for his aircraft. He hovered his aircraft over the bow of the moving ship and successfully completed the evacuation of the injured man under the most hazardous conditions. He then flew the casualty to awaiting medical attention at Vinh Long Airfield and quickly rearmed returning to the scene of contact to press his attacks on the enemy positions. Forced to rearm once again at Vinh Long, Lieutenant Walker again returned to the ambush scene and succeeded in breaking the fiercely-resisting insurgents and suppressing all their planned fire. Through his tenacious and courageous attacks, he turned a well-planned enemy ambush on United States naval forces into a disastrous enemy rout. Lieutenant Walker's composure under fire, outstanding professionalism and valorous dedication were in keeping with the highest traditions of the United States Naval Service.

ALLEN E. WESELESKEY, Lieutenant Commander, USN, citation for extraordinary heroism on March 9, 1968 while serving as an Attack Helicopter Fire Team Leader with Helicopter Attack (Light) Squadron THREE in the Mekong Delta region of the Republic of Vietnam. While attempting to rescue two United States Army advisors who had been critically wounded when their Vietnamese battalions engaged communist insurgent (Viet Cong) forces, Lieutenant Commander Weseleskey and his helicopter fire team were caught in an intense cross fire during the attempt to land. Signaled to abort and clear the area by ground troops, the fire team departed the zone, machine guns blazing. When his wingman's aircraft commander and gunner were wounded Lieutenant Commander Weseleskey ordered them to return to base while he remained on station to complete the mission alone. Witnessing a Vietnamese aircraft receive several hits which forced it to depart station, Lieutenant Commander Weseleskey renewed his determination to complete a successful rescue of the Americans. Joined by an Army AH-IG gunship to cover his attempt, he led his crew into the combat zone, again receiving intense enemy automatic-weapons and .50 caliber fir. He landed his helicopter on target, in an extremely confined zone and brought aboard the two critically wounded US Army advisors and a seriously wounded Vietnamese soldier. Lifting his heavily laden helicopter out of the zone, Lieutenant Commander Weseleskey maintained absolute control of his aircraft despite adverse flying conditions. By his professional leadership and courageous fighting spirit he served to inspire his crew to perform to their utmost capability, thus ensuring the success of the mission. His heroic actions were in keeping with the highest traditions of the United States Naval Service.

WARREN R. WESTPHAL, Boatswain's Mate First Class, USN, citation for extraordinary heroism on Nov. 24, 1968 while serving with River Division 572 during combat operations against enemy aggressor forces on the Mekong River in the Republic of Vietnam. As Patrol Officer for River Patrol Boats (PBR's) 138 and 55, Petty Officer Westphal was conducting a routine mission on a narrow branch of the Mekong River when his patrol encountered a communist battalion crossing southward. The enemy force took the two PBRs under increasingly intense fire from at least twenty positions. Realizing that they were caught in the kill zone of a hostile force vastly larger than their own, the patrol boat crewmen accelerated to full speed and headed for the open river. Suddenly, a rocket detonated directly in front of the lead boat, PBR 138, in which Petty Officer Westphal was embarked, seriously wounding the forward machine gunner. Believing that PBR 55 was in more serious trouble, Petty Officer Westphal gave the order to turn toward it and then personally manned the forward gun battery in PBR 138 until his craft received three additional hits which wounded the entire crew, including himself, flooded the boat and rendered its weapons useless. After transferring two seriously-injured crew members to PBR 55 and ordering the cover boat to proceed out of the canal he beached his own craft on the far bank and personally provided medical assistance for another injured man. Petty Officer Westphal's crew received no additional enemy opposition and he was then able to request a medical evacuation helicopter and vector outside assistance to engage the retreating enemy. By his exemplary courage and outstanding professional ability, he prevented a large enemy force from crossing the river and was directly responsible for saving the lives of eleven of his comrades. Petty Officer Westphal's heroic actions in the face of almost overwhelming enemy opposition were in keeping with the highest traditions of the United States Naval Service.

JAMES E. WILLIAMS, Boatswain's Mate First Class, USN, citation for extraordinary heroism on Jan. 15, 1967 while serving with River Section 531 and friendly foreign forces during combat operations against communist insurgent (Viet Cong) forces on the Mekong River in the Republic of Vietnam. As Patrol Officer of a combat River Patrol Boat (PBR) patrol, Petty Officer Williams interdicted a major enemy supply movement across the Nam Thon branch of the Mekong River. He directed his units to the suspected crossing area and was immediately taken under intense hostile fire from fortified positions and from along the river banks. After coordinating Vietnamese artillery support and US Air Force air strikes, Petty Officer Williams courageously led his three PBR's back into the hazardous river to investigate and destroy the enemy sampans and supplies. Blistering fire was again unleashed upon his forces.

Frequently exposing himself to enemy fire, he directed his units in silencing several automatic-weapons positions and directed one PBR to investigate several sampans which could be seen, while the other PBR's provided cover fire. Almost immediately, the enemy renewed their fire in an effort to force the PBR's away from the sampans. Petty Officer Williams ordered the destruction of the sampan and the extraction of all his units. During the fierce firefight following the temporary immobilization of one of the units, Petty 0fficer Williams was wounded. Despite his painful injuries, he was able to lead his patrol back through the heavy enemy fire. His patrol had successfully interdicted a crossing attempt of three heavy-weapons companies totaling nearly four hundred men, had accounted for sixteen enemy killed in action, twenty wounded the destruction of nine enemy sampans and junks, seven enemy structures and 2,400 pounds of enemy rice. By his courage in the face of heavy enemy fire and his utmost devotion to duty, Petty Officer Williams upheld the highest traditions of the United States Naval Service.

LLOYD T. WILLIAMS JR., Aviation Machinist's Mate First Class, USN, citation for extraordinary heroism on April 28, 1969 while serving as a crew chief and door gunner with Helicopter Attack (Light) Squadron THREE, Detachment THREE, during a strike mission against enemy sampans in the Republic of Vietnam. When the wing-aircraft was struck by ground fire and crashed and his own aircraft was also struck and forced to land, Petty Officer Williams calmly directed the preparations for the forced landing while continuing to return enemy fire. After his aircraft had landed and the crew had abandoned it, he advanced toward the enemy under heavy fire and established a defensive position on the path leading to the enemy positions. Observing a crew member from the crashed wing-aircraft moving in the midst of the wreckage, Petty Officer Williams exposed himself to the blistering fire and ran across an open field to rescue the casualty. After carrying the severely injured man back across the open field to an area near the defensive perimeter, Petty Officer Williams returned to the wreckage in an attempt to find others from its crew. Obliged to suppress enemy fire in order to conduct his search, he persisted in his rescue attempts, despite the heat from the fire and the dangers of the exploding ammunition until his ammunition was exhausted Petty Officer Williams then ran to the defensive perimeter to report that the enemy had started using mortars and proceeded to assist a casualty aboard a rescue helicopter before boarding the craft himself to render first aid to the other wounded. Petty Officer William's determined efforts, his indomitable courage under fire and his inspiring devotion to duty were in keeping with the highest traditions of the United States Naval Service.

Vam Co Dong Patrol, PBR 19, River Division 591, Spring 1969. (Courtesy of Keith DeClercq)

(Courtesy of John Kirk Ferguson)

West Coast Memorial Monument for T.F. 116 River Patrol Force - Gamewardens of Vietnam. Louis C. Duty, president of the West Coast Chapter, giving a memorial service and wreath laying at the Naval Training Center in San Diego, CA. Memorial has the names of 25 servicemen killed in Vietnam. Memorial has since been moved to the Naval Amphibious Base, Coronado due to the closure of the Naval Training Center.

An Emotional Tribute from a Survivor and Friend

by BMCS Louis C. Duty, USN (Ret.)

Ladies and gentlemen, fellow warriors and distinguished guests, welcome. This is a sad time for me and if I get a little emotional and shed a few tears and get choked up, please bear with me. It only proves that I care and I have feelings. We remember and give thanks — from the Gamewardens of Vietnam, Inc.

We are here today to pay tribute to our fallen comrades. We dedicate this wreath to the memory of our 256 shipmates who were killed in action, while serving with the US Navy River Patrol Force in South Vietnam, known as "Operation Gamewarden" — Task Force #116. They gave their tomorrow for our today. Freedom is not free. We know that the road to freedom is paved with Purple Hearts. These brave men sacrificed their lives in defense of our freedom and ideas, and they were awarded every decoration this country has to offer, including more than one Medal of Honor.

They are under a different Command now;
One that knows no rank — only love,
One that knows no danger — only peace.

We, who remain to carry on, should not think of our shipmates as departed from us, but rather as having been transferred to a great "Celestial Ship" or "Station" in the heavens, where we hope all of us may be shipmates again someday.

"We do not lose the ones we love, they only go before

Where there is everlasting life, where sorrow is no more.
And there the soul will always live, and peace is everywhere.
We do not lose the ones we love. God takes them in His care."

We remember and give thanks for the services rendered to the US Navy and a grateful nation. Our shipmates died in a far-off, distant land, a long ways from home. They are enshrined in our hearts, and as long as any of us survivors remain alive, they will never be forgotten.

God bless America, God bless our POWs and MIAs, and God bless these brave men who gave their all for their country. May they rest in peace. We salute you. ("Taps" is played.) Let's all observe one minute of silent prayer for our departed comrades and our POWs and MIAs. May the blessing of Heaven rest upon us and brotherly love prevail. Until we meet again, God bless you.

Thank you.

BMCS Duty, with River Section 531, Vietnam 1967-69, is past president of Game Wardens of Vietnam, Inc., West Coast Chapter, San Diego, CA.

48 Hours with a Gamewarden LST, Jan. 19-20, 1969

by CDR A.L. Van Horne, USN (Ret.)

Sirens blared piercingly through the early-morning haze and brightly-colored flares filled the sky. This farewell salute was rendered to the large, gray LST on the brown waters of the upper Mekong River as the swift river patrol boats departed for a new base after being attached to Jennings County (LST-846) for some four months.

Jennings County is a Game Warden LST. She is a unit of the naval forces patrolling the intricate waterways of the Mekong Delta in pursuit of the elusive Viet Cong. The primary mission of the "T" is support — a term which is synonymous, in this application, with diversity. It includes providing berthing, food and relaxation for personnel of embarked units and visitors; rearming, refueling and repair of the boats and helicopters operating from the ship; acting as a communication center for all routine message traffic; coordinating, from a Tactical Operations Center, operations of a myriad of forces against the enemy; and serving as a landing platform for helicopters.

Departure of the River Division was part of a standard ship-base/shore-base rotation. The same day, another division of 10 PRBs embarked on Jennings County. Preparations for this turnover had begun weeks in advance, as foresight is essential to successful support. Spare parts were ordered, loaded, sorted and stowed; ammunition was procured; berthing spaces were prepared; and repair equipments were modified to respond to the needs of the newer model of boats to be attached. As a result of the advance preparation, embarkation went smoothly. The CO, LCDR A. Van Horne, briefed the newly-embarked personnel on facilities available to them, and the shipboard routine. Officers and loading petty officers were briefed on the tactical and geographical situation, then all were served a welcome-aboard steak-to-order dinner.

Patrols began at once in the canal assigned to the PRBs, and it was not long before Jennings County was called upon to exercise all phases of her capabilities. Heavy contact was made with the enemy before four hours of the patrol had passed.

From Jennings County, efforts began immediately to call in assisting units. All units were coordinated from the ship's voice communication center. Through the night, helicopters were guided in through the black sky to land on the red-illuminated deck, receive fuel and ammunition, and launch repeated attacks on the VC forces. Other helicopters were directed to the battle area to remove the wounded to hospitals. Supporting boats were checked out alongside and dispatched to the scene of action.

Eventually the situation quieted, and arrangements were made to feed and berth the weary helo crewmen. Their planes waited, ready at a moment's notice, on deck.

Morning brought new challenges. Damaged PRBs were returned to Jennings County and hoisted from the water to the large well deck repair area where the maintenance division immediately commenced work. Plans were laid for the next patrol. While this activity progressed, Jennings County hosted a visiting admiral for lunch, a briefing of operations and a tour of facilities.

As afternoon came, the second patrol set out for the canal. Once again the enemy struck. Again all available units were called to action;

again activity on the flight deck continued well into the night. One helo, struck by an enemy rocket, crash-landed in enemy-held territory, guided safely down by a highly-skilled pilot. In a heroic effort, the pilot of the companion aircraft dropped down to rescue the four downed fliers. They, along with a casualty from the River Division, were flown back to the LST where skilled hospital corpsmen waited, stretcher teams alert, to receive and treat them. Before the action ceased, US Navy and Army and Vietnamese forces all had been positioned to trap the enemy and provide security for the downed aircraft.

In days to come, as in days past, similar actions would take place. As always, the men of Jennings County would respond — quickly, eagerly, professionally — to the challenge of the moment, proud in the role of support, aware of and firm in belief in the motto of their fine ship: "We Can Handle It."

Naval Support Activity Detachment Resurrects Stricken PBR

by JO1 William H. Maisenhelder, USN

SAIGON, Aug. 12, 1968 — A USN river patrol boat (PBR) slips down the launching ramp into the Bassac River at Binh Thuy in South Vietnam's Mekong Delta. For PBR-130, it is the second trip down the ways, a second chance to prove herself in combat.

Less than three months before, the heavily-armed fiberglass speedboat lay helpless in the water, her guns on the muddy bottom 60 feet below the river's surface. A third of her crew had been killed, and more than three-fourths of the boat destroyed by enemy recoilless rifle fire.

As the boat backs slowly into the river, then turns to come alongside her sister PBRs, men of the Naval Support Activity Detachment, Binh Thuy, grin with the pride of having done what others had said was impossible.

They had built a boat, virtually from the hull up.

Early in the morning of May 5, the city of Chau Doc on the Upper Bassac River had come under attack by an unknown-sized enemy force. PBR-130 was directed to investigate reported enemy 75mm recoilless rifle positions six miles southeast of the city. As the boat approached the reported positions, a 75mm round plowed into her bow, wounding the forward gunner. In the ensuing action, the PBR was pounded by recoilless rifle and automatic weapons fire. Two men were killed and two wounded.

The battered and burned vessel was towed upside-down to Long Xuyen, then righted and towed to Binh Thuy.

Although the boat was 80 percent destroyed, the NSA detachment requested permission to restore her in tribute to the two men who lost their lives. The detachment repair officer, LT Phillip S. Thompson of Chicago, set a completion date of July 31. All hands participated in the reconstruction.

Since the Binh Thuy detachment has complete PBR fiberglass molds, the task of rebuilding the hull could all be done locally, although many parts had to be ordered and others completely manufactured.

The first step was to cut away and clean the damaged sections of the hull and replace them with complete molded patches. One of the main braces in the frame had to be reshaped, repaired, renewed. The entire electrical had to be stripped from the boat and replaced.

As new parts rolled in, the shipfitters started making new engine and gun mountings. The gun mounts were specially constructed to give the boat a more rapid fire capability. All the best features of both the Mark I and Mark II were incorporated to make this boat the best on the river. Meanwhile, newly-molded sides and deck sections were fastened in place and the hull sanded down. New engines, pumps, radar and radio gear were installed prior to painting.

In less than three months' time, NSA Detachment, Binh Thuy, had build a boat from the hull up. The detachment's officer-in-charge, LCDR Francis E. Glaser of Fresno, CA, stated that his men could build an entire PBR from scratch, if so authorized.

The detachment has been doing all types of repair for Game Warden unites in the Delta. Because of its repair facilities, fewer vessels need to be stricken from the lists and replaced.

When PBR-130 was first brought to Bin Thuy, she was considered a hopeless repair task. Now that the rebuilt boat has returned to combat, the detachment looks forward to newer and greater challenges which their pervading "Let's do it" spirit and Navy teamwork will just as surely accomplish.

Visions from Vietnam

by (former) LTJG Clayton H. Stone

I had been in South Vietnam about two months. It was starting to get hard. My new position was exciting enough: the first administrative officer on the staff of Commander River Patrol Force, Commander Task Force (CTF) 116. Operation Gamewarden seemed like the right thing to do relative to its mission of disrupting lines of communication and supply in the counter-insurgency operations in Vietnam.

My first exposure to the excitement of this new adventure was the landing at Tan Son Nhut Airport on the outskirts of Saigon. The plane took a precipitous drop in its approach to the landing strip. I later found out that was to avoid being fired upon by the "unfriendlies." Fortunately, the scotch put some control to the fear factor.

The Southeast Asian Pre-deployment course (12 weeks) was behind me. The academic training, the weapons training, the field training at Pendleton, the survival training at Warner Springs, and the Vietnamese language training made me the skilled, counter-insurgent USN advisor to the Vietnamese Navy. Junk force, here I come!

But the billets were filled, and the Coastal Surveillance Centers didn't much appeal to me. The staff job at Commander Naval Forces, Vietnam, at Phan Dinh Phung and Doan Thi Diem, Saigon, sounded great. That initial impression of excitement was growing thin.

It was my turn for duty that night. The Command Duty Officer had to sleep overnight at HQ, responding, as needed, to emergencies from our small but rapidly-growing operational forces in the Rung Sat Special Zone and Mekong Delta. As every night, the darkness was filled with the distant sounds of war. Everywhere was fire: Lights of fires, automatic weapons fire, tongues of fire (from the C-130 gunships), and the internal fire of a dissolving wall of invulnerability.

It is easy to be unafraid in the day time, with the sound and movement of active people doing real things in honest emotion. At night, there are only shadows, forms and occasional sirens of wailing spirits departing this war-torn land. Sometimes, the only life was the darting geckoes on the dark blue glass, snatching the insets which were attracted to the light within.

But the light within me was diffused and indistinct from the visible. Letters helped a lot. I wrote to several people other than the sometimes-obligatory missives to my parents. Even second cousins were prey to my wandering thoughts and remembrances of more pleasant moments back in Wisconsin. Melrose may be considered by some sophisticates to be pretty hick, but to me, then, it was Eden, far away, too surreal.

I was to survive Vietnam. I got shot at. I shot back with my "handy-dandy" M-79 grenade launcher. We killed, and were killed. Once, the local Republic of Vietnam Regional Force HQ requested that the PBRs perform a med-evac of one of the local rice farmers who was wounded in one of the artillery shellings that the RVNRF had showered on some suspected VC stronghold. I accompanied this patrol, though it wasn't my primary function. Our staff had moved to the Mekong Delta, near the provincial capital of Can Tho, at a base near the VAF base at Binh Thuy.

The farmer's wife came with her husband, sobbing, almost hysterical. His head was crudely bandaged, with the blood caking on the sides. His breathing was slow, deep and rasping. The sound was guttural and feeble. His wife kept sputtering strange sounds of a language which I barely understood, despite the language training. Perhaps it was the dialect. He died. His breathing just stopped. His wife lost it, as one could only expect. Fortunately, now, I understood her words, her depth of grief, her loss. She wanted to go home, home with her husband.

As we made our turn away from the dock where we dropped them off, I saw people carrying him away on an old discarded door. I guess it served the purpose. Thank God, there was only one month to go fighting these insurgents. Life will never be innocent again.

Long Night's Ambush

by Richard A. Stengel

One day the CO, LT Donaldson, learned we had a large VC compound in our area. The following is a brief account of what happened. This was the worst night I ever spent in ambush in Vietnam, and I spent a few bad ones, believe me.

The camp was located up a narrow ditch, off a main canal. The trick was to get in there and see what was going on. Both my boats were tied up to a monitor (MSR) on one side with slip knots to the cleats, and with that monitor making so much noise going up that canal, everyone could hear us.

As we passed close to the ditch, we slipped the knots, and slowly with power, went into the ditch, and into night ambush as soon as we tied up to the tree branches. You could still hear that monitor, making so much noise, but we were in the ditch halfway up and ready.

Around 9 o'clock that night it started. The VC were whooping it up, dancing and raising Cain, drinking rice wine and having a blast. We could smell them and their pot pipes. The smell was thick. I had been shot at before, and crawled on my belly to that radio mike to call for cover, but this ambush was something else. I just felt so insecure, felt like a sitting duck. All night, all we did was listen to them and smell the pot they were smoking. Anyone who says they were not scared is a liar, or plain nuts. I was wet, sweating through my clothes as usual, but worse this night.

Nothing happened, with the exception of them raising hell all night. We were able to keep a good watch on it with the starlights. At 0440, the CO said, "Let's break," and I was one glad son of a pup to get out of there — but I wasn't the only one.

A short story:

I am still looking for that Army colonel who said we would get the Army Commendation Medal for helping that night, and putting in firepower for his ski boats, and for turning over all the items to them that we picked up. We did get a "meal" at the base camp from the Army; even our CO was invited.

'Iron Butterflies' Pack a Powerful Sting

by Frank Re III, with Riv Div 593

Jumping from his PBR, the young gunner's mate and two other River Division 593 sailors dashed up the night-shrouded riverbank and into the dense undergrowth, firing as they ran.

Dodging a hail of VC rocket-grenade and machine-gun fire, they found the entrenched and battered US Army Reconnaissance team, three dead and three wounded, and carried them back to the PBRs.

An enemy element almost 50 strong had hit the recon troopers only minutes after their midnight insertion on the upper Saigon River, some 25 miles north of the capital city. They were only seconds away from being overrun when the sailors pulled them from the jungle to safety. Now the two boats, reinforced by four more RivDiv 593 PBRs, were firing into the bank, suppressing the enemy fire. Artillery fire was called in, and the helos arrived to med-evac the Army casualties.

This was an unusual action for RivDiv 593, but it's indicative of the courage found in the men of the division known as the "Iron Butterfly"; seven Bronze Stars were awarded for that night. The 54 officers and enlisted men of RivDiv 593 won a combined total of 131 Silver Stars, Bronze Stars, Navy Commendation Medals, Navy Achievement Medals and Vietnamese Crosses of Gallantry after their formation May 1968. The men also have received 57 Purple Hearts, five of them posthumously.

Obviously the RivDiv 593 sailors, easily recognized by their yellow-and-black Iron Butterfly shoulder patches, are a combat unit in which heroic action is the rule, not the exception. As in any such unit, individuals stand out:

Appropriately, Chief Monzingo, one of several RivDiv 593 "old-timers," was involved in the division's first official contact with the VC, back in May 1968. His sailor killed five enemy soldiers in a fire-fight on the Long Tau River, the twisting shipping channel southeast of Saigon, only a few days after the unit was formed. The Long Tau runs through 593's official home, the treacherous Rung Sat Special

Zone, a humid maze of jungle and water where the division killed 40 elusive enemy residents.

Other 593 campaigns include "Operation Giant Slingshot," where Iron Butterfly patrols helped suppress enemy infiltration along two strategic rivers running north of Saigon, the Vam Co Dong and Vam Co Tray. RivDiv 593 sailors counted 95 fire-fights with the enemy there, and killed 70 VC in the process. Twenty-one large enemy weapons caches were uncovered.

But RivDiv 593 always will be remembered for its relentless campaign against the enemy along the upper Saigon River, where they accounted for 134 VC dead. They assisted US 1st Infantry Division and 5th ARVN Division troopers in killing 50 more. Like all in-country Navymen, the sailors of the 593 were planning ahead for the day when their assets — nine battle-proven PBRs — would be turned over to the RVN. Iron Butterfly sailors trained 61 Vietnamese Navymen after receiving the first "class" of 11 seamen in March 1969, and another 21 trainees were with the division.

The Vietnamese sailors ate, slept, worked and fought alongside their American counterparts, sharing the victories and hardships of men at war, while proudly wearing the famous Iron Butterfly shoulder patch.

"The Brown Water Navy March"

"The Brown Water Navy March" was selected by ADM Elmo Zumwalt in 1970 as the official theme song of the Riverine forces of the Vietnam region. MUC Wallace Q. Roderick was assigned to the Navy Band-Great Lakes as the staff arranger and associate conductor when he was asked by ADM Zumwalt's staff to develop a fight song to pay tribute to the men and women of the forces serving the shallow waters and rivers in the Delta regions of Vietnam.

Chief Musician Roderick premiered the march as he conducted his former high-school concert band in Portage, WI, in early 1970. Seemingly forgotten after the Vietnam era, there were few requests for the march to be performed. However, in 1979 Senior Chief Musician Roderick, while assigned to Navy Band-San Diego, performed the Brown Water Navy March at numerous ceremonies and anniversaries at bases along the West Coast and especially at the NAB in Coronado, CA.

The Brown Water Navy March may not be as well-known as the great marches by Sousa, but it is an exciting and spirited piece of music dedicated to the valiant people who served in one of the Navy's most difficult and demanding forces of the Vietnam campaign. *Courtesy of Wallace Q. Roderick*

The Godbehere Patrol

by Jere A. Beery Jr., USN (Ret.)

(Author's Note — There was no such thing as "just another day" in Vietnam. All the preparation in the world couldn't prepare you for survival in a war zone where the enemy had no rules, maintained no constants and wore no uniform. Anything was possible; therefore, ev-

Mark II PBR on Van Co Tay River, River Division 594 in Rung Sat Zone - 1969. (Courtesy of Bill Curtis)

erything was probable. For some of us, the ability to survive depended entirely on one's will to live, one's belief in God, and the "above and beyond" capabilities of one's shipmates. The following story reflects the epitome of what can happen when these three elements merge in a combat zone.)

Friday, 1 March 1968; payday at the USN's river patrol base, River Section 511, Task Force 116 at Binh Thuy, South Vietnam. Earlier that day I'd gotten paid, and Otto and I had gone to Morley's (an off-base East Indian tailor) to pick up my new pair of custom-made fatigues. They were made out of a camouflage poncho liner, and I had decided to wear them for he first time on that night's patrol.

When I showed up at the dock wearing my new uniform, the rest of the crew began teasing me about my new look. "Hey, Beery, where are you? I can't see you with those camis on," Otto said. Sherman called me "a walking tree." Even LT Godbehere got into the act, saying, "If Beery doesn't show up for patrol, he's going on report." The teasing didn't last long, since we had a patrol to get ready for.

Bravo Patrol was preparing for another night patrol on the Bassac River. Bravo and Bravo One were both 31-foot Mark I PBRs. The two high-speed patrol boats were being checked out and loaded by their crews. Bravo always operated with the same crew members. Bailey, Otto, Sherman and I had been together since December 1967. We were one of the very few crews that had not suffered any personnel losses since the first of the year. Sherman and I were both E-3, seamen. We were the lowest in rank aboard Bravo. In January, we both had taken our test for PO3, but we hadn't received the test results as yet.

We were both looking forward to the advance in pay and rank to E-4. In his early 20s, Sherman was one of the very few black men to volunteer for the river patrol force. He was a rather quiet man, but you always knew he was there. He stood about 6-2 and weighed in somewhere around 235 lbs. He definitely could intimidate the Vietnamese with his presence, which came in handy on occasion when searching suspected VC sampans. Sherman was quite effective with the M-60 machine gun, as well.

This night was to be Sherman's last patrol with Bravo, as he had been reassigned to duty in the front office of River Section 511 starting the following day. We always looked for excuses to have a party, so we agreed we'd all meet at the base bar after our patrol to give Sherman a proper send-off.

Otto and I provided the wit and humor aboard Bravo. Our exchange of one-liners and puns was never-ending, and on occasion even clever. This in itself was a very valuable contribution to the morale of the crew. If it was ever to be said that I had a good time while serving in Vietnam, it had to have been with Otto.

Our boat captain, Bailey, was probably our best audience. The 26-year-old 1C boatswain was senior man aboard Bravo when we weren't carrying a patrol officer. He knew the river like the back of his hand. He could handle a boat as well as, if not better than, anyone in our river section. This night was about our 60th patrol together for the crew of Bravo.

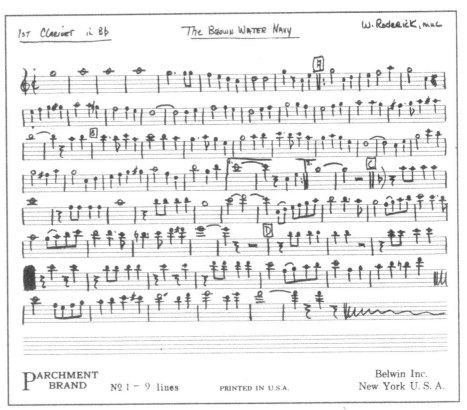

(Courtesy of Wallace Q. Roderick)

Our patrol officers would rotate. Every time we went out, our two-boat patrol would be commanded by a different patrol officer. Some officers we preferred over others. Tonight we were under the command of one of our favorites, LT Richard Godbehere. The lieutenant was in his early 30s and had been with River Section 511 for about eight months. During that time, the lieutenant had encountered the VC many times, including having one boat shot out from under him, sunk. Because he was a "mustanger," we all felt a little closer to him than some of the other officers.

A "mustanger" works his way up through the ranks to become an officer; in other words, he once was, as we were, an enlisted man. We had been out many times with LT Godbehere and had survived quite a few fire-fights under his leadership. He always took great care in not putting his men, or the boats, in unnecessary danger, and he was well-respected by all the crews. In addition, because of his name, Godbe-here, he was considered something of a good-luck charm. The running line around the dock was, "I'd rather have God-be-here than anyone." We all echoed that sentiment.

We tried to take the boat out on every patrol. The #60 boat was the fastest boar in the River Section, but we had to share it with other patrols. Otto, 21, was a third-class gunner's mate, and was very meticulous about our boat and *his* forward guns, "the Twins." The Twins were a pair of .50-caliber machine guns mounted in the bow of the boat. Together with the .50-cal gun I manned on the stern, these guns were the heaviest standard firepower on a PBR. This day, Otto was pretty upset about the fact that the twins had been left dirty, and Otto knew how to cuss.

Bailey was checking out the engines, and

Sherman and I went to get C-rations and ammo. LT Godbehere checked out the radios and radar. Then he looked over his map, planning our patrol. After we were all loaded, we had a brief meeting with both boat crews, conducted by LT Godbehere. The boat captain of Bravo One was a PO2 by the name of Lucidi. He, along with three other sailors — Ellis, Larrimore and Cole — made up the crew of our cover boat. All together, Bravo Patrol consisted of nine men and two boats.

During our briefing, LT Godbehere informed us that we'd be transporting two sailors to an LST (landing ship, tank) located about a mile downriver. Then he shared the latest military intelligence with both boat crews. He told us to be on our toes at all times, because Charlie was still taking this "Tet thing" very seriously. He said the number of night river crossings were on the increase, and the VC were depending heavily on the waterways to transport arms and supplies.

He reminded us that the other patrols had been taking a lot of hits, and we were losing men every week. When he had completed his briefing, we cast off and pulled away from the dock. Otto loaded the forward Twins; Sherman set up and loaded the M-60. I loaded the after-50s and put C-rations on the engine covers so we would have hot food later. Bravo was to operate as lead boat, with Bravo One as cover boat. LT Godbehere would be using his personal radio ID name, "Handlash Delta," to communicate with the base back at Binh Thuy and the other boat.

Once we had cleared the base and were in the middle of the river, we opened the boats up to full-bore. This seemed to impress our two passengers, the "T" sailors. However, the crew of Bravo was looking forward to dropping off the excess weight and getting the boat back up on-step. This is the point when a boat achieves minimum draft, or drag, and maximum speed. When a boat reaches this point, you feel like you are skimming across the top of the water, occasionally even feeling airborne. No one talks; you just hold on and enjoy the ride.

The LST was one of the smaller 542-class landing ships used in Vietnam. The sight of the LST reminded me of my previous two years of duty aboard the USS Westchester County, LST-1167, in the waters of Vietnam. The Westchester County, an 1156-class LST, was somewhat larger than this one. Their operating capabilities, however, were virtually the same. I couldn't help but think about my former shipmates, and wondered where they and the ship were now.

The words of my former CO, LCDR Norman T. Hansen, were echoing through my head: "Beery, I strongly recommend you retract your request for duty with the river patrol. This is very dangerous duty, and you're just going to get yourself hurt or killed." Other members of the crew suggested I extend for another two years aboard the Westchester County, as this was considered "safe" Vietnam duty. I had carefully considered all my options before making my final decision. It had made me feel pretty damn good to know of their concerns, though.

When you live aboard a ship for two years, you become attached not only to the crew, but to the ship as well. A lot of fond memories of my time aboard the "Wesco" were going through my head as we approached the LST's port beam. A ladder was dropped over the side, and without mooring, we came alongside, discharged our passengers and cast off. Once we had cleared the T, both boats were put up on-step. Things were pretty relaxed at this point, as we were on our way to our assigned patrol area, and the sunset was incredible.

By dark, we had to navigate by radar. In a short while, radar had picked up two contacts headed straight for us. Although we had a good idea what the two were, we manned our battle stations anyway. As we suspected, it was just the patrol we were relieving. They were on their way back to the base. The two patrols acknowledged each others' presence by flashlight, then proceeded on their way.

Both boats of Bravo Patrol were operating with no running lights to avoid visual detection. The boats were traveling at full bore, 25 knots, 100 yards apart. After another 15 minutes or so, we were coming up on Cu Lao May Island, dead ahead. Cu Lao May was approximately 10 nautical miles long and about 2 miles across at its widest point. It was located about 25 miles inland from the mouth of the Bassac River.

When coming up on Cu Lao May, we had the option of passing to the right or left of the island. This time we chose a course to port, our left. The river bottle-necked at this point, making the distance between the two banks about 125 yards. Because a large sandbar was located between us and the mainland, we always had to pass close to the north end of the island. Three weeks earlier, the crew of Bravo had spent eight tense hours grounded on this particular sandbar.

The northern tip of the island was about 1,000 yards off our starboard stern, when suddenly, without warning, we began taking rocket fire from the treeline on the island. We all scrambled for our flak jackets and helmets. I jacked back my 50 and looked forward to LT Godbehere for permission to return fire. All guns were manned and ready. The lieutenant was on the radio: "Bravo One, this is Handlash Delta. We are receiving rocket fire from Cu Lao May Island. Reduce speed to half-throttle and hold your fire! We don't want to give away our position until we know what we are up against!"

"Bravo One at the ready and standing by," came the reply.

The lieutenant sensed Charlie was holding something back. We slowly approached the island in the darkness, being careful not to give away our exact position. For the next two minutes or so, rockets were launched blindly in our direction. Several struck the water and exploded just short, and some on the other side of our boat. Charlie then confirmed LT Godbehere's suspicions by opening fire with at least six positions of .30-cal machine guns and an undetermined number of rifles. Their fire was accurate, hitting both boats.

LT Godbehere ordered the two boats to open fire and commence a full-speed firing run. As the two boats of Bravo Patrol leaped up on-step, the darkness erupted in a barrage of red and green tracer fire. There were many positions of heavy automatic weapons fire. RPG-2 and RPG-7 rockets were coming out of the treeline, two and three at a time. Otto and I were pounding the island with our 50s.

I didn't know which way to aim! There were more targets than I could shoot. The treeline was riddled with enemy muzzle flashes. Sherman was lighting up the night with his M-60, and LT Godbehere was dropping M-79 grenades into the treeline. Otto began having trouble with his Twins, and he stopped firing. I thought he was hit at first, but then I saw his silhouette frantically trying to get the Twins to fire.

A bright flash to our stern caught my eye as a rocket hit the cover boat and exploded. I just knew we had lost somebody. It became obvious very rapidly that these were not your run-of-the-mill VC dirt farmers. We were up against an undetermined number of heavily-armed mainforce VC Regulars, and there was no turning back. Because of the sandbar to our port, we had to maintain a distance of only 40 or 50 yards from the island.

We were committed to the firing run, which had by this time turned into one hell of a firefight. Otto had given up on the malfunctioning Twins and was returning fire with his M-16. The events were unfolding so rapidly that there was no time to call for additional support. I had just emptied my first canister of ammo when I saw two reddish-orange fireballs leave the island. Because of our speed and the darkness, I thought the chances of a direct hit were slim. I started to reach down to pick up another canister of ammo.

Before I had a chance to pick one up, I realized that one rocket had my name on it. I reached up as fast as I could and grabbed hold of my gun. Just as I did, the rocket hit the starboard side of the boat, right in front of me. In a split second, I saw the rocket come through the side of the boat, explode, and hit me in the right side and stomach. The heat and brightness of the explosion were overwhelming, and the impact knocked the breath out of me. Red-hot pieces of the rocket ripped into my body. The concussion sent my head spinning, and I was totally disoriented. I held onto my gun for dear life, for one of our greatest fears was to be blown overboard at night.

I lost all sense of direction. The only way I knew which way was up was because I assumed my gun still was standing upright. I was night-blind from the blast and unable to see anything. My ears were ringing, and what sounds I could hear were muffled and distorted. After a couple of minutes, my sight began coming back slowly. Although I was unable to focus, I could tell we still were under fire.

I tried to remember if I had been successful in reloading my gun. I tried to jack it back, but didn't have the strength. I pulled the trigger; nothing happened. I was standing on my left leg, and couldn't put any weight on my right. At first I thought my leg had been blown off. It was as if it wasn't there. I ran my hand down my right side and felt it was all wet. I knew I was hit bad.

LT Godbehere was hit by shrapnel in the right arm and right leg, and was blown to the deck. He quickly recovered and returned to the fight. When the lieutenant didn't see Sherman beside him any more, he was sure that the seaman had been blown out of the boat.

Bailey was hit in the right hand, but still maintained control of the boat. The lieutenant looked back at me and assumed I was OK because I still was standing up at my gun. Otto finally got the Twins working again, and for a period of time he was the only firepower the boat had.

Then a second rocket slammed into the starboard side of the boat, right in our grenade locker. The second explosion set off several grenades, and set the boat on fire. I was hit again, this time in the left eye and left leg. The left side of my head felt like it had been hit with a hammer, and I could feel blood running down my face and neck. Somehow, again I managed to hang onto my gun and remain standing, but that's all I could do.

LT Godbehere was blown to the deck for a second time, this time receiving serious wounds to both legs. The lieutenant pulled himself back up, and looked around to assess the situation. The light provided by the fire in the grenade locker enabled LT Godbehere to relocate SN Sherman. The seaman was obviously in a great deal of pain as he struggled to get to his feet. The force of the first explosion had blown Sherman across the boat and to the deck on the port side, behind Bailey's position. The seaman reappeared with a large piece of metal sticking all the way through his right foot, and a big chunk missing out of his left arm above the elbow.

Unexploded grenades were visible in the flames in the grenade locker, and the possibility of additional explosions was undeniable. After several attempts and in spite of his wounds, Sherman somehow managed to beat the fire out with his bare hands. He threw all the hot unexploded grenades over the side.

The second rocket also knocked out the starboard engine, and Bailey was trying frantically to get it restarted. LT Godbehere looked back at me, and again assumed I was OK because I still was standing up at my gun, but he couldn't understand why I wasn't firing. The lieutenant instructed Sherman to make his way aft to check on me. When Sherman returned, he told the lieutenant that I was badly hurt. LT Godbehere ordered the boats to continue south, clearing the immediate area in order to assess damages and evaluate the wounded.

The entire fire-fight lasted all of five or six minutes. Bravo One radioed, "Have taken two rocket hits, three men with minor wounds, boat and guns fully operational, standing by." LT Godbehere then made his way back to my position. I still was standing up with a "death grip" on my gun when LT Godbehere and Sherman got to me. The lieutenant asked me where I was hit. I could barely get it out: "In the gut." That's when LT Godbehere saw how badly I was hurt. My stomach had been sliced open and my intestines were hanging all the way to the deck. LT Godbehere grabbed me by the shoulders. "Let go of the gun, Beery! We've got you! Let go of the gun!" he said.

I turned loose and the lieutenant and Sherman laid me down on the deck. LT Godbehere began placing my guts on top of my stomach. He told Sherman to get one of those big battle dressings out of the first-aid kit. He instructed Bailey to head for the US Army outpost at Tra On. Then he placed the battle dressing over my belly and tried to keep the blood inside. I also had a big piece of shrapnel sticking out of my back on my right side. The lieutenant held his hand around it to keep the blood from coming out. In addition to my stomach wounds, my left eye was hanging half-out and my legs were peppered.

My new camouflage fatigues were full of holes from the many shrapnel wounds that covered both of my legs and stomach. LT Godbehere handed Sherman his personal hunting knife and told him to cut away my pants and assess my many wounds. There was not doubt in my mind that I was dying. The pain was becoming very intense, and at times dying seemed like an

acceptable option. I could feel myself getting weaker by the second, as the blood left my body.

I knew we were a long way from help, and my only chance of surviving was not to panic. I had to stay calm. If I let myself get upset, my pulse would increase and I would bleed faster. I tried to relax as much as I could. This wasn't easy, but I had no choice. I figured as long as I was aware of what was going on around me, I could make some contribution toward whether or not I died. Everything had become very seriously real.

A lot of things were going through my head. I remember thinking about my upcoming birthday in 12 days, and how I wasn't going to live to see 20. My main concern was getting a message to my parents. I tried to talk, but didn't have sufficient breath to be heard over the sound of our remaining engine.

In an act of desperation, I grabbed LT Godbehere's flak jacket and pulled him down to me. I whispered in his ear, "If I don't make it, tell my Mom and Dad what happened, and I love them."

The lieutenant seemed to get upset. "Now you listen to me, Beery! You're going to be all right! You aren't missing anything! Your intestines just fell out. They can put them back in. They do it all the time! Goddammit, Beery, you're going to be all right!"

In an effort to make me more comfortable and at my request, LT Godbehere and Sherman picked up my shattered right leg and moved it to the other side of the gun mount. This seemed to ease the pain somewhat. LT Godbehere then instructed Bailey to get on the radio and call for "Pedro," the USAF med-evac helicopter. "Have them meet us at Tra On with blood plasma standing by," he said. Bailey radioed. Otto kept watch in the forward guns while nursing a minor wound to his right hand. Shrapnel holes the size of baseballs had penetrated the forward gun turret, missing Otto by fractions of an inch.

I was still very aware of what was going on around me, even though I was on the brink of

passing out from the loss of blood. "Stay awake, Beery! Don't go to sleep! It won't be long now! We're almost there," the lieutenant said as he shook me.

I remember looking up at the lieutenant and Sherman as they worked on me, and seeing the amount of concern in their faces. I remember seeing both men covered with blood as they bent down over me, totally unconcerned with their own wounds. I remember thinking how ironic it was to have a man named God-be-here at my side when I was dying. I was having the ultimate religious experience as I prayed to God for my very existence.

I remember the dim light from the battle lantern, seeing the flag of the USA flying in the wind behind the two men. I remember thinking that if I were to die, at least I died for a good cause, in good company....

It seemed like it would take us forever to get to Tra On, since we were operating with one engine and could obtain less than half-speed. Tra On was about 5 miles downriver on the mainland side. At 15 or 20 mph, it would take 15 or 20 minutes to get there and dock, and another 30 to 45 minutes to reach a field hospital by chopper. We were looking at at least an hour before any of us could get medical attention other than first aid. LT Godbehere was worried about the amount of blood I had lost.

Bravo limped its way toward Tra On, with Bravo One close behind acting as cover and ready to assist. At no time did LT Godbehere or Sherman leave my side. Between the five of us on Bravo, we must have caused our boat's bilge pumps to pump a lot of American blood into the Bassac River that night.

After about 20 minutes, our patrol arrived at the US Army outpost at Tra On. A US soldier came aboard Bravo and started the blood plasma IV in my arm. I'm sure I was in shock by this time, but I still was very aware of what was happening around me. Soldiers then came aboard with a stretcher for me. One of my legs was on one side of the gun mount and one was on the

These five men were glad to see each other at the Gamewardens Association of Vietnam reunion in 1991. It was the first time all five had been together since a night in 1968 when they were barraged by enemy fire in Vietnam. From left are Richard Godbehere, Jere Beery, Harold Sherman, Dallam Bailey and Dave Otto.

other side. In order to get me on the stretcher, they had to move my wounded leg around the mount. This was very painful, but once it was accomplished, I was taken off the boat.

Nobody was saying much of anything, so I tried to break the silence by cracking a joke. "I don't know how they hit me. I look like a tree," I said. No one laughed. LT Godbehere and Sherman were unable to stand on their own, and had to helped off the boat. Both men were in a great deal of pain from their wounds. As I was loaded into the back of a Jeep, LT Godbehere and Sherman were placed on the hood. Bailey was transferred to Bravo One, where first aid was administered to a deep wound in his right hand.

The lieutenant, Sherman and myself were driven about a quarter-mile outside the outpost to a rice paddy, where a helicopter landed to take us aboard. LT Godbehere and Sherman put their arms around each other and were able to hop the short distance to the chopper from the Jeep by using their better legs. From there we were flown about 45 miles to the US Army's 3rd Surgical (Mobile) Hospital at Dong Tam. At some point, Lucidi, the boat captain of Bravo One, also was med-evac'd out. The extent of his wounds were unknown.

Otto stayed with Bravo at Tra On. Later that night, he had the depressing duty of nursing the crippled #60 boat back to the base at Binh Thuy, alone. Bravo One acted as escort.

After-action report: LT Godbehere reported the size of the opposing forces to be at least 100 men, six to eight positions of heavy automatic weapons, two or three positions of RPG-2/B-40 and RPG-7/B-50 rocket launchers, and 25 to 30 positions of rifle/light automatic weapons. Estimated combat ratio: 11 to 1.

Of the nine men on Bravo Patrol, eight were wounded: Four minor, three seriously, one severely, four med-evac'd. No fatalities. Two PBRs seriously damaged. Enemy KIAs unknown; damage to enemy positions unknown. Recommendations were made by LT Godbehere to LT Carl Kollmeyer, OIC of River Section 511, that the four crew members of Bravo be recognized for their individual contributions of heroism and bravery on the night of 1 March 1968. Kollmeyer was killed in action 5 May 1968, and had processed only one of the recommendations at the time of his death: SN Sherman's.

It wasn't until 18 Sept 1990, after Godbehere resubmitted his recommendations, that the other three crew members were recognized for their actions on that fateful night. Bailey and Otto were awarded the Navy Commendation Medal with combat-distinguishing V; Beery was awarded a Bronze Star with combat-distinguishing V. The Chief of Naval Operations recommended that Godbehere be decorated as well, and on 21 Jan 1991, he was awarded a Bronze Star and V.

LT Richard G. Godbehere never saw combat in Vietnam again. He recovered from his wounds and remained in the Navy, retiring after 20 years of service as LCDR. He was awarded his second Purple Heart for wounds received on 1 March 1968. In 1988, he retired

after four years as sheriff of Maricopa County, AZ, and now lives in Hawaii with his family.

PO1 Dallam Bailey also received his second Purple Heart for the above-described action. He retired from the Navy in 1988 with 28 years of service as LCDR. He is the harbormaster at the Port of Brownsville, Bremerton, WA.

PO3 David G. Otto was discharged from the Navy after his second TOD at the rank of PO2. He is an AC motor technician with Reliance Electric Co. and lives in Jefferson, Ohio.

SN Harold W. Sherman Sr. was awarded a Silver Star and a Purple Heart for his actions

on 1 March 1968. He retired from the Navy after 20 years of service as Boatswain's Mate 1C. He works at Trane AC Co. and lives in Tyler, TX.

SN Jere A. Beery Jr. never saw combat in Vietnam again. He spent the next year and a half in the hospital, where he received his Purple Heart. PO3 Beery was retired from active duty on 14 May 1969. He has personally thanked Godbehere, Otto, Bailey and Sherman for saving his life. He is a special effects assistant with Bob Shelley's Special Effect International Inc., and lives in Newnan, GA.

Vietnam Service Medal

U.S. Naval Support Base Exhibit
"Somewhere, South Vietnam"

★★★★★★

Dedication

★★★★★

20 February 1993

PATRIOTS POINT
Naval & Maritime Museum

U.S. Naval Support Base

In 1966, sailors from the United States Navy were committed to the interior regions of South Vietnam to provide both general support to ground troops, and specific assistance to the counter-insurgency operations being conducted in the region's waterways. Their primary mission was to block the movement of supplies, while preventing the Viet Cong from entering South Vietnam. This was the first time since the American Civil War that naval forces had operated *within* a hostile country.

Nicknamed "Game Wardens" by General William C. Westmoreland, these special naval warfare groups operated from a series of strategically located base camps. Though often coming under fire, the naval support bases served as relatively secure areas for resupplying and rest.

It is our sincere hope that visitors to the Vietnam Naval Support Base Exhibit will not only feel a deep appreciation for those who served, but will also gain a better understanding of the living and operational conditions under which they existed. We believe this exhibit is a first of its kind - a true hands-on learning experience that accurately reflects a time in our nation's history that many Americans will never forget.

Program

Michael McDermott, Master of Ceremonies

I. Presentation of Colors....U.S. Navy Color Guard

II. National Anthem ....282nd Army Band

III. Pledge of Allegiance ......J. Elliott Williams, President Congressional Medal of Honor Society Member, Patriots Point Development Authority

IV. Retirement of Colors

V. Invocation ....E. B. "Buzz" Purcell Member, Game Wardens of Vietnam Association, Inc.

VI. Welcome ....Charles G. Waldrop, Executive Director Patriots Point Development Authority

VII. Remarks ....John F. Floyd, Chairman Patriots Point Development Authority

J. Elliott Williams

Gen. William C. Westmoreland, USA (Retired)

VIII. Opening of Exhibit

Dedication program. (Courtesy of Ron Laratta)

"VC gator" in the Rung Sat, 1969. (Courtesy of William H. Curtis)

EN2 Jim Davy, River Division 593. Taken on Operation Giant Slingshot in March 1969. Two enemy flags captured on patrol with an AK-47 Chinese assault rifle. Photo taken at Fire Support Base Barbara. (Courtesy of James Davy)

The Fastest Boats On The Delta

by Cmdr. John Kirk Ferguson, USN (Ret)

The first rays of morning light cast shadows on the still slumbering NVA campsite along the Mekong tributary. In an instant the silence was broken by the flash of M-60 machine gunfire and a barrage of .50 caliber machine gun bullets slicing through smoldering hooches set on fire by 40mm low velocity grenades. All of this fire power coming from a pair of high speed boats skimming along the river in front of the campsite. The devastated NVA troops had been taken completely by surprise.

The two Chinook helicopters lowered the two high speed strike assault boats into the waterway within striking distance of the VC base. Within minutes, the boat crews were pouring machine gun fire and grenades into the totally surprised base defenders, destroying the fortifications. The two boats returned to rendezvous with the Chinooks and were lifted to safety.

The NVA troops and VC guides were busy boarding sampans to cross the canal into South Vietnam. In the mist of daybreak they did not see nor hear strike assault boats inching their way toward the boarding site. Suddenly, heavy machine gun fire and grenades took the NVA and VC completely by surprise, scattering and sinking the sampans and annihilating the enemy troops.

If these scenarios sound like something out of "Apocalypse Now," then guess again. These were scenes as envisioned by the staff of Commander, Naval Forces Vietnam (COMNAVFORV) soon after Vice Admiral Elmo R. Zumwalt, U.S. Navy, took command of the organization at the end of September 1968. He and his staff were most impressed with the Light SEAL Support Craft (LSSC) operations in An Xuyan Province and decided that a modification of the LSSC could improve riverine strike warfare operations in the upper delta. Other than for the overall dimensions and the aluminum hull, the Strike Assault Boat (STAB) was considerably modified from its original LSSC configuration.

Under a $2.2 million dollar U.S. Navy contract, the Grafton Boat Company, Grafton, Illinois, built 22 STABS. The boats were 26 feet, 2 inches long, with a 10 foot, 4 inch beam, a 3 foot, 9 inch draft, and each boat weighed about 15,000 pounds. The aluminum hull had an inner liner of ceramic armor which stopped small caliber bullets and caused larger projectiles to fragment. Inside the crew's cockpit was a flak blanket of many layers of nylon, on both port and starboard sides, for the shrapnel to imbed itself. It worked very effectively.

Each STAB was completely foam filled from bow to stern to prevent capsizing if damaged. The boat, if holed, would sink to the gunwale and no further. Several damaged boats sank only to the gunwale, as predicted in the builders specifications.

Each boat had two 350 horsepower gasoline powered Mercruiser III, 427 cubic inch engines located in nearly sound-proof, separate, watertight compartments; each engine had an out-drive and propeller. The STAB could accelerate from dead-in-the-water to 40 knots in about 15 seconds.

Every STAB had two 150 gallon, foam filled, self-sealing, rubber, gasoline bladders located under the floor plate in the crew's cockpit, below the waterline. The advantage of this design included little chance of fire or explosion. There were several instances in which enemy machine gunfire and in one instance, an enemy antitank rocket, penetrated the bladders; no fire nor explosions resulted.

All STABs had an LN-66, relative bearing, Pathfinder, radar and a fathometer installed. The radar was removed from the boats in Vietnam due to space limitations (more space was needed for storing ammunition), the shrapnel hazard of the dome-shaped antenna if hit by a projectile, and the fact that riverine and canal navigation did not require the use of a radar. The fathometer provided accurate depths even with only one foot of water under the keel.

All 22 STABs had four pintle mounts, one on each or the four corners of the crew's cockpit. The normal armament consisted of two M-60 machine guns on the port and starboard pintle mounts forward, and either two M-60s aft or one M-60 and one MK-20 automatic grenade launcher (firing 40mm low velocity grenades) on the side nearest the shore. Occasionally, when it was anticipated that growths of bamboo would have to be penetrated, .50 caliber machine guns were substituted for one or more of the M-60s forward.

Each boat crew also took a Starlight Scope (night vision device) on every night patrol. Each boat also had FM radios with frequencies both in the clear and secure voice.

All 22 STABs had three unique characteristics no other boat in the Republic of Vietnam had: (1) fast acceleration and high speed capability (between 40 and 45 knots); (2) very quite operations at slow speeds due to the soundproofing of the engine compartments; and (3) a very low silhouette since there was no canopy. Frequently, the slap of the water on the hull would identify the location of the boat before the noise from the engines would be heard. These three assets made them a unique weapon platform for strike operations.

The mission of these boats, as envisioned by the COMNAVFORV staff, was multi-faceted: (1) fast attack gun boat to conduct strike warfare; (2) resource control operations for daytime boarding and search of questionable sampans/junks; (3) Waterborne Guard Post operations to ambush the enemy at night; (4) SEAL platoon daytime strike warfare; and, (5) SEAL Team night insertion and extraction operations.

Each STAB was assigned a four-man crew: a coxswain, a boat engineer, a gunner's mate, and a line handler. The boat captain was generally either the gunner or the coxswain, since these were the only petty officer rates assigned to the squadron when the boats arrived in-country Vietnam. Generally, a patrol officer was assigned to every three or four boats on patrol, for coordination purposes.

STABRON 20 was a unique entity, since we grew together into a cohesive unit at NIOTC before leaving the United States and remained together with the STABs during their one year in-country Vietnam tour of duty.

Upon arrival in-country, the personnel organization was chaotic at the "White Elephant," the nickname given to the whitewashed building housing the U.S. Naval Support Activity, Saigon. No one knew about the STAB organization, and after two or three days of being cooped-up in the uncomfortable White Elephant, I arranged for the STABRON 20 personnel to be flown to Binh Thuy in CH-46 Sea Knight helicopters. Commander River Patrol Flotilla FIVE (COMRIVPATFLOT 5) and his staff were located in Binh Thuy and STABRON 20 was to work for him. The accommodations for our personnel weren't exactly like the Hilton, but each man had a bunk and the mess hall was air-conditioned with a swamp cooler.

During the first meeting with COMRIVPATFLOT 5 and his staff, it did not take long for me to figure out they knew nothing about the STAB, its characteristics, capabilities, nor its mission. I educated them as best I could without a boat to show them.

COMRIVPATFLOT 5 was concentrating on the SEALORDS (Southeast Asia Lake, Ocean, River, and Delta Strategy) Campaign of barrier patrols along the RVN waterways paralleling the Cambodian border. Two of these barrier areas were Tran Hung Dao I and Operations Barrier Reef, each with PBRs and RACs assigned to the barrier. Tran Hung Dao I extended from the eastern town of Ha Tien, on the Gulf of Thailand, following the Vinh Te canal system on the south side of the Cambodian border, to Chau Doc, to the west on the upper Bassac River. Operation Barrier Reef, in the Plain of Reeds, extended in an east-west barrier along the

Seal Team 1 STAB boat after insertion during Bold Dragon mission in January 1968. (Courtesy of Thomas P. Stiller)

STABs preparing to get underway. (Courtesy of Don Mirkovich)

Kirk Ferguson, center with glasses, in STAB ready to get underway. (Courtesy of Don Mirkovich)

Grand Canal, a 40 mile long canal from the northern Mekong River village of An Long, on the west, eastward to Tuyen Nhon on the Vam Co Tay (river).

Since we had no STABs and there was no mission for them anyway, both I and COMRIVPATFLOT 5 agreed that STABRON 20 patrol officers and all enlisted personnel be assigned to augment the boat crews on Tran Hung Dao I and Operation Barrier Reef until such time as the STABs arrived at Dong Tam. During this period, I became COMRIVPATFLOT 5's Mekong Delta equivalent to Perry Mason, investigating cases of misconduct and also deaths of Vietnamese civilians who had been killed accidentally during combat operations. These diversified assignments continued from the latter part of November 1969 until the STABs arrived at Dong Tam in early January 1970.

STAB underway at slow speed. (Courtesy of Don Mirkovich)

All STABRON 20 personnel participated in the activation of the 20 boats at Dong Tam and we were motivated to complete the job as quickly as possible, since the military base was mortared every night by the enemy. In about a week we were ready to transit the Mekong River north, about 90 miles, to An Long and Operation Barrier Reef.

The logistics of the 20 STABs were simplified by shipping from the United States two of each item installed on each boat. For example, since there were two engines per boat, four engines were shipped as spares. Spare parts for commonly used items in Vietnam were obtained from the logistics center at the Naval Support Activity, Binh Thuy. The Achilles' heel of the STAB was its need for gasoline; at high speeds the boat would consume about 50 gallons of gasoline per hour. Since there were no other combat boats in the Mekong Delta with gasoline engines installed, the STABs had to have an especially configured pontoon barge, filled with gasoline and resupplied by the tugs which made the trip up river each week with supplies from Nha Be. The gasoline pontoon barge was anchored in the center of the Mekong River near the STAB pontoon maintenance facility.

From January until mid-June 1970, the 20 Stabs augmented PBRs and RACs assigned to night Waterborne Guard Post (WBGP) ambush sites along the 40 mile long Grand Canal in Operation Barrier Reef.

The WBGPs severed the Communist resupply, from the north, in the region near the capitol and the Plain of Reeds. Every night prior to sunset a fully manned and armed boat would establish a WBGP by securing itself to the northside of the eastwest canal, each boat one kilometer apart, along the entire length of the canal. The boats would remain in that position all night to interdict enemy troops attempting to cross the Grand Canal from north to south. Combinations of electronic sensors and night vision devices were employed to alert boat personnel of approaching enemy troops. Claymore mines on the canal banks were used to protect boat personnel from direct attack.

As a result of a U.S. Presidential order, on 9 May 1970, 10 of the STABs accompanied a flotilla of combined Vietnamese-American combat units transited the northern Mekong River, across the Cambodian border to Neak Luong, a strategic ferry crossing linking Highway 1 between Phnom Penh and Saigon. This push into Cambodia was intended to place further pressure on Communist military forces by hitting their base camp areas just inside the Cambodian border. I was on board the lead STAB during the transit to Neak Luong. Enemy forces must have been advised of the flotilla's intended transit plans, because no enemy personnel were sighted, nor was there any gunfire during the transit to Neak Luong. It is of interest to note that during the few days at Neak Luong, U.S. Navy divers refloated a vehicle/personnel ferry that had been sunk by Communists several years before.

From June through July 1970, I commanded Operation Barrier Reef along with my STABRON 20 organization. On 1 August 1970, the command of Operation Barrier Reef was shifted from the U.S. Navy to the RVN Navy and renamed Tran Hung Dao NINE. Since there were still 30 or more boats under U.S. Navy command, I continued through September to coordinate those boats with the Vietnamese lieutenant commander who was in command of the operation.

On 5 July 1970, LT Gorman and LTJG Barnes were designated by COMNAVFORV as Commander Strike Assault Boat Divisions 201 and 202 respectively. Each division had 10 boats and on 13 August both divisions departed from the Upper Mekong River to Dong Tam, where COMSTABDIV 201 commenced operations in Tran Hung Dao EIGHT and COMSTABDIV 202 continued on to Nha Be to operate in the Rung Sat Special Zone (RSSZ) and the Long Tau shipping channel. The two STAB Divisions operated in those respective areas until early October 1970.

LT Gorman, with his executive officer, LTJG Carpien, and the 10 boats of STABDIV 201 conducted night WBGP duties, and daylight troop/SEAL platoon insertion/extraction operations along the canals which fanned out from Dong Tam.

LTJG Barnes, with his executive officer, LTJG Mirkovich, and the 10 boats of STABDIV 202 operated out of the support activity at Nha Be. They provided security escort for deep draft shipping on the 25 mile Long Tau shipping channel between the open ocean and Saigon. Since the channel bordered the RSSZ, there were frequent enemy attacks on these ships, but the STABs acted as a deterrent. Additionally, the STABs set WBGPs in the small tributaries of the RSSZ, including insertion/extraction of troops.

On 17 October 1970, both STAB Divisions ceased all operations in their respective areas and all of us returned to Dong Tam to deactivate all 20 boats. The STABs were then loaded on board USS *Wexford County* (LST-1168) for transshipment to Boat Support Unit ONE, located at Coronado, San Diego, California. And, after their year in-country was completed, all STABRON 20 personnel returned to the United States for some well deserved leave and relaxation.

Our squadron did suffer four fatal combat casualties. The first casualty was Seaman Daniel Case, USN, shot while his Strike Assault Boat was in waterborne guardpost on the Grand Canal, on the night of 20 March 1970. He, of course, was wearing his flak jacket and battle helmet, however, the bullet entered his body under his armpit and tore its way through his torso. A medical "dustoff" helicopter evacuated him to the Third Surgical Hospital in Binh Thuy, and he was subsequently transferred to a hospital in Saigon where he died of a cardiac arrest while suffering from renal failure.

Our other three casualties were killed in action in the same boat, on Friday, April 3, 1970. These three men, Engineman Third Class Edward J. Baker, USN; Gunner's Mate Third Class George R. Crabtree, USN; and FN Joseph D. Johns, USN were killed instantly while their Strike Assault Boat was in waterborne guardpost on the Grand Canal. The Viet Cong initiated a firefight against the STAB, firing three B-40 rockets and automatic weapons fire which struck them down. The Patrol Officer, Boatswain's Mate Chief William Curtis Spencer, USN, was wounded during the attack, and he survived.

Our superb "circuit riding" chaplain, LT Lester L. Westling Jr., USN, who rode Seawolf from one base of operations to another in the Delta, flew aboard USS *Benewah* on 4 April 1970 and conducted an unforgettable memorial service on the ship's helicopter deck for me and my assembled squadron personnel. Besides Psalm 130, the Gospel of St. John 14:1-6, and the Apostles' Creed, Chaplain Westling presented these stirring words:

"We are assembled to pay tribute to our comrades who gave their lives in the service of their country and of freedom. Words cannot describe what they have given to the United States of America and to our Navy. They answered the highest call and gave the greatest amount without hesitation.

We are here to honor them and to thank God for having had their comradeship, and for the knowledge that they are in the good hands of our divine Master.

It is now our responsibility to redouble our efforts to carry on their tasks and our own in the highest professional manner in tribute to them proving always that our mission will bring an end to suffering to all in a righteous peace.

These men are our comrades, our friends. A part of each of us has gone with them. They are American sailors who met the test."

I recall another event which will, in turn, provide some personal insight into the dynamic Vice Admiral Zumwalt. This naval officer was one of the rare few who could, while leaning over the cover of a boat engine, discuss the problems of the malfunctioning engine with a pay grade E-3 engineman, and a few minutes later sit down with senior officers and discuss the problems encountered with the combat operations against the VC and NVA.

Several times before our the STABs arrived, Admiral Zumwalt visited USS *Benewah*. On each occasion his helicopter, with several chase helos providing protection, would arrive on board *Benewah*.

While I was doing my duty as the Delta's "Perry Mason," investigating fatal accidents in which Vietnamese civilians were killed as a result of combat operations, an incredible event occurred which never would have happened except for the snowballing of natural and man-made circumstances.

Earlier, I mentioned the Mekong River depth during the various seasons of the year. The melting snows in the Himalayas flood the Mekong and its tributary, the Bassac, during the spring and summer. The level of the rivers rise 20 to 40 feet, flooding the rice fields throughout the Delta. During the fall and winter, after the summer monsoonal rains, the rivers drop 20 to 40 feet and the previously swift current drops from 10 or more knots to zero. There are occasions during the winter months when the current in the Bassac and Mekong Rivers actually reverses itself; there is, in fact, a current upriver due to the effects of the South China Sea tide.

During the winter months of 1969, one of the crews of a PBR, stationed with USS *Benewah*, at An Long, decided to make up an excuse to take their PBR north about five miles, to another YRBM located at Tan

STAB shoulder patch. (Courtesy of John Ferguson)

A Cambodian fort along the VN border after the VN raid into Cambodia, 1970. (Courtesy of J. Warnoch)

Tha Cambodian invasion fleet up the mighty Bassoui River, 1970. (Courtesy of J. Warnoch)

Memorial Service for Gamewardens Killed in Action, July 1969. Nha Be Vietnam. (Courtesy of James Davy)

Chau, in order to enjoy some refreshments at a beer barge moored alongside the YRBM. Predictably, the short stay turned into a longer stay and, when it was becoming dusk one of the crewmen suddenly remembered they had to get back to the *Benewah*. What none of the crew knew was that while they were enjoying their liquid refreshment, the ocean's tide had worked up the Mekong River far enough to turn the YRBM around 180 degree in the river. Since the outpost of Tan Chau was located at the Cambodian border, it only took the PBR a few minutes to be moving at full speed across the border into Cambodia, while the not completely sober crewmembers thought they were enroute down river to the *Benewah*. It didn't take long for several Cambodian gunboats to intercept and capture the PBR and the crew members.

The PBR was reported missing in the late afternoon and by the time radio contact was made with the YRBM at Tan Chau, we knew it had left the YRBM, but we didn't know where it was located. Later that night we received a report in *Benewah's* command center from Saigon indicating the Cambodian government had reported it had captured a U.S. PBR in the Mekong River which was headed upriver from the Vietnamese border.

Early the next morning the *Benewah* was advised that Vice Admiral Zumwalt was enroute to the ship in his helicopter. There was no need to ask the reason for the visit, since we knew it was because of the missing PBR. About mid-morning, the lookouts sighted the admiral's helicopter with several chase helos following behind. The ship's skipper, myself and several other PBR and RAC squadron commanders greeted the admiral as he stepped off his helicopter onto *Benewah* helo deck. He asked the skipper if he could sit down with all of us in the ship's wardroom to discuss the missing PBR. Of course, the skipper said yes, and the following hour or so demonstrated the calm, quick and decisive mind of the admirals. I've known many senior officers who would fly into a rage, castigating everyone and threatening court-martial with such an event as this, but not Admiral Zumwalt. He wanted to know from the PBR squadron commander the details of the boat's loss, as much as he knew. The admiral indicated that the Cambodian government hadn't yet placed any demands for the return of the PBR crewmen, but he felt the demand would be heavy equipment and farm machinery. As it turned out, Admiral Zumwalt was correct; several weeks later a shipload of farm machinery and heavy earth-moving equipment was off-loaded at Phnom Penh in exchange for the PBR crewmen. The PBR was never returned.

Admiral Zumwalt appointed me as the informal investigating officer to inquire into the facts of this incident and report them to him along with my opinions and recommendations. He told us to tighten up our procedures to preclude an incident like this occurring again. We knew without being told that an international incident like this was casting a poor light on the U.S. Government, and one of our PBR sailors had caused it.

In my investigation, I pointed out all the facts, as we knew them, explained the 180 degree reversing of the YRBM's position in the river, and recommended that the PBR crew be disciplined upon their release.

We never saw the crew members again. I heard by word of mouth, but not substantiated in writing, that after their release in Phnom Penh to U.S. government authorities, they were flown to Saigon where they were

Sunday Services, Riv Div 514, 1969. (Courtesy of J. Warnock)

disciplined under Article 15 of the Uniform Code of Military Justice, and received some non-judicial punishment for their actions.

After our STABs were finally operational, Admiral Zumwalt visited *Benewah* several times to see them and talk to the crewmen. He was most interested in knowing from the crewman their opinion as to how the STABs performed in combat and the ease or difficulty in maintaining the boats. The subject of the PBR in Cambodia never came up in our conversations again.

The esprit de corps of STABRON 20 was exemplified in several ways. Prior to departing for Vietnam, we had a contest to design a shoulder patch for our in-country green, camouflage uniforms. The winning design had a light blue background with S.T.A.B.S. written across the top in white on a black banner. A yellow dagger in the center split two red thunderbolts with two olive branches crossing each other in the lower portion of the patch. The dagger and thunderbolts denoted warfare and the olive branches symbolized peace. Everyone wore this squadron shoulder patch.

There were always at least two metal tubs on the deck of the maintenance pontoon filled with cans of coke, cooled by chunks of ice. The profits from the coke fund bought Zippo lighters for each member of the squadron with the shoulder patch design on one side and on the other a drawing, by Don Mirkovich, of a STAB in action. The men also received a squadron plaque with the STAB design drawn by Don Mirkovich. We sent a plaque to each of the families of our deceased shipmates and I also sent a plaque to Admiral Zumwalt after he had been selected for four stars and assigned to the top job in the Navy, the Chief of Naval Operations.

A Chaplain's Tale

by Lester L. Westling Jr., CAPT, CHC, USN (Ret)

While serving in the Delta as Chaplain, I developed a three week circuit that took me from Ha T'ien, Chau Duc and the An Long Canal on the north to My Tho, the Cho Gao Canal and Bien Tre on the south. Sa Dec was my base camp as the center of the geographic

The business end of a 144. (Courtesy of R. Morgan)

Jewish personnel were ministered to also. Lieutenant Arnold Resnicoff, Comm Officer in USS *Hunterton County* (now CAPT, CHC, USN), acted as my Jewish "Lay Reader" by providing liaison with the Jewish Welfare Board. He loaded my pack with scriptures, readings and "Solo Seder Kits" when I made regular stops on board his ship. Jewish sailors on the canals and in remote Advisory Teams were thus kept in contact with their faith through my traveling presence.

Near the end of my tour, I rode the Tangos up the Mekong to Neak Leong, Cambodia, escorting the VN Navy LSTs that far, as they went beyond our allowed 21-mile limit to Pnom Penh to rescue 100,000 of the Chinese and Vietnamese families who were otherwise being eliminated. Bodies of many who were not fortunate enough to leave by these ships were floating down the river or on the shore being eaten by wild dogs. When the ships passed through our lines returning down river loaded to the gunnels with Asian civilians, we gathered the Tango boats in midstream to offer a Eucharist of thanksgiving for the success of this mission.

MADNESS!

by Sherman Pridham

Four boats were patrolling a small river southeast of Nhe Be about December 1968. Not many of us had ever been in a firefight before. A B-40 rocket shot out of the bushes passed through the bow of the second boat and exploded on the opposite side of the river. Everyone on all four boats mashed down on their triggers and just started blasting away! Twelve 50 calibers, four M-6O machine guns and whatever else we could shoot or throw at them! No one aimed, just started shooting where guns were pointed. I was in the lead boat in the front gun tub. There were so many tracer bullets flying over my head, I thought it was WWII. Bullets were hitting the water all around us, all from the boats behind us. The man on the engine covers on the second boat started firing towards where the rocket blew up and realized that it must have come from the other side. He picked up the M-60 and swung it down to bring it up pointing in the other direction. The only problem was that he was still firing! He shot out both engines and put a bunch of holes in the bottom of the boat, which of course, started to sink. One round hit him in the big toe, which was the only injury of the firefight. As far as we know, the one rocket was the only enemy round. It is absolutely amazing that we didn't all kill each other!

A LETTER HOME

River Division Five Three One
FPO San Francisco 96601
1 February 1969

Dear Folks,

First, I hope you will forgive me for not having written to you since I came to River Division 531 in late September, but I think as you read these pages you will understand just how busy all your sons and husbands have been. My intention here is just to relay to you a short history of events covering the last three months, a history which your loved ones have made.

As most of you know, we left My Tho on 1 October and went to the Ham Luong River aboard the USS *Jennings County* (LST-846), a tank landing ship converted to a floating home base for PBRs. During the first few weeks we were quite busy adjusting to the changes in our routine aboard a ship instead of a shore base. Of course, all during this time we still had to continue our 12 hour patrols and learn the new river. There were times when some of the people were out on the river as much as 18 to 19 hours before they could get back to the ship, then would have to go back on patrol after only seven hours of rest. However, before Halloween, we adjusted to our new surroundings and our daily routine. We would check as many as 300 sampans and junks in one day and 2,500 people. At night we prevented any movement on the river as curfew was in effect.

Then just as we had settled down, we were ordered to move with the LST to the Bassac River and start patrolling a small canal which started at a small town on the gulf of Siam called Rach Gia. Since this town was about 35 miles down the canal from the Bassac River, we had to stage six of our 10 boats in Rach Soi (a smaller town near Rach Gia), as the LST could not go down the canal. This meant that many of us had to sleep and eat C-rations on the boats, out in the open, for periods up to 10 or 12 days.

figure eight I pursued, and where I reorganized my resources for my next "rounds" of the circuit. Sixty-five combat units and advisory teams were served, which included four support LSTs, four YRBMS and personnel at the NSA support bases at My Tho, Dong Tam, Sa Dec, and Ha T'ien, Army support units at Chau Duc, Tan Chau and various Advisory Teams.

I traveled through "Indian Country" from place to place by Navy Seawolf helicopters, Army fixed wing and helicopters, Canadian aircraft, river supply craft, Boston Whaler, or by daisy chain" from one PBR or Tango boat squadron to the next squadron's units down the canal for the next day's sleep, worship, and night on patrol. Before departure on night patrols in the field, or on the support YRBMs or LSTs, worship services (including Holy Communion) would be offered, and the Chaplain would always be available for informal chats and counseling. Much time was devoted to the Vinh Te Canal boat units and Army Advisory Teams, with my "base" there at Vinh Gia on the Charlie Boat. I served occasionally as translator for the Chinese "Nung" mercenaries who drove the airboats for the Army "Green Berets" on flooded rice fields at the westerly end of the Vinh Te.

On Christmas Eve and Day and likewise during Easter, HA(L)-3 "Seawolfs" provided me with a helo for two day "marathons" so that I could provide 18 Christmas communion services for isolated units and 14 Easter communion services, with the helo circling the perimeter while the men were assembled. On Christmas Eve, we flew the canals where water-borne guard posts (PBRs and Tangos) were presumed hidden under the canopy, and played Christmas Carols directed toward the ground using the psy-ops speakers under the aircraft.

We rotated the boats back to the LST as much as possible but there were times when this was impossible. Bathing, shaving, and bathroom facilities were crude to say the least. However, as most of you know, we were trained for much like this back at Mare Island in California. The training sure came in handy for the six weeks in November and December.

On 7 November six of our boats proceeded down the canal to Rach Soi to set up a forward base camp at the Vietnamese Junk Repair Base. We then started our 24 hour patrol of the canal with three PBRs and our larger craft called an ASPB (Assault Support Patrol Boat) on 12 hour shifts. During daylight we conducted operations designed to show the local people that the PBRs were there to help them and help make their life a little easier. At night, we stopped the VC from using the canal to transport large amounts of supplies and provided additional security to the scattered Vietnamese outposts on the canal.

The canal was lined on both banks with heavy jungle foliage and made detection of people impossible, even in day light. Three other Navy boats that carried Vietnamese troops worked with us conducting sweeps of the banks during the day. The first action involved these boats on 11 November taking some rocket and machine gun fire from the VC, however our PBRs were not in the area at the time and were, therefore, not involved. The first two weeks we conducted our patrols and the PBRs had no direct contact with the VC.

Then, on 21 November, our luck changed. PBR 110 with Mineman Cecil H. Martin, Boat Commander and Engineman Harry R. Jones, Engineer Seaman William T. O'Donnell and Gunner's Mate Seaman Vernon B. Lucas, Engineman Hartwell A. White. crewmen and PBR-109 with Signalman Donald P. McClemons, Commander, Engineman Keith L. Erntson, Gunner's Mate Jackie D. Touchstone, Seaman James W. Drennan and Michael J. Eckhardt crewmen, were proceeding together to Rach Gia. Martin's Boat was ahead and going around a cutoff in the canal when Mac's boat came under attack with rockets and machine guns. PBR-109 went out of control and beached. Mac's crew opened up on the VC and Martin came back to help. After several minutes of heavy fire the VC retreated and PBR-110 left the area to meet other PBRs speeding to assist. McClemons and his crew were on Martin's's boat as 109 was still beached but was only left for a few minutes, as other boats came and towed 109 back to Rach Soi. Bravery and heroism during this action was displayed by members of both crews. Some men, even though wounded, still returned and suppressed the enemy fire. Others returned fire and rendered assistance while still under fire.

Let me pause here and explain my policy concerning wounds of our men received in action. A man is considered wounded in action if he takes any injury from enemy fire, from a broken ear drum or a scratch which is fixed up with a Band Aid and Mercurochrome, to serious wounds which cause evacuation of the man to Japan or the United States. During these six weeks almost one half of our guys did receive wounds of some type, but the only names I will mention are those who have been evacuated out of Vietnam. About one fourth of our people have been evacuated due to wounds sustained during these weeks. Drennan and Eckhardt on PBR-109 were the first to be evacuated, however, we heard that they are doing O.K.

Our patrols continued night and day as normal with little enemy activity. Occasionally, one or two VC would shoot a short burst at the boats, then run or hide as the return fire from the boats was fast and furious. On 26 November Aviation Boatswain's Mate Eugene E. Davis was patrol officer for PBR-29 and 39. PBR-29's commander was Yeoman Oliver E. Durham with Seaman Don A. Dennis, Engineman Donald S. Thrash and Gunner's Mate Alan B. Olson as crew and 39 had Gunner's Mate Donald J. Minick as commander with Seaman Thomas D. Coble, Engineman Edward L. Markham and Gunner's Mate Wayne D. Maxwell as crew. Just after dark the VC attacked with rockets and machine gunfire as the boats went by, again the boats responded with heavy fire. Fortunately, none of the boats were hit.

The next night, 27 November, we were not so fortunate. LTJG Bradford M. Dixon and Chief Kenneth L. Carwile had a four boat patrol again with Durham's boat (29), Minick's Boat (39), and PBR-101 with Boatswain's Mate Frank D. Henning as commander, Boatswain's Mate Seaman Larry D. Garamillo, Gunner's Mate Donald R. Morris, and Engineman Kenneth W. Freeman as crew and one of the ASPBs. The boats went into an ambush with the VC spread along both banks for 800 yards. All boats came under heavy rocket and machine gunfire at the same time.

All three PBRs were hit and returned fire immediately and continuing until the area was cleared. Durham's boat (29) took one hit and as he fought to control the boat, it took another resulting in the boat beaching. LTJG Dixon, in Henning's boat, which was not badly hit, and the ASPB went immediately to the assistance of PBR-29 and helped suppress fire. It was at this time we found that Oliver E. Durham, YN1 had made the ultimate sacrifice for his country. I know of no words which can express the feelings we experienced at the loss of this fine man. I'm sure that I speak for every man in the Division in that we all wished there was some way we could stand as one with his family.

Durham was the epitome of the spirit of River Division 531 and we intend to carry on with that spirit. Dennis and Thrash were also wounded and have been evacuated out of Vietnam and are doing well.

Chief Carwile was on Minick's boat (39), which was also hit, and proceeded to an outpost from which Chief Carwile helped direct medical helo evacuations for others who were wounded. Ensign David L. Funk and Signalman Ralph T. Morelli scrambled Martin's PBR-110 and the other ASPB and helped guard the area for the remainder of the night.

When daylight came, Warrant Officer Jerry G. Hine and I went to the outpost to help with salvage, but found that all boats were temporarily fixed so that they could be taken back to the LST. Jerry Hine and Bradford M. Dixon took charge of these boats, and Chief Louis C. Duty and I proceeded on down the canal with four PBRs. 110, Martin's boat, Engineman Charles H. Sagar commander of 103, with Gunner's Mate James H. Stefanik, Engineman Charles F. Hienbuck and Seaman Benny R. Scurlock as crew; 105, Gunner's Mate Mose M. Bailey commanding, with Engineman Salvador F. Perales, Gunner's Mate George R. Embrey and Engineman Raymond E. Kerr as crew; and 56, Signalman Norman T. Brown commanding with Gunner's Mate Michael F. Adams, Seaman Ronald J. Paris and Engineman William M. Ellard as crew.

As we proceeded down the canal, one or two VC shot automatic weapons, and I think he must have regretted it as all four boats opened up with all guns and we heard nothing further from "Charlie."

For the next several nights, when the boats went into the canal, they fired into the banks to offset any ambush attempts. It was during one such night on 6 December when Stefanik evidently detonated a booby trap on the bank with his machine gun and was wounded by the shrapnel. He was a gunner on PBR-103 with Sagar as commander, Heinbuck, and Scurlock as crew. We have heard that he went to Philadelphia and is doing fine.

Two days later on 8 December, "Charlie" ambushed another patrol. Chief Alfred P. Pereia was patrol officer with one ASPB and three PBRs, 110 Martin, 105, Gunner's Mate Mose M. Bailey commander, with Engineman Salvador G. Preales, Gunner's Mate George R. Embrey and Seaman Keith M. Jackson; 56 Signalman Norman T. Brown commander, with Gunner's Mate Michael F. Adams, Seaman Ronald J. Paris, and Engineman William M. Ellard as crew. This time Martin's boat (110) and Brown's Boat (56) were hit with rockets and small arms. All returned fire instantaneously. Engineman Harry R. Jones emptied his machine gun although wounded. Jones is now in Yokohama, Japan hopefully enjoying the U.S. nurses.

T.K. Anderson with PBR 110 Boat Captain Cecil Martin, 1968. (Courtesy of T.K. Anderson)

Our patrols continued. On 12 December, at the request of local Army personnel, a patrol stopped at an outpost to help mortar suspected VC positions. During the firing of the mortar, one of the rounds exploded; wounding Ensign David L. Funk, Chief Louis C. Duty and one other man who will be returning to us very soon. ENS Funk is now at the Naval Hospital in Great Lakes, Illinois and Chief Duty has been transferred as his tour of duty here was finished. Chief William E. Keene took over as our leading chief.

Our last serious action took place on 13 December. The patrol was with Lieutenant Samual S. Hurd and PBR-110, Martin's, Bailey's 105 and PBR 127 with Hubbard F. Reeder, Boatswain's Mate, as commander and Gunner's Mate Harry T. Dawkins, Seaman Robert D. LA Brode, and Engineman Richard H. Ries as his crew. The VC again attacked with rockets and automatic weapons, Reeder's boat (127) was the only one hit but was able to continue patrol. Earlier that same day came one of the high points. LTJG Dixon with MC Clemons' 109, Morelli's 32 and Henning's 101, discovered a sunken sampan full of automatic weapons and rifles. Capturing weapons such as these is one of the ways we really hurt "Charlie."

According to high ranking sources, I have been told that River Division 531's action in that area really hurt the VC. Not only did they sustain casualties but also their supply route was cut to ribbons. Prior to our arrival large quantities of supplies crossed this area and we were responsible for cutting this flow to a trickle.

Seven of our 10 boats were hit with rockets as described above, but all were involved in firefights at one time or another. The only boat crew I haven't mentioned so far is that of PBR-32 with Signalman Ralph T. Morrelli as commander, with Gunner's Mate David O. Rodrigues, Engineman Carroll S. Cathy, and Gunner's Mate Mark C. Evans as crew, had several firefights but were fortunate enough not to get hit with rockets. Our senior patrol officer, LTJG Frank G. Duserick, as well as Gunner's Mate Elby J. Billeaudeau and Seaman Keith E. Gottschall was also involved in several of these type incidents.

The maintenance gang during this period did an outstanding job in repairing the damaged boats in record time, putting in many long hours so that the boats could be ready again for patrol and could relieve other boats in need of repair. This team headed by Warrant Officer Jerry G. Hines consisted of Engineman Hartwell A. White, Engineman Robert W. Kohn, Engineman Thomas A. Wuellner, Engineman Michael J. Eckhardt, Engineman Raymond E. Kerr and Gunner's Mate Lawrence P. Noel; all of whom were down in the canal at various times on some patrols and on-scene repairs. I might also mention that Yeoman Wayne L. Clark, our division yeoman, did a fine job of handling the administrative matters, at times alone as during certain periods all officers were down in the canal.

We were relieved of our area in the Rach Gia Canal by River Division 514 on 17 December, and all boats returned to the LST. After a couple of days at Binh Thuy we moved up on the Mekong River, where we began patrols. We enjoyed a quiet Christmas with outstanding food provided by the *Jennings County*. At the turn of the year, we started patrolling another canal off the Mekong River but at this time we are still based on the LST. Also, this time there is no jungle on either side of the canal. I do not believe this patrol area will give us as much trouble as the last as "Charlie" has few places to hide.

Fortunately, this area is not to be our permanent home as we recently received orders to move 531 to Nha Be, a large city 15 miles south of Saigon. We plan to move around the end of January, and needless to say we are looking

Riv Div 593, Nha Be, Vietnam. Pictured are Weeks, Hickey, Temple, Persico, Bodiford, Williams, Owens, Randall, Sutter, and Madden. (Courtesy of Ronald J. Weeks)

Riv Div 514 mascot, 1969. (Courtesy of J. Warnock)

Riversection 511, 1967-68; John Myers, Jon A. Wisth, Steve Aznoe, John Elliot, Bill Sullivan, Richard Green.

forward to the change. We did encounter the VC three times in the canal, but believe we got the best of them. None of our boats were hit with rockets. We are now at Nha Be enjoying the facilities of the Naval Station.

I would like to take this opportunity to compliment our new arrivals to River Division 531. Since 15 December, we have received three new patrol officers including Chief Reginald P. Ewers, Chief Louis H. Kent, and Boatswain's Mate Max C. McCleod, who was initiated into Chief's Quarters shortly after his arrival. Engineman Osmond K. Lipps arrived to assist Jerry G. Hine as maintenance supervisor. Replacing some of our casualties, we received a group of experienced crewmen from other divisions, including Gunner's Mate Thomas E. Jones from River Division 524 and Seaman David M. Prevette from River Division 533. Engineman Kenneth D. Lourash from River Division 523 and Seaman James R. Coleman from River Division 573. Also checking into the division are a number of recent graduates of the Naval Inshore Operations Training Center in Mare Island, California: Signalman John W. Conner, Gunner's Mates David L. Edwards, Dennis H. Ledoux, Merle

Seal Team 1 members with VC prisoners from Tan Dinh Island during Bold Dragon mission, January 1968. (Courtesy of Thomas P. Stiller)

A. Pocholec, and Gary Polmanteer; Enginemen David B. Anderson, Ronnie J. Connon, Lloyd S. Syverston; and Seamen Billy L. Kell, Jerry W. Newman, and David E. Schmidt. They have adapted themselves well into the fine spirit of this division. The names of all personnel and their assigned duties are listed as an enclosure to this letter. Many members of this command have been nominated for awards but are not yet approved. I might add that the entire division is under consideration for the Presidential Unit Citation for the Rach Gia Campaign. There is no doubt in my mind that this is the most courageous, and finest group of men with whom I have served in almost 10 years of service. These men bear the same badge of courage as our more respected fore fathers and are true Americans of the highest standards. I am more than proud to have the opportunity to serve with them for their remaining time in-country. You can count on all of us to take care of each other and hopefully 1969 will see us all return home to our loved ones.

I hope to write to you more often but perhaps not quite as lengthy next time. Please do not hesitate to write to me as letters from the families will be most welcomed. Here's wishing you all the best of the New Years from River Division 531.

Respectfully
T.K. Anderson
LCDR, USN
Commander, River Division 531
FPO San Francisco, CA 96621

OPERATION NEW LIFE

by James D. Davy

It was April 1975, and the war in Vietnam was ending. Many of the Vietnamese people who had worked for the U.S. Government or U.S. civilian firms wanted out before the Communist take over. But where? Where do you relocate several hundred thousand people in a hurry? After the inquest was made and after much consideration, the answer came from Washington and the answer was Guam. Thus began "Operation New Life." On Guam the Commander in Chief U.S. Pacific Representative received word on 23 April 1975 to execute "Operation New Life," a plan designed specifically for the evacuation of Southeast Asia. Camp Asan Guam, the current site of the war in the Pacific Park, was readied for use in 24 hours by (U.S. Navy Seabees and Marines working around the clock. Next came the end of the Island known as Orote Point. The WWII Japanese airstrip was selected for most of the refugees, and before Operation New Life was complete, over 100,000 Vietnamese were processed through the Orote Point camp. Several of the Naval Station

Guam Staff Civil Engineers were in on the planning for the Orote Point project, and related that over 600 acres of jungle and undergrowth had to be cleared and tents set up for the in coming refugees. Volunteers from every military command on the island, including the Navy ships USS *Hector* and USS *Proteus*, aided the Seabees in constructing this city of tents. Not only were 350 tents per day put up, but miles of water line, power and phone cables were laid. By the end of May, 50,000 people were living on Orote Point in 3,600 tents. Many Island residents remember the days without sleep when everyone working for the Government was assigned to help after regular working hours. Many of these volunteers worked at Anderson Air Force Base and the Naval Air Station, where terminals and hanger areas were manned 24 hours a day with U.S. servicemen, servicewomen and volunteers. Planes arrived every 10 to 20 minutes, bringing in over 5,000 refugees a day. Buses would take the refugees to the assigned camps after processing. The next phase of the operation began on May 7 when ships began arriving at Apra Harbor Guam with refugees aboard; over 13,000 Vietnamese were processed that day. Many refugees were sick. All were hungry and tired. Again, volunteers were called on to meet the ships at dockside and help in any way possible. During the height of "Operation Frequent Wind," the name given the airlift and ship arrivals, over 800 people per hour were processed. One of the ships that arrived in Apra Harbor with refugees and planes overflowing her decks was USS *Midway*. *Midway* stayed just long enough to offload and then steamed back to the South China Sea.

During the time the refugees were on the island of Guam, child care was provided, recreation equipment was set up, and insecticide spraying was started to control disease. Fire trucks were used for the first showers in camps and the Navy Exchange set-up small stores in the camps for the refugees. Seabee cooks worked 24 hours a day seven days a week with eight field kitchens trying to feed the long lines that never seemed to end. Medical units from the Navy, Army and Air Force set up field hospitals to provide care and immunizations for the refugees. Emergency dental care was also provided for many.

Over 2,000 Army personnel from Hawaii were ordered to Guam to aid in the administration and processing of the refugees and to provide much needed security. Fifteen camps in all were established on Guam. The Tokyo Hotel was rented by the Navy, and used to house nearly 1,000 people. Then Governor Ricardo J. Bordallo met with many of the refugees at a native Chamorran Fiesta planned by the village of Merizo in a gesture of friendship.

After the refugees had cleared all processing at Orote Point or Camp Asan, they were moved to Anderson Air Force Base to await a flight to their new home on the mainland. This also took a great deal of effort on the part of service personnel and volunteers, but everyone joined in and the job was done.

On 25 June 1975 the Orote Point Camp was closed; 23 October the Tokyo Hotel Refugee Camp closed; and 1 November Camp Asan closed, terminating Operation New Life on Guam. Not many signs are left from Operation New life. The jungle has covered Orote Point again and all the buildings at Camp Asan are gone. But many of the island residents remember those hectic days, and recall with a smile of satisfaction the hard work and long hours put into a critical and worthwhile cause. They smile because many people were given a chance for a new life by the efforts of the people of Guam.

COMBAT HISTORY OF RIVER DIVISION FIVE ONE TWO

22 November 1968 - 31 March 1970
by Frank Henning

As time marches on the world's great combat units cease to exist due to the end of a war, the demobilization of the unit or, as in the case in the Republic of Vietnam, the turning over of the unit's combatant equipment to the South Vietnamese. On 31 March 1970 River Division 512 was turned over to the Vietnamese Navy, thus ending a long and commendable record. The dates and instances recorded in this brief history are only the highlights of the division's combat record. To record every contact and firefight would be to write a book and not a brief history. The divisions combat strength came from the 10 River Patrol Boats (PBRs) assigned and from the valorous sailors who manned and maintained them. If the reader can understand the nerve-wracking strain of a patrol or night ambush when an attack by the enemy could come at any time, then he will truly appreciate this history.

On 22 November 1968 the division operated from Binh Thuy Naval Base, RVN on Operation Sealords, a blockade of Dung Island on the Lower Bassac River. The blockade consisted of River Divisions 512 and 511, River Assault Division 113, and four Swift Boats (PCFs). The land force was composed of U.S. and Vietnamese Army units. The combined Army force swept the island hunting Viet Cong, arms caches and intelligence. This week-long operation resulted in numerous Viet Cong captured and killed plus documents and many arms caches.

On 28 December 1968, the division moved its base of operations to a PBR support ship, the USS *Hunterdon County* (LST-838). The ship was to provide PBR support for the division and gunfire support for the various commands. within range of her big guns.

On 14 January 1969 the division operating in conjunction with the U.S. Army trapped a company or reduced battalion of Viet Cong in an open field on the mainland side of the Bassac River. With the division acting as a blocking force, the Army swept the field calling on the division for fire support. This action resulted in the annihilation of the entire force and large numbers of documents and arms captured.

On 21 January 1969 the division inserted a company LRRP troops in Foxtrot Straights on Dung Island. The patrol then moved a short distance away, ready to move instantaneously should the LRRP team need quick extraction or fire support. The LRRPs made contact and when they had completed their mission, called the boats requesting pickup and fire support. The patrol quickly returned to the extraction site and laid down a heavy cover of fire for the team. As they scrambled aboard the boats, one soldier was wounded by a sniper, but they had completed their mission. They had captured a Viet Cong village chief, freed a Hoi Chanh's family and discovered an arms cache large enough to fill an LCU boat.

The beginning of February brought the division's first casualty in six months. During a patrol on 1 February in Foxtrot Straights on Dung Island, heavily infested with Viet Cong, the patrol came under heavy automatic weapons fire. Unable to suppress the fire, the patrol moved out of the kill zone and quickly made a 180 degree turn to return. This second firing run resulted in the after .50 caliber machine gun gunner on PBR-897 being wounded by shrapnel. The crewmembers checked on the injured man and seeing he needed to be medevaced, quickly returned to the LST where he was Dusted Off to Binh Thuy Naval Hospital. USN casualties: Culbertson, GMGSN (minor, medevaced to Binh Thuy).

The next casualty occurred on 28 March 1969 while a patrol was near the Vietnamese Junk Base on the Lower Bassac River. The boats noticed a suspicious object on the beach. As they moved in to investigate the object, the patrol was taken under fire by small arms and rocket fire. As the patrol cleared the kill zone, it was discovered that the M-60 ma-

chine gunner was hit in the leg and in extreme pain. He was taken to the LST for immediate evacuation to Binh Thuy Naval Hospital, and later was returned to the United States for further medical treatment. USN casualties: Fielden, EN2 (Serious medevaced to U.S.)

April found the division on the move once more. This time it was to Tra Cu on the Vam Co Dong River in support of Operation Giant Slingshot. The division's support facility was to be the YRBM-18 located at the mouth of the Vam Co River. Tra Cu was an Advanced Tactical Support Base (ATSB) and it was necessary for our boats to transit the Vam Co Dong River to the YRBM-18 in order to have major maintenance work accomplished. ATSB TRA CU was situated just south of the Parrot's Beak, the border between Vietnam and Cambodia, and right on the Ho Chi Minh Trail leading to Saigon. Everyone knew the importance of this operation and that the enemy would attempt to keep the needed supply route open.

The division reported to Tra Cu on 6 April 1969 and was immediately embroiled in a fierce firefight in the infamous Horseshoe, the extreme southern end of the AO. There were no casualties and the enemy casualties were unknown, but it was indicative of the heavy fighting yet to come.

A Navy correspondent visited Tra Cu on 10 April 1969, and requested that he be permitted to go on a normal combat patrol. He was collecting data for a story on the Navy's fighting "Brown Water Sailors." He was granted permission to join the day patrol which was about to head on their southern leg. The boats were just inside the Horseshoe when the enemy opened up with a deadly barrage of automatic weapons and rocket fire. The cover boat, on which the correspondent was riding, took a direct rocket hit in the coxswain's flat, immediately killing the boat captain. The rocket continued through the splinter shield seriously wounding the correspondent. A second rocket struck the boat in the engine compartment, putting both engines out of commission. The boat then veered wildly out of control and grounded itself on the beach opposite the enemy's position. With the reminder of the crew wounded, the M-60 gunner seriously, they were still able to keep up the return fire into the enemy's position. The lead boat made an instant 180 degree turn speeding to the stricken boat's side and firing furiously. The other day patrol only a short distance away, hearing a call for assistance on the radio and seeing the myriad flashes, hurried to the aid of the stricken patrol. Arriving at the scene, they quickly took the enemy position under fire and soon subdued the return fire. The lead boat then went to the aid of the stricken boat to give aid to the wounded. They were loaded on board the lead boat and rushed to base camp for Dust Off while the remaining two boats took the damaged boat under tow and brought her to Tra Cu. A week hadn't gone by and the toll was beginning to mount. USN casualties: Clerkin, SM1 (KIA); Bilderback, GMG2 (serious, medevaced to U.S.); Conklin, EN3 (minor, retained on board); Dyson, GMGSN (minor, retained on board); Yelinek, LT (serious and medevaced to U.S.)

On 12 April 1969, the enemy opened fire with a mortar attack that lasted 15 minutes, doing little or no damage to the camp. On 14 April 1969 a patrol had just left base camp and headed south on a daytime patrol when the enemy opened with a barrage of small arms and rocket fire. In the ensuing firefight the enemies fire was suppressed, but they delivered two more of the division's sailors to the list of the wounded. USN casualties: Ussery, GMG3 (minor, retained on board); Culbertson, SN (minor, retained on board).

Between 15 April and 15 May 1969 the enemy suffered heavy losses. Numerous nighttime crossings were disrupted by the chatter of the division's machine guns. Only the river knew how many of the enemy it hid. The division also set the enemy back with the discovery of huge arms caches. In one such cache, 54 Chinese Communist sidearms were found, the largest single discovery to date, Also found were dozens of B-40 rockets, mines, dynamite blasting caps, small and large mortar rounds, and a .51 caliber machine gun. The only revenge the enemy was able to get was on the evening of 21 April 1969, when at approximately 1900 hours they opened with a heavy mortar attack and this time were on target. PBR-8105 took a direct hit in the engine compartment virtually demolishing the boat. PBR-897 moored alongside 8105 suffered severe shrapnel damage and in the ensuing scramble these two boats were unable to get underway. The rest of the division's PBRs and the River Assault Boats (Tangos, Zippo, 105 Monitor and Alpha Boats) scrambled out to the river so that if the base were hit by a ground probe they could provide supporting fire. The enemy ceased mortaring and followed up with a ground probe in strength. The base's defenders plus the now boatless crews of 8105 and

897 went to work repelling the attackers. In less time than it takes to tell about it, the enemy was reeling in full retreat from the demonical ferocity pouring out of the sailors weapons. Soon all enemy fire had ceased and an alert watch was maintained by the entire base should the enemy attempt another attack. A daylight sweep by CIDG troops in the nearby compound found many blood trails and three bodies and other indications that the enemy had indeed suffered heavy losses. But the enemy once more added to our wounded. USN casualties: Costa, EN1 (minor, retained on board); Kuhn, GMG2 (minor, retained on board); Banks, GMG2 (Minor, retained on board; Barnes, GMG3 (minor, retained on board).

The enemy seemed now to decide that in order for them to operate with any degree of safety they must wipe out the River Rats of River Division 512, and they started that task the late afternoon of 17 May 1969. The daytime patrol was on its final leg of its northern perusal and headed for base camp, when the enemy opened with a barrage of rockets and machine gunfire. The lead boat, 8102, was hit in the port engine, destroying it immediately. The cover boat hovered behind the stricken lead boat, providing a heavy return fire and keeping the enemy's head down, enabling the crippled boat to leave the kill zone without further injury. The patrol officer called the Tra Cu NOC requesting immediate assistance and also an immediate Dust Off Helicopter. USN casualties: Bennett, RM1 (serious, medevaced to Cu Chi); Bruehl, GMG2 (minor, retained on board); Davis, EN2 (minor, retained on board.)

The following days were action-packed with the enemy once more getting the worst of it. The tables turned again on 29 May 1969. In the early morning hours, a patrol broke ambush when relieved by the midnight patrol. As they started passing the local village, HIEP Hoa, the enemy struck with shocking savagery. The air was suddenly filled with rockets and heavy automatic weapons and small arms fire. The lead boat, PBR-8102, was hit in the starboard engine with the opening fire, putting it out of commission. Then both boats unleashed their own tremendous firepower. The stricken lead boat, with three wounded aboard, struggled to maintain steerage and headway when a second rocket struck. Keeping up the heavy return fire the boats, continued moving through the kill zone calling for assistance. The midnight patrol only five minutes away rushed to the aid of the stricken patrol. As the rescue patrol came to the ambush area, the stricken boats finally cleared the kill zone and the enemy fire ceased. Not taking any chances, the rescuing patrol came on through the kill zone with all guns blazing. When they reached the stricken patrol, the cover boat had already taken the lead boat under tow. The lead boat then came alongside the stricken boat and took off the three wounded and detailed the cover boat to stay with the boat under tow, then rushed the wounded to base camp and called for a Dust Off Helicopter. The wounded column was adding up. USN casualties: Buckingham, LT(jg) (serious, medevaced to U.S.); Bennett, RM1 (serious, medevaced to Cu Chi); Davis, EN2 (serious, medevaced to U.S.)

There was to be no slacking on the enemy's initiative. On 31 May 1969 the day patrol had been blowing bunkers when suddenly they were hit from the opposite bank with small arms and RPG rocket fire. The patrol cleared the kill zone and made a 180 degree turn and came back on a firing run. The enemy seemed undaunted and returned the fire. Suddenly they ceased firing and it was then that the cover boat, 898, boat captain discovered that he was wounded in the leg. He refused to be medevaced at the time and the patrol retired to the U.S. Army Advisor camp at the Sugar Mill. Upon arrival the boat captain began to feel some pain in his leg. The rest of the boat crew checked the boat over and found numerous small arms holes and shrapnel holes in the hull. The patrol officer then got the patrol underway, radioing ahead requesting that a Dust Off be awaiting their arrival. Another divisional sailor was added to the ever growing list of wounded, USN casualties: Beaudoin, GMG1 (serious, medevaced to Cu Chi).

On 3 June 1969 the enemy struck again. This time it was just south of the base camp. The patrol had just got underway, heading for the Horseshoe, when the enemy opened fire with a heavy barrage of machine gun and small arms fire. As the boats were clearing the kill zone preparatory to returning on a firing run, the forward gunner on PBR-8103 was wounded by flying shrapnel. The boat captain ordered the M-60 machine gunner to look at the forward gunner and determine the extent of his injuries. The gunner reported that the forward gunner had better be medevaced immediately. He had suffered a severe head wound from the flying shrapnel. Immediately informing the patrol officer, the boats made a 180 degree and headed back through the kill zone for base camp. A Dust Off was

Riv Div 531, December 1968, PBR 101 part of Rach Gia Interdiction Group, Operation Sea Lord. Boat Captain BM2 Frank Henning, BMSM Larry Garamillo, EN3 Ken Freeman, and EN2 Robert Henry with weapons cache found by 101 boat crew. (Courtesy of Frank Henning)

waiting and another of the division's sailors increased the casualty figures. USN casualties: Byrd, GMG3 (serious, madevaced to Cu Chi).

In the early morning hours of 6 June 1969, the enemy mortared the base camp. As the boats scrambled to get underway the enemy found the range damaging the mess hall, NOC bunker and various buildings in the vicinity. The flying shrapnel also wounded two division sailors attempting to reach their boats. The enemy ceased the barrage but did not follow up with the expected ground probe. USN casualties: McCullock, BMC (minor, retained on board); Bauer, EN2 (minor, retained on board).

In the early morning hours of 7 June 1969, the U.S. Army Advisor Team at the Sugar Mill radioed Tra Cu requesting immediate assistance. They were under attack by an enemy ground probe in force and the enemy had already penetrated their outer defenses of concertina wire with bangalore torpedoes and were starting to blow the inner defenses. Two patrols of three boats each got underway immediately. As the second patrol got underway the Army team radioed that the attack seemed to be slackening. The patrols continued on their way and radioed the Army they were 10 minutes out and requested information on the enemy positions. The Army radioed back to the boats that the enemy had suddenly broken off the attack. By this time the lead patrol was only five minutes from the Sugar Mill and continued despite the ominous radio message hoping to catch the enemy possibly crossing the river. The lead patrol was entering the ever dangerous HIEP HOA area when the entire western bank erupted with rockets, machine gun and small arms fire engulfing the entire patrol. They immediately returned fire from all their guns and continued twisting and turning through the heavy enemy fire. The second patrol seeing their comrades fighting valiantly, raced on into the kill zone just as the lead patrol broke with only minor damage to the men and the boats. The enemy immediately opened fire on the second patrol this time with deadly accuracy. The lead boat, PBR-8104, took a rocket hit in the port engine almost immediately. As the stricken boat struggled to continue on through the kill zone, another rocket struck the port side forward just below the waterline. As the boat started sinking, the boat captain headed his boat to the opposite beach. The remaining two boats fired furiously to cover the stricken lead boat. The first patrol, hearing the disaster on the radio, made a 180 degree turn and racing back into the kill zone to the aid of the second patrol. The patrol officer radioed his two covering boats as they continued firing, and directed his lead boat to the side of the stricken boat. Upon arriving at their side they immediately took off the crew and weapons, pulled out and back toward the Sugar Mill. Directing the remaining four boats to follow they gave a covering fire and cleared the kill zone. Arriving at the Sugar Mill the patrol officer radioed for Dust Off Helicopter and loaded the seriously wounded to be sent to Cu Chi. When all wounded had been medevaced, the patrol radioed NOC that they were going to attempt to reach the now abandoned boat and return it to base camp. NOC radioed that the River Assault Craft were on the way to assist. The boats entered the kill zone once more and again were met by a vicious barrage of enemy fire. Unable to suppress the fire, they retreated. The River Assault Group reported their arrival and the PBRs again entered the kill zone and again met heavy enemy fire. The enemy evidently not aware of the arrival of the Assault Group, were taken under fire from two Tango Boats and a 105 Monitor. The Monitor firing 105mm rounds at the enemy soon suppressed all enemy fire, and the boats rushed to the side of the stricken boat, fashioning a makeshift patch to prevent the boat from sinking while they towed it off to base camp. The night had been long and the enemy had once more taken a toll of the division's sailors and another boat was damaged. USN casualties: Allen, TDC (minor, retained on board); McCullock, BMC (minor, retained on board); Delena, BM1 (minor, retained on board); Costa, EN1 (minor, retained on board); Bauer, EN2 (minor, retained on board); Collins, SN (serious, medevaced to Cu Chi); Collins, SN (serious, medevaced to Cu Chi); Cannon, GMG3 (minor, retained on board); Amoroso, GMG3 (serious, medevaced to Cu Chi).

On the night of 11 June 1969, a patrol at the extreme northern portion of the AO was attacked with rockets and machine guns. A rocket struck the cover boat, PBR-8105, in the fuel tanks and started a fire. The lead boat made a 180 degree turn to come to the cover boat's aid while suppressing the enemy's fire. The cover boat beached and the lead boat took off the crew and all the weapons that could be salvaged. Another patrol in the next AO hearing the fight immediately came to the aid of the stricken patrol. A Tango Boat in the vicinity also arrived offering the use of her helo deck so the Dust Off could take the wounded. With the departure of the wounded, the remaining boats maintained a watch on the burning boat. In the early morning hours the fire had finally burned out and the boat sunk leaving only the bow out of the water. The Tango attached a tow line to the bow and drug the boat along the river bed to base camp. USN casualties: Caldwell, EN3 (serious, medevaced to U.S.); Kuhn, GMG2 (minor, retained on board); Bostain, GMGSN (minor, retained on board.

The division was now in dire straights. The remaining boats, of which there were only five in operation, four down due to battle damage, one down due to mechanical failure, were constantly on patrol. The engineers at base camp were working night and day to keep those remaining boats in operating condition so that the division might be able to meet any commitment. On 10 June 1969 a Navy Seal Team reported to the base. The division was to insert the SEALs in a dangerous place just south of Hiep Hoa after full dark and then extract them at 0100 hours. With two Tangos and a Zippo to mask the sound of the PBRs engines, a three boat patrol got underway with the Seal's on board and inserted them at a point previously decided upon. The PBRs then pulled into the Sugar Mill while the Heavies continued on a nighttime patrol. At the prearranged time, the Heavies came down past the Sugar Mill heading south and the PBRs pulled in behind them. Just across from Hiep Hoa the enemy opened fire on the Heavies with rockets and machine guns. The enemy fire ceased as the Zippo ignited her flame and a deadly stream of fire spewed forth engulfing the entire enemy position. The enemy's fire was suppressed immediately and the PBR's continued on to the pickup point. Once there, the SEALs radioed that they had decided to

remain overnight. In the early morning light the PBRs returned for the SEAL Team who reported many new bunkers, booby traps and fighting slit trenches in the area.

On 11 June 1969, it was decided to try to leave a large LCM-8 tow the damaged 8104 boat to the YRBM-18 for repairs. A tow line was attached to her and with another boat alongside to pump out any incoming water, the LCM headed downstream with an escorting patrol. Just before reaching the Horseshoe, the patch on 8104 started coming loose and the boat pumping the water reported this to the escorting patrol and NOC. They ordered the units to return to base camp at best possible speed and another method would be found to take the damaged boat down for repairs. As the boats made a 180 degree turn the enemy opened fire. The escorting patrol exploded into action spraying the enemy's position. A patrol of Black Pony aircraft were overhead and noticed the action and called the patrol and requested they depart the area so that they could place a strike. The boats complied with the request and the Ponys went to work completely shattering the enemy's attack. One man on the LCM was wounded and the NOC was requested to have a Dust Off waiting. On their arrival the wounded man was medevaced to Cu Chi.

On 19 June 1969, a three boat patrol headed toward the YRBM-18, for hull work to repair battle damage. In the middle of the Horseshoe the enemy struck once more with a withering fire of rockets and machine guns. PBR-8103 took a rocket hit forward. Paying no attention to the damage done to the boat, the three boats turned immediately and came back into the kill zone on firing runs. When the enemy's fire was subdued, the patrol continued on their way to the YRBM-18. There were no personnel casualties, but another boat was to be out of commission for a longer time than expected.

On 20 June 1969, three boats were headed back to Tra Cu from the YRBM-18, replacing the three boats that had left the base the day before. As they reached the Horseshoe the enemy struck again. PBR-8101 in the lead position took a rocket hit in the fuel tanks, starting a fire. The boat captain, blinded by the smoke, beached the boat to put out the fire as the cover boats fired wildly into the enemy positions. A nearby day patrol, hearing the trouble, raced to the aid of the boats under attack, the enemy fire was soon suppressed and the fire put out on the stricken boat. The boat was then taken under tow by the rescuing patrol and the remaining two boats took the wounded and raced to base camp, awaiting Dust Off Helicopter. The toll of wounded continued to mount. USN casualties: Freeman, EN3 (serious, medevaced to Cu Chi); Henning, BM2 (minor, retained on board); Polmanteer, GMGSN (minor, retained on board).

The day finally arrived and we were relieved by River Division 552. After packing personal belongings, the division loaded onto the remaining boats and departed Tra Cu for the last time. Heading south, all guns were manned and the air was filled with apprehension. As the division neared the Horseshoe, they waited breathlessly for the orangish red flash followed by the blast of a rocket and the high whine of bullets whipping by close overhead. Fingers tightened on triggers, breathing quickened. Finally the boats were out of the Horseshoe. Now the tension was not as great, but danger was still all around. Finally, after about three hours tran-

Operation Giant Slingshot, PBR101 is beached after taking direct rocket hit in fuel tanks in the portion of patrol area called the Horseshoe, June 1969.

sit time, Ben Luc loomed just a short distance away. The boats were now out of the dangerous area. The division stayed the night at Ben Luc, hosted by River Division 534 and 591. It was the 22nd of June 1969.

In the morning of 23 June 1969, with the arrival of the Mike boat carrying the division's maintenance tools and personnel from the YRBM-18, the division started on its way, heading for the YRBM-20 on the upper Mekong River. The division moved a little way north on the Vam Co Dong River to a small canal that connected the Vam Co Dong with the Vam Co Tay rivers. After transiting this small canal, they turned right on the Vam Co Tay heading up to the Grand Canal. Upon reaching the Grand Canal, the division turned and a few hundred meters up the canal they stopped for the night Thuyen Nhon, hosted by River Division 595. The evening found everyone able to relax for the first time in many months. A few of the personnel decided this would be the perfect time for a division party, and implemented an immediate plan. Refreshments were obtained and soon a roaring party was in progress. The previous months of fighting were momentarily forgotten as everyone began to think of the future and the prospect of the big river. The night progressed with various members of the division performing acts of strength and dexterity. As the never to be forgotten party came to a close the 512 legacy of being the best at everything was upheld. The morning found many aching heads and churning stomachs as the XO gave the word to get underway. At 1700 hours on 24 June 1969 the division finally arrived at An Long and turned north on the Mekong River toward the nearby YRBM-20 where the division was to spend the next eight months.

After two days on the YRBM, the division started Patrolling the Upper Mekong and Bassac rivers, checking for curfew violators false ID cards and providing fire support for any outpost under attack. The division also received its first Vietnamese sailors who were the first of many the division would receive prior to turn-over in March 1970. The only time the weapons were fired was on a day when we took the Vietnamese sailors up a small canal into an area known to be a VC training ground. We taught our counterparts how to fire every weapon onboard. This idyllic period was soon to end, however.

On 26 July 1969, orders were received to cease patrolling the Mekong and Bassac rivers and commence patrolling the Vinh Te Canal in support of Operation Tran Hung Dao. The canal was located off the Chau Doc River, which emptied into the Upper Bassac River. The Vinh Te Canal stretched clear to the Gulf of Thailand and was an excellent location for the division boats to interdict the enemy supply route from Cambodia.

The night of 18 August 1969 was an exceptional night in that it did not rain! Two boats had set an ambush just east of Tinh Binh when the boat on the south bank suddenly spotted movement 300 meters away. The boat captain immediately radioed the lead boat who in turn radioed and requested permission to fire. This was a highly populated area and unless you had actually been fired upon you could not fire without permission. NOC radioed back that they were attempting to get permission to take the VC under fire. The boat on the south bank acknowledged the message and continued to watch the enemy who by now were much closer to the boats and getting still closer. Suddenly the enemy was on top of the boat and started shooting. The boats immediately returned fire not needing the permission now. The boat on the south bank, R 8102, took a rocket in the fuel tanks and many shrapnel hits. The boat on the north bank was taking numerous small arms rounds. They got underway immediately from the area, as many were wounded and they were facing a numerically superior force. The boats raced to a Popular Force outpost, nicknamed Fort Apache, and called in a Dust Off Helicopter. Once more men of the division were added to the list of the wounded. USN casualties: Henning, BM2 (serious, medevaced to U.S.); Brazythis, GMG3 (serious medevaced to U.S.); Polmanteer, GMGSN (minor, retained on board); Men, VNN (serious, medevaced to Saigon).

On 4 October 1969, the division received an emergency call to muster all available boats and scramble to Lac Quoi, the town at the extreme western end of the AO, and aid in the medical evacuation of a number of Vietnamese soldiers and civilians. The VG had attacked a CIDG outpost with the intention of teaching our valiant allies a lesson, made no discretion between fighting men and noncombatants. Soon a number of seriously wounded men, women and children poured into the town. The division then took the more seriously wounded and put them on waiting medevac helicopters and the less seriously wounded were loaded on the boats and sped to nearby medical facilities. This medevac is the largest single medevac by River Patrol Boats in the history of the Vietnam War.

River Division Five One Two responded magnificently with maximum participation, minimum confusion and customary aplomb.

The night of 6 November 1969 was another night of heavy leaden skies. Soon after full dark, the clouds opened up and the rains came pouring down. Visibility at its best that night was only a few meters. Shooting a flare was little help. PBR-8103 was sitting in a night ambush position approximately halfway through the AO. In the sudden clearing of the rain clouds the VC struck hard and fast. A rocket struck the stanchion just aft of the coxswain flat, wounding the boat captain in the head. He whirled out of the flat and attempted to reach his after .50 caliber machine gun. Another rocket hit the boat directly amidships, this time fatally wounding the boat captain. All hands had manned their stations but the clouds closed once more reducing visibility. The NVA fire had stopped as one man applied artificial respiration to the ailing boat captain and another member of the crew went for assistance. Another boat came to the aid of the stricken boat and immediately called for a Seawolf in the area. The boat captain was loaded on the helicopter and whisked away to Binh Thuy Naval Hospital. In the morning the division learned the tragic news. USN casualties: Cain, QM1 (KIA).

3 January 1970 was a clear night with no moon. In the early morning hours the enemy opened up with a mortar barrage on the base camp at Vinh Gia. One of the crewmembers on watch in ambush just west of the base camp suddenly noticed a movement on the north bank. He passed a night vision device to his boat captain then opened fire on the movement. The enemy must have been ready to fire at the same time for return fire from the enemy was almost instantaneous. Soon the patrol was embroiled in a fierce dual of rockets and. machine gunfire. Two boats were sprayed with the shrapnel from the enemy's rockets. Ignoring their wounds, the patrol poured fire into the enemy's positions in an attempt to suppress the return fire. Soon all enemy fire ceased. At this point a boat immediately got underway and came to the side of the two boats that had the wounded on board and took them to the base camp to be medevaced immediately. The remaining boats, with reduced crows, got underway to return to base camp to re-arm and possibly to get additional men to replace the wounded. This done, the boats also picked up some M-Force soldiers and returned to the ambush site to insert the m. Dawn broke and the soldiers made a sweep of the area. The information gathered by this sweep indicated that the boats had encountered an enemy sapper team of an unknown number, but had inflicted casualties indicated by the empty first aid packs, grenades and camouflage gear. This time the enemy scored heavily. USN casualties: Finley, GMG3 (serious, medevac to Binh Thuy); Ashmore, ENFN (serious, medevac to U.S.); Emery, SN (serious medevac to U.S.); Gumpf, SN (serious medevac to YRBM-20); McCoy, EN3 (minor, retained on board); Khanh, VNN (serious, medevac to YRBM-20); Muon, VNN (serious, medevac to Saigon). This same night there were many firefights in our area. The enemy seemed to have planned an attack on all the ambushes along the canal in addition to mortaring the base camp. Another of the division's ambushes was attacked, but suffered no casualties and came to the aid of the patrol that was in distress.

Once more the division received orders. This time it was to report to USS *Benewah* (APB-35). This would be the final move for the division, and took place on 19 February 1970. The division was to move to the *Benewah* to prepare the boats for the turn over to the Vietnamese Navy. This was supposed to be a period of repair and training, but, operational commitments on the Grand Canal in support of Barrier Reef West meant that the upkeep and training would have to be done as a sideline. The division had to keep eight boats in the canal nightly, as did River Division 514 and 592 The division and River Division 514 were to turn over all boats to the Vietnamese on 31 March 1970, and the engineers of the division had their work cut out for them. With eight boats in the canal, they had to work day and night to put the already hard worked boats into their original shape. Like the old pro's that they were, they completed the job with the skill, ease and professionalism that has characterized River Division Five One Two.

The long awaited day of 31 March 1970 arrived. Tomorrow River Division Five One Two would no longer be carried on the active roles of the United States Navy. As the entire division stood stiffly at attention, the boat captains marched aboard their boats with infinite sadness. They grasped the flagstaff that had flown the colors into battle so many times and lowered them for the last time. Although the Stars and Stripes will never fly on 512's boats again, the memory of the valiant sailors who rode them with courage and devotion will never be forgotten. For the man of

512, 31 March will not mean the end of 512. No, we will never forget the division or its great combat record. The proud sailors who wrote the division's history will be remembered for writing new pages into the annals of the United States Naval Service and even more so into the History of the American Fighting Man.

MINED IN THE MEKONG DELTA

by Petty Officer 2ⁿᵈ Class G.W. Frederickson,
U.S. Navy (ret)

Originally designed to transport and land troops directly onto a beach, in late 1968 *Westchester County* was serving as a temporary home and base to 175 soldiers of the 9th Infantry Division's 3rd Battalion, 34th Artillery, and to the crews of Navy River Assault Division 111. Assigned as support ship for Mobile Riverine Group Alpha, *"Wesco,"* as she was known throughout the fleet, was anchored midstream on the muddy My Tho River, 40 miles upstream from the coastal seaport of Vung Tau. Clustered in a rough semicircle around the LST were the Brown Water Navy command ship USS *Benewah*, the repair vessel USS *Askari*, two large barracks barges, a small salvage vessel and scores of squat, green armored assault craft. All were fully loaded with fuel and ammunition.

Tied to *Wesco's* starboard side and cushioned from the ship's hull by a 50-foot-long teakwood log called a "camel" were three "ammis," huge aluminum pontoon barges linked together that served as combination pier, loading dock and ammunition and gasoline storage depot. The 25 monitors, assault support patrol boats and armored transports a River Assault Division 111 were moored to the ammis. On the ship's main deck were five fully fueled Army helicopters; below, on the tank deck more than 350 tons of high explosives and ammunition were stored.

Operating out of Yokosuka, Japan, the 384-foot-long LST was one of many World Ware II and postwar amphibious workhorses pressed into service with the Brown Water navy. She was no stranger to the coffee-colored rivers of the Mekong Delta, and on the night of November 1, the ship was almost at the midpoint of her fifth combat deployment to the Republic of Vietnam. So far, the cruise had been routine—for a combat tour- filled with hot, humid, seven-day workweeks, little liberty time ashore and the always-present chance of VC attack.

Nevertheless, morale was high. The ship's engineering department had recently taken the coveted Squadron "E" for excellence, and the award was now proudly displayed on her bridge. With only one month left in the delta, Wesco's 132-man crew looked forward to offloading their mobile riverine "guests" and sailing for Singapore and a well-deserved period of rest and recreation.

It was a typical night on the river. The ship was darkened, with only navigation lights showing. Forward and aft, 3-inch rapid-fire guns were loaded and ready, manned by reduced crews. Armed lookouts were posted on deck. A roving petty officer made sure that gun crews and sentries remained alert. A full watch was in place on the bridge, and in the engineering spaces the "snipes," as engine room personnel were known, stood ready to answer all bells. In the distance muffled thumps could be heard as picket boats made their rounds, dropping concussion grenades to ward off enemy frogmen. Below decks, in the crowded berthing compartments, the silence was disturbed only by the whir of air-conditioning fans and the murmurs of sleeping men.

But as the crew slept, a team of VC frogmen evaded the picket boats and silently approached the ship. The messenger of the watch had just gone below to wake the oncoming duty section when two enormous explosions ripped into *Wesco's* starboard side. A pair of swimmer-delivered mines, each estimated to contain between 150 and 500 pounds of explosives, had been simultaneously detonated directly beneath the camel.

Compressed between the pontoons and the LST's hull, the force of the explosions was driven upward, shredding steel plating, rupturing fuel tanks and blasting into the berthing compartments. One of the ammis seemed to leap out of the water as a huge spray of oil, water and hardwood splinters were thrown into the air. In an instant, visibility within the ship was reduced to zero as lighting was knocked out and the air filed with clouds of choking steam and vaporized diesel fuel.

In the crowded sleeping areas, the blasts rolled an entire deck upward and back, like the tongue of a shoe, leaving only a cramped crawl space jammed with twisted mental and mangled bodies between the deck and bulkhead. Below, in the Army berthing spaces, men, bedding, weapons, ammunition and personal gear were hurled across the compartment as two gaping holes opened the interior of the ship to the muddy waters of the My Tho.

Shock waves reverberated across the water, and *Wesco* began listing to starboard. General Quarters was sounded throughout the ship as men groped in the tangled darkness to reach battle stations or aid wounded shipmates. The LST's commanding officer, Lt. Cmdr. John Branin, had been pitched from his bed by the blast. Thinking his ship was under rocket attack, Branin picked himself off the deck struggled into his pants and dashed for the bridge.

USS Westchester County (Courtesy J.D. Davy)

Just beneath the main deck a volcano waited to erupt. Two-thirds of the tank deck, running nearly the entire length of the ship was being used for ammunition storage. More than 10,000 rounds of Army 105mmm and 155mmm high–explosive ammunition were stored there, closely stacked alongside pallets of 20mmm ammunition, boxes of C-4 plastic explosive Claymore mines, white phosphorous ammunition and cases of flares and pyrotechnics. In the wake of the explosions, loose and damaged ammuntion lay scattered about the deck. Clouds of highly flammable vaporized fuel hung in the air. With just one spark, the entire contents of Westchester County could easily go "high order".

On the bridge, Commander Branin and his executive officer, Richard Jensen, faced a grim situation. Early reports indicated sever damage amidships and suggested heavy casualties, especially among the senior petty officers. Movement about the ship was extremely hazardous on oil-slick decks. Communications between repair parties and damage control central was almost negligible. On the tank deck, clouds of vaporized fuel and tons of ammunition provided the potential for an explosion of hellish dimensions. And while it was now clear that the LST was not being rocketed, there was a very real possibility that the VC had planted more than two mines.

But for the moment, Branin's attention was occupied by a more immediate problem. Wesco's list was increasing as tons of river water continued to flood into ruptured compartments. As the ship heeled, charts, publications shattered class and overturned equipment began to slide across the bridge deck. For an instant Branin thought, "She's going all the way over!"

If the LST was to be saved, the list had to be corrected—and corrected fast. Twenty-four years of navel service and an intimate knowledge of the Wesco's unique capabilities gave Branin his solution. Designed for amphibious assaults, the landing ship was equipped with a sophisticated ballasting system. By flooding a series of huge internal tanks, the ship was designed to be able to partially sink herself onto a beach and offload her armored cargo through a set of massive bow doors. After that, it was simple to pump out the ballast, refloat the ship and back away. Since depth on the tidal rivers of the Mekong Delta can change rapidly and become quite shallow, Wesco's forward ballast tanks were already flooded as a precaution when the mines exploded. Branin knew that if the hull in the forward part of his ship was still watertight, he could "deballast" the LST's forward starboard tanks and, therefore, theoretically, offset the tons of water flooding in amidships.

With so many of the senior petty officers killed or wounded, many of the ship's vital stations had to be quickly reorganized. Junior petty officers and nonrated men stepped up, instinctively taking charge at battle stations suddenly undermanned and without leaders. As watertight doors were being closed throughout the ship, 22-year-old Petty Officer 2nd Class Rick Russell found himself alone in the LST's forward pumping station. Discovering little damage in the forward section of the ship, Russell made contact with the bridge by sound-powered phone, reported and stood by for orders. Over 30 years later, Branin still gives his youthful shipmate credit for reversing Wesco's list by "doing exactly as he was told."

Miraculously, there was still electrical power to the pumps and, with Branin's damage control officer relaying precise instructions, Russell began the complex process of deballasting the forward starboard tanks. While the captain held his breath, instructions were passed, valves opened and pumps started. As water was forced from the tanks, the rate of list began to decrease. Groaning, Wesco straightened herself out and slowly started rolling back.

Because of the darkness and devastation, a detailed investigation of the ship's conditions was still extremely difficult, but with an hour and a half before first light, damage control and rescue efforts continued. Soundings indicated that the flooding was being brought under control as compartments next to the devastating areas were sealed off.

By now, every crew member still able was hard at work. As soon as it became evident the ship was not under sustained attack, Captain Branin released nonvital men from their topside battle stations to assist with rescue and casualty evacuation. Until blowers could clear the lower decks of vaporized fuel, the use of cutting torches was out of the question. Chain falls, pry bars, come-alongs and screw jacks were used to free men trapped in the wreckage. Battle lanterns and portable lighting equipment provided illumination. On the ammunition-laden tank deck, an attentive fire party stood by with hoses at the ready while sailors gingerly went about the work of collecting damaged ammunition, gently setting it aside until it could be disposed of.

In the flooded fourth-deck troop compartment, the inrush of river water and diesel oil finally abated, stabilizing at a depth of 6 feet. But inside the 88-man berthing area was a scene out of Dante's Inferno. Rescue teams were held up by an impenetrable tangle of debris. Sheets, blankets, pillows, M-16 rifles and duffel bags were intermingled with shredded metal lockers, bunk stanchions and an incredible jumble of personal gear. Another hazard facing the rescuers was a bewildering assortment of grenades, mines and ammunition, brought back aboard the ship in violation of regulations by soldiers returning from the field. Once all the trapped and injured survivors were evacuated, the compartment was abandoned until a complete investigation could be conducted. The next day, salvage divers removed the remains of five soldiers who had been crushed in the explosions.

At first light, as boats shuttled rescue equipment and wounded men to and from the scene, the scope of the VC attack and the damage resulting from it became obvious. Wesco's hull was scarred by a pair of gaping, 10-foot holes, and the ship still listed 11 degrees to starboard. On the oil-soaked main deck, two of the Army choppers were wrecked beyond repair. The inboard ammi, miraculously still afloat, was grotesquely crumpled. Its forward third punched inward by the force of the blasts. Dozens of damaged light anti-tank rockets, Claymore mines, blocks of C-4 plastic explosive, flares, grenades and other loose ordnance lay strewn across the ammi's twisted deck. The pontoon's guard shack was a jumble of splintered timber; Petty Officer 3rd Class Harry Kenny, the sailor who had been manning this post, was missing. Several armored assault craft moored to the ammi were severely damaged and in danger of sinking. The teakwood camel was no longer in the water. The forward half of the enormous log had been vaporized, and a telephone-pole-sized chunk of the remaining 25 feet had been driven through the ammi's aluminum hull with the splintered remainder scattered over the decks of the pontoon and LST.

Several days later, after unsuccessfully attempting to assess the full damage to his ship where she lay, Branin reluctantly gave orders to beach Wesco, and the LST was gently run aground on the bank of the My Tho near Dong Tam. At low tide, enough of the hull was exposed to enable the captain to plan temporary repairs.

With the help of a repair division from Askari and a team from Naval Support Activity, Dong Tam, Wesco's crew worked around the clock for the next 14 days, building a cofferdam to keep the river at bay, cutting away mangled steel and binding up the LST's wounds.

But before the temporary repairs could be completed, Branin and his men faced one more challenge. A local shortage of structural steel plating and I-beams threatened to keep the ship in its vulnerable riverbank position until a shipment of the critical materials could arrive from a repair base in Japan or the Philippines. Not willing to wait, Branin decided to follow a time-honored Navy tradition and sent a party ashore for a little "midnight requisitioning." That evening at an Army engineer compound near Dong Tam, Branin's men located a stockpile of portable bridging equipment, complete with assorted I-beams and plenty of steel plating. Within hours the "borrowed" I-beams and patches were cut to size and welded into place on Wesco.

On November 14, 1968, with the help of a large Navy tug, the crew of Westchester Country refloated their ship and steamed down the My Tho, outbound for the South China Sea and a 2,500-mile voyage home to Yokosuka for dry-docking and permanent repairs. Wesco's passage home was not to be an easy one. Along the way, the wounded LST lost a race trying to outrun a typhoon. Rough seas caused cracks and ruptures in the temporary repairs, and the ship's damaged holds began taking on water. By the time the LST entered Tokyo Bay on November 25, flooding from the hole in the aft part of the ship had overwhelmed pumps capable of pumping 3,200 gallons per minute. Once again, parts of the damaged areas were flooded to the waterline.

This time the crew was ready. Watertight doors and well-braced bulkheads sealed off flooded compartments from the rest of the ship. Well-tested damage control parties stood by, confident of themselves and of Wesco's ability to take whatever was thrown at her.

At 1000 hours the next day, battered but unbowed, Westchester Country passed the Yokosuka breakwater and steamed into her home port. Obvious patches marked where the VC mines had torn into her side, and her main deck was still piled high with debris cut away during the repair effort. But topside, the ship sported a fresh coat of haze-gray paint, and while the special sea–and–anchor detail scrambled to make her fast to the pier, a veteran crew manned Wesco's rail.

When the final casualty figures were tallied, they showed that 17 crew members of Westchester County had been killed in the explosions; five 9th Infantry Division soldiers died in the wreckage of the troop compartment. Also killed in the attack were one sailor from River Assault Division 111, one South Vietnamese "Tiger Scout" interpreter. Twenty-two crewmen had been wounded. The 25 KIAs lost in the mining of Westchester County represent the U.S. Navy's greatest single-incident combat loss of life during the entire Vietnam War.

Following repairs in Japan, *Westchester County,* continued to make regular deployments to Vietnam until the end of the American involvement. By the time she was decommissioned in 1973, *Wesco* had been awarded three Navy unit commendations, two Meritorious Commendations and 15 Engagement Stars, a combat record matched by only two other LSTs. More than 36 awards and commendations were awarded to the ship's crew for its performance during and immediately after the November 1 attack.

In 1974, USS *Westchester County* was turned over to the Turkish navy, where she continues to serve as TCG *Serdar* (L 402).

Night patrol on Vinh Te Canal, 1969. (Courtesy of Jeff Warnock)

RIVER RATS

submitted by James D. Davy
The words to this song were allegedly written by a machine gunner with the 101st Airborne Division in 1970. The original title was "Boonierat". The writer was killed in action, and the song has been modified many times…in this case, it reflects the life of a Brown Water Navy River Rat.

I landed in this Country,
One year of life to give,
My only friend a weapon,
My only prayer, to live.

I walked away from freedom
And the life that I had known,
I passed the weary faces
Of those going home.

River Rats, River Rats,
Scared but not alone,
300 days, more or less
Then I'm going home.

The first few days were hectic
As they psyched my mind for war,
I often got the feeling
They're trying to tie the score.

The first night with my unit
We set an ambush with much skill,
To surprise old Victor Charlie,
To capture, wound or kill.

River Rats, River Rats,
Scared but not alone,
200 days, more or less
Then I'm going home.

The air was hot and humid,
The river shined like glass,
Ten times I cures the war
and wished that I could pass.

I learned to look for danger
In the trees and on the ground,
I learned to look for cover
When I heard a rocket round.

River Rats, River Rats,
Scared but not alone,
100 days, more or less
Then I'm going home.

Iron Butterfly is our motto,
Sat Cong is our cry,
Freedom is our mission,
For this we do or die.

River Rats a legend
For now and times to come,
Wherever there are sailors
They'll talk of what we've done.

They say there'll always be a war,
I hope they're very wrong,
To the River Rats of Vietnam
I dedicate this song.

River Rats, River Rats,
Scared but not alone,
Today I see my Freedom Bird,
Today, I'm going Home.

TO THE BRAVE MEN OF
TASK FORCE 116 WHO DIED
FIGHTING TO PRESERVE A NATION

Lest We Forget (Courtesy of J. Warnock)

Photo courtesy of Carl A. Nelson.

Editor's note: All members of the Gamewardens Veterans Association were invited to write and submit biographies for inclusion in this publication. The following are from those who chose to participate. The biographies were printed as received, with only minor editing. The publisher regrets it cannot accept responsibility for omissions or inaccuracies within the following biographies.

GAMEWARDENS VETERANS' BIOGRAPHIES

RICHARD E. ABBOTT, born on May 4, 1940 in Tooele, UT. He joined the USN on May 29, 1959 as a yeoman and served in Hawaii, San Diego, Port Hueneme and Vietnam.

Some of his memorable experiences include Staff of CTF-116 from 1966-67, where he served as aide and writer for Captains Witham and Gray. He was the first to water ski in Vietnam (1967); also participated on several combat patrols and operations.

Discharged in 1969 with as YN1. Awards and medals include three Vietnam Service Medals, Navy Commendation Medal, Navy Achievement Medal with Combat V and three Good Conduct Medals.

Abbott is married to Valasi Aupiu and they have 10 children. He is a retired chiropractor and enjoys surfing. They reside in Laie, HI.

ROBERT B. ADAMS, born in Hampton, VA. He enlisted in the USN on April 21, 1967. His military stations include Moc Hoa and Chau Duc. Adams participated in the following battles: Riv. Div. 511; May 1969-January 1970; advisor from January-May, 1970 at Chau Duc.

He is still active and attached to Special Boat Sqdn. Two, NAB Little Creek, VA. Achieved rank of CWO4. Awards and medals include the Navy Commendation Medal with Bronze V, Navy Achievement Medal with Bronze V and Combat Action Medal.

Adams is married to Linda Osborne from Maine.

RODGER D. ALSTON, born in Casa Grande, AZ. He joined the USN on Sept. 22, 1964 and served in Chou Duc, Ben Luc and Moc Hoa.

Some memorable experiences include patrolling the Vihn Tay Canal out of Chou Duc with Riv. Div. 551 from June-August 1969 and serving with NOC Staff at Ben Luc, Moc Hoa and Tan An from September 1969-May 1970.

Discharged July 21, 1970 as gunnersmate 3rd class (had a grandson born same day and month in 1991). Received the Combat Action Ribbon, National Defense, Vietnam Service with one Silver and two Bronze Stars, Republic of Vietnam Campaign, Navy Unit Commendation with Bronze Star, Good Conduct Medal, Republic of Vietnam Meritorious Unit Citation, Gallantry Cross and Civil Action Medal.

He and wife, Sharon, have a married daughter (whose husband is stationed at USN Coronado) and one grandson. Alston is a Job Service Veterans Employment representative and is also commander of VFW Post #1704.

ROGER D. ANDERSON, born on Aug. 19, 1949 at Scottsville, KY. He entered the USN in April 1969; received basic propulsion and engineering and Engineman A School, Great Lakes, IL; counter-insurgency and survival, evasion, resistance, escape, NAB Coronado, CA; weapons training at Camp Pendelton, CA; ambush, outer perimeter defense, booby trap detection and enemy bunker design with the USA's 1st Inf. Div., Cat Li, RVN.

Anderson served in TAD at Cham Rhan Bay Naval Air Facility and at Cat Li with the Big Red One; permanent duty was at Nha Be, RVN where he was first assigned to the Packard engine shop, then the outboard engine shop. He was on swimmer patrol watch and was also a member of the "Filthy Few."

Discharged in 1971; his awards include the National Defense Medal, Vietnam Service Medal, Vietnam Campaign, Presidential Unit Citation, Cross of Gallantry with Palm and Civil Actions.

A disabled mechanical maintenance technician, diagnosed PTSD, since 1992. He married Sue Kingrey on Dec. 21, 1975.

STEVEN NELSON AZNOE, born on June 12, 1945 in Sturgeon Bay, WI. Enlisted in the USN on Aug. 30, 1965. He served with the PBRs, Riveron Five, River Section 511, Can Tho, Mekong Delta, 1967-68. Military locations and stations included NAS Corpus Christi, TX; River Section 511 Can Tho; LST 1073, Outagamie City, Home Port, San Diego; Special Boat Unit 11, Mare Island.

His most memorable experience was after six months "in country," he received word that his twin daughters were born. Discharged on Sept. 15, 1990 as EN/1. Received Combat Action, Vietnam Service Medal and Vietnam Campaign.

Aznoe is divorced and has three daughters: Stephanie, Margaret and Leah. He is an electrician at St. Mary's Hospital in Green Bay, WI.

JOHN BABCOCK (JACK), born on April 14, 1939 in Westerly, RI. He joined the Navy on April 17, 1956 and served on various MSOs, YOs and YPs before Naval inshore training (Class 75), Mare Island, CA.

Arrived "in country" in April 1969 as engineman 1st class and was assigned to Riv. Div. 511 as boat captain PBR 36 in Binh Thuy, SVN. Three weeks later, Riv. Div. 511 was transferred to Moc Hoa, SVN for Operation Giant Slingshot on the Van Co Tay River. He "returned to the world" in April 1970 for various duties onboard MSO, Iceland, DD, Comm. 2nd Fleet, Admiral's Barge, before retiring in June 1975, Newport, RI.

His awards include the Navy Commendation Combat V, Navy Achievement, Combat Action, National Defense, Good Conduct, Vietnam Service, Republic of Vietnam Campaign and Armed Forces Expeditionary.

He has three children: Mark, John and Tami. Currently living in Stonington, CT with wife, Julie, and step-children, Sera and Sam. He is employed with the Coast Guard Foundation.

MICHAEL H. BAILEY, born on May 14, 1939 in Dayton, OH. Joined the USN on June 21, 1956. Military locations and stations included MSO 440, SS 408, SSBN 625, Riv. Div. 532 and SSBN 627.

His memorable experiences include serving in Vietnam with Riv. Div. 532 as patrol officer, 1969-1970; Tra-Cu, Sadec, Tay Ninh, Tan An and Ha-Tien; 142 combat patrols; 42 engagements and 13 major fire fights; but most of all, the bonding friendships that still exist.

Retired on Oct. 21, 1975 as MMCS (SS). Awards include the Bronze Star with Combat V, Purple Heart, Good Conduct Medal (4th Award), Combat Action Ribbon, Presidential Unit Citation Ribbon, Navy Unit Commendation Ribbon, Meritorious Unit Commendation Ribbon, National Defense Service Medal, Vietnam Service Medal, Vietnam Cross of Gallantry (Army) with Star, Republic of Vietnam Meritorious Unit Citation (Civil Action Color), Republic of Vietnam Campaign Medal with four stars, Small Boat Command Device, Dolphins, SSBN Patrol Pin with 13 stars, and Italian Mine Sweeping Device.

Bailey married Bonda R. on April 1, 1960. They reside in Charleston, SC. They have one son, Robert J. and one daughter, Holly A.

COLUMBUS W. BAKER JR. (C.W.), born on Nov. 3, 1941 in Ft. Worth, TX. He joined the Navy in February 1959 to November 1963; re-enlisted in August 1965. Baker served in numerous billets and commands, including USS *Ticonderoga*, USS *Newport News* and USS *Sierra*.

Received amphibious training, Pacific, USNAB Coronado, CA, January 1968; Cos. Div. 13, Catlo Republic of Vietnam, March 1968; Naval Act. Detachment, An Thoi, RVN, August 1968; USN Sta., Subic Bay, Naval Advisor Group 159, October 1970-1971; Republic of Vietnam, Harbor Clearance Two, USS *Recovery* ARS-43; NAVSTA Roosevelt Rd., San Juan, PR; Fighter Sqdn. 51, Amphibious Construction Bn. Two (Seabees), USS *Newport*, LST 1179, USS *El Paso* LKA-117.

Retired on Oct. 31, 1983 as BMC. Received the Purple Heart, Navy Commendation Medal with Combat V, Presidential Unit Citation, Navy Unit Commendation with star, Good Conduct Medal (4), Battle Efficiency E, National Defense Service Medal, Navy Marine Expeditionary Medal, RVN Meritorious Unit Commendation (Civil Action) Medal with Palm, RVN Meritorious Unit Citation, Gallantry Cross with Palm, Vietnam Service Medal with two Bronze Stars, Vietnam Campaign Medal with Device and Combat Action Ribbon.

Latest marriage was to Joyce on Nov. 4, 1988. He has one son, Richard.

EDWARD H. BAKER, born on Jan. 18, 1927 in Milan, MI. He enlisted in the Navy on June 11, 1943 and served two years and seven months in WWII in England, Scotland, Russia and the Mediterranean as a member gunner of the armed guard on merchant ships.

He left the Navy in 1946 and re-entered in 1950. After serving onboard APD-89, LST-1159, DDE-446, LST-1169 and LSD-35, he attended the Vietnam Language School in Coronado, and the evasion, resistance and escape training in California. In 1967, he attended PBR training in Vallejo, CA and jungle training in Subic Bay, PI. Baker arrived in Saigon, RVN in July 1967 and was assigned to RIVERSEC 542, Nha Be. Serving on combat patrols on Long Tau and Soi Rap rivers, he was wounded in ambush in December 1967. After seven months hospitalization, he returned to Vietnam in October 1968 onboard LST-1169. As a result of wounds suffered in RVN, he was placed on limited duty in Yokosuka, Japan in 1969.

Retired from the Navy in 1973 while stationed at NTC Orlando, FL. BMCS Baker was awarded the following honors: Bronze Star with Combat V, Purple Heart, Combat Action Ribbon, Presidential Navy Unit and Meritorious Unit Commendation, VN Cross of Gallantry, VN Service Medal, Occupation Medal, EAME Medal, Expeditionary Medal, WWII Victory Medal, Good Conduct Medal and Small Boat Device Emblem.

He married his Navy nurse, Deirdre, and resides in Memphis, TN.

CHARLES EDWARD BAXTER, born on Jan. 23, 1938 in Bay City, Matagorda County, TX. Enlisted in the USN on Dec. 16, 1956 in Albuquerque, NM. Duty stations included RTC NTC, San Diego, CA; TG 7311, Amphibious Base, Coronado, CA; Stockton Group,

PACRESFLT, Stockton, CA; USS *Leader,* MSO-490, LB, CA; NAS Moffett Field, CA; Amphibious Base, Coronado, CA; NIOTC, Vallejo, CA; COMRIVRON, RVN, RIV, SEC 512/531/533; DLIEC, Washington, DC; CHNAVADVGRU, RVN, Nha Be, South Vietnam; NAVRES TRG CEN, Austin, TX; USS *Illusive*; USS *Holland*; INACTSHIPFAC, PSNS, Bremerton, WA.

His most memorable experience was serving in a River War Fare Unit and becoming a PBR boat commander. Retired on Feb. 10, 1976 at Bremerton, WA. Awards include the Combat Action Ribbon, Presidential Unit Citation, Meritorious Unit Commendation, Good Conduct (4), National Defense Service, Vietnam Service, Civil Action 1/C Vietnam and Republic of Vietnam Campaign.

Civil Service work includes naval acoustic range, Fox Island, Gig Harbor, WA; Puget Sound Naval Shipyard, Shop 03/Pumpwell Crew. Retired on April 30, 1993 after 36 years of combined naval and civil service time.

Has been married 14 years to Charlotte Irene. From previous marriages, they have nine children and 15 grandchildren.

REYNOLDS BECKWITH, born on Aug. 9, 1924 in Coral Gables, FL. He graduated from the USNA in 1949 and received his wings in February 1951. As a member of VP-871, he flew ASW patrols in the Japan Sea and night missions over North Korea during the Korean War. Graduated from Naval Postgraduate School in Monterey, CA, 1956, with an MS in electronics engineering and was designated helicopter pilot at HT-8 in 1958.

He served three years in VX-1 as sonics engineer and project officer; was operations officer in VP-24, then attended Armed Forces Staff College. As executive officer and commanding officer of HS-7, he participated in Task Group Alfa ASW exercises; served onboard the USS *Princeton,* then reported to HS-10 as commanding officer; then reported to HA(L)-3 as commanding officer in 1969.

Left Vietnam in April 1970 and reported to OPNAV where he became director, Air Division (OP-951C); moved to ASWSPO (PM-4) in 1973 as director, Systems Planning Office.

Retired in 1975 as a captain. Received DSC, DFC and air medals. Capt. Beckwith worked as consultant to the Navy and defense contractors;

led a Washington office for Bendix Oceanics and still consults for that Allied Signal Division. He is presently president of Objective Interface Systems, Inc. of Reston, VA.

He and wife, Mary E. (Bette), have one daughter Karen, one son Bill and four granddaughters.

ROBERT O. BEER JR., born on July 23, 1940 in Bremerton, WA. He graduated from the USNA in 1962 and entered the USN on June 6, 1962. Was captain of Navy Supply Corps; served as Logistics officer, RIVRON 5. His most memorable experience was bringing the first 120 PBRs into RVN and operating out of crude tent bases, 1966-1967.

Retired on Aug. 1, 1991 with rank of captain. Received the Defense Superior Service Medal, Defense Meritorious Service Medal, Navy MSM with star, Navy Commendation, PUC, MUC, JMUC, Battle E (2), Combat Action, National Defense with star, Vietnam Service and Vietnam Campaign Medal.

Beer has one daughter and two sons. He resides in Burke, VA and works as a consultant.

JERE A. BEERY JR., born on March 13, 1948 in Orlando, FL. At the age of 17, Beery quit school and joined the Navy in 1965. His first duty station was onboard the USS *Westchester County* LST-1167, home ported in Yokosuka, Japan. He spent the next 23 months onboard *Westchester County* and was involved in many operations in the waters of Vietnam.

In 1967 Beery volunteered and was accepted for duty with the River Patrol Force, TF-116, Vietnam. After completing a number of special warfare schools, Beery was assigned to River Section 511, Binh Thuy, South Vietnam. On March 1, 1968, as a crew member of the Godbehere Patrol, he was critically wounded by a direct hit from a B-40 rocket and medivaced out of country. He credits his survival that night to the "above and beyond" actions of his wounded shipmates: LCDR Richard Godbehere, LCDR Dallam "Bill" Bailey, BM/1 Harold Sherman, and GM/3 Dave Otto.

As the result of Beery's injuries, he was medically retired from the USN at the rank/rate of signalman, 3rd class petty officer, and was evaluated at 100% disability by the VA.

On Nov. 1, 1968, the USS *Westchester County* was mined near My Tho, RVN, killing 25. Many of the KIAs were friends and former shipmates of Beery. This incident has gone down in naval history as the USN's greatest loss of life in a single incident as the result of enemy action during the entire Vietnam War.

Beery's service records reflect five military campaigns of service in Vietnam, one Bronze Star with V, three Purple Hearts and the Combat Action Ribbon.

Jere Beery and his wife, Donna, currently live in Newman, GA, where he works with special effects for motion pictures and commercials. He and his wife also spend a great deal of their spare time working on ways to better the systems that serve veterans.

BARRY C. BENNER, born on Aug. 29, 1950 in Port Jervis, NY. He completed recruit training in the USN at Great Lakes, IL on June 20, 1969; graduated from Class 2537-A, Enginemen A School, on Oct. 31, 1969. This class was nicknamed the "Filthy Few" by one of the instructors at Great Lakes.

Additional training was received at Coronado NAVPHIBASE and Camp Pendleton, CA before going to Vietnam. The units to which he was assigned in Vietnam were NAVSUPPACT Saigon, Cat Li, Vihn Gia (ATSB), Nha Be, Nam Can (Solid Anchor) and Bihn Tuy, RVN.

His decorations include the National Defense Medal, Vietnam Service Medal, Vietnamese Campaign Medal, Navy Unit Commendation Ribbon and the Republic of Vietnam Meritorious Unit Citation.

He married Aleece, and they have a daughter Trina Marie, and a son Jason Alan. Benner is employed by the U.S. Postal Service as a rural mail carrier. They now reside in Milford, PA.

MONTE LeROY BLACKWELL, born on April 1, 1932 in Indianapolis, IN. He enlisted in the USN on June 22, 1951 and served on various ships. In 1969 he volunteered for PBRs; attended NAVINSHORETRACEN Vallejo, CA; Language School in Coronado; SERE in Washington.

Arrived "in country" on Aug. 18, 1969 and assigned to River Division 511 at Moc Hoa on the Van-Co-Tay and Tuyen Nhon on Thu-Tua Canal. When Div. 511 and 395 combined to form RPG-56, he remained as an advisor to the RVN navy. On May 6, 1970, RPG-56 entered Cambodia on Rach Cai Cay. In two days, RPG-56 had 15 of its 20 boats hit, and sustained one VNN KIA, 15 VNN WIA and nine USN WIA.

Decorations include the Bronze Star with Combat V, Navy Commendation Medal with Combat V, Combat Action Ribbon, Navy Unit Commendation, Good Conduct, Vietnam Campaign, Expeditionary Medal, European Occupation, National Defense, RVN Gallantry Cross, RVN Civil Actions and Small Boat Insignia.

Blackwell married Sue E. Vaughan in 1972, and they reside in Chesapeake, VA.

ROY H. BOEHM, born on April 9, 1924 in Brooklyn, NY. He enlisted in the Navy in April 1941 and saw action in WWII; fought in the Pacific Theater of Operations from February 1942 until the conclusion of the war in 1945.

LCDR Boehm is a survivor of one of the largest all surface sea engagements of WWII, the Battle of Cape Esperance at Guadalcanal. While serving onboard the destroyer, *Duncan* (DD-485), the ship received 58 eight-inch and six-inch shell hits at point blank range before going down. He also participated in Battle of Coral Sea, Bougainville, Truk, Green Island, Emirau, Saipan, Tinian and Guam; participated in supplying ammunition to the guerrillas in the Philippines, and saw action in Kerama-retto and Okinawa; also saw action in the Korean Conflict and Vietnam.

Boehm is a graduate of airborne and ranger training. In early 1960s, under a Presidential Two priority received from President John F. Kennedy, he developed, designed, implemented and led the Navy's Commando organization known as SEALS. He was the first officer in charge of SEAL Team Two; also assisted in design and implementation of the Navy's first counterinsurgency course, after which he was made head of the Navy's River Patrol Craft Div.

Medals: Meritorious Service, Bronze Star with Combat V, Air Medal, Navy Achievement, Purple Heart, Presidential Unit Citation with Bronze Star, Good Conduct with four stars, American Defense with A, American Campaign, Asiatic-Pacific with six Battle Stars, WWII Victory, Navy Occupation, China Service, National Defense Service with one Bronze Star, Korean Service with two Bronze Stars, Armed Forces Expeditionary, Vietnamese Campaign with one Bronze Star, United Nations Service, Philippines Liberation, Philippines Presidential Unit Citation, Korean Presidential Unit Citation, RVN Campaign, Meritorious Unit Commendation and Expert Pistol Medal.

Roy Boehm and Chuck Sasser are currently writing Roy's autobiography.

PAUL R. BOHN (BON), born on Aug. 12, 1939 in Decatur, IL. He enlisted in the Navy in September 1956 at Great Lakes, IL; USN, AMS and SAR aircrewman. Was detachment chief of Rowell's Rats, November 1966-July 1967, the fourth detachment deployed by HC-1 to participate in "Operation Gamewarden." Unit's designation changed to HAL-3, DET 4, upon the commissioning of HAL-3 in April 1967.

Prior to his assignment to Rowell's Rats, Bohn served as a rescue aircrewman and detachment petty officer of HC-1, DET B (Hell's Angels) deployed on the USS *Ticonderoga* in the South China Sea. Received his gunner and crew chief training with the Army's 101st Abn. Gunship Platoon (Thunder Birds) in-country (Soc Trang, RVN). His tour was cut short by a leg wound received in action near the lower Ham Loung River while operating with River Section 513 and LST-821. He returned to HAL-3 in February 1969 as the aircrew training and assignment chief at Bihn Thuy, RVN.

Honorably discharged in March 1970. Eleven years later he re-enlisted and was promoted to master chief and retired as the command master chief of the Naval Aviation Maintenance Office at NAS Patuxent River, June 30, 1990. He is now retired and resides in Norfolk, VA.

RAYMOND R. BOLLINGER JR., born on March 12, 1927 in Glen Rock, PA and joined the USN on March 27, 1944. Received boot training at Bainbridge, MD, and was stationed onboard the USS *Harry E. Hubbard* (DD-748). Bollinger saw action in WWII in the Pacific, earning four Battle Stars.

In May 1966, he went to California for Vietnamese language and survival training. Upon arriving in Vietnam, was assigned to  Riv. Div. 543 and later transferred to Riv. Div. 533 where he was boat commander of PBR-160, leaving in May 1967. Returned to Vietnam on Sept. 19, 1968, serving as advisor to the Vietnamese navy on PBRs.

Retired from the Navy in 1972. Awards include Combat Action Ribbon, Navy Commendation with Combat V, American Defense, Asiatic-Pacific with four stars, WWII Victory Medal, Good Conduct with four stars, China Service, National Defense, PUC, MUC, Antarctica, Vietnam Service, Vietnam Medal of Honor Two Grade, Vietnamese Cross of Gallantry and Republic of Vietnam Campaign Medal.

Married Rose Marie in 1968 and has a son, Trey. Since he already had combat training, he is a school bus driver.

ROBERT W. BRANDT, born on Dec. 12, 1948, in Cleveland, OH. He entered the Navy on March 18, 1968. Attended the SERE and Vietnamese Language School from November 1970 to April 1971. Vietnam "in-country" service from April 1971 to November 1972. Assignments include River Patrol Div. 54 Ben Keo, Logistics Support Base Dong Tam, Intermediate Support Base Nam Can, Naval Advisory Unit Cat Lo, Engineering Advisor, Vietnam Radar Ship Ba Dong.

Decorations earned include Navy Commendation with Combat V, Navy Achievement, Combat Action, Presidential, Navy and Meritorious Unit Commendations, Good Conduct Medal; National Defense, Armed Forces Expeditionary, Vietnam Campaign, Humanitarian Service, Sea Service, Vietnam Civil Action First Class, Vietnam Service, Vietnam Tech First Class, Vietnam

Training First Class, Expert Rifle and Pistol, Navy Small Craft Device, Enlisted Surface Warfare Specialist.

Brandt retired in 1988 as chief engineman (SW). Resides in Madison, OH with his wife, Yvonne. He is a life member of VFW and Gamewardens of Vietnam and "Ready to serve again; anytime, anywhere."

GERALD BURTON BROOKS (JERRY), born on Sept. 21, 1944 in Dayton, OH. He enlisted in the USN on May 27, 1965 and received boot camp training at Great Lakes, IL. Was stationed at Sandia Base, Albuquerque, NM; Chase Field, Beeville, TX; USS *Yorktown* (CVS-10); and arrived in RVN on April 2, 1968 and was assigned to Riv. Div. 535 as a GMG/3 forward gunner on boat 724.

On his first patrol, he was in a fire fight at the Bottle Neck by *Snoopy's Nose*. What a way to get broke in and also get your hat (black beret) loop cut. He was in more fire fights than he can remember, but he can still remember all their boat crews and the professionals that manned them.

Participated in Operation "Giant Slingshot, Barrier Reef" and "TET 69." Their boat never missed a patrol. Departed RVN on March 29, 1969. Over the next 24 years he had 11 different duty stations and moved six times. Retired from active duty on June 30, 1993 as a master chief machinist mate (SW) and now resides in Fort Calhoun, NE with his wife, Master Chief Operations Specialist (SW) Sherry, and their two children, Grayce and Tommy. Decorations include the Navy Commendation, Navy Achievement (2), Combat Action, Vietnam Cross of Gallantry, Vietnam Campaign (7), Sea Service (6), Battle E (2), Armed Forces Expeditionary, Presidential Unit Citation, Navy Unit Commendation, Meritorious Unit Commendation, Good Conduct (6), National Defense (2), Expert Rifle and Expert Pistol.

He now grows Christmas trees on their farm in a town of 548 people.

LARENCE H. BROWN, born on April 15, 1934 in Washington, DC. He enlisted in the USN on Sept. 17, 1951; received boot training at NTC San Diego, CA and served onboard USS *Prairie* during the Korean Conflict, 1951-1954, in optical shop and NAS Great Lakes, IL, January-

April 1955. Re-enlisted and served onboard USS *Everglades*, in optical shop, July 1955-December 1959, making several Mediterranean and Caribbean cruises; Naval Training Command, Great Lakes, IL, Class C Periscope School, July-August 1956; Submarine Base, New London, CT, optical/periscope shop, January 1960-October 1963.

Commissioned ensign in November 1963 and attended Officer Orientation School, Newport, RI; Officer Engineering School, San Diego, CA; served onboard USS *Maunakea* and USS *Regulus*; COMFOUR Staff, Philadelphia; Naval Inshore Operations Training Center, Mare Island; Gamewardens, RVN, Riv. Divs. 552 and 513, Van Co Dong, and Van Co Tay Rivers, Tra Cu, Ben Luc and Hot Tien near Cambodian border; USS *Arco*, XO, Guam, M.I.; Naval Training Publications Detachment, Navy Yard, Washington, DC; NS Annapolis, MD; USS *Coral Sea*. Transferred to Fleet Reserve in 1975 with 24 years of active service. Retired in 1975 with rank of lieutenant commander. Awarded Navy Commendation Medal with Combat V for meritorious combat service in the Mekong Delta.

Married Gloria J. of Annapolis, MD on July 14, 1988. Fully retired and does volunteer work in the county public school system. He is a member of FRA Branch 24. Also has BS degree in mechanical engineering and MS in marine engineering.

NOEL W. BROWN (SKIP), born on April 25, 1937 in Attica, IN. He entered the USNA in 1958; USN, 1630 Intelligence specialist. Military locations and stations included Vietnam, 1967-1968; Nilo Vinh Long, Naval Intelligence liaison officer; USS *Courtney*; ASWFORPAC; COMTHIRDFLT; FICEURLANT; SALLANT. Battles include TET 1968; MANG TIT 1968; and BING LOC 1968.

Discharged on July 1, 1984 with rank of commander. Received the Bronze Star with Combat V, Joint Services Commendation, Air Medal, Combat Action, Navy Achievement, National Defense, Vietnam Service Medal and Vietnam Campaign Medal.

He and wife, Linda, have three children: Mike, Katie Forwalder and Debbie. Their son-in-law, Lt. Bob Forwalder, USN, was lost at sea in an E2C crash in over Bosnia waters in March 1993.

Brown is an engineer/specialist at Newport News Shipbuilding, Newport News, VA.

THOMAS L. BROWN, joined Riv. Div. 593, "The Iron Butterfly," in September 1968 at Nha Be, RVN. He was awarded the Purple Heart for wounds received in action on Jan. 19, 1969, during "Operation Giant Sling Shot."

The division was patrolling the Rung Sat special zone when, on April 9, 1969, Petty Of-

ficer Brown's patrol came under heavy automatic weapons and rocket fire. During the action, Brown was mortally wounded when hit by an enemy rocket.

Petty Officer Brown had been with the division seven months. During that time, he was engaged in several firefights and proved himself to be reliable under fire and true to his unit. Brown was an excellent gunner and was, and is, missed by all that served with him.

ZANE L. BROWN, born Sept. 1, 1950 in Topeka, KS. He joined the USN on Feb. 27, 1969 with TDY at Vietnam. Had general duties and some firefights at night.

Discharged Feb. 27, 1971 as EM3. Received the National Defense Service, Victory Service Medal with 12 stars, RVN Cross of Gallantry, Armed Force Medal (Korea), Combat Action Ribbon, Presidential Unit Commendation Ribbon and VCM with Device.

Brown is retired from Good Year.

JACK CAMPBELL, born in Hollywood, CA on April 17, 1942. Upon graduation from college in June 1967, he entered the USN and served in Operation Market Time patrolling the waterways from Phu Quoc Island in the Gulf of Thailand around the Ca Mau Peninsula to the Mekong Delta.

He was wounded at Can Tho in July 1967 and then was buried in a rocket attack at Vinh Long during the TET Offensive in early February 1968. Upon return from Vietnam, he was assigned to the USS *Nereus* (AS-17) at Point Loma (San Diego), CA and then was released from the Navy by Presidential Mandate in November 1968, after having served 16 months active service.

Jack remembers the value of the time served in Vietnam as the experiences he shared with courageous and compassionate men and women of the military service.

He married in 1971 and has two sons, born in 1971 and 1977. He resides in Diamond Bar, CA and is employed by the city of Los Angeles.

WALTER D. CAMPBELL, born Aug. 14, 1929 in Albany, NY. He joined the USN and his duty stations include: NTC Newport, RI; USS *Kula Gulf, Terawa,* and *Roanoke;* Boston Reserve Fleet; Norfolk Reserve Fleet; USS *Brownson*; Navy and Marine Corps RTC, Huntington, Long Island, NY; River Section 512 Vietnam (1968-69); USS *Milwaukee*; Construction Bn. CT, Davisville, RI; USS *Manitowoc*.

Of his 26 years of naval service, the year served in Vietnam was the most memorable. Arriving "in country" during the TET Offensive of 1968, he was leading Chief of River Section 512 and patrol officer. River patrol duty molded them into a tightly knit family of young sailors, old sailors, officers and enlisted. He will always remember the fire fight while towing his cover boat.

DOD: Aug. 16, 1976; he achieved the rank E-8, BMCS. His awards/medals include the Bronze Star with V, Navy Achievement, Combat Action, Presidential Unit Citation, Good Conduct Medal, Navy Expeditionary, China Service, National Defense Service, Korean Service, Armed Forces Expeditionary, Vietnam Service, Korean Presidential Unit Citation, Gallantry Cross, United Nations Medal and RVN Campaign Medal.

Employed by the Massachusetts State Police for the past 14 years as a maintenance man and supply driver. He married Marilyn on Dec. 5, 1960.

FORD L. CARNES JR. (SKIP), born Aug. 27, 1947 in Harrisburg, PA. He joined the USN and was stationed in Saigon, Ben Tre, Can Tho and Cat Lo. His memorable experiences include: when YRBM-16 was blown up on Thanksgiving Day in 1967 and TET Offensive in January 1968.

Discharged Aug. 29, 1969 as E-3. His medals include the Good Conduct, Vietnam Campaign, National Defense and Vietnam Service.

Activities director for Pennsylvania American Legion, he lives in Middletown, PA with his wife, Patricia. They have three sons: Paul, Michael and Andrew.

LAWRENCE C. CARTER (LARRY), born in Oakland, CA on Oct. 28, 1924. He joined the USN on July 24, 1942 and served on the USS *Kendrick, Epperson, Sablefish* and *Des Moines*. During his active duty, Larry had many noteworthy duties some of which were: instructor, electronic maintenance, sonarman, commissioned an officer in 1957, OIC of MOTU Eight USNB Newport, RI and his

last overseas assignment was OIC Air Transportable Comm. Unit 100A in Can Tho, Vietnam.

After retirement in 1967, he worked at Wright Patterson AFB, Dayton, OH, until his death on March 6, 1986, from lung cancer. He earned the following medals and commendations: EAME Campaign, American Theater, Asiatic-Pacific, WWII Victory Medal, Navy Good Conduct (3), Navy Commendation with Combat V, National Defense Medal (Bronze Star), Vietnam Campaign, Vietnam Service Medal and Navy Occupation (Europe).

He married Marion in 1963 and retired in 1967 to live in Cincinnati. He was a loving father to Michael, Jeffrey, Susan and Lisa-Anne and, as of 1993, a grandfather to three granddaughters and seven grandsons.

His love of the USN and his country were clearly evident in his everyday actions and conversation.

WILLIAM W. CATER, born Nov. 24, 1948 in Centerville, IA. He joined the USN on March 28, 1969. Duty stations include: basic training at San Diego; Engineman "A" School, Great Lakes; NIOTC, Mare Island; SERE training, Whidbey Island, WA; River Division 571, Ahn Long; Chau Doc; Moc Hoa; and Phouc Xyuen, South Vietnam and his last duty station, chief engineer, USS *Mankato*, Groton, CT.

Some of his memorable experiences include fighting the North Vietnamese army on the Vihn to canal; at Moc Hoa in "Giant Sling Shot" on the Van Co Tay River; participating in the Allied invasion of Cambodia.

His awards include the National Defense, Navy Commendation with Combat V, Vietnam Service, Vietnam Campaign, Combat Action Ribbon, Vietnamese Cross of Gallantry and Good Conduct. He was discharged as engineman second class.

Married in 1980 to Jayne; they have one son Jeffrey and live in western Nebraska where he is a locomotive engineer for the Burlington Northern Railroad.

TERRY S. CHELIUS, born Oct. 14, 1939 at Golden, CO. He enlisted February 1957 in the USCG and served active and reserve until 1966. In January 1966, he joined the USN and served three tours in Vietnam. He served with Riv. Sec. 511 at Binh Thuy, participated in "Crimson Tide" operation as well as numerous covert PBR/SEAL operations throughout the Mekong Delta.

Left Vietnam as boat captain of PBR 58 in 1968 with rank of BM2. His decorations include: three Purple Hearts, Navy Commendation Medal with Combat V, Combat Action Ribbon, two Presidential Unit Commendations, Navy Unit Commendation, Meritorious Unit Commendation, Vietnamese Medal of Honor 1st Class, Vietnamese Campaign Medal, Vietnamese Service Medal, Good Conduct, Antarc-

tic Service, Armed Forces Expeditionary Medal, two National Defense, three Armed Forces Reserve Medal, Meritorious Reserve Medal, Sea Service Ribbon, Overseas Service Ribbon, Expert Rifle Medal and Expert Pistol Medal. After discharge from active duty, he remained in the Naval Reserve until his retirement in 1993. With 36 years of service, he retired as a chief petty officer.

Served as a police officer since his discharge. He graduated from the University of Northern Colorado with a BA in history while serving as a state trooper, later went to work for the Denver Police Dept. Currently serving with the Colorado Dept. of Corrections in Buena Vista, CO.

He raised two daughters: Shana, a nurse in Denver, and Terri, a Gulf War veteran who just re-enlisted in the regular Navy. Chelius and Terri are both life members of the VFW.

GREGORY M. COFFMAN, born Dec. 13, 1942 at Connellsville, PA. Entered the USN on Dec. 10, 1960 and was stationed at Vietnam from December 1966 to January 1970; TF-116 River Div. 551; TF-117; T131-5; Tutuica ARG-4; USS *Lauaerne Cty* LST-902; GMG-1 Amphib. Gp. 3, San Diego.

Left the service Aug. 1, 1986. His awards include the Good Conduct (5th awd.), Combat Action, Purple Heart, Bronze Star with Combat V, MUC (3rd awd.), PUS (2nd awd.) Vietnamese Medal of Honor First Class, Vietnamese Gallantry Cross with Palm, Vietnam Service Medal, Service Deployment Ribbon (8th awd.), Surface Warfare Insignia, National Defense Service Medal, Navy "E" Ribbon, Expert Rifle and Pistol, Patrol Boat Pin and RVN MUC.

Married Rose Wilson on Aug. 13, 1983; his profession is apartments management.

RUDOLPH V. COFIELD, born in Philadelphia, PA on Dec. 9, 1945. He joined the USN in July 1965 and was stationed on board the USS *Keppler* (DD-765) out of Newport, RI on his first tour of duty off the coast of North Vietnam. He volunteered for PBR duty in 1967 and was the twin fifty gunner on PBR-138 out of Vinh Long. He served with the River Division 523/572.

He received the Purple Heart and Bronze Star with Combat V for bravery for his action on

Nov. 24, 1968. When they encountered a main force communist battalion crossing southward on a narrow branch of the Mekong River. He is a life member and a two year trustee with the MOPH Chapter 63 in Philadelphia, PA.

Married to Janice Randall in 1970; they have one son, Jayson; two daughters, Janise and Janie; and one granddaughter. "Remember the men of the PBRs who are no longer with us."

CLARENCE G. COOPER, born May 23, 1933 at Fort Worth, TX. He joined the USN on July 11, 1951 and served on submarines and small craft. His memorable experience was serving "in country" without earning a Purple Heart.

Left the Navy Sept. 13, 1973 as E-8, transferred to Fleet Reserve. His awards/medals include the Navy Achievement, Combat Action, PUC, Good Conduct Medal, National Defense, NUC, Vietnam Service and Vietnam Campaign, Fleet and FBM Dolphin Devices, Sorall Boat and Craftmaster Device.

Married Evelyn Davey, Portsmouth, NH in 1957; they have a daughter Vicki and a son Eric. He is a former merchant seaman; instructor at a maritime school.

DAVID B. CROCKETT, born Feb. 28, 1941, in Nassawadox on the eastern shore of Virginia. He was raised in Portsmouth and graduated from Churchland High School, Class of '61. He enlisted in the Navy Reserve Dec. 3, 1958 and went on active duty June 27, 1961 at Great Lakes, IL. He graduated from Hospital Corps School in December 1961.

After serving at the Naval Hospital, Portsmouth, VA, he volunteered for service in Vietnam. He was first sent for duty aboard the USS *Cacapon* (AO-52). In June 1965, he arrived at Naval Support Activity Det. Binh Thuy, RVN serving as a medical representative, HM3, assigned to LCM-63 in support of Operation Bold Dragon I. Supported and participated in Medical Civil Action Program (MEDCAP).

Member of the Vietnamese American Assoc., teaching English to the Vietnamese adults in Can Tho. During TET of 1968, he was wounded the night of January 31 by shrapnel from a 57mm recoiless rifle round. Although wounded, he persisted in remaining to tend the injuries of other injured personnel, ignoring his own condition and proceeding tirelessly in treating others wounded. Reluctant to leave the scene where he was needed, he was eventually evacuated by helicopter to the Army hospital at Binh Thuy.

For the above action, he was awarded the Bronze Star Medal with Combat V and the Purple Heart. Following medical treatment, he completed his tour of duty in Vietnam. Upon returning to the U.S., he served at NAS, Moffett Field, CA; U.S. Naval Hospital, Guam, M.I. and 2/9, 3rd Mar. Div., Okinawa, Japan.

From April 1974 to May 1975, he was assigned to the Pre-com unit Nimitz (CVN-68) and became a plankowner. He was in charge of medical equipment and supplies. There was a North Atlantic cruise, acquainting him with Germany, France, Scotland, and England.

In 1975 he served at the Naval Reserve Center, Brockton, MA as the Command LPO, Medical/Dental Dept. Head. In March 1977 he went on to the Navy Occupational Task Analysis Program, Washington, DC. During this time he functioned as a technical writer for the HM Program. For exemplary performance of his duties he was awarded the Navy Achievement Medal. Next he served with the 2nd FSSG, Camp Lejeune, NC as career counselor. Dave was initiated chief petty officer here in 1979.

In June 1981 Chief Crockett arrived at the Naval and Marine Corps Reserve Center, Norfolk, VA where he functioned as the command senior chief, Medical Dept. Head, and coordinated and participated with Marine Forces for evacuation and rescue of local civilians during a northeaster at Willoughby Spit. He served on the Advisory Committee for the CPO Club Little Creek. Advanced to senior chief in 1982.

Went on to Naval Environmental Health Center, Norfolk, VA in July 1983, serving as the assistant fleet liaison officer for mobilization of preventive medicine personnel worldwide.

After departing this command, he went on to the Senior Enlisted Academy, Newport, RI in 1986, and on to another tour in Okinawa with 3D FSSG. He served as senior enlisted advisor to the commanders of the 3D FSSG, the Dental Battallion, and the Medical Logistics Co. He combined three separate chiefs associations into the 3D MAF CPO Assoc. and served as its first president.

Returning Stateside, he reported to the USS L.Y. *Spear* (AS-36), Norfolk, VA. He was responsible for the overall operation of the Medical Dept. during a difficult overhaul period in Norshipco Shipyard, Berkely, VA. This shipyard now occupies the area of the old St. Helena Annex, which was the location of Dave's weekly Naval Reserve meetings for Division 514 (L) while still attending high school.

October 1987 he returned to Naval Hospital, Portsmouth, VA as the program manager for Special Services. His scope of duties included organizing and coordinating all special recreational events; responsible for operation of indoor/outdoor pools, bowling alley, gymnasium, weight room, and recreational gear issue. Served as the administrative assistant to the comptroller.

In October 1989 he retired with 28 years of active duty service with the following awards: Bronze Star Medal with V, Navy Achievement Medal, Navy E, Good Conduct Medal (6th awd.), Armed Forces Expeditionary Ribbon, Sea Service Deployment Ribbon, RVN Meritorious Unit Citation, RVN Campaign Medal, Purple Heart, Combat Action Ribbon, Navy Fleet Marine Force, National Defense Service Medal, Vietnam Service Medal, Overseas Service Ribbon, RVN Meritorious Unit Citation and Expert Pistol Shot Medal.

Dave is presently employed by Sentara Enterprise as a health benefits advisor at NAVCARE Norfolk. While serving in this capacity, Dave has been recognized as Employee

of the Month for his willingness to assist fellow employees and patients. He received special recognition in the *Sentara News* for his efforts to obtain housing and medical care for a disabled veteran who came into the clinic. Although the veteran did not qualify to be treated by the clinic, Crockett coordinated through the Veteran Center in Norfolk to arrange transportation and medical care at a civilian facility.

Crockett has served as a member for three years on the Tri-care Developmental Task Force and the Tidewater Regional Health Benefits Advisory Council.

He is a member of the VVA Tidewater Chapter 48, the FRA Branch 40, NCOA, and the Moose Lodge #898. He currently serves as secretary/treasurer of the German European Assoc. of Virginia, Inc., and East Coast Vice President-Gamewardens of Vietnam, Inc. He is asked to speak to students of local colleges on his experiences as a Vietnam veteran and has been featured in the *Navy News*. He and his wife, Barbara, have two grown sons and five grandchildren.

JIM CRONANDER, in Vietnam was operational commander who brought the PBR's into the Mekong Delta. Established headquarters in Can Tho as advisor and Binh Thuy as Commander Task Group 116.1. Established curfew patrols on Mekong and Bassac rivers immediately after leaving similar duties in Venezuela. Mekong Delta River Patrol establishment meant bringing 80 PBRs, two support landing craft, and two helicopter fire teams into operational status. When these were in place CTF-116 moved from Binh Thuy and he left shortly after.

His previous service was in submarines ultimately commanding USS *Sea Fox* (SS-402). Shore duty as head of submarine and antisubmarine firecontrol research.

His medals include the Legion of Merit (combat), Air Medal, Cross of Gallantry (Palm) and shared a Presidential Unit Citation with the Task Group 116.1.

Presently a registered professional engineer in private practice, Cronander resides at Redwood City, CA.

THOMAS R. CROWDER II, born Nov. 15, 1946 at Moline, IL. He entered the USN in June 1966 and served with PBR Riv. Div. 514 from September 1968 to August 1969. He was stationed in USS *Lorain County* (LST-1177), Norfolk, VA; Binh Thuy, Vietnam.

Participated in 246 patrols, 17 hostile fire fights, Mekong Delta and was made boat captain in July 1969.

Discharged Oct. 10, 1969 as GMG/2. His awards include the Vietnamese Cross of Gallantry, Vietnam Service, Vietnam Campaign, Combat Action, National Defense and Bronze Star with V.

Systems Tech. Ameritech Service, Moline, IL; Crowder is single.

MICHAEL H. CURRY, born Feb. 6, 1945 in Ottawa, IL where his father worked in the Seneca, IL Ship Yards building LSTs. He joined the Navy in July 1965. After ENA School he served on the USS *William C. Lawe* (DD-763) making a Med. cruise and was there during the six day war between Israel and Egypt in 1967.

He was an EN/2 when he went to Vietnam in July of 1968. He served with River Patrol Div. 513 on PBR-82 boat. They were operating from the USS *Harnett County* (LST-821) on the Bassac River. They moved to Binh Thuy a short time later.

He was awarded the Navy Commendation Medal with Combat V, Combat Action, National Defense, Vietnam Service Medal and Vietnam Campaign.

Married Mary Adams in 1967; they had a daughter Kelly Ann in May 1968 (she died a few hours after birth); daughter Dawn was born March 29, 1969 while Curry was in Vietnam; son Scotty; and son Shawn. Curry returned home in July 1969 and went to work as a steamfitter on construction in Peoria, IL. He lives with his wife at Metamora, IL.

GLEN G. CURTIS, born Oct. 30, 1948, Staten Island, NY, enlisted in the USN, TF-115 and served with the Coastal Forces in Da Nang.

His memories are keeping his fallen brothers in his mind. He was discharged June 10, 1969 as BM3. Auto Mach Con Edison, he lives with his wife Carol Ann.

WILLIAM H. CURTIS (CURT), born Oct. 13, 1948 (USN's 173rd anniversary) at Aiea Heights Naval Hospital, HI, the son of Chief Corpsman Donald J. Curtis who served in the South Pacific with the 4th Mar. Div. during WWII. He joined the Navy Oct. 10, 1966; with boot camp at San Diego; GM "A" School, Great Lakes, 2nd in class; USS *Camp* (DER-251) "Market Time" June-1967 to May 1968.

"In country" Aug. 4, 1968, Riv. Sec. 523, Riv. Div. 572 Co Chien River, USS *Garret County,* Vinh Long, Sadec. Riv. Div. 594 Rung Sat Zone, Moc Hoa, 259 patrols, five "official" firefights. First and last boat captains, RM1 Gray and "Terrible Tom" Larry Thomas.

Most recalled incident was the "Exploding Egg Basket" on the 55 Boat (MK1), Co Chien River, Aug. 27, 1968. Remembered, Rudy Cofield, Riley, Chief Church, Hamilton from Riv. Sec. 523. Pachecano and Skeet (594) and still has the fan.

Retired Chief from Reserve, December 1992 with 26 years. Married Cindy in 1972; they have two daughters Shanon and Tanya. He has been a postal letter carrier since 1980.

HENRY M. DAVIS JR., born Sept. 16, 1948, Longview, TX. He enlisted June 6, 1966 in the USN. Stationed at Binh Thuy, Giant Slingshot and Rach Ghia Canal. He served in the National Guard seven years as a tank commander from May 1980 to May 1987. He served in Vietnam September 1966-67 on LST-15 USS *Caddo Parish*. Served on PBR-102 from August 1968-69. He was wounded in action May 17 and again on May 29, 1969.

Participated in 225 patrols and 90 fire fights. His memorable experience was going through Hiep Hoa May 29, 1969 at 11:00 p.m., boat took several rocket hits and small arms, knocking out both engines and boat was sinking. He was M-60 gunman. M-60 and armor plate was blown from boat. He used M-79 grenade launcher while wounded in both legs and thighs. The boat captain was hit in ribs and patrol officer was shot in leg. They had to be towed 20 miles to be medivaced to Cu Chi Army Hospital.

Awards and medals include VSM, VCM, Purple Heart with cluster and NC with Combat V. Was discharged Oct. 21, 1971 as EN2.

An auto auction operator in Longview, TX. He has two sons and a daughter: Ricky, Michele Marie and David Allen.

JAMES DEAN DAVY, born Feb. 28, 1948, in Anaconda, MT. He enlisted in the USN in September 1965. Following basic training in San Diego, CA, he was assigned to the USS *Independence* CVA-62. In early 1967 he was ordered to Commander Naval Forces Vietnam, and following a course of intensive training at the Naval Amphibious Base, Little Creek, VA, he reported to Naval Support Activity Saigon for further assignment in the Mekong Delta region. Completing his first tour of duty in September of 1968, then Petty Officer Davy volunteered for another year in the war zone and was sent back to the States for additional training at the Naval Inshore Operations Warfare Training Center at Mare Island, CA.

Upon completion of training in Mare Island and a course in Vietnamese, Petty Officer Davy reported to ComRivPatFlot 5, Vietnam for assignment to River Division 593 (the Iron Butterfly). Petty Officer Davy was a boat captain of PBR 756 and made over 200 total combat patrols.

His decorations and awards include four Bronze Stars with Combat Vs, two Purple Hearts for wounds in combat, the Meritorious Service Medal, four Navy Commendations Awards, Army Commendation with Combat V, the Navy Achievement Medal, Combat Action Ribbon, two Presidential Unit Citations, two Navy Unit

Commendations, Meritorious Unit Commendation, five Good Conduct Awards, Navy Expeditionary Medal, three Navy Battle E Awards, four Vietnam Service Awards, Sea Service Deployment with three stars, Overseas Service with two stars, Vietnamese Gallantry Cross, Individual Award, RVN Civic Action Unit Citation and RVN Campaign Ribbon.

James remained in the Navy for 24 years retiring as a master chief petty officer in 1988. He completed his BS degree, taught NJROTC for the Chief of Naval Education and Training following his retirement and now works for the Department of Veterans Affairs. He is very active in veterans activities and in addition to being a life member of Gamewardens, he is a life member of both the Disabled American Veterans and the MOPH. He is also a member of the Veterans of Foreign Wars, American Legion, Fleet Reserve Assoc., Vietnam Veterans of America, National Association for the Uniformed Services, Veterans of the Vietnam War and the Battleship New Jersey Historical Society.

KENNETH A. DELFINO (DEL), born July 6, 1945, Chicago, IL. He was inducted in the USN in June 1964. Stationed at NTC San Diego, USS *Seminole* AKA-104, August 1964-June 1966; PBR training June 1966-October 1966; Riv. Div. 533 October 1966-July 1968; christening crew member of PBR 152.

His memorable experience was hitchhiking from Saigon to My Tho armed only with a .38 and K-bar when their convoy left early without a roll call. Also memorable was the USO Christmas 1967 visit to My Tho by Johnny Grant, Diane McBain, Melody Patterson and Sabrina Scharz.

Discharged Jan. 17, 1969 on medical disability; his left leg was amputated due to wounds received. His awards/medals include the Navy Commendation with Combat V, Purple Heart, Armed Forces Expeditionary, Citation from Philippine Civic Action Group, Presidential Unit Citation, Combat Action Ribbon, Vietnam Service, Civic Action, Cross of Gallantry, Vietnam Campaign and "Gedunk" Medal.

A reservations supervisor for United Airlines for 24 years. He joined Kiwanis International in 1987 and served as club president and last year 1992-93 as lieutenant governor of his 15 Club Division. He enjoyed skiing until he ruined his only knee, now he just golfs when he can and enjoys visiting this beautiful country. He has kept in touch with several members of 533 over the years and participated in the Pointman Project run by the New Jersey Agent Orange Commission. He visits NIOTC every once in a while. The guys now wear their beret flash on the wrong side! It was a great 22 month stint, and yes, he would do it again.

THOMAS BALFE DE MOTT JR., born Oct. 31, 1948 in Santa Barbara, CA. He entered the USN despite originally being classified as a 1-Y (permanent medical reject) due to eye problems. Despite this, he fought for entry and entered the Navy on Feb. 19, 1968. After boot camp and Service School training as a Radioman, he transferred to NAVCOMMSTA Guam where he served until 1970.

He volunteered for Vietnam and was sent to COMNAVFORV on Adm. Zumwalt's staff in April 1970. He later transferred to NSA Nha Be working with PBR squadrons involved in RSSZ ops. In July 1971 he was discharged from the USN. Three months later, he re-enlisted again requesting duty in Vietnam. He was assigned to Chief Naval Advisory Group where he was sent to NSU Cho Moi for interdiction and comm. relay operations.

Six months later he was re-assigned to Vietnamese HQ and assigned as a RM advisor to RVN. He completed his tour assisting in the closing of USN communications sites and retrieving communications/crypto equipment throughout the delta prior to the pullout. During this second tour, he was meritoriously advanced to petty officer 2nd class, transferring to NAF Atsugi, Japan in October 1972.

Chief De Mott's later career took him to Midway Island, JUSMAAG Thailand, Guam, Norfolk, VA and back to NAVCAMS WESTPAC Guam where he retired on his 40th birthday, Oct. 31, 1990 after 22 and a half years service. He is currently serving as the data base manager for NCTAMS WESTPAC Guam.

During Chief De Mott's career, he was awarded three Navy Achievement Medals with Combat V, the Vietnam Service Medal with four Bronze Stars, Combat Action Ribbon and numerous other campaign and service awards. Tom and his wife Mamie have two children, Jason and Yoko. In addition to Gamewardens, Chief De Mott is active in VFW Post 1501, American Legion Post 503 and Vietnam Veterans of America plus Fleet Reserve Assoc. He is the Gamewardens area rep. for Guam and the Marianas Islands.

JAN PHILLIP DIAL, born in Brady, TX on Aug. 2, 1947. He enlisted in the USN in August 1966. After training as an aviation electronic technician, he served in VF-111 aboard USS *Oriskany* and USS *Intrepid*. He joined HAL-3 Seawolves in October 1969 and served from December 1969 to July 1970 as doorgunner/ crew chief Seawolf Det-9 stationed aboard YRBM-21 on the Mekong River three miles from Cambodian border.

He separated from the USN August 1970 as ATN-2. He was commissioned 2nd lieutenant USAR April 1977 and served with 313th Mash. Transferred USNR May 1990 and served with Fleet Hospital 9. Completed 20 years service and transferred to IRR as lieutenant commander USNR.

His awards include the Distinguished Flying Cross, Air Medals (2-S/A) (14 F/S), Navy Good Conduct, National Defense (2), Vietnam Service Medal, Presidential Unit Citation, NUC, Vietnam Cross of Gallantry Unit Citation, Vietnam Civil Action Unit Citation, Vietnam Campaign Medal, Armed Forces Reserve Medal, Army Reserve Achievement Medal, Expert Rifle, Expert Pistol and Air Crewman Wings.

Currently employed as OR nurse manager, he married Donna in 1973 and they have one son, Steven.

AULDREG R. DISMUKE JR. (SONNY), born in Oakdale, CA on Jan. 22, 1947. He joined the USN on Sept. 1, 1966 and went to boot camp training in San Diego and then was transferred to the USS *Galveston* CLG-3 where he served two years. He did a tour in the Middle East in 1967 and Vietnam on board the *Galveston*.

Completing school at Mare Island, he was assigned to Riv. Div. 531 in Vietnam as forward gunner on PBR 105. He was 3rd class gunners mate for four months and then field promoted to 2nd class and made a boat captain of PBR 32.

After PBR 32 was sunk by enemy fire, he was assigned to PBR 98 which was heavily damaged at Giant Sling Shot. His next boat was PBR 57 which took a rocket starboard engine. My last and best boat was once again PBR 105.

He received the Bronze Star, two Navy Commendations, Purple Heart all with Combat V, VSM, CAR, VCM and NDSM.

A quality control and training manager for Toyota, he and wife, Carole, have sons: Don, Dean and Brian; daughter, Kristy; and two granddaughters, Bailee and Brooklynn.

JOSEPH J. DIZONA JR., born in Omaha, NE on April 29, 1947. He joined the USN May 5, 1964 and was a radioman/crypto repairman. He attended PO Leadership School and Radio School in San Diego. He went aboard the *Gunston Hall* LSD-5 in March 1966; went to NAVSCOLCOM M.I., Vallejo, CA, April 1966;

then to USNAB Coronado, CA, June 1966; then to survival training. He was transferred to Delta River Patrol Group TF116.1 and TF117 NSA Nha Be/Go Cong, October 1966.

He was discharged Sept. 28, 1968 as RM3. His primary job was operating, repairing and installing communication gear, and teaching others to use it. He received the National Defense Service Medal, Vietnam Service Medal with three Bronze Stars, Republic of Vietnam Campaign Medal and the Good Conduct Medal.

He is a real estate appraiser, married to Arleen since May 28, 1971, and has two sons, Nick and Paul.

PATRICK DOYLE (PAT), born Dec. 15, 1944, Waterbury, CT. He joined the military service in June 1962.

Stations/Locations include: USS *Kearsarge* (CVS-33), NAVSTA Kodiak, AK; NSA DET Nha Be, RVN, USS *Poncono* (LCC-16), Fleet Intelligence Center Atlantic, Assault Craft Unit 2, USS *Sam Houston* (SSBN-609) Naval Security Group Det. Pearl Harbor, USS *Finback* (SSN-670).

Left the service Jan. 1, 1984 as SKC (SS). Awards/ Medals: Navy Achievement with Combat V, Vietnam Campaign, RVN Meritorious Unit Commendation, Vietnam Service (4), Navy Unit Commendation, Meritorious Unit Commendation, Armed Forces Expeditionary, Enlisted Silver Dolphins and SSBN Patrol (4).

He and his wife, Linda Jean, have two daughters, Shannon Marie and Christine Erin.

WILLIAM EVERETT DuBOIS, born July 8, 1933 in Deuel County, NE. He enlisted in the USN in the Spring of 1951 and participated in every conflict since WWII and was a member of the recovery crew for three of the space flights.

CPO DuBois spent 20 years of his lifetime in the USN and passed away May 9, 1971, at the naval hospital in Newport, RI from injuries received in an auto accident on April 19.

At the time of his death he held the following medals: Good Conduct (four stars), Bronze Star, Presidential Unit Citation, Navy Unit Commendation, National Defense, Armed Forces Expeditionary, Navy Forces Expeditionary, Vietnam Service, United Nations, Korean Service, Korean Conflict and Vietnamese Medal of Galantry.

Survivors include his parents, Mr. and Mrs. George DuBois, Cave Junction, OR; sisters: Mrs. Dale Stockham, Mrs. Harold Greenwald, Mrs. Glen Carlock and brothers: Bob and Jim DuBois. Funeral services were held May 15 in Boston, MA with burial in Mt. Hope Cemetery with military honors.

LOUIS C. DUTY SR., born April 3, 1924 in Temple, TX. He joined the military service in January 1942; served on destroyers, APAs, guided missile cruisers, EOD, UDT and Commando units; was deep sea diver, explosives expert, captain of tugs and tankers.

Served in WWII, Korea and Vietnam, was a patrol officer with the River Patrol Force, Task Force 116; PBR River Section 531 from 1967-1969; served three tours in Vietnam. Engaged the "Viet Cong" and NVA units in 42 battles and fire fights. Served as a PBR patrol officer during the TET Offensive, Jan. 31, 1968, at the Ben-Tre Canal incident where we saved the city of Ben-Tre from being overrun by enemy assault forces and destroyed a lot of Viet Cong and NVA units. "Sat Cong"

He was wounded in action five times (three in Vietnam) and awarded 37 medals, commendations and citations during three wars. He was in seven major battles in the Pacific, European and African, and Normandy Campaigns during WWII. Released from the service in August 1974 as senior chief boatswain, USNR.

Past president of FRA, BR 103, Yokosuka, Japan Tokyo Commandry #1, member of Normal Heights Masonic Lodge 632 F&AM, Al Bahr Shrine, Legion of Honor, life member of DAV Chapter #2, MOPH Chapter 49#, VFW, Branch 9512, San Diego, CA, past president and life member of Gamewardens of Vietnam Inc. (West Coast) San Diego, CA.

Now living the easy life with wife, Elizabeth, in San Diego, CA. They have two children, Louis C. Duty Jr. of Temple, TX and Kathy M. Harrison, and grandson, Justin "Boots" Harrison, of Bryan, TX.

DON ENGLISH, born June 14, 1931, in Williamsport, PA. He enlisted in the USN in June 1948 and served aboard the USS *Midway* CVB-41 after boot camp at Great Lakes, IL.

After leaving the Navy in 1953, English rejoined in 1958 going aboard the USS *Gurke* DD-783 out of San Diego, then was transferred to the USS *Gridley* DLG-21 out of Long Beach, then went to shore duty to NAVCOMSTA Greece, then volunteered for PBR  duty in 1968, in country at Nha Be, Vietnam with River Div. 541/591 on Mark I PBRS, medivaced out of country in January 1969, transferred to Philadelphia Naval Hospital, released to full active duty to Naval Training Center, SD for shore duty. Back to sea again aboard the USS *Sterett* DLG-31.

English retired on Feb. 4, 1974. He was awarded the National Defense Service Medal, Vietnam Service Medal with one Bronze Star, RVN Campaign Medal, Combat Action Ribbon, Com. 7th Flt Letter of Commendation, Navy Unit Commendation, Navy Unit Citation and Purple Heart.

He now works as steel sales rep. and lives with his wife, Helen, at San Diego, CA.

NEDWARD CLYDE ESTES JR., joined Riv. Div. 593 only two weeks prior to being mortally wounded by a B-40 rocket when PBR-755, on which he had been assigned as engineer and M-60 gunner, came under heavy attack.

PBR-755 was part of a two boat patrol on the upper Saigon River during Operation Ready Deck/Tran Hung Dao V.

Although with the division only a short time fireman Estes had seen considerable combat and had proven himself to be a solid reliable member of the patrol and the division. He was and is remembered and missed by those who served with him.

RICHARD J. FALCONE SR., born Nov. 13, 1950, Rome, NY. He enlisted in the USN in April 1969. During Engineman "A" School, he volunteered for Vietnam. He served in River Divs. 571 and 573 patrolling the Mekong Delta.

His awards include Navy Commendation Medal with Combat V, Combat Action Ribbon, two Purple Hearts, Expert Rifleman Medal, Pistol Marksmanship, Vietnam Campaign, Vietnam Service Ribbon and the Good Conduct Medal.

After returning to the States, he finished his enlistment aboard the USS *Desoto County* in Little Creek, VA an the USS *Ponce*, at Norfolk Naval Station. He was honorably discharged in April 1973.

Rick married Pamela McCoy in December 1969, five days before leaving for Vietnam. They have two children, Richard Jr. born August 1971 and Kristi born August 1975, and a grandson, Nicholas James, born October 1993.

He is the founder and president of VVA Chapter #708 and a member of the American Legion. Falcone and his daughter, Kristi, are very involved in the POW/MIA issue and spend every Memorial Day in Washington riding in "Rolling Thunder." His hobbies include hunting, gun collecting and Harley's. He works as a frame and unibody technician.

JOHN KIRK FERGUSON, born April 17, 1935, in Great Falls, MT. He joined the Naval Reserve in 1953 and received his baccalaureate degree from the University of California, Riverside, California in June 1957. He was commissioned an ensign at OCS, Newport, RI, Nov. 1, 1957.

After duties as the operations officer, USS *Tingey* (DD-539) and XO USS *Diachenko* (APD-123) and USS *Eaton* (DD-510). Ferguson was ordered to Commander, Strike Assault Boat Sqdn. 20 (STABRON 20), the fastest boats on the Mekong Delta; these 20 boats and their crews, though capable of so much more, performed

admirably during their year in country (1969-1970).

He served as commanding officer, USS *Flint* (AE-32), enjoying two deployments to WESTPAC and participated in Operation Frequent Wind, the evacuation of Saigon through the port of Vung Tau. After retiring a commander, USN, on May 31, 1981, he joined the Standard Missile organization at General Dynamics, Pomona Div., retired a design engineer in May 1990 and is now enjoying the good life in Southern California.

JOSEPH LLOYD FINDLEY, born Nov. 7, 1947, Andalusia, AL. He enlisted in the military service Jan. 23, 1968, Brown Water Navy, LST-838 E-3 M.R. Stationed at Charleston, SC; Corpus Christi, TX; Galveston, TX; Phnom Phen; and Cambodia.

Participated in battles from mouth of Baasac River to Cambodia border, all of Mekong River from Delta to Phnom Phen, Cambodia Invasion (1970) and coastal patrol Cau Mia Peninsula to Ha Tinh. A memorable experience was carrying SEAL team eight miles up Mekong River, went deeper into Cambodia than anyone else.

Discharged from the service Oct. 24, 1970 as E-3 M.R. He was a union pipe fitter for 16 years; retired at age 40, 100% PTSD. He owns a house in the country with seven acres where he lives with his 4th wife. His hobby is riding a 1991 orange and white Harley. Findley has two teenage sons.

RALPH DONALD FLORES, born in Los Angeles, CA on June 21, 1942. He enlisted Aug. 26, 1960 and reported to NTC San Diego, CA for boot camp. Since that day, he has served faithfully aboard seven ships and eight shore stations concluding with four and a half years FLETRAGRU WESTPAC, Yokosuka, Japan. In 1968 he reported to PBR Mobil Base II at Tan Chan and later at Tan An, RVN. Reported to CHNAVADVGRU-MACV for his second tour from March 1970-71 and served as a patrol officer advisor for RPG-52.

Among his personal decorations are Navy and Marine Medals for heroism, Bronze Star with Combat V, two Purple Hearts, Combat Action Ribbon, Combat Small Craft Insignia, Presidential Unit Citation, Navy Unit Commendation, Meritorious Unit Commendation, Pistol

Expert Medal, National Defense Medal, Philippine Presidential Unit Citation, RVN Armed Forces Meritorious Unit Commendation (Gallantry Cross), RVN Meritorious Unit Citation (civil actions col. with Palm), Vietnam Service Medal with Silver Star, Vietnam Campaign Medal, Battle E, Sea Service Deployment Ribbon and six Good Conduct Awards.

After his retirement in December 1986, he is still serving the Navy by working at Puget Sound Naval Shipyard, Bremerton, WA where he enjoys his exotic birds and his Harley-Davidson Motorcycle (he says he deserves it).

THOMAS G. FORREST, born on March 22, 1946, Philadelphia, PA. He joined the USN on Sept. 28, 1964; served onboard the USS *Ernest G. Small* (DDR-838) from 1965-67 as radarman.

Memorable Experience: In May of 1968, on a routine patrol with another PCF, they were running the coast line down in the Cau Mau and spotted a sanpan making a run into the Bode River. They went in after him, not knowing that it was an ambush. Once inside the mouth, they didn't see the sanpan, so started up river checking the banks. They were in about a mile when they started to see the bunkers. The next thing was the RPGs coming out. They got a direct hit on the lead boat in the gun tub. They came in behind with guns blazing to get out of the ambush. Once the smoke cleared, they had three wounded who needed to be medivaced. There was a LST sitting out about five miles, so ran them out there. On their boat, they had morphine and Forrest went over to the other boat to administer it to the gunners mate, James Akers, who was from Ohio. All the man wanted was a drink of water. His left shoulder was blown apart, shrapnel down both legs and a 50 cal. slug in the back from the ammo that blew after the RPG hit. The other guys weren't so bad off. One had shrapnel wounds and the other had an AK-47 wound. They were medivaced to the field hospital at Can Tho. When they arrived by chopper and had landed, the VC mortared the base and the one of the guys was hit again. He did come back to Cat Lo before he left, but Forrest never did see the other two again; although, he suspected that Jim would not make it.

Years later, when the Vietnam Veterans Memorial was dedicated in Washington, Forrest was in attendance with his best friend and future wife. He looked, but never found Jim's name. In the year that followed, Forrest was on the job installing transformers. They had riggers putting up I-Beams about 15 feet off the floor. One shifted and a man came down and received a severe compound fracture of the right arm. They took him to a hospital where they put his arm back together. The next day it turned black because of a pinched artery. He came very close

to losing his arm and was out of work for a total of eight months. While he was out, another electrician that Forrest worked with asked him if he knew him and Forrest said no that he had just met him on the job when he was hurt. He told Forrest that he was in the Navy in Vietnam and on the boats. After the man finally got back to work, Forrest went over to talk to him, and it turned out he was Jimmy Akers. He had been medivaced to Philadelphia Naval Hospital and was there for two years where he met his wife, and they married and settled down in Philadelphia.

To end my story, he moved two years ago and now lives down the street from me. Just think of it, 12 guys at 12,000 miles from home, ambushed in the Bode River in the Cau Mau and one of them living around the corner from me.

Forrest is member of Bristol Memorial Chapter United Vietnam Veterans Organization; VFW; was a founder of Vietnam Vets Assistance Fund UVVO in 1980 and elected as assistant regional vice commander and national second junior vice commander (UVVO was eventually dissolved); was founding member Delaware Valley Vietnam Veterans; invited guest to the internment of the Vietnam Unknown Soldier; Member of the board of directors for the construction of the Bucks County Vietnam Veterans Memorial; assisted in raising thousands of dollars for the Philadelphia Vietnam Veterans Memorial; life member, Gamewardens; member, American Legion; established a Vietnam Veterans Honor Guard at company post; and member of the Mobil Riverine Force Association.

His decorations include the National Defense, Vietnam Campaign with 60 Device, Vietnam Civic Action, Vietnam Presidential Citation, Vietnam Service Medal with seven Battle Stars, Navy Meritorious Unit Commendation, two Navy Unit Commendations, Vietnam Unit Gallantry Citation, Vietnam Cross of Gallantry, U.S. Presidential Unit Citation (2), Combat Action and Navy Commendation Medal (Valor). Discharged March 19, 1969 as RD2. Forrest is married, no children.

In memory of Gerald Pochel, KIA Sept. 4, 1968; John McDermott, KIA Sept. 7, 1968; Steve Luke, KIA Dec. 6, 1968 and Danny Boy, KIA Dec. 18, 1968. "It is up to us survivors to ensure that the memories of our brothers who gave it all they had are never forgotten."

RENAL FOUST, born Sept. 9, 1937, Hughes, AR. He joined the USN on Nov. 15, 1955 and served onboard the USS *Harnett*, Ham Luong, Vam Co Dong, Bassac River and Co Chien River.

His memorable experience was going home. Released from duty June 5, 1974 as operations specialist. His awards include the China Service, Navy Commendation, Armed Forces Expedi-

tionary, Good Conduct with five stars, Vietnam Service Medal with five stars, Cross of Gallantry, two Presidential Unit Citations, two National Defense and others.

Foust is medical retired and lives in Gautier, MS with his wife, Jeannett. They have a son, Robert, and two daughters, Harriet Foust Imaino and Jo Ann Foust Canfield.

EDWARD GARY FREDA, born March 16, 1934, Fitchburg, MA. He enlisted September 1951 in the USN and was stationed in Newport, RI and Norfolk, VA. He served one year on USS *Davis* in Vietnam and 18 months PBR Sq. TF-116, stationed at Binh Thuy and participated in the 1968 TET Offensive.

Released from duty in April 1972 as BM1. His medals and awards include the Combat Action Ribbon, National Defense Medal, RVN Campaign, Purple Heart, Navy Good Conduct Medal and Vietnam Service Medal.

Retired, he lives in Fitchburg, MA with his wife, Betty A. Rozgonyi, who he married on April Fool's Day 1967.

BASIL J. FRI, born Nov. 16, 1928, Lacygne, KS. He enlisted Sept. 26, 1947 in the USN. Served in AO-52, DE-419, AF-10, NAS Key West, FL, LST-1177, PA-36, AKN-260, AF-10, Riv. Sect. 523, NIOTC, AO-147, Korea 1951-54, Lebanon 1958, Cuba 1962, Vietnam 1966-67 and Suez 1970.

His memorable experiences include Vietnam on PBR, 1966-67 and being an instructor on PBRs 1967-70.

Released from duty March 1, 1972 as BMC (E-7). His awards and medals include the Korean Service Medal with seven stars, Good Conduct Medal with four stars, Meritorious Commendation with two stars, Navy Occupation with two stars, UN, Navy Unit Commendation, China Service with two stars, National Defense, Vietnam Service with two stars, Vietnamese Cross of Gallantry, Presidential Unit Citation and others.

He and his wife, Doris, have two daughters, Debby and Lisa, and son, Dan, in the USAF.

LEONARD G. FRIEDEL, born March 9, 1945, New York. He was commissioned in June 1967, USN; served in USS *Harnett County* (LST-821) 1967-68; NILO Soc Trang, 1969-70; Operation Sea Lords clearance of Cu Lao Dung Island in lower Bassac River. His memorable experience was supporting Seal team one and TF-116 operations in the lower Bassac River.

Discharged in June 1971 as lieutenant. He received the Bronze Star with V, Purple Heart, Air Medal, Silver Lifesaving Medal, Navy Commendation Medal, Vietnamese Staff Honor Medal, and Combat Action Ribbon.

Friedel is married with two children. He is Venture capital fund manager.

DAN T. FULLER, born in Toledo, OH on Dec. 13, 1948. He joined the USN on Oct. 9, 1968 and after boot camp, was assigned to Honor Guard duty on the USS *Constitution (Old Ironsides)* which was one of the first USN ships to visit Vietnam in May 1845 at Hue. In December of 1969 he volunteered for boat duty in Vietnam and was sent to Counterinsurgency School, arriving in Vietnam in March 1970.

After one week in country, he was assigned to ATSB Tuyen Nhon upper Delta about one mile south of Parrots Beak on the Cambodian border. About three days after arriving, two Army Mike 8 boats hauling 59 tons of small arms ammunition tied up for the night about 20 yards from my hooch on the Grand Canal. At 01:15 there was a large explosion on the stern of the Mike 8s sinking them, but not setting off the cargo. The next thing he knew the guy in the bunk next to him was throwing a flak jacket at him and said "welcome to Vietnam."

Discharged July 14, 1972 as gunners mate E-3. His awards include the National Defense, Vietnam Service, Vietnamese Campaign and Combat Action.

Fuller is a locomotive engineer. He married Patty Ross on Aug. 17, 1973; they have two children, Benjamin and Patrick.

NEIL A. FULTON, born Sept. 13, 1938, Luther, MI. He joined the USN on June 21, 1956; spent one year at Great Lakes; four months in USS *Hampdon* (LST-803); seven and a half years on the USS *Okanogan* (APA-220) where he went from seaman to BM2; four years on recruiting duty in Detroit where he advanced to BM1.

He was proud to serve in Riv. Div. 531 and had a total of four tours in country spanning 10 years (1959, 1963, 1964 and 1969-70 with 531). While on patrol March 20, 1970, "Charlie" set off one of their 750# bombs under the boat as they went up river.

Received medical discharge in March of 1971. His awards include the National Defense, Good Conduct (third with Gold Hash Marks), Rifle Marksman, Vietnam Service with three stars, Vietnam Cross of Gallantry, RVN Campaign, Bronze Star with Combat V and Purple Heart.

Married Eileen in May of 1991. Between them they have seven adult children: Kris, LaVendee, Matthew, Corey, James Templin III, Paul Templin and Anita Templin; and four grand-daughters.

GALE E. FURTHMILLER, born Aug. 6, 1947, Warsaw, IN. He entered the USN in September 1965. Following 15 months aboard USS

Pyro (AE-24), he attended Vietnamese language survival evasion and operation (PBR) training in California, and extended survival training in P.I.

He arrived in Vietnam on April 6, 1968, assigned to River Division 543 Nha Be with a follow-on assignment to Cua Viet. One night while on patrol, his boat was struck by a RPG, knocking out both engines, and received an array of small arms fire, amazingly no one was injured.

His awards include the Navy Commendation Medal with Combat V, two Navy Achievement medals, two National Defense Medals, RVN Campaign and the aviation and surface warfare specialist and small craft insignias.

Presently on active duty following broken service from 1969 to 1978. He married Shirley Saucier and they have two daughters, Kari Ann and Karen, two boys, Matthew and Jay.

GODFREY GARNER, born March 10, 1947, in Columbus, MS. He entered the USN GMG in August 1964. His duty stations included Great Lakes; Adak, AK; USS *Firedrake*; and in August 1967, Sa Dec, Vietnam, as a gunner's mate 3rd class, assigned to Riv. Div. 513, PBR Sec.

He will never forget his experiences in Vietnam. He was never wounded or seriously hurt, although he saw several of his shipmates killed in action. He often wonders if his thoughts and memories would be the same had he been unfortunate enough to have been one of those who returned to a life in a wheelchair or some other confinement.

He received the National Defense Service Medal, Vietnam Service Medal and Vietnam Campaign Medal. He was discharged in September 1968 as an E-4.

After his tour in Vietnam, he returned to his home in Jackson, MS. He has been a police officer, teacher, counselor and, now, director of the Criminal Justice Program at a College in Mississippi. He is also working on a Ph.D. in counseling and is counseling Vietnam veterans through his studies at Mississippi State University. In working with these veterans, he is constantly reminded of how many of them have not yet returned home. He often wonders if their experiences in that far away land somehow confused them to the point that they couldn't recognize "home" even if they could return.

Garner and his wife Vickie have a two sons, Tony and Glenn, and a daughter, Temple.

THOMAS V. GARRISON, born Sept. 22, 1945, in Jerseyville, IL. He entered the USN on Sept. 23, 1964. Duty stations/assignments: RTC USNTC San Diego, CA; USS *Furse* DD-882; SSC USNTC Great Lakes, IL; USNS Subic Bay; COMRIVRON 5, Riv. Div. 533; USNS Subic Bay; NAVSTA Annapolis, MD; PHiBCB 2 Little Creek, VA; USS *Pensacola* LSD-38; NAVSTA Norfolk, VA; USS *Hoist* ARS-40; NAVSEC Grp. ACT Northwest Ches, VA. He participated in the 1968 TET.

Awards include the National Defense Service Medal, Vietnam Campaign Medal, Vietnam Service Medal with Bronze Star, Combat Action Ribbon, Expert .45 Caliber Pistol, Navy Achievement Medal, Navy Expeditionary Medal, Sharp Shooter Navy Rifle, Sea Service Deployment Ribbon, Third Expert .38 Caliber Pistol, Battle Efficiency Award, fourth Good Conduct Award and RVN Meritorious Unit Citation. He was discharged April 30, 1986, as an EN-1.

Garrison is married and has three children and three grandchildren. He is working for PWC Norfolk, VA, Little Creek site.

ROBERT DOUGLAS GEDDES (DOUG), born in Wichita, KS, on Aug. 3, 1947, and entered the Navy in September 1965. After completing PBR training, he was assigned to the "Delta Dragons," Riv. Sec. 531, My Tho, Vietnam, from May 1967 to May 1968. He was involved in combat operations conducted from My Tho and off the USS *Harnett County* (LST-821).

He separated from the Navy in 1968 but returned to active duty and was commissioned in the Air Force in 1975. His Air Force career included: missile operations in the U.S. and Europe; working nuclear security and survivability issues for NATO; and developing contingency plans and counter-intelligence operations at the major command level.

Lt. Col. Geddes retired from the Air Force in 1994 and entered the School of Theology, University of the South, Sewanee, TN, to complete studies required for ordination as a priest in the Episcopal Church.

His military decorations include the Defense Meritorious Service Medal, Meritorious Service Medal with three OLCs, Air Force Commendation Medal, Combat Readiness Medal, Combat Action, Navy Presidential Unit, Air

Force Outstanding Unit, Air Force Organizational Excellence, Navy Unit Commendation, National Defense Medal, Vietnam Service Medal, Air Force Overseas Short and Long Tour, Air Force Longevity, Small Arms Expert, Air Force Training, RVN Civil Action Unit, RVN Gallantry Cross, RVN Campaign Medal.

He married Karen in 1969; they have a son, Scott, who was born in 1972.

GENE GLASCO, born in Los Angeles, CA, on Feb. 10, 1948, and joined the USN on May 1, 1967. He underwent counter-insurgency training and Vietnamese Language Instruction School at the Naval Amphibious Base in Coronado, and combat weapons training at USMC Camp Pendleton, CA, before arriving in South Vietnam, April 19, 1969. He was first attached to naval support activity, Saigon, as a radioman in the communications center at Nha Be, located 15 miles southeast of Saigon near the Rung Sat Special Zone.

Having expressed his desire for a more active roll in fighting the communist infiltration of the Mekong Delta, Glasco was reassigned in November 1969 to a distant and primitive Advanced Tactical Support Base with River Div. 532, 150 miles west of Saigon just inside the Vietnam/Cambodian border town of Ha Tien. While there, Glasco qualified as a Navy Operation Center watch stander and helped direct Seawolf helicopter cover attacks in support of his river divison's nightly patrol and ambush activities. When not calling in air strikes, Glasco often times accompanied regular PBR crew members on ambush/river patrols.

His decorations include the National Defense Service Medal, Navy Expert Rifleman, Republic of Vietnam Campaign Medal, Vietnamese Cross of Gallantry and the Vietnam Service Medal with one Bronze Star.

Today, he is a food broker for Glasco and Associates in Southern California representing national and regional food manufacturers.

RICHARD G. GODBEHERE (DICK), born Aug. 24, 1935, in Globe, AZ. He enlisted in October 1952 and served in the USS *Zelima* (AF-49) 1953-54; USS *Paricutin* (AE-18) 1954-56; commissioned (OCS) Nov. 22, 1963. He served in the following commands: USS *Conquest* (MSO-488) 1964-66; Defense Intelligence School 1966-67; River Patrol Force (TF-116, Riv. Sec. 511, Binh Thuy) 1967-68; U.S. Naval Destroyer School 1968-69; USS *Cone* (DD-866) 1969-71; COMNAVLOGPAC 1971-73; CRUSDESFORPACREP SUBIC 1973; COMUSFKOREA 1973-74; CINCPACFLT 1975-76; operations and coordinator Hawaiian area 1976-79.

He served aboard ship in the following areas: Pacific, China Sea, Sea of Japan, Gulf of Tonkin, Atlantic, Caribbean, Adriatic and Mediterranean. The highlight of his career was the privilege and honor to have served with the men of the USN River Patrol Force in Vietnam. Their courage and audacity while engaged with the enemy in close combat affirms the fighting spirit of the American Bluejacket. Their calling can be looked upon with great pride in the annals of USN history.

Godbehere was awarded 22 decorations, including two Bronze Star Medals with Combat V, Navy Commendation Medal with Combat V, Joint Service Commendation Medal, two Purple Heart Medals, Presidential Unit Citation and Combat Action Ribbon. He retired as a lieutenant commander at Pearl Harbor, Nov. 30, 1979.

He served as Veterans Advisory Committee chairman for Senator John McCain's first congressional campaign. Godbehere was elected sheriff of Maricopa County, Phoenix, AZ, 1985-88. Currently, he is a general building contractor and commercial fishing boat owner. He is a 32° Mason.

ROBERT LOUIS GRAETER, born Dec. 25, 1948, in Enosburg Falls, VT. He joined the USN on June 25, 1966; graduated from Radioman "A" School, Bainbridge, MD; assigned to USS *Spiegal Grove* (LSD-32), Little Creek, VA. Reported to USS *Harnett County* (LST-832), Aug. 10, 1968, via NAVSUPPACT Saigon, Binh Thuy PBR Base, Bassac Dong River. On Dec. 12, 1968, LST-821 reported for duty to Vam Co Dong River, Ben Luc, Operation Giant Slingshot.

Graeter was awarded the Presidential Unit Citation, Combat Action Ribbon, Navy Unit Commendation Ribbon and Vietnam Service and Campaign Ribbons. He was discharged as RM-3 from Treasure Island, San Francisco, July 30, 1969.

He served five years with the USCGR and 10 years with the VTARNG. He worked 14 years for the telephone company, nine years with U.S. Immigration and Customs Service and was declared disabled in June 1993 from effects of Agent Orange. He ia a member of: VFW, American Legion and Vietnam Veterans. His and his wife Patricia reside in Enosburg Falls, VT.

GARY ROBERT GRAHN, born Sept. 22, 1948, in Bridgeport, CT. He joined the USN in March 1967 and reported to the Mobile Riverine Forces on Assault Support Patrol Boat 111-7 in April 1968. The boat was transferred to the RVN navy in April 1969. Other commands include USS *Whipple* (FF-1062) and USS *Dwight D. Eisenhower* (CVN-69). He retired in 1989, after 22 years of active duty, as a chief warrant officer.

His decorations include the Navy Commendation Medal, Navy Achievement with Combat V, Combat Action Medal, Presidential Unit Citation, Navy Unit Commendation, Navy Expeditionary, Vietnam Service and Campaign Medals, and Rifle and Pistol Expert.

Since retiring, he has earned a bachelor of arts degree in business administration (technology management) and is a telecommunications analyst with C-Cubed Corporation. He resides in Chesapeake, VA, with his wife, Michele, and step-son, David. Two daughters, Tracy and Lori, reside in Illinois and two sons, Gary Jr. and Jason, reside in Washington.

LORENZO GRANADOS (LARRY), born in El Paso, TX, Nov. 14, 1939. He entered the the USN, GMG in November 1947 and served in the Mekong Delta. His memories are painful; his most memorable experience was coming home after being in "hell." He took a medical retirement Dec. 7, 1976, with the rank of petty officer.

Granados is single and works in agriculture management.

GREGORY C. GREEN, born March 3, 1949, in Chicago, IL. He enlisted in October 1967, and as an SM-3, attended CI/SERE and weapons training in Coronado and Camp Pendleton, and Small Boat School in Long Beach, CA. On his second tour (1969-70) with Inshore Undersea Warfare Group One (IUWG-1), supporting Market Time and Gamewardens, he was involved in "Operation Coconut Grove."

As a six-man recon/ambush team member, he spent three memorable days and nights, two clicks inside the tree line with 164 tribal Montagnard Mercenaries. Not many have captured, boiled and eaten a six-foot giant lizard or listened to a 12-year-old mercenary describe how he acquired his collection of ears. Like his fellow river rats, Green has enough memories to last two lifetimes.

His awards include the Vietnamese Gallantry Cross, Civil Action, Combat Action, Navy

Unit Citation and Navy Achievement Medal with three stars. He was recalled during Desert Storm and retired July 10, 1993, from the Navy Reserve, after 25 years.

Green served seven years as treasurer of the California Vietnam Veterans Memorial Commission. The Memorial is the second most visited venue in Sacramento. He is employed by TRW Incorporated and resides in Diamond Bar, CA, with his wife, Sharon; children, Greg and Kimberly; and their dog, Major, a German shepherd.

JAMES B. GUTHRIE JR. (JIM), born in Somerset, KY, July 5, 1947. He joined the USN on his birthday, July 5, 1967, and went through NIOTC in California, Vietnamese Language School in Coronado and SERE training in Washington.

He arrived in Vietnam Feb. 1, 1969, and was attached to Riv. Div. 533. Served as gunner's mate on PBR-147; made 138 combat patrols; and survived seven firefights in six months. His last firefight was Aug. 1, 1969, when his fellow gunner's mate, GMG3 John D. Muir, was killed in action.

Guthrie became an adviser, teaching English at the Small Boat School in Saigon. On October 10, he helped turn over 40 PBRs to the Vietnamese navy and received a Certificate of Thanks from the VN navy.

As for his records, like so many other Vietnam combat veterans, they don't reflect the horror of war. His DD-214 only shows the standard awards everyone received. He states, however, that he is a USN Vietnam veteran and a proud American.

Guthrie had to have his left heel amputated as the result of an injury received while on a PBR patrol in the not so friendly rivers of Vietnam. After learning to walk again, he went to school and became an engineering draftsman. While going to school, he met and married Georgia Steele of Bowling Green, KY, Dec. 29, 1973. His very understanding wife is the owner of VV-WAR (Vietnam Veterans Wife and Relatives), a mail order business.

DON I. GUY, born Nov. 21, 1935, in Monahans, TX. He entered military service June 2, 1954, serving in the USN. Military stations included NAS New Orleans, VX-6 Deep Freeze, USS *Hornet* (CVA-12), USS *Rancer* (CVA-61), NAAS El-Cen, MD, USS *Iwo Jima* (LDH-2), FASDAN-118, Okinawa/Formosa. He served in Riv. Div. 592, October 1968-October 1969; Nha-Be and Go Dau Ha (Giant Slingshot), as boat captain and patrol officer.

Memorable Experiences: In 1991 he attended the West Coast Chapters reunion in San Diego (his first) and ran into a few old "Rats" from the past. They had the moveable "wall" at

NTC where a memorial service and picnic were held.

His awards include Bronze Star with Combat V, Combat Action Ribbon, Navy Achievement Medal, National Defense Medal, Navy Unit Commendation (2nd awd), Combat Action Ribbon, Vietnam Campaign Medal, Vietnam Service Medal, Antarctica Service Small Craft Insignia and Good Conduct Medal (fifth).

He an his wife, Sandra, have three children and three grandchildren. He is in real estate and enjoys fishing and hunting.

JOEL B. HAGAN, born June 27, 1941, in Brewster, FL, Polk County. He joined the USN July 11, 1958; served aboard USS *Lookout* (AGR-2), USS *Skywatcher* (AGR-3), USS *Mills* (DER-383) prior to Vietnam. In Vietnam he served in Riv. Div. 534 and VN River Patrol Group 53, My Tho; USS *Hunterdon* CTY, Ben Luc, Tra Cu, Go Da Hau, Ben Keo.

He received the Bronze Star and Navy Marine Corps Medal while in country. After Vietnam he served at Orlando RTC, USS *Roosevelt* (CV-42), COMSECFLT staff, detailer to quartermaster community and back to Orlando to retire on June 30, 1981.

Since the Navy, he has lived with his wife in Florida, presently in Lake Worth. They have eight children and 13 grandchildren. He works as an inspector for Grinnell Fire Protection.

JESSE F. HARTLEY JR., born July 1, 1947, in Houston, TX. He entered the USN Nov. 21, 1968, and served at GMA, Great Lakes, IL; Vietnam 1969; USS *Thomaston* (LSD-28). He was a gunner's mate on a PBR with Riv. Div. 554, USN Support, Binh Thuy, RVN, from October 1969 to July 1970.

His mmemorable experiences include the all night patrols, firefights, rain, mosquitoes, heat, his boat crew, the equipment they left

during the turn-over and his buddy, Jay Swayser.

Awards/Decorations: National Defense Service Medal, Vietnam Service Medal with four Bronze Stars, Vietnam Campaign Medal with 60 Device, Navy Commendation Medal, Expert Pistol and Expert Rifleman.

Hartley is a single parent with two daughters and one son. He is regional sales manager for Crane Company, Chem Pump Division.

BRUCE HARTT, born Feb. 12, 1950, in Boston, MA. He entered military service Oct. 12, 1968, at Beverly, MA, and served as a USN radarman, naval advisory group. Military locations/stations: RVN 1969-70; MSO 421 1970-72; NAS Gitmo 1972-74; instructor, USNA 1974-77.

Memorable Experiences: SERE School, Little Creek, October 1969; PHYOPS from HELO and water-borne guard post in the Rung Sat Special Zone, March 1970; the Iron Butterfly; sensor implants outside of Rach-Gia, August 1970.

His awards include the Navy Achievement Medal with Combat V, Presidential Unit Citation, Combat Action Medal, Good Conduct Medal and service medals. He left military service as an E-6, first class operations specialist, on June 12, 1980.

His wife, Susan MacDonald Hartt, is a registered nurse; his son, Bruce, is a pilot; daughter, Vickie, National Honor Society. Hartt is with Combat Systems Engineering for Navy AEGIS Program in D.C.

RAYMOND E. HAYWOOD enlisted in St. Louis, MO, Feb. 6, 1959; re-enlisted six years for PBR duty. Assigned duties as the boat captain of MK-1 PBR #55 in Riv. Div. 572 on the Grand Canal, April 1, 1969. Moved in July to My Tho to patrol the Cho Gao Canal; spent September in Binh Thuy overhauling the boats; and started Operation Breezy Cove on the Song Ong Doc in October.

Awarded the Bronze Star with V, two Purple Hearts, Combat Action Ribbon and the usual Vietnam and U.S. medals. He retired from Keyport, WA on Feb. 28, 1986, as a master chief torpedo man.

Haywood married the former Juanita Amelia Garcia, from Denver, in Orlando in 1970. They have two sons, Kenneth (born April 1971) and Jonathon (born February 1973). They reside in Poulsbo, WA. He is interested in any blood disorders diagnosed soon after return to CONUS and VA response.

EVERETTE P. HEBERT (YOGIE), born Sept. 13, 1946, in Houma, LA. He enlisted in the USN April 24, 1964; attended boot camp at San Diego, CA; En. A School, Class 9-65, Great Lakes, IL, August to November 1964. Served in USS *William R. Rush* (DD-714) EN FA to EN 3, December 1964 to June 1966. Arrived in Vallejo CA, June 30, 1966, PBR Det., Mare Island; August 1966, SERE training and Vietnamese Language School, Coronado, CA; September 1966 JEST training, Cubi Point, Philippines.

Arrived in Saigon, South Vietnam, TF 116

Riveron 5, Operation Gamewarden, September 1966. Helped organize PBR Sect. 532 in Cat Lo. When 532 moved to My Tho, he stayed in Cat Lo to start PBR Section 533. Section 533 moved to Nha Be in November 1966. They patrolled the Long Tau and Soirap Rivers. In April 1967, moved with Section 533 to LST on the Co Chin River. He lost a friend, Wilber Cosson, RD-1 patrol officer, to a VC sniper's bullet.

In September 1967, he returned to the States to Treasure Island NAVSTA, CA. Separated from service Sept. 12, 1967.

Hebert married Evelyn in 1968 and they have two boys, Everette Jr. and Andrew, and three grandchildren.

RAYMOND F. HELBLING JR., born Oct. 24, 1936, in Pittsburgh, PA. He entered the USN in January 1956; served as chief engineman, Riv. Sections 531, 533, 552 and RPG 59. He served in USS *Cascade* (AD-16), USS *Becuna* (SS-319), AFDB 7, *Thomas Jones Gary* (DER-326), USS *Detroit* (AOE-4), NRD Pittsburgh, PA. Helbling served three tours in Vietnam from April 1966 to February 1971.

He received the Navy Commendation Medal with V, Navy Achievement Medal with V, Purple Heart, Combat Action Ribbon, National Defense Service Ribbon, Armed Forces Expeditionary Medal, Vietnam Service Medal and RVN Campaign Medal. He was discharged in September 1976.

Married to Virginia (Kessler) Helbling USNR Ret., and they live in Triadelphia, WV. He owns and operates a ceramic studio.

FRANK D. HENNING, born Aug. 14, 1943, in North Platte, NE. He served in the USA, Jan. 16, 1961 to Dec. 31, 1963, serving in Germany; and served in the USN, Feb. 3, 1966, to Nov. 30, 1969, Navy Sup. Act Det., Chu Lau, Vietnam, Riv. Div. 531 and 512.

Henning spent 34 months on the ground in Vietnam and participated in a lot of fire fights. He found four large weapons caches Dec. 13, 1968; May 27, 1969; May 29, 1969; and May 31, 1969. He had one successful ambush on the VC, shot up several sanpans and captured the weapons, June 14, 1969.

He was awarded the Bronze Star with V, Navy Commendation with V, two Purple Hearts, Combat Action Medal, National Defense Ser-

vice Medal, Vietnam Service Medal, Vietnam Gallantry Cross with Palm, Vietnam Service Medal, Expert Rifle, Expert Pistol and Small Boat Device. He was a BM-2 when he took disability retirement Nov. 30, 1969.

He married Terry in 1985 and they have one son, Frank. He is a coal mine superintendent in Grass Creek, WY.

RICHARD LEE HICKS, born June 11, 1932, in Little Falls, WI. He entered the USN in March 1952; graduated from Machinery Repairman School; was promoted to ensign; and assigned as the maintenance, weapons and logistics officer in RPB Div. 514 of River Patrol Boat Flotilla-5 operating from YRBM-16 in Chau Duc-Vinch Canal, 4th Corps, Mekong River.

In January 1970, he was reassigned to staff HQ, Binh Thuy, as maintenance and logistics officer. He was the chief engineer officer and plankowner on the USS *Mt. Whitney* (LCC-20). He was promoted to lieutenant commander, assigned to the USN Safety Center, Norfolk, VA, until his 1974 retirement.

His awards include the Meritorious Service Medal, Navy Commendation Medal with Combat V, Navy Achievement Medal, Combat Action Medal, National Defense Service Medal, Navy Good Conduct Medal, Vietnam Service Medal, Vietnam Gallantry Cross, RVN Campaign Medal, Vietnam Training Medal, First Class, the Surface Warfare Device and Small Boat Device Emblem.

Hicks married Gloria in 1953, and they have two daughters, Cheryl Lee and Leann Patricia, and a son, Richard Lee Jr.

ALAN R. HILL (AL), born in Milwaukee, WI, Jan. 15, 1947. He enlisted in the USN on June 18, 1965, and retired as chief petty officer on March 31, 1985. His PBR training began at Vallejo, CA, and continued with SERE School in 1966. Hill served in Riveron 5, Sec. 531 as the after machine gunner on PBR 103 on combat patrol on the Mekong and Ham Luong Rivers, from August 1966 to August 1967. PBR 103 completed 175 combat patrols on the Mekong, 17 under hostile fire.

He received the National Defense Service Medal, Vietnam Service Medal with Combat Insignia, Vietnam Campaign Medal, Combat Action Ribbon, Presidential Unit Citation, two

Navy Unit Commendations, Navy Expeditionary Medal, Sea Service Deploy Ribbon and others. He was recommended for the Purple Heart but it was never awarded.

He married Linda in 1971. Hill was diagnosed with an inoperable brain tumor in December 1989, shortly after his 43rd birthday, and died on Feb. 3, 1990. He had been employed at the Charleston Naval Weapons Station and was active with the local chapter of Boy Scouts of America.

His widow resides in North Charleston, SC. Their son, Victor Alan, attends Winthrop University where he majors in English and hopes to eventually earn a Ph.D.

CLARENCE E. HOAGLAND, born Oct. 19, 1938, in Dayton, OH. He entered military service May 29, 1956, and served in the USN, QM1-0161 and 911.

Awards/Decorations: Bronze Star with Combat V, two Purple Hearts, four Navy Commendations with Combat V, two Navy Achievements with Combat V, Presidential Unit Citation, Vietnam Campaign Medal, Vietnam Service Medal with 14 stars, Combat Action Ribbon, Vietnamese Cross of Gallantry, Vietnamese Technical Service Medal, one Unit Award, Navy Expeditionary Medal, National Defense Service Medal, five Good Conduct Medals, Small Boat Device Emblem and Craft Master Insignia. He was discharged Aug. 28, 1975.

Hoagland and his wife, Mary, have one daughter, Linette, and a granddaughter, Tara. He is a mechanic at a division of Navistar.

WILLIAM R. HOGAN (JINX), born Jan. 5, 1946, in Newark, NJ. He joined the USN, Aug. 18, 1964, and served in Iceland and Vietnam. As a member of River Squadron 5 operating PBRs, he participated in 250 patrols, 30 of which were under hostile fire, from April 1968 to March 1969.

His awards included the Navy Commendation Medal with Combat V, National Defense Service Medal, Vietnam Service Medal and Vietnam Campaign Combat Action Medal.

William Hogan was an Irvington, NJ, police officer. He passed away April 6, 1994, and is survived by a son, Timmy; sister, Dolores; and three brothers: Tom, Dan and Pat. Tom was in the USNR, Dan was in the USN and served on the USS *Guam*, and Pat was in the USA and served in An Khe, Vietnam, 4th Bn., 60th Arty. (Dusters) from 1968-69.

JULIUS HORNYAK, born Dec. 15, 1940, in Cleveland, OH. He served in the USA, September 1958-June 1961; and in the USN, September 1962-October 1967, GMG2, YFNB-21, YRBM-16. Military stations included New Foundland, USS *Shangri La*, USS *Randolph*.

Memorable experiences are of the fire missions almost every night from the deck of YRBM-16.

His awards include the Army Good Conduct Medal, Expert Infantry Badge, four National Defense Service Medals, Navy Vietnam Service Medal, RVN Campaign Medal and Unit Commendation Medal.

Hornyak and his wife, Judy Morton, have no children. He has been a machine operator for the GM Auto Plant in Parma, OH, for 27 years.

MARSHALL ALAN HUNT (HARLEY), born in Dayton, OH, on June 16, 1947. He joined the USN on Aug. 2, 1966; went through boot camp, Co. 483, BP&E School, and EN/A School at Great Lakes, IL. He was assigned to the USS *Sutter County* (LST-1150) from April 1967 to October 1968. He pulled market time and hauled troops, supplies and vehicles throughout South Vietnam. He was assigned to the USS *Gunston Hall* (LSD-5) from November 1968 to April 1969 and from April 1969 to June 1969. He went through NIOTC in Vallejo, CA, for PBR training; survival, evasion, resistance and escape training in Washington; and Vietnamese Language School in Coronado, CA.

He again served time in Vietnam from June 1969 to June 1970, assigned to PBRs, Riv. Div. 535, TF 1165, RIVPATFLOT 5. He was the engineman on PBR 726 and, later, boat captain of PBR 726 and then boat captain of PBR 729. He made 226 combat patrols and had 120 hostile fire fights. He was instrumental in training over 150 Vietnamese sailors at Binh Thuy at the Vietnamese PBR Training School which began Jan. 19, 1970.

His decorations include the National De-

fense Service Medal, Meritorious Unit Commendation Ribbon, Vietnam Service Medal with one star, Vietnam Campaign Medal with device (1960-), Combat Action Ribbon and Navy Commendation Medal with Combat V. He was discharged July 2, 1970.

He works for Chemineer Inc., Dayton, OH, as a parts' inspector and group leader. He is a life member of VFW Post 4986, a member of American Legion Post 762, Vietnam Veterans of America Chapter 97, Mobile Riverine Force Association, S.E. Region Chapter of Gamewardens of Vietnam, West Coast Chapter of Gamewardens of Vietnam, the U.S. LST Association and the USS Gunston Hall (LSD-5) Association.

He was married in 1976 and divorced in 1986. He has one daughter, Jessica Denae, born Dec. 7, 1976. Hunt resides in New Lebanon, OH.

ROBERT BRIAN HUNT, born Jan. 17, 1946, in Seattle, WA, and entered the USN in January 1963. He graduated from QM A School and served 20 years in the Navy. He served on three destroyers, one destroyer tender and one ammunition-oiler. He graduated from Submarine School and served aboard one of the last diesel boats and Submarine Group, San Francisco. He had a tour in Assault Craft Unit One, the Deep Sea Diving School, the Torpedo Station and Guam.

Highlights of his tour were the USS *Plainview*, the world's largest experimental hydrofoil, and three years of drug suppression while assigned to the U.S. Customs Service on Guam.

Hunt's re-enlistment bonus was to be a gunner on a river boat in Vietnam and his first tour was with River Sec. 533 (February 1967) in the Rung Sat Special Zone and, later, the Co Chien River. Because he had shipped for six years, his XO would not allow him to have a battlefield promotion (Ho Chi Minh) to QM2, but required him to take the exam. Upon advancemen, he was assigned to the newly forming Riv. Sec. 534 in Nha Be and later on the Ham Luong River; 534 was the first of the Mark II river patrol boat sections. The three officers that came to Vietnam with his class suffered one death, one lost hand and one minor wound.

April of 1969 saw Hunt in training with Patrol Craft Fast (swift boats). Arriving in country in August 1969 with three officers in his class, his boat officer was KIA, the second wounded, and the third (Elmo Zumwalt Jr.) died of Agent Orange two decades later. After placing a Vietnamese crewman on report for cowardice in the face of the enemy, QM2 Hunt accidentally shot him and pleaded guilty to a Special Court Martial, where he was reduced-in-rate 10 days before being promoted to QM1. He shipped out of country and finished his career in the Navy.

Awards include the Navy Commendation with Combat V, PUC, MUC, NUC, Combat Action, National Defense, Good conduct Medal, Humanitarian Medal, Vietnam Service Medal, Vietnam Gallantry Medal and Vietnam Campaign Medal with eight stars, Small Boat Device Emblem and Craftmaster Insignia.

Hunt's first daughter died of Agent Orange, although it can not be proven beyond a doubt. Second daughter was born healthy and married in 1971 and was divorced in 1977.

Upon retirement from the Navy, as a QMC, in March 1983, he went to school full time and earned a BS in business administration from Columbia, an MBA in management and an MPA in government. Married Commander Marilyn R. Rose in 1979. Upon her retirement from the Navy in 1992, they moved to a log home in Post Falls, ID. Between 1985 and 1992, he worked as a substitute elementary school teacher (specializing in the learning disabled) in Vallejo, CA; Los Angeles and Waukegan, IL.

JOHN D. HURT, born in Dudley, MO, on Aug. 9, 1947. He joined the USN on June 5, 1965, and went to boot camp in San Diego, CA. He attended Gunner's Mate School in Great Lakes, IL; the Naval Inshore Operations Training Center in California; Vietnamese Language School in Coronado; and survival, evasion, resistance, escape training in California. He arrived in Vietnam on Dec. 2, 1966, being attached to Riv. Sec. 533 as a gunner's mate on a PBR. In the later months of 1967, he was chosen as one of the members to form the new Riv. Sec. 534.

During a month-long leave in Missouri, he married Connie Medley on Jan. 5, 1968, and within the week returned to Vietnam. He arrived back in Vietnam directly into the TET Offensive of January 1968.

He was awarded the Navy Commendation Medal with Combat V for meritorious conduct on April 24, 1968. He was also awarded the National Defense Service Medal, Vietnam Campaign Medal, Vietnam Service Medal and Certificate of Achievement.

On May 28, 1968, he returned to civilian life in Poplar Bluff, MO. On Feb. 10, 1971, daughter Debra Denise was born and in August 1971, he began his employment with Rowe Furniture Corporation in Poplar Bluff. He is presently departmental manger of three departments with that company.

JERRY R. IRVINE, born Sept. 27, 1934, in Seattle, WA. He entered the USN Dec. 7, 1951. Duty stations included eight ships and two stations; SAR captain 1963; AVR 1970, Midway Island; was part of Riv. Sec. 523 and 521. Participated in Korea, Vietnam and in the Cuban Missile Crisis.

Memorable Experience: Being hit by RPG

fire two times in TET '68 (Hue City) and being shot at by 8" shore batteries in Swato, China, 1952.

Awards include the Bronze Star with V, Presidential Citation, Navy Unit Commendation, Gold Star (two), and Cross of Gallantry. BMC Irvine was discharged in 1971.

Irvine is retired. He is partially disabled from a construction accident and had a stroke in 1989.

FRANK JACARUSO was from New York State. He joined the USN in early 1969, and after basic training and Gunner's Mate School, he reported in October to Riv. Div. 593 at Nha Be, RVN. He saw some very heavy combat patrolling both the upper Saigon River on Operation Ready Deck and the Rung Sat Special Zone.

On March 12, 1970, Jacaruso's patrol was operating on the upper Saigon River in an area of heavy Viet Cong and NVA concentration when he was mortally wounded by sniper fire. Petty Officer Jacaruso was a good gunner's mate and a solid shipmate in a fire fight. He was and is missed by all of those with whom he served.

EDWIN L. JAY (NED), born in South Bend, IN, July 21, 1925. He served during WWII, July 1943-May 1946, USNR.
He was an associate member of Gamewardens, and was not in the USN during the Vietnam era. He served on PT boats (Sqdn. 40) in the Atlantic and Philippines.

Electronics Technician's Mate First Class Jay was discharged in May 1946. He received the Atlantic and Pacific Theater Ribbons.

He and his wife, Jeanne, have two sons, John and Jeffrey. After a TV career with Storer and Turner Broadcasting, he is retired and makes Navy documentaries on patrol boat subjects and Naval Aviation for USS Yorktown Association.

HOWARD L. JOHNSON, born March 3, 1936, in Cabarrus County, NC. He enlisted in the USN on Oct. 19, 1954, after graduating from Navy Boot Camp at Great Lakes, IL, then transferred to USS *Windham Bay* LPH-92. During his Navy career, he served aboard numerous surface ships and submarines.

Johnson volunteered for duty in Vietnam in August 1968 and served there from January 1969 to January 1970 as a patrol officer with Riv. Div. 593. Some of his more interesting activities was the excitement in carrying out night-time waterborne guard post duty.

His decorations include the Presidential Unit Citation, Combat Action Ribbon, four Bronze Stars, Purple Heart, Vietnamese Cross of Gallantry, Good Conduct, Vietnam Service Medal, and RVN Campaign. Retired from the USN

aboard the submarine *Cashmer Polawski* SSBN-633 on Aug. 20, 1974.

He graduated from UNC Charlotte with a BA in accounting. Married the late Carol J. Overcash on May 25, 1957, and has four children: Jerry, Michael, Mary Ann and Jimmy. Remarried to Betty M. Johnson and now has five step-children: Donna, Cathy, Neal, Carolyn and Debbie and 12 grandchildren. Employed by the U.S. Postal Service since February 1978, he resides in Charlotte, NC.

CHARLES RAY JONES, born Dec. 15, 1943, in Rockingham, NC. He was commissioned NROTC in November 1965 at the University of North Carolina at Chapel Hill. He served in the Supply Corps, in the USS *Tom Green County* (LST-1159). Supported U.S. Marines (3rd MAF), USA Riverine Forces, USCG, swift boats, market time, all coasts of Vietnam, all major rivers, Dong Ha, Vung Tau, Cam Ranh Bay and My Tho.

Memorable Experience: The terror of a live mortar round landing at his feet, it was smoking but did not explode after tearing through the ships hull.

He received combat action-related awards. He was discharged in July 1968, selected for lieutenant.

Jones has a wife, Hilda H. Little, two daughters, Alyson L. Jones (1971) and Megan H. Jones (1977). He is the Gulf States Region Manager for the Navy Exchange.

WALLACE K. KANAHELE, born April 26, 1938, on the island of Molokai, HI. He joined the USN in 1956 and received his training in San Diego. He served on vessels in the Pacific, from China to Alaska, and was in Vietnam from October 1968 to October 1969. There, he was attached to Riv. Sec. 541, Riv. Div. 591 and was boat captain and patrol officer with four boats on the Long Tau River in armed combat against the Viet Cong.

He participated in over 240 combat patrols in the Rung Sat Special Zone. For action there, he received the Bronze Star with Combat V. He also received the Navy Achievement Medal with V.

Kanahele retired in 1975 as chief boatswain's mate. Later, during his 10-year employment with the National Oceanic, he was awarded the Department of Commerce Gold Medal for rescuing a shipmate from drowning. He and his wife now reside in Renton, WA.

WILLIAM E. KEENE, born in Meridian, MS, Dec. 17, 1931. After Vietnam, the "chief" continued his Naval career, completing 36 years of active naval service. He retired in 1986 as command master chief (E-9), a title he held for the last 10 years of his career.

SMC Keene's awards include two Bronze Stars with Combat V, two Navy Commendation Medals with Combat V, two Purple Hearts, Combat Action Ribbon, Presidential Unit Citation, seven Navy Unit Commendations, Meritorious Unit Commendation and two Vietnamese Crosses of Gallantry. He is enlisted surface warfare qualified.

He married the former Ann Mutter of Portsmouth, VA. They have three children: one girl, Barbara, two boys, William III and Frederick. All are married. He and his wife currently reside in Columbia, SC.

DANE KENNETH KELLER, born in Louisville, KY, Sept. 29, 1947. He entered military service in October 1966, and served in the USN as a gunner's mate. He served a nine-month tour in 1967, West-PAC, Korea, 1968, aboard USS *Brooke* DEG-1, Saigon, Nha Be, Sa Dec, Tra Cu, Binh Thuy, Ha Tinh, Vam Co Dong, Chau Doc, Vinh Long, Vinh Te Canal, Dong Tam. He was boat captain of PBR 121, also forward gunner.

Memorable experience was while patrolling the Vinh-Te Canal and a B-40 rocket entered the port side, passed through below his gun tub, left via starboard side, hit the bank and exploded.

Awards/Medals: Navy Commendation Medal with Combat V, two Purple Hearts, Combat Action Ribbon, National Defense Service Medal, Armed Forces Expeditionary Medal, Vietnam Service Medal with four Bronze Stars, RVN Campaign Medal, Presidential Unit Citation, Meritorious Unit Citation, Vietnam Civic Action Ribbon, Vietnamese Cross of Gallantry with Palm. GMG-3 Keller was discharged in October 1970.

Keller is a single parent and has a son, Kenneth (20), and a daughter, Jennifer (19). He is an ordnance mechanic for the Defense Department, Naval Ordnance Station, Louisville, KY.

JAMES T. KESLER joined the Navy at age 18 in 1952. Between 1965 and 1972 he did tours on bases in Puerto Rico and Guantanamo Bay, Cuba. He joined the Gamewardens in Vietnam in 1966, Group 511. He was there for one year, then returned in 1969-70 for another tour as YU boat captain in Da Nang. During this tour, he received the Navy Achievement Medal.

One of his most memorable experiences is from his first tour of Vietnam in 1966. High school girls from his hometown had made and sent goodie packages. It was from Pam Ward of Nicholson, GA, a neighbor and friend. When the mail call came, he received the package; but they had to go on patrol, so decided to wait to open it when he could take his time and enjoy it more. They were a couple of days out and no activity had been reported; it was a nice "quiet evening." He got the care package out and the crew, all four of them, gathered round like ants to candy. They could just taste those sweet cookies from home. All of a sudden both banks opened fire. It was like the fourth of July. Whatever happened to those cookies will never be known.

He retired in 1972 as BMC. He now resides in Nicholson, GA.

JAMES L. KEYES (JIM), born in Clinton, MO, on Sept. 11, 1935, and was raised in Yuma, AZ, and joined the USN on Feb. 1, 1954. He graduated from AT(A) School and served as NAAS Whiting Field before appointment as a naval aviation cadet in 1956. In June 1957. he was commissioned in the USNR and designated a naval aviator. He served in HU-1, VT-1, NAAS Saufley Field and HU-1, where he was commissioned in the USN and promoted to lieutenant commander.

He was assigned to staff, COMCRUDESLANT. He served in HA(L)-3 Det. 3 and Staff CTF117 from February 1969 through January 1970. He was promoted to commander and served as NAS Corpus Christi, TX; NAS Agana, Guam; NAS Chase Field, TX; and USS *Franklin D. Roosevelt*.

His awards include the Silver Star, Distinguished Flying Cross, Air Medal with two stars and Numeral 6, Combat Action Ribbon, Presidential Unit Citation, Navy Unit Commendation, Vietnam Service Medal, Vietnam Gallantry Cross and RVN Campaign Medal. He retired July 1, 1980.

He married Melba Walker in 1957 and they have one daughter, Kendal Lane, and one son, Kevin Lawrence.

ROBERT W. KILKELLY, born Sept. 20, 1946, in Newburyport, MA. He entered military service Sept. 1, 1964 to September 1967. He served a second enlistment from February 1968 to October 1969 as a USN engineman. He served in the USS *James C. Owens* (DD-776); NAS Coronado, CA; USMC Camp Pendleton, CA; Nav Suppact Da Nang, Vietnam; USS *Perkins* (DD-877); USS *Cadmus* (AR-14); USS *Butte* (AE-27), plankowner; engineman 2/c, Oct. 31, 1970.

Served in Vietnam on small craft LCM 8s, 1965-66. He received combat training at Coronado Naval Base; weapons training at Pendleton Marine Base, CA; ERE training, Washington State.

His awards include the Navy Unit Commendation with star, Combat Action Ribbon, Good Conduct Medal, National Defense Service Medal, Vietnam Service with three stars, Vietnam Cross of Gallantry with Palm, Vietnam Civil Action Medal first class with Palm and Vietnam Campaign Medal with Bar.

JEROME H. KING JR., born in 1919 in Youngstown, OH. He attended school there through 1937; then Yale University, graduating in 1941 with a bachelor of engineering degree and NROTC commission as ensign, USNR. In the Pacific Fleet, cruisers—communication and gunnery billets, August 1941 throughout WWII; many battles. Transferred to the USN in 1943.

Post-war, commanded, successively, a destroyer, destroyer division, destroyer tender, and destroyer squadron, interspersed with shore duty tours in various schools, staffs afloat and commands ashore. Attended USN Post-Graduate School, graduated from Massachusetts Institute of Technology in 1951 with a master of science degree in nuclear physics, and attended U.S. Naval War College. He was a 7th Fleet plans officer, 1963-65; executive assistant and senior aide to the Chief of Naval Operations, 1966-68.

Promoted to rear admiral in 1968; commanded ASW Group ONE with flag in CVS KEARSARGE, in WestPac; returned to Pentagon as chairman, Ship Characteristics Board; then was director of Strategic Plans and Policy Division, Office of the CNO. Promoted to vice admiral in 1970; relieved Vice Admiral Zumwalt as Commander Naval Forces, Vietnam; Chief, Naval Advisory Group, Vietnam; and Senior Gamewarden. Returned to Washington to serve as deputy CNO, Surface Warfare, then as director for Operations, Joint Staff of the JCS, from 1972 until retirement from the Navy in 1974.

Decorations include the Distinguished Service Medal (on three occasions), Legion of Merit (two), Bronze Star Medal with Combat V, Commendation Medal (two), and numerous unit, campaign, service and foreign decorations and awards.

He and Annette married in 1985 and have, between them, three daughters, two sons, several grandchildren and lots of happiness. They live in Palos Verdes Estates, CA.

Today, twenty some years later, his most memorable experiences from the ComNavForV tour are the moments of decision in combat action planning sessions, and later, reviewing the searing after-action reports. These generally reflected progress toward U.S. objectives in Vietnam but the occasional costs in casualties were always and will always be, anguishing.

FLOYD R. KIRKEY (RON), born in Massena, NY, on Feb. 23, 1939. He joined the Navy in May 1956, serving aboard the following

ships: USS *Roosevelt* (CVA-42), USS *Argonaut* (SS-475), USS *Chikaskia* (AO-54), USS *Rigel* (AF-58) and USS *Tutuila* (ARS-4). Upon his completion of shore duty at Naval Instructor School, Norfolk; attended PBR Training School, Norfolk.

He volunteered for Vietnam and attended PBR training in Class 49, Vallejo, CA. In March 1968 he was assigned to Riv. Sec. 531, operating out of the city park in My Tho. He qualified as patrol officer in late April and transferred to Riv. Sec. 544 in Nha Be, where he was promoted to warrant office (Bosn.). On August 2, while on day patrol in the Rung Sat Special Zone, his patrol was ambushed by a VC rocket team. Everyone aboard PBR 843 was wounded and medivaced to the 3rd Field Hospital in Saigon. Kirkey was later transferred to the Naval Hospital in Japan where he underwent lung surgery.

He returned to Portsmouth Naval Hospital and was assigned to NAS Corpus Christi, TX. In 1970, as CWO-2, he was assigned to the USS *Forrestal* (CVA-59) as ship's Bosn. Here. he qualified as fleet officer of the deck. In 1974 he was assigned to Coastal Riv. Sqdn. 21 as combat craft officer. In 1976, he was assigned to the USS *Opportune* (ARS-41) as salvage and weapons officer.

His awards include Navy Achievement Medal with Combat V, Purple Heart, Combat Action Ribbon, Presidential Unit Citation, Good Conduct (three awards), Navy Expeditionary, National Defense Service Medal, Armed Forces Expeditionary, Vietnam Service with three stars, Vietnam Cross of Gallantry with Bronze Star, Vietnam Civic Action, Vietnam Campaign with Clasp, Surface Warfare Officers Insignia and Small Boat Device. He retired in September 1977 with 22 years as CWO-3. He is a professor at J. Sargeant Reynolds Community College in Richmond, VA. He and Pat, were married in December 1960, and have one son, Christopher.

JOHN R. KITCHURA (JACK), born Jan. 17, 1947. He joined the Navy Aug. 4, 1966, and made GMG-3 on his first tour while participating in Operation Market Time in 1968. Received further training at Mobile Riverine Base, Mare Island. Began second tour as GMG-2, May 1969, with Riv. Div. 153 out of Tuyen Nhon. Participated in Operation Giant Slingshot as boat captain of ASPB, running from Parrots Beak through Plain of Reeds, to Rung Sat Special Zone.

Kitchura participated in over 230 patrols and 21 fire fights. Most memorable occurred on April 7, 1970, while transiting Vam Co Tay River. Their patrol came under heavy attack. They took rocket and automatic weapons fire, caught fire with three wounded crew. They fought back until they could suppress enemy fire and be towed clear. Everyone did their job and survived to fight again.

Decorations: Bronze Star with Combat V, Commendation Medal with Combat V, Good Conduct Medal, National Defense Service Medal, Vietnam Service Medal with one Silver Star, Presidential Unit Commendation, Navy Unit Commendation, RVN Meritorious Unit Citation (two) and RVN Campaign Medal.

Following his 1970 discharge, Kitchura earned a BA and entered international shipping. His oldest daughter, Tina, was born Oct. 1, 1969. He is now married to Patricia Reichley Kitchura, with a daughter, Caitlin (July 27, 1990), and son, Clay (Sept. 24, 1991).

ROBERT J. KLEIMAN, born Feb. 14, 1938, in Kewaunee, WI. He entered the USNR in June 1955. Military Locations: NAS Glenview, NAS Seattle, NAS Da Nang, USS *William R. Rush* (DD-714), Riv. Div. 533, Riv. Div. 573, Riv. Div. 535, USS *Enterprise* (CVAN-65), NAS Whidbey Island, USS *Wabash* (AOR-5), AD Com Great Lakes, USS *Vancouver* (LPD-2). He was a boat captain on the river patrol boats in Vietnam. Turned over 533 and then transferred to 573, turned it over, then went to Riv. Div. 535.

Awards/Medals: Breast Insignia Boat Captain River Patrol Boat, Meritorious Unit Commendation, Navy Achievement Medal, Navy Unit Commendation, Sea Service Deployment Ribbon, RVN Cross of Gallantry. Left the service in October 1982 as senior chief boatswain mate.

He married Gloria Jimenez in August 1983. He works at Camping World in El Cajon doing maintenance.

DONALD E. KORMAN JR., born in Bellefont, PA, Oct. 11, 1946. He joined the USN April 5, 1966; went to RTC Great Lakes, IL. Then went to USS *Tattnall* (DDG-19) out of Charleston, SC. Made two Mediterranean cruises, then received order to go to NIOTC California for PBR training, survival training, language, etc.

Arrived RVN Sept. 2, 1968, attached to Riv. Div. 533. He was gunner's mate on PBR 21, which was later sunk in the Cho-Gao Canal when it came under heavy rocket and small arms fire, from both banks of the canal. Two good friends were lost and all were wounded. If it hadn't been for their cover boat, he might not be here today. Thanks guys!

Korman was awarded the Bronze Star, Purple Heart, two Navy Achievement Medals, Navy Commendation Medal, Presidential Unit Citation, Navy Unit Commendation Ribbon, Combat Action Ribbon, Vietnam Campaign Medal, Vietnam Service Medal, Vietnam Counteroffensive and National Defense Service Medal.

He now resides in Grand Island, NY, with his wife Shelagh; son, Shawn; and daughter, Kim.

JIMMIE L. LAMBERT (JIM or LAMBCHOPS), born in Cardwell, MO, on Dec. 8, 1938. He spent his formative years in St. James, MO. Following his brother's footsteps (Bill was a Navy Korean War veteran), Lambert enlisted in March 1956. Until 1974, Lambert was an aviation parachute rigger who served three tours in Vietnam.

He knows of only three other PRs that served as boat captains and, like himself, all were survival instructors that volunteered for PBRs. He had the privilege of meeting most of the brown-water sailors from 1965 to 1969 at Whidbey Island, WA. Most will not remember him by his real name, but will remember Sgt. Maj. Lambrowski during the POW phase of SERE training (both are the same).

In 1969, he requested PBR duty and was assigned to ACTOV-3. In December 1969, at age 31, he reported to the proud, brave reliables of Riv. Div. 543 at Da Nang. He was boat captain of PBR-91 until it was literally blown out of the water in January 1970. He took over PBR-29 until turnover and remained with RPG-60 as an advisor until rotation in December 1970. Two things stand out during his career: 1) Everything he did in the Navy required him to volunteer, and 2) He had the honor to serve with the greatest group of men in the world, the sailors of the PBRs!

Having credit for over 24 years' active service, he retired on Dec. 10, 1979, as a senior chief. At his retirement, he wore 23 medals or citations, plus the Small Craft Insignia of a PBR boat captain and the Wings of an enlisted navigator in jet bombers.

He and his wife, Mary, have two daughters, Melinda and Sharon.

ROBERT R. LANGEVIN, born Dec. 30, 1947, in Boston, MA. He was inducted Nov. 24, 1966, into the USN and served as a communica-

tions technician. Military stations included NTC Great Lakes, IL; NCTC Pensacola, FL; NSGA Homestead, FL; NAB Little Creek, VA; NSGA San Mieguel, RPI, Co. L, Det. A, RVN.

His awards include the National Defense Service Medal, Vietnam Campaign Medal, Vietnam Service Medal, Combat Action Ribbon and Purple Heart. Discharged Sept. 11, 1970, as CTR2/c.

Langevin is divorced and has two children, Beverly and Robert Jr. He has been a firefighter for the city of Newark, NJ for 20 years.

FRED LEON LANGUELL, born July 30, 1929, in Ft. Wayne, IN, and entered the USN in October 1948. He served on numerous ships, attaining boiler tender chief petty officer in July 1959; successfully completed nuclear power surface program in 1961. Promoted to ensign in March 1965 and assigned to Riv. Div. 593 in 1970 and after turnover to Vietnam navy, was reassigned to Riv. Div. 594. While a member of Riv. Div. 593, he participated in the invasion of Cambodia in April 1970. He served as chief engineer on USS *Sagamore* (ATA-208); USS *Shanadoah* (AD-26) and was on two turnover crews to foreign navies. Languell was assigned to a U.S. military group to Chile from 1973 to 1977. He was promoted to lieutenant commander on July 1, 1973.

His awards include the Bronze Star Medal with Combat Device, Combat Bronze Star, Vietnam Service Medal, Pistol Sharpshooter, Vietnam Campaign Unit Citation (first class with Palm), Meritorious Unit Citation, Armed Forces Expeditionary Medal, Good Conduct awards (five) and Rifle Marksman.

He married Carol in 1956 and they have two children, a son, Michael, at Vanderbilt University as a Ph.D. candidate, and a daughter, Joyce, who is a graduate of East Carolina University. Languell now lives in North Carolina.

RON LARATTA, born Jan. 6, 1946, in Newark, NJ. He was RCPO of Recruit Co. 251; GMG3 on USS *Tattnall* (DDG-19), Charleston. Arrived in RVN August 1968, Riv. Sec. 532 in My Tho. He was forward gunner on PBR 140; was in Tra Cu, Vam Co Dong River for Operation Giant Slingshot. His 13th and last fire fight was on February 18, 1969. He saved many lives.

Awards include the Silver Star, Purple Heart,

Combat Action Ribbon, two Presidential Unit Citations, Navy Unit Citation, Meritorious Unit Citation, Navy Expert Rifleman Medal, RVN Civic Action Medal, RVN Cross of Gallantry and five others. He was discharged in January 1970.

He attended photography school in New York City; received a business administration degree from the University of Miami. He served as president of the Professional Photographers Guild of Florida in 1985. He is a certified professional photographer (CPP). Laratta married his high school sweetheart, Denise, in 1976. He and his wife live in Roswell, GA. He is a professional photographer in the Atlanta area.

Laratta is a life member of the DAV and Atlanta Vietnam Veterans Business Association; Gamewardens National: "Life+" since 1982, board of directors since 1985; Southeast Region Chapter: vice president/secretary, charter member, and newsletter editor. He and his wife have traveled most of the world and look forward to more locations. They toured Vietnam in June 1994.

MILTON BRYANT LARKIN JR., born
Oct. 1, 1934, in Washington, D.C. and raised in Falls Church, VA. He joined the USN on March 3, 1954; stations and duties included six old DDs, one CVA, various staff duties, training group, NROTC Ohio State, Riv. Sec. 542, Riv. Sec. 524. He was stationed in Nha Be, My Tho and Sa Dec, Vietnam.

Between August 1967 and August 1968, he participated in over 200 combat patrols in the Rung Sat Special Zone and Mekong River, from the South China Sea to the Cambodian Border. He boarded and searched over 7,000 junks and sampans in search of enemy munitions and supplies.

His awards and medals include the Bronze Star Medal with Combat V, Navy Achievement Medal with Gold Star (2nd awd.), Coast Guard Achievement Medal, Combat Action Ribbon, Presidential Unit Citation, Navy Unit Citation, Coast Guard Meritorious Unit Commendation, Navy Good Conduct Medal (8 awds.), Naval Expeditionary Medal, National Defense Service Medal (2nd awd.), Armed Forces Expeditionary Medal, Vietnam Service Medal (5th awd.), RVN Civil Actions Unit Citation and RVN Campaign. QMC Larkin retired Dec. 1, 1983.

Married Norma Fox in Bermuda on June 9, 1958; they have one daughter, Carol Lynn; five sons: Michael, Steven, Richard, David and Andrew; seven granddaughters; and six grandsons. Currently, he works at NAB Little Creek Country Store Warehouse.

DAVID LARSEN, born in Parsons, KS, on June 18, 1947, and joined the USN in September 1966. He went to the Naval Inshore Operations Training Center, Vallejo, CA, and the Vietnamese Language School in Coronado, and survival evasion resistance escape training. He arrived in Vietnam Sept. 13, 1968, attached to Riv. Div. 593. He was a gunner's mate on several different boats.

His decorations include the Navy Cross, Bronze Star with Combat V, Navy Achievement (Gold Star two awards with Combat V), Purple Heart, Combat Action Ribbon, National Defense Medal, Meritorious Service Award, Vietnam Service Medal, RVN Campaign Medal and Armed Forces Expeditionary Medal. He was discharged in June 1972 as gunner's mate third class.

He married Mary in June 1968 and they have one son, Ken. Larsen is a concrete contractor.

JAMES M. LAWHORN (MIKE), born March 27, 1948, at Greenville, WV. He entered the USN on Oct. 9, 1968; graduated from Engineman A School on April 11, 1969. Attended NIOTC at Mare Island, CA; survival, evasion, resistance and escape training in Washington state; and Vietnamese Language School in Coronado, CA.

Arrived in RVN last week of July 1969, and was attached to Riv. Div. 515. Served as the boat engineer on "8" boat, a Mark II type of PBR. He survived over 260 patrols on the "Grand Canal," and several other canals in the Chau Due, Ha Tien and Rach Gia areas. He helped train South Vietnamese naval personnel until Riv. Div. 515 was turned over to the South Vietnamese navy during June 1970.

Memorable Experience: While on liberty to Rach Gia (about 10 or 12 miles out of Rach Soi), there was an MACV unit, plus other points of interest to sailors looking for a little in country R&R. While at Rach Gia they were required to carry either a sidearm or an M-16 rifle. Curfew

was 6:00 p.m. Sometime about 11:00 p.m., Lawhorn found himself alone on the streets. He went to the MACV unit, but it was all locked up. Everything was locked up. Having observed Viet Cong in the town at night before (don't ask), his only option was to hike back to Rach Soi. So he started out, with only an M-16 and one clip (18 rounds). He was a little worried, but then, after walking for a couple of miles, a boy of about 10 or so came up behind him on a small Honda motorcycle. He stopped and asked Lawhorn if he needed a ride. What a question! Lawhorn climbed on behind the boy and off they went. Going about a mile, the boy turned off the main road and drove up to a small cluster of hooches. The boy got off and took some groceries into one of the hooches, leaving Lawhorn alone on the motorbike. A lot of things were going through Lawhorn's mind. But his fears were unfounded. The boy soon came out again, hopped on the bike and down the road they went. They made it back to the base at Rach Soi without further incident.

As Lawhorn got off the bike and reached for his wallet to pay him, the boy grinned real big, waved at him and drove off. Lawhorn has often wondered what ever happened to that boy, and what would have happened to him if it weren't for the boy.

After leaving Vietnam, he served on USS *Preserver* (ARS-8) out of Little Creek, VA. Awards include the National Defense Service Medal, Combat Action Ribbon, Navy Commendation Medal with Combat V, Vietnam Service Ribbon and RVN Campaign Medal. He ended his four-year enlistment as engineman second class petty officer.

He has been working at a textile plant in Narrows, VA, as an electrician since 1972. He was married, but is now separated, and has three children: Jennifer K., Ted Wayne (now in USN) and Debra Lynn; and a grandson, Austin Micheal. Lawhorn is proud to have served on PBRs.

ROBERT A. LEBLANC (FRENCHY), born Aug. 6, 1947, in Newport, VT. He entered military service in June 1966, serving in the USN. He completed river patrol craft training at the Naval Inshore Operations Training Center, CA, in August 1968. He later attended Vietnamese Language School in Coronado, CA, and from there he completed survival, evasion, resistance and escape training.

He arrived in Vietnam Sept. 15, 1968, and was attached to Riv. Div. 573 in Sa Dec. He was an engineman second class and later became boat captain on PBR 745 "Charlie Patrol." He was involved with "Operation Giant Slingshot," December 1968-January 1969 in Sa Dec. He'll never forget the time "Mad Dog" Jimmy Madox, Buddy Wilson and he went wading in the river to recover a VC sanpan full of enemy weapons smuggled from Cambodia. After being seven months in country, under the command of officer Vincent Rambo out of Tan An on April 9, 1969, his patrol came under intense enemy rocket and automatic weapons fire while patrolling the Vam Co Thy River.

His awards include the Purple Heart, Vietnamese Campaign Medal, Navy Citation and Navy Commendation Medal with Combat V. He was discharged in September 1969 as an E-5 petty officer second class engineman.

Married Sherry Searles, April 3, 1971, and they have two children, Jamie and Judson. They reside in Barre, VT. LeBlanc has been a sales manager for the past 24 years with John Hancock Financial Services. He is a life member of the Gamewardens of Vietnam Association.

STEVE QUINT LO PRESTI, born March 25, 1947, in Tulare, CA. He joined the USN May 17, 1967; received training at NIOTC Mare Island, CA. Arrived in Vietnam in September 1968; attached to Riv. Div. 592; gunner's mate, PBR 70.

Memorable Experience: One night, on patrol out of Go Dau Ha, they engaged in an intense fire fight. Their boat captain, Norman Slimmer, decided to get into the action by pulling out his 45 pistol and firing all the rounds into the river "to help out." Jeff Bartholomew, their engineman, always brought something back with him from liberty. You never knew what would show up next. For instance, an old Indian motorcycle in perfect condition. One liberty brought them a pet monkey. They named him Charlie and he became their mascot, never missing a patrol. Charlie was one of the guys, even got drunk with them. He learned all the trouble spots on the river and was as good as radar. Good old Charlie hated the VC also!

Lo Presti received the National Defense Service Medal, Vietnam Service Medal, Vietnamese Campaign Medal and Combat Action Ribbon.

On coming home, Lo Presti took over the family business of making cemetery gravestones and monuments. In 1982 he met and later married JoHanna, who now works with him in the monument shop.

JAMES L. LOVE served in Vietnam from June 1968 to June 1969. He was rear gunner on PBR 140, attached to Riv. Div. 532 in My Tho. They transferred to Tra Cu in January 1969 with Operation Giant Slingshot. He was wounded on Feb. 18, 1969. His awards include the Purple Heart, Bronze Star, Navy Commendation with V and Navy Achievement with V.

His son, John, was born in August 1968 while Love was in country. Love divorced in July 1969 and was granted custody of John, then 11 months old. He worked as manager of an auto parts warehouse until 1976 when he opened his

own parts store. He went out of business three years later. He changed careers and became a chef. He was working as food service manager at Primary Children's Medical Center when, on Sept. 1, 1990, he was in a motorcycle accident which blew off his left leg. After three and one-half years recuperating, he entered Salt Lake Community College and is now working on a degree in occupational therapy.

RODNEY C. LYNCH, born in Camden, ME, on July 9, 1945. He graduated from Ricker College in 1967 with a BA degree and joined the Navy, May 31, 1967. After attending Storekeeper A School in San Diego. Ordered to Vietnam, he served with River Boat Support Det. YRBM-16 on the Bassac River in the Mekong Delta near Cho Duc on the Cambodian border.

After leaving Vietnam he served aboard the USS *Graffias*. He recieved an early-out on Oct. 15, 1969, and returned to graduate school at the University of Maine at Orono, where he received his master's in public administration in 1972. His Vietnam awards include the Vietnam Service Medal, Vietnam Campaign, Navy Unit Commendation, Vietnam Unit Commendation for Combat Gallantry, Vietnam Civic Action and National Defense Service Medal.

After getting off active duty, he stayed in the Naval Reserves. Presently, he is a master chief storekeeper with 27 years of service. Assignments have included command senior and master chief and senior enlisted advisor. There are few Vietnam Navy veterans still in the Reserves.

Since 1972, he has worked as a professional city planner and town manager. Currently, he is town manager of Norridgewock, ME. Professional and civic organizations include American Institute of Certified Planners, Rotary, Masons and International City Managers Association.

He has recently been in contact with the family of SK-3 Glenn Howard who died in December 1969 while serving aboard the YRBM-16, and in contact with SK-3 Mike Snidow, YRBM-18 at Tan Chu. Lynch lives in Skowhegan, ME, in the home of Senator Margaret Chase Smith, who was on the Armed Services Committee during the Vietnam war. She is 96 and he occasionally sees her.

LEONARD S. MARKASKY (SKI), born in Brookfield, OH on March 14, 1933. He en-

listed in the USN on June 12, 1950. He arrived in Vietnam in late July of 1968 and was assigned to Riv. Div. 512 as a patrol officer on PBRs. He was later transferred to Riv. Div. 553.

One of the scariest moments of his in country tour occurred on the evening of Jan. 11, 1969. His two-boat patrol departed base camp at Hiep Hoa on the Van Co Dong River. Near the northern section of "Blood Alley," they were ambushed and the lead boat took a B-40 rocket hit in the stern and began taking on water rapidly. Swift action by the crew enabled them to use one engine as a pump and the other for propulsion and keep afloat. Added to this, they were in a "dead spot," and could not communicate with anyone. Later, he found out that the entire Delta could hear him but he couldn't hear anyone. Fortunately, they were able to make it to Go Dau Ha and beach the damaged boat.

Some of his decorations include the Bronze Star with Combat V (two awards), Combat Action Ribbon, Presidential Unit Citation, Vietnam Gallantry Cross and the Small Boat Command Device.

He retired from the USN in August 1974, attended college and received a BS in business administration. He currently resides in Charleston, WV and is a production supervisor for Appalachian Power Co.

CECIL HARVEY MARTIN, born Nov. 6, 1940, Yale, IL. He enlisted in the USN July 23, 1958 and attended Minewarfare School. He served in Vietnam from May 1968 to May 1969. He was assigned to Riv. Div. 531 as boat captain PBR-110.

MN1 Martin was awarded the Navy Cross for action on the night of Nov. 21, 1968. He remained in the USN and retired a lieutenant on May 1, 1979. After retirement, he returned to Illinois and earned a BA and MA in Art under the GI Bill. He is now a wildlife artist and part-time carpenter.

Martin and his wife, Kazuko, have been married since 1962 and have a daughter, Regina, and a son, Toby.

In addition to the Navy Cross, his awards and decorations include the Bronze Star with V, Purple Heart, Navy Commendation Medal, Combat Action Ribbon, Presidential Unit Citation, Navy Unit Commendation (2), Good Conduct Medal (3), National Defense Service Medal,

Vietnam Service Medal, RVN Cross of Gallantry with Bronze Star Device, RVN Presidential Unit Commendation, RVN Meritorious Unit Citation, Vietnam Campaign Medal and Small Craft Insignia.

JOSEPH MAZARES JR., born in Newark, NJ on April 29, 1943. He joined the USN in 1965 and after GM-A School and PBR training, he reported to RIVPATSEC 523 in Long Xuyen and later Vinh Long. He was a gunner's mate assigned to PBR 52 and later 141.

Following the USN in 1969, he enrolled at San Diego State University, earning a master's degree in political science in 1975. From 1969-1976, he boxed as a professional in the featherweight class under the ring name Joey Vincent. He boxed throughout the U.S., South Africa and Philippines. He taught for San Diego Community College District, 1977-81, later working for a Navy contractor.

He now sails as an able seaman with the Government Merchant Marine and resides in San Diego with his wife, Gloria; they have two sons, Joe III and Florio.

C.A. McCAFFERTY was KIA on Feb. 17, 1969. He joined the Iron Butterfly, River Division 593 in December 1968. He took part in some of the heaviest combat of the war during Operation Giant Slingshot.

He was mortally wounded on Feb. 17, 1969 when his patrol, while working on the upper Vam Co Dong River, came under heavy automatic weapons and rocket attack. Petty Officer McCafferty was the boat captain of the cover boat in a two boat patrol. His boat, during the action, took a direct hit in the coxswains flat.

Although with the division only a short time, boat Capt. McCafferty had proven to be a very reliable man in a firefight and was highly respected by everyone in the outfit.

WALTER McLAUGHLIN, born June 6, 1948, Niles, MI. He enlisted in the USN on Feb. 14, 1967; attended PCF training (gunner) at Coronado, CA Amphib. Base. He arrived in RVN on Jan. 31, 1968 and served in Anthoi COSDIV 11, Feb. 4, 1968 to April 1968; COSDIV 12 Chu Lai on PCF 79 April 1968 through September 1968; Da Nang from September 1968 to January 1969 aboard PCF 79 and PCF 81.

During his first three days in February 1968, along with his crew, was in transit to Anthoi. TET was in full swing. They were billeted at the Annapolis overnight awaiting a flight to Anthoi when they came under attack. First the mortars and rockets came in. The Navy in its infinite wisdom decided that rather than issue them weapons, they should lay on the floor under mattresses. His friend Jerry Peterson gave him one of his buck knives. They watched helplessly

from their second floor balcony as a Vietcong unit of about 12 men advanced door to door toward them. Luckily they were taken out by the guards positioned below them. After a sleepless night, they were flown in a "Vintage" S-2 to Anthoi. Welcome to the war.

Separated Nov. 2, 1970 as GMG3. He earned his associate of arts degree in 1972 and his BS in 1976, since 1991 he has been on VA disability compensation and civil service disability retirement.

In 1969 he married his high school girl friend, Mary; they have two children, Michael and Erin.

RICHARD A. McMURRY, born Oct. 11, 1944, Lynchburg, VA. In 1966 he joined the USN and served with Riv. Pat. Sec. 531, My Tho from 1967-68. He will always remember the people, the Delta, the job and the PBR-105.

Discharged in 1970 as GMG3. He received all the regular medals plus the Navy Commendation with Combat V.

McMurry is married and has a stepson. He is in the profession of heat, a/c, refrigeration contracting.

HARLAN McPHERSON (MAC), born July 4, 1947, Memphis, TN. He joined the USN, May 16, 1966 and was stationed at My Tho Riv. Sec. 533, Coronado Boat Support V-1, NAVCOMSTA Greece and engineman. His memorable experience was the TET Offensive of 1968.

McPherson was discharged Feb. 27, 1970 as engineman second class. He received the Silver Star, Purple Heart, National Defense, Vietnam Cross of Gallantry, Meritorious Unit Commendation, Presidential Unit Commendation, Combat Action Ribbon, Vietnam Service and Vietnam Campaign.

A journeyman electrician, he and Sue were

married in April 1972; they have two sons, Adam and Chris.

JOHN G. MELLIN, born in Stamford, CT. He joined the USN on Nov. 15, 1951 and was stationed in numerous ships, shore stations and Vietnam, 1966-68 PBR Sect. 512 and 513.

Memorable Experiences: petty officer, Vinh Long Navy Base; TET 1968; ducking mortars and ground fire; VNs throwing children under truck wheels, etc.

Mellin left the service on April 15, 1974. He received the Purple Heart, Combat Action Ribbon, Presidential Unit Citation, etc.

Works for the VFW post adjutant. He lives with his brother in Maryland; also has a brother in New York and a sister in Connecticut.

JAMES RICHARD METZGER (JIM), born Sept. 16, 1947 in Detroit, MI. He joined the USN on Jan. 6, 1967 and went to boot camp at NTC/RTC San Diego. He completed Gunner's Mate A School at NTC Great Lakes, IL. He was stationed at Naval Ordinance Facility, Yokosuka, Japan until being transferred to Naval Support Activity Sa Dec, Vietnam attached to Riv. Div. 573 in July of 1968.

In July 1969 he was transferred to the USS *Alamo* LSD-33 and was honorably discharged from active duty with the rate of gunner's mate guns second class in January 1971. His decorations include the Navy Achievement Medal, Combat Action Ribbon, National Defense Medal, Navy Good Conduct Medal, Vietnam Service Medal and RVN Campaign.

He is a safety manager for a national truck leasing and logistics company. He married Susan on the beach in Maui, HI on Valentines Day in 1991. He has a daughter Shannon Michelle and two sons, James William and Joshua Richard. He currently lives in the southern California area with Susan and Joshua.

JAMES W. MILDENSTEIN (JIM), born in Ida Grove, IA on Dec. 18, 1938. He joined the USN in February 1956 and served on CVA-14; DD-937; NAVRECSTA Brooklyn, NY; MCAS Iwa Kuni, Japan; DDG-12. He attended the Naval Inshore Operations Training Center, Mare Island, CA; Vietnamese Language School, Coronado, CA; SERE training, Warner Springs, CA.

He arrived in Vietnam October 1968 as torpedoman's mate first class and was assigned to Riv. Div. 593 as boat captain. His patrol was ambushed on a tributary of the Song Thi Vai River, and patrol officer, QMC Theodore Smith of St. Louis, MO, was mortally wounded.

In January 1969 he was assigned to Riv. Div. 554 as boat captain. His patrol was ambushed at the High Banks on the Kinh Dong Tien Canal and AFT .50 gunner, Paul A. Holtz of Falls City, NE, was mortally wounded, and Mildenstein had his left hand amputated as a result of a B-40 rocket hit during ambush.

His awards include the Bronze Star Medal with Combat V, Purple Heart Medal, Meritorious Unit Ribbon, National Defense, Good Conduct, Vietnam Service and Vietnam Campaign.

He works in electronics at the Naval Undersea Warfare Engineering Station, Keyport, WA with the metal hook replacing his left hand (he's also quite popular at BBQs). Resides with his wife, Frances, in Bremerton, WA.

JOHN C. MILLER, born Nov. 1, 1947, Hampton, IA. He joined the USN on Nov. 2, 1966. Military Locations/Stations: Co. 123 Great Lakes, IL, March 1967; EN A School, Great Lakes, June 1967; USS *Grant* CO LST-1174, September 1967; NIOTC January 1970; PCF-37 COSDIV 11 An Thoi RVN, March 1970; PCF-694 COSDIV 13 Sea Float, June 1970; turned over last 14 PCFs Cat Lo RVN, Dec. 1, 1970; USS *Garrett* CO APG-786, January 1971.

His memorable experience was swift turnover ceremony on Dec. 1, 1970.

Discharged USN, EN2 on Feb. 25, 1971, and continued his career in Navy Reserve. Retired as chief engineman in October 1993. His awards and medals include the Navy Commendation Medal with Combat V, Navy Achievement Medal, Combat Action Ribbon, Navy Unit Commendation, Navy Meritorious Unit Commendation, Navy "E" Ribbon, Good Conduct Medal, Naval Reserve Meritorious Service Medal, National Defense Service Medal, Vietnam Service Medal, Naval Reserve Sea Service Ribbon, Armed Forces Reserve Medal with Hour Glass, RVN Gallantry Cross Unit Citation, RVN Training Medal second class, RVN Campaign Medal, Expert Rifleman Medal and Pistol Sharpshooter Ribbon.

Miller is a maintenance supervisor for Cooper Industries, Houston, TX. He is married with five children.

MICHAEL E. MOREHEAD (MIKE), born March 28, 1947, Wenatchee, WA. He joined the USN on April 23, 1968, River Sqdn. 15, Dong Tam, Message Center, Pearl. Dec. 1, 1969, transferred Monitor 6 Ha Tien Fire Support for SVA Base on Cambodian border at Grand Canal where it comes into Yang Tang River.

Memorable Experiences: Heavy T-151-9 Tango Boat, June 9, 1969; Operation Giant Sling Shot; Vam Co Tay and Vam Co Dong Rivers; home base Go Dau Ha and Tay Ninh.

Discharged as RM3 in January 1972, Whidbey Island, WA; his awards/medals include the National Defense Service Medal, Meritorious Unit Commendation, Combat Action Ribbon, Vietnam Service Medal, Vietnam Campaign Medal, Navy Commendation Medal with Combat V and Presidential Unit Citation.

He lives with his wife, Barbara, in the country near Pilot Rock, OR, where he enjoys hunting, fishing, gardening and raising a few cows.

RODNEY MORGAN (THE WEASEL), born Jan. 18, 1947, San Francisco, CA. Joined the USN on Aug. 1, 1966 and graduated from Engineman A School, NIOTS and SERE training. Arrived in country on June 17, 1967 and was assigned to Riv. Div. 532 stationed at My Tho.

He eventually became the snipe on PBR-144, frequently the finest running boat in the fleet. Of his 19 month tour, his most memorable experience was when relocating from My Tho to the "T" Harnett County during TET, and on the same day, the evacuation from Ben Tre of all remaining friendlies, by all boats in the division.

His awards include the Purple Heart, Bronze Star with the Combat V and OLCs, National Defense Medal, Vietnam Service Medal, Vietnam Cross of Gallantry with Combat V and the Vietnam Campaign Medal.

He married Linda Serna on New Year's Eve 1972 and has a son, Matthew. He makes his living as a professional sailor, doing yacht consulting, contracting and racing. He is still on the river.

DANIEL G. MORRIS, born April 9, 1947, Hemet, CA and joined the USN on April 14, 1964. Duty Assignments: 1964-90, USS *Washtenaw County* (LST-1166), Yokosuka, Japan; USS *Proteus* (AS-19), Guam; Riv. Div. 544, 593 and 515, RVN; Harbor Tugs, Long Beach, CA; TAD to FAA as a sky marshal Operation Grid Square; COMPHIBRON 3 Staff SD, CA; Company Commander RTC SD; USS *Albert David* (FF-1050) SD; *USS Dixie* (AD-14)SD; CC RTC SD; SEA; USS *Doyle* CMC FFG-39.

Retired 1990, Fleet Reserve, ENCM(SW).

His medals/awards include two Purple Hearts, Combat Action Ribbon, Navy Commendation with V, VSM, RVN Campaign Medal, NDSM, VPUC, UN Meritorious Unit Citation, MUC, PUC, Navy Expeditionary Medal, six Good Conduct Awards, Armed Forces Expeditionary Medal, USCG Special OPS Service Ribbon (2), Sea Service Deployment Ribbon (5), Surface Warfare Specialist and Master Training Specialist.

Became a councilor NCOA upon retirement. He and PNC Suzzanne Desha were married in 1984. There are no children.

MICHAEL K. MORRISON, born on Jan. 16, 1944 in Battle Creek, MI. He entered the Navy OCS in 1967 after graduation from Michigan State University. He was trained as an explosive ordnance disposal officer and served aboard USS *Chara* (AE-31) in WESTPAC prior to becoming officer in charge of EOD Mobile Unit 45, assigned to TF-116 in October of 1969.

He participated in 69 combat operations with the River Patrol Force, 5th Special Forces, Seal Team One and RAG and Junk Force units throughout the Mekong Delta. He was involved in the transition from sea float to solid anchor. He was awarded the Bronze Star with Combat V for actions at Ba Xaoi Special Forces Camp in the Three Sisters area. Other awards included the Meritorious Service Medal and Navy Unit Commendation.

Following separation from active duty in 1970, he remained active in various Naval Reserve EOD and harbor clearance units until his retirement with the rank of commander in 1986.

Morrison has been married to the former Pauline Monti since 1966. Their sons, Dan and Justin, are grown and independent. He is currently executive director of corporate communications for Chrysler Corp. and lives in Rochester Hills, MI.

GARY W. MOSS lives in Pensacola, FL with his wife, Yasuko, and teaches high school Navy Junior ROTC. His first tour was 532. After six months back in the fleet, he came back for a second tour and one extension. This time in 571. After turnover, he became advisor in RPD 63 (old 532 and 571). Then went to RPD 53 to get back to My Tho. He had a falling out with their gallant allies and was sent to be close to the Commodore down in Binh Thuy.

Worst time was the nights on the Van Co Dong, especially when his cover boat got hit. Also the night in the My Tho M.P. conex box jail (with cuffs).

Best time was back in My Tho, when they drew Chief Clouse for patrol officer. Weasel, my snipe, took a dump in an individual C rat box and placed it near where we knew Chief Clouse would sleep that night on the engine cover. He slept with his head about 12 inches from that box, but never said a word. The next morning, when they got back to the park, they met BM1 Sprouse and his crew coming down for day patrol. #144 had been in the shop and we'd used their boat that night. When Chief Clouse saw them, he hollered "get down there and get that boat cleaned up, it smells like sh..."

NICK MOTT, born July 13, 1944, and grew up in St. Paris, OH. He joined the USN April 13, 1965. After duty on the USS *Yorktown* CVS-10, he went to fleet training at San Diego, then to the Naval Amphibious Base at Coronado. Evasion resistance, escape training and moc POW camp training followed at Whidbey Island, WA.

Assigned as gunner's mate to Nha Be Support Base on Feb. 28, 1967, he armed and fueled Hueys and Cobras, and made ammo runs to Long Binh to supply ammo for gunships, PBRs and the Seal Team.

He married in 1969 to Darlene Becker; they have two daughters and two grandchildren. In 1988 he was severely injured on his job, but God spared his life. Although, on disability retirement, he praises God for watching over him.

He would like to locate Robert Dennis Scott, formerly of New York, who was in the Navy with Mott for four years. If anyone knows about Robert, please call Mott at 513-339-3643.

STEPHEN A. MUNGIE (STEVE) is a native American Indian and was born in Keego Harbor, MI on Jan. 16, 1947. He joined the USN on April 15, 1964 and in July 1968, he arrived in Vietnam at the USS *Hunterdon County,* supporting River Section 533 near Ben Tre on the Ham Luong River.

On Sept. 12, 1968, he distinguished himself during an attack on the *Hunterdon* and was nominated for the Congressional Medal of Honor. Unfortunately lost paperwork and time has denied him this award; but new information to Congress may allow its award though 25 years late.

He left the USN in 1970 and went into the Army as a helicopter pilot, retiring as CWO in 1986. He has been awarded 31 combat awards between Navy and Army service.

Mungie lives with his wife, Brenda, and daughter, Samantha, in Colorado Springs, where he DJ's at a local country-western radio station.

JOSEPH TONY MUSETTI JR., born in Hall Quarry, ME on Jan. 17, 1943. He enlisted in

the USN in 1964. His first duty assignment was aboard the USS *Lake Champlain* as EN3 was to be on hand to effect recovery of both Gemini 2 and 5 space crafts.

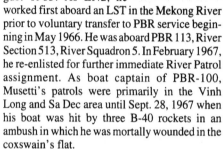

Musetti volunteered for duty in Vietnam in August 1965. As EN2, he worked first aboard an LST in the Mekong River prior to voluntary transfer to PBR service beginning in May 1966. He was aboard PBR 113, River Section 513, River Squadron 5. In February 1967, he re-enlisted for further immediate River Patrol assignment. As boat captain of PBR-100, Musetti's patrols were primarily in the Vinh Long and Sa Dec area until Sept. 28, 1967 when his boat was hit by three B-40 rockets in an ambush in which he was mortally wounded in the coxswain's flat.

While in Vietnam, he earned a Purple Heart, the National Defense Service Medal, Vietnam Service Medal and the RVN Campaign Ribbon Bar. His outstanding courage was an inspiration to all of his associates.

CARL A. NELSON, born in Pittsburgh, PA, on Oct. 11, 1930. He enlisted in the USN in April 1949 and rose from apprentice to captain by way of Annapolis, 33 years of service, five surface combatant commands and four tours of duty in the Vietnamese War.

He served his in country tour as the last senior advisor of the Rung Sat Special Zone (RSSZ) Naval Advisory Unit Nha Be. Reduced from hundreds to a final team of 24 Navy and Marine advisors, his unit turned over the Nha Be complex and flew home on Feb. 11, 1973, one day before the first 115 POWs were released.

He was awarded more than 20 personal and campaign decorations including the Legion of Merit, Bronze Star, Air Medals, Combat Action and various commendations and unit citations. As a civilian, he earned his doctorate and is author, consultant and professor of international business.

He married Barbara in 1956 and they have three grown children.

AL O'CANAS (PANCHO), born Dec. 6, 1942, LaJunta, CO. He joined the USN on Oct. 29, 1963 and was stationed at My Tho, Vietnam, Riv. Sect. 533 from 1967-1968.

Memorable Experience: He was assigned as M-60 machine gunner aboard PBR-112. The PBR-112 and 153 were transiting the My Tho River 11 miles west of My Tho en route to station when the crew of PBR-153 spotted an evading sampan near the south bank and gave chase while PBR-112 provided cover as they closed the bank. PBR-153 was ambushed from the south bank by an estimated Viet Cong platoon with B-41 rockets, 57mm recoilless rifle, automatic weapons and small arms fire. They were set on fire and every man onboard was wounded. After one firing pass, PBR-112 went alongside the 153 under fire in order to render assistance and evacuate the wounded. O'Canas and another crewman entered the burning cockpit to free the wounded coxswain. For this he is authorized to wear the Combat V.

Discharged June 17, 1968 as SN. His awards include the Navy Marine Corp Award, National Defense, Navy Commendation with V, Purple Heart, Good Conduct, Vietnam Service, Vietnam Campaign and Armed Forces Expeditionary Medal. He and wife, Nelda, have two daughters, Sherry and Monica.

VINCENT J. O'CONNOR, born Oct. 27, 1948, Cleveland, OH, but moved to a small farm at a young age. He enlisted in the USN February 1967 on the delayed entry program. His father was a WWII veteran and served on a merchant ship.

After boot camp in Great Lakes, IL, he attended basic electricity and electronics, then Electrician's Mate Class A School, Great Lakes, IL. Was transferred to Adak, AK and spent a year in the Aleutians. Attended Survival Evasions, Resistance, Escape and Survival School, Coronado Island, CA.

While in Vietnam, his YRBM-20 was on the Bassac and Mekong Rivers. His job was to repair electrical systems on PBRs, ALPHA boats, Tango boats, monitor boats and set up generator and electric for Special Forces. He made patrols and set up ambushes with the PBR Divisions 573, 515 and 552.

He was blown up by a sachel charge in Chau Doc on the Cambodian border on Sept. 24, 1969, and air evacuated to Binh Thuy, then to Saigon, to Japan, to Bethesda Naval Hospital. Four months later he was assigned as brig chaser at the Naval Station, Washington, DC. Nine months later, transferred to Charleston, SC to Ship Company AD-27 USS *Yellowstone* to finish out his enlistment.

Discharged March 17, 1971 as EM3/c. Received the Purple Heart and Combat Action Ribbon.

After the service, he attended Kent State University, OH; worked for the National Park Service as electrician; rode with the Sly Fox Motor Cycle Club; bought a 30 acre farm in

Ashtabula, OH and currently a self-employed electrician and raises beef, hogs and North American Game Cocks. He is divorced.

JAMES D. OLSON

DANIEL PALMER, born Aug. 6, 1949, in Bethesda, OH. He enlisted in the USN in February 1969. After completing Engineman A School and PBR School, he was assigned to Riv. Div. 553 as boat engineer on PBR-8134 at Kien Son. After turning the division over to the Vietnamese, he was transferred to naval support activity, Dong Tam. Assigned to Mine Flotilla Three in Long Beach, CA on board USS *Endurance* MSO-435 and MSL-32.

Honorably discharged Dec. 1, 1972. He entered the USNR in January 1977 and is currently serving with Naval Reserve Center, Moundsville, WV as an engineman first class. His awards include the Navy Commendation Medal with Combat V, Combat Action, Navy Unit Commendation, Meritorious Unit Commendation, Good Conduct, Naval Reserve Meritorious Service Medal, National Defense Medal, Vietnam Reserve Meritorious Service Medal, National Defense Medal, Vietnam Service Medal, Armed Forces Reserve Medal, Expert Rifle Medal, Expert Pistol Medal and Republic of Vietnam Campaign.

He now works on road construction, driving heavy offroad trucks. He married Erin on Jan. 24, 1976; they have one daughter, Amanda.

KEITH J. PECHA, born Aug. 17, 1931, in Mosinee, WI. He entered the USN July 14, 1949; was assigned to recommissioning crew on USS *Ingersoll* (DD-652); was first messenger of the Watch on recommissioning. As a BM3 in USS *Monrovia* (APA-31), landed with Marines in Beirut, Lebanon during 1958 crisis. Trained six companies as company commander RTC, San Diego, CA.

In 1968 he was assigned to Riv. Sec. 533 at My Tho, aboard USS *Hunterdon County* (LST-838) on lower Ham Luong; plankowner, Riv. Div. 553 on the Vam Co Dong at Hiep Hoa during Operation Slingshot. He left country from Chau Doc. Assigned to commissioning crew USS *Peoria* (LST-1183), as its chief boatswain's mate and stood the first JOOD watch.

Retired Aug. 10, 1970. His awards include the Bronze Star with Combat V, Combat Action Ribbon, Good Conduct, National Defense, WWII Occupation, Navy Expeditionary, Vietnam Campaign and Vietnam Service.

He married Patricia Bacon in 1958 and has two stepchildren, Elizabeth and William.

RONALD L. PERRY, born April 7, 1941, in Eugene, OR. He joined the USN in July 1959. He arrived in Vietnam in January 1967 and was attached to Riv. Div. 541 for a few months. He was the boat commander on PBR 26 and was also attached to Riv. Div. 514 for a few months. He left Vietnam in February 1969.

Perry's awards include the Bronze Star with Combat V, Navy Achievement Medal with Combat V, Combat Action, Presidential Unit Citation, Meritorious Unit Medal, Navy Good Conduct Medal, National Defense Service Medal and medals for Vietnam service, Vietnam Campaign, Vietnam Gallantry as well as small boat device emblems.

He married Donna Kidder in 1972. He retired from the Navy in April 1979 as a chief quartermaster and is now a mail carrier in San Diego, CA.

MICHAEL F. PERSICO, born Aug. 8, 1948, in Waterbury, CT. He entered the service July 26, 1966 to Feb. 28, 1969 and from Oct. 20, 1977 to present.

Duty Stations from 1966 to 1990: USS *Ranger* (CVA-61); forward gunner river sections 543/544 and Riv. Div. 593 located at Nha Be in the Rung Sat Special Zone; USS *Dyess* (DD-880); COMNAVSURFGRU Four staff; USS *Miller* (FF-1091); NAVRESREDCOMREG One staff; COMNAVRESFOR staff; PSA Norfolk staff; and from November 1990 to present, Bureau of Naval Personnel staff.

His awards include the Navy Commenda-

tion Medal with Combat V and three Gold Stars, Navy Achievement Medal, Combat Action Ribbon, Presidential Unit Citation, Navy Meritorious Unit Commendation Ribbon, Battle E Ribbon, Good Conduct Medal, National Defense Medal with Bronze Star, Vietnam Service Medal, Naval Reserve Sea Service Ribbon, Armed Forces Reserve Medal, RVN Meritorious Unit Citation Civil Action, RVN Campaign Medal, Navy Pistol Marksman Medal and the Enlisted Surface Warfare Specialist Device.

Currently, a master chief personnelman attached to BUPERS as the assistant for Reserve matters for PASS programs. He married Audrey Rund on Oct. 24, 1970; they have three daughters: Tara, Dina and Jena.

CARL JERROLD PETERSON, born Oct. 31, 1936, in New York City. He entered the Naval Academy in Annapolis in 1954 and was commissioned ensign in 1958. He served on the destroyer, *McCaffery,* and then for two years on *Arneb* (AKA-56), engaged in resupply missions to the Antarctic.

Following a tour in OPNAV, he became communications officer on the staff of Commander Middle East Forces. As operation officer of Ogden (LPD5) from 1966 to 1968, he participated in amphibious landings in Vietnam, developing new and very successful landing procedures. When detached in 1968, he requested further duty in Vietnam and was made commander of River Patrol Sqdn. 57, assuming command in December 1968 after his predecessor was killed on his last patrol.

Carl Peterson was KIA on April 2, 1969. The Spruance destroyer (DD-969) has been named *Peterson* in tribute to his memory.

EDWARD E. PIETZUCH, born Feb. 24, 1947, in Cincinnati, OH. He joined the USN on April 18, 1967, and attended AD Jet School at Memphis. He was assigned to NAS Imperial Beach, CA; transferred to Helicopter (light) Attack Sqdn. 3, at Binh Thuy and arrived in country in May 1970.

He was discharged on April 19, 1971. His awards include the National Defense, Vietnam Service and Vietnam Campaign.

Pietzuch attended Riverside City College in Riverside, CA; worked in the automotive field as a tech; then at General Electric on jet engines in the test cells. In 1982 he became self-employed as a dealer for Snap-on Tools. He is divorced and has two sons, Jason and David.

RALPH F. PINEGAR (FRANK), born in Indianapolis, IN on Dec. 31, 1948. He joined the USN on May 8, 1968 and took SERE training at Little Creek, VA. Was sent to Vietnam in February 1969 and assigned to Naval Support Activity Det. Binh Thuy. His first four months there, he was part of security. Later, he was assigned to the base armory where he repaired and routined small arms. Occasionally, he would make boat runs to forward PBR bases: Chau Doc, Kien Son, Rach Gia, YRBM 16, etc.

He left Vietnam in February 1970 and was

awarded the Vietnam Service Medal, RVN Service, National Defense, Navy Unit Commendation and two RVN Meritorious Unit Citations. Upon return to the States, he was assigned to the USS *Coronado* (LPD-11) homeported out of Norfolk, VA.

Pinegar was discharged on March 16, 1972. He married Nancy Simms on Feb. 24, 1973; they have a son, Joshua F., and a daughter, Abbi S. He works for Indiana Bell Telephone Co. in Lebanon, IN.

MARK C. POLLONI, born Oct. 18, 1947, in Fort Wayne, IN. He volunteered for the USN on Oct. 21, 1964. Duty stations: MST-2 (Seal support); Det. Echo at PBR MSB-2 Tan Chau; Quin Nhon; Rach Giang Thanh Canal; Bien Thuy; Nha Be; short tour Rach Soi/Rach Gia and Saigon; Lanship Ron 9 out of Yoko; LSMR 525; LST 1169; LST 1165 and LPD-7; 18 months MCB-10 at Diego, Garcia, Huneme and Guam.

Memorable Experiences: Sharks Den at Bien Thuy; five days at Vung Tau; and everything west of Hawaii. If TF 116 goes back to the Delta with boat, he hopes to go back.

Discharged Dec. 15, 1975 as GMG2. His awards include the NUC, MUC, CAR and four Vietnam Service Medals.

Married and divorced twice; he has one adopted son (Thai) and one granddaughter. Polloni has security jobs all over San Francisco.

JAMES W. RANDALL (JIM), born Aug. 15, 1947, in Connersville, IN. He entered the USN on Sept. 22, 1966. Military duty stations include: base security at Little Creek AMPHIB, VA; Engineman A School, Great Lakes, IL; PBR School, Valleyjo, CA; Vietnamese Language School, Coronado, CA; SERE Training, Warner Springs, CA; River Section 544, Nha Be, Vietnam; Riv. Div. 593, Nha Be, Vietnam; Operation Sling Shot, attached to USS *Harnett County*; Vietnam 1968-69; USS *Sioux* (ATF-75) NOB San Diego, CA, 1969-1970.

His memorable experience was taking PBR up Saigon River for a memorable day at Saigon Zoo. He was discharged June 9, 1970 as EN3. His awards include the National Defense Service Medal, RVN Campaign Medal, Vietnam Service Medal with one Bronze Star, Purple Heart w/A, Bronze Star w/V, Vietnamese Cross of Gallantry and Combat Action Ribbon.

He has worked at ABB (formerly Westinghouse) transfer plant for the past 27 years. He has two daughters, Lori and Shawn; three sons: Richi, Jim and Jeff; and one grandson, Christopher. He and Gloria were married on June 30, 1990. They enjoy attending Union

Chapel Ministries and a weekly Bible Study on end of time Bible prophecy. He looks forward to the return of Jesus Christ.

DONALD L. RASMUSSEN, born Aug. 6, 1948, in Madison, WI. He joined the USN and served in Nha Be, Vietnam with River Division 593.

Memorable Experience: In December of 1969, he and a friend (after a few drinks) got the idea of taking the Christmas tree from the EM Club. They moved closer to the tree, but it was chained down; so they threw a beer bottle (to distract attention) and when it hit the table, a fight started; they cut the chain, grabbed the tree and ran out the door. When they got back to their barracks, they decided to return the tree; so dressed in their undershorts, they carried the tree through the door, singing *O Christmas Tree*. The SP thanked them for returning the tree and told them to get the hell out of there because they were out of uniform.

He was discharged June 27, 1970 and GM E-3. He is disabled.

H. FRANKLIN RAWL (FRANK), born Nov. 20, 1935, in Johnston, SC. He joined the USN in March 1954, and after boot camp in San Diego, he attended QM School, graduated, and was assigned COMNAV for Japan staff, followed by USS *Rupertus* (DD-85), then duty on USS *Mars* until ordered to MINRON 11 DET A.

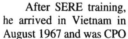

After SERE training, he arrived in Vietnam in August 1967 and was CPO in charge of MSB 18, sweeping Long Tau River for Mings from Nha Be to Vung Tau until August 1968. Chief Rawl then served as instructor in Survival School at Little Creek, VA, followed by assignment to COMPHIBGRU 2 staff on *Mount Whitney* (LCC-20).

He then was Navy recruiter in Charlotte, NC until he retired in September 1977, as senior chief quartermaster. His awards include the Combat Action, Presidential Unit Citation, Meritorious Unit Citation, Good Conduct, Vietnam Service Medal, Vietnam Cross of Gallantry, RVN Campaign and Small Boat Device.

FRANK RE III, born in White Plains, NY on July 7, 1948. He joined the USN on Aug. 25, 1966. His first duty station was the USS *Bon Homme Richard* (CVA-31). He made two Vietnam cruises before volunteering for service with river patrol boats. He underwent training for PBRs at Naval Inshore Operations Training Center, California and Vietnamese Language School in Coronado, CA.

Assigned to Riv. Div. 593, Iron Butterfly, March 8, 1969 to Jan. 1, 1970. He transferred to the Naval Advisory Group MACV on Jan. 1, 1970 and completed tour of duty Feb. 18, 1970.

His rank at time of discharge was GM3/c. He received the Bronze Star with Combat V, Navy Commendation Medal with Gold Star and

Combat V, Vietnam Service Medal with one Silver and five Bronze Stars, Presidential Unit Commendation Ribbon, RVN Meritorious Unit Citation (Gallantry Cross Medal Color with Palm), RVN Meritorious Unit Citation (Civil Actions Medal, first class color with Palm).

He now owns and operates PBR Services, a printing company established in July of 1987, and he resides in Bedford, NY with his wife, Nancy, and son, Joseph.

WILLIAM H. REICHERT (BILL), born Jan. 6, 1942, in Philadelphia, PA. He entered the USMCR in 1959 and went to boot camp at Parris Island, SC and artillery training at Camp Lejeune, NC. In 1961 he enlisted in the USAF and served as an aircraft control and warning operator in Labrador, TX, Colorado, Spain, Vietnam, and Bangkok, Thailand.

During the next two years, he worked as a police officer, advertising salesman and surf shop manager before enlisting in the USN. His next stop was Coronado for PBR training with a side trip to the notorious SERE School at Whidbey, then to Vallejo.

Arrived in RVN in June 1967 and was assigned to River Patrol Section 531 (PBR 101) My Tho. Patrolled the Co Chien, Ham Luong and My Tho Rivers. The section spent five months aboard the USS *Harnett County* LST-821, trouble-shooting the Delta. On the first day back at My Tho, he was given the task of making purchases for the crew in town. An hour after PBR-101 got underway, TET 1 commenced and Reichert was attached to the Seal Team Det. until he and his crew were re-united. Departed RVN in June 1968 and was assigned to the USS *Orion* AS-18, Norfolk, VA.

He was affiliated with the Naval Reserve in January 1970 and retired in October 1994 after 31 years of service and attaining the rank of master chief boatswain's mate. A total of 17 awards were attained during those years, including the Purple Heart, Navy Commendation with Valor Device, Combat Action, Presidential Unit Citation, Gallantry Cross with Bronze Star, etc.

Reichert affiliated with the Jupiter (FL) Police Dept. in 1970 and retired in 1992 at the rank of captain. He is currently the director of administration for the Martin County Sheriff's Office in Florida and holds the rank of major.

In 1972 he married Carol Eastwood of Philadelphia; they have two children, Billy and Brooke; the family resides in Hobe Sound, FL.

FRANCIS J. REILLY was from Chatham, NJ. He joined the USN in 1968 and attended basic training at Great Lakes, IL. After A School, he joined Riv. Div. 593 at Nha Be, Vietnam in late October 1969, transferring in from another in country command.

He returned to the States in March of 1970

and reported to the USS *Lasalle* in Norfolk, VA. In 1971 the *Lasalle* moved to the Philadelphia Shipyard for an overhaul.

Petty Officer Reilly was killed in a motorcycle accident on Oct. 12, 1971. He was awarded the Bronze Star Medal for Action on Operation Ready Deck conducted on the upper Saigon River. He also received the Purple Heart award for wounds received in combat while serving with the Iron Butterfly.

His mother, Winifred Reilly, still lives in Chatham and is a memorial member of Gamewardens.

JAMES RICHARD RENICK JR., born on

Oct. 27, 1946, in Jefferson City, MO. He arrived June 29, 1966, at Great Lakes Naval Training Center. He was assigned to the USS *Fort Marion* (LSD-22), San Diego, CA as seaman, assault boat coxswain. During the West Pack in 1967, he directed and led two U.S. Marines amphibious assaults just north of the Cua Viet River.

He volunteered for PBR School and reported to Mare Island, CA. In July 1968 he arrived in Vietnam reporting to Riv. Div. 535 on Home Base YRBM-18. Most of his in country time was the after gunner on PBR-725 which gave him over 259 patrols, 172 engagements and nine major fire fights, with many TET Offensives in 68-69. PBR 725 took him to the South China Sea, to the Van Co Tay River in the Parrots Beak, Ham Luong, My Tho Rivers and many canals. Villages: Vin Long, Meto, Moc Hoc. Places: Snoopy Nose, Bottleneck, VC Island in the Mekong Delta.

He became a PBR boat captain at the rank of boatswain's mate 3/c petty officer and received a Purple Heart. He cannot express in words the honor he feels to have served with Riv. Div. 535 and all boat crews and staff, also the loss of special sailors: Ford, Cline, Eastman and others.

Single, he lives in Jefferson City and works for the Missouri Dept. of Correction.

WILLIAM A. RETZ, born in Blauvelt, NY
and attended the University of New Mexico as an NROTC scholarship student. He graduated with a degree in mechanical engineering and was commissioned in June 1963. He later earned a master of science degree from George Washington University.

His first assignment was in USS *Taylor* in which he made three Western Pacific deployments. Subsequent at-sea assignments included USS *Borie*, the River Patrol Forces (TF-116) in Vietnam, USS *Ainsworth* and CO of USS *Stump*. The highlight of his sea duty was as Commander, Destroyer Squadron 22.

He participated in the 1973 Middle-East crisis, Operation Gamewarden in Vietnam, the hostage crisis off Beirut, Tomahawk cruise missile tests and Battle Group Operations. His shore duty included tours as student, Cruiser-Destroyer Force Engineering School, Naval Destroyer School, Naval War College, and placement officer, Bureau of Naval Personnel, Washington, DC.

Additionally, he served at USNA, NWC, Offices of the CNO and Chief of Naval Personnel. He was deputy director for Operations, U.S. Central Command, with responsibilities for Persian Gulf escort and retaliatory strikes during the Iran/Iraq War. His flag assignments included assistant chief of Naval Personnel. Rear Admiral Retz assumed command of NAVSURFGRU MIDPAC and NAVBASE Pearl Harbor in July 1992.

His awards include the Defense Superior Service Medal, Legion of Merit (with two Gold Stars), Bronze Star (with Combat V), Purple Heart, Meritorious Service (with Gold Star), Navy Commendation, Combat Action Ribbon, Presidential Unit Citation, Meritorious Unit Citation and various campaign and service awards.

He and his wife, Julia, reside in Pearl Harbor, HI; they have five grown children on the mainland.

WILLIAM C. ROBINSON, born Aug. 22,
1931, in Lancaster, SC. He joined the military service in March 1949 and served in Korea, USS *E.A. Greene;* USS *R.A. Owens* and Mt. Baren.

His memorable experiences include the 212 patrols, 18 firefights, seven months as sky marshal and the 12 months in Korea.

Left the service on April 1, 1979, as BMCM. His medals and awards include the Bronze Star, Korean Service, Presidential Unit Citation, Combat Action, United Nations Service, Occupation of Japan, Good Conduct, Vietnam Service, National Defense, etc.

He married in 1992 and is a rigger at Charleston Naval Shipyard.

WALLACE Q. RODERICK, born in Portage, WI on Oct. 13, 1942. He auditioned and joined the USN on June 24, 1960. He graduated from the Navy's assistant bandleader's course in 1968 and was promoted to chief musician in 1969.

He was commissioned chief warrant officer on April 2, 1980 and retired in 1986 after serving as the 7th Fleet Bandmaster, OIC of Navy Band Fleet Support Unit and Training Support Officer for the School of Music.

Throughout his career, CWO Roderick lead bands at Guantanamo Bay, Cuba, on carriers in both the Atlantic and Pacific fleets and, with ships of the Atlantic amphibious forces, toured the South Pacific on the USS *Horne*. He also served on the public affairs staff for the United States Navy Band in Washington, DC.

He was with Navy Band Great Lakes when he was called upon to write *The Brown Water Navy March*. CWO Roderick now resides in Janesville, WI.

STEPHEN J. RODGERS (DOC), born July 10, 1943, in Philadelphia, PA. He joined the Reserves June 5, 1965, and was activated on June 3, 1968. He served as senior medical officer in the Medical Corps at NSA Binh Thuy.

He recalls with fondness MEDCAPS, isolated villages and the providence orphanage at Can Tho. He recalls, with terror still fresh, flying backseat with CDR Bob Porter (skipper of the Black Ponies).

He returned to the Reserves on Sept. 30, 1975 as full commander; was captain in the Reserves in 1980. So far, he has earned six rows of ribbons. Rodgers had some severe injuries while on active duty, but was permitted to stay in the Reserves and now is awaiting the determination of a physical evaluation board.

He married Bobbi Rhine on Sept. 21, 1974. Children, Abigail and Rebecca, are joys to their father's heart. He is a medical/legal consultant.

CARL A. ROSCHETZKY, born in Mathis,
TX on Dec. 30, 1942. He lived in Corpus Christi, TX until 1975, then moved to Odem, TX. He enlisted Feb. 9, 1965 in the Navy S.A.; enlisted CCTEX Rectd. training SDNB, TI, San Francisco, CA; Coronado, CA; CPTP-USNAB-Coro.Ed student. COM RVRON 5, Vietnam SN. Came out GMG3. Back to NAS CORPC, TEX and commenced tour of Feb. 9, 1969 (793-93-47).

He participated in about 30 battles, made three runs into Cambodia to pick up downed pilot and POW that escaped, and made two search and destroy runs during the monsoon season. Roschetzky was in Cat Lo for six weeks, Vinh Long for almost a year, and six months at Vung Tau. His boat run was the Co Chien River out of Vinh Long for one year, then spent six months at Sa Dec.

Roschetzky received the National Defense Service Medal, Vietnam Service Medal, Vietnam Campaign Medal and Navy Unit Commendation Ribbon Bar. PBR-III was his home away from home most of the time.

He works for Koch Refinery in Corpus Christi and is an A-1 class mechanic; he also works with honey bees and does part-time ranching. His family consists of his wife, Carolyn, whome he married Dec. 22, 1972. He has a stepson, Joe D. Simpson, of College Station, TX; step-daughter, Tracy A. Simpson Bark, of Corpus Christi; daughter, Beth E; and son, Gary W., both of Odem.

JOSEPH A. ROY, born April 12, 1944, in Kaplan, LA. He enlisted in the USN on Aug. 19, 1962; River Section 543, Nha Be, Cua-Viet, two and a half miles from DMZ. His memorable experiences include Med Cap for the people, TET, Nha Be and shelling of Cua-Viet base.

Discharged Oct. 8, 1968 as BM3. His awards include the National Defense Medal, Vietnam Campaign Medal, Vietnam Service Medal and Armed Forces Expeditionary.

After discharge, he went to a reserve unit (Coastal Riv. Div. 22 which became SBU-22 in 1980) in Orange, TX. He helped to train active and reserve personnel until Congress passed a law that if anyone had served 28 years as E-7, they had to retire or go into IRR, which he did. He misses working with the personnel of Special Boat Unit 22 and all the other services, and all the traveling he did with SBU-22.

He was married to Phyllis for 20 years; now divorced, he has two children, Joseph Ray and Michelle Ray.

ROBERT RUBIO, born in El Paso, TX on May 5, 1949. He was drafted into the USA in March of 1969; took basic training at Fort Bliss, TX; advanced infantry training and military intelligence at Fort Gordon, GA.

He arrived in Vietnam in September 1969 and was sent to MACV Advisory Team 55 and Navy Riv. Div. 532 at Ha Tien on the Cambodian border. There, he and his team members worked with the ARVNs and PFs as well as Navy PBR and Swift boats in and out of Hatien.

His awards include the Distinguished Service Medal, Army Commendation Medal, National Defense Medal, RVN Gallantry Cross with Palm, Unit Citation Badge, Combat Infantry Badge, Vietnam Service Medal, Good Conduct Medal and RVN Campaign Ribbon. He left Vietnam Oct. 10, 1970, as sergeant E-5.

He married Joy Cannon in 1975 and has three daughters: Jo Ann, Angela and Jennifer, and one granddaughter, Amali. He is a diesel mechanic for a freight company.

WILLIAM ROBERT RUSTH (RUSTY), born Aug. 18, 1945, in California. He joined the

USN and served with U.S. Forces engaged in riverine assault operations against the Viet Cong communist in the RVN from November 1968-August 1969. He served as a gunner on board a craft attached to River Assault Sqdn. 15. He participated in numerous combat missions which struck deep into enemy infested waters of the Mekong Delta and he also participated in Operation Giant Slingshot. For the above he received the Navy Achievement Medal.

He received the Navy Commendation Medal for meritorious service while serving as a gunner attached to Riv. Div. 532 and participating in 165 combat patrols from March to October 1970. In addition, he conducted psychological warfare operations and civic action programs.

Also received the National Defense Service Medal, Vietnam Service Medal with Silver Star, Navy Expert Rifle and Pistol Medals, Combat Action Ribbons, Navy Commendation Ribbon Bar, RVN Meritorious Unit Citation (Gallantry Cross Medal Color with Palm), RVN Campaign Medal with Device and Small Boat Device Emblem.

His father served in WWII and his grandfather in WWI. Rusth is a life member of VFW, DAV and Gamewardens. He has a son, William, and daughter, Tammi.

CHARLES E. SCHMITZ (RED BARON), born Nov. 4, 1947, in New York City. He joined the USN on Nov. 24, 1964, and was stationed in Da Nang from 1965-67. He was assigned with the Riv. Div. 534 from 1967-68.

Memorable experiences include: at age 20, he was the youngest boat captain on the river; the battle of Ben Tra (TET 68); and first 20mm to be mounted on PBR Mark II.

Discharged Nov. 6, 1970 as GMG3, boat captain E-6. His awards include the Navy Commendation Medal with Combat V, Presidential Unit Citation, National Defense, Vietnam Campaign with four stars, Vietnam Service and others. (Awarded Bronze Star, but never received it.)

A retired police officer, he is currently a private detective. He and wife, Kathy, have a son and a daughter.

SAYRE A. SCHWARTZRAUBER, born in Illinois in 1929. He was drafted during the Korean War, chose to serve in the USN and attended OCS in 1952. After serving in amphibs, destroyers, and carriers, he was accepted into the Regular Navy.

His Vietnam service was as commander, and it started with the TET Counteroffensive, February 1968, Binh Thuy. His job was

COMRIVRON 5, with administrative responsibility for the five RIVDIVs and their 25 RIVSECs. After RIVRON 5 became RIVPATFLOT 5, he was reassigned to the DMZ as Commander Task Force Clearwater, based in Cua Viet, with PBRs and minecraft assigned, and with responsibility for the Cua Viet and Perfume Rivers.

After Vietnam, 1969, he was detailed to American University for a Ph.D. Then followed destroyer, Pentagon, and recruiting duty and a promotion to rear admiral. Retired in 1983, he and Beryl live on Cape Cod where he writes.

DENNIS J. SCULLY, born Aug. 13, 1948, in Taunton, MA. He entered the USN on Oct. 14, 1965. His duty stations include: NTC Great Lakes (basic Co. 624); USS *Currituck* AV-7; Vietnam Language School, Coronado, CA; SERE training, Warner Springs; NIOTC, Vallejo, CA; survival training, Subic Bay, P.I.; Riv. Sec. 534; and USS *Sacramento* AOE-1.

Riv. Sec. 534 was assigned the first MKII PBRs in Vietnam. These PBRs were designed to carry a standard gun tub forward with twin 50 caliber machine guns. While assigned as gunner's mate aboard PBR-12 during the Spring of 1968, Scully was involved with the modification of the forward gun tub, consisting of the removal of one .50 caliber and replacing it with a 20mm cannon. When firing the 20mm off the beam, the recoil was so tremendous that it pushed the boat sideways. It also had the problem of malfunctioning, and jammed often after firing only 10 to 12 rounds. On April 24, 1968, PBR-12 was the last boat in a column of six PBRs, which made a run through the Ben Tre Canal. The intense attack by enemy recoiless rifle, B-40 rocket, and automatic weapons fire sank PBR 12. All possible equipment was removed from the PBR except for the 20mm cannon.

He received the National Defense, Vietnam Service Medal with three stars, RVN Campaign Medal, Purple Heart, Navy Commendation Medal with Combat V and Gold Star in lieu of second award, Navy Combat Action Ribbon and Navy Unit Commendation.

Scully graduated from Bristol Community College with an associate degree in science of criminal justice; currently attending University of Massachusetts/Dartmouth; and employed as a patrolman on the Taunton Police Dept. He is a life member of Gamewardens Assoc. and active member of Northeast Chapter of Gamewardens. He married Kathleen McRae on Oct. 15, 1976; they have one son, David.

MICHAEL D. SHARP, born March 28, 1948, in Ponca City, OK. He joined the USN in October 1968. After boot camp, he attended Gunnery A School at Great Lakes Naval Training Station. His next assignment was Naval Inshore Operations Training Command, Mare Island, CA. Upon completion of small boat training, he was sent to Camp Roberts, CA for sniper training and then to Vietnam.

He arrived in Vietnam as a GMGSN and was assigned to Riv. Div. 512 stationed near Chau Doc at the mouth of the Vinh Tey Canal. After serving as a forward gunner on interdiction patrols for several months, the division was turned over to the Vietnamese Navy and he was reassigned to Riv. Div. 572 at Song Ong Doc near the U Minh Forest. The Riv. Div. was also turned over in June of 1970 and he was transferred to Naval Support Activity, Nha Be, after serving as a station armorer there with a TDY period at ATSB Moc Hoa.

He left Vietnam in April of 1971. He served on the DDG USS *Henry B. Wilson* for a WestPac cruise and then on the USS *O'Callahan* before getting out of the Navy in 1972. He was awarded the Vietnam Service Medal, Combat Action, Navy Commendation with Combat V, Vietnam Campaign and Purple Heart.

He earned an associate degree from Northern Oklahoma College, worked as a machinist and tool and die maker for five years, then earned a bachelor's degree from Oklahoma State University. He is now employed as a manufacturing engineer and resides with his wife, Cheryl, and their two mules, in Tuttle, OK.

ROBERT SHENK, born on April 10, 1943, and after graduating from the University of Kansas, he was commissioned in 1965. He served as Communications Officer in USS *Harry E. Hubbard* (DD-748) and then as patrol officer in Riv. Div. 535 from mid-1968 to mid-1969. In the middle of that tour he participated in Operation Giant Slingshot on the rivers flanking the Parrot's Beak of Cambodia.

After leaving the USN, Shenk married the former Paula Elshire who he first met while in PBR training near Vallejo. He studied for a Ph.D in English literature, and then was recalled to active duty for three years service each, in the English departments of the Air Force Academy and the Naval Academy.

He now is a professor at the University of New Orleans, and has authored two books for the U.S. Naval Institute: *Guide to Naval Writing* (1991) and *The Left-Handed Monkey Wrench* (1985), the latter being a collection of the shorter works of the author of *The San Pebbles,* Richard

McKenna. Shenk retired from the Naval Reserve as a captain early in 1994.

DON SHEPPARD, born Feb. 8, 1930, in Chicago and grew up in the Midwest. Enlisting in the USN in 1948, he became an electronics technician and was promoted to chief petty officer at the age of 25. He was commissioned an ensign in the Regular Navy in 1958 and served aboard his first destroyer for four years, most often as the ship's chief engineer. Later, he served as executive officer, and as commanding officer of other destroyers.

After Vietnam, he served in Japan with a joint service intelligence command. He retired as a commander in 1977. During his naval career, he earned the Silver Star, Legion of Merit with Combat V, three Bronze Stars for Valor, two Purple Hearts, two Vietnamese Crosses of Gallantry, a Vietnamese Honor Medal and the Presidential Unit Citation.

He holds a bachelor's and two master of science degrees. Since his Navy tour, he has worked as a stock broker and held various upper management positions with companies in the Midwest and in Long Beach, CA. He resides in Huntington Beach, CA.

H.W. SHERMAN SR., born March 31, 1945, Cuney, TX. He joined the USN on Feb. 15, 1965; went to Naval Inshore Operation Training Center, NAB Coronado, San Diego, CA; two weeks Vietnamese Language School at NAB Coronado; survival, evasion, resistance and escape training at Whidbey Island, WA; PBRY weapons training at NS Vallejo, CA and jungle training in Republic of Philippines.

Arrived in RVN in August 1967; was assigned as Commander, Riv. Sqdn. 5; and to PBR-60 as M-60 machine gunner. While on patrol, he was wounded in March 1968. PBR was the best duty he had while in the Navy. He stands ready to do it all over again, if needed.

Left the service Nov. 30, 1984 as BM E-6. His awards include the Silver Star, Purple Heart with Gold Star, National Defense Service Medal, Combat Action Ribbon, Navy Good Conduct with three stars, Vietnam Service Medal with two Silver and one Bronze Star, Republic of Vietnam Campaign Ribbon and Meritorious Unit Commendation.

He married Stella L. Williams on Nov. 4,

1968. He works for the Trane Air Conditioning Co.

JAMES A. SHRECKENGAUST, born in McFall, MO on Sept. 12, 1937, and graduated from Pattonsburg High School and from the University of Missouri, Class of 1960, with a BS degree in mechanical engineering. He entered the USN through the NROTC Program.

After serving three years aboard USS *Mitcher* as gunnery officer and anti-submarine warfare officer, he was assigned as assistant professor of naval science at Oregon State University from 1963-65. Capt. Schreckengaust was assigned to USS *Jonas Ingram* as weapons officer in 1965 and 1966, then as Commander, Riv. Div. 521 in Vietnam during 1967 and 1968.

Capt. Schreckengaust earned an MS/MBA in computer systems management at the Naval Postgraduate School, Monterey, CA, in 1969; returned to sea as XO, USS *Waddell*; graduated from the Naval War College in 1972; assumed command of USS *Dupont*; then served in the Bureau of Naval Personnel from 1974-77 as surface commander detailer, then as director of automation for officer development and distribution.

He next served as XO, USS *Oklahoma City* from 1977-79, relieved as CO and steamed the ship to San Diego for decommissioning. From January 1980-May 1981, he was chief, Navy Section, U.S. Army Command and General Staff College, Fort Leavenworth, KS. Capt. Schreckengaust then completed a one year tour as commanding officer, Military Sealift Command Office, Indian Ocean and Commander, Task Group 73.7, commanding the 13 ships of the Near Term Prepositioning Force operating out of Diego Garcia in 1981 and 1982.

Capt. Schreckengaust completed a two year major shore command tour at Navy Manpower and Material Analysis Center, Pacific, followed by a one year tour as deputy director, Total Force Information Systems Division, Office of the Chief of Naval Operations. Prior to reporting for a three year tour of duty as the deputy inspector general, commander in chief, U.S. Atlantic Command and U.S. Atlantic Fleet, Capt. Schreckengaust served a one year tour as Commander of Maritime Prepositioning Ships Sqdn. 1. He retired June 1, 1990.

His decorations include the Legion of Merit, Bronze Star (with Combat V), Meritorious Service Medal (fourth award) and the Navy Achievement Medal. He is married to the former Shirlene Huntsberger of Enid, OK. They have three daughters: Jill, married to a Navy Seal; Robyn, a medical doctor with the USAF; and Karen, a grade school/Spanish teacher.

TERRY CLEO SIMONSON was from Lansing, MI and had joined the USN in 1965. He began his tour in Vietnam with River Section 544 in May 1968. He was awarded the Silver Star and Purple Heart for action on Aug. 2, 1968 when his patrol came under heavy attack and he aided his wounded shipmates while still under fire.

125

On Sept. 1, 1968, River Section 544 was redesignated as River Division 593, a unit of River Patrol Flotilla 5, Petty Officer Simonson was part of this transition and continued the tradition of the Iron Butterfly. On Jan. 17, 1969, he was mortally wounded by an AK-47 round in the neck, when his patrol came under heavy automatic weapons and rocket fire while on patrol on the Vam Co Dong River as part of Operation Giant Slingshot. He was highly regarded by all in the division and was, and is, missed by those he served with.

NORMAN H. SLIMMER JR., born June 27, 1943 in Millville, NJ. He enlisted in the USN in 1961 and was assigned to the USS *Charles S. Sperry,* then to the U.S. Naval Base Subic Bay in Harbor Patrol. After being relieved of command of the main gate, he was assigned to Riv. Div. 592 at Nha Be and Go Dau Ha, RVN.

He had assignments as a federal air security specialist in Brunswick, ME; subsequent tours on USS *America*; joint service tours in Germany and Iran. His final tour was at Amphib School, Little Creek, VA.

Presently, works as a corrections officer at Ionia Michigan super maximum facility. He resides in Saugatuck, MI with his bride, Chick.

THEADORE SMITH (TED), reported to River Section 544 in May of 1968 as the unit was forming. He came from another in country command at Long Vinh. Chief Smith was assigned as a patrol officer and began patrolling the Rung Sat Special Zone as soon as the unit was operational.

On Nov. 8, 1968, Chief Smith's patrol left Nha Be at first light en route to the Thi Vai/Go Ghia area. This area was known as a Viet Cong strong hold. During the patrol he was directed to enter a small canal with his two boats and act as a blocking force for a land unit sweeping the area. Chief Smith's patrol was ambushed coming out of the small canal and his cover boat took a direct hit, wounding all onboard.

After clearing the kill zone, Chief Smith transferred to the cover boat to assist the wounded and maneuver the boat out of the ambush. As Chief Smith started to move the boat out of the kill zone, it took another direct rocket, killing him instantly. For this action he was awarded the Silver Star and a second Purple Heart for his mortal wounds. He had earlier received a Bronze Star for bravery and aggressiveness under fire.

WILEY F. SMITH, born in Oklahoma City, OK on Jan. 29, 1948. He enlisted in the USN, at the age of 17, on Feb. 8, 1965. After serving two and a half years aboard the ocean going tug, USS *Mataco,* and graduating from Engineman A School at Great Lakes, IL, he was transferred to the Naval Inshore Operations Training Center at Mare Island, CA. He attended SERE training and

Vietnamese Language School at the Naval Amphibious School, Coronado, CA.

He arrived in Vietnam on Aug. 4, 1968; assigned to Riv. Sect. 544; and was stationed at Nha Be, RVN. He became a plankowner of Riv. Div. 593 when the sections were changed to divisions in 1968. He served aboard PBR-752 as boat engineer and M-60 machine gunner. Participated in Operation Giant Sling Shot and, while on patrol south of Ben Luc, he was wounded on March 9, 1969 by a B-40 rocket.

PO3/c Smith was honorably discharged on Oct. 31, 1969 at Coronado, CA. His awards include the Purple Heart, Navy Commendation with Combat V, Presidential Unit Citation, National Defense, Vietnam Service Medal with three stars, Vietnamese Cross of Gallantry Medal with Palm, Vietnamese Civil Actions Medal first class, and RVN Campaign Medal with 1960 Device, and Combat Action Ribbon.

Smith has worked as a maintenance technician for the U.S. Postal Service for the past 20 years and lives in the small town of Yukon, OK. He has two children, Jeffrey (in the USAF) and Jennifer.

RAYMOND G. SNOW, born Oct. 2, 1934, in St. Johnsbury, UT. He joined the USN on Nov. 16, 1951. His duty stations include: USS *T. Sherwood, Shelton, Paul Revere,* APA-248, USS *Taylor* and *Newell.* He served with Riv. Sec. 542 from 1967-68 and Riv. Div. 574 from 1968-69.

He left the service on Oct. 2, 1972 as boatswain's mate chief. His awards include two Bronze Stars with V, Purple Heart, Meritorious Service Medal, Combat Action, National Defense, Navy Good Conduct, Navy Occupation, China Service, Vietnam Service, Meritorious Unit Citation, Vietnamese Cross of Gallantry, Armed Forces Expeditionary, Combat Action, RVN Campaign and Enlisted Button.

Married Gayle in 1984 and has two stepchildren, Gary and Wanda, and five grandchildren: Heather, Megan, Dustin, Jeremy and Jason. He manages a glass shop.

ROBERT W. SPENCER, born Oct. 28, 1929, in Columbus, GA. He joined the USN in August 1949 and was awarded his wings and commission in May 1951. He reported to VA-65, A-1 Pilot, and had two tours to Korea aboard *Boxer* and *Yorktown.*

His career spanned duties as flight engineer (fixed and rotary wing), catapult/arresting gear officer (CVA-9), HU-2, air officer (LPH-8), chief of staff & operations (COMNAVFORCARIB) and served as CO of HA(L)3 "Seawolves" and CTG-116 from May 1967-68.

Retired in August 1978 as captain. His awards include the Distinguished Flying Cross, Bronze Star, 10 Air Medals, two personal Commendation Medals, Ground Combat Action, two Presidential Unit Citations, National Unit Citation, Meritorious Unit Citation and Korean Unit Citation.

Second marriage was to Patricia Meehl in 1985. He has nine children and 16 grandchildren. Currently, he is retired and lives in Richmond, VA.

JERRY STAPLES, born Oct. 24, 1937, Marceline, MO. He joined the USN in 1955 and served with Riv. Div. 593, TCF-116, LST-209, MSC-197, AN-91, DD-761, MACV Vietnam, BSU-1, TCF-116 and NAVSTA Adak. His memorable experience was Giant Sling Shot.

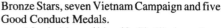

Left the service in June 1975 as E-7. His awards include two Navy Commendation Medals, two Bronze Stars, seven Vietnam Campaign and five Good Conduct Medals.

Married, he and his wife, Phyllis, have three children and five grandchildren. He works for the Missouri Highway and Transportation Dept.

LEON G. STARCK (LEE), born on Oct. 3, 1946, in Providence, RI. He enlisted in the USN in September of 1965 and arrived in Long Xuyen in August of 1966. He was assigned to PBR-63 for three months, then was transferred to Riv. Sec. 543. The section patrolled out of Cat Lo, Nha Be, and Cau Viet.

Most of the patrols were in the Rung Sat Zone (Forest of Assassins) southeast of Saigon. After nine months in country, and only 19 years old, he was promoted to boat captain of PBR-42. He was also field promoted, under fire, two times to GMG2. His PBR crew, all younger than him, were great. Frank and Dale were with him for 18 months and they still get together today.

Although he had many scrapes with death during his 700 plus patrols, his closest encounter was at Cau Viet, Northern I Corps. During one of the many artillery attacks on the base, he alone took a PBR away from the pier, and about 200 yards away, it was hit by a 10" shell.

He was sent back to the States in April of 1969. He received many medals, Presidential and Meritorious Citations, and Letters of Accomodations. He is a proud volunteer. Today he has own brick laying company.

ROBERT PAGE STARK, born in Lansing, MI, on April 21, 1942. He joined the USN in August 1960 and had submarine duty until June 1968. He attended Naval Inshore Operations Training Center, Vietnamese Language, and survival, evasion, resistance and escape training in California.

Assigned to Nha Be, Vietnam (Rung Sat Special Zone) as PBR-18 boat captain, Riv. Div. 541 and 591. He participated in Operation Giant Sling Shot. Stark was stationed at Sasebo, Japan as gas station/garage manager from 1969-73. He returned to submarine duty in 1973 until retirement as chief of the boat MMCM(SS) in October 1983.

His awards include the Bronze Star with Combat V, Purple Heart, Navy Commendation with Combat V, Navy Achievement, Combat Action, Good Conduct, Navy Expeditionary, National Defense, Vietnam Service Cross of Gallantry, Civil Action and Vietnam Campaign.

He currently owns and operates Starks NW Enterprises. Married almost seven years, he and wife, Darlene, have three sons.

DONALD L. STEIGEL, born Sept. 22, 1949, in Calgary, Alberta, Canada. He became a U.S. citizen on July 23, 1957. Enlisted in the USN on Dec. 26, 1968. Steigel completed GMG School, River Patrol Craft and SERE training in 1969. He reported to the RVN where he was assigned to Riv. Div. 593, PBR 841 which operated from Nha Be into the Run Sat Special Zone, the Saigon River, the Ven Te and Grand Canal, as well as on the Mekong River far into Cambodia.

Personal Story: After setting waterborne guard post, they settled into their normal nightly routine. Around midnight there were noises off to their northwest and they were all on their guard. At the stroke of midnight, the entire sky lit up with pop flares: red, white, blue and green. The light and color were spectacular! Then, they realized it was Christmas! They sat there, basking in the glow of all that light, recalling their favorite Christmas stories. Pulling up and heading in was their present priority, as they became sitting ducks lit up by the lights of Christmas. They all tried to find a little Christmas cheer to share with one another. Maybe one day, there will be "Peace on Earth."

Steigel was awarded the Navy Commendation with Combat V, Combat Action, Presidential Unit Citation Vietnam Service, Vietnam Campaign and National Defense Award. He was honorably discharged on Dec. 9, 1972.

He is presently a member of the SCNG where he is a staff sergeant, tank commander in Co. C, 2nd Bn., 263rd Armor, Clover, SC. He is also a member of the Metrolina Vietnam Veterans, VFW and St. Luke's Catholic Church.

He married June A. Cheney on July 26, 1969; they have two daughters, Donna Jean and Diana Marie. He received his bachelor's degree from Fort Lauderdale University in 1978; has over 10 years' experience in retail lumber and is now a carpenter/cabinet maker. He and his family reside in Charlotte, NC.

RICHARD A. STENGEL (CASEY), born in Buffalo, NY on Sept. 9, 1927. He enlisted in the USN on Sept. 24, 1944. After boot camp at Great Lakes, IL, he was assigned to Pacific Fleet, mostly on cargo ships: USS *Scania* (AKA-40) and *Arequipa* (AF-31). The Air Force supplied fresh provisions to the Army at the islands during the A bomb test called Sandstones Operation. He also placed the USS *Newport News* in commission and the USS *Little Rock*. He spent four years aboard the USS *Iowa,* then on to destroyers USS *W.C. Lawe* and USS *Zellars*.

He decided to volunteer for Vietnam in 1968 and attended Naval Inshore Operation Training Center in California, Vietnamese Language School in Coronado, and survival, evasion, resistance and escape training in Washington. He arrived in Vietnam in November 1968 and was assigned as patrol officer in Riv. Div. 571. They had the Mark One's PBRs and moved to many different areas of Vietnam (ditches, canals and rivers) mostly night ambush. They inserted Seals and Grunts in ambush duty with the Army and protected ski boats in ambush at night.

His last year in service was at Orlando Training Center. He retired in 1974. His awards include the Bronze Star with Combat V, Navy Commendation Medal with Combat V, Combat Action Ribbon, Vietnam Service Medal with one star, Vietnam Campaign Medal, Presidential Unit Citation (571), National Defense with one star, Good Conduct Medal with Silver Star, Asiatic-Pacific, WWII Victory Medal, China Service Medal, American Theater, and Navy Occupation Medal.

A widower, he lives in Atlantic Beach, FL and has a daughter, Patricia Foss, and two grandchildren.

HERB STEPHAN, born in Koln, Germany on Dec. 19, 1939. He entered the USN in January 1958 in Salina, KS and achieved his commission on Aug. 1, 1969 through the CWO/LDO Program. Upon completion of Recruit Training and

QM A School in San Diego, CA, his initial assignment was aboard the USS *Graffias* (AF-29).

Subsequent duty took him to USS *Guadalupe* (AO-32), USS *George Washington* (SSBN-598), USS *Tench* (SS-417), USS *Angler* (SS-241), USS *Irex* (SS-482), USS *Grouper* (SS-417), USS *Sea Robin* (SS-407) and USS *Blenny* (SS-324). From December 1965 until November 1967, he was attached to the NAS Brunswick, ME.

In November 1966, he was promoted to chief petty officer and reported to PBR training. He attended SERE and Language School which led him to duty as the leading chief petty officer/patrol officer for RIVSEC 541//RIVDIV 591 in 1968-69. He operated mainly in the Rung Sat area and was involved in many offensive operations during this tour.

He was selected as a warrant officer and reported to USS *Wasp* (CVS-18) in August 1969, where he served as the ship's boatswain. From July 1972-June 1974 he was an instructor at OCS, Newport, RI. Selected as a limited duty officer, he reported to USS *San Jose* (AFS-7) in August 1974, where he served as deck department head. He assumed command of the USS *Recovery* (ARS-43) from May 1980-August 1982. Next was as assistant chief of staff for Underway Replenishment for Commander, Service Group 2. In November 1984, he was assigned as operations officer aboard the Naval Amphibious Base, Little Creek, VA.

Next was USS *Concord* (AFS-5) in November 1987, where he served as XO in April 1989. He was commanding officer of the Naval Amphibious Base, Little Creek, from June 1989 until June 1991. Prior to reporting to Naval Beach Group 2, he was commanding officer, Fleet Training Center, Norfolk, from June 1991 to July 1993.

His awards include Legion of Merit with Gold Star, three Bronze Stars with Combat V, three Purple Hearts, Meritorious Service Medal with three Gold Stars, Navy Commendation Medal with Combat V, Navy Achievement Medal, Good Conduct Award with Bronze Star, Combat Action Cross of Gallantry, Vietnam Service Medal, Vietnam Meritorious Unit Citation, Armed Forces Expeditionary Medal and the Vietnam Campaign Medal.

Still on active duty and presently assigned as commander, Naval Beach Group 2 at Little Creek, VA, he plans to retire from the Navy in March of 1996. He is married to the former Lorie Allore of Ludlow, MA. They have three children: son, Adam, and two daughters, Kristen and Mrs. Kimberly Morgan.

CLAYTON H. STONE, born Sept. 2, 1940 in La Crosse, WI. He entered the USN in July 1963, and after attending OCS, Newport, RI, he was commissioned in February 1964 and served on the USS *Thomaston* (LSD-28).

LTJG Stone volunteered for Vietnam duty and attended counterinsurgency pre-deployment course and Vietnamese Language Training, Coronado, CA; survival, evasion, resistance and escape training, Warner Springs, CA; and jungle environmental survival training, Philippines. LTJG Stone was assigned as the first administrative officer, CTF-116 Staff, in June 1966.

He separated from the Navy at Communication Station, Naples, Italy in September 1969 as a lieutenant. His awards include the Navy Commendation Medal with Combat V, Presidential Unit Citation, Vietnam Service Medal with four Bronze Stars, RVN Campaign Medal, Armed Forces Expeditionary Medal, Combat Action Ribbon, and National Defense Service Medal.

He married Karen Jean in 1986; they have two sons, Christopher and Justin.

EWELL G. STURGIS JR. (BUDDY), born Sept. 9, 1947, in Rock Hill, SC. He joined the USNR on Jan. 16, 1967 and served with Riv. Div. 592, COMNAV FORV (staff security). His memorable experience was as special security for Adm. Zumwalt, commander of Naval Forces, Vietnam (23 years later). He developed and constructed first U.S. Naval Adv. Tactical Support Base exhibit at Patriots Point Museum, Charleston, SC.

Discharged in December 1970 as BM2. His awards include the Purple Heart, Combat Action Ribbon, National Defense, Vietnam Campaign and Vietnam Service. CW2 South Carolina National Guard and deputy curator of Patriots Point Museum.

He and his wife, Judy, have son, E.G. Sturgis III (Chip)

JAMES R. TALLEY, born July 26, 1947, in Concordia, KS. He enlisted June 6, 1966, and was assigned to USS *Ozbourn* (DD-846) on June 23, 1967, and to RIV PAT FLOT 5 on June 9, 1969, with RIVDIV 551.

Separated June 12, 1970, as GMG3; reafilliated with USNR as BU2 with NMCB 15, Sept. 18, 1976; advanced to BUC on Sept. 16, 1983 to present.

Memorable Experience: The expression and tears of pride and happiness in his father's face

when his end of tour award and commendation were read and presented at the American Legion Post where his dad was a past commander. His dad passed away four years later as a result of a stroke.

His awards include the Navy Commendation Medal with V, Navy Achievement Combat Action, Navy Unit Commendation, Navy E, Naval Reserve Meritorious (4th), National Defense (2nd), Armed Forces Expeditionary, Vietnam Service, Armed Forces Reserve Medal, RVN Gallantry, Cross Unit Citation, RVN Campaign Medal, Vietnam Training Medal, Expert Rifleman, Pistol Sharpshooter, CB Combat Warfare Specialist and Small Craft Device.

Second marriage to Vicki; he has two children, seven step-grandchildren and two grandchildren. He is proprietor of a local hardware store, Sunnyside Hardware).

JON D. TEHAN, born May 20, 1936, in Milwaukee, WI. He enlisted in the USN on June 14, 1954. After two breaks in service and 10 years of sea duty, he volunteered for duty in Vietnam. A signalman first class, he reported to Riv. Div. 551, a plankowner and was assigned boat captain of PBR-779 at Nha Be, May 1968. He completed 242 patrols while attached to Nha Be, Mobile Support Base II and YRBM-16. The high point during one patrol as patrol officer, he detained 21 violators, 11 confirmed VC from black list. His call sign was Azalea Blossom 8.

His awards include the Bronze Star with Combat V, Meritorious Service Medal, Navy Achievement Medal (three awards), Combat Action Ribbon, Good Conduct Medal (seven awards) and numerous others. Authorized Small Craft Command Device, earned and designated air warfare specialist while command master chief of VS-41 "Shamrocks" at NAS North Island. He retired a master chief Navy counselor with 30 years service in February 1988.

Now retired, he is part-time employed at the Tinder Box tobacco/gift shop, El Cajon, CA. Retirement interests include wood carving, collecting military Zippo cigarette lighters and decorating worn out life rings brought to life as quality works of art.

He is married to Iiosdada Santos from Anda, Bohol, Philippines. They have four children: Josephine, Jean, Jessica and Jon Gabriel (serving with the USMC). He resides in El Cajon, CA.

JAMES PATRICK THOMAS (JIM), born in Chicago, IL on Sept. 24, 1946. He joined the USN, at the age of 17, on June 11, 1964. He served on the USS *Savage* (DER-386) in Operation Market Time RVN from April 1966-May 1967. He volunteered for Patrol Craft Fast (PCF) (Swift Boat) crew duty. On Nov. 27, 1967, he reported to Coastal Sqdn. 1, Cam Ranh Bay, for assignment to An Thoi, Phu Quac Island, RVN.

He served on PCFs 10, 73, 43, and 45. Jim extended eight months in Vietnam in order to receive an early out. Thus, he served on the PCFs from November 1967 through August 1969. He spent 15 months at COSDIV 11, An Thoi and the last five months at COSDIV 14, Cam Ranh Bay. While at Cam Ranh Bay, he served as the leading petty officer and bow gunner of a recon Boston whaler with an M-60 mounted on the bow. He also served as an instructor for training new crews in country and served as a liaison/instructor for the new Vietnamese crews. He was heavily involved in training the Vietnamese crews for the Vietnamization Program. Finally, he served as COSDIV 14 senior radarman.

High points of his tour include TET 68 (he was wounded on Feb. 16, 1968 while on PCF-10 on a night recon on the Song On Doc River); SEALORDS Operations (he was on Sealords #1 through #198); Operation Silver Mace; Operation Giant Sling Shot; and the establishment of SEAFLOAT.

He left Vietnam in August 1969 and started college. He was asked to become a plankowner of a new unit that became Coastal Riverine Div. 21 at Great Lakes, IL. There, Jim was assigned to Nasty Class PTF-17 and made RD1.

In 1973 he graduated from Drake University in Des Moines, IA, with a degree in political science and history, then was commissioned in the USAF. He served in various assignments as a Minute Man III Missile Launch officer and a Signals Intelligence officer until his retirement as a major in October 1990.

His awards and decorations include the Purple Heart, Defense Meritorious Service Medal with OLC, Meritorious Service Medal, Air Force Commendation Medal, Air Force Achievement Medal, Navy Combat Action Ribbon, National Defense Medal, Vietnam Service Medal with eight Campaign Stars, Vietnam Campaign Medal, and he is authorized to wear the Senior Missile Launch Officer Crewmember's Badge and the Basic Non-rated Air Crewmember Wings.

In 1994, he received a master of science in Special Education from the Johns Hopkins University. He is now pursuing a new career working with children who have severe and profound handicapping conditions.

Currently, he lives in Ellicott City, MD; he has one son, Nicholas, who also lives in Ellicott.

PATRICK NEVILLE THOMPSON, born Aug. 23, 1949, in Sandusky, OH. He enlisted in the USN on June 6, 1968 and served on board the USS *Tanner* in Vietnam with Harbor Clearance Unit 1, and later, on board USS *Kansas City* in Vietnam (Da Nang, Vung Tau and An Thoi).

He participated in Project Jenny, Operation Market-Time, Operation Gamewarden, TF-116, and for a short period, with Task Force Clearwater TF-117. His memorable experiences include: first time under fire; first time on a run with the PBR; being scared almost all the time.

Left the USN in June 1980 as CWO4. He retired from Ohio Naval Militia as Commander (0-5) after 12 years in 1992. His awards and medals include the National Defense, Armed Forces Expeditionary, Combat Action, Meritorious Unit Commendation, Vietnam Service, Vietnam Campaign with three stars, Navy Achievement, Vietnam Cross of Gallantry, Expert Rifle and Pistol, USCG Special Operations Ribbon, Ohio Meritorious Service Medal and Ohio Distinguished Service Medal for rescue of a civilian from a crashed and sinking amphibian aircraft in Toledo.

Presently employed with the U.S. Army Corps of Engineers, Buffalo, NY District, as a tug skipper and merchant mariner. He is married to Denice Louise (Kline) Thompson of Alpena, MI, who had worked part-time for him as a deckhand onboard U.S. EPA research ships on the Great Lakes when he was mate.

PHILLIP S. THOMPSON, born April 7, 1931, in Chicago, IL and entered the USN in April 1948. Upon completion of recruit training, he was ordered to Submarine School and subsequently completed 25 years of submarine service. While stationed at Portsmouth Naval Shipyard, he earned a BS degree in Marine engineering and naval architecture and was ultimately designated a Submarine Engineering Duty Officer (EDO).

He was ordered to PBR School in 1967. Shortly after his arrival in Vietnam, NAVSUPPAC requested that he be transferred from PBR duty to NSA Binh Thuy, where he assumed the duties of detachment assistant officer-in-charge and detachment maintenance and weapons officer.

Awards: Bronze Star Medal w/Combat V, Good Conduct Medal, Navy Occupation Medal, National Defense Medal, Korean Service Medal, Vietnam Service Medal, Navy Unit Commendation, Combat Action Ribbon, Korean Campaign Ribbon, and RVN Campaign Ribbon.

LCDR Thompson was medically retired from the naval service in 1973. He then worked for Ingalls Shipbuilding as a senior nuclear engineer before starting a successful yacht design business in Mobile, AL.

RODNEY K. THOMPSON (TOM), born in Pittsburgh, PA on Aug. 13, 1941. He joined the USN in 1958, served in RVN in Riv. Div. 552 from November 1968 to November 1969. During his first Vinh Te Canal fire fight, Lt. Bierrable and a CIDG were KIA aboard PBR-868.

Later, QM Thompson was assigned as PBR-868 boat captain of literary Charley Patrol with PBR-864. That boat was destroyed in January 1969 by a command detonated mine near the Canal's French Cemetery. Miraculously, the crew survived the explosion and small arms fire and were rescued by the crew of PBR-868. She, while patrolling the Vam Co Dong River, was raked by a 50 caliber, killing Joe Milano.

In October 1969, RMC Norman Green (later KIA) relieved QM1 Thompson of PBR-868. His awards include the Bronze Star and Navy Commendation Medal.

He retired in 1980 and survived a heart-attack on Aug. 8, 1988. He married Eileen MacFee in 1966, and they have two married daughters.

BUDDY L. TOWNSEND, born July 1, 1946 in Banner Elk, NC. He joined the USN in October 1965; stationed at San Diego, CA; SERE training at North Island, CA; river patrol craft training at Valley, CA; Vietnamese Language School at Amphibious Training Command, San Diego, CA.

He served aboard the USS *Delta* AR-9, Riv. Div. 552 - 515 and Small Boat School in Saigon. When the Vietnamese took over the PBR, he retired from NCNG as E-7 with 22 and a half years. Townsend was activated in November 1991 for Dessert Shield and Storm for eight months with the Army.

His awards include the National Defense with Bronze Star, Vietnam Service Medal, Vietnamese Campaign Medal, Navy Achievement Service Medal with Combat V, Combat Action Ribbon, NCO Professional Ribbon, Armed Forces Reserve Medal, Army Service Ribbon and Vietnam Cross of Gallantry.

Married Daphine Hamby on April 26, 1970. They have two daughters, Tammy Nelson and Michelle Cox. He works for Greene's Furniture Co., Boone, NC and is a member of DAV Chapter #90.

D.L. TUCKER was KIA on July 6, 1969. PO Tucker joined Riv. Div. 593 in May of 1969. He completed 17 combat patrols during the time left that month. He was assigned as a boat captain

after only a short time in the division because of his cool nature under fire.

On July 6, 1969, his patrol was conducting operations in the Rung Sat Special Zone when they came under heavy rocket and AK-47 fire. PO Tucker was mortally wounded when a rocket struck the port side of the coxswain's flat where he was operating the PBR.

He was a great shipmate and a good man to have in a firefight. He was, and is, missed by those he served with.

MARTIN W. VICE (MARTY), born in Chicago, IL, on Jan. 5, 1948. He attended Kelvyn Park High School (Chicago), McHenry High School (McHenry, IL) and Paramount High School (Paramount, CA), graduating in 1966. He enlisted in the USN in October 1966; attended Counter Insurgency/Survival Schools in Little Creek, VA; Vietnamese Language School in Coronado, CA; PBR School in Mare Island, CA.

He arrived in Vietnam May 20, 1967, attached to Riv. Sec. 542 at Nha Be. He was reassigned to newly formed Riv. Sec. 534 in August 1967 and relocated to the Mekong Delta operating near My Tho and Ben Tre. Riv. Sec. 534 was the first to receive new Mark-11 PBRs.

Under the command of Lt. R.M. Wolin, Riv. Sec. 534 chalked up a remarkable combat record in a very short period of time. Boats from 534 were the first on the scene, Jan. 31, 1968 (the beginning of TET), to defend the city of Ben Tre from a massive Viet Cong attack. During the 18 hour battle, the VC suffered heavy casualties while 534's losses of men and material were minimal. The city of Ben Tre was virtually destroyed during the siege.

GMGSN Vice received the National Defense Service Medal, Vietnam Service and Vietnam Campaign Medals and a Certificate of Achievement Award from W.C. Westmoreland, Commanding General, U.S. Forces, Vietnam.

Married to Diane, he has a son, Richard; daughter, Tamara; stepsons, Gregory and Garret Parker; and two granddaughters, Sadie and Shelby Vice. He is a supervisor for Santa Fe Pacific Pipelines, Los Angeles, CA and resides in Upland, CA.

CLARENCE J. WAGES JR., born in New Orleans and attended public schools there and in Monroe, LA. In 1947 he enlisted in the Naval Reserve and was called to active duty during the Korean War in 1951. He served aboard the USS *McCord* and *Richard E. Kraus* in the Atlantic and Pacific Fleets.

Released from active duty in 1953, he attended Louisiana State University, graduated in 1957 with bachelor's degree and was commissioned an ensign, USNR and returned to active duty. Attended CIC Officer and Air Control courses at NATTC Glynco, GA; reported in

1957 to USS *Calcaterra*; reported to Naval Schools, Mine Warfare in Charleston, SC (1959); sent to USS *Exultant* as XO; served as Aide and Flag Lieutenant to Commander, Mine Force, Atlantic Fleet; attended COMCRUDESPAC Engineering School; and assigned to USS *King*.

Completed tour at the Bureau of Naval Personnel; graduated from U.S. Naval War College in 1967; served as XO of USS *Cochrane*; reported to Commander Naval Forces Vietnam in 1969; attended United Kingdom Joint Services Staff College, Latimer, Buckinghamshire, England; was personal aide to Adm. Zumwalt; attended Destroyer School at Newport, RI; was CO of USS *Josephus Daniels* (1972); commanded Destroyer Squadron 26 (1973); served as director, Surface Warfare Manpower and Training Requirements Div. in the office of DCNO (1975); and his final assignment on the staff of the Chief of Naval Reserve as Chief of Staff.

Retired from the Navy July 1, 1981. He received the Silver Star, Legion of Merit with V, Bronze Star with V, Purple Heart, Air Medal, Navy Commendation with V, two awards of Vietnam Cross of Gallantry and others.

Married the former Cynthia Caldwell and they have two daughters, Zoe Wages Dillard and Paris Caldwell Wages, and two granddaughters, Ashley Faye and Phoebe Francis Dillard. They reside in Panama City, FL.

LEE R. WAHLER, born and raised in Washington, DC. He was commissioned Oct. 11, 1968. His first sea duty assignment was as auxiliary division officer onboard the USS *Graffias* (AF-29) on which he deployed to WESTPAC.

After training in riverine operations at NIOTC Vallejo, CA, in late 1969, he served a one year tour in Vietnam on river patrol boats. He served both as a USN patrol officer in Riv. Div. 513 based at Rach Gia on Vietnam's West Coast and later as an advisor to the Vietnamese Navy RIVPATGRU 62 on the Song Ong Doc River. As a result of his actions while in country, he was awarded a Bronze Star with Combat V, Combat Action Ribbon and Navy Unit Commendation, as well as several Vietnamese Campaign and Service Ribbons.

After Vietnam, he was 1st lieutenant and navigator on the USS *Francis Marion* where he was promoted to lieutenant, making several Caribbean deployments. He was designated a surface warfare officer in February 1972. His next ship was the USS *Newport* where he served as the Operations Officer until July 1975.

For overseas duty, he was assigned as XO, Military Sealift Command Office, Naha, Okinawa from 1975 until 1978. He reported to Military Sealift Command Pacific at Oakland, CA as assistant to the engineering officer.

After being released from active duty in June 1979, LCDR Wahler joined the Naval Re-

serve in October 1979 with the Military Sealift Command Office West MED 406 at NRC Baltimore, MD and with Naval Control of Shipping Office Texas/So. America 406 at NRC Adelphi, MD until his retirement in April 1989.

JAMES H. WALKER (JIM), born Jan. 25, 1939, in West Pelzer, SC. He joined the USN on June 8, 1956 and served with Riv. Div. 573 in the Mekong Delta. Was hotel patrol officer from September 1968 to April 1970. He completed 360 combat patrols.

Retired May 27, 1981 as EMCS (E-8). His awards include the Bronze Star with Combat V, CAR, Presidential Unit Citation, Meritorious Unit Citation, National Defense, Good Conduct, Vietnam Service Medal, Vietnam Cross of Gallantry and VCM.

He was Southeast Region Chapter Treasurer of Gamewardens. He and wife, Terry, have two daughters, Trudy and Tonni, and one son, Mitchell.

JEFFREY JOHN WARNOCK, born May 27, 1944, in Brooklyn, NY. He joined the USN in May 1968 and graduated from OCS in February 1969. He arrived in Vietnam in June 1969 and was attached to Riv. Div. 514 as patrol officer. He operated along the Vinh Te Canal during Operation Tran Hung Dao, and remained as an assistant senior naval advisor to RPG-55 from April 1970 through October 1970 when the USN turned River Divisions over to VNN. Assigned to USS *Luce* (DLG-7) as MPA in October 1970.

Discharged from active duty in October 1972, he remained in the Naval Reserve as an engineering duty officer (1445) and was promoted to captain in June 1990. His awards include the Bronze Star with V, Navy Commendation with V, Navy Achievement with V, Air Medal, Combat Action, National Defense, Vietnam Service, Vietnam Cross of Gallantry, Vietnam Staff Service, Vietnam Training Service, Vietnam Civil Action, Small Boat and Surface Warfare Devices.

Married to Ann Sherry and they have three children: Meghan, Timothy and Kevin. They currently reside in Exeter, NH. His fondest memory of the Navy is serving with the men of the Brown Water Navy, a unique and singular experience in naval history and his personal career.

BILL DANIEL WATTS, born June 14, 1943, in Port Orchard, WA. He joined the USN on Nov. 24, 1962. His military stations/locations include: USS *Vega* (AF-59); Vietnamese Language School, San Diego, CA; Survival School, Whidbey Island, WA; PBR Training, Mare Island, CA; Jungle Survival School, Subic Bay, P.I.; River Section 541, Nha Be; River Section 514, Binh Thuy, Vietnam.

He was assigned as M-60 machine gunner of River Patrol Boat 17 on combat patrol of the Long Tau River, Rung Sat Special Zone, and received the Navy Commendation Medal with Combat V for heroic achievement during an ambush on Dec. 6, 1967.

Discharged March 3, 1973 as GMG3. His awards include the Purple Heart, Combat Action Ribbon, National Defense, Vietnam Campaign, Vietnam Service and Vietnam Cross of Gallantry.

Married Gwinny Watts in August 1972; they have five children: Danielle, Stephen, Elisha, Torrey and Joshua. He is retired.

ROBERT WEINSCHENK (BOB), born Oct. 26, 1946, in Madison, IN. He joined the USNR on July 17, 1967, and served with Riv. Sec. 541, Nha Be, Rung Sat.

His memorable experience was being in Vietnam with guys like "B.T., Mad Dog and Dirty Dan" and surviving.

Discharged July 5, 1972 as GMG3. His awards include the National Defense, Vietnam Service, Vietnam Campaign, Purple Heart, and Navy Commendation with Combat V.

Married Dec. 9, 1978, to Mary; they have three daughters: Sara, Kim and Kelli. He is regional sales manager for a veterinary pharmaceutical company in the southeast U.S. He recently joined Gamewardens Assoc., and looks forward to being active in it.

MITCHELL ALLEN WENTZ, born on Oct. 10, 1946, in Pensacola, FL. He was the son of a career naval officer, CDR Charles A. Wentz, and spent his formative years living aboard many Naval Air Stations stateside and in Hawaii. After graduation from Lompoc High School in California, he joined the USN in November 1965. He was sent to boot camp in San Diego and upon graduation was assigned to the USS *Betelgeuse* and the USS *Peregrine*.

He arrived in Vietnam in October 1967 and was assigned to Riv. Sec. 541, Nha Be. He patrolled the Rung Sat Special Zone until he was transferred to Riv. Sec. 514, Binh Thuy in April 1968. He patrolled the North Bassac and served as boat captain of PBR 747. Mitchell made second class in two and a half years of service.

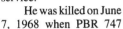

He was killed on June 7, 1968 when PBR 747 came under fire on the Bassac at Tan Dinh Island. He was awarded the Purple Heart, National Defense Medal, Vietnam Service Medal and Vietnam Campaign Medal.

His many friends will remember him as an avid surfer. He is survived by his mother, Rita M. Wentz, and his sister, Dale Wentz Drake.

JOSEPH EDWARD WHERRY, born Oct. 9, 1948, in Chicago, IL. He joined the USN on Oct. 20, 1966 and served in Vietnam. He received a gunshot wound in his knee on Jan. 4, 1969.

Was given a citation for work done with Vietnamese children during his recuperation. Discharged April 17, 1970. He received the Purple Heart, Vietnam Service Medal with two Bronze Stars, RVN Campaign Medal with Device, Combat Action Ribbon, RVN Meritorious Unit Citation (Gallantry Cross Medal 1/C Color with Palm) and Civil Actions Medal with 1/C Color with Palm.

National Service Representative for VVA, Nov. 22, 1988 NSO of MOPH, Pen and Sword Society, UNO Vice President, Disabled Student Agency, Knights of Columbus, BSA, Sons of Italy, Men's Club of St. Patrick's Church and Boystown Alumni.

ALAN LEWIS WHITE, born April 13, 1947, near Cullman, AL. He joined the USN in November 1965; attended basic training at Great Lakes; Class A Gunner's Mate School at NTC, Great Lakes; PBR School, Mare Island, CA; POW and Survival School, Coronado, CA; and transferred to Subic Bay, Philippines for more Survival School.

Arrived at Long Xyen, Vietnam in August of 1966 to form a new River Patrol Boat Section 523. Was with that unit until September 1968 when he was sent home on emergency leave because his father had been in a bad car accident (recovered). In November 1966, he was re-assigned to the USS *Aludra* out of Oakland, CA; then went back to Vietnam and re-supplied ships off the coast, and once, pulling into Saigon Harbor.

GM2/c White was discharged in September 1969 when the *Aludra* was decommissioned and put in the Moth Ball Fleet. He received the Presidential Unit Commendation Medal, RVN Campaign Medal, Armed Forces Expeditionary Medal, two Bronze Stars with Combat V and Vietnam Service Medal with star.

Worked a couple of jobs before starting with a caterpillar tractor dealer in Birmingham, AL. He retired in 1990 (after 17 years) on disability, with a neuro muscular disease. Currently, living in a motorhome and traveling the country with his wife, Connie. He would like to hear from anyone in his old unit, the 523.

NEAL R. WILLARD, born Oct. 28, 1934 in New York. Joined the U.S Navy in 1951 at age 17 and served in Korea. Neal reported to River Division 593, The Iron Butterfly, in September, 1969 while the Division was on Operation Ready Deck. He saw action on the Upper Saigon River and in the Rung Sat Special Zone.

On the Rivers of Vietnam or on the Roads of America, Neal Willard was a Shipmate and a Friend. After returning from Vietnam and retiring from the Navy, Neal became a long haul trucker and would try to find fellow warriors on his many trips across America. Finally poor health and a bad fall took Neal off the highway; but he never gave up looking for or staying in touch with fellow members of Gamewardens.

Neal received his last set of orders on Monday, Aug. 15, 1994 and is now serving on the staff of the Supreme Commander. Neal, we miss you, keep your powder dry and don't forget your cover boat will always be there.

Neal left behind his wife Margaret, two sons, four daughters and several grandchildren.

JOHN CLYDE WILLIAMS, born in Sedalia, MO on May 19, 1936. He joined the Naval Reserve in June 1953, graduated from Osawatomie, KS High School in 1954, and began active duty at NAS Olathe, KS in January 1955. He transferred to the Norfolk, VA area.

He served one uneventful year in Can Tho/ Binh Thuy, RVN as part of the original River Patrol gang in RIVRON 5/RIVDIV 51 from April 1966-67, rear echelon warrior. He received no significant medals. During 30 years active duty, he served in three ships: *Arcturus*, *Connole* and *Mount Whitney*, with lots of shore duty and ending up at Little Creek.

Retired in January 1985 and is now mail handler in the main post office in Norfolk. He is active in Masonic activities and is 33° assistant secretary of Norfolk Scottish Rite Bodies.

Married to Christine; they have five children and four grandchildren. He is original secretary/treasurer of Gamewardens of Vietnam Assoc. and is now president.

WILLIAM B. WILSON, born March 16, 1946, in Jackson, TN. He joined the USN on April 3, 1963; trained for PBRs and Vietnam in Coronado; and jungle survival in Manila.

He arrived in Vietnam in February of 1966 and was assigned to Riv. Div. 511 as engineer, after gunner and relief coxswain on PBR-37. In October of 1966, he took a PBR into Juliet to rescue Ratliff and lost crewmember, T.J. Freund, during a three hour firefight. He was wounded on Jan. 27, 1967 during an ambush at Long Phu.

His awards include the Bronze Star with Combat V, Purple Heart, Navy Achievement Medal with Combat V, Vietnam Service, Vietnam Campaign, Vietnam Presidential and National Defense.

Married Carol in 1977; he has four children from a previous marriage and seven grandchildren. Today, he is disability retired from PTSD and has isolated himself in the woods in Alabama.

BURTON BROOKS WITHAM JR., born March 18, 1923, Portland, ME. He joined the USN in July 1942 and was commissioned in 1945. Was Commander, River Patrol Force, CTF-116; Command LST-822; MSO-424; COMINDIV 82; Command USS *Rushmore*; and USS *Spiegel Grove*.

Left the service Aug. 1, 1973 as captain. His awards include the Legion of Merit, Presidential Unit Commendation, Korean Action, Vietnam Service, WWII Victory, DOD Meritorious Service, Vietnam Naval Distinguished Service Order 1/c, and Vietnam Gallantry Cross with Gold Star.

Married Caroline in 1945 (deceased in 1992). He has two daughters, Anne Kilpatrick and Mary Huddleston. He is retired.

RONALD M. WOLIN, born in Burlington, VT and enlisted in the USN after high school. He was an AT2, flying as a crewmember on seaplanes. After discharge, he graduated from Bos-

ton University and accepted a direct commission, serving on various ships and staffs.

He volunteered for Vietnam and was assigned as OIC to form up the first unit to employ the MK II PBRs, RIVSEC 534, which was activated at Nha Be on Sept. 11, 1967. The unit was then assigned to the Ham Luong River area operating from APL 55. RIVSEC 534 was heavily involved in the Ben Tre area during the 1968 TET Offensive.

His awards include the Silver Star, Bronze Star with Combat V w/2nd awd., Purple Heart w/ 2nd awd., Combat Action Ribbon, Presidential Unit Citation and the Vietnam Cross of Gallantry with Bronze Star.

Retired as lieutenant commander in 1978. He is self-employed.

HARRY L. YORK III, born Dec. 27, 1950, in Keene, NH. He joined the USN in November 1968; went to boot camp at Great Lakes; served in USS *Jason* (AR-8), in San Diego, CA; units in Nha Trang and Cam Ranh Bay; Operation Seafloat IV Corps; Groton Submarine Base; VA-81 and Commander, Light Attack Sqdn. (staff clerk); and USS *Saratoga*.

The most memorable experiences he had in Vietnam were the frequent sapper attacks; the people he met; and always traveling alone when going from base to base.

Discharged Nov. 22, 1972, he re-enlisted

and attained the rank of BM3/c. His awards include the Vietnam Service, Vietnam Campaign, Combat Action Ribbon and National Defense Medal.

Single, he lives in Keene, NH and works for Ossiam/Sylvania in Hillsboro, NH. He earned a bachelor of arts in history from Keene State College in 1986. He has one daughter, Casey Marie York.

ELMO RUSSELL ZUMWALT JR., born in San Francisco on Nov. 29, 1920. He graduated from the Naval Academy and was commissioned an ensign in June 1942. He was assigned to the USS *Phelps* and in November 1943, detached for instruction in the Operational Training Command, Pacific at San Francisco.

In January 1944, he reported to the USS *Robinson*. Succeeding posts include: prize crew officer of the HIJMS ATAKA; XO of the USS *Saufley*; XO and navigator of the USS *Zellers*; tour with the Naval Reserve Officers Training

Corps Unit of the University of North Carolina; CO of the USS *Tills*.

During the Korean Conflict, he was navigator of the battleship, USS *Wisconsin*; attended the Naval War College, Newport, RI; reported as head of the Shore and Overseas Base Section, Bureau of Naval Personnel, Washington, DC; served as officer and enlisted requirements officer and as action officer on medicare legislation; CO of the USS *Arnold J. Isbell*; tour at Bureau of Naval Personnel; served as special assistant, executive assistant and senior aide for Naval Personnel.

In July 1959, commanded USS *Dewey*; was student at National War College; assigned to the Office of the Assistant Secretary of Defense; and served as executive assistant and senior aide to the Secretary of the Navy. Became Commander, Cruiser-Destroyer Flotilla 7; director of the Chief of Naval Operations Systems Analysis Group in Washington; Commander, USN Forces, Vietnam.

Vice Admiral Zumwalt is married to the former Mouza Coutelais-du-Roche of Harbin, Manchuria. They have two sons, Elmo R III and James G, and two daughters, Ann and Mouza C. His awards include Legion of Merit and Gold Star in lieu of a second Legion of Merit.

THE FOLLOWING BIOGRAPHIES HAVE BEEN
NEWLY SUBMITTED FOR THIS SECOND EDITION.

THOMAS KING ANDERSON, born Jan. 27, 1938, Petersburg, VA. After graduation from Davidson College, NC, enlisted in the Naval OCS program and commissioned ensign in November 1959. His first tour was on the USS *Springfield,* Sixth Fleet Flagship in the Mediterranean, followed with tours on the USS *Galveston* and USS *King* with deployments in the Tonkin Gulf.

From 1965 to 1968, he and his family had a great tour with the NROTC in Moscow, ID. The "payback" orders were as CO, RIVDIV 531 from September 1968-69. Anderson made patrols on each of the boats of the "Delta Dragons" and developed a deep respect for the patrol officers and crews of those boats.

He made LCDR while in-country and was asked to give up his division to become a CTE commander in charge of 45 assorted boats near Tay Ninh City. In view of the strong bond formed with 531, Anderson convinced his superiors to

let him stay as CO in the river division as well as taking the other "hat." Upon completion of this tour, Anderson served as a department head on the USS *Wainwright* with another Tonkin Gulf tour, XO, USS *Jonas Ingram* and CO, USS *Mullinix* with a couple of tours in Washington, DC mixed in between.

He retired as commander in 1979 to become an algebra teacher in the Moscow, ID public school system. After 15 years in education, Anderson retired again with Claire, his wife of 35 years, to their 15 acre "dream spread" on a hill overlooking Moscow.

After 30 years of interactions with all kinds of people since the RIVDIV 531 days, he now has and will always have an even higher degree of respect for the men known as the "River Rats" of the Mekong Delta!

THOMAS W. "GUNS" ARMSTRONG, born Feb. 17, 1948 in Liberty, TX. Entered the service August 1968 and trained at Mare Island, CA, October 1969. Served with RIVDIV 553, NAG Ben Luc.

Arrival in Vietnam was stark reality; first ambush: stark, intense anxiety and heightened senses; first kill: cold objectivity, this guy was go-

ing to kill him! He lost six friends and experienced depression and anger. Man at his best, man at his worst.

Discharged October 1974 as GMGSN. Awarded Presidential Unit Citation, Combat Action Ribbon, NDSM, RVN Service Medal, UN Campaign Medal and Purple Heart.

Owner of Enterprise Network Integration, TECH Genesis Consulting, INC. He is a life member of Gamewardens and was the key engineer of the largest computer acquisition project ever, $4.5 billion by US Air Force with Sperry Universe.

Married to Peggy, his father is F.W. Armstrong, USNR, and brother James.

STEVEN NELSON AZNOE, born June 12, 1945, Sturgeon Bay, WI. Enlisted in the USN Aug. 30, 1965. Attended basic at Great Lakes, IL. JEST training in the Philippines, SERE at Coronado and PBR Class 23 at Mare Island.

Served with PBR's RIVRON 5, RIVSEC 511, Can Tho, Mekong Delta, 1967-68. Military locations and stations included NAS Corpus Christi, TX; RIVSEC 55, Can Tho; 1st 1073; Special Boat Unit 11.

After being in-country for six months, he received word his twin daughters were born. Discharged Sept. 15, 1990 as EN1. Awarded Combat Action, Vietnam Service Medal and Vietnam Campaign.

Employed as chief electrician at St. Marys Hospital in Green Bay, WI. He is divorced and remarried to Marge Liberski. Together they have three girls: Stephanie, Margaret, Leah and three boys: Mark, Peter and Joel.

C. W. BAKER JR.,

C. W. BAKER JR., born Nov. 3, 1941 in Fort Worth, TX. Enlisted in the USN February 1959. Ten ships later on March 1968, he voluntarily joined the Inland Shore Warfare and River Groups. Training including PCF (patrol craft fast) at Colo, CA; Viet languages, internal security, market time survival, evasion and resistant training.

He was stationed in Cat Lo March-August 1968 on US PCFs. He ran PCF 103-104-98-97 during TET 1968. It was an all out push for the Viet Congs to over run the south and all forces. The boats patrolled about 20 miles each, or wherever they were needed in the Mekong Delta, also called Nam Can, after base was moved to shoreline. During the first tour Baker received the Purple Heart during a heavy firefight. He recouperated 1-1/2 years later in Subic Bay, Philippines only to volunteer another year back on the rivers. He could not stay away; he wanted more action; wanted to finish some of whatever he didn't finish the first time.

After renewed and advanced training Colo, CA, his second tour consisted of being an adivsor in ADV. 159, along with internal security guard in Anthoi, Phoc Qua, Hatien, N Ha Bea, 3rd and 4th Delta Zone teaching South Vietnam Navy officers and crew how to run the patrol crafts, navigate, gunnery, market time, roundup and rivers; while gathering intel information from village chiefs and from boats, junks, sanpans on waterway traffic on rivers and canals.

Baker was taken off the rivers October 1972 to return to the US. After two tours he has a few memories of while he was on US patrol and VN advisor. He had 69 combat patrols with the first tour and 80 with the second tour.

Retired as chief, basemate Oct. 30, 1983. Awarded Purple Heart, Navy Commendation Medal w/Combat V, Combat Action Ribbon, Navy Expedition Medal, Armed Forces Expedition Medal, four Good Conduct Medals, Vietnam Service Medal w/2 Bronze Stars, RVN Gallantry Cross w/Palm, Meritorious Service Medal, Civil Action Medal First Class w/Palm, two Vietnam Campaign Medals and several others.

RONALD GENE BIRCHFIELD

RONALD GENE BIRCHFIELD, born Sept. 22, 1944 in Nordheim, TX. The firstborn son of Kathleen and Charles Birchfield, he had two brothers, Kenneth and Arlen and two sisters, Charlene and Susan.

The summer before his junior year, he moved with his family to Port Lavaca where he graduated in 1963. While still in school he made a decision that would map out his next 25 years of life, he joined the Naval Reserves.

After high school he attended college for a semester or two and then decided to forgo college and complete his required two years of active duty in the Navy. Stationed in New Orleans for those two years, he decided he liked the Navy, and re-enlisted for another four years. Requested a transfer to San Diego or Pearl Harbor, the Navy gave him Saigon. Spent two years in Vietnam, he was only required to spend 12 months there, but he volunteered for two more six month tours of duty.

When he finally came home from Vietnam, it was to a new wife and daughter. Married Dewana Dixon August 1968 and adopted her daughter, Alex. Moved to new assignment in Orland, FL. They were divorced shortly after the birth of their second daughter, Elizabeth.

Married Marge Sawyer in 1971 and acquired a family of two boys, George, Sherman and two daughters, Sharon and Janet in Norfolk, VA.

Birchfield spent the rest of his Naval career stationed in Norfolk, except for two years in Sardinia. Promoted to master chief petty officer, he spent much of his last several years in the Navy traveling up and down the eastern seaboard, inspecting ships when they docked in various ports. Retired in 1987 after 25 years of service.

Moved to California and finished his college education by receiving his diploma, then moved to Nevada. Enjoyed spending time with his grandchildren Eirik and Amanda. Ronald passed away July 3, 1997.

LARRY BISSONNETE

LARRY BISSONNETE, born June 16, 1940 in Rhinelander, WI. Entered the Navy 1962. Attended NROTC at Oregon State University and commissioned ensign in 1962.

Served on USS *Rogers* (DD-876), USS *Carpenter* (DD-825), MAAG Germany, USS *William H. Standley* (DLG-32), NAVSEASYSCOM, USS *Mullinix* (DD-944) and Surface Warfare Officers School.

He remembers CO RIVDIV 593, January-December 1969. Completed over 125 patrols on Van Co Dong in Giant Slingshot; Rung Sat Special Zone and the upper Saigon River at PhuCvong.

During 1972-75, while with the 1200 PSI improvement program at NAVSEA, the program was the sponsor of a propulsion plant being installed at Surface Warfare School in Newport, RI. Eventually a computerized simulator was installed. Later in 1978 he became the director of Engineering Training at SWOSCOLCOM in charge of the 1200 PSI propulsion plant simulator.

Discharged in 1982 as CDR. Awarded Silver Star, Bronze Star w/V, Purple Heart, two Presidential Unit Citations, RVN Gallantry Cross w/star and Palm, Meritorious Service Medal as well as others.

He is self-employed in insurance sales, funeral plans and long-term care policies.

MARK J. BOWERS

MARK J. BOWERS, born Jan. 31, 1947 in Twin Falls, ID. Entered the service in 1965. Trained at the usual places as a member of USN and a member of the River Patrol Force, RVN.

Served with RIVSEC 544, RIVDIV 593 and 594.

There were too many memorable experiences to name, but he was bit by a snake while on PBR 756 in 1968 and hit by B-40 in February 1969 while on patrol out of Moc Hoa.

Discharged in 1969 as PO3. Awarded Bronze Star w/Combat V, Presidential Unit Citation, RVN Gallantry Cross, Navy Achievement and others.

Currently is the captain of the Carson City Fire Dept, NV and has three sons. He was a member of the Navy Reserve from 1969-93 and retired as chief petty officer.

LEWIS RAYMOND BRITTON

LEWIS RAYMOND BRITTON, born April 7, 1945 in Burbank, CA. He went in the Navy June 1966. Attended boot camp at San Diego and went aboard the USS Waddell (DDG-24), A Gang. Two days after Christmas in 1966 they went on a west Pacific cruise. While off the coast of Vietnam, they got hit by an air burst and received about nine holes in the ship. Returned to Long Beach early June 1967.

Transferred to the USS *Bridget* (DE-1024) in 1968. The ship went to Seattle, WA and he got orders to Vietnam in May 1968. The word was if you had less than a year left in the hitch, you did not go to Vietnam. He had one year and two weeks left and went to Vietnam June 1969. His first station was NSA Det My Tho as EN 3rd class and worked on engines for the PBRs stationed there. In August 1969 he received a Bronze Star w/Combat V for fighting a fire on two ammo trucks and a building. The fire was caused by a mortar attack.

He was transferred March 1970 to NSA Det Dong Tam and worked on ALFA boat engines. The end of April he was sent to Naval Advisory Group A, PL 27, Saigon River Det.

Discharged June 1970 at the age of 25. Awarded NDSM, Vietnam Campaign Medal w/service ribbon and Vietnam Service Medal.

Currently he is a maintenance person for low income housing. Founder and past president of VVA Chapter 355.

Married Lynn June 25, 1967. He has two daughters and four grandchildren.

LARENCE H. BROWN, born in Washington, DC. Enlisted in the Navy at Roanoke Rapids, NC, September 1951. Received boot training at NTC, San Diego, CA. Served onboard USS *Prairie* (AD-15) during the Korean Conflict 1951-54 in the deck department and the Optical shop.

Re-enlisted Navy and served onboard USS *Everglades* (AD-24) Optical shop, July 1955-December 1959, making several Mediterranean and Carribean cruises; Naval Training Command, Great Lakes, IL, Class C Periscope School, July-August 1956; Submarine Base, New London, CT in the engineering and repair department of the Optical/Periscope Shop, January 1960-October 1963.

In November 1963, commissioned ensign, USN and attended Officer Orientation School, Newport, RI; Officer Engineering School, San Diego, CA January-March 1964. Served onboard USS *Maunakea* (AE-22), main proplusion assistant, April 1964-March 1965 and USS *Regulus* (AF-57), chief engineer, April 1965-June 1967.

COMFOUR Staff, Philadelphia, material/logistics officer, July 1967-June 1969; NIOTC, Mare Island, CA, July-August 1968; Gamewardens, RVN, RIVDIV 552 and 513, Van Co Dong, Van Co Tay Rivers, Tra Cu, Ben Luc and Hot Tien near Cambodian border August 1969-July 1970; USS *Arco* (ARD-29), executive officer, Guam, MI, August 1970-July 1971; Naval Training Publications Detachment, Navy Yard, Washington, DC, August 1971-January 1974.

Naval Station, Annapolis, MD, executive officer/small craft department head, February-December 1974; served onboard USS *Coral Sea* (CV-43), auxiliary officer, January-September 1975, assisting in the retrieval of Miakez and the evacuation of civilians from RVN. Transferred to Fleet Reserve Sept. 17, 1975 with 24 years of active service.

Employed ARINC, Research Corp., systems engineer, Annapolis, MD, 1977-84 then went to work for Anne Arundel County Public Schools in Maryland, 1984-91. Academic credentials: BS in mechanical engineering and MS in marine engineering.

Married former Gloria Jean Brown July 14, 1988. Member of FRA, Branch 24 since May 1974. Member of the Mayor's Conservancy Board, Annapolis, MD since 1993. Full-time health and fitness consultant with four different gyms and member of the Annapolis Mall Power Pacers, 1991-97.

Awarded highest Navy Award, Navy Commendation Medal w/Combat V for Meritorious Combat Service in the Mekong Delta while serving with friendly Foreign Forces engaged in armed conflict against the North Vietnamese and Viet Cong communist aggressors in the RVN.

THOMAS L. BROWN, born July 30, 1946 in Lawrence KS joined the Navy July 30, 1963 on his 17th birthday. After basic in San Diego, spent most of his first hitch on the USS *Ticonderoga* (CV-14) and USS *Ranger* (CVA-61).

Re-enlisted 1967 and volunteered for duty in Vietnam. After completing training he joined RIVDIV 593, Iron Butterfly, September 1968 at Nha Be. First saw action in the Rung Sat and then operation Giant Slingshot.

He was awarded the Purple Heart for wounds received in action Jan. 19, 1969. The division was back patrolling the Rung Sat again when on April 9, 1969 Petty Officer Brown's Patrol came under heavy automatic weapons and rocket fire on the Dong Tranh River 7-1/2 miles east of Nha Be. During the action he was mortally wounded when the forward gun tub on PBR-756, that he was manning, was hit by enemy rocket fire.

PO Tom Brown had been with Iron Butterfly for seven months and had made over 100 combat patrols and engaged in many firefights. A true shipmate, one that could be totally depended on in action. He was an excellent gunner and crewman and is missed by all his friends who served with him and his family. He was posthumously advanced to GMG2, awarded a Bronze Star and another Purple Heart.

Tom was proceeded in death by his brother and parents. He left behind a young wife, Fay and brothers George and James. Fay Brown is in contact with members of Iron Butterfly.

PAUL WAYNE "ICE MAN" CAGLE, born Aug. 14, 1946 in Florence County, SC. Entered the service August 1967. Trained from June-August 1967 at Coronado, Mare Island and Cubic Point, Philippines.

Served with RIVDIV 532, made over 250 combat patrols and participated in operation Giant Slingshot.

His achievement was surviving TET and Tra Cu. Personally knowing four close friends

who were killed in action; knowing them has helped him realize the true meaning of life.

Discharged April 1969 as GMG3. Awarded Bronze Star w/V, three Purple Hearts, Navy Achievement w/V and Presidential Unit Citation among others.

Retired on VA disability. He is a life member of DAV, Gamewardens; member of FRA, PBR, FVA and USBA.

Married for 31 years to Myrle Herin, they have no children.

DAVID L. "BUTCH" CARTER, born Oct. 19, 1946 in Newport News, VA. Joined the Navy in 1963. Attended boot camp at Great Lakes, IL. Spent four years in the Navy and re-enlisted.

Ordered to Coronado, Vallejo, CA and the Philippines. Reported for duty at Na Bay May 24, 1968, RIVDIV 544, later changed to 593 as engineer and gunner.

Served 10 years in the Navy and was awarded four Bronze Stars w/V, Purple Heart, Unit Citation, Navy Commendation and Combat Medal for one year in Vietnam.

In civilian life he was employed as an engineer on cruise ships in the Virgin Islands and Dutch West Indies; engineer on tog boats in Baton Rouge, LA and for 10 years he was self-employed as a plumber. He sold the business in 1997. A member of the VFW.

Married for 18 years to Mary, he has six step-children.

RALPH W. CHRISTOPHER SR., born Feb. 3, 1950 in Richmond, VA. Enlisted Feb. 3, 1967 on his 17th birthday, Kiddy Crusser. Attended boot camp at Great Lakes, IL.

Served on USS *Vega* (AF-59) MM3; Tonkin Gulf, three Westpacs, Korea. Special Warfare School, Coronado, CA, Navphibase; Nav Sup Pact, Anapolis Hotel Saigon; YRBM21, boat repair mechanic, engineman mikeboat, supported firebases; Cambodian Invasion, withdrawal of refugees; Advance Tactical Support Base Bay Keo Van Co Dong River, Tay Ninh, Slingshot supported Vietnamese River Patrol Group 53, RIVDIV 15.

Captain M-60 team and released at Treasure Island. Awarded Vietnam Service Medal w/ Silver Star, three Bronze Stars, Navy Unit Commendation Ribbon, Presidental Unit Citation, Metorious Unit Citations, Armed Forces Expeditionary, Combat Action, RVN Gallantry Cross and Civil Action.

Received degree at Musicians Institute, Los Angeles, CA. He is a professional musician at Veselys Music, Las Vegas, NV. He was the co-builder of Nevada Veterans Memorial Wall in 1992.

Married to Deborah Bordsal and has four children: Sean, Brandon, Kayli and Alysia.

GERALD D. COLE, born Norristown, PA. Enlisted USN 1947 at Philadelphia, PA. Served in the following ships/stations: USS *Missouri, Albany, Des-Moines, Columbus, Helena, Los Angeles,* Fleet Act., Yokosuka, Japan, ACB-One-Westpac, Admirals Barge Coxswain, Newport, RI, RIVDIV 513 1968-69, St. Francis River.

Three tours in Vietnam: boat captain, RIVDIV 513, ACB One and St. Francis River.

Awarded Bronze Star w/Combat V, Purple Heart, RVN Gallantry Cross w/Bronze Star, Armed Forces Expeditionary, Good Conduct Medal w/2 stars, Korean Service w/3 stars, Vietnam Service w/2 Bronze Stars and Silver Star, Vietnam Campaign, Vietnam Civil Action Medal, Navy Occupation, China Service Medal, UN Service Medal, Combat Action Ribbon, Korean PUC, Navy Unit Commendation w/star, NDSM w/star and Meritourius Unit Commendation.

Transferred to Fleet Reserve in 1970. Employed by US Customs as boat commander/investigator (drug smuggling branch). He retired in 1985.

DAVID F. CONKLIN SR., born Nov. 9, 1946 at Elmira, NY. Entered the service May 1966. Trained at Great Lakes, IL and Mare Island. Served with the USS *Taluga* (A-062), RIVDIV 512 (PBR).

Served as after 50 gunner and boat captain. Made 195 combat patrols from October 1968-December 1969. He was on Joe Clerkins boat when Joe was killed in action in 1969.

Discharged December 1969 as ENS 3rd class. Awarded Bronze Star w/Combat V, Purple Heart and Navy Commendation Medal w/Combat V.

He is supervisor of customer service, US Postal Service, Elmira, NY.

Married for 29 years, he has five children and seven grandchildren.

ROBERT R. "BOB" COOK, born Nov. 24, 1931 in Ute, IA. Entered the service December 1950. Attended Instructor School in San Diego August-October 1966 and Coronado for boat training. Served in Vietnam with RIVDIV 593 for six months and (RPN 61) Vietnamese advisor for one year.

His memorable experience was being with NIOTC from October 1966-January 1970 and

with Lt. Boehm and Chief Penn. He will never forget his duty as Vietnamese advisor and being on the rivers for four or five days at a time.

He is married to Marie.

JAMES DEAN DAVY, born Feb. 28, 1948 in Anaconda, MT. He enlisted in the USN September 1965. Following basic training in San Diego, CA, he was assigned to the USS *Independence* (CVA-62). In early 1967 he was ordered to Commander Naval Forces Vietnam and following a course of intensive training at the Naval Amphibious Base, Little Creek, VA he reported to Naval Support Activity Saigon for further assignment in the Mekong Delta region. Completing his first tour of duty in September 1968, Petty Officer Davy volunteered for another year in the war zone and was sent back to the States for additional training at the NIOTC, Mare Island, CA.

Upon completion of training at Mare Island and a course in Vietnamese, Petty Officer Davy reported to COMRIVPATFLOT 5, Vietnam for assignment to RIVDIV 593, Iron Butterfly. He was a boat captain of PBR 756 and made over 200 total combat patrols.

His decorations and awards include four Bronze Stars w/Combat Vs, two Purple Hearts for wounds in combat, Meritorious Service Medal, four Navy Commendation Awards, Army Commendation w/Combat V, two Presidential Unit Citations and RVN Gallantry Cross, among others.

He remained in the Navy for 24 years, retiring as master chief petty officer in 1988. Completed his BS degree, taught NJROTC for the Chief of Naval Education and Training following his retirement. Now works for the Department of Veterans Affairs. He is a life member of Gamewardens, DAV, MOPH, VFW; a member of the American Legion, FRA, Vietnam Veterans of America, National Assoc. for the Uniformed Services, Veterans of the Vietnam War, NCOA, Retired Enlisted Assoc. and the Battleship New Jersey Historical Society.

KEITH L. DECLERCQ, born Sept. 12, 1937 in Georgetown, NY. He enlisted in USN in February 1955. Following basic training in Bainbridge, MD he attended Radioman School and served on various ships and shore stations before being selected for the "Seaman to Admiral" program in 1962. After graduating from OCS in August 1962, Ens. deClercq was assigned to  the USS *Brownson* (DD-868) and participated in the Cuban missile crisis. After various assignments and graduation from the USNPGS

Monterey, CA in June 1968, Lt. deClercq volunteered for duty in Vietnam.

Lt. deClercq reported September 1968 to RIVDIV 593 operating near Saigon. He assumed command of RIVDIV 591 January 1969 and commanded the division in the Mekong Delta until turned over to the RVN Navy in October 1969.

Awarded two Bronze Stars w/Combat Vs, two Purple Hearts, Navy Commendation Medal w/Combat V, Armed Forces Expeditionary Medal for Cuba, Dominican Republic and Vietnam. He earned various campaign ribbons and unit citations among other awards.

Retired as LCDR March 1975 after 20 years of service. He then worked as an engineer/project manager and later became president/GM of EG&Gs, Washington Analytical Services Division.

He now lives and works on his family farm in upstate New York and is a life member of Gamewardens and VFW.

RONALD WALTER DERING, born Nov. 17, 1939 in Coatesville, PA and graduated in 1957 from S. Horace Scott High School. Enlisted in the USN July 6, 1957 and completed basic at Bainbridge, MD.

Following a short tour at Earle, NJ he attended Submarine School at New London, CT. Served on the USS *Robin* (SS-407) 1958-60; USS *Sequoia* (AG-23) 1961-62 and USS *James Madison* (SSBN-627) 1963-68. In 1968 he volunteered for duty in Vietnam and following PBR School at Vallejo, he reported to RIVDIV 593 in late March 1969. He was boat captain of PBR-842 for his full year with Iron Butterfly and made over 300 combat patrols.

Awarded five Bronze Stars for bravery in combat and among his many other awards was the Army Commendation Medal w/Combat V for heroism. Dering was also one of six men from Iron Butterfly awarded the RVN Navy Gallantry Cross for action in September 1969.

In March 1970 he left Vietnam and reported to the USS *Puffer* (SSN-652) were he served until April 1972; shore tour at Fleet ASW School and FTG, San Diego until December 1974 and the last tour was USS *Fort Fisher* (LSD-40) where he served until transferred to Fleet Reserve Oct. 1, 1976.

Ron worked for San Diego Fire Systems until his battle with cancer forced him to retire in 1997. He died Feb. 6, 1998 at the age of 58.

He was a true shipmate, one that could be depended on in firefight or any type of fight.

Ron Dering left behind a family and many close friends. He is survived by a son, three brothers and four sisters. Several of Ron's family are in touch with members of RIVDIV 593. He was a life plus member of Gamewardens, West Coast Chapter and very active in several chapter activities including PBR resoration and maintenance. He is missed.

BRUCE FREDERICK DE WALD, born Dec. 7, 1938 in Everett, WA. Enlisted in the Navy Reserve in December 1955, completed recruit training June 1956 and went on active reserve duty at NAS Seattle.

Re-enlisted USN in 1957 and served in USS *Renshaw* and USS *Savage*. Wintered over at McMurdo Station, Antarctica in 1963 and 1966 with USS *Springfield* in between. Graduated AGB School in 1957 and CI-3 enroute to Vietnam. Served as staff meterologist, Commander Naval Forces Vietnam from October 1967-August 1968 and assistant staff meterologist until April 1969.

Made chief aerographer's mate Nov. 16, 1967. Flew to Da Nang and reported aboard USS *Valley Forge* in Vietnamese waters October 1969. Participated in Operation Bold Dragon VII and VIII, a SEAL operation against the VC, while TAD in USS *Weiss*, October-November 1968 and Operation Brave Aramada, the last USMC regimental combat assault in Vietnam.

He subsequently made chief warrant aerographer and LDO meterology, served in USS *Okinawa* and remained in the Navy for 30 years, retiring as lieutenant commander in 1986. Awarded Navy Commendation Medal w/Bronze V and Gold Star, Navy Achievement Medal and RVN Armed Forces Meritorious Unit Citation w/Palm.

He was a security countermeasures and counterintelligence officer for the Army for 10 years, retiring in 1996.

JAMES T. "JIM" DUBOSE, born Oct. 5, 1936 in Rock Hill, SC. Joined the Navy in 1954. Attended boot camp NTC San Diego; Nuclear Power School 1961; PBR training NAB Coronado 1967 and Instructor School, Norfolk 1971.

Served as E-1 through MMC; commissioned February 1967 as WO-1 retired as CWO-3. Served on the ships USS *Menard, Regulus, Buck, Enterprise, Fort Snelling, Noxubee* and *Seattle*.

During Vietnam service in-country he served with TF 116, RIVDIV 52, RIVSEC 522 as maintenance officer from June 1967-June 1968. Operated off YRBM-16 until it was blown up while anchored at Ben Tre in the Ben Tre River. Transferred to Garret County at mouth of Bassac River. At the beginning of 1968 TET Offensive, RIVSEC transferred to Vinh Long.

Retired January 1976 after 22 years of service. Awarded Naval Achievement Medal w/Combat V, four Good Conduct Medals, NDSM, Vietnam Service Medal w/Silver and Bronze Star, RVN Meritorious Unit Citation (Gallantry Cross w/Palm), Combat Action Ribbon, Navy

Unit Commendation w/Bronze Star, PUC, Small Craft Insignia and RVN Campaign Medal.

After retiring he worked at Colorado State University as trades service manager. Retired in January 1996 after 20 years.

Married over 40 years, he has two sons and one granddaughter.

HAMILTON A. DUNCAN JR., entered the Navy June 15, 1951 and took his recruit training at USNTC Bainbridge, MD in Co. 144. On Feb. 1, 1978 he retired from the Navy while serving in Air Borne Early Warning Squadron 123 (VAW-123) NAS Norfolk, VA after 24-1/2 years service.

The majority of his Naval service was in aviation with the exception of his tour in the Riverine Forces. During the Vietnam era he made two cruises to Southeast Asia. In 1966-67 in VS-38 aboard the USS *Bennington* (SVC-20) and as ships company in the USS *Intrepid* (CVS-11) from 1968-69. Also during this time he served a short while as an advisor to the Royal Thia Navy.

In country he served in RIV DIV 593/RPD-593 from February 1970 until turnover to the VNs at Chau-due, then on to serve in VN RPG-57.

While in 593, he operated on the upper Saigon River (Phu-Coung), the Grand Canal, Cambodian Incursion and Venti Canal, with RPG-57 he operated in the Rung Sat out of Nha-be.

He made 116 patrols and was in seven firefights with 593, in RPG-57 he made 30 patrols and had no firefights.

Awarded Navy Commendation Medal w/Combat V, Combat Action Ribbon and Small Craft Device (PBR). Prior to retiring, he obtained an AA degree from Geroge Washington University.

He is now fully retired and resides in Springfield, VA. A life member of the Gamewardens Assoc., Springfield Lodge No. 217, AF:Am and the Alexandria Scottish Rite.

NEDWARD CLYDE "BUSTER" ESTES JR., born Dec. 26, 1948 in Dallas, GA. Graduated from Matthews Consolidated High School in 1966 and joined the USN October 12 of the same year. After basic training and short ship tour, he volunteered for duty in Vietnam and was ordered to NIOTC for PBR and SERE training. He joined RIVDIV 593, Iron Butterfly, on the upper Saigon River at Phu Cuong in December 1969.

Fireman Estes was with the division for only a short time when he was killed in action Jan. 16, 1970 when PBR-755 which he had been assigned as engineer and M-60 gunner came under heavy attack.

PBR-755 was part of a two boat patrol on the upper Saigon River during Operation Ready Deck (Tran Hung Dao V), when the patrol came under heavy enemy automatic weapons and

rocket attack. Nedward was stuck in the chest by a B-40 rocket and killed instantly.

Although with the division only a short time, he had seen considerable combat and had proven himself to be a solid reliable member of Charlie Patrol and the Iron Butterfly. He was and is missed by those who served with him.

Buster is survived by his parents, two sisters and two brothers. The Estes family resides in Hiram, GA and are in touch with members of Iron Butterfly.

CARL L. "FLETCH" FLETCHER, trained at NIOTC, Vallejo, CA in 1969. In Vietnam he served with RIVDIV 593, Iron Butterfly as a patrol officer. Served on several ships before and after Vietnam and with other units.

He will always remember July 6, 1969, the patrol was ambushed in the Rung Sat, Petty Officer Darrell Lee Tucker was killed and others were wounded.

Awarded Bronze Star, PUC, Vietnam Service, Vietnam Campaign and various other awards.

Retired Navy and now just retired. Work on Gamewardens West Coast PBR and keeping the Memorial at NAB, Coronado. He is a life plus member in Gamewardens.

A husband, father and grandfather.

RALPH DONALD FLORES, born June 21, 1942 in Los Angeles, CA. Enlisted Aug. 26, 1960 and reported to NTC San Diego, CA for boot camp. Since that day, he has served faithfully aboard seven ships and eight shore stations concluding with 4-1/2 years FLETRAGRU WESTPAC, Yokosuka, Japan. In 1968 he reported to PBR Mobil Base II at Tan Chan and later at Tan An, RVN. Reported to CHNAVADVGRU-MACV for his second tour March 1970-71 and served as patrol officer advisor for RPG-52.

Among his personal decorations are Navy and Marine Medals for heroism, Bronze Star w/Combat V, two Purple Hearts, Combat Action Ribbon, Combat Small Craft Insignia, PUC, Navy Unit Commendation, Meritorious Unit Commendation, Pistol Expert Medal, NDSM, Philippine Presidential Unit Citation, RVN Armed Forces Meritorious Unit Commendation (RVN Gallantry Cross), RVN Meritorious Unit Citation (civil actions col. w/Palm), Vietnam Service Medal w/Silver Star, Vietnam Campaign Medal, Battle E Sea Service Deployment Ribbon and six Good Conduct Awards.

After his retirement in December 1986, he is still serving the Navy by working at Puget

Sound Naval Shipyard, Bremerton, WA where he enjoys his Harley-Davidson motorcycle (he says he deserves it). He is married to the love of his life, the former Irmgard Regina Schlembach, a native of Germany. Together they live on 2-1/2 acres in a house they built together in Kingston, WA. They both have a passion and love for animals and share their home and land with two retired Greyhounds, two Dobermans, three exotic birds and two cats. He plans to retired from the Naval Shipyard in 2005.

CHARLES F. "RICK" FOSTER III, born
Aug. 6, 1945 in Sioux Falls, SD, but grew up in Cushing OK. Rick graduated from Southeastern Oklahoma State University in 1968 with a degree in accounting.

He entered the Navy April 1968 and after graduation from OCS in Newport, RI he was ordered to Naval Amphibious Base, Coronado, CA for intensive training in language, first aid, small unit tactics, SERE and Vietnam orientation. Then sent to NIOTC, Mare Island, CA for boat training. Upon completion of training he was assigned to COMRIVPATFLOT 5, Vietnam for assignment to RIVDIV 573, stationed at Sa Dec. His duties included patrol officer, senior patrol officer and psychological warfare officer.

After his tour in Vietnam, served as operations officer aboard the USS *Exploi* (MSO 440) home ported in Charleston, SC. He left the Navy in July 1971. A few years later, he earned his degree in geology from Oklahoma State University.

Both Rick and his wife, Vicki reside in Cushing, OK. Rick is employed with an engineering company, Stewart & Bottomley of Tulsa, OK as a construction manager. He has two children, Amy and Charles and has been a life member of Gamewardens since 1990.

RALPH J. FRIES, born July 19, 1937 in
Brewster, WA. He attended and completed the Tacoma Vocational Technical School in diesel and heavy equipment me-

chanics course in May 1957 and enlisted in USN May 17, 1957. After recruit training, in August 1957 with Co. 169 he attended Machinery Repairman A School and reported onboard the USS *Hamul* (AD-20). In March 1961 he re-enlisted for six years of service. Transferred to USS *Bryce Canyon* (AD-36). In 1962 he was shipped to Japan and after many assignments, returned to the States April 1965. Upon completion of several training schools, he departed from Travis AFB, CA for Saigon, Vietnam River Squadron 5 June 1, 1967 for duty as logistics/maintenance officer for RIVSEC 543.

At the start of TET 1968, a four boat patrol departed Binh Thuy for operations in the Chau Doc Area for patrolling and supporting Allied Forces. He departed RIVSEC 535 on May 31, 1968 by PBR to Vinh Long, flying from there to Saigon to turn in his side arms and check out of River Squadron 5 for departure to the States, arriving at Travis AFB, CA June 1, 1968.

Served onboard the USS *Cascade* (AD-16) 1968-70 and was promoted to CWO-2; he became

main propulsion officer onboard the USS *Tulare* (LKA-112) April 3, 1972. During his tour of duty, he was promoted to CWO-3 and made two Western Pacific cruises during his three years onboard. He departed the ship April 1, 1975 and reported for his last tour of duty in the Navy as director, Machine Repairman Schools, Service School Command, San Diego, CA. It was where he received his first professional knowledge of becoming a machinery repairman 17-1/2 years earlier.

Retired from active duty as CWO-3 June 1, 1977. Awarded Navy Commendation Medal w/Combat V, Combat Action Ribbon, PUC, Meritorious Unit Citation, Good Conduct Medal w/3 Bronze Stars, NDSM, Armed Forces Expeditionary Medal, VSM and RV Campaign Medal.

Retired in Aug. 3, 1993 from an independent owner operator trucker with his own ICC operating authority. He is a member of various asociations and organizations, serving in various capacities.

He and his wife reside at Escondido, CA. He has two sons, Gary, Glen and three granddaughters: Marissa, Ella and Eva.

GLEN FRY, born Sept. 9, 1943 in San Antonio, TX. Enlisted in the USN October 1960. After basic training at San Diego, CA he reported to the USS *Sirius* (AF-60). In 1962 he graduated from Radar Class A School at Treasure Island and was assigned to the USS *Dennis J. Buckley* (DDR-808) and in 1964 to the USS *Walke* (DD-723).

In 1967 he was assigned as an instructor at the US Naval Academy, Annapolis, MD. He volunteered for duty in Vietnam in 1965 and was called in 1969. He trained with ACTOV-3 at NIOTC and reported to COMRIVPATFLOT 5 where he was assigned to RIVDIV 514 as boat captain of an all Vietnamese crewed boat.

In 1970 RIVDIV 514 went through turnover and became RPG-55 where he was an advisor. He also served as an advisor with RPG-59 until the expiration of his enlistment in October 1970.

Married, he has 15 year-old daughter and lives near San Antonio, TX. Fry retired from Civil Service at Randolph AFB in 1995 and is now working on his master's degree in history at the University of Texas.

WILLIAM JACKSON "BILL" GAINEY, born June 7, 1934 in Wilmington, NC. Joined the USN in 1955 and went to basic training in San Diego. Bill served on several ships out of Norfolk including the USS *Canaberra* and was off Cuba during the Bay of Pigs and again for the missile crisis. He also did a tour in New Foundland and Gitmo and then volunteered for duty in Vietnam.

He first served with RIVDIV 511 and then joined RIVDIV 593, Iron Butterfly, in January 1970 as a patrol officer.

On Feb. 12, 1970 Chief Gainey was the patrol officer for PBRs 752 and 841 in ambush at the intersection of the Saigon and Thi Tinh Rivers. Heavy movement was dedected on the beach and the patrol was poised for action when suddenly a grenade bounced on the canopy and landed on one of the boats. BMC Gainey grabbed the grenade and tossed it overboard before it exploded saving the crew from injury. The boats then broke ambush and reconned by fire. For this action Chief Gainey was awarded the Silver Star. He was also awarded the Bronze Star and two Purple Hearts while with 593.

Bill did a tour on the USS *Guadalcanal* and Annapolis where he retired in 1981. After retiring he owned and operated two service stations until diagnosed with cancer in 1989. Bill passed away in 1995 after a long battle.

He was a member of the VFW, FRA and the DAV where he did volunteer work at the Perry Point Veterans Hospital. He left behind Margaret, his wife of 38 years, three daughters, three grandchildren, four brothers and a sister. He is missed! Margaret is in touch with members of Iron Butterfly.

MICHAEL THOMAS GALINDO, born
May 19, 1947 in Vallejo, CA. Wanting to embark on an USN career (like his father), Michael enlisted in the USNR in May 1964. After completing basic training (during the summer) in San Diego, CA, Mike became bored with civilian life and enlisted in the regular USN in October 1964. His first assignment was the USS *Floyd B. Parks* (DD-884).

In late 1965, Mike volunteered for duty in Vietnam. In March 1966, after completing "in-country preparatory-training" at both the Naval Amphibious Base, Coronado, CA and Camp Pendleton Marine Corp Base, CA, Michael was assigned to Naval Support Activity, Da Nang (White Elephant). In April 1966, he was transferred to Naval Support Detachment, Chu Lai.

While in Vietnam, BMSN Galindos duties included security, deck seaman on pusher boats, deck seaman on a warping tug and deck seaman on a "mike-eight" boat (which transported US Marines up and down rivers in the I Corps area. In December 1967, BMSN Galindo extended for additional "Nam-time."

Awarded Navy Achievement Medal, three Good Conduct Medals, RVN Gallantry Cross and Vietnam Service Medal w/Silver Star, among others.

Michael stayed in the Navy for 22 years, retiring as a yeoman first class petty officer in 1986. He is an annual member of Gamewardens and a life member of DAV.

ROBERT L. "BOB" GEORGE, born Oct.
5, 1945 in Portland, OR. Enlisted in the USN January 1965. Following basic training in San

Diego, CA he was assigned to the USS *Mansfield* (DD-728). Served off the coast of Vietnam for six months.

In December 1965 he volunteered for shore duty in Vietnam, March 1966 reported to Naval Amphibious Base Coronado, CA for training and Camp Pendleton for weapon training. Was assigned to Naval Support Activity Da Nang on mike boats in the Da Nang Harbor. Volunteered for duty on a mike boat going to Naval activity Tan-My, to escort and mine sweep the Perfume River from Tan-My to Hue City.

In 1966 he volunteered for duty in country again. Late 1967 was reassigned to Naval Support Activity Da Nang as a MAA at Camp Tien-Sha until leaving country.

Discharged in 1969 from the Navy. Awarded Boatswain's Mate 3rd Class by an act of Congress, Navy Unit Citation, Medal of Defense, Vientam Service Ribbon w/4 stars and Marine Corps Anchor and Vietnam Ribbon w/ Year Bar.

Employed by the Transit District, Portland, OR for 31 years in tire shop maintenance. He is a life member and state officer of the VFW, member of Vietnam Veterans of America and the USS *Mansfield* Assoc.

Married to Jean, he has three sons, two stepsons and nine grandchildren.

EDWARD F. "GOLDY" GOLD, born April 20, 1926. In 1943 he was sent to Little Creek, VA where he was trained in underwater demolition, using re-breathers. Completing this training he went to Fort Pierce, FL for advanced explosive training. Upon his return to Little Creek he was tasked to train in amphibious landings. Appointed to coxswain on an "LCM" landing craft mechanized. He finally was sent by ship to England and spent the winter at the Dartmouth Royal Naval College in preparation for D-Day. During the invasion of Normandy, he was tasked to make the landing on Omaha Beach. Carried 125 infantry men into the beach on the 1st wave. Returning to the transport to assault the beach on the 3rd wave. During this time frame, enemy fire was very heavy and they were ordered to go to the left of the previous landing spot. When his seamen dropped the ramp, it hit a mine that wiped out half of the crew and infantry.

During the Vietnam Conflict, he participated in 298 combat patrols and 29 firefights in RIVSEC 544, RIVDIV 593. His many decorations include two Purple Hearts, Bronze Star w/ Combat V, two Navy Unit Commendations, Presidential Unit Citation, Combat Action Ribbon, VSM, five RVN Campaign Medals, Navy Expeditionary Medal, two NDSM, WWII VM, American Area Campaign Medal, EAME, Navy Occupational Service Medal, American Defense Service Medal, RVN Civil Action Medal, Navy Achievement Award, Vietnam Presidential Unit

Medal, RVN Gallantry Cross Medal (meritorious), Armed Forces Expeditionary Medal (Cuba) and five Good Conduct Medals.

Married for over 51 years, he has three sons, one daughter and one grandchild.

PETE GONZALEZ, born Sept. 29, 1946 in Weslaco, TX. Enlisted Feb. 12, 1965. Attended basic training at San Diego, CA. Assigned NAVCOMSTAPHIL. Assigned TAD to VP50, who first introduced him to Vietnam in November 1965.

Cruised the Gulf of Tonkin twice onboard the USS *RK Turner* DDG-20. Assigned to the Riverine Force in 1968 and served with RIVRON 13, RIVRON 15 Staff, Tango, RIVDIV 152 and Mike 1. Last sited RVN December 1970.

Other assignment IUWG 1, MIUW 13, BCT Whibey Island, WA, NAVCRUITCOM SAN FRAN, USS *Waddel* DDG-20, USS *Paul F. Foster* DD-924. Joined the submarine force and made five patrols, USS *Ulysses S. Grant* SSBN-963.

Retired RM 1 (SS) at COMNAVSUBLANT in 1986. Awarded Ribbon 13th Award, Vietnam Campaign Ribbon w/ clasp, RVN Gallantry Cross w/Palm, Battle E Ribbon, RVN Civil Actions Citation, Combat Action Ribbon, Navy Commendation w/Combat V, Navy Expeditionary Medal, Marine PUC, Armed Forces Expeditionary Medal, NDSM, Sea Service Deployment Ribbon 5th Award.

He has one daughter and one son.

CHARLES DEWALT "CHUCK" HAMILTON, born Dec. 14, 1942 in Pittsburgh, PA. Entered the service 1967. Trained at Amphibious Base, Coronado, CA and NIOTC, Vallejo, CA. Served with River Squadron 5, RIVDIV/Sec 523/544.

Lt. Hamilton searched 5,000 junks and sampans; TOC watch officer during TET Offensive initial attack and planned ambush of NVA regulars returning from mortar attach on Vung Tau; 19 KIA.

Awarded Bronze Star w/Combat V, Vietnam Campaign and Vietnam Service Medals.

He is employed as civil engineer, Director of Public Works for city of Gulf Shores, AL. Served as officer in Civil Engineer Corps, USN for 15 years. Retired with rank of commander.

Married to Melinda, he has a son Chad and daughter Melinda.

ALAN LEE HARRIS, born in Poughkeepsie, NY. Entered the service Nov. 9, 1965. Attended NCT, Great Lakes, IL, Nov. 9, 1965; Shipfitter A School, SSC, NTC, San Diego, CA Jan 14-June 10, 1966; Kenitra, Morocco, June 29, 1966-Sept. 16, 1967; USS *Lexington* CVS-16, October 1967-June 1968. Served with NAVPHIBASE June 1968, Coronado, CA SERE, NAVSUPPTACT, Da Nang, RVN, July 1968-August 1969. Small craft repair facility, Mon-

key Mountain, NAVSTA TI, San Francisco. He was instrumental in refurbushing all metal hull boats; helped design .50 cal. gun mounts.

Discharge Sept. 16, 1969. Awarded NDSM, VSM, VCM, NUCR and Good Conduct Medal.

Employed 21 years with Metro Dade Fire Department, Aviation Div. ARFF/CFR, Miami Internal Airport Station 12-B. He is a life time member of DAV.

Married May 30, 1975; post hurricane Andrew divorce in 1994. He has two daughters, Meghan and Kayla.

THOMAS JOSEPH HEKELE, born July 17, 1947 in St. Paul, MN. Enlisted in US Naval Reserve Sept. 5, 1967 at St. Paul, MN. Started boot camp Feb. 4, 1968 at Great Lakes, IL. Active Reserve until Feb. 15, 1969 then active duty. Upon completion of transfer to the NIOTC at Mare Island, CA for eight weeks PBR training. Included was one week of SERE training at Whidby Island NAS.

Reported to COMRIVPATFLOT 5, Vietnam for assignment to RIVDIV 574, June 27, 1969 as boat engineer. Reassigned to RIVDIV 514 on Nov. 8, 1969 due to RIVDIV 574 being turned over to the Vietnamese Navy. On Jan. 1, 1970 he was reassigned to Naval Advisory Group MACV to Vietnamese River Patrol Group 54 until June 22, 1970 as Naval advisor to VN Navy.

Served active Naval Reserve 1967-69; active duty 1969-70 and inactive Naval Reserve 1970-73. Held rank of petty officer 3rd Class-EN 3.

Awarded Bronze Star w/Combat V, NDSM, Vietnam Campaign Medal, Vietnam Service Medal and Combat Action Ribbon.

He is employed as project manager for Amclyde Engineered Products Division of Halter Marine, Gulfport, MS. A member of VFW Post 1782, White Bear Lake, MN and Gamewardens.

Married to Jackie since October 1971, he has two daughters and one son.

FRANK D. HENNING JR., born Aug. 14, 1943 in North Platte, NE. He served in the Army Jan. 16, 1961 to Dec. 31, 1963 serving in Germany. Served in the Navy Feb. 3, 1966 to Nov. 30, 1969, Navy Sup. Act Det., Chu Lau, Vietnam, RIVDIV 631 and 512.

Henning spent 34 months on the ground in Vietnam and participated in a lot of firefights. He made 301 combat patrols and found four large weapon caches Dec. 13, 1968; on May 27, 1969; May 29, 1969 and May 31, 1969. One successful ambush on the VC, shot up several sanpans and captured the weapons June 14, 1969.

Awarded two Bronze Stars w/V, Navy Commendation w/V, two Purple Hearts, Combat Action Medal, NDSM, Presidential Unit Citation w/2 stars, Navy Unit Commendation w/4 stars, Vietnam Service Medal w/6 stars, RVN Gallantry Cross w/Palm, Expert Rifle, Expert Pistol and Small Boat Device. He was a BM-2 when he took disability retirement Nov. 30, 1969.

He is employed as a coal mine superintendent in Grass Creek, WY. Married Terry in 1985 and has one son Frank.

HUGH MARVIN HIGHLAND, born Oct. 29, 1943 in Jordan, MT. Began Naval OCS at Newport, RI in July 1966 and was commissioned November 1966. He was first lieutenant with USS *William C. Lawe* (DD-763) in the Sixth Fleet in the eastern Mediterranean throughout the six day war crisis of June 1967.

In May 1968 he went to NIOTC at Vallejo, CA to prepare for river patrol boat operations, his first river patrol boat/PBR command in Vietnam in August 1968. Over the next 3-1/2 years, he served in a series of riverine combat units in I, III and IV Corps participating in 307 patrols, 35 of which experienced major combat with NVA/Viet Cong forces.

Served with RIVSEC 523, RIVDIV 521, COMNAVFORV Staff (NOC WO) Saigon, Driver Patrol Division 58.

His career experiences were June 1970-November 1971, senior advisor River Patrol Division 58, 2,200 combat patrols; February 1972, US Navy Flag Plot at the Pentagon, specialized in submarine intelligence; July 1978, returned to Naval service as historian for US Navy's Nuclear Test Personnel Review; May 1982-June 1984, served as historian and Navy liaison officer for the US Army Agent Orange Task Force; July 1984-October 1985, administration officer for commander, Iceland Defense Force; October 1985-July 1987, Navy liaison officer, US Embassy, Bahamas.

Awarded Legion of Merit w/V, Bronze Star (Gold Star in lieu of 4th award) w/Combat Distinguishing Device, Defense Meritorious Service Medal, two Meritorious Service Medals, Navy Commendation Medal w/Combat V, Army Commendation, Coast Guard Commendation, Navy Unit Commendation, VSM w/6 Bronze Stars, Combat Action Ribbon, RVN Gallantry Cross w/Bronze Star, RVN Campaign Medal and Ribbon w/Device, RVN Armed Forces Meritorious Unit Citation (Gallantry Cross), Vietnamese First Class Training Service Medal Certificate, Viet-

namese Medal of Honor (1st class) and Vietnamese Staff Honor Medal (1st class).

CDR Highland was in the Navy for over 21 years until his passing in 1987. He was laid to rest at Arlington National Cemetery. His final assignment was to be a history instructor at the Naval Academy. He had completed his MA in world history at Georgetown in 1975 and was a Mason with Alexandria-Washington Lodge No. 22. Survived by his children Jennifer, Juliette and Howard; his wife, Hyunsook; his mother, Geneva and three brothers and a sister.

LARRY R. HONE, a graduate of the University of Missouri. Entered the Navy through Aviation Officers Candidate School. After receiving his wings May 1969, he reported to VS-41 in San Diego for OV-10A transition and weapons training. He then joined the "Black Ponies" of VAL-4 in Binh Thuy, RVN September 1969. Under the operation command of CTF-116, then Lt. (jg) Hone flew 376 combat missions in support of the riverine forces, SEALS and ARVN. After a year with VAL-4, he reported to VT-7 in Meridian, MS for a two year tour as a basic and advanced jet flight instructor.

Hone affiliated with the Naval Reserve upon leaving active duty in 1970, retiring as a captain in 1997. His reserve assignments include VA-203, VA-204, CINCLANT, CINCLANTFLT and commander, Naval Forces Eastern Atlantic, where he served as chief of staff.

Awarded DFC, Meritorious Service Medal, 30 Air Medals, eight Navy Commendation Medals, Presidential Unit Citation, Meritorious Unit Citation, RVN Gallantry Cross, Vietnamese Presidential Unit Citation and Combat Action Ribbon among others.

LONNIE ELWOOD HOOPAUGH, born July 11, 1947 in Candor, NC. Enlisted July 30, 1965 and after training at Great Lakes, he was assigned to the USS *Page County*, LST-1076. Volunteered for river patrol boat duty and after intense training was assigned to RIVDIV 532. His tour commenced Aug. 5, 1968 until his death. EN2 Lonnie Hoopaugh was killed in

action Feb. 11, 1969 in an ambush attempting to save their cover boat.

While patrolling the Vam Co Dong River, just two miles north of Tra Cu, as part of operation Giant Slingshot, the lead patrol boat was attacked by heavy enemy machine-gunfire and B-40 rockets. Approaching the initial ambush site, PBR 40 was decimated when a second wave of enemy fire and B-40 rockets came from the other side of the river bank. The boat captain beached the PBR to keep from sinking. Lonnie and two others died.

Awarded Bronze Star w/V, Purple Heart, Navy Combat Ation Ribbon, two Presidential Unit Citations, Navy Unit Citation, Meritorious Unit Citation, NDSM, Vietnam Campaign Medal w/3 stars, Vietnam Service Medal, RVN 1st class Civic Action Medal w/Gold Frame and Palm, RVN Gallantry Cross w/Gold Frame and Palm and Small Boat Command Device.

Lonnie is fondly remembered by his shipmates and is survived by his brother, Wade who is seeking additional information about his brother's River Patrol combat service in My Tho and Tra Cu and especially his final patrol. Wade resides in Candor, NC.

FRANK JACARUSO, born in New York state, he was raised and attended school in Spring Valley, NY. He joined the Navy Nov. 27, 1958 and following basic training, Gunnersmate School and PBR training at Mare Island, he reported to RIVDIV 593, Iron Butterfly in October 1969 at Nha Be, Vietnam. He saw some very heavy combat patrolling both on the upper Saigon River on operation Ready Deck and the Rung Sat Special Zone.

On March 12, 1970, a three boat patrol from 593 consisting of PBRs 761, 756 and 842 were patrolling 20 miles northwest of Phu Cuong in an area of heavy Viet Cong and NVA concentration when they were ambushed by a large enemy force firing B-40 rockets and automatic weapons fired from the west bank of the river. Several crewmembers were hit and Gunnersmate Jacaruso was fatally wounded.

Frank was a good crewman and gunner. He was a solid shipmate in a fire fight and a friend to many. He was and is missed by his family and those with whom he served.

Frank left behind a family including his parents, Franklin and Alberta, brothers Wayne and Robert and a sister, Donna. Robert is a life memorial member of Gamewardens and is in touch with several members of Iron Butterfly.

WAYNE D. JANOUSEK, born July 13, 1947 in Twin Falls, ID. Enlisted in the Navy June 1965 and entered active service in June 1966. After basic training in San Diego, CA he was assigned to the USS *Point Defiance*. In July 1967 he received orders to Commander Naval Forces Vietnam following intensive training at Naval Amphibious Base, Coronado, CA., NIOTC at Mare Island, CA and jungle environmental survival training at Subic Bay NS, Philippines. After completion of training, he was transferred to RIVRON 5 Saigon and was assigned to River Secion 544 which later became RIVDIV 593.

Seaman Janousek was assigned to boat 761 as the boat seaman. During the 15-1/2 months as a member of Iron Butterfly, he made over 200

combat patrols and was promoted to gunners mate third class.

Awarded Bronze Star w/Combat V, Purple Heart, Navy Achievement Medal w/Combat V, Navy Commendation Award, Meritorious Service Medal, Presidential Unit Citations among others.

Wayne Janousek later converted his gunners mate rating to data processing technican and retired January 1987 with 20 years active service. After retiring he worked as a computer programmer and started a successful software consulting business in Dallas, TX. He resides on a small farm just outside Jarrell, TX with his wife and two children. Currently works as a software engineer for Dell Computer Corp. in Austin.

RICHARD LEE JIMENEZ, born April 15, 1947 in Anthony, KS. He enlisted in the USN in May 1964. Attended basic training in San Diego where he volunteered for submarine duty. After Submarine School in New London, CT, he was stationed aboard the USS *Remora* SS-487 out of Pearl Harbor. In May 1968 he re-enlisted for six more years and volunteered for PBR duty in Vietnam.

Upon completed of training at Mare Island, Petty Office Jimenez was sent to Vietnam and assigned to RIVSEC 544 which later became RIVDIV 593, Iron Butterfly. He served as an engineman aboard PBR 756 and made over 250 combat patrols, engaging the enemy of 12 separate occasions.

During his tour he was awarded two Bronze Stars, Navy Commendation Medal, Navy Achievement Medal all w/Combat V, Purple Heart, Navy Unit Citation and Presidential Unit Citation.

After leaving Vietnam, he served two years aboard tug boats in Sasebo, Japan. Later served aboard the USS *Blackfir* (SS-322) until she was decommissioned. He spent the last two years in the Navy aboard the USS *Tang* (SS-563).

Richard left the Navy in May 1974 and worked in the air conditioning and refrigeration industry for 25 years and now works for the Burlington Northern and Santa Fe Railroad as a pipefitter.

ALBERT FRANK "JOHN" JOHNSON, born Jan. 12, 1947 in Denver. Enlisted USN June 6, 1966 following San Diego boot camp, was assigned Gunner's Mate A School, Great Lakes, IL. Stationed aboard USS *Mispillion* (AO-105) spent six months on South China Sea. Volunteered for PBR duty late 1967, trained for patrol craft, Vietnamese language, counterinsurgency, SERE, small arms, West Coast, thence Cubic Point, Philippines and JEST School. Reported RIVSEC 523, Delta Gypsy, Vinh Long before TET 1968. Completed over 30 patrols. Transferred to Nha Be to aid activation RIVSEC 544, RIVDIV 593, Iron Butterfly as forward gunner. Later became Boat No. 841 captain made 345 patrols and extended six months. Mid 1967, extended again and transferred to CTU 1941. Team 2, Duffelbag, to train with electronic surveillance team. Afterwards,

traveled III/IV Corps scouting and sniping. Separated Dec. 12, 1969.

Awarded Silver Star, two Navy Commendations w/V, 10 Vietnam Service Medals, three Presidential Unit Commendations, Meritorious Unit, RVN Gallantry Cross and Civil Actions.

After the service he went to college and was a welder/engineer for over 20 years. Currently a leather smith/artist.

BOBBY GENE JOHNSON, born March 3, 1948 in Panama City, FL and entered the service July 1968. Trained at Great Lakes, IL May 1967. Joined RIVDIV 552 July 1968 at Nha Be; assigned to YRBM 16 October 1968 and moved to Chau Duc November 1968 for operations in Vinh Te Canal. He was wounded Nov. 18, 1968.

Awarded Purple Heart and Navy Commendation w/Combat V.

Currently he is a sales manager at Arizona Chemical. He has two sons and one daughter.

TIMOTHY MATTHEW "SKI" KARWOSKI, born Sept. 23, 1950 in Ferndale, MI. Attended basic training September-December 1968 at San Diego, CA.

Served on USS *Navarro* (APA-215), USS *Terrell County* (LST-1157) and USS *Shields* (DD-596). He survived an over 50 day cruise from home port in Yokosuka, Japan to Bremerton, WA for decommissioning on perhaps one of the slowest vessels in the Navy; an LST, "Long Slow Target" as they called them!

Discharged in 1972 as BT3. Awarded Vietnam Service, Vietnam Campaign and Navy Achievement Medals. He received the Navy Achievement Medal for meritorious service while attached to the USS *Terrell County* (LST-1157) during three deployments to the combat zone in the Mekong Delta in support of operation Market Time.

Married to Janice, he has three daughters and one son who has been in the USAF since January 1998.

JOHN RICHARD KEIPER, born Sept. 26, 1932 in Hazelton, PA. Entered the service Jan. 7, 1952. Completed NIOTS training at Vallejo, CA Sept. 1, 1967. Reported to Command Naval Forces Vietnam Sept. 7, 1967. Assigned to RIVSEC 543, Rung Sat Special Zone. Later he helped form Section 544. Patrolled Rung Sat until

leaving country in September 1968. He served with top sailors on PBRs.

He remembers giving toys to the kids on the river sent from Eugene, OR collected by his wife.

Retired from the Navy March 1, 1974 as BMC. Awarded Bronze Star w/Combat V, Combat Action Ribbon, Navy Unit Commendation, Good Conduct Medal (5th award), European Occuptaion Medal, NDSM w/star, Armed Forces Expeditionary Medal, Vietnam Service Medal w/4 stars, RVN Gallantry Cross and Campaign Ribbon.

Retired USO after 23 years. He was married to Lorenah, deceased; has two children, Sherri and Patricia and one grandson, Devon.

ROBERT JEFFREY "JEFF" KELLEHER, born Sept. 28, 1945. Entered the service in 1967 and attended training at NIOTC, Mare Island, July-October 1969.

He served with Naval liaison, 25th ARVN Div.; RIVDIV 535 and was a senior patrol officer and executive with the division.

Discharged in 1970 as lieutenant J6. Awarded Combat Action Ribbon and Bronze Star w/V.

Currently he is a lawyer.

R. L. KIRK, born Aug. 31, 1937 in Dayton, WA. He re-enlisted in the Navy November 1967, eight years after his first tour. Classification and outfitting at Treasure Island, San Franciso. Requesting and receiving orders to PBR training. Transferred to Amphibase, Coronado December 1967. He joined PBR Class 49, undergoing language, counter insergency and related training, SERE at Warner Springs, CA.

Class 49 under went PBR indocmentation and training at Mare Island NS, NIOTC. Completing boat training, Kirk reported to COMRIVPATFLOT 5, Siagon, Vietnam. He was assigned to RIVDIV 531 in My Tho in April 1968 patrolling lower Mekong.

In November 1968 he received orders to NSA Det Nhabe, where he joined new RIVDIV 553 patrolling Vam Co Tay and Vom Co Dong from the sugar mill, later based at Mac Hou.

He completeted his tour in March 1969 and extended his tour joining RIVDIV 511 patrolling the upper Bassac. He was transferred in June 1970 to special forces B camp, Camp Sylvester, returning to CONUS in September 1970.

Kirk served 22 years in the Navy with eight years Naval Reserve and one year USMCR. With over 28 years of military service he was medically retired in January 1986 as E-7 gunnersmate.

Awarded Purple Heart, Bronze Star w/Combat V, Navy Commendation w/V, Combat Action Ribbon, Good Conduct Medal w/4 stars and Vietnam Service Medals.

He now travels extensively, living part-time in Marysville, WA, the mountains of the northwest and part-time in the deserts of Arizona.

DOUGLAS H. KOENIG, born July 24, 1949 in Detroit Lakes, MN. Enlisted June 1968. Attended basic training in San Diego, Engineman A School at Great Lakes and NIOTC, Mare Island, CA Class 76 in February 1969.

Served with COMRIVPATFLOT 5, RIVDIV 534 April 1969. Transferred to swift boats, Coastal Division #11 October 1969 and then to Coastal Divsion #14 March 1970.

Awarded National Defense Service Medal, Vietnam Service Medal, Combat Action Ribbon, Meritorious Unit Commendation and Navy Achievement Medal w/Combat V.

RON LARATTA, born Jan. 6, 1946 in Newark, NJ. Joined the Navy April 1966. Appointed recruit chief petty officer of award winning Co. 251, 1966. Served on USS *Tattnal* (DDG-19), out of Charleston, SC. Worked on 5"/54 guns and missile launcher. Visited the Mediterranean as a NATO host ship. Toured the Caribbean and East Coast ports. Volunteered for PBRs in Vietnam for the "adventure" and to "blow things up." Assigned to RIVDIV 532 after training with NIOTC Class 60. Arrived August 1968, based out of My Tho, in the IV Corps Delta, then Tra Cu, in the III Corps area of combat. Served as a forward "twin 50" caliber machine gunner on Mk-1 PBRs. Severely wounded in action just south of Tra Cu in an ambush at Horeshore Bend on the Vam Co Dong.

GMG2 Laratta received the Silver Star, Purple Heart, Navy Combat Action Ribbon, two Presidential Unit Citations, Navy Unit Citation, Meritorious Unit Citation, NDSM, Navy Expert Rifleman Medal, Vietnam Campaign Medal w/ 2 stars, RVN Civil Action Medal, RVN Gallantry Cross and RVN Service Medal.

After almost a year of recuperating from wounds inflicted (he has limited hearing and limited use of his left arm) discharged January 1970. He went to the New York Institute of Photography in New York City. Received two AA degrees in commercial and advertising photography in 1974 and a bachelor's degree in business administration in 1978 from University of Miami, FL and owned a professional photography studio in Fort Lauderdale. He served as president of the Professional Photographers Guild of Florida in 1984 and won the President's Outstanding Service Award in 1985. Attained a prestigious Certified Professional Photographer degree (CPP) and taught photography at the Art Institute of Florida.

Ron serves as life member of the DAV and DAV Honor Society and UDT/SEAL Assoc. A member of American Legion, Atlanta Vietnam Veterans Business Assoc. and Mobile Riverine Force Assoc. In the US Navy Gamewardens Assoc. he is a lifeplus member, has served in various chairs on the National Board of Directors since 1982 and had a term as national treasurer and history book chairman. Ron is also an officer and charter member of the Southeast Region Chapter of Gamewardens. He is a Georgia State Representative and serves on the board of his Spring Ridge Homeowners Assoc.

Married to high school sweetheart Denise since 1976. Retired in 1997, he and his wife have

traveled the world extensively and plan to continue their worldwide trek to exotic places. Visited Vietnam in 1994, an emotional return to a beautiful country. He could finally show his wife the places and things he always talked about. The trip took them to Hanoi, Hue, Da Nang, Saigon and Ch Chi. A memorial ceremony was held on a bridge crossing near the infamous Vam Co Dong River. They reside in Roswell, GA near Atlanta.

RODNEY CORNELIUS "ROD" LYNCH, born July 9, 1945 in Camden, ME. Attended Ricker College in Houlton, ME where he graduated 1967 with BA degree in social sciences. Enlisted in USN June 1, 1967 and attended recruit training at Great Lakes, IL followed by Storekeeper A School in San Diego, CA. After graduation in May 1968 ordered to Vietnam arriv- ing July 26, 1968. Assigned to River Patrol Boat Det YRBM-16. Areas of assignment included Rung Sat Special Zone and on the Bassac River in the Mekong Delta near Chau Duc on the Cambodian border. Left Vietnam July 22, 1969.

Served aboard the USS *Graffias* out of San Francisco. Received an early-out Oct. 15, 1969 as a result of a RIF. Following separation attended Graduate School at University of Maine, Orono, where he received master's degree in public administration June 1972.

Remained in Naval Reserves retiring Jan. 1, 1998 as master chief petty officer with a total of 30 years and seven months combined Navy and Naval Reserve service. Naval Reserve assignments included USS *Perry*, Seabees, Military Sealift Command, Ship's Intermediate Maintenance Activity, Newport, RI and NAS Brunswick, ME (where he formally retired) and command senior and master chief and senior enlisted advisor for NRC, Augusta, ME. Awarded two NDSM, RVN Meritorious Unit Citiation (Gallantry Cross w/Palm), Vietnam Campaign, Vietnam Service w/3 Campaign Awards, Veitnam Civil Action Citation w/Palm, Navy Unit Commendation, Meritorious Unit Commendation, Naval Reserve Service w/7 Awards and Armed Forces Reserve w/Gold Hour Glass for 30 years of service. When he retired he was one of the last in-country Navy Vietnam veterans, either still on active duty or in the Naval Reserves.

Since 1972 he has worked as a professional planner and town manager. Positions have included city planner for Auburn, ME; town manager for Bethel, ME and Norridgewock, ME. Presently employed as economic and community development director for city of Rockland, ME where he resides.

Active professional and civic organizaitons include American Institue of Certified Planners, secretary Maine Assoc. of Planners, Rotary and Scottish Rites 32 degree Mason. Main hobby is his classical 1930s federal style house.

In June 1998 he was visited by members of the family of SK3 Glenn Howard who died December 1969 while serving aboard the YRBM-16. Also, he is in regular contact with SK3 Mike

Snidow who served with RBM-18 at Tan Chu. Master Chief Lynch (Ret.) has two nephews who are career Navy enlisted personnel.

J. PATRICK MADDEN, born Sept. 28, 1945 was commissioned an ensign, USN June 1967 upon graduation from Brown University, Providence, RI. Following a tour on USS *O'Bannon* (DD-450), including a deployment to Vietnam, he volunteered for PBRs in 1968 and joined RIVDIV 593 Oct. 3, 1968 as LTJG Madden. Served with RIVDIV 593 until Oct. 3, 1969. Following training under the leadership of RDC Ron Weeks and SMC Bob Monzingo, Madden served as a patrol officer and made over 200 combat patrols.

His Vietnam decorations include two Bronze Stars w/Combat V, Navy Commendation Medal w/Combat V, Combat Action Ribbon, two Presidential Unit Citations, RVN Gallantry Cross Individual Award and RVN Gallantry Cross Unit Award. His best memories are those of the RIVDIV 593 officers and men he served with.

Madden remained in the Navy for 21 years and retired as LCDR. Obtained his master's degree while teaching NROTC at the Unversity of Washington in Seattle. Post Vietnam assignments included tours on other destroyers, frigates and various staff assignements including COMIDEASTFOR and NATO HQ. His last assignment prior to retirement was on the OPNAV staff in Washington, DC.

WILLIAM MARAUGHA JR., born Feb. 14, 1933 in Indian head, PA. Enlisted in USN November 1951. Following basic training at Great Lakes, IL assigned to NATTC, Norman, OK. In 1953 assigned to USS *Randolph* (CVA-15); 1954 assigned to USS *Midway* (CVA-41) to take it from Norfolk, VA around the world to Bremton, WA. Delayed to help evacuate Tachon  Island in Formosa; 1956 assigned to USS *Johnnie Hutchins* (DE-360) reserve training out of Boston; 1958 USS *Robert A. Owens* (DD-827). Served 5-1/2 years and was the first ship in Cuban missile crisis. Sent to Argentia in 1953 and in 1968 assigned to NAS Brunswick, ME. After a short tour in Maine, volunteered for Vietnam. Trained at Mare Island and Language School at Coronado, CA. Assigned RIVDIV 593 as patrol officer. Evacuated in 1969.

After six months at Annapolis, MD, Naval Hospital, released and went aboard (DLG-16) *Lehay*. He volunteered in 1970 for Vietnam again and assigned RPG 53 as leading chief. He made over 150 patrols in two tours.

Awarded two Purple Hearts for wounds in combat, three Bronze Stars w/Combat V, three Navy Commendation Medals w/Combat V, two Presidential Unit Citations, RVN Gallantry Cross among others.

Retired MMC in December 1971 out of Vietnam. Worked in Building Inc. until he retired in 1998.

"I want to give all the praise and glory to the young men who served on my boats, putting their young lives on the line on every patrol. Thank you all."

CORNELIUS A. "MAC" MC CAFFERTY,
born Sept. 24, 1940 in Mansfield, OH. Enlisted in Marine Corps Reserve while still in high school and did his basic training at Parris Island. Leaving the Corps he joined the Navy in August 1960 and served onboard ship out of Norfolk, making a Westpac in 1968. Volunteered for duty in-country and following NIOTC, SERE and Language School he joined Iron Butterfly, RIVDIV 593 in December 1968. Took part in some of the heaviest combat of the war on operation Giant Slingshot.

On Feb. 17, 1969 Mac was boat captain of the cover boat of a two boat patrol working on the upper Vam Co Dong River when the patrol came under heavy automatic weapons and rocket fire. His boat took a direct hit in the coxswains flat mortally wounding PO McCafferty and wounding all other crew members.

Although with the division only a short time he had proven to be a very reliable man in a firefight and was highly respected by everyone in the outfit.

PO McCafferty was survived by his widow Susan, two daughters, Julia and Kasey, a son, Michael Patrick, his parents and two sisters. His son Michael was killed in a car accident Feb. 19, 1987.

His mother Elsie said the only heartache he ever caused was losing him and she will grieve for him until she dies. The family is in touch with members of Iron Butterfly and they, in turn, have added to the division family. Mac was awarded the Bronze Star and Purple Heart posthumously for the action that took his life; he is missed.

BOB A. MONZINGO,
born July 14, 1937 in Hollis, OK. Raised in Fort Worth, TX and grew up in the USN. Joined the Navy June 1956 and retired March 1975. Served on two heavy cruisers, two destroyers, Comfirst Flight staff, COMPHIBRON one staff, recruiting duty "Indiana," SERE instructor, manager CPO mess open, NASNI.

The chief went in-country Vietnam from May 1968 to July 1970. Assigned to RIVSEC 544/RIVDIV 593, COMNAVFORV and RIVDIV 535 as a patrol officer. He made 426 combat patrols and over 100 firefights. The first to use ambush/waterborne guard post tactics.

Awarded two Silver Star Medals, five Bronze Stars w/Combat V, Navy Commendation w/Combat V, Army Commendation w/V for Valor, Purple Heart, Combat Action Ribbon, China Service Medal, three Good Conduct Medals, two Presidential Unit Citations, two Navy Unit Commendations, Meritorious Unit Commendation, Vietnam Service Medal, Vietnam Campaign Medal (11 campaigns), NDSM, Vietnam Meritorious Unit Citation, Civil Actions Medal First Class color w/Palm, Expert Rifle, RVN Gallantry Cross w/Silver Star, RVN Gallantry Cross w/Bronze Star, both for Valor, Small Craft Insignia and Naval Parachutist.

Now living the good life with wife Janice in southern California.

CHARLES E. "CHUCK" MORGAN,
born March 7, 1942 in Laurens County, SC. Trained at Amphib Base, Coronada and Vallejo, CA. Served with Unit 542, 1967-68 as engineman 2nd class. Boat captain on boats 70 and 94, also on maintenance. Call sign Porpoise 72.

Received Navy Commendation w/Combat V, Presidential Unit Citation, Meritorious Unit Commendation, NDSM, Vietnam Service and Small Boat Device Emblem.

Currently retired pipefitter and steamfitter and refrigeration and heating.

Married to Dianne they reside in the Pine Forest of central Oregon with dog and two horses. Numerous toys! Interest are all water activites, canoeing and rafting particularily.

RODNEY "THE WEASEL" MORGAN,
born Jan 18, 1947 in San Francisco, CA. Joined the USN Aug. 1, 1966 and graduated from Engineman A. School, NIOTS and SERE training. Arrived in-country on June 17, 1967 and was assigned to RIVDIV 532 stationed at My Tho.

He eventually became the sniper on PBR-144, frequently the finest running boat in the fleet. Of his 19 month tour, his most memorable experience was when relocating from my My Tho to the "T" Harnett County during TET and on the same day, the evacuation from Ben Tre of all remaining friendlies, by all boats in the division.

Awarded Purple Heart, two Bronze Stars w/Combat V, Presidential Unit Citation, Combat Action Ribbon, RVN Gallantry Cross w/ Bronze Star among others.

Married Linda Serna on New Year's Eve 1972 and has a son, Matthew and a beautiful

granddaguther Camille. He makes his living as a professional sailor, doing yacht consulting, contracting and racing, still on the river.

JAMES E. "GUNNER" MORRISON,
born 1943 in Washington, DC of CQM Charles G. Morrison Sr., USN.

As a "Navy brat" he didn't relish military service but was force to enlist in the Navy Reserve (yes, he was a &*!# Reservist) while attending college in Long Beach, CA. Ironically, he chose the Navy to avoid being a "Polish mine sweeper" in the Army but "found" a mine Jan. 6, 1969 during Giant Slingshot and was medivaced to NNMC, Bethesda, MD where he recovered fully with all orginal parts intact.

Tired of being poor, he separated from the Navy in September 1969 and attended a computer school. In November 1976 he moved to Knoxville, TN where he eventually completed his college education and obtained a BSEE in 1998.

THOMAS R. "SKI" OLEZESKI,
born July 8, 1948 in Jersey City, NJ. Entered the service August 1966 and attended training February 1967 at Ream Field, Pendelton, Coronado Beach and went in-country. Served with HAL 3 (Seawolves) Det l, two tours.

He made some great friends with whom he is still in touch.

Discharged November 1969 as E-5. Awarded Navy Unit Citation, RVN Gallantry Cross, three Purple Hearts, 72 Air Medals, Navy Commendation Medal w/ Combat V, two DFCs and Bronze Star.

Currently owner and operator of a construction company. Married with four children: John, Thomas, Tara and Nicole.

LYNN "HUN" PARSHALL,
born Aug. 16, 1946 in Marianna, PA. Entered the service in 1969. Trained at Mare Island August-October 1969. Served with RIVDIV 552, Tra Cu and Vietnam River Group 59 at Tuyen Nhon. His memorable experiences include serving on PBR 869 as engineman, training Vietnamese sailors and being wounded during TET 1970 at Tra Cu.

Discharged 1973 as E5. Awarded Navy Commendation w/V and Purple Heart.

He received a BA in history from the University of Pittsburgh. Currently maintenance superintendent for a local housing authority and part-time farmer.

Married Shirley and has a son, George and daughter, Roslyn.

JOHN ARMOUR PHILLIPS, born Aug. 20, 1949 at Aransas Pass, TX. Enlisted in USN August 1968. Following training at Naval Training Center, Dan Diego, CA he was assigned to USS *Ranger* (CVA-61) in November 1968. Served on the USS *Ranger* until August 1969 in which he completed a Westpac Cruise in the Tonkin Gulf as a seaman, helmsman, rigger and coxswain of the captain's gig. Received river patrol craft/riverine warefare training at Vallejo, CA September-November 1969.

Reported overseas in Vietnam to RIVDIV 593, Iron Butterfly, November 1969. He participated in 223 combat patrols and was under hostile fire on 16 patrols as boat seaman and gunner until June 30, 1970 until RIVDIV 593 was transferred to the South Vietnamese government. From July-September 1970, he served as English instructor at a Vietnamese Riverine Warfare Training Center in Saigon, Vietnam. Assigned to USS *Coronado* (LPD-11) at Norfolk, VA November 1970. Served as boatswains mate second class petty officer in charge of all deck operations for First Division and participated in Caribbean and Mediterranean cruise until his honorable discharge August 1972.

Awarded Navy Commendation Medal w/ Combat V, Combat Action Ribbon, Presidential Unit Citation, Expert Rifleman Medal and RVN Gallantry Cross.

John graduated with honors from New Mexico State University (BS in agriculture) at Las Cruces, NM and began a career with the Department of Interior for the Bureau of Land Management in 1976. He is currently serving as an associate district manager in Farmington, NM responsible for managing public lands.

Married Rebecca Ann Weber on his return from Vietnam Oct. 3, 1970 in Rockport, TX. They are happily married in Bloomfield, NM with two grown children. A son, William Erik who lives in Boise, ID with his wife, Rebecca and their daughter Amber and a daughter, Georgia Ann Johnston who lives in Bloomfield, NM with her husband, Todd.

FELIX PIN'A JR., born May 18, 1937 in Cotulla, TX. Entered the service January 1956. Trained April 1971 at Coronado, CA. Units served with: *St. Paul* (CA-73), *Fort Marion* (LSC-20), Corpus Christi NAS, *Bradley* (DE-1041), *Fort Fisher* (LSD-40), Det. C, San Diego, Naval Support Vietnam Det. YRBM21.

He remembers receving fire in the summer of 1971. Eleven rounds were fired at YRBM, first hit PBR, second hit YRBM officer wardroom, third hit helicopter on deck.

Discharged September 1975 as MMC. Awarded Combat Action, Vietnam Service, RVN Gallantry Cross and others.

He is certified in surface water production, back flow testing and repair. Currently senior water plant operator Trinity River Authority of Texas.

Married to Toni, he has two daughters, Maria, Virginia and two sons, Felix Ira and Humberto.

SHERMAN PRIDHAM, born Sept. 30, 1949 in Rockland, ME. Enlisted in USNR, Albuquerque, NM Dec. 7, 1966. Active duty May 1968. Volunteered for PBRs twice! Trained at Mare Island July 1968. Arrived in Vietnam September 1968.

Served at Nhd Be, RIVDIV 592 until March 1969 and transferred to Tra Cu, RIVDIV 532. The division transferred to Sa Dec about May 1969 and then transferred to Can Tho, RIVDIV 574 July 1969, back to Go Dau Ha, RIVDIV 592 August 1969. He went on 213 combat patrols and was in eight firefights.

Awarded Combat Action Ribbon, Navy Unit Citation, Presidential Unit Citation and Navy Commendation Medal w/Combat V. He is a life member of Gamewardens.

After Vietnam he became a Christian and attended Baptist Bible College in Springfield, MO. Served as a missionary in Norway from 1981-88. Now he is a tile contractor in Albuquerque.

Married the former Joan Alls in 1974, he has three boys.

FRANCIS J. "FRANK" REILLY, was from Chatham, NJ. Joined the USN in 1968 and attended basic training at Great Lakes, IL. After A School, he joined RIVDIV 593 at Nha Be, Vietnam in late October 1969, transferring in from another in-country command.

He returned to the States in March 1970 and reported to the USS *LaSalle* in Norfolk, VA. In 1971 the *LaSalle* moved to the Philadelphia Shipyard for an overhaul.

Petty Officer Reilly was killed in a motorcylce accident Oct. 12, 1971. He was awarded Bronze Star Medal for action on operation Ready Deck conducted on the upper Saigon River. Also received Purple Heart for wounds received in combat while serving with the Iron Butterfly.

His mother, Winifred Reilly still lives in Chatham and is a memorial member of Gamewardens.

KENNETH R. "ROSY" ROSENBERGER, born March 18, 1948 in Culver City, CA. Entered the service 1968. Attended boot camp at San Diego, CA GMG A School, Great Lakes, IL and NIOTC.

Served with RIVDIV 591, operation Giant Slingshot March-October 1969; RIVDIV 572

October 1969-July 1970 and RPG 62 July 1970-May 1971.

His achievements include surviving the destruction of ATSB Song Ong Doc; over 400 patrols and 47 firefights and spent 18 months on Song Ong Doc.

Discharged 1971 as GMG2. Awarded Bronze Star/w V, Navy Commendation w/V, Navy Achievement w/V, Purple Heart, Combat Action, Navy Unit Commendation, Vietnam Service, Vietnam Campaign w/4 Battle Stars.

He has been a crane operator at Alco Smelter for 25 years.

KENNETH HENRY RUECKER, born Nov. 18, 1922 in Cornelius, OR. Entered the service 1941 and trained at San Diego, CA; 1942, Bremerton; 1943, UCLA; 1944 University of Southern California; 1949 San Diego; 1951 Barbers Point; 1962 Virginia Beach and 1966 Coronado.

Served with USS *Gillis* (AVD-12); *Hulbert* (AVD-6); *Catalpa* (AN-10); Columbia River Group, PACRESFLT; *Helena* (CA-75); *Kalmia* (ATA-184); CO *Samoset* (ATA-190); NAVHYDROOFC Washington, DC; CO, *LaMoure County* (LST-883); CO, *Jerome County* (LST-848); COMSERVPAC staff; CO, OceanDet 1; LANDSHIPRON 9 staff; COMRIVRON 5; Repose AH16; FleActs Sasebo; JointUSMilAdvGrp Korea; PhibGrp 1 staff; NavBase Subic Bay.

His memorable experiences include Battle of Midway, Aleutian Campaign, Korean War and Vietnam War. He was the most junior commander in US Fleet; most junior LST commander in US Fleet; three other commands-at-sea and 1st COMRIVRON 5.

Discharged in 1978. Awarded Legion of Merit w/V, Joint Services Commendation, Navy Commendation w/V 2nd award, Combat Action, Navy Unit Commendation, Meritorious Unit Commendation, 2nd award; Good Conduct, 2nd & 3rd awards; Vietnamese Honor Medal 1st Class; plus 14 service and campaign medals from China, Japan, Korea and Vietnam.

Married with two children.

RICHARD D.W. "DUTCH" SCHULTZ, born Aug. 17, 1934 in Buffalo, NY. Entered the service August 1951. Attended basic, Bainbridge, MD; AB School, Coronado; Vietnam language; PBR, Mare Island; ordered to Vietnam July 1969.

Served with RIVDIV 592, leading chief and patrol officer RPG # 56 advisor. Served aboard USS *Tarawa*; Mobile Fasron 121 and numerous crash crews before Vietnam. He lost capture of only PBR during Vietnam conflict to Cambodia while leading chief met

Zumwalt personally, second RPG into cambodia, after leaving Vietnam, three year tour in Antartic as loadmaster.

Discharged September 1975 as ABCM. Awarded Bronze Star w/Combat V, plus 15 others during Vietnam service and career of 24 years.

Retired from Navy and Federal Civil Service with a combination of 38 years. Employed with Civil Service in 1976, he advanced from gate guard to general foreman before retiring in 1989. A life member of DAV, VFW, Gamewardens and a member of American Legion, Fleet Reserve, SERE Instructor Assoc., VFW Cooties and Am. Legion 40+8.

Married to Alice, he has five children and 11 grandchildren.

THOMAS JOHN "TJ" SHERIDAN, born Aug. 27, 1944. Entered the service September 1967 and trained in 1969 at Mare Island. Served with RIVDIV 592 from 1969-70. The whole 12 months tour was an experience that he cannot put into words, that can describe the best of times and the worst of times.

Discharged May 1970 as GMG2. Awarded all the usual medals involving the Navy Commendation w/Combat V, Combat Action Ribbon, Vietnamese Service w/Silver and four Bronze Stars.

Received his BBA from Southest Texas State University, ASE master auto repair technician. He is owner of TJ's Auto Repair Service.

Married to Nancy for 31 years, he has a son John and daughter Jamie.

LLOYD WAYNE SHRINER, born March 11, 1947 in Marion, IN. Enlisted USN October 1966. Following basic training and GMG A School at Great Lakes, he was assigned to the USS *Samuel Gompers* AD-37. Upon completion of NIOTC training, Mare Island; SERE training, Whidbey Island (who could forget that?), PO Shriner reported to RIVDIV 592 Nha Be, Vietnam February 1969. In July 1969 he was transferred to RIVDIV 593 as gunner on PBR 842.

He finished his tour of Vietnam and USN February 1970. Awarded four Navy Commendations w/Combat V.

Shriner attended Purdue and worked in government electronics for 22 years including Magnavox, ITT and Memcor as an electronics technician. Presently at United Technologies Automotive, Huntington, IN.

Married to Samia, they are kept busy with three sons, two daughters, eight grandchildren and activities at Freedom Assembly of God Church, Alexandria, IN.

TERRY CLEO SIMISON, born April 2, 1947 in Lansing, MI. He attended St. Casimir School and graduated from Everett High School. Enlisted in USN April 21, 1965 while still in high school and attended basic training in Great Lakes. After completion of basic, he attended Submarine School in New London and was then assigned to the USS *Sailfish,* from there transferred to submarine rescue ship USS *Kittywake* until April 1968 when he volunteered for duty in Vietnam.

After completion of training at NIOTC he reported to RIVSEC 544 at Nha Be Vietnam May 1968. He was in action within days of reporting and was awarded the Silver Star and Purple Heart for action on Aug. 2, 1968 when his patrol came under heavy attack and he aided the wounded while still under fire, although wounded himself.

On Sept. 1, 1968 RIVSEC 544 was redesignated RIVDIV 593, COMRIVPATFLOT 5. PO Simison was part of this transition and continued the tradition of the Iron Butterfly. On Jan. 17, 1969 he was mortally wounded by an AK-47 round in the neck when his patrol came under heavy attack on the Vam Co Dong River as part of operation Giant Slingshot.

He was highly regarded by all in the division and was, and is, missed by those he served with and his family. Terry was survived by his mother Reath and father Riley. Also two brothers, a sister and two step brothers. Terry's family is in touch with members of the Iron Butterfly.

THEADORE "TED" SMITH, reported to RIVSEC 544, later re-designated as RIVDIV 593 in May 1968 as the unit was forming at Nha Be. He came from another in-country command at Long Vinh. Chief Smith was assigned as a patrol officer and began patrolling the Rung Sat Special Zone as soon as the unit was operational.

On Nov. 8, 1968 Chief Smith's patrol left Nha Be at first light en route to Thi Vai/Go Ghia area. This area was known as a Viet Cong strong hold and had been the location of many enemy ambushes in the past. During the patrol he was directed by higher authority to enter a small canal with his two boats and act as a blocking force for a landing party sweeping the area. His patrol was ambushed coming out of the canal and his cover boat took two direct hits, wounding all aboard.

After clearing the kill zone, Chief Smith transferred to the cover boat to assist the wounded and maneuver the boat out of the ambush. As he started to move the boat out of the kill zone to medivac the wounded, it took another direct hit from a rocket killing him instantly. For this action he was awarded the Silver Star and second Purple Heart postumously for his mortal wounds. He had earlier received a Bronze Star Medal for bravery and aggresiveness under fire.

Chief Smith was a true professional and took the well being of his crew as a first priority. He gave his life trying to help those crewmen that were wounded. He left behind a wife Eiko, now deceased, and a son Rick. His devotion to

duty and courage earned him wide reknown throughout the Rung Sat Special Zone. We all miss him.

DOUGLAS L. SPREY, enlisted in the Navy 1950. His seagoing career spanned amphibious ships, aircraft carriers and three submarines. During the 28 years he saw duty in all ranks from fireman apprentice through chief petty officer and warrant to lieutenant commander.

In the submarine force, Sprey had duty aboard the diesel submarine Sarda and put the nuclear-powered *Seawolf* and *Andrew* Jackson in commission.

Newly appointed Ens.Sprey made his first in-country Vietnam tour as maintenance and patrol officer in 1969 with RIVDIV 543 in Cua Viet, six clicks south of the DMZ in I Corps. Two years later he returned as an advisor to an RVN Coastal Division at An Toi, Phu Quoc Island.

Between patrol, maintenance and salvage work, the Riverine and Coastal Division jobs called for all out effort even drawing on Sprey's Navy diving qualifications.

Awarded a Bronze Star, two Navy Commendation Medals (all w/Combat V), Purple Heart and other personal and unit awards.

After his Navy retirement in 1979, it took 14 more years of shipboad life to get the sea out of his blood. Doug retired as a US Merchant Marine engineer in 1993 and only goes out on his sailboat now.

RICHARD A. "CASEY" STENGEL, born Sept. 9, 1927 in Buffalo, NY. Enlisted in USN Sept. 24, 1944. After boot camp at Great Lakes, IL he was assigned to Pacific Fleet, mostly on cargo ships: USS *Scania* (AKA-40) and *Arequipa* (AF-31). The Air Force supplied fresh provisions to the Army at the islands during the A bomb test called Sandstones Operation. He also placed the USS *Newport News* in commission and the USS *Little Rock*. He spent four years aboard the USS *Iowa,* then on to destroyers USS *W.C. Lawe* and USS *Zellars*.

He decided to volunteer for Vietnam in 1968 and attended NIOTC, Vietnamese Language School in Coronado and SERE in Washington. Arrived in Vietnam November 1968 and was assigned as patrol officer in RIVDIV 571. They had the Mark One's PBRs and moved to many different areas of Vietnam (ditches, canals and rivers) mostly night ambush. They inserted Seals and Grunts in ambush duty with the Army and protected ski boats in ambush at night.

His last year in service was at Orlando Training Center. He retired in 1974. Awarded Bronze Star w/Combat V, Navy Commendation Medal w/Combat V, Combat Action Ribbon, Vietnam Service Medal w/star, Vietnam Campaign Medal, Presidential Unit Citation (571), NDSM w/star, Good Conduct Medal w/Silver Star, ACPM, WWII VM, China Service Medal, American Theater and Navy Occupation Medal.

A widower, he lives in Atlantic Beach, FL and has a daughter, Patricia Foss and two grandchildren.

THOMAS P. STILLER, born April 10, 1947 in East Chicago, IN. Attended basic training, Great Lakes, IL, August 1966; Gunners Mate A School, Great Lakes, October 1966; Naval Amphibious Base Coronado, CA March 1967 for Vietnamese Language School and SERE training and NIOTC, May 1967 at Mare Island, CA. In June 1967 he reported to RIVRON 5 and assigned

to PBR Section 512. He was forward gunner on PBR and served in other areas as needed. He went on 180 combat patrols, 26 patrols in which a firefight occurred.

His memorable experiences include C rations and heating them on the exhaust manifolds of the PBR's engines; fishing for the locals using percussion grenades; duck hunting on the Bassac estuary using the aft organ grinder (40mm grenade launcher) and M60; red light conditions before night patrol; skiing bhind the PBR, trying to get over the enormous wake it made and enjoying hot bread stolen from the galley of the LST Jennings County.

He received the usual awards reeived in a combat area of Vietnam. The one he treasure mosts is the Presidential Unit Citation, it best rewarded what they as sailors were all about, a great team.

Stiller was hospitalized for wounds inflicted during the war and subsequently medivaced to Japan and finally to Great Lakes Naval Hospital for more surgery. Tom was medically retired from the Navy August 1970 after undergoing two years of rehabilitation.

Receved a BA degree from Indiana University in 1975 and now sells real estate in Loveland, CO. He retired from AMOCO in 1999 where he worked as a chief operator at the refinery in Whiting, IN for over 20 years. A life member of DAV and member of UDT-Seal Assoc. and Gamewardens.

Married his high school sweetheart Monica in June 1969. He has two daughters, two sons-in-law and two grandchildren.

JAMES A. STOVER, born Aug. 18, 1946 in Grand Rapids, MI. Entered the service Oct. 20, 1965. Attended CYN A School, Norfolk, VA May 1967 and CI School, Littlecreek, VA June 1967.

Served at NSA Det Binh Thuy, TAD CTF 116 Comm. Center Active duty NRSD9-96(M),

NR telecombat 113 NRDD982, Nicholson, NR NSC Norfolk 2113.

Discharged March 1, 1989 as 4N1. Awarded Navy Unit Commendation, Navy Reserve Meritorious Service (five awards), two Armed Forces Reserve Medals, three Vietnam Service, Vietnam Campaign, Vietnam Meritorious Unit Citation w/Palm and NDSM.

He is an equipment service employee with Northwest Airlines. A life member of NERA, Navy Memorial Foundation and MRF. He received the Gerald R. Ford chapter NERA Memorial Award.

Married to Kathryn, he has a son, Andrew and daughter, Merry.

NEIL E. "RED" STUMMER, born Dec. 24, 1947 in Goshen, IN. Joined the USN Aug. 7, 1968.

First duty station was USS *Hornet* (CVS-12), anti-submarine warfare aircraft operating in the Gulf of Tonkin off the coast of North Vietnam and Yankee team mail carier. Additional duty in North Korea waters after North Korea had show down USN EC-121 reconnaissance plane killing all 31 USN personnel aboard. Shorty after return to Long Beach, CA, *Hornet* was designated prime recovery ship for the Apollo 11 astronauts; also recovered second group of men to land on the moon, Apollo 12 astronauts. USS *Hornet* was decommissioned June 1970.

Volunteered for in-country duty in Vietnam and took SERE instruction in the classroom at the Coronado Naval Amphibious and Small Arms Weapons Training Center at USMC Base, Camp Pendeleton, CA.

Second duty station, August-November 1970, stood fire watches, filled sandbags, rode garbage trucks at Camp Tien Sha, Da Nang, RVN, I Corps.

Third duty station at Annapolis Base enlisted quarters, Saigon; transferred to USS *Hunterdon County* (AGP-838), which was the first major vessel to cross the line during the Cambodian incursion. Ship was decommissioned July 1971 and turned over to the Singapore navy.

Fourth station was from August 1971-April 1972, Nam Can/Solid Anchor, Ca Mau Penninsula, An Xuyen Province, Tran Hung Dav IV. He was shot down on a return flight from Saigon to Nam Can on Thanksgiving Day 1971; five men wounded in the attack; crash landed in a rice paddy.

Left Saigon April 1972 for separation at Treasure Island Naval Base in San Francisco as E-4, petty officer third class. Awarded NDSM, VSM w/3 stars, VCM w/60 Devices, NVCW w/ Bronze Star, AFEM, MVCR w/2 Bronze Stars.

He is a life member of Veterans of the Vietnam Wars, Inc., #0378; American Legion (PUFL), Post 30, Reno, NV; VFW, Battle Born Post 9211, Reno, NV; DAV, Chapter 3, Indianapolis, IN; VVA, 1217, Chapter 295, Indianapolis, IN; AMVETS, Post 9936, Nevada-California; Gamewardens; River Patrol Force, Task Force 116-117, Brown Water Navy, San Diego, CA; NCOA, San Antonio, TX; and annual USS *Hornet* Club, Inc., North Port, FL and Mobile Riverine Force Assoc., Inc., Elkhart Lake, WI.

He works with VAVS (VA Hospital escort service and West Nevada Cemetary Memorial Honor Guard. He has never married.

JOHN A. "COMBAT YEOMAN" SULLIVAN, born May 9, 1948 in New York City, NY. Entered the service April 1967. Trained at Great Lakes, IL; NAS Lemoore, CA and attended Survival School at Coronado in September 1968. Served with VA-122, July 1967-September 1969 and RIVDIV 543 September 1969-April 1970 in RVN. While on ambush with five other PBRs on Ba Rein River in I Corps, across on the other bank was a company of RNV soldiers unaware of them. They opened up from 50 yards across. Poor guys didn't know what hit them. Boo Coo KIA. He was wounded in Vietnam, amputation of tongue but is able to speak.

Discharged July 1970 as YN2. Awarded Navy Commendation w/V, Combat Action, Vietnam Campaign, Vietnam Service and Good Conduct Medal.

Currently he is a mailman for US Postal Service. Married for 23 years and has four children and two grandchildren.

MICHAEL PETER "SPLASH" SULLIVAN, born March 22, 1945 in Santa Barbara, CA. Entered the service in April 1968. Enlisted NOC School, Newport, RI November 1967-April 1968; PBR School, Vallejo, CA May-August 1969.

Served with USS *Taylor* (DD-468), RIVDIV 593 September 1969-June 1970; COMNAVFOR V June-September 1970.

Discharged February 1971 as LTJG. Awarded NDSM, Vietnam Service Medal w/4 Bronze Stars, Army Commendation Medal, Combat Action Ribbon, RVN Campaign Medal w/Device.

He received his BS in math in 1967, MA in math in 1972 from Cal Poly San Luis Obispo, CA. Employed as math teacher at Bakersfield, CA for 18 years. Went on 15,000 mile camper trip around USA in 1971.

Currently unmarried, he has a son and daughter.

HOWARD E. "HANK' SWAIN, born Sept. 1, 1940 in Boone County, IA. Enlisted July 1958 and attended basic in San Diego. After basic he completed MM A School in Great Lakes and Sub School in New London. His first assignment was USS *Diodon* (SS-349) out of San Diego. Volunteered for Vietnam in 1968 and received orders to NIOTC, Vallejo for PBR School. After completing PBR training and a course in Vietnamese Language at NAB Coronado. He reported to COMRIVPATFLOT 5 for assignment to RIVDIV 593, Iron Butterfly. Chief Swain was assigned as a patrol officer and made over 200 combat patrols.

His decorations include Bronze Star, Purple Heart, Navy Commendation, RVN Gallantry Cross, Vietnam Service, Vietnam Campaign and Combat Action.

He remained in the Navy for 30 years retiring as a master chief in 1988. After completing college he signed on with the California Department of Corrections and is a correctional officer at San Quentin prison. He is a life member of Gamewardens and DAV. Also a member of the Fleet Reserve Assoc.

Married to the former Diane Rusk of Vallejo.

JOHN SYDOW, born March 15, 1944 in Dayton, OH. Served with PBR Mobile Base One. Military locations: I Corps Vietnam, Perfume River; Hue Tam My Vietnam; NSA Da Nang, Vietnam; NAS Olathe, KS; Long Beach; SERE/CI training Amphib Base, Coronado, CA; National Rifle Matches, Camp Perry, OH; CINCLANTFLT, Norfolk, VA and NTC San Diego, CA. He remembers the TET in 1968 (Hue).

Awarded Navy Unit Citation, Good Conduct Medal, NDSM, RVN Campaign Medel and Vietnam Service Medal w/star.

Employed as functional unit manager, Department of Corrections, Missouri.

Married to Bernadine, he has a daughter, Dyna, and two sons, Harold and Bernard.

DON CAMERON THOMSON, born Oct. 14, 1941 in Kansas City, KS. He completed six years of college and was sworn in the USNR Oct. 2, 1966. He reported to Aviation Officer Candidate School in Pensacola, FL Feb. 7, 1967 receiving his commission there April 28, 1967. Received his Navy wings of gold there July 21, 1968 and assigned as a SAR pilot at NAS Cecil Field and NAS Jacksonville, FL before receiving orders to HAL-3 in Vietnam. Arrived in Saigon Aug. 7, 1970 and was at HQ in Binh Thuy before reporting to Det 1 at Solid Anchor at Nam Can in October 1970. He transferred to Det 3 in Cau Mau for April and May returning to Binh Thuy for June and July. He received his helicopter aircraft commander (HAC), attack helicopter aircraft command (AHAC), fire team leader (FTL) and post maintenance test pilot (MTP) pilot ratings which were all that were recognized in HAL-3. He departed Saigon Aug. 4, 1971 after flying 494 combat missions. Departing Vietnam on special circuitious travel orders he circled the globe westward arriving back at NAS Jacksonville, FL 60 days later.

Left active Navy duty Dec. 21, 1971 rejoining the Navy Reserves Oct. 1, 1977 eventually reaching the rank of commander, USNR. On Nov. 17, 1986 he received an interservice transfer to the Missouri Army National Guard as a chief warrant officer second (CW2). He flew Cobra gunship helicopters for seven years and

has been back on active duty (full-time) for five years as a CW4 Missouri Army National Guard Counterdrug (RAID) pilot. He wears Master Army Aviator Wings.

His decorations include 18 Strike Flight Air Medals, Navy Combat Action Ribbon, Navy Presidential Unit Citation, Army Commendation Medal, Navy Meritorious Unit commendation, Reserve Components Achievement Medal, NDSM, VSM, Armed Forces Reserve Medal w/Silver Hourglass, Army Service Ribbon, RVN Gallantry Cross, Vietnam Campaign Medal, Navy Rifle Marksmanship w/E (Expert), Navy Pistol Marksmanship Ribbon w/E and Missouri National Guard 10 year Ribbon.

He is a life member of the Gamewardens, Navy Reserve Assoc., National Guard Assoc., Missouri National Guard Assoc. and the Hal-3 Seawolf Assoc. He is a co-founder of the latter group and has served as their historian/curator since its formation in 1985. Also a member of the Vietnam Helicoper Pilots Assoc. and is a plank owner in the US Navy Memorial Assoc.

CONLEY ROBERT TIPTON JR., born at home in the moutains of Johnson City, TN Dec. 24, 1946. His father had served in the USN SEALS in the Pacific during WWII, so in November 1964 Conley Jr. enlisted in the USN too.

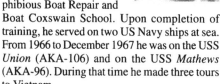

After basic boot camp training in San Diego, CA, he was sent in March 1965 to Coronado Amphibian Base for Amphibious Boat Repair and Boat Coxswain School. Upon completion of training, he served on two US Navy ships at sea. From 1966 to December 1967 he was on the USS *Union* (AKA-106) and on the USS *Mathews* (AKA-96). During that time he made three tours to Vietnam.

After completing his first tour of duty in December 1967, Tipton re-enlisted in early 1968 and was sent to San Diego, CA for PBR training and Vietnamese language training. In 1968 he was given orders to go to Task Force 116, RIVDIV 593, Iron Butterfly in Nha Be, as EN3 and then EN2 on boat #761. Participated in operation Giant Slingshot and operation Gamewarden. During that time he also made over 250 combat river boat patrols.

Discharged in 1969 and awarded two Bronze Stars w/Combat V and two Naval Commendations w/Combat V. Again he re-enlisted in 1974 and ordered to USS *Sellers* (DDG-11), where he worked in A gang and AC&R group for two years. Discharged in 1976.

Tipton now lives in Jacksonville, FL and has his own construction and remodeling business. A member of AM-Vets and other veteran groups, he feels very proud and honored to have served his country with such a well trained and elite group as the RIVDIV 593 and SEALS group 1 and 3. May God Bless all the Vets!

JOHN TROIA, born Oct. 19, 1937 in Brooklyn, NY. Enlisted Oct. 25, 1957. Trained at Great Lakes, January-June 1958; duty at Underwater Ordnance Station, Newport, RI. June 1958-June 1959 duty aboard USS *Norris*. From July 1959-

April 1962 duty aboard USS *Charles Berry*. Discharged April 1962.

Re-enlisted September 1964 for Sub School and assigned to USS *Henry Clay* December 1964-July 1968. Transferred to NAVINSHOPTRA, NIOTC, Vallejo,CA. Assigned to PBR Class 64, 1968 and Language School, San Diego, CA. From October 1968-69 in-country with RIVDIV 543 at Cua Viet, RVN Northern I Corps as boat captain, then patrol officer. Made 237 patrols and seven major firefights.

He served aboard USS *Trumpetfish*, USS *Pickerel* and USS *Francis Scott Key*; and with COMSUBRON 18 staff, Naval Intelligence, COMSUBGRU 6 staff and at Recruiting District, New York and Naval Reserve Training Center, Brooklyn, NY, retiring in 1984.

Awarded BSM w/V, two NAMs, CAR, PUC, two NUCs, NMUC, four Battle Efficiency Es, four GCMs among others.

Having helped save a Marine forced recon team(7 UP) under fire by NVA regulars. They called for backup and helo support and provided cover fire and illumination. Four Marines were wounded, one critically, the team corpsman performed a tracheotomy to open the airway. They sent two men to resupply the Marines. Backup help and helos arrived and the NVA left; eight NVA killed in action body count. They medivaced the Marines to waiting ambulances in Dong Ha and later learned they recovered. It felt really good to have helped. It still feels as good today as 30 years ago.

DARRELL LEE TUCKER, born April 29, 1947 in Spokane, WA. Grew up in the Washington/Idaho area calling Connell home when he enlisted in the USN Oct. 6, 1965. After basic training in San Diego, assigned to USS *England* for his first tour of duty. Sent to RD School from there and then reported to USS *Constellation* (CVA-64).

Tucker volunteered for Vietnam while on the *Constellation* and had to extend in the Navy for the orders. He completed NIOTC and then reported to RIVDIV 593 in early May 1969 at Nha Be. Completed 17 combat patrols in the remainng days of May and assigned as boat captin of PBR-841 after only a short time in the division because of his leadership ability and cool nature under fire.

On July 6, 1969 Tucker was part of a two boat patrol working in the Rung Sat Zone when they came under heavy enemy rocket and automatic weapons fire. PO Tucker was mortally wounded when a rocket struck the port side of the coxswains flat where he was standing to operate the boat.

Darrell was a natural leader and a good man to have in a firefight. Although in the division only a short time, PO Tucker had made many lasting friends as can only be done in combat. The Iron Butterfly lost a friend and a shipemate on July 6, 1969. He will always be remembered. Darrell's father Clarence and younger brother Tim are in touch with members of the Iron Butterfly.

CHARLES RICHARD "CHARLIE" VANCE, born July 9, 1947 in Oxnard, CA. Entered the service November 1965. The units he served with USS *Proteus*, RIVDIV 593, RPG 54, NIOTC, NAS Alameda, USS *San Jose*, USS *Racine*, NAS North Island, USS *San Bernardino*, service craft, Subic Bay.

He was discharged from the Navy January 1986 as ENC.

HENRY DANIEL "DANNY" WADE, enlisted in the Navy in Passaic, NY 1966. On Jan. 29, 1967 he reported to the Great Lakes NTC,

Co. 58. Even though his first name was Henry, all his friends called him Danny. Upon completion of boot camp he was designated as airman and sent to NAS, Alameda, CA, assigned to VAW 13. After a nine month cruise on the USS *Coral Sea*, he was promoted to aviation electricians mate 3rd class (AE3) and received orders to Survival School in Coronado, CA and then to Naval Air Facility Cam Rahn Bay.

Assigned to the avionics shop, tried his best to get transferred to Market Time a few miles away. The closest he got was one patrol on PCF 45. Transferred to Saigon to a unit that had so many names he still doesn't know what unit he was in. It went by Naval Suport Activity Saigon Det Ton Son Nhut, AirCoFat, White Hat Airlines and NAF Cam Rahn Bay Det Ton Son Nhut.

Assigned crew chief on the old green helicopters (UH34D) that delivered mail and transported personnel. He has landed on every LST, YRBM and every base in the Delta, Godaha, Sadec, Binh Thuey, Long Xuyen, Tan An, Can Tho and many more.

They lived in the Battle Creek Hotel on Plantation Road just down from the Annapolis Hotel. Saigon was the best time he had in all four years in the Navy and they still get together once a year with old friends for their annual barbecue.

Discharged, he was hired by US Customs Service as sky marshal and retired August 1998 after 27 years service as supervisory special agent. Over those years he served at numerous duty stations. Currently he is a part-time police officer in Auburn, NH and part-time deputy sheriff, Rockingham County Sheriff's Department assigned to Manchester Airport unit.

Being associated with the Brown Water Navy was the most memorable and best part of his life and he will never forget it.

RONALD ROBERT WALTON, born Jan. 10, 1946 in Canandaigua, NY. Graduated Hamburg High School in 1965. Enlisted in USN October 1965. Went to basic training in February 1966 at Great Lakes, IL. After basic reported to USS *Paul Revere* (APA-248). Volunteering almost immediately for Vietnam, entered PBR training NIOTC at Mare Island, Vallejo, CA in September 1968.

Entered Vietnam during TET New Years 1969. Assigned to RIVDIV 593, Iron Butterfly. Assigned to couple of make shift patrols, before being assigned to PBR 756 under James Davy boat captain and Patrol Officer Bob Monzingo. On Sept. 15, 1969 he was wounded and medivaced to Cu Chi field hospital. Eventually sent to St. Albans Naval Hospital in Queens, NY.

Medically retired from USN in April 1970. Awarded Bronze Star w/V, two Navy Meritorious Medals, "V," Purple Heart, two Presidential Unit Citations among others.

He has held numerous jobs until finding out in 1989 diagnosed with PTSD. Currently 100 percent retired.

Married and has two step-children and one grandchild. Involved with AMVETS, held county position and worked his way up to commander of post.

JEFFREY JOHN WARNOCK, born May 27, 1944 in Brooklyn, NY. Joined the USN May 1968 and graduated from OCS in February 1969. He arrived in Vietnam June 1969 and attached to RIVDIV 514 as patrol officer. He operated along the Vinh Te Canal during operation Tran Hung Dao and remained as an assistant senior Naval advisor to RPG-55 from April-October 1970 when the USN turned River Divisions over to VNN. Assigned to USS *Luce* (DLG-7) as MPA October 1970.

Discharged from active duty in October 1972, he remained in the Naval Reserve as an engineering duty officer (1445) and was promoted to captain June 1990. His awards include the Bronze Star w/V, Navy Commendation w/V, Navy Achievement w/V, Air Medal, Combat Action, NDSM, Vietnam Service, RVN Gallantry Cross, Vietnam Staff Service, Vietnam Training Service, Vietnam Civil Action, Small Boat and Surface Warfare Devices.

Married to Ann Sherry and they have three children: Meghan, Timothy and Kevin. Currently reside in Exeter, NH. His fondest memory of the Navy is serving with the men of the Brown Water Navy, a unique and singluar experience in naval history and his personal career.

STEPHEN B. WATSON, born Dec. 27, 1943 in Niagara Falls, NY. Enlisted April 10, 1961. After boot camp was sent to USS *Edmonds* (DE-406) then on to USS *Weiss* (APD-135) where he made his first visit to Vietnam. The next duty station was USS *Midway* (CVA-41) for a long second trip to Vietnam. When the *Midway* returned from the western Pacific, he volunteered for Vietnam and was sent to Naval Amphibious Base, Coronado, November 1965 for PBR training. He attended JEST School, Subic Bay RP, then on to be a "Plank Owner" in RIVSEC 511 located in Can Tho on Bassac River. As the after gunner on PBR 40 (the only slow PBR), he participated in numerous firefights.

In October 1967 he was transferred to RIVSEC 533 at Nha Be as boat captain of PRB 149. At the end of the tour, he again volunteered to stay in-country and transferred to RIVSEC 512 in the lower Bassac River and served as boat captain on two different PBRs. While attached to the River Patrol Force he served as radio operator for the MACE team.

He made over 400 combat patrols and was in over 150 firefights. Advanced from EN3 to EN2. At the end of his tours, transferred to USS *Austin* (LPD 4), Norfolk, VA.

Awarded Navy Accommodation Medal, Navy Achievement Medal w/V, Purple Heart w/ Gold Star, Combat Action Ribbon, two PUCs, Meritorious Unit Award, two Battle Es, five Good Conduct Medals, NDSM, RVN Service, four RVN Campaigns, RVN Gallantry Cross and various others.

Steve retired as master chief engineman with 28 years of service. He is a life member of Gamewardens and was national president 1998-2000. A member of USS *Weiss* Assoc. Employed as a general foreman by SAIC/AMSEC.

Married to Pat, he has two daughters and six grandchildren.

RONALD J. WEEKS, born Sept 10, 1937 in Topponish, WI. Enlisted in the USN Dec. 7, 1954. In 1955 he volunteered for an Antarctic expedition aboard the USS *Arneb* AKA-56, he was a part of operation Deep Freeze I. Adm. Richard E. Byrd, the American who insisted the territory be explored, was also aboard. This expedition entailed 38,000 mile around the world cruise. Chief Weeks

volunteered for PBR duty in 1968. After attending PBR training at the NIOTC, Vallejo, CA, he attended Vietnamese Language School in Coronado, CA. He underwent survival training in Warner Springs, CA. Upon his arrival in-country Chief Weeks was assigned to RIVSEC 544 in the Rung Sat Special Zone. He took command of Bravo patrol consisting of two, mark two, PBRs. This river section was soon changed to RIVDIV 593. In November 1968, RIVDIV 593 was pulled from the Rung Sat and sent to the Ben Luc area on the Vam Co Dong River as part of the Giant Slingshot operation. He was one of the pioneers of the PBR ambush tactic. This manuever proved to be highly successful. He was wounded in 1969 and medivaced out of country shortly thereafter.

Awarded two Bronze Stars w/Combat V, Purple Heart, Presidential Unit Citation, Navy Unit Citation, Meritorious Unit Citation, RVN Gallantry Cross, Combat Action Ribbon and the Antartic Service Medal among others.

Married to Carol for 43 years, he has three daughters, one son and six grandchildren.

LESTER LEON "PADRE" WESTLING JR.,

born Oct. 19, 1930 in Oakland, CA. Entered the service June 27, 1966. Attended Field Medical Service School, Camp Pendleton, CA September 1966; Defense Language Institute (Vietnamese language course) Feb. 13, 1969-May 8, 1969.

Served with 3rd Marine Div. (Medical Battalion and Infantry), 3rd Bn., 9th Mar. Regt. October 1966-September 1967; Naval Support Activity, Saigon as circuit rider chaplain to approximately half of IV Corps combat units to all services May 24, 1969-May 28, 1970.

In February 1974 he wrote Doctor of Ministry Dissertation: "Ministry to POW Returnees and their Families in the Long-term Readjustment Period."

Discharged May 31, 1987 as captain, CHC, USN. Awarded Bronze Star Medal w/Combat V, Purple Heart, Navy Commendation w/Combat V, Navy Achievement Medal, Combat Action Ribbon, Sea Service Ribbon (three awards), Submarine Deterrent Patrol Pin, two Presidential Unit Citations, three Navy Unit Commendations, Meritorious Unit Commendation, Vietnam Presidential Unit Citation, Vietnam Meritorious (Civil Action) Unit Citation, NDSM, Vietnam Serice w/6 stars and Veitnam Campaign.

He is an Episcopal Priest (retired from Parish and Chaplain ministries) licensed marriage and family therapist with country mental health and in private practice.

Married to Marjorie Clark of Mobridge, SD since Nov. 1, 1958 he has three children in professional positions.

JOSEPH EDWARD WHERRY, born Oct.
9, 1948 in Chicago, IL. Joined USN Oct. 20, 1966. Served in Vietnam. Wounded Jan. 4, 1969 with gunshot wound to right knee. Given citation for work done with Vietnamese children during his recuperation. Sent to Vietnam three times.

Discharged April 17, 1970 from Seal Team I. Awarded Purple Heart, Vietnam Service Medal w/2 Bronze Stars, RVN Campaign Medal w/ Device, Combat Action Ribbon, RVN Meritori-

ous Unit Citation (Gallantry Cross Medal w/1/ C color w/Palm) and Civil Actions Medal w/1/ C color w/Palm.

He is now a National Service Representative for VVA, member of MOPH, Pen and Sword Society, UNO vice president, Disable Student Agency, Knights of Columbus, BSA, Sons of Italy, Men's Club of St. Patrick's Church and Boystown Alumni.

DAVID ALLEN WHITE, born Jan. 1, 1947
in Savannah, TN. Entered the service 1966. Attended training at Mare Island, Vallejo, CA May-June 1968 and Coronado, CA June 1968. Served with PBR RIVSEC 544, RIVDIV 593.

Discharged in 1970 as GMG2. Awarded two Purple Hearts, Silver Star, two Bronze Stars, Navy Achievement, Navy Commendation, Combat Action, RVN Campaign, Meritorious Unit Citation and Navy Unit Citation.

Currently he is a pipefitter with Local 760 in Muscle Shoals, AL. Married to Deborah for over 25 yers, he has one son, Jimmy and one daughter, Kimberly.

NEALE R. WILLARD, born Oct. 28, 1934
in New York. Joined the USN in 1951 at the age of 17 and served in Korea. Neal reported to RIVDIV 593, Iron Butterfly, in September 1969 while the division was on operation Ready Deck. He saw action on the upper Saigon River and in the Rung Sat Special Zone.

On the rivers of Vietnam or on the roads of America, he was a shipmate and a friend. After returning from Vietnam and retiring from the Navy, he became a long haul trucker and would try to find fellow warriors on his many trips across America. Finally poor health and a bad fall took Neal off the highway, but he never gave up looking for or staying in touch with fellow members of Gamewardens.

Neal received his last set of orders Aug. 15, 1994 and is now serving on the staff of the Supreme Commander. Neal, you are missed, keep your powder dry and don't forget your cover boat will always be there.

Neal left behind wife Margaret, two sons, four daughters and several grandchildren.

ROBERT M. WILLAUER JR., born May
25, 1947 in Chester, PA. Enlisted in the USN July 1966. After basic training at Great Lakes, IL NTC (Co. 470), he was assigned to the gunnery division of USS Bon Homme Richard (CVA-31), San Diego, CA. Following a Westpac cruise off the coast of Vietnam (Yankee Station) and returning to Long Beach,

CA, he received orders to USN Amphibious School, Coronado, CA then NIOTC, Mare Island, PBR Class 49.

After jungle warfare training at Subic Bay, PI, he arrived in Vietnam March 1968. PO Willauer reported to RIVDIV 512 at Binh Thuy on the Bassac River. His first patrol aboard PBR-40 was April 6, 1968. The worst day in-country was May 24, 1968 when he was informed his cousin SP/4 Andy Brinzo, serving with the 9th Inf. at Dong Tam, was listed as killed in action. In October 1968 he was transferred to RIVDIV 594, Nha Be, to start a new river division, which patrolled the Rung Sat Special Zone, the Vam Co Tay and Vam Co Dong Rivers. Being one of the original crew members, he is a fiberglass Plank Owner or RIVDIV 594. After 225 combat patrols he departed Vietnam March 1969. His new assignement was aboard the USS Richard E. Kraus (DD-849) out of Charleston, SC, where he finished his enlistment as GMG2.

Separated April 1970, he received Navy Commendation w/Combat V, Combat Action Ribbon, Presidential Unit Citation, Navy Unit Commendation, Vietnam Service Ribbons, NDSM and RVN Gallantry Cross.

Currently he resides in Bethel Township, PA and is employed by Sun Oil Co. His hobbies are drag racing, old car restoration (he has a '57 Chevy convertible), Harleys and Naval reunions. He is a life plus member of Gamewardens and VVA Chapter 708.

Married to Jeannie for over 28 years, he has a son, Rob and daughter Dani.

He is proud to have served as a PBR sailor, which he considers to be one of the finest bunch of sailors ever assembled by the Navy.

WILLIAM ANDREW "ANDY" WINTERS,
born May 17, 1947 in Lonaconing, MD. Enlisted in April 1966 and attended basic training at Great Lakes, IL. Reported to USS Dyess (DD-880) at Newport, RI and received Gun Operation and Maintenance, 5"/38 cal. School. Advanced to GMG3 while on the destroyer. Even though he did not volunteer as many had, he received orders

for PBR training at Mare Island, language training at Coronado and SERE training at Warner Springs, CA.

Served with RIVDIV 593 TF116 and USS Hector (AR-7). Assigned to RIVDIV 593 at Nha Be from August 1968-August 1969. Part of operation Giant Slingshot. Before the end of tour he was sent to Phu Loi and operating out of base camp. He was made boat captain after Giant Slingshot, being the only GMG3, due to heavy losses and for his experience in Rung Sat area.

Discharged January 1970 as GMG2. Awarded NDSM, Purple Heart, Navy Commendation Medal w/Combat V, RVN Service, RVN Campaign, Bronze Star for 252 combat patrols in-country and others.

Currently employed as supervisor with Alliant Tech Systems for over 25 years. Life member, past commander and current finance officer, Post 189 American Legion with 31 years continuous membership, also, life member VFW Post 5280.

Married to Sharon, he has a stepson Robert Hopkins and daughter, Christine.

JAMES H. WOODS, born Nov. 26, 1949 in Grand Forks, ND. After attending trade school in Fargo, ND, he enlisted in the Navy July 1968.

Following basic training at Great Lakes, IL, he was sent to Engineman A School and to NIOTC, Mare Island, CA for river boat training. After a course in Vietnamese language, PO Woods reported to COMRIVPATFLOT for assignment to RIVDIV 593, Iron Butterfly as engineman.

James returned Stateside and served with Harbor Clearance Unit 2 until being discharged April 1970. Awarded two Navy Commendations, RVN Campaign Medal and Purple Heart for wounds in combat, among others.

After leaving the Navy, he attended the University of Illinois at Chicago Circle, where he earned a BS degree in mechanical engineering. Since earning his bachelors he has worked for various manufacturing and consulting firms until 1994, when he started his own engineering consulting firm called Howe-Woods Technical Services, Inc.

JOHN W. WOODY, born Sept. 26, 1938 in Big Spring, TX. Entered the service in 1962. Attended OCS, commissioned 1963 ensign, USNR. Served on USS *Rellatrix* (AF-62), USS *Mattoponi* (AO-41) and with Boat Support Unit One, Amphib Base, Coronado, CA.

His memorable experiences include Mobile Support Team One, Da Nang; Mobile Support Team Two, Can Tho as officer in charge.

Discharged 1989 as captain he was awarded Bronze Star w/Combat V.

Currently he is employed as a computer consultant; received MBA at Seattle University and is a life member of Gamewardens.

Married and has two children.

MMC William Maraugha repairing Mark I after firefight. (Courtesy of William Maraugha Jr.)

River Division 591 leaving Cho Dao Canal, July 1969. (Courtesy of Keith DeClercq)

ROSTER

THE FOLLOWING IS THE ROSTER AS IT WAS PROVIDED BY THE GAMEWARDENS HISTORY BOOK COMMITTEE. THE PUBLISHER REGRETS IT CANNOT ASSUME LIABILITY FOR ERRORS OR OMISSIONS.

JOHNNY B. ADAMS
DAVID LEE AJAX
ROBERT S. ALLEN
WILLIAM E. ALLISON
RODGER D. ALSTON
ARNE ERIC ALTONEN
STEVEN AMOROSO
JIM ANDERSON
RICHARD W. ANDERSON
SCOTT A. ANDERSON
THOMAS K. ANDERSON
CHARLES E. ARDINGER
GERALD B. AREA
USS TUTUILA ARG-4
DENNIS W. ARMSTRONG
THOMAS W. ARMSTRONG
ALEXANDER L. AUTHER
STEVEN N. AZNOE
JOHN S. BABCOCK SR.
GARY E. BABEL
MICHAEL T. BAGETIS
DALLAM BILL BAILEY
MICHAEL H. BAILEY
EDWARD H. BAKER
JOHN D. BAKER
COLUMBUS W. BAKER JR.
CHARLES BALLENTINE
STEENY C. BANKS
THE BARGAIN SHOP
MARVIN R. BARNES
STEPHEN BARRY
STEPHEN BARRY
DOROTHY BASS
CHARLES BAXTER
HENRI L. BAXTER
JOHN S. BEACHY
ARTHUR BEATTY
JERE A. BEERY
STEVEN N. BELL
WILLIAM H. BELL
PAUL E. BELLMORE
BARRY C. BENNER
MICHAEL BERRY
BUD BESSEY
RONALD G. BIRCHFIELD
JAMES BIRD JR.
STEPHEN BISCHOFF
GEORGE BISHARDT
SAM BISHOP
WILLIAM B. BISHOP
GEORGE BISSETT
LAWRENCE A. BISSONNETTE
MONTE L. BLACKWELL
CHRISTOPHER BLAKE
RONALD C. BLEEMER
JOHN A. BLUST
COM SPEC BOAT RON TWO
ALFRED BODWAY
ROY H. BOEHM
DELBERT BOERNER
PAUL R. BOHN
GARY J. BOLLINGER
RAYMOND R. BOLLINGER JR.

FRANK BOONE
GARY BORODAEFF
LOUIS BOUSQUET
LAWRENCE B. BOVAT
MARK J. BOWERS
JOHN T. BOYD
HAROLD BOYDSTUN
ROBERT W. BOYLE
JOHN J. BRADBURY
GLEN A. BRADEN
LE ROY G. BRAGG
ROBERT W. BRANDT
W. J. BRAZELL
HAROLD R. BRENNEMAN
WILLIAM J. BRINGMAN
ED BRISBIOS
MELVIN BRITAIN
LEWIS R. BRITTON
ARTHUR BROOKS
SAMUEL L. BROWINING
JOHN E. BROWN
JOHN R. BROWN
JOHN W. BROWN
LARENCE H. BROWN
LAWRENCE V. BROWN
NOEL W. BROWN
DR. ROBERT BROWNING (G-CP/H)
THOMAS BRUGMAN
DAVE BUCKERT
THOMAS D. BUCKLEY
JAMES A. BUKOSKIE
MICHAEL J. BURCHAM
LIONEL C. BURNS
DAVID BUTCHER
EUGENE BUTLER
NORMA BYRD
PAUL W. CAGLE
RUSSEL CALKINS
WILLIAM R. CALVERT
WALTER D. CAMPBELL JR.
EDMUND B. CANBY
DAVID CAPOZZI
CLINTON S. CARPENTER
JOHN CARR
MAX R. CARROLL
STUART W. CARSON
ARTHUR G. CARTER
COLIN H. CARTER
MARIO CARTER
WILLIAM K. CARTER
WILLIAM W. CATER
DOUGLAS CATES
ARTHUR C. CATES SR.
R. M. (MIKE) CHAMBERS
M. J. CHARPENTIER
TERRY S. CHELIUS
J. THOM CHIRURG
RALPH W. CHRISTOPHER JR.
MIKE CLARK
ROBERT L. CLARK
WILLIAM CLARK
ROBERT CLIVER
KEN COEN

GREGORY M. COFFMAN
GERALD D. COLE
MICHAEL B. COLE
EVERETT COLLIER
MICHAEL L. COLLINS
WILLIAM D. COMBS
ROBERT H. COOMBS
CLARENCE COOPER
JAMES J. COPASS II
JACK A. COPENHAVER
ARTHUR A. CORBETT
DONALD E. CORN
ROBERT COSGROVE
TRACI L. COUNTRYMAN
RICHARD COUPE
WILES C. COX
TRAVIS COX JR.
DAVID R. CRAWFORD
GARY CREST
DAVID B. CROCKETT JR.
JAMES H. CRONANDER
DAVID W. CRONIN
EDWIN C. CROSS
EDWARD P. CULLIGAN
EUGENE P. CULLIGAN
DAVID CUPP
MICHAEL H. CURRY
WILLIAM H. CURTIS
ROBERT CZARKOWSKI
BERT DAHL
ORVIE M. DAHL
GORDON A. DANIELS JR.
LAURENCE J. DARLAND
THOMAS R. DAUGHERTY
PAUL DAVIDSON
BENNY DAVIDSON SR.
JACK B. DAVIS JR.
KWAME (EDWARD) DAVIS JR.
RICHARD A. DAVIS JR.
JAMES D. DAVY
KENNETH A. DELFINO
THOMAS B. DEMOTT JR.
RONALD W. DERING
JOSEPH M. DESERIO
STEVEN E. DEWITT
JAN P. DIAL
LOWELL W. DICKEY
NANCY DIERKS
JAMES (DOC) DILDINE
DR. STEVE DIMOND-SMITH
JOHN F. DISKO
SONNY DISMUKE
KENT N. DIXON
STEPHEN W. DIXSON
JOSEPH J. DIZONA JR.
PAUL DONALDSON
JOHN J. DONOVAN
JOHN T. DOOLITTLE
JOHN M. DORSO
JOHN F. DOYLE
PATRICK F. DOYLE
PATRICK J. DRAIN
DALE DRAKE

RONALD G. DREDGE
LARRY DU BOIS
JAMES T. DU BOSE
ARNOLD W. DULANEY
PAUL L. DUNBAR
RICHARD DUNBAR
HAMILTON A DUNCAN JR.
ROBERT B DURRETT
LOUIS C. DUTY SR.
ROBERT S. DWINELL
JOHN B. DWYER
CARTHEL R. DYSON
VERNON K. EATON
FRANK X. EDGELL
JOHN F. EDWARDS
WILLIAM L. EDWARDS
MATTHEW E. EGAN
JAY C. EICHHORN
A. ELLIOT
ALVIN K. ELLIS
RICHARD EMERY
DONALD G. EMMONS
FREDERICK ENGLE
DONALD ENGLISH
J. DANIEL ENNIS
ROBERT FAINELLI
GEORGE FAIRFAX
ANDRES N. FAJARDO
DONALD FALLON
WALTER FANTON
GEORGE F. FARNAN
MICHAEL FARNEY
MICHAEL O. FAUGHN
JOHN K. FERGUSON
WILLIAM FERGUSON
WILLIAM M. FINDLAY
JOSEPH L. FINDLEY
DAVID V. FISHER
CARL FLETCHER
RALPH D. FLORES
JACK M. FOGEL
WAYNE A. FORBES
WAYNE A. FORBES JR.
THOMAS FORREST
CHARLES F. FOSTER III
ROBERT FRED
FRANK FREE
BASIL / DORIS FRI
RALPH J. FRIES
GLEN E. FRY
MALCOLM W. FULLAM
DAN T. FULLER
FRED A. FURLAN
JOHN GAINEY
MARGARET GAINEY
G. G. GAITAN
MICHAEL GALINDO
RITO M. GALLARDO
WILLIAM GAMBRELL
GERALD GANDY
ROBERT C. GARNO
BRADFORD J. GARRETT
MELCHOR V. GARZA

WILLIAM W. GASKINS JR.
NORMAN J. GEIST
JERRY L. GENTILE
CARL A. GERKEN
MICHAEL GERVAIS
DELBERT GIBSON
MCPO JIM GIRARDIN
EUGENE B. GLASCO
RICHARD J. GLAZESKI
RICHARD G. GODBEHERE
ED GOLD
WYNN GOLDSMITH
PETE GONZALEZ
WILLIAM C. GORDON
ROBERT L. GRAETER
HOWARD GRAHAM
RONALD J. GRALEWICZ
LORENZO GRANADOS
GARY D. GRASSI
PAUL N. GRAY
SIDNEY GREAK
GREGORY C. GREEN
GORDON GREENWELL
WALLACE J. GROVES
WILLIAM B. GRUNDY
PAUL GUAY
JAMES B. GUTHRIE JR.
DON I. GUY
JAMES N. GUY
DENNIS C. HAAS
MICHAEL D. HAECKER
KENNETH HALE
ROSS H. HALL
THOMAS O. HALL
CHARLES D. HAMILTON
HOOD C. HAMPTON III
ALBERT M. HAND JR.
JOSEPH L. HANRATTY
DALE HARDIE
MAX E. HARKSEN
BRIAN HARLAN
BUDDI C. HARLAN
JAMES T. HARRELSON
ALAN LEE HARRIS
RAYMOND W. HARTZ
PAUL W. HAWKINS
WILLIAM E. HAYENGA JR.
TIMOTHY J. HAYES
H. FRANK HAZELWOOD
WILLIAM M. HEDRICK
ROBERT C. HEINEY
THOMAS J. HEKELE
RAYMOND F. HELBLING
FRANK D. HENNING JR.
JOHN HERKE
DR. JAN K. HERMAN
DANIEL F. HICKEY JR.
RICHARD L. HICKS
HYUNSOOK HIGHLAND
GORDON K. HILLESLAND
HOWARD HINDS JR.
DIRECTOR NAVAL HISTORICAL
CENTER
LEWIS H. HITCHCOCK
CLARENCE HOAGLAND
VICTOR HOARD
BOB HOLLINGSHEAD
JAMES C. HOLT
PHILIP R. HOOD
JULIUS HORNYAK JR.
CHARLES L. HORTON JR.
JAMES D. HORVATH

JAMES HOTT
JOHN H. HOWE
LAWRENCE G. HOWE
NORMAN HOWELL
ROBERT A. HUGHES
MARSHALL A. HUNT
ROBERT B. HUNT
JAMES S. HUNTER
VETERANS OF ILLINOIS
JONATHAN INSKEEP
JERRY R. IRVINE
STEVEN C. IVIE
ROBERT JACAURSO
STUMP JACKIE D.
DANA JACKSON
MICHAEL JACKSON
WAYNE JANOUSEK
WAYNE D. JANOUSEK
EDWIN L. JAY
BRUCE C. JAYNE
KENNETH J. JENDA
CLAUDE JERNIGAN
RICHARD L. JIMENEZ
CHARLES L. JOHANN
ALBERT F. JOHNSON
BILLY J. JOHNSON
HOWARD L. JOHNSON
KENNETH M. JOHNSON
LARRY M. JOHNSON
DAVID M. JONES
JAMES A. JONES
KEITH JONES
RODNEY F. JONES
KENNETH K. KALISH
WALLACE KANAHELE
PAUL KANE
WILLIAM E. KEENE
JOHN KEIPER
JOHN R. KEIPER
JAMES W. KEITH
R. KELLEHER
EARL KENNEDY
JAMES E. KENNEDY
RAYMOND KENNEY
WILLIAM F. KENNEY
ROBERT J. KERMEN
JAMES T. KESLER
JAMES KEYES
MICHAEL J. KILEY
ROBERT W. KILKELLY
JEROME H. KING JR.
JAMES P. KINSEY
RUSSELL J. KIPKOWSKI
RICHARD L. KIRK
RON KIRKEY
ROBERT J. KLEIMAN
BILLY R. KLINKEFUS
NORWOOD KOONCE JR.
ROBERT L. KORN
BRADFORD T. KOWHAN
ROBERT A. KREYER
MELVIN M. KRINES
JAMES J. KUZNICKI
ROBERT D. LABRODE
DAVID LAFFERTY
JIM L. LAMBERT
ALBERT LAMBINUS JR.
ROBERT R. LANGEVIN
W.T. LANGHAM
STEPHEN P LANGLEY
FRED L. LANGUELL
WILLIAM K LANNOM

RONALD F. LARATTA
MILTON LARKIN JR.
DAVID R. LARSEN
EDWARD H. LAVILETTA
BOB LEBLANC
RANDALL LEE
JERRY R. LEEDS
FRANK D. LEHR
PATRICK K. LELAND
O.P LENT III
EARNEST L. LEONARD
W. T. TIM LINDENZWEIG
DENNIS R. LINGO
DONALD C. LITZENBURG
STEVEN Q. LO PRESTI
DOUGLAS LOTT
CLYDE W. LOVELL
ALLAN J. LUDI
JERRY I. LUGAR LUNTSFORD
ERICK DOC LUOMA
RODNEY C. LYNCH
KENNETH MAC DONALD
FRED MAC LEOD
J. PATRICK MADDEN
JIMMY RAY MADDOX
MICHAEL J. MADRID
NORMAN D. MAITLAND
JOHN M. MALOVIC
WILLIAM MANTOOTH
WILLIAM MARAUGHA JR.
RICHARD MARCINKO
PERRY MARK
GERD W. MARKER
MICHAEL MARRERO
DETLO MARTHINSON JR.
BOB MARTIN
CECIL H. MARTIN
JACK MARTINEZ
DONALD W. MATHEWS
BERT MAXFIELD
TED MC CALL
BRUCE MC CAMEY
ARTHUR A. MC CLAIN JR.
DONALD P. MC CLEMONS
FREDERICK H. MC DAVITT
GERALD L. MC DERMOTT
HARRY J. MC DERMOTT
FRED L. MC DONALD
PAUL E. MC DONALD
THOMAS F. MC DONALD
FRED MC ELROY
JOHN D. MC GOVERN
TERRY MC HENRY
GEORGE MC HORSE
LEONARD MC KETHAN
RICHARD A. MC MURRY
HARLAN E. MC PHERSON
FREDRICK J. MCGAVRAN
KENNETH MEEK
JOHN G. MELLIN
PHILIP E. MENDOZA
WARD L. MERRILL
STAN PETE MESTON
RONALD P. METTERT
LESTER METTS
JAMES R. METZGER
HAROLD MEYERKORD
JAMES W. MILDENSTEIN
ANDREW G. MILLER
JOHN R. MILLER
JAMES S. MILLS
NORRIS MILSTEAD

ROBERT G. MITCHELL
JOHN H. MIXON
ROBERT MOASE
JOSEPH A. MOCERI
SAMUEL MONK
MICHAEL L. MONROE
BOB A. MONZINGO
EDWARD MOODY JR.
ROBERT E. MORAN
CHARLES E. MORGAN
RODNEY DEAN MORGAN
WILLIAM J. MORGAN
JAMES F. MORGAN JR.
MIKE MORGAN-OLSON
DANIEL G. MORRIS
FRED S. MORRISON
STEPHEN B. MORRISON
ROGER J. MOSCONE
GARY W. MOSS
JOHN W. MUIR
BRIAN L. MULLEN JR.
UDT/SEAL MUSEUM
CO NAVSPECWARGRU ONE
CARL A. NELSON
KENNARD F. NELSON
NOLAN NELSON
RONALD NEUMAN
WILLIAM D. NEWCOMB
GERALD NOLAN
GAMEWARDENS OF VIETNAM
NORFOLK
JOHN T. NUGENT
ALBERT L. O'CANAS
JOSEPH M. O'CONNOR
DONALD W. O'DELL JR.
AUDREY O'DONNELL
THOMAS O'MALLEY JR.
MILTOMN P. O'NEAL
VIETNAM VETS OF MASSACHU-
SETTS
FRED OLDS
MICHAEL E. OLSON
ADRIAN A. ONDERDONK
CHARLES R. OREFICE
JOHN A. ORR
JOSEPH OSMAN SR.
EDWIN L. OSWALD
DAVID G. OTTO
VETS OUTREACH
JAMES PAFIAS
LEONARD H PAINE
DANIEL G. PALMER
WAYNE E. PALMER
WILLIAM P. PARK JR.
DENNIS L. PARRISH
FRANK P. PARRISH
JAMES E. PASTERNAK
W. A. PATNAUDE
DORLAND PAYNE
NORMAN E. PEARSON
KEITH J. PECHA
ALAN R. PERRY
RONALD L. PERRY
THOMAS L. PERRY
MICHAEL F. PERSICO
LANNY C. PETERSON
THOMAS MAX PEVEY
JOHN PHILLIPS
J.E. PICKENPAUGH
C. A. PICKETT
PETER J. PINI
PETER J PINTO

RAYMOND P. POKORNY
DENNIS G. POLEDNA
GERALD A. POLISKEY
ANDY POLLARD
MARK C. POLLONI
ROBERT B. POTTER
PAUL H. POULSON
ARTHUR W. PRICE JR.
SHERMAN D PRIDHAM
LAVERNE PRINE
STEPHEN M. PRINGLE
PAUL R. PRITCHARD
BRADLEY N PROFFITT
WILLIAM PUNCH JR.
PAUL QUINLAN
VINCE RAMBO
FIDEL RAMIREZ II
HARRY D. RAMSDEN
JAMES A. RAMSDEN
JAMES W. RANDALL
DONALD L. RASMUSSEN
ROBERT B. RATLIFF
H. FRANK RAWL
GARY L. RAYMOND
FRANK RE III
MICHAEL L. REBOULET
RICHARD REEDY
WILLIAM H. REICHERT
FRANK J REILLY
PAUL H. REILLY
MICHAEL J. REILLY JR.
HERBERT REMMERS
JAMES R RENICK JR.
DON RHEA
DANNY RICE
DAVE RICE
LISTER RICES
CHARLES RICHEY
ARTHUR L. RICHMOND
JERRY RINEHOLD
R. LYNN RISHEL
RONALD K RITTER
RICHARD RITZ
JAMES O. ROAHEN
BILLY J. ROBERTSON
PHELPS E. ROBINSON
STEPHEN J. RODGERS
DAVE ROEVER
JOHN J. ROGERS
RONALD D. ROLATER
GEORGE L. ROPER
CARL A. ROSCHETZKY
ROBERT A. ROSE
ALDO F. ROSSI JR.
FRANK E. ROUGH
ERNEST L. ROY
JOSEPH ROY
KENNETH H RUECKER
EARL RUSSELL
WILLIAM R. RUSTH
FREDERICK SABINE
STEPHEN SAHM
HENRY C. SALA JR.
FRANK SALIVE
JOHN O. SALONEN
BILLIE J. SANDERS
JAMES SANDERS

JESSE C. SANDLIN
PATRICK C. SANDOVAL JR.
RODERIC SANGSTER
GERALD SAXTON
RON SAXVIK
VINCENT SCANDOLE
PETER J. SCHIFF
DAVID H. SCHILL
MERLE E. SCHLOTTERBACK
CHARLES E. SCHMITZ
EDWARD SCHNEIDER
KENNETH A. SCHNEIDER
JOSEPH SCHREIBER JR
STEPHEN F. SCHRIENER
RICHARD SCHULTZ
WILLIAM P SCHULTZ
WILLIAM I. SCHWARTZ
SAYRE A. SCHWARZTRAUBER
GEORGE SCOTT
DENNIS SCULLY
MARCUS E. SEAGERS
HAL-3 SEAWOLF ASSOCIATION
ERIC L. SEDLACEK
RICHARD C. SEMON
PAUL D. SENECAL
NORMAN J. SHACKELTON
MICHAEL D. SHARP
JOHN E. SHAW
EUGENE SHEA
DONALD SHEPPARD
THOMAS J. SHERIDAN
H. W. SHERMAN
JOHN F. SHERRED
JOHN F. SHERRED
RICHARD SHIRK
JAMES SHRECKENGAUST
LLOYD W. SHRINER
RICK SILVEIRA
WILLIAM H. SIMMONS
DENNIS L. SIMPSON
JEAN SIMPSON
LARRY SINGER
BRAD SLEPICKA
NORMAN SLIMMER JR.
RICHARD T. SLOANE
DANIEL M. SMILEY
CHESTER B. SMITH
CLIFFOR A. SMITH
HERMAN SMITH
JAMES L. SMITH
JERRY W. SMITH
WILEY F. SMITH
RAYMOND SNOW
VIRGIL SNYDER
HAROLD J. STANTON
ROBERT M. STANTON JR.
JERRY STAPLES
LEON G. STARCK
ROBERT P. STARK
JAMES W. STEFFES
DONALD L. STEIGEL
ROBERT A. STEIN JR.
HERBERT A. STEPHAN
CHARLES STITHEM
DAVID STOCKLEY
JAMES STODDARD
EDWARD STOLLE JR.

CLAYTON H. STONE
CURTIS W. STONE
EDWIN STONE
WILLIAM STRAIGHT
CENTER FOR THE STUDY OF
VIETNAM
NEIL E. RED STUMMER
BUDDY STURGIS JR.
WALTER F. SUAREZ JR.
MICHAEL J. SUNTAVA
RONALD A. SWAFFORD
HOWARD SWAIN
JOHN J. SWAYSER
WEYMOUTH D. SYMMES
JAMES DEAN TABOK
JAMES D TABOR
SALVATORE TALLARICO
JAMES R. TALLEY
JOHN P. TANNER
KENNETH TAYLOR
GRANT R. TELFER
FREDERICK W. TEMPLE
LEWIS H. THAMES
JAMES P. THOMAS
GARY H. THOMPSON
JIMMIE L. THOMPSON
RODNEY THOMPSON
DON C. THOMSON
WARREN K. TOM THOMSON
PAUL THUEMMLER
CLEMON TIERCE
DANNY TINGEN
ROBERT TIPPINS
CONLEY TIPTON
FRANK J. TODARO
MORTON E. TOOLE
BUDDY L. TOWNSEND
IVAN TRAVNICEK
GERRI TRUETT
CLARENCE TUCKER
TIM TUCKER
WILLIAM F. TURNBULL
EDMUND TURNER
MAURICE TURPIN
JAMES ULLRICH
JIM T. VAGENAS
RAYMOND VAN DER MEER
ALFRED L. VAN HORNE SR.
CHARLES R. VANCE
MICHAEL J. VENEZIA JR.
MARTIN W. VICE
EDWARD H. VICK
FRIENDS OF THE VIETNAM
VETERANS MEM
GAMEWARDENS OF VIETNAM
ASSOC.
GERRY VOGT
C. J. WAGES JR.
FERNLEY WAGNER JR.
LEE R. WAHLER
JAMES H. WALKER
RAYMOND R. WALKER
THOMAS C WALLACE
ROBIN C. WALTER
WILLIAM BILL WALTERS
VICTOR WANDRES
OF THE VIETNAM WAR INC.

DENNIS M. WARD
JAMES L. WARD
N. G. WARD
PETER L. WARD
EDD WARREN
WILLIAM J. WARREN
DONALD WATERS
STEPHEN WATSON
HARRY B. WATTERS
JACK D. WEAVER
BMCM KELLY WEBB
LOWELL WEBB
RONALD J. WEEKS
ROBERT WEINSCHENK
BERT H. WELLS
RICHARD M. WELLS
WALTON E. WELLS
RITA WENTZ
CRAIG WERT
MARK WERTHEIMER
ALLEN WESELESKEY
TIMOTHY R. WEST
REV. LESTER WESTLING JR.
WILLIAM C. WESTMORELAND
VICTOR WESTPHALL
ALAN LEWIS WHITE
CHARLES WHITE
PHILIP WHITNEY
EVERETT R. WIEDERSBERG
S.J. WIGGINS
MICHAEL A. WILEY
NEAL WILLARD
ROBERT M. WILLAUER JR.
CHARLES W. WILLIAMS
CLARENCE F. WILLIAMS
J. ELLIOTT WILLIAMS
JOHN CLYDE WILLIAMS
WILLIAM G. WILLIAMS
WILLIAM S. WILLIAMS
WYLIE W. WILLIAMS
ALAN J. WILSON
ALAN L. WILSON
THOMAS A. WILSON
WILLIAM B. WILSON
THOMAS L. WINKLESS
WILLIAM A. WINTERS
BURTON B. WITHAM JR.
WILLIAM WITTING
MICHAEL WOLFE
RONALD WOLIN
LEONARD O. WOLTERSDORF
PAUL A. WOOD SR.
JAMES WOODS
PETER WOODWARD
JAMES WOODWARD JR.
JOHN W. WOODY
MICHAEL D. WORTHINGTON
DAVID WRIGHT
WILLIAM F. WYCKOFF
JAMES T. YOUNG
JAMES W. YOUNG
WILLIAM V. YOUNG
LARRY YOUNGBLOOD
R. MATTHEW ZIMMER
ELMO R. ZUMWALT JR.
ROBERT C. CARPENTER

(Courtesy of W.F. Kenney)

River Division 514 Liberty Boat to Binh Tuey, 1969. (Courtesy of J. Warnock)

Hugh M. Highland during the late 1960s.

Assault Support Boat, ASPB, September 1967. (Courtesy of W.F. Kenney)

(Courtesy of W.F. Kenney)

River Division 594, Nha Be, 1969. (Courtesy of Robert M. Willauer)

Strong stuff on the Vinh Te. (Courtesy of J. Warnock)

YR-26, River Division 514 maintenance time. (Courtesy of J. Warnock)

OV-10A "Broncos" in flight. Usually flying in teams of two, provided close-in air support for Brown Water Navy river patrols and for allied ground operations near waterways. (Courtesy of James D. Davy)

A U.S. Navy River Patrol Boat cruises slowly down a canal during an operation Gamewarden patrol. (Courtesy of W.F. Kenney)

(Courtesy of W.F. Kenney)

Assault Troop Carriers in the waterlogged fields of Tong An, June 1967. (Courtesy of W.F. Kenney)

A

Abbbott, Richard E. 14
Abrams, Creighton 60
Abrams, J.L. 61
Adams, Michael F. 85
Agazzi, D.M. 61
Ajdukovich, George 64
Albrecht, J.A. 61
Alcock, R.G. 61
Allen, TDC 90
Alspaugh, Timothy D. 64
Amoroso, GMG3 90
Anderson, BM1 5
Anderson, David B. 87
Anderson, F.E. 61
Anderson, T.K. 85, 87
Andrews, R.W. 61
Antone, F.G. 61
Apolinar, F.J. 61
Arnold, R.J. 61
Ashmore, ENFN 91
Ashton, C.M. 61
Atkins, W.L. 61
Aydelotte, Sam 42
Aznoe, Steve 86

B

Babcock, John 59
Bacon, Charlie 48
Bailey, Dallam 77, 78
Bailey, Michael H. 62
Bailey, Mose M. 85
Baker, C.A. 61
Baker, E.J. 61
Baker, Edward J. 82
Baker, Harold L. 65
Baker, W.S. 49
Banks, GMG2 89
Baratko, Robert E. 65
Barden, A.W. 61
Barnes, Bill 43
Barnes, GMG3 89
Barnes, LTJG 81
Barney, Eugene 17
Bartholomew, Jeff 32
Barton, J.B. 61
Bassac River 15, 26, 28, 30, 50, 53, 65, 73, 88
Batchelder, W.K. 61
Bauer, EN2 89, 90
Baxter, Charles E. 30
Beaudoin, GMG1 89
Beckwith, Reynolds 21, 43
Beery, Jere 33, 53, 74, 76, 77
Belcher, H.E. 61
Belford, J.A. 61
Ben Tre 27, 39, 42, 43
Bennett, RM1 89
Berkebile, J. 61
Bernique, Michael 58
Bilderback, GMG2 88
Bill Mackie 42
Billeaudeau, Elby J. 86

Binder, Rubin 10, 51
Binh Thuy 27, 43, 45, 73
Birky, H.E. 61
Black Ponies 43, 44
Blais, R.L. 61
Blandino, H., 61
Bodiford 86
Bomar, F.W. 61
Bordallo, Ricardo J. 87
Bostain, GMGSN 90
Boston, D.E. 61
Bowers, James S. 47
Bowles, L.L. 61
Braden, T.L. 61
Brandt, Robert 132
Branin, John 92, 93
Brazythis, GMG3 91
Brewton, J.C. 61
Brock, Harry 49
Brooks, C.E. 61
Brooks, Dwayne 56
Brown, E.J., Jr. 61
Brown, H.E., Jr. 61
Brown, Norman T. 85
Brown, R.L. 61
Bruehl, GMG2 89
Buckingham, LT(jg) 89
Bucklew, Philip 24, 58
Burgess, R.H. 61
Burke, Arleigh 24
Burke, J.R. 61
Buzzell, R.H. 61
Byrd, GMG3 89

C

Ca Mau Peninsula 15, 60
Cain, J.R. 61
Cain, QM1 91
Caldwell, EN3 90
Cam Lo 15
Cam Ranh Bay 38, 48
Can Tho 27, 30, 45, 50
Cancilia, N. 61
Cannon, GMG3 90
Canur, F.H. 61
Cape Batangan 49
Carpien, LTJG 81
Carr, M.P. 61
Carriveau 61
Carter, G.L. 61
Carter, T.E. 61
Carwile, Kenneth L. 85
Cary, W.A. 61
Case, D.C. 61
Case, Daniel 82
Castle, H.C. 61
Castleberry, R.L. 61
Cat Lo 26, 28, 44, 49
Cater, William W. 160
Cathy, Carroll S. 86
Cau Hai Bay 35
Center, R.L. 61

Chapman, Rick 18
Chau Doc 45
Childers, R.D. 61
Childress, G.H. 55
Cho Chin River 20,
Cho Gao 56
Chon, Adm. 12
Claiborne, D.R. 61
Clark, Gary 61
Clark, Wayne L. 86
Clerkin, J. 61
Clerkin, SM1 88
Clifford, M.J. 61
Cline, M.E. 61
Co Chien River 17, 26, 28, 42
Coble, Thomas D. 85
Coker, B.L. 61
Cole 75
Coleman, James R. 87
Collins, R.M. 61
Collins, SN 90
Cone, L.A. 61
Conklin, EN3 88
Conner, John W. 87
Connon, Ronnie J. 87
Cosson, W. 61
Costa, EN1 89, 90
Cota, E.K. 61
Cover, L.L. 61
Cowen, H.E. 61
Cozad, John 132
Crabtree, G.R. 61
Crabtree, George R. 82
Craghead, TJ. 61
Croizat, Victor 29
Crone, C.R. 61
Crose, R.A. 61
Cua Dai River 15, 36
Cua Viet 15, 37, 39
Culbertson, SN 88
Curtis, Bill 15, 16, 20, 27, 29, 38, 46, 55, 61, 74, 79
Cutler, Thomas 17, 19, 52

D

Da Nang 37, 38, 45
Dam Doi River 60
Damrow, O.P. 61
Davis, EN2 89
Davis, Eugene E. 85
Davy, James D. 2, 11, 36, 39, 79, 83, 87, 92, 94, 132, 156
Dawkins, Harry T. 86
Day, O.A. 61
Dean, Paul 26
Deckert, J.C. 14
DeClercq, Keith 69
Dees, E.A., Jr. 61, 37, 39, 40, 41, 49, 50, 63
Delena, BM1 90
Delfino, Kenneth 32, 33, 41, 54

Delph, S.C. 61
Dennis, Don A. 85
Dennis, W.E. 61
Dennis, W.R. 61
Devine, D.E. 61
Dixon, Bradford M. 85
Dixon, LTJG 85, 86
Dizona, Joseph 44, 132
Dock, R.L. 61
Donaldson, LT 73
Donavan, P.J. 61
Dong Tranh River 18
Doty, G.W. 61
Douglas, H.J. 61
Drako, Dale Ms. 14
Drennan, James W. 85
Dunn, Gil 48
Durham, Oliver E. 61, 85
Duserick, Frank G. 86
Duty, Louis C. 72, 85, 86
Dyson, GMGSN 88
Dyson, R.D. 50

E

Easton, R.G 61
Eckhardt, Michael J. 85, 86
Edwards, David L. 87
Edwards, F.L., Jr. 61, 62
Egbert, D.E. 61
Eldridge, TC. 62
Ellard, William M. 85
Elliot, A.J. 52, 62
Elliot, John 86
Ellis, F.M. 62
Embrey, George R. 85
Emery, SN 91
Emory, TH. 62
Enoch, Barry W. 65
Erntson, Keith L. 85
Estes, N.C., Jr. 62
Eugene Rosenthal 42
Evans, L.B. 62
Evans, Mark C. 86
Ewers, Reginald P. 87

F

Faulk, Capt. 132
Fee, D.F. 62
Ferguson, John 82
Ferguson, John K. 19, 71, 80
Ferguson, Kirk 81
Finley, GMG3 91
Flowers, W.N. 62
Flynn, W.V. 62
Forbes, John 34
Ford, BM1 62
Ford, P.O. 62
Ford, Patrick 53, 65
Fortino, J.A. 62
Frahm, W.D. 62
Fraley, E.F. 62
Frederickson, G.W. 92

Freeman, EN3 91
Freeman, Ken 89
Freeman, Kenneth W. 85
Freund, T.J. 62, 65
Fries, Ralph 11
Fuller, Dan 22
Funk, David L. 85, 86
Funk, H.L. 62

G

Gage, N.G. 62
Gallagher, Gary G. 65
Gallagher, Robert T. 46, 65
Gallery, Daniel 21
Gallo, S.F. 57
Garamillo, Larry D. 85, 89
Gates, Michael 56, 66
Giant Slingshot 58
Gilliam, TE. 62
Giovannelli, G.L. 62
Glaser, Francis E. 73
Godbehere, Richard 50, 53, 75,
  76, 77, 78
Godines, M.M. 62
Goff, Del 132
Goldbin, C.H. 62
Gollahan, J.D. 62
Gorman, LT 81
Gorshe, Joe 56, 132
Gottschall, Keith E. 86
Graber, Hal 18
Graham, G.J. 62
Green, J.E. 62
Green, R.L. 62
Green, Richard 86
Guest, D., A01 62
Guest, D., BMC 62
Gulf of Thailand 15
Gulf of Tonkin 25
Gumpf, SN 91
Guthrie, Jim 11, 23, 32, 56,
  61, 132

H

Hagerich, W.C. 62
Haines, C.W. 62
Hall, D.C. 62
Ham Luong 15, 27, 28, 39,
  42
Hampton Gregory O. 66
Hangan, J.A. 62
Hardcastle, Bill 17
Hart, J.F. 62
Hartzell, D.F., Jr. 62
Hayenga Jr., William E. 66
Heintz, R.A. 62
Henning, BM2 91
Henning, Frank D. 85, 88, 89
Henry, Robert 89
Hick, Dick 12
Hickey 86
Hickey, Eugene 49
Hicks, Dick 31, 33
Hienbuck, Charles F. 85
Highland, Hugh M. 154
Hines, Jerry G. 85, 86, 87

Hodkins, Chuck 56, 132
Hoffman, David P. 62
Hoffman, Roy 58, 60
Hoi An 36
Holloway, L.D. 62
Holmes, H.B. 62
Holtz, P.A. 62
Hoopaugh, L.E. 62
Hooper, B.W. 62
Hornyak, Julius 38
Hou Giang 15
Houck, E.F. 62
Howard, Commander 52
Howell, Norm 5
Hunt, J.R. 62
Hurd, Samual S. 86

I

I Corps Tactical Zone 15
Ismay, Arthur 48

J

Jacaruso, F. 62
Jackson, D.M. 62
Jackson, Keith M. 85
Jamison, J.D. 62
Jensen, Richard 93
Johns, J.D. 62
Johns, Joseph D. 82
Johnson, A.D. 62
Johnson, R.D. 62
Johnson, S.A. 62
Jones, Harry R. 85
Jones, J.C. 62
Jones, L.E. 62
Jones, M.M., Jr. 62
Jones, Thomas E. 87

K

Kamps, Charles T Jr. 29
Kearney, D.G. 62
Keene, William E. 86
Keith, R.B. 62
Kell, Billy L. 87
Kenney,W.F. 150, 154, 155,
  156, 157
Kenny, Harry 93
Kent, Louis H. 87
Kerr, Raymond E. 85, 86
Kerrey, Bob 46
Kerrey, Joseph R. 46
Khanh, VNN 91
Kinnard, Donald C. 66
Klien, H.I. 62
Kohn, Robert W. 86
Kollmeyer, Carl 62, 78
Koshmaul, R.E. 62
Kuhn, GMG2 89, 90
Kurz, D.L. 62
Kushmaul, R.E. 62

L

LA Brode, Robert D. 86
Lake, R. R. 62
Larafta, Ron 2, 11, 78, 132
Larrimore 75

Larsen, David R. 66
Lassiter, Jerry 42
Lavell, Kit 43, 44
Leazer, TF. 62
Ledford, S.D. 62
Ledoux, Dennis H. 87
Lehman, D.J., III 62
Lewis, J.C. 62
Lipps, Osmond K. 87
Long Tau 15, 18, 38, 40, 74
Long Xuyen 27
Lopresti, Steve 32
Lourash, Kenneth D. 87
Lucas, Vernon B. 85
Lucidi 75
Luckeft, L.J. 62
Luntsford, J.E. 62

M

Machen, B.W. 62
Mackie, Bill 42
Madden 86
Mahner, L.A. 62
Maisenhelder, William H. 73
Maner, H.J. 62
Mann, D.M. 62
Market Time 47, 49
Markham, Edward L. 85
Marquis, W.D. 49
Martin, Aubrey G. 62
Martin, Cecil H. 67, 85
Mathis, W.G. 56, 132
Matthews, RAdm. 12
Mattingly, H.A., Jr. 62
Maxwell, Wendell 42
Maxwell, Wayne D. 85
McCaffety, C.A., Jr. 62
McClemons, Donald P. 85
McCleod, Max C. 87
McCoy, EN3 91
McCullock, BMC 89, 90
McDavitt, Fred 10
McGuinn, E.C. 62
McKinley, S.W. 62
McLeod's Navy 18
McLeod, Kenneth L., III 18
McMurry, R.A. 46
McNamara, Robert 17, 25
Mekong Delta 14, 15, 17, 18,
  25, 29, 35, 36, 39, 42, 45, 50,
  51, 73
Mekong River 10, 64, 67, 68,
  72, 81, 86
Men, VNN 91
Meute, H.M. 62
Meute, J.M. 62
Meyer, L.W. 62
Meyerkord, Harold Dale 17
Milamo, J.S. 62
Minick, Donald J. 85
Mirkovich, Don 81, 82, 83
Moe, L.J. 62
Monzingo, Chief 74
Moore, R.D. 62
Moore, TM. 62
Morelli, Ralph T. 85, 86

Morgan, D.E. 62
Morgan, Jim 24, 57
Morgan, R. 84
Morrelli, Ralph T. 86
Morris, Donald R. 85
Moultine, C.R. 62
Muir, John D. 56, 57, 61, 62
Mulcahy, J.M. 62
Mulford, Mike 33, 132
Mulrooney, G. 62
Munsey, R.C. 62
Muon, VNN 91
Murray, Eldon 61
Musetti, J.T 62
My Tho 15, 26, 29, 42, 45
Myers, John 86

N

Neal, R.K. 62
Nelson, Carl 96
Nelson, D.R. 62
Newman, Jerry W. 87
Nha Be 26, 28, 38, 40, 45
Nha Trang 38, 46
Nickerson, G.B. 62
Niemi, J.A. 62
Nitze, Paul H. 9
Noel, Lawrence P. 86
Norris, K.E. 62
Norris, Thomas R. 46
Nunes, Robert 42

O

O'Dell, M.C. 62
O'Donnell, William T. 85
O'Mara, Richard 48
Oberdorfer, Don 51
Olson, Alan B. 85
Ong Doc River 60
Operation Barrier Reef 80
Operation Clearwater 35
Operation Frequent Wind 87
Operation Gamewarden 26, 73
Operation Giant Slingshot 74,
  88, 90
Operation Green Wave 35
Operation Market Time 25
Operation Monster 44
Operation New Life 87
Operation Quai Vat 44
Ortiz, A.O. 62
Ott, E.L. 62
Otto, David G. 77, 78
Ouellet, David G. 53, 62, 64
Owens 86

P

Pace, R.E. 62
Pack Vee 44
Paddock, G.C. 62
Paddock, Gary 40
Padgett, Oscar Jr. 17
Page, G.M. 62
Page, Tim 49
Paris, Ronald J. 85
Parrot's Beak 56

Paulson, W. 62
Pawlowski, E.W. 62
Peddicord, D.G. 62
Pederson, W.A. 62
Perales, Salvador F. 85
Pereia, Alfred P. 85
Perfume River 36
Persico 86
Peters, Mike 42
Peterson, C.J. 60, 62
Pocholec, Merle A. 87
Poe, J.R. 62
Polmanteer, Gary 87, 91
Pope, W.G. 62
Porter, Robert O. 67
Potter, W.V. 62
Preales, Salvador G. 85
Prendergast, A.0. 62
Prevette, David M. 87
Price, Arthur 58
Pridham, Sherman 84
Prince 47
Proffer, G.F. 62

Q

Quant Tri 15
Qui Nhon 38, 47, 48
Quinn, M.C. 62

R

Rach Giang Thanh River 58
Rambo, Lieutenant 54
Ramos, J. 62
Ramos, R. 62
Randall 86
Rankin, K.D. 62
Ratliff, J. 62
Re, Frank, III 74
Reardon, R.J. 62
Reeder, Hubbard F. 86
Resnicoff, Arnold 84
Rice, A.W. 62
Rickli, R.H. 62
Ries, Richard H. 86
Risher, C.T., III 62
Ritch, E.E. 62
Ritter, J.L. 62
Roberts, Paul 33
Robertson, D.R. 62
Robertson, R.D. 62
Robinson, R.D. 62
Rockwell, William 41
Roderick, Wallace 0. 74, 75
Rodrigues, David O. 86
Roever, Dave 23, 31, 34, 50, 54
Romanski, J.H. 62
Ronald J. Weeks 86
Roper, Jim 33
Rosenthal, Eugene 42
Rossignol, R.W. 62
Rost, J.F. 62
Roster 151
Rubio, Robert 28
Rucker, Kenneth 26
Rung Sat 16, 18, 25, 26, 28, 35, 38, 41, 43, 45, 73

Rush, G.H. 62
Russell, P.F. 62
Russell, Peter 44
Russell, Rick 93

S

Sa Dec 27, 34
Sa Ky River 49
Sagar, Charles H. 85
Saigon River 59, 74
Sandberg, J.A. 62
Sander, J.K. 62
Santoli, Al 43
Saporito, R. 62
Schafernocker, M.E. 62
Schlote, L.C. 62
Schmidt, David E. 87
Schreadley, R.L. 37
Schwarztrauber, Sayre 37, 50
Scurlock, Benny R. 85
SEALs 45
Seawolves 42, 43
Seery, J.L. 62
Seven Mountains 29
Sheppard, Donald 34
Sheridan, TJ. 32
Sherman, Harold 54, 75, 76, 77, 78
Sidote, Richard 26
Sikkink, R.D. 62
Sillett, D.H. 62
Simison, T.C. 62
Simmers, G.W. 62
Simon, J.L. 62
Slane, Willis 19, 25
Slimmer, Norman H., Jr. 32
Smith, Chester 10, 67
Smith, G.W. 37
Smith, P.T. 62
Smith, T. 62
Soi Rap River 18, 49
Spencer, William Curtis 82
Stafford, T S. 62
Stayton, Norman B. 67
Stefanik, James H. 85
Stengel, Richard A. 73
Stiller, Thomas P. 80, 87
Stone, Clayton H. 73
Stone, Guy E. 67
Stone, J.L.J. 62
Suhr, A.H. 62

Sullivan, Bill 86
Summerhill, Robert B. 20
Sutter 86
Swanson, Leroy V. 26
Swartztrauber, S.A. 28, 29, 32
Syverston, Lloyd S. 87

T

Tan An 34
Tan Chau 27
Tan My 37
Tan Son Nhut 28
Taylor, Maxwell 45
Temple 86
Thames, J.F. 62
Thomas, Robert J. 67
Thompson, Phillip S. 73
Thompson, Tom 11
Thompson, W.J. 62
Thompson, William 55, 56
Thomson, Tom 132
Thrash, Donald S. 85
Timmons, B.A. 49
Tinnin, E.S. 62
Toole, Morton E. 10
Touchstone, Jackie D. 85
Tozer, E.W. 62
Traini, F. 62
Truett, Quincy 55, 60, 62, 68
Tucker, D.L. 62
Tuey Nhon 33
Tuller, E.L. 62

U

U Minh Forest 29, 60
Uhlig, Frank, Jr. 28
Underwood, P.L. 62
Ussery, GMG3 88

V

Vam Co Dong 56, 60, 74
Vam Co Tay 56, 60
Van Horne, A.L. 72
Van Hoy, K.E. 62
Vinh Long 68
Vinh Long 17, 27, 41, 68
Vung Tau 41

W

Walt, Lewis 36
Walker, James R. 68

Wall, J.A. 62
Wampler 62
Ward, Norvell G. 18, 25
Warnock, J. 12, 30, 31, 33, 82, 83, 86, 94, 95, 132, 154, 155
Watson, Stephen 5, 11
Weaver, G.R., Jr. 62
Webb, D.D. 62
Weeks, Ronald J. 86
Wendell Maxwell 42
Wentz, M.A. 62
Weseleskey, Allen E. 68
Westervelt, J.B. 62
Westling Jr., Lester L. 82, 83
Westover, D.E. 62
Westphal, Warren R. 68
White, Hartwell A. 85, 86
Wilbourne, David 49
Willauer, Robert M. 155
Williams 86
Williams Jr., Lloyd T. 69
Williams, A.G. 62
Williams, James Elliott 7, 10, 51, 53, 64, 68
Williams, John C. 2, 11, 132
Williams, Robert 34
Williamson, Jack 42
Wilson, D.A. 62
Winters, W.R. 62
Wisth, Jon A. 86
Witham, B.B., Jr. 26
Witham, Burt 6, 62
Witham, Burt, Jr. 40
Witt, C.D. 62
Wobbe, D.M. 62
Woodward, James F. Jr. 132
Worth, R.E. 62
Wright, F.E. 62
Wuellner, Thomas A. 86
Wukovitz, John 34, 59

Y

Ycoco, G.R. 62
Yelinek, LT 88

Z

Zumwalt, Elmo Russell, Jr. 7, 8, 9, 15, 45, 49, 57, 74, 80, 82, 83
Zumwalt, Elmo, III 60

Courtesy of William W. Cater

Printed in the USA
CPSIA information can be obtained
at www.ICGtesting.com
JSHW060054150824
68134JS00032B/2730